IFIP TC 2/WG 2.6 Working Conference on
Visual Database Systems
Tokyo, Japan, 3–7 April, 1989

NORTH-HOLLAND
AMSTERDAM • NEW YORK • OXFORD • TOKYO

VISUAL DATA

VISUAL DATABASE SYSTEMS

Proceedings of the IFIP TC 2/WG 2.6 Working Conference on
Visual Database Systems
Tokyo, Japan, 3–7 April, 1989

edited by

Tosiyasu L. KUNII

Department of Information Science
The University of Tokyo
Tokyo, Japan

1989

NORTH-HOLLAND
AMSTERDAM • NEW YORK • OXFORD • TOKYO

PREFACE

Information processing has been evolving from numerical computation to character handling, and now to visual information processing. Likewise, database systems as the means for information sharing are also progressing along this line. Fairly large amount and complex structure of visual information make visual database systems both storage and computation intensive. Now, the storage and processing power barrier is removed by the recent advancement of workstations with very large memory and files and powerful processors. Also rapidly increasing social demand for multimedia databases is putting visual databases in a position of indispensability for everybody.

Considering the situation mentioned above, visual database systems now worth serious studies for basic understanding and for practical applications. The volume is the result of IFIP TC-2's effort to initiate the studies by sponsoring a working conference on the subject, organized by IFIP WG 2.6 on database, and co-sponsored by Information Processing Society of Japan and Department of Information Science, Faculty of Science, The University of Tokyo. It contains 4 invited and 19 submitted papers by the researchers working in this field, all peer reviewed.

The areas covered include pictorial database, multimedia databases, object-oriented databases, visual structures, visual data models, model-driven approach, solid model-based databases, database design, prototyping and user-interfaces. Organizing the working conference and editing the proceedings volume have given me the pleasure of looking into these rapidly progressing and changing areas in detail after almost 20 years of my own research on the subject. As you observe after reading the papers, the size and complexity of visual databases still leave many somewhat obscure parts for understanding the subject. It is also true that such obscurity of the subject is a source of attraction for further research.

Tosiyasu L. Kunii
Editor

TABLE OF CONTENTS

ORGANIZATION AND SPONSORSHIP

Organized by IFIP Working Group WG 2.6

Sponsored by IFIP TC-2

Co-sponsored by
Information Processing Society of Japan
and
Department of Information Science, the University of Tokyo

Organizing Committees

Honorary Chairperson

Dr. Masanori Ozeki

Organizing Chairpersons

Tosiyasu L. Kunii
University of Tokyo

R.A. Meersman
Tilburg University

Program Co-Chairpersons

Tosiyasu L. Kunii
University of Tokyo

R.A. Meersman
Tilburg University

Local Arrangements Chairman

Yasuto Shirai
University of Tokyo

Program Committee

Shi-Kuo Chang
University of Pittsburgh

Alejandro P. Buchmann
CCA

Jose Encarnacao
Technische Hochschule, FRG

Tadao Ichikawa
Hiroshima University, Japan

Yahiko Kambayashi
Kyushu University, Japan

Allen Klinger
UCLA

Tosiyasu L. Kunii, Co-Chair
University of Tokyo

R.A. Meersman, Co-Chair
Tilburg University

Enrique H. Ruspini
SRI International

Daniel Thalmann
Ecole Polytechnique, Lausanne

Paul Thompson
CDC

Tony C. Woo
University of Michigan

Akinori Yonezawa
Tokyo Institute of Technology

EXTERNAL REFEREES

J. Andre	M. Maekawa
M. Azmoodeh	M. Managaki
M. Azuma	X. Mao
P. Boursier	S. Shimada
W. Cao	S. Mori
R.S. Davis	Z.M. Ozsoyoglu
M.J. Duerst	A. Rosenfeld
J.D. Foley	Y. Shirai
R.D. Hersch	Y. Shirota
D.K. Hsiao	Y. Takai
Y. Ichitawa	M. Tanaka
I. Fujishiro	N. Nakajima
K. Kanasaki	T. Noma
A. Kemper	S. Uemura
N. Kin	D. Woelk
H. Kitagawa	C.T. Wu
D. Krishnan	G. Wyvill
H.S. Kunii	K. Yamaguchi
Y.J. Lou	M.J. Zyda

Session 1

VISUAL STRUCTURES

Visual Database Systems
T.L. Kunii (Editor)
Elsevier Science Publishers B.V. (North-Holland)
© IFIP, 1989

Visual Structure and Data Bases

Allen Klinger and Arturo Pizano

Computer Science Department
University of California, Los Angeles

ABSTRACT

This paper deals with the interface between image data and descriptive files by identifying structure in visual data. We describe a range of image indexing methods usable in an interactive mode, and present examples relative to two problem areas, "geographic" and "sketch", that have different processing requirements. "Geographic" refers to map and satellite image data, and "Sketch" to any simplified picture that models a more complex image. The results in this last area concern basic principles useful for general visual databases, because they present ways to create representations intermediary between the source data and a string index.

1. INTRODUCTION

This paper addresses the interface between visual images and language, to develop principles for storage and retrieval in image databases. We show that converting image data to descriptive files begins with identifying structure in visual data. We propose a standardized means to develop image-indexing methods: indices for keys to picture objects that will be aides facilitating the use of computer-stored pictorial records. We base this on a human directing computer-indexing, and call this process "identifying visual structure."

Previous computer literature described picture-indexing [1] through abstract concepts, including zooming. Recent work on specifying the human-computer interfaces emphasizes state transition diagrams [2], and graphics: menus, user interaction [3]. All three references utilize organization methods known as "chunking," [4], i.e., a type of hierarchical data organization that condenses information so that it can be recalled. We combine these approaches in the following discussion of using visual structure to index image databases. This research concerns methods for computer-addressable visual databases. We cover several related issues, not all in equal depth:

1.   Principles for transforming images into indices.

2.   Measures of search and retrieval efficiency.

3.   High level image descriptors.

4.   Systematic use of pictorial information.

5.   Standardization methods.

Since efficiency concerns speed, recall size set, and relevance of retrieved items, and this paper is not about an actual implementation, it is not possible to present experimental measurements. Clearly we need to measure the relation of index selection to these items, to evaluate database designs, especially for their effectiveness in different data domains.

Another method for data condensation is called level abstraction or semantic description. We need to know how analogous visual database indexing, condensing and abstracting methods impact recall relevance. Finally, we need to determine how to merge the following database design with the area based, string encoding, and descriptive language methods, discussed in [5-8]. The design draws upon the Entity-Relationship model [9] for database organization.

This paper presents our views of these issues based on investigations in two application domains. We began analyzing the problem of computer representation of visual structure by considering a field where there are several ways that real objects are described pictorially. For example, maps and satellite photographs both represent geographic regions: e.g. sections of cities and states. After examples based on geographic data we considered the general problem of stylized representation which involves the development of a simplified pictorial representation of an image, i.e., a sketch.

2. STRUCTURE AND SELECTION OF SYMBOLIC REPRESENTATION

Symbolic picture representations, i.e., encodings useful for retrieval queries, involve structure detail and relationships that meet human needs. This section concerns ways that they can be closer. We consider the geographic picture types and illustrate varied manners for composing indices. These indices are intermediaries between a human and a visual database, consisting of actual images.

In any database there must be a multiplicity of referencing mechanisms. Thus at one level this paper explores how to build strings able to convey several kinds of data. Specifically, we need to include descriptors of structural relationships (adjacency, inclusion, etc..), class membership (colors, materials, etc.), and symbol types (as in maps, signs, or schematic designs).

The above issues are complicated by the way humans aggregate and condense data. Compound name items are recalled by initials of individual words - UNESCO for United Nations Education Scientific and Cultural Organization. In [4] Miller discusses simplification by "... formation of chunks, ... groups of items that go together, until there are few enough chunks so that we can recall all the items," originating the concept of chunking. Chunking is made difficult by the visual image to computer storage interface. For example, general word strings may include text like "blue region (sky) above [green area (forest) next to grey zone (road)]." In this set of words parenthesis separators give likely interpretations of prior text, and brackets denote grouping or inclusion. This is a structure, an organization we will build on in this paper. Picture data has a wide range of complexity. Yet simple organization forms enable significant image database organization.

We will organize pictorial data to enable retrieval from queries, basing our approach on geographic data examples. Geographical databases need to describe real objects in several ways. For example, states, counties and cities, are presented as regions in maps and satellite imagery

Users must be able to describe classes of picture objects in the database. However, this also requires use of non-pictorial objects i.e., representations of real world entities that must be included in the database. For example, an official, say a governor of a state, is a non-pictorial object associated to one or several pictorial records.

An object must have attributes that distinguish it from other objects. These attributes may be pictorial (e.g. color, position, dimensions,...), or non-pictorial (e.g. names, dates, amounts,...). Objects described by the same set of attributes are grouped into classes. Typical object classes likely to be found in a geographic environment include: states, cities and roads. Attributes for these classes are (name, boundaries, population), (name, location, mayor), and (road-number, capacity and path) respectively. Clearly the symbolic representation should have a distinctive format. We propose a format based on a tripartite decomposition of the data, that involves many linguistic elements.

Every pictorial attribute has a non-pictorial representation. For example, the color of an object may be encoded in strings such as pair of integers (X,Y); and pixel values are seen as triplets (X,Y, grey-level). Encoded values providing non-pictorial descriptions of pictorial data may be included directly as qualification fields in a symbolic description of a picture. The "blue region", the "green area" and the "grey road" above are expressions that can be mapped directly into the database by associating the values 'blue', 'green' and 'grey' with the color attribute of the objects being qualified. We will further exploit this property in section 5.

Non-pictorial representations of pictorial attributes may be unsuitable for symbolic picture descriptions. For example consider state boundaries in a digitized map. Boundary coordinates, describing a polygon, complete a state description but at too low a level, i.e. the detail obscures the concept. It is possible to map the polygon coordinate values to strings of the form $"(X_1,Y_1),(X_2,Y_2),...,(X_n,Y_n)"$, but this is not useful for high level descriptive expressions. Nevertheless this data is needed for fine discrimination. Hence our overall design allows both high-level (text) descriptors and detail (coordinate values, picture elements, etc). We now describe the basic design in some detail.

2.1. Conceptual Model

Visual structure is so varied that the only way to create a model that is uniformly applicable is to focus on solely geometric relationships. Although extensions to [1] found in [4, pp. 121-260] and elsewhere provide useful approaches to image indexing, we believe that another starting point is needed. This section provides the background for the indexing techniques to be discussed in the remainder of the paper. It describes the conceptual model, an abstraction of the database that presents users a picture view that is independent of its physical organization.

Briefly, conceptual models are rooted in database design. They consist of regularly organized logical records or headers associated with the contents of a database. In this work, these records capture any aspects of a picture useful for retrieval queries. Thus for both the geographic and the sketch cases, we can use a conceptual model based on pictorial entities, relationships and attributes. *Entities* are abstractions of real world objects as seen by the user; *relationships* are associations between entities; and *attributes* are abstractions of the properties that describe an entity or relationship. Entities or relationships that are described by the same set of attributes are grouped into entity-sets or relationship-sets respectively. The basic constructs in this model are pattern after Chen's Entity-Relationship (ER) Model [9]. However, as will become apparent in the remainder of this paper, there are important extensions needed to satisfy the needs of pictorial data management. These extensions were not considered in the original proposal.

To illustrate this idea consider the region map shown in shown in Fig. 1. A conceptual view of this picture would involve three entity-sets: cities, counties and roads. Relationships between entities in these sets could be grouped into the following relationship sets: "[city] located-in [county]", "[road] crosses [city]", and "[road] intersects [road]". The following table shows some typical attributes for these entities and relationships, with attribute types indicated in parentheses.

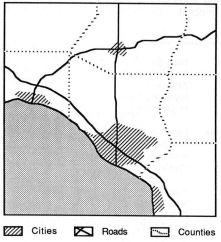

    Cities   Roads   Counties

Figure 1. A Digitized Region Map.

From Table 1 (maps example), the conceptual model of a picture does not correspond to the way it is internally organized. This conceptual view contains information external to the picture, e.g. the names and populations of the cities and counties, and the types of the roads. It also contains information not directly available in the picture but that can be derived from it, e.g. the area of a city or county, the path of a road, or the crossing point of a pair of highways.

We now turn to representation issues.

2.2. Symbolic Header Structure

A symbolic header is a data structure that establishes a liaison between: 1) the conceptual model of a picture, 2) external information provided by the user, and 3) the picture itself. Note that item 2) places the user's preferences in the underlying computer records governing future image retrieval. This is an essential step in our view; it provides an essential difference between this work and past efforts.

Symbolic headers serve as maps between the internal structure of a picture and high-level concepts understandable by the end-user. This is seen with reference to a conceptual model of a pictorial database. The conclusion that we present new methods is supported by the data structure or symbolic header detail. As we shall see this support answers to queries by mappings from text to indices.

Symbolic headers provide a top down characterization of visual data that enables database queries to retrieve only a limited subset of pictorial records from a file. A top down characterization of a set of pictures requires time consuming human input for each item. This is less of an obstacle than it seems because for many applications much of what is needed is already present in noncomputer records. In order to make the best possible use of existing information we have designed our headers to contain slots for three basic kinds of information: entities, relationships, and auxiliary knowledge.

A block diagram presenting an overview of the symbolic header appears as Fig. 2. There, each basic kind of information shown is allotted a set of contiguous words. Subsequent sections discuss these in detail.

Cities	Name (string)
	Boundaries (polygon)
	Area (real)
	Population (integer)
	Mayor (string)
Counties	Name (string)
	Boundaries (polygon)
	Area (real)
	Population (integer)
Roads	Number (integer)
	Type (constant e.g. 'interstate', 'state', 'divided',...)
	Path (line set)
	Length (real)
Intersects	Road_1 (Road)
	Road_2 (Road)
	Crossing point (point)
Crosses	Road (Road)
	City (City)
	Crossing_segment (line set)

Table 1. Conceptual View of a Digitized Regional Map.

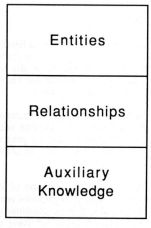

Figure 2. Symbolic Header.

3. ENTITIES AND ATTRIBUTES

In this section we describe methods for including query oriented information concerning picture objects. Specific objects are isolated entities and their attributes. We chose to emphasize them in our design by placing them at the beginning of the symbolic header data organization. This section continues with a detailed presentation of methods we propose to use to organize this information. We indicate the concepts through a design that is presented by a series of figures. The first of these, the entity block of the symbolic header detail, is shown in Fig. 3. We now turn to presentation and discussion of the specifics of the entity block itself.

The entity block first contains sub-blocks associated with distinct entity-sets: see Fig. 3a. Each sub-block corresponds to a conceptual model entity-set. A single entity-set sub-block has an internal organization that displays both user-oriented descriptions (entity-set headers) and individual occurrences (entity-detail): see Fig. 3b. To make this concrete, one distinct entity-set is cities. That term appears in the subsequent header and it in turn is followed by several named cities (San Diego, Santa Barbara, Los Angeles).

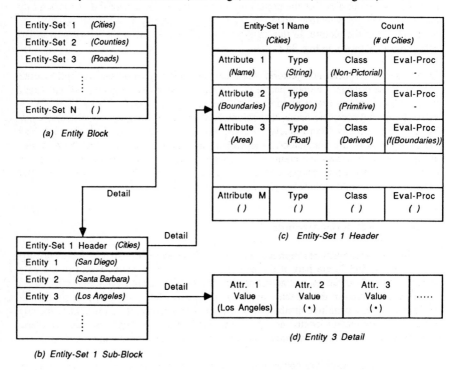

Figure 3   Entity Record Structure

The entity-set header is itself a user-oriented record. This item is broken into detail in Fig. 3c. It contains an entity-set name, an occurrence count, and a list of attribute descriptions. Specific records follow this format and give detail of each occurrence. Fig. 3d shows detail of the L.A. entry.

We distinguish four kinds of attribute description fields: names, types, class, and complexity. *Names* are human coinages that identify the property represented by the attribute. *Types* are geometric extensions of the common program term. Some particular kinds are string, integer, polygon, and point. *Class* refers to conceptual (non-pictorial), primitive, and derived information. For an example of conceptual class we have "metropolis", i.e., a city of several million people. A primitive item is directly observable in an image. They are discussed in the sections below in some detail; for a rough idea, think of the image conveyed by "twin cities". Derived data are found from functions of images.

3.1. Non-pictorial Attributes

Non-pictorial properties like the population of a city, the year a road was built, or a city mayor's name are valuable image indices, whose values are provided by the user separately from the picture. In this design these values are stored as the first part of the entity detail, as shown in Fig. 3d.

Entity labels are special non-pictorial attributes that uniquely associate real world names with database objects. The city name, county name, and highway number all are labels that could be used to select picture records containing the specified item. Their values may a be formal complete name, its abbreviation, or an informal equivalent (nickname). For example, the city "San Francisco" is also named by "S.F." and "SF"; likewise "San Fran" or "'Frisco" are understood to represent that place. "Boundary" and "population" are other attribute names less commonly used but serving equally well as identifying picture indices. Only a few images would be retrieved if either of them were specified, and very likely one would include the place sought.

3.2. Primitive Pictorial Attributes

Primitive pictorial attributes represent properties that can 1) be found in the picture by simple means, and 2) are part of the physical organization of the picture. For example county and city boundaries, and actual road paths, are all primitive attributes; they would be physically stored in the database as either polygons or line sets. A human could indicate presence of a primitive attribute in an image. For instance, the statements: "the city center is approximately located at (x,y)," "the line begins near (x,y)," or "a circle of radius r, centered near (x,y) lies entirely inside blob B," all describe primitive attributes.

Real world image primitives correspond exactly to pictorial attributes in an ideal map or design drawing; they are distinguished from those that a human could not directly locate, but that could be computed.

Primitive pictorial attribute values are not stored in the symbolic header. Instead the corresponding entity detail attribute field contains a pointer to their location in the physical picture. The exact form of this pointer depends on the type of picture being represented. For example, if the picture is internally organized as a grid, the pointer could be any set of values that determine the boundaries of the entity in the picture.

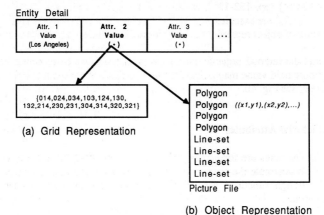

(a) Grid Representation

(b) Object Representation

Figure 4. Primitive Attribute Representation.

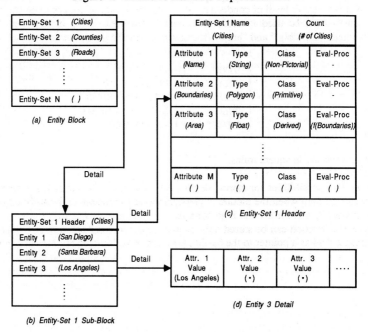

Figure 5. Quadtree Representation of a Region.

Fig. 4a depicts a pointer into the city of "Los Angeles" using a linear quadtree representation of the city boundaries. This string is an encoding of the black leaf nodes of the quadtree that describes the region occupied by the city in the image; see Fig. 5. This technique, described in [4] (pp. 133-135), is based on a location code, a base 4 number in which the values 0,1,2,3 are associated with the NW, NE, SW and SE quadrants. A more in-depth discussion of object representation techniques is given in [6].

If we assume that the internal organization of the picture follows an object-oriented approach, the attribute field value may point directly to the location in the picture file where the entity is stored; see Fig. 4b.

3.3. Derived Pictorial Attributes

Derived pictorial attributes are formed by applying mathematical functions to primitive attribute values. For example the area of a city and the length of a road are derived attributes obtained through functions applied to the boundaries and path values of the corresponding entities.

We believe it would be useful to define derived pictorial attributes in user-oriented terms. Such terms could be achieved by applying mathematical functions to derived attributes. This obtains a further level of condensation of pictorial information. For example, county area values could be used to create text county size descriptors of the form "tiny," "small," "medium," "big," and "huge". The following formula serves this purpose:

$$Size = \begin{cases} \text{'TINY'} & \text{if } area < 100 \\ \text{'SMALL'} & \text{if } 100 < area < 1000 \\ \text{'MEDIUM'} & \text{if } 1{,}000 < area < 10{,}000 \\ \text{'BIG'} & \text{if } 10{,}000 < area < 100{,}000 \\ \text{'HUGE'} & \text{if } area > 100{,}000 \end{cases}$$

where all areas are in square miles.

There are two possibilities for storing derived attribute values in a symbolic header. One is to compute them when the picture is loaded, storing the results in the attribute field of the entity detail; and the second is to store the function that generates the value. In this last case, the function can be stored only once in the entity-set header, using the value of the attribute field as a pointer to the header field where the function is defined; see Fig. 6.

Entity-Set Header

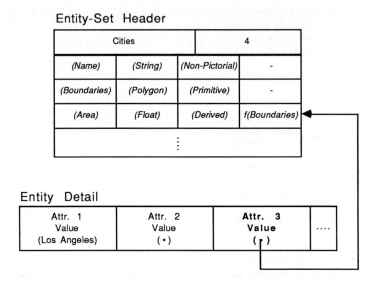

Entity Detail

Attr. 1 Value (Los Angeles)	Attr. 2 Value (•)	Attr. 3 Value (ρ)	....

Figure 6. Derived Attribute Representation.

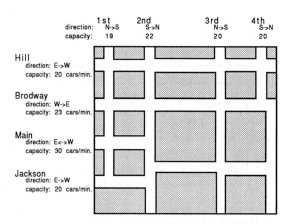

Figure 7. City Street Map.

3.4. Uninstantiated Entity-Sets

In some cases, the number of occurrences in a pictorial entity-set is so large that it becomes impractical to have every single occurrence identified separately. Yet, those entities exist in the picture, and have properties of interest in the application domain. We propose using uninstantiated entity-sets to deal with this problem. This section describes that process.

We illustrate the idea be considering the street map depicted in Fig. 7. The map displays two types of entities: streets and blocks. Streets form a regular entity set because their occurrences must be stored as part of the picture. On the other hand, blocks may be defined as uninstantiated entities. Block occurrences are found by the procedure presented in Fig. 8.

```
Find-Block(North-Street, East-Street, West-Street, South-Street) {
    return( Intersection(North-Street, West-Street)
            Intersection(North-Street, East-Street)
            Intersection(South-Street, West-Street)
            Intersection(South-Street, East-Street)
        ) }
```

Figure 8. Block-Finding Procedure.

To the user, and at the database conceptual level, uninstantiated entity-sets are regular entity-sets. Internally, however, the entities in these sets have no distinguishable attributes. Instead, they are given by means of pattern recognition procedures. In other words, the entity detail part of the symbolic header is used for an algorithm, replacing the observed attributes otherwise there. This is shown in Fig. 9.

```
Entity-Set  Header    (Blocks)

Find_Block (N_St, S_St,...){
      return (Intersection(...)
              Intersection(...)
                        ⋮
    ) }
```

Figure 9. Uninstantiated Entity-Set Detail.

Note that the procedure returns values that define the position of the block in the picture. In general, this is a requirement of all pattern recognition procedures associated with uninstantiated entity-sets. Values locating a pictorial entity will be considered primitive attributes and will be declared as part of the entity-set header. Furthermore, these attributes can be used to compose derived attributes. For examples of derived attributes, consider "block area", "perimeter", and, more generally, "shape".

4. RELATIONSHIPS

In this section we discuss the means to organize information concerning associations between entities in the picture. We discuss in detail the relationship block of the symbolic header, using for this purpose the diagram shown in Fig. 10. Several sub-blocks, each associated with a different relationship-sets, are distinguished in Fig. 10a. Each sub-block corresponds to a conceptual model relationship-set. The relationship-set sub-block organization is similar to that for entity-set. Fig. 10b shows that this plan supports both user-oriented set descriptions (relationship-set headers), and individual relationship occurrences (relationship detail).

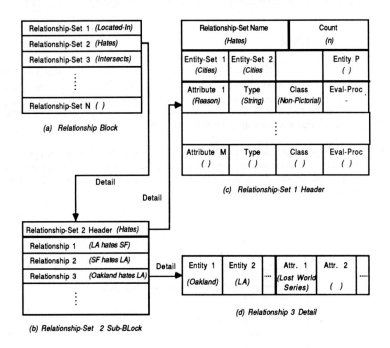

Figure 10.   Relationship Record Structure.

The relationship-set header is a user-oriented record. It consists of name, count, list (participating entity-sets), and attribute fields; see Fig. 10c. The remaining records in the sub-block contain details of actual relationship occurrences.

Relationship attribute definitions follow the same structure of their entity counterparts. Names associate attributes with the real world property they represent. Types describe internal attribute structures. Attribute classes are again non-pictorial, pictorial primitive and pictorial derived. Evaluation procedures describe non-pictorial attributes. However we find it necessary to classify two kinds of relationships: (1) non-pictorial, and (2) spatial (pictorial). Both are described in the following.

4.1. Non-pictorial Relationships

Non-pictorial relationships are associations between entities that exist independent of their position in the picture. For example: "[city x] shares-police-departments-with [city y]," "[city x] (natives) hate [city y] (natives)," or "[city x] receives-money-from [county y]." Non-pictorial relationships are established by the user. They are recorded in the symbolic header as part of the relationship detail. For an example refer to Fig. 10d.

4.2. Spatial Relationships

Spatial relationships are associations that exist between pictorial entities because of their relative position in the picture. For example, "left," "right," "above," "below," "close," "far," "distance," "intersection," "overlap," etc. Spatial relationships are built-in the picture. For instance the fact that Anaheim "is-located-in" Orange County may be deduced from the picture; it does not have to be recorded separately.

Because of this property, the definition of spatial relationships must be accompanied by a function describing how their occurrences are found in the picture. This function is stored in the detail portion of the relationship-set sub-block, replacing individual entity occurrences otherwise located there, as shown in Fig. 11.

```
┌─────────────────────────────────────────────────┐
│ Relationship-Set  Header          (Blocks)       │
├─────────────────────────────────────────────────┤
│   Above (E1, E2) {                               │
│       if (E1.center.y > E2.center.y              │
│           return (TRUE)                          │
│       else                                       │
│           return (FALSE)                         │
│   }                                              │
└─────────────────────────────────────────────────┘
```

Figure 11. Spatial Relationship Detail.

We note that there are several kinds of functions that define spatial relationships: 1) Boolean functions, 2) attribute functions, 3) entity functions, and 4) entity-attribute functions. We explain these below.

4.2.1. Boolean Functions

Boolean functions are used to determine the existence of a relationship among a given set of entities. The general form of these functions is:

$$f(E_1, E_2, \ldots, E_n) = \begin{cases} TRUE & \text{if the relationship exists} \\ \\ FALSE & \text{otherwise} \end{cases}$$

where E_i is an entity identifier.

The following function, describing the relationship "[city] north-of [city]," illustrates this case. We assume that a new derived attribute "center" has been defined for city entities. City centers correspond to the centroid of the region occupied by the city in the picture.

$$north\text{-}of(City_1, City_2) = \begin{cases} TRUE & \text{if } City_1.center.y > City_2.center.y \\ \\ FALSE & \text{otherwise} \end{cases}$$

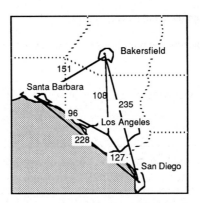

Figure 12.   City Names and Distances.

Table 2 illustrates how the relationship "north-of" would be perceived at the conceptual level. The entries in this table are based on the labeling of city entities shown in Fig. 12. Notice the transitivity property of the relationship reflected in the table.

City_1	City_2
Bakersfield	Santa Barabara
Bakersfield	Los Angeles
Bakersfield	San Diego
Santa Barbara	Los Angeles
Santa Barbara	San Diego
Los Angeles	San Diego

Table 2.   "North-of" Relationship.

4.2.2. Attribute Functions

Attribute functions are extensions of Boolean functions in which particular properties of the relationship are determined in addition to its existence. The values returned by these functions become attributes of the relationship. When the relationship among the given entities does not exist, the attribute set is empty. Attribute functions have the following general form:

$$f(E_1, E_2, \ldots, E_n) = (A_1, \ldots, A_n)$$

where E_i is an entity identifier, and A_j is an attribute.

The relationship "distance-between-city-centers," described by the following formula illustrates this case.

$$Distance(City_1, City_2) = \sqrt{(City_1.x - City_2.x)^2 + (City_1.y - City_2.y)^2}$$

City_1	City_2	d
Bakersfield	Santa Barabara	151
Bakersfield	Los Angeles	108
Bakersfield	San Diego	235
Santa Barbara	Los Angeles	96
Santa Barbara	San Diego	228
Los Angeles	San Diego	127

Table 3.   "Distance" Relationship.

Table 3 shows the conceptual view of this relationship. Notice that the previous function computes the distance between two points based on the Euclidean formula. Other metrics, e.g. city-block, or parameters, e.g. the closest point, could also have been used.

In general, the number of relationships that exist in a picture is too large to be predefined. The symbolic header provides an extensible mechanism that allows tailoring visual structure to the needs of a particular user or application domain.

4.2.3. Entity Functions

Boolean and attribute functions determine the existence of a relationship given a complete list of participating entities. Entity functions find entities that satisfy a relationship given a partial list of participating entities. The values returned by these function are identifiers of relationships that satisfy the relationship. Entity functions have the following general form:

$$f(E_1, E_2, \ldots, E_k) = (E_{k+1}, E_{k+2}, \ldots, E_n)$$

where E_i is an entity identifier.

For example the relationship "[city] nearest [city x]" can be defined by the formula:

$$Nearest\_City(City_1) = (City_2)$$

where the actual implementation of the formula is chosen by the user. Table 4 illustrates the materialization of this relationship in the conceptual model.

City_1	City_2
Bakersfield	Los Angeles
Santa Barbara	Los Angeles
Los Angeles	Santa Barbara
San Diego	Los Angeles

Table 4. "Nearest-City" Relationship.

4.2.4. Entity-Attribute Functions

Entity-attribute functions are an extension of entity functions that allow the definition of relationships with attributes. The general form of these functions is given by the following formula:

$$f(E_1, E_2, \ldots, E_k) = (E_{k+1}, E_{k+2}, \ldots, E_n, A_1, A_2, \ldots, A_m,)$$

where E_i is an entity identifier and A_j is an attribute.

As an example of entity-attribute functions consider the relationship "[city] farthest-to [city x]" and assume that the distance between the cities is a property of interest. The following function, materialized in Table 5 for the map in Fig. 12, defines this relationship:

$$Farthest\_City(City_1) = (City_2, d)$$

City_1	City_2	d
Bakersfield	San Diego	235
Santa Barbara	San Diego	228
Los Angeles	San Diego	127
San Diego	Bakersfield	235

Table 5.   "Farthest-to" Relationship.

4.3. Choosing a Function

Relationships can be described by more than one type of function. For example, Nearest_City was represented earlier in this section with an entity function. It could have also been represented by the following Boolean function:

$$Nearest\_City(City_1, City_2) = \begin{cases} TRUE & \text{iff } d(City_i, City_j) , \, d(City_i, City_k) \text{ for each } k \neq i, j \\ \\ FALSE & \text{otherwise} \end{cases}$$

where $d(City_i, City_j)$ is the Euclidean distance between two city centers.

There are advantages and disadvantages to the use of each definition. For example, a query that requests the name of the nearest city for a given city can be answered more efficiently if Nearest_City is implemented as a entity function. On the other hand, a query that only tests if two cities are nearest neighbors would be better answered by the Boolean function defined above. This selection of the function should not be noticed at the conceptual level, except for possible performance effects.

Another performance motivated element would be the implementation of pre-evaluated functions, that could be stored as look-up tables in the symbolic header. This feature would be specially useful in dealing with pictures in which entities seldom, or never, change positions. Some important types of pictures that would fall into this category include LANDSAT images and digitized X-ray charts.

5. AUXILIARY KNOWLEDGE

There is knowledge about picture contents that is independent of entities and relationships. We call such knowledge *auxiliary,* and place it in a third block of the symbolic header. An example of auxiliary information is about the contents of a picture. This information includes aggregated values, that is, any data summarizing overall picture contents. Examples are: geographic: number of cities, largest county, average city area; design: number of gates, average fan-out, number of subsystems; sketch: number of straight lines, number of enclosed areas, area of largest size region. We store such information as auxiliary knowledge, that is, as items located by traversing pointers located in the third block of the symbolic header.

Significant research on converting pictorial data to strings appears in a variety of sources. Two references to that literature, [5] and [7], present this via the term *visual language;* for example, see [5, Ch. 7, pp. 262-300]. In section 5.2 we discuss the inclusion of descriptive strings, that locate icons or actual image entities in a pictorial record, in the auxiliary information category.

5.1. Aggregation

There are two picture aggregation data types: overall, and localized. The first refers to measures that are derived from an entire image, as the number of cities in a (map) scene. The second, may be area-based, as in either half or quadrant decompositions, e.g., "the left part contains no tumors, the right has a small one at ..."; in other words, localized picture aggregates describe the contents of restricted regions. The connection of the second data type to quadtree data structure is readily apparent.

We believe that aggregate information can be obtained by automatic generation methods. In doing so, we make use of default conditions. For example the entity count included in the entity set header. We also employ user defined functions to develop aggregate information. This functions employ a series of standard operations (e.g SUM, COUNT, MAX, MIN, AVG,...) that are applied to specific attributes of entities or relationship sets. In other words, many of the aggregate information items are found by employing elements of a set of restored procedural rules: picture functions.

5.2. Labeling

Practical differences regarding internal labels for image data arise that cause a need for specifying two possible modes for string generation. These modes are preexisting, and iconic. The first refers to the existence of entities that are already labeled. One instance, that explains the nature of the design question, is the case of a city whose name is the most appropriate string to associate to portions of an aerial photograph that includes the city area. Clearly, there is no intrinsic reason (within the actual photograph) for the city name to be available to a computer as a string, so making that association requires a user's input. Alternatively, in the case of a sketch, items may be present that are immediately identifiable. Coke bottles, highway stop signs, crescent moons are all sufficiently distinctive shapes that their presence in an image can be identified. This can give rise to "specific icon j is present" triggers, and such flags can be the basis of strings labels that are best located in our view in sub-blocks reached from the symbolic header by pointers from its auxiliary data region.

The following are some specific instances and characteristics of each of these kinds of auxiliary data. In the situation where preexisting labels are known, the individual has the duty to use them. Some such cases where entities are specifically labeled are those we have been using in the geographic case. For example, cities and counties, labeled by their names, and highways labeled by their numbers, are entities usually associated with concrete objects in the picture. They have a potentially large number of occurrences (there are certainly a hundred cities in a US map), and therefore any string descriptors of the pictures that contain them must be based on aggregate information such as that described in section 5.1.

By contrast, when there are no preexisting names, it may be necessary to decide whether a generic term is useful. For instance, a dirigible may be well represented by a database string that simply says "elliptical" since that is a fairly uncommon shape. Thus, the name of a pictorial icon is an example of a generic term useful for strings that describe sketches. Such strings may involve several terms of that sort and their relationships. As a general image is reduced to a sketch, or a stylized sketch is included in a pictorial database, entities may be assigned generic labels; some examples are car, house, person. The usual situation is that there will be only a small number of entities, in a sketch, and usually very few from the same class.

We will now illustrate how database access to sketch pictures is supported by the symbolic header. In particular we will show how uninstantiated entity-sets and spatial relationships can be used to build strings that serve as global indices. These indices are stored as part of the auxiliary knowledge block.

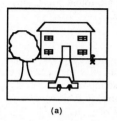 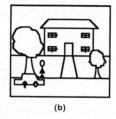 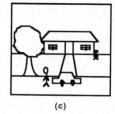

(a) (b) (c)

Figure 13. Sample Sketches.

Fig. 13 presents three sketches of digitized photographs. Internally, these pictures are represented as sets of lines without any structure. To a human, however, they may symbolize scenes based on the following conceptual model:

Entities (attributes):

Houses (shape, type)
Trees   (shape, area, size)
Cars   (shape, color)
People   (shape, height, complexion)

Relationships:

[trees] located (with respect to) [houses]
[people] near [cars]
[cars] in_front_of [houses]
[people] close-to [houses]

There are two ways in which symbolic headers may be used to support this conceptual model: 1) assign a symbolic header to each picture in the database, as we did in the geographic examples; or 2) define a generic symbolic header associated with a collection of sketches described by the same conceptual model.

The first alternative is appropriate, and indeed necessary, whenever individual instances of an entity or relationship set must be explicitly identified. In other words, when there are concrete indices into the contents of the sketch. The second alternative is adequate only if every entity-set is uninstantiated, and the only relationships allowed are spatial or can be computed. We pursue here the latter approach, assuming that in our example sketches are the highest level of pictorial indices that have a concrete representation in the database.

Figures 14 and 15 illustrate the entity and relationship blocks of the symbolic header for our sample sketches. Notice that both entity and relationship details contain procedures and functions instead of actual occurrences. The point of constructing this type of structure is that a systematic evaluation of the entity-finding procedures and spatial relationship functions can be used to generate strings of the form:

(qualifier) [ENTITY] "relationship" (qualifier) [ENTITY]

to be stored in the auxiliary knowledge block. These strings form a catalog of user-oriented indices into the original pictures. Although they are not complete scene descriptions. The following are strings generated from the sketches in Fig. 13. We assume that derived attributes are as shown in Table 6.

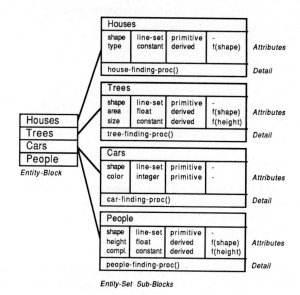

Figure 14. Sketch Entity Block.

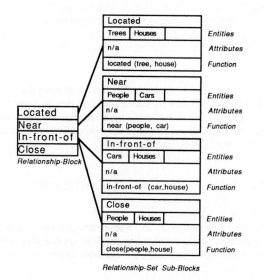

Figure 15. Sketch Relationship Block.

From Fig. 13a:

(big) [TREE] "located" (left-of) (two-story) [HOUSE]
(red) [CAR] "in-front-of" (two-story) [HOUSE]
(short) [PERSON] "close-to" (two-story) [HOUSE]

From Fig. 13b:

(big) [TREE] "located" (left-of) (two-story) [HOUSE]
(small) [TREE] "located" (left-of) (two-story) [HOUSE]
(tall) [PERSON] "near" (red) [CAR]

From Fig. 13c:

(big) [TREE] "located" (left-of) (one-story) [HOUSE]
(red) [CAR] "in-front-of" (one-story) [HOUSE]
(short) [PERSON] "close-to" (one-story) [HOUSE]
(tall) [PERSON] "near" [CAR]

Entity	Attribute	Source	Values
House	type	shape	"ONE-STORY" or "TWO-STORY"
Tree	area	shape	
Tree	size	area	"BIG" if area>X; "SMALL" otherwise
People	height	shape	
People	complexion	height	"TALL" if height>6 ft.; "SHORT" otherwise

Table 6.   Derived Attributes for the Sketch Example..

6. CONCLUSIONS

Visual structure is central to database indexing, and to user interaction via computers with pictorial data. further research and development on the indexing issue is needed to make image databases useful to broad classes of users. Language can introduce patterns and methods for creating image indices. Computer representation of the complexities of real imagery require string-encodings of both property (feature) and relationship (structure) data. It also involves high-level textual descriptors that serve as global indices into the contents of an image.

In this paper we discussed visual structure at two different levels. First, the conceptual model provides the means for users to view images and related textual data in terms of the real world objects and relationships of the application domain. Then we showed visual structure at the representation level, through the symbolic header data structure that supports the mapping of the conceptual view into physical organization.

In building the symbolic header we considered the mismatch that exists between the level at which data is viewed by the user and its actual internal representation. Thus we described the use of derived attributes as a form of pictorial "chunking" in which very detailed pictorial data (e.g. pixel intensities) is condensed into human understandable concepts (e.g. area). Through the use of uninstantiated entity-sets we incorporated certain pattern recognition mechanisms are part of the indexing mechanisms in a manner that is transparent to the end user.

In geographic data we saw the need to handle pictures with potentially large numbers of specifically labeled entities, that were concretely represented in the pictures. In sketches we addressed pictures with small numbers of entities associated with generic labels. The conceptual model and symbolic header were equally applicable in both realms.

There are several directions in which this research may be extended. Three of the most promising, in no particular order, are: 1) building a conceptual language interface on top of the symbolic header; 2) studying the use of the symbolic header as a vehicle for providing transparent access to pictorial data from conventional database systems; and 3) extending the symbolic header to support conceptual models involving multiple pictures.

References.

[1] Chang, S.K. and Liu, S.H., "Picture Indexing and Abstraction Techniques for Pictorial Databases," *IEEE Trans. on Pattern Analysis Mach. Intell., PAMI-6,* 1984, 475-484.

[2] Jacob, Robert J.K., "Using Formal Specifications in the Design of a Human-Computer Interface," *C. ACM, 26,* April, 1983, 259-264.

[3] Myers, B. A., "Creating User Interfaces by Demonstration," Ph. D. dissertation, Univ. of Toronto, TR CSRI-196.

[4] Miller, G. A., "The Magical Number Seven Plus or Minus Two: Some Limits on Our Capacity for Processing Information", *The Psychological Review, 63,* 1956, 81 - 97.

[5] Chang, S.K., *Principles of Pictorial Information Systems Design,* Engelwood Cliffs, New Jersey: Prentice Hall, 1989.

[6] Rosenfeld, A., "Image Analysis: Problems, Progress and Prospects," *Pattern Recognition, Vol. 17,* No.1, 1984.

[7] Chang, S.K., Ichikawa, A. and Ligomenides A., (Eds.), *Visual Languages,* New York Plenum Press 1986.

[8] Minsky, M. "Steps Towards Artificial Intelligence," *In Computers and Thought,* E.A. Feigenbaum and J. Feldman (Eds.), McGraw-Hill, New York, 1963.

[9] Chen, P., "The Entity-Relationship Model: Towards a Unified View of Data," *ACM Transactions on Database Systems, Vol. 1,* No. 1, March 1976.

Session 2

PROTOTYPING ENVIRONMENT

Visual Database Systems
T.L. Kunii (Editor)
Elsevier Science Publishers B.V. (North-Holland)
  IFIP, 1989

IMAGE-PROCESSING APPLICATION GENERATION ENVIRONMENT:
A LABORATORY FOR PROTOTYPING VISUAL DATA-BASES

P. Stucki and U. Menzi
Department of Computer Science
University of Zurich
8057 Zurich/Switzerland

1. INTRODUCTION

A Visual Data-Base (VDB) is defined as an indexed set of
text/image information representations covering a predetermined
application field. Unlike in the well established area of conventional Data-Base (DB) design, there is relatively little experience available in how to model and implement VDB systems.

In order to master this new level of sophistication, a VDB pro-
totyping-activity has been initialized at the Computer Graphics
Laboratory of the University of Zurich, with the objective of
acquiring knowledge for the design and the implementation of
VDB-systems in general. The test-bed used is the Image-Processing Application Generation Environment (I-PAGE), a hardware and
software laboratory-outfit that provides main-frame and distributed system services to build and design working models of
new text/image application scenarios [1].

A general-purpose VDB system that uses advanced terminals
and/or workstations, input/output raster periphery and appropriate software components for storage and retrieval of compound text/image documents can be structured around the following functional units:

Input: - Image Data Capture

              Digitizing documents and natural scenes and sto-
              ring their images using scanning and video frame
              grabbing subsystems.

              - Synthetic Image Generation

              Creating synthetic images using text processing
              and computer graphics tools.

Processing: - Text/Image Document Indexing and Data Filing

              Assigning catalog information to each text/image
              file and archiving the composite data structure in
              a storage subsystem.

Output: - *Text/Image Document Retrieval and Display*

Searching the catalog and selecting the compound
document file of interest for presentation at a
terminal or a workstation.

- *Text/Image Document Transmission and Printing*

Distributing compound document files over Local
Area Networks (LAN) and Wide Area Networks (WAN)
as well as to shared image printing subsystems.

The requirements to be met by the individual functional units
are very much VDB application dependent. This is true for the
requirements concerning the physical parameters of the various
data objects as well as for the conception of the VDB management system itself. For example, the quality requirements for
images may range from low-resolution, bi-level achromatic
representations to high-resolution, multi-level RGB color images, and the VDB management system requirements may span from
simple index structure models to very elaborate sets of pertinent information descriptions.

The purpose of this paper is to describe the approach taken and
the results obtained by using I-PAGE as a test-bed to develop
host-based VDB prototypes for application in the field of natural sciences.

2. HARDWARE AND SOFTWARE COMPONENTS OF I-PAGE

The hardware core of the I-PAGE based test-bed environment is a
main-frame system running under IBM´s Multiple Virtual System /
Time Sharing Option (MVS/TSO) and providing Graphical Data Display Manager (GDDM) services to drive a wide variety of IBM peripheral devices such as the 3179G color graphics terminal, the
3270 PC/AT-GX workstation and the 3852 color ink-jet convenience printer. The I-PAGE hardware also includes several to-
ken-ring host attached PC/AT-based imaging subsystems that support a video camera frame grabber, a color scanner for document
capture and a 640 x 560 x 24 Bit RGB controller unit for high
quality image display. A main-frame environment guarantees data
security through Remote Access Control Facility (RACF) features
and provides host-to-host data-communication based on System
Network Architecture (SNA) protocols.

The software core of I-PAGE is the Image Manipulation Application Generation Environment (IMAN/AGE) program product [2] that
consists of two independent software packages, the Image Manipulation Subsystem (IMSS) and the Application Definition Subsystem (ADSS), both running on the main-frame system.

The IMSS is used to prepare achromatic and color image data for
storage, retrieval and output on All-Point Addressable (APA)
displays and printers. The IMSS software is written in PL/1 and

requires the GDDM based Presentation Graphics Feature (PGF) package for the rendition of text/image documents on raster displays and printers as well as the Virtual Storage Access Method (VSAM) to access the image library.

The ADSS is a menu and panel-builder for interactive data entry and information retrieval applications, covering alphanumeric data and images. The ADSS software is written in APL (A Programming Language) and its prerequisites are the installation of the APL2 compiler, the APL Data Interface (DI) and the Application Prototype Environment (APE) packages [3]. The latter is an advanced application modeler that consists of a set of menu driven design tools to build sophisticated software applications quickly and at low cost.

In addition to these standard software components, I-PAGE includes a large number of self developed main-frame and imaging subsystem programs to perform a variety of data transfer and digital image processing operations like geometric transforms and digital halftoning [4], linear and nonlinear filtering [5] and data compression [6].These programs are predominantly coded in PL/1 and C.

3. DOCUMENT MODELING

The design of appropriate data structures for the administration of documents in a VDB system is of primary importance. Compared with the structure of objects in conventional information retrieval systems, the structure of so-called multi-media documents are more elaborate as they contain a number of components that carry different types of information. For example, a multi-media document can be composed of data, text, graphics and image and perhaps even contain features to accommodate voice annotation. Currently, a substantial amount of research is being conducted into the understanding of multi-media document-handling requirements and the development of corresponding architectures [7,8,9].

In general, the various components of a multi-media text/image document can be classified into active and passive components.

Active components, like for example text, may be used in queries that are provided by the access methods of the system. They serve to select and retrieve text/image documents from an archive. Passive components, like for example scanned and/or synthetic images, do not appear in any query process yet as today's technique for real-time pattern recognition is not sufficiently developed.

In practice, active components are further subdivided into structured and unstructured information.

Structured information is composed of features that describe the text/image document using the concept of attributes that are manually assigned or indexed. In practice, the content and the configuration of attributes generally varies according to the nature and the application origin of the text/image document. It is therefore important that the corresponding data structures can be adapted accordingly.

The model of the text/image documents used for the VDB application prototyping effort described in this paper is shown in Figure 1.

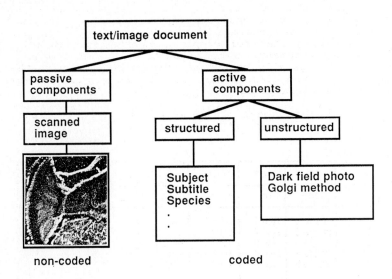

Fig.1   Text/image document model.

4. INFORMATION RETRIEVAL AND THE RELATIONAL DATA MODEL

The choice of an appropriate information retrieval system can be based on quantitative and qualitative criteria. Enumerations with respect to the first group are statements concerning the system response behavior and the number of stored objects. Related to the second group is primarily the response quality of a query. The precision of a response is defined as the ratio between the selected number of relevant data objects and the total number of selected data object. The ideal situation exists whenever this ratio gets as close as possible to one. This can be obtained with perfectly defined criteria for attribute selection and assignment during the indexing operation and a well defined formulation of the query.

The attribute selection or indexing that describes a document is a key operation in any VDB application. There exists techniques that allow the automatic assignment of indexes [10]. However, such an approach requires the implementation of text/image understanding or pattern recognition concepts, i.e.

artificial intelligence techniques which proof not yet feasible
in practice. Therefore, the attribute selection in VDB´s remains still a truly manual operation that uses a dictionary
containing a predefined attribute list. In the case of scientific applications, the creation of an appropriate thesaurus is
a process that generally requires deep professional knowledge.

Today, the conventional DB-designer has basically the choice of
four different logical data models [11]. They all represent a
different form of a data system, i.e., they underlay a hierarchical, network, relational or object oriented structure. A
careful study of the characteristics of the different logical
data models shows that for proper exploitation of VDB´s in a
scientific environment, where sophisticated information retrieval queries usually cannot be formulated à priory, the implementation of the classical relational data model [12] proves
to be a reasonable approach.

The relational data model of documents that contain images can
be represented in form of a two-dimensional table (Tab.1).

Row#1	Row#2	Row#3	Row#4	Row#5	......	Row#n+3
Doc#	Image	Text	Attr#1	Attr#2		Attr#n
1	Image 1	Text 1	val.1.1	val.1.2		val.1.n
2	Image 2	Text 2	empty	val.2.2		val.2.n
3	Image 3	Text 3	val.3.1	empty		empty
4	Image 4	Text 4	val.4.1	empty		val.4.n
5	Image 5	Text 5	empty	val.5.2		val.5.n
.	.	.	.	.		.
.	.	.	.	.		.

Tab.1 Relational data model for VDB documents.

Each document is described by a n-tupel vector that contains
the various attributes, where the row assignment is as follows:

>   Row #1   Doc#   Document number (key)
>
>   Row #2   Image   Scanned R,G,B image (uncompressed)
>
>   Row #3   Text   Text string (comment)
>
>   Row #4   Attr#1   Attribute number 1
>
>   Row #5   Attr#2   Attribute number 2
>   .   .   .
>   .   .   .
>   Row #n+3   Attr#n   Attribute number n

5. VDB APPLICATION PROTOTYPING UNDER I-PAGE

The realization of a VDB storage and retrieval application requires the implementation of the following main tasks: Application building, image capture and document indexing.

5.1 Application Building

Prior to the capture of document related data, appropriate display fields need to be defined that carry the attributes or indexes and their values of the individual text/image documents
stored on the main-frame system. The ergonomy of the man-
machine interface-design in VDB applications is very important
as, once in production, these systems will also be used by VDB
service and data entry operators without specific data processing skill and motivation.

The APE package provides a Menu-DESIGN tool (MDESIGN) that allows the creation of menu selection systems consisting of one
or more menus that are automatically linked to each other. Once
created, there are a number of different ways of navigating
within a menu selection system. APE also provides a Panel-
DESIGN tool (PDESIGN) that allows the creation of panels containing attribute fields, numeric and alphanumeric value
fields, as well as a graphics/image field. The creation of panels consists of a series of steps, the most important of which
are the layout definition, the field type selection, the color
specification and the assignment of attribute values or descriptors (Figure 2 and 3).

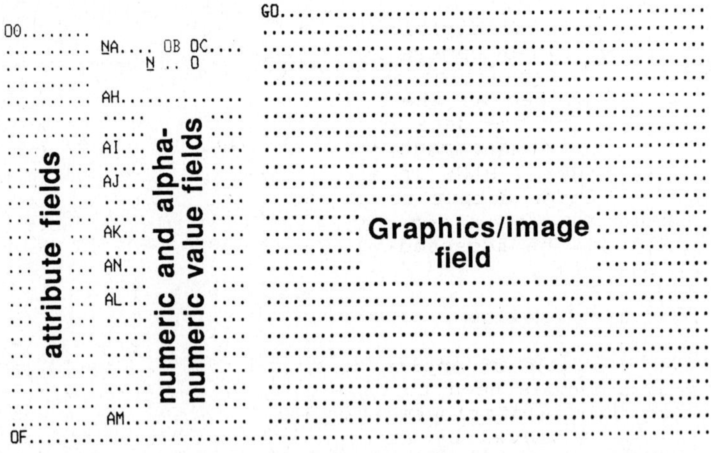

Fig.2   Layout definition, field type selection and
         color specification (N: numeric and A: alphanu-
         meric value fields, G: graphics/image field).

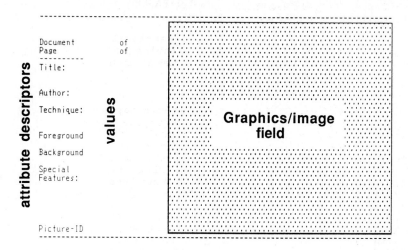

Fig.3   Attribute value assignment.

Upon completion of the menu and panel design by the application developers, the pertinent information such as document and page number, title, author, technique, etc. is entered through the text/image data entry operators. APE provides space to accommodate up to nine A4 document pages.

5.2 Image Capture

The pictures to be digitized under I-PAGE are processed in the PC/AT based video camera or scanner imaging subsystems. The corresponding data files obtained are then formatted, transmitted to and stored at the main-frame system. Depending on the ultimate use of the data files, image processing such as scaling, contrast enhancement, halftoning and data compression is performed under I-PAGE in a batch-oriented mode. GDDM is used to provide image output to the main-frame system periphery and the IMSS maintains a sequential and keyed VSAM file organization that can be accessed by ADSS to build the actual VDB application.

5.3 Document Indexing

In order to get an application operational, numeric and alphanumeric values need to be assigned in the predefined fields relating to the attribute values or descriptors. Document retrieval is achieved by entering specific selection criteria. Basically, ADSS provides two standard retrieval options: ´Select a Query´ and ´Search for Documents´. The first standard retrieval option allows the selection of a query tuple from a wide range of predefined search parameter combinations. The second standard retrieval option allows the entry of any arbitrary, e.g. one or more, search parameters. In this case, how-

ever, the user needs to know the content of the numeric and alphanumeric value fields and their corresponding attribute values in advance.

6. VDB APPLICATION SCENARIOS

In order to gain experience with the use of I-PAGE as a laboratory for prototyping VDB, the following application scenarios
have been implemented and evaluated:

6.1 VDB in Neurobiology

In this application, special emphasis has been placed on the
problems of the large variety of pictures and quality as well
as the image processing requirements as they are encountered in
natural science disciplines. An example of a light micro-scopic
dark field photograph of an bee´s eye together with its
descriptors is shown in Figure 4.

The operational parameters, the technical VDB system specifications required by neurobiological experts and the resulting key
design values of this application are summarized in Table 2.

Image types	Photographs, video-frames, graphs
Purpose of VDB	Archive, slide-show, publishing
# of docs/application (Ni)	$100 < Ni < 10'000$
Capture-time/doc (Tc)	$60 < Tc < 240$ s
System response time (Ts)	$1 < Ts < 2$ s (browse mode) $1 < Ts < 15$ s (high-quality mode)
Reproduction requirements	Low-quality for proofing High-quality for publishing
Data vol. before compression (Rd)	250 KByte $< Rd < 12$ MByte
Data vol. after lossless compr. (D1)	125 KByte $< D1 < 4$ MByte
Data vol. after lossee compr. (D2)	50 KByte $< D2 < 1$ MByte
# of instr. for number crunching (In)	1 MInstr. $< In < 1$ GInstr.

Tab.2   VDB in Neurobiology - operating parameters,
        technical system specifications required and
        resulting VDB key design values.

6.2 VDB in the State Archive of Zurich

In this application, special emphasis has been placed on the issue of handling art work and the required aspects for its preservation. An example of an antique color seal dated 1695 with its descriptors is shown in Figure 5. Extreme care had to be taken in removing such a valuable and fragile document from a well guarded archive and taking it into a computer test-bed environment for digitization. This procedure is very time consuming and there is no indication that this process can be substantially accelerated when going into real production.

The operational parameters, the technical VDB system specifications required by museum experts and the resulting key design values are summarized in Table 3.

Image types	Photographs, antique facsimiles
Purpose of VDB	Archive, slide-show, preservation
# of docs/application (Ni)	$1000 < Ni < 1'000'000$
Capture-time/doc (Tc)	$300 < Tc < 1800$ s
System response time (Ts)	$1 < Ts < 2$ s (browse mode) $1 < Ts < 60$ s (high-quality mode)
Reproduction requirements	Low-quality for proofing High-quality for publishing
Data vol. before compression (Rd)	500 KByte $< Rd < 12$ MByte
Data vol. after lossless compr. (D1)	250 KByte $< D1 < 4$ MByte
Data vol. after lossee compr. (D2)	unacceptable
# of instr. for number crunching (In)	1 MInstr. $< In < 1$ GInstr.

Tab.3   VDB in the State Archive of Zurich – operating parameters, technical system specifications and resulting VDB key design values.

7. REQUIREMENT ANALYSIS AND RESULTS

Characteristic of both scenarios described above is the very broad document quality spectrum required, the extremely time consuming document acquisition and the users high expectations with regard to system response, cost and reliability. These requirements can only partly be satisfied with the current I-PAGE test-bed environment. The VDB key system design parameters needed to properly fulfil these requirements are very large and their implementation has to make use of very advanced system components such as high-speed signal-processors and multi-processor computer architectures, wide-band communication facilities, low-cost and large capacity storage devices, high-fidelity peripheral equipment and, last but not least, programs that are developed using modern software engineering tools. Together with the required reliability, availability and serviceability features, the present development of such a supersystem is not easy to be met under economical constraints. Also, the costly document acquisition process is an important factor in the overall system design. Therefore, careful application planning, in particular with respect to a very long term strategy for storage and retrieval of text/image documents, becomes mandatory.

Nevertheless, technology continues to advance at a steady pace, making the implementation of VDB systems more and more become realistic. Taking into account the art preservation requirements expressed by many experts involved in the various prototyping efforts, the VDB prototyping team has come to the conclusion that the image data captured needs to be stored with the best possible quality; e.g. 24 Bit amplitude resolution for color pictures, 8 Bit amplitude resolution for achromatic pictures and array sizes ranging from 250 KPixel to 4 MPixel. Figure 6 shows a high-fidelity display of the image-master ´color seal dated 1695´.

Any lower resolution quality will be derived from the high-quality image-master using appropriate image processing functions. Most of the parameters enumerated in Table 2 and 3 are self explanatory, except perhaps the fact that the museum experts will not tolerate any image quality loss whatsoever, and therefore, the consideration of any lossee data compression scheme has to be ruled out for this application.

The ever changing and cost-performance improving computer technology as well as the high acquisition cost to build VDB applications already experienced are the driving forces to justify the high-quality image-master approach. Experiments based on the implementation of dynamic data structures to optimize the management of lower-resolution derivates of high-fidelity masters are subject to further research using the I-PAGE laboratory-outfit.

8. CONCLUSIONS

I-PAGE has proved to be a valuable test-bed environment for prototyping potential VDB applications and to gain first experience on key design issues. Getting it right the first time and guaranteeing data portability seem to be the two major requirements that need to be considered by application designers. This in order to find the necessary acceptance amongst experts wanting to use advanced VDB tools to improve their daily work.

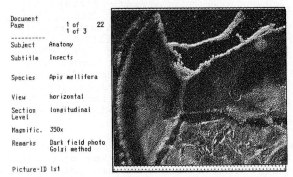

```
Document
Page         1 of    22
             1 of 3
----------
Subject    Anatomy

Subtitle   Insects

Species    Apis mellifera

View       horizontal

Section    longitudinal
Level

Magnific.  350x

Remarks    Dark field photo
           Golgi method

Picture-ID ls1
```

Fig.4 Neurobiology: Light microscopy picture. Raw-data: 512x512x24 RGB byte-map. Rendering: 3179G terminal, 360x240x3 RGB bit-map.

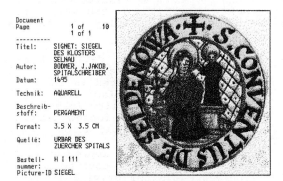

```
Document
Page         1 of    10
             1 of 1
----------
Titel:     SIGNET: SIEGEL
           DES KLOSTERS
           SELNAU
Autor:     BODMER, J.JAKOB,
           SPITALSCHREIBER
Datum:     1695

Technik:   AQUARELL

Beschreib-
stoff:     PERGAMENT

Format:    3.5 X 3.5 CM

Quelle:    URBAR DES
           ZUERCHER SPITALS

Bestell-   H I 111
nummer:
Picture-ID SIEGEL
```

Fig.5 State Archive of Zurich: 'Color seal dated 1695'. Raw-data: 1024x1024x24 RGB byte-map. Rendering: 3179G terminal, 360x240x3 RGB bit-map.

Fig.6 State Archive of Zurich: 'Color seal dated 1695'. Raw-data: 1024x1024x24 RGB byte-map. Rendering: 640x 560x24 RGB bit-map (PC/AT based imaging subsystem).

ACKNOWLEDGMENTS

This research is being supported by IBM´s Academic Computing
Information Systems (ACIS) division. The authors wish to thank
P. Tedaldi from the Computing Center of the University of
Zurich and M.Schaerli from the Zurich State Archive for their
help.

REFERENCES

[1]   Menzi, U. and Stucki, P., Image-Processing Application
       Generation Environment (I-PAGE): Softwarewerkzeuge für
       die Gestaltung offener Text/Bildanwendungssysteme, In-
       formatik-Fachberichte, 149, Mustererkennung, E. Paulus,
       Ed., Springer-Verlag, Berlin-Heidelberg-New York-London-
       Paris-Tokyo, 1987.

[2]   IMAN/AGE - Image Manipulation and Application Generation
       Environment, IBM Program Offering 5785-WBE.

[3]   Application Prototype Environment, General Information,
       IBM Publication # GH19-6526-01.

[4]   Stucki, P., Image Processing for Document Reproduction,
       in Advances in Digital Image Processing, P. Stucki, Ed.,
       Plenum-Press, New York, 1979.

[5]   Pratt, W.K., Digital Image Processing, John Wiley &
       Sons, New York, 1978.

[6]   CCITT Recommendations Terminal Equipment and Protocols
       for Telematic Services, Vol. VII, Geneva, 1985.

[7]   Meynieux, E. et al., Office Paper Document Analysis, ACM
       Transactions on Office Information Systems, Vol.2, No.6,
       Oct.1984.

[8]   Bever M. and Ruland D., Aggregation and Generalization
       Hierarchies in Office Automation, ACM SIGOIS Bulletin,
       Vol.9, No.2&3, April&June 1988.

[9]   Roukens, J., ESPRIT and the Office Subsystems Subpro-
       grams, Office Automation Symposium, IEEE, April 1987.

[10]   Mresse, M., Information Retrieval, Teubner, Stuttgart,
       1984.

[11]   Zehnder, C.A., Informationssysteme und Datenbanken,
       Teubner, Stuttgart, 1985.

[12]   Codd, E.F., A Relational Model for Large Shared Data
       Banks, Communications of the ACM, Vol.24, No.6, June
       1970.

Session 3

DATABASE DESIGN

Visual Database Systems
T.L. Kunii (Editor)
Elsevier Science Publishers B.V. (North-Holland)
© IFIP, 1989

EXTENSIBLE SEMANTIC AUTOMATA FOR MODULAR DESIGN SYSTEMS *

John R. BEDELL and Fred J. MARYANSKI

Computer Science and Engineering Department, U-155
University of Connecticut
Storrs, Connecticut, U.S.A. 06268

Computer-aided design of modular, hierarchical systems has database needs that conventional schemes do not fill. A design process centered on components requires an object-oriented structure defined by a layer of semantic metadata. The resulting self-knowledge provides the flexibility to extend the system to any number of different design environments whose interfaces are specified by the user as networks of nested state machines.

1 Introduction

The design process of an engineering system calls for features not found in conventional database schemas. The user must be able to create and manipulate a system's components individually over a wide range of developmental tasks and environments as the design passes from general schematics to final manufacturing plans. To achieve this flexibility, the database must have an underlying level of semantic metadata that gives it complete self-knowledge, particularly concerning the subtyping and subcomponent relationships embodying different levels of detail within a hierarchical structure. The most formidable problem of a design system is the creation of its user interface; therefore these semantic concepts are applied in detail to the modeling of an interface as a collection of nested state machines, each corresponding to a window or other screen entity.

Binnacle, the database environment under development at the University of Connecticut, supports engineering system design with an underlying model applicable to custom-built user interfaces. Building on previous research in engineering design systems and extensibility features, notably the object-oriented semantics of [1,2] and the state machines of [3,4,5], the fundamental concepts of the semantic database are introduced below. These lead into a discussion of the Binnacle data model and its extensibility, an emphasis on the interface model with an example, and the project's contributions to its research area.

*This research was partially supported by grant IRI-8704042 from the National Science Foundation

2   Previous Engineering Databases and Interfaces

Modeling and design of engineering systems constitute one of many areas of application not adequately addressed by conventional relational databases. The instinctive approach of the designer and the natural structure of systems call for a representation allowing access to individual components at variable levels of detail. An entire system can thus be split into many subsections for individual solution, while at the same time parts of the design can be temporarily glossed over without premature concern for detail. Thus a discrete, object-oriented database allows both top-down and bottom-up approaches to system design.

2.1   Engineering Databases

Numerous schemes for general-purpose databases have the object-oriented structure required for engineering system design; examples are DASDBS [6], EXODUS [7,8], POSTGRES [9], PROBE [10,11], and Starburst [12,13]. They offer a high degree of adaptability, but no particular support for the engineering design process or for modeling of system dynamics. Some, such as POSTGRES, PROBE, and CACTIS [14], incorporate a degree of functional knowledge into database entities. PROBE in particular has extended its object-oriented system to model spatial data, including composite objects such as those found in databases for engineering design [15]. Following a similar approach, [16] presents a formal object-class model for spatial knowledge.

Databases formulated especially for system design and simulation, such as [17], provide the user with additional design support. Such models contain built-in object types allowing connections between components, behavioral constraints and other aspects of control systems, and constructs for the preservation of distinct versions of the same subsystem.

One semantic CAD/CAM model, SAM* [18], is fairly general in application. This object-oriented schema defines seven different *association types* to form various structures and constraints from its atomic elements. For example, the *composition* association defines is_part_of relationships between a complex object and its subcomponents or subdatabases that represent alternative versions, while *generalization* unites the common characteristics of different concept types to form a more abstract type. These building blocks of SAM* are similar to those of the semantic model of [1], described later as a foundation of Binnacle. In both cases, abstract relationships bind elements into complex objects, and objects into semantic networks of classification, type inheritance, component structure, and other pertinent features of modular assemblies. Such concepts can transform an engineering database from mere specialized data storage to a system directly aiding the user's design process.

2.2   Interfaces

The most common means of interaction between a conventional database and its user is a data manipulation language (DML) or query language which allows the user to issue commands to the database in something resembling his own language. This suffices so long as the database remains a simple collection of records–a computerized filing cabinet–and the requested actions consist of straightforward insertions, modifications and retrievals. As databases grow in complexity to accommodate intricate networks and hierarchies with enormous numbers of individual entities, a strictly defined language is no longer practical as a direct interface. A special purpose language such as EXODUS's E or the Data Model Specification Language [2] may be necessary at a higher level to provide a complete database specification. The DML, however, should be hidden behind a front end efficient and friendly enough to satisfy the engineer's need to grasp both the details and the general structure of any complicated system design.

Graphical interaction is among the easiest to use, and can be implemented at various levels of complexity. An interface combining forms and graphs, such as SeaWeed and related projects [19,20,21,22], is an effective tool for building systems of interrelated entities as long as their properties can be clearly expressed at the lowest level of detail using only text, numerals, and other conventional data formats that can be represented on forms. The simpler type of pictorial interface uses icons to represent components of a structure or participants in a relationship, for example the circuit elements of [23] or anatomical features of [24]. Icons cannot directly show the internal structure of the systems they represent, but can be helpful as nodes in a graph or as elements of a diagram showing a single level of a hierarchy. Finally, a full pictorial interface such as that of Scrimshaw [25] will display a level as an assembly of its subtrees, each visible down to its leaf nodes.

Several systems have provided tools to help users design interfaces; many are object-based, but organize their objects in different ways. The Peridot system presented in [26] generates code for an interface by abstracting sample values given to it in a demonstration session conducted by the designer, while the grammatical approach of [27] uses a special-purpose language to define a (possibly nested) series of dialogue entities.

More commonly, systems are event-driven or based on state transition. In Sun-View's multi-window environment [28], windows and their components are defined as objects with procedures that are triggered by specified input events. The HutWindows of [29] follow the more traditional model of finite state machines. These approaches suit interaction in which the system responds to input from the user, but both have disadvantages. State transition requires the specification of all paths out of the current state, so that the addition to the machine of a generally available feature such as an abort/commit panel requires that new next-state paths be appended onto all states from which the feature can be invoked. This proliferation of transition arcs is cumbersome for other than rigidly structured dialogues. As opposed to this "departure-oriented" transition specification, an event-based model can be considered an "arrival-oriented" state machine, where event-triggered procedure calls are like paths into the current state. These reduce the clutter of the first model, but because they specify no previous state, they must be completely redefined whenever the dialogue must follow a particular restricted sequence of states. Binnacle allows both "pre-state" and "post-state" arcs in its state specifications, and thus has the advantages of both models. The format of these states is described in detail in Section 5.

3   The Binnacle Model

3.1   Semantic Entities

Binnacle is an object-oriented model whose components and interrelationships are embodied as individual structures, each accessible through a strictly defined set of operations. These structures, or *entities,* are defined similarly to those of SeaWeed [2], the Meta-database design tool of the Data Model Compiler (DMC) project [20,30]. Entities with attached attributes and operations are used to model both objects and relationships among other entities.

3.2   Basic Objects and Relationships

The initial DMC Model [1] defined several semantic relationships which have been adapted for the Binnacle model. These include the *aggregate,* which groups attributes into a single entity to serve as the semantic equivalent of the conventional data relation; the *nest,* a one-to-many correspondence that allows one entity to "own" a collection of subentities; and the *reference,* a many-to-one correspondence that allows several entities to share a relationship with one other entity. In the many-to-many *association,* all participant entities are of equal status, none having a dominant owning or referenced role.

Aggregate relationship:
      attributes: (<key and non-key attributes>)
      operations: (<methods for insertion, deletion, modification>)

Nest relationship
      attributes: (owner, ownedEntity)
      operations: (<system-defined methods>)

Reference relationship:
      attributes: (referrer, referredEntity)
      operations: (<system-defined methods>)

Association relationship:
      attributes: (participantEntity1, participantEntity2)
      operations: (<system-defined methods>).

The *is_a* or *subtype* relationship allows one entity to be a specialized version of a general type, inheriting the latter's properties while possibly adding or refining its own.

IsA relationship:
      attributes: (superType, subType)
      operations: (<method for property inheritance>).

3.3   Modules

The fundamental unit in a Binnacle database is the *module*; this object represents a component, at any level of complexity, of the system being designed. The module may be structured, implying a composition of several submodules, or atomic, needing no lower levels of representation. Following the general form for objects,

Module Aggregate:
    attributes: (name, revisionDate, editor, comment)
    operations: (<methods for revision, duplication, etc.>).

Specialized subtypes of modules would have additional attributes for their own particular properties, as well as functional components that describe their behavior within the larger system.

4   Extensibility to New Data Types

Binnacle includes new data types and seeks to isolate the issues of data Representation and display. This approach, it is hoped, will increase the versatility of the database system while reducing the problems involved in specializing it for a particular application.

4.1   Semantic Arrays

It is difficult to imagine a multi-media data model without some provision for compound data entities, allowing a single unit to be made up of numerous elements of a single type. One previous approach to implementing this feature has been the long field or "blob", as in [31,22]. Its universally adaptable but formless nature makes its contents meaningless to a general semantic data model, since any interface must be custom-made to understand the data's particular structure.

A compound entity may be more accessible if treated as an array [7], perhaps defined as an aggregate containing size and type specifications:

Array Aggregate:
    attributes: (dimensionality, <dimensions>,
                 element type, <element value limits>)
    operations: (<methods for rescaling, block access>)

while individual elements form a nest belonging to this aggregate. Operations defined on semantic arrays could redefine their size, access their elements, and load elements into a single block of primary memory to exploit the traditional array's access speed. A hierarchy of array subtypes can be set up that includes data structures suitable for many different uses, from the familiar character string to image bitmaps to equation sets specifying dynamic behavior.

4.2 The Semantic Rule

A degree of logical intelligence can be incorporated into a semantic data model by
defining the *clause* as an association between two *predicate* aggregates.

Predicate Aggregate:
    attributes: (name, <arguments>)
    operations: (<method to check true/false status>)

Clause Association:
    attributes: (condition, conclusion).

Rule types are established using these definitions and two fundamental "true" and
"false" predicates. CLAUSEes whose CONDITION roles are filled by the "true" predicate are asserted facts; those whose CONCLUSIONs are "false" indicate known fal-
lacies, leading to complete knowledge where untruth is as certain as truth. Several
CLAUSEs having the same CONCLUSION unite into a Horn clause, while AND and
OR relationships are used to form conjunctions. When the CONCLUSION of one
CLAUSE is the same as the CONDITION of another, the two resolve to a single
CLAUSE; this is a logical analogue of the composition of modules from interconnected
submodules.

5   Building User Interfaces

To take advantage of the variety of systems that Binnacle's semantic data model can
represent, there must be facilities to create appropriate interfaces for the display and
modification of any system's information. The nature of an interface is roughly similar
to that of the system it accesses in that it is hierarchical and modular, enabling the
necessary degree of complexity and ease of design. Here, however, each component represents both a visual aspect (e.g. a display window) and a dynamic aspect–a procedural
structure that helps drive the interaction.

5.1   The Pod Structure

The fundamental element in the Binnacle interface model is a combination of dialogue
entity and procedure called a *pod*. Each pod contains attribute data and a state transition machine, and is one of an arbitrarily deep is-part-of hierarchy of pods forming
a complete interface. This tree is traversed as interior pods successively invoke their
subpods according to user input; control eventually reaches the leaf nodes where most
graphical output occurs. An interface is thus a structure of nested state machines
somewhat like those of [3,4], except that at any particular level, actions are situated in
the state nodes rather than on the arcs that mark transitions between nodes. The pod
hierarchy perhaps more closely resembles the tasks and subtasks generated internally
by SeaWeed [5].
     The pod definitions seen below are implemented in Servio Logic's GemStone [32],
an object-oriented database system whose programming language, OPAL, resembles
Smalltalk. This means that a pod class's data and methods can be defined and stored

together, reflecting its dual nature as an object and a procedural entity. The pod's data is kept in its instance variables (attributes), its functional aspect in its *invoke, display,* and *transit* methods:

Object subclass: #Pod
    instVarNames: #(#name #superPod #subPods #origin #popsUp)
    defaults: #[#[popsUp, true]].

method: Pod
invoke
    | returnValue |
    (popsUp) ifTrue: [self display].
    returnValue := self transit.
    (popsUp) ifTrue: [self erase].
    ↑returnValue.

method: Pod
display
    subPods do: [:subPod | (subPod popsUp) ifFalse: [subPod display]].

method: Pod
transit
    | states |
    states := #[<states>].
    ↑perform state transition>).

5.2   Pod Invocation

A pod is called by sending it the "invoke" message. Subsequent display of this subtree of the interface depends on the pod's "popsUp" flag: if true, the subtree is transitory, displayed whenever, and only as long as, the pod is activated; if false, the subtree has already been displayed on activation of its closest pop-up ancestor and remains onscreen as long as the latter is active. If called, the recursive display method descends each branch of the subtree until a subPod is found that itself pops up. Thus a pop-up command menu will appear whenever invoked and disappear after use, simultaneously with its choice boxes that do not pop up on their own. On the other hand, a scrollbar forming part of a window does not pop up but will remain onscreen, active or not, as long as does the window.

While all pods share this hierarchical invocation structure, some distinction is required. Most interface components such as menus and their choice boxes, control panels and their pushbuttons, scrollbars, textports, canvases, and dialogue boxes can be opened and entered as windows; drawings and other irregularly shaped graphics, however, do not form such nested, well-defined regions. These graphics, atomic or compound, must ultimately be displayed by more specialized drawing methods.

Pod subclass: #WindowPod
      instVarNames: #(#width #height #foregroundColor #backgroundColor).

method: WindowPod
display
      <open window>.
      super display.

Pod subclass: #GraphicPod
      "Handles item drawn in a window pod"
      instVarNames: #(#graphic)
      defaults: #[#[popsUp, false]].

method: GraphicPod
display
      (subPods isEmpty)
            ifTrue: [superPod draw: graphic]
            ifFalse: [subPods do: [:subPod | subPod display]].

5.3 Pod State Machinery

The functional component of a pod is defined as a set of states within its transit method; this allows the states' action blocks to share local variables and access parameters passed to the pod through its invoke method. Besides the action block containing arbitrary code, each state has a name, an *on* attribute containing arrival paths (event triggers), and a *then* attribute containing departure paths (next-state transitions). Each path indicates an object class, an instance of which found at the head of the event stream will cause entry into the indicated state. An action block can push any object onto the event stream, allowing the pod to influence directly the course of the dialogue; the block can also invoke subpods or call the transit method of its pod's superclass. Sending the pod a "return" or "return: returnValue" message will pass control back to the superpod or subclass that called the current state machine.

5.4 Specifying an Interface: An Example

The following pod definitions describe the interface for a simple drawing program (the "states" arrays shown appear inside transit methods in an actual specification). On the screen of a workstation with a keyboard and one-button mouse, the user sees a blank window representing the root pod of the interface. To add an item to the drawing, he moves the cursor to any location and pushes the mouse button, at which point a pop-up menu appears offering a choice of a line, box, or circle. When a choice is made, the appropriate item is drawn starting at a point selected by pushing the button a second time. To leave the program, the user hits any key.

WindowPod subclass: #RootPod
    "Root pod for single-menu design interface"
    instVarNames: #().


```
states := #[
      name: 'selectCmd'
          on: #[MouseButtonDown]
          action: [(subPods at: 1) invoke.],
      name: 'doCmd'
          on: #[GraphicPod]
          action: [ subPods add: thisEvent.
                    (subPods last) invoke.],
      name: 'exit'
          on: #[KeyStroke]
          action: [self return]].
```


theInterface := RootPod new.

A single instance of a RootPod waits for choices from its first subPod, the command menu, and adds each chosen drawing component, a GraphicPod, to its collection of subPods before invoking it. When accepted as a trigger, an event is automatically pulled off the eventStream and assigned to thisEvent.

WindowPod subclass: #MenuPod
    "Generic menu offers choice from subPods"
    instVarNames: #().


```
method: MenuPod
display
      origin := Cursor location.
      super draw.
```

```
states := #[
     name: 'consider'
         on: #[Entry]
         action: [ (subPods includes: (thisEvent pod))
                        ifTrue: [thisEvent pod invoke.]],
     name: 'wander'
         on: #[Exit],
     name: 'select'
         on: #[ChoicePod]
         action: [ eventStream push: ((thisEvent classChosen) new).
                    self return],
     name: 'giveUp'
         on: #[MouseButtonUp]
         action: [self return]].


theMenu := MenuPod new.
theInterface subPods: #[theMenu].
```

The menu's subPods are command choices that are invoked on entry; when one is chosen, the appropriate GraphicPod is pushed onto the eventStream. If the cursor wanders outside the menu, it is ignored until it re-enters.

```
WindowPod subclass: #ChoicePod
    "Menu component"
    instVarNames: #(#classChosen)
    defaults: #[#[popsUp, false]].


method: ChoicePod
display
    self clear; print: name.


method: ChoicePod
invertColors
    | tempColor |
    tempColor := foregroundColor.
    foregroundColor := backgroundColor.
    backgroundColor := foregroundColor.
```

```
states := #[
     name: 'start'
          action: [self invertColors; display.],
     name: 'select'
          on: #[MouseButtonUp]
          action: [eventStream push: self. self return.],
     name: 'reject'
          on: #[Exit]
          action: [self invertColors; display. self return.]
```

theMenu subPods: #[ChoicePod new, ChoicePod new, ChoicePod new].

A ChoicePod's classChosen attribute determines the type of object created if that ChoicePod is selected. The LinePod class defined below, along with similarly defined BoxPod and CirclePod classes, are placed in the classChosen attributes of the menu's ChoicePods.

```
GraphicPod subclass: #LinePod
     "Draw a line from selected point"
     instVarNames: #().
     defaults: #[#[popsUp, false]].
```

```
states := #[
     name: 'start'
          on: #[MouseButtonDown]
          action: [ origin := (Cursor location).
                         graphic := (Line new) begin: origin end: origin.
                    self display.],
     name: 'stretch'
          on: #[MouseDragged]
          action: [ self erase.
                         graphic end: (Cursor location).
                         self display.],
     name: 'exit'
          on: #[MouseButtonUp]
          action: [self return: graphic.]].
```

((theMenu) subPods at: 1) classChosen: LinePod.
((theMenu) subPods at: 2) classChosen: BoxPod.
((theMenu) subPods at: 3) classChosen: CirclePod.

6 Research Contributions

The Binnacle system is intended to allow the creation of customized engineering databases for modular system design. To achieve the needed flexibility, its semantic data
model must define a basic hierarchical system structure adaptable to the user's own
application. This is a common approach, but most research has proceeded from this
point to consider lower-level issues of storage and retrieval raised by the variability of
databases with user-definable data classes. The flexibility of such a system's user interface rarely extends beyond its data definition or manipulation languages, while more
sophisticated front ends such as those of CAD systems are usually developed from start
to finish with a narrow range of application in mind. Binnacle seeks an extensible semantic model with sufficient diversity of application, emphasizing issues of interaction
rarely touched on by previous research:

1. Binnacle considers especially the problems of creating interfaces that communicate with the user employing forms, graphs, pictures, and other efficient media.

2. Tools for the production of these interfaces are defined as much as possible according to the data model. Thus their structures remain accessible and meaningful
   to other semantically based components of a complete engineering development
   system, yet are detachable from particular hardware and system constraints.

3. Unconventional data types such as those mentioned in Section 4 are defined in
   semantic terms, making them consistent with existing types as well as subtypes
   and complex types created by the user.

4. The functionality of interface components is defined in a format having the advantages of both conventional state machines and event-triggered procedures.

The Binnacle system is an extension of the Data Model Compiler, building especially
on the SeaWeed entity specification tool developed by [2]. Binnacle consists of an
object-oriented language for defining semantic data structures and database interfaces,
along with a library of predefined primitives. We plan to implement the system using
Gemstone, Servio Logic's version of Smalltalk with persistent objects.

References

[1] Peckham, J., *A Formal Model for the Design of Semantic Databases,* M.S. Thesis,
     Electrical Engineering and Computer Science Department, University of Connecti-
     cut (1985).

[2] Hong, S., and F. Maryanski, "Representation of Object-Oriented Data Models",
     Information Sciences, accepted for publication.

[3] Olsen, D. R., "Pushdown Automata for User Interface Management", *ACM Trans-
     actions on Graphics,* Vol. 3, No. 3 (July 1984) pp. 177-203.

[4] Wasserman, A. I., "Extending State Transition Diagrams for the Specification of
     Human-Computer Interaction", *IEEE Transactions on Software Engineering,* Vol.
     SE-11, No. 8 (Aug. 1985) pp. 699-713.

[5] Hong, S., and F. Maryanski, "Database Design Tool Generation via Software Reusability", *IEEE COMPSAC* (Oct. 1988) pp. 361-368.

[6] Paul, H.-B., et. al., "Architecture and Implementation of the Darmstadt Database Kernel System", *Proceedings of SIGMOD '87 International Conference on Management of Data* (May 1987) pp. 196-207.

[7] Carey, M.J., et al., "The Architecture of the EXODUS Extensible DBMS", *Proceedings of the 1986 International Workshop on Object-Oriented Database Systems* (Sept. 1986) pp. 52-65.

[8] Richardson, J. E., and M. J. Carey, "Programming Constructs for Database System Implementation in EXODUS", *Proceedings of SIGMOD '87 International Conference on Management of Data* (May 1987) pp. 208-219.

[9] Stonebraker, M., "Object Management in POSTGRES Using Procedures", *Proceedings of the 1986 International Workshop on Object-Oriented Database Systems* (Sept. 1986) pp. 66-72.

[10] Manola, F., and J. A. Orenstein, "Toward a General Spatial Data Model for an Object-Oriented DBMS", *Proceedings of 1986 International Conference on Very Large Data Bases* (Aug. 1986) pp. 328-335.

[11] Manola, F., and U. Dayal, "PDM: An Object-Oriented Data Model", *Proceedings of 1986 International Workshop on Object-Oriented Database Systems* (Sept. 1986) pp. 18-25.

[12] Schwarz, P., et al., "Extensibility in the Starburst Database System", *Proceedings of the 1986 International Workshop on Object-Oriented Database Systems* (Sept. 1986) pp. 85-92.

[13] Lindsay, B., J. McPherson, and H. Pirahesh, "A Data Management Extension Architecture", *Proceedings of SIGMOD '87 International Conference on Management of Data* (May 1987) pp. 220-226.

[14] Hudson, S.E., and R. King, "CACTIS: A Database System for Specifying Functionally-Defined Data", *Proceedings of the 1986 International Workshop on Object-Oriented Database Systems* (Sept. 1986) pp. 26-37.

[15] Orenstein, J. A., and F. A. Manola, "PROBE Spatial Data Modeling and Query Processing in an Image Database Application", *IEEE Transactions on Software Engineering*, Vol. 14, No. 5 (May 1988) pp. 611-629.

[16] Mohan, L., and R. L. Kashyap, "An Object-Oriented Knowledge Representation for Spatial Information", *IEEE Transactions on Software Engineering*, Vol. 14, No. 5 (May 1988) pp. 675-681.

[17] Batory, D.S., and W. Kim, "Modeling Concepts for VLSI CAD Objects", *ACM Transactions on Database Systems*, Vol. 10, No. 3 (Sept. 1985) pp. 322-346.

[18] Su, S. Y. W., "Modeling Integrated Manufacturing Data with SAM*", *IEEE Computer*, Vol. 19, No. 1 (Jan. 1986) pp. 92-100.

[19] Hoelscher, S., and F. Maryanski, "COMPASS: A Computerized Office Management Package and Semantic System", *Proceedings of Conference on Human-Computer Interfaces* (Aug. 1987) pg. 328.

[20] Maryanski, F., and S. Hong, "A Tool for Generating Semantic Database Applications", *IEEE COMPSAC* (Oct. 1985) pp. 368-375.

[21] Maryanski, F., and D. Stock, "SURF: A Semantic Update and Retrievel Facility", *Proceedings of National Computer Conference* (June 1987) pp. 367-373.

[22] McDonald, L., *TugBoat: A Tool for Generating Software Engineering Database Systems,* M.S. Thesis, Computer Science and Engineering Department, University of Connecticut (1988).

[23] Walker, M. G., and J. McGregor, "Computer-Aided Engineering for Analog Circuit Design", *IEEE Computer,* Vol. 19, No. 4 (Apr. 1986) pp. 100-108.

[24] Frasson, C., and M. Er-radi, "Principles of an Icons-Based Command Language", *Proceedings of SIGMOD '86 International Conference on Management of Data* (May 1986) pp. 144-152.

[25] Bedell, J.R., and Maryanski, F., "Semantic Data Modeling Support for CAD", *Proc. ACM/IEEE Fall Joint Computer Conference* (Oct. 1987) pp. 498-504.

[26] Myers, B. A., "Creating Interaction Techniques by Demonstation", *IEEE Computer Graphics and Applications,* Vol. 7, No. 9 (Sept. 1987) pp. 51-60.

[27] van den Bos, J., "Abstract Interaction Tools: A Language for User Interfaces", *ACM Transactions on Programming Languages and Systems,* Vol. 10, No. 2 (Apr. 1988) pp. 215-247.

[28] Sun Microsystems, Inc., *SunView Programming Guide* (1986).

[29] Koivunen, M.-R., and M. Mantyla, "HutWindows: An Improved Architecture for a User Interface Management System", *IEEE Computer Graphics and Applications,* Vol. 8, No. 1 (Jan. 1988) pp. 43-52.

[30] Maryanski, F., et al., "The Data Model Compiler: A Tool for Generating Object-Oriented Database Systems", *Proceedings of 1986 International Workshop on Object-Oriented Database Systems* (Sept. 1986) pp. 73-84.

[31] Haskin, R. L., and R. A. Lorie, "On Extending the Functions of a Relational Database System", *Proceedings of SIGMOD '82 International Conference on Management of Data* (May 1982) pp. 207-212.

[32] Servio Logic Corporation, GemStone system documentation (1988).

Visual Database Systems
T.L. Kunii (Editor)
Elsevier Science Publishers B.V. (North-Holland)
© IFIP, 1989

ERDDS - the intelligent E-R-based Database Design System with Visual Semantics Knowledge Base Prototype

Po-Jen Chuang and Frederick Springsteel *

The University of Missouri at Columbia

Department of Computer Science

218 Mathematical Sciences Bldg

Columbia, Missouri 65211 USA

(314) 882-4480; 882-3842

BitNet: csfreds @ UMCCSL

KEYWORDS AND PHRASES: Entity-Relationship Diagrams; Graphical data model representation; Efficient PROLOG database design; Visual database designer interface; ERD layout & logical schema heuristics

ABSTRACT

Earlier graphical data models - hierarchial and network - were computer oriented and unsuited to express users requirements. Chen's E-R model has natural, visual data semantics, seen in its E-R Diagrams (ERDs). It is useful for rapid prototypes in the data-independent relational model, the modern choice for most applications.   ERDDS aids the process by exploiting **ERD-visible semantics (keys and domains)**, expediting the ERD layout, and helping the user/designer <u>see</u> the schema!   ERDDS **has E-R analysis built into its PROLOG knowledge base** which favors E-R diagrams with more **robust relational schema**. The latter are assured by rigorous checks for desirable properties of <u>**regular, well-formed**</u> ERDs, efficiently represented as PROLOG "databases" of **facts**.   After the designer's ERD passes all these tests, it is laid out breadth-first via **prioritized object placement heuristics**. Simultaneously, the designer is warned of any detected ERD "loops".   **Loop-free ERDs have many fewer transaction anomalies, because they enjoy Boyce-Codd Normal Form**.   Finally, ERDDS translates semantic information from its **PROLOG graph representation** into **SQL-coded logical schema** for the robust relational database so obtained.

* This research was supported in part by the USA National Science Foundation under its DB programs' grants IST 8503082 & IRI 8709726.

I.   INTRODUCTION AND RELATION TO PRIOR RESEARCH

**Earlier graphical data models - hierarchial and network - were computer
oriented and unsuited to express users requirements.** Over the decade
since the entity-relationship (E-R) approach to database design was
introduced (or named), as a "unified view of data" by Chen [5], it has
undergone significant development. There has been much research
interest, evidenced by several international conferences on the E-R
approach, e.g., [6], [9], [7], [21]. **This great interest is due to the
clearly defined <u>visual</u> semantics of the E-R model and to its utility as a
<u>visual</u> database design tool, as this paper hopes to show in concrete
implementation.**

The concepts of entity and relationship sets are easily learned and used,
and yet provide powerful and natural insights for defining the logical
view of a database. **The model is pictorially represented by an E-R
diagram (ERD) that is translatable into any of the major data models -
hierarchial, network, or relational - enroute to any given database
implementation** [27]. Thus many authors have begun to use the ERD as a
<u>visual</u> language for their various conceptual models: [2], [8], [18],
[23], [28]. **It is very useful for rapid prototypes in the data-
independent relational model, the modern choice for most applications.**
[Newer, "nested" relations are special cases.]

**Despite this "visible" interest in the E-R model, most of the work with
it has focused on practical aspects, with some research on its visual
development and assumptions.** The main goal of our analysis is to examine
more closely some precise versions of these assumptions and the reputed
benefits of using ERDs for database modeling. **We find that such analyses
provide knowledge which is useful for our database design system ERDDS;
it is based on the concept of "regular" ERDs.**

**ERDDS speeds DB design by exploiting ERD-visible semantics (keys and
domains), expediting the ERD layout, and helping the user/designer <u>see</u>
the schema!** The reported work applies previous research knowledge, some
of it by the second author, about "extended regular" ERDs and their
relational schemas, especially the normal form implications for this
larger family of ERDs, which have Inclusion Dependencies as well as key

dependencies [27]. Algorithmically, we find these results important to our prototype system for robust database (DB) design, which uses several important principles:

a) interactive construction of (extended) regular ERDs from user-input description of a planned information system, in the spirit of [12] with a test of whether the ERD is "well-formed" [20]:

b) automatic translation from an acceptable (well-formed, regular) E-R diagram to its canonical relational schema (CRS), with all embedded key dependencies and existence constraints derived from the ERD:

c) advising the designer if parts of the CRS satisfy certain normal forms, as determined by results discussed below:

d) re-design of the current relational database schema, perhaps to fit better an enterprise's changing environment, as represented by the dynamic E-R design diagram.

Among the features of ERDDS are the familiar automatic layout criteria of the pioneering GIOTTO and GINCOD systems [1; 11; 26]. Besides their grid standard and layout criteria which minimize edge crossings, bendings, path lengths and total diagram area, ERDDS uses (second priority) diagonal edges to further reduce edge crossings and to group up to eight "objects" (nodes) around a given node. Lower conceptual domain information is often kept hidden, at a pop-up level.
The interactive package is "designer-friendly" and menu-driven, but acts swiftly to input the objects - entities, attributes (with domains) and relationships - and to output user-understood specifications: keys and existence constraints.

Our system checks whether the ERD is: well-defined (i.e., "well-formed"), regular, loop-free (in $O(|E|)$ time), and it also translates the ERD graph's listing $EG = (N, E)$ into its CRS (R, K, I) of relational database schema R, set K of key dependencies, and set I of inclusion constraints, as defined below.

II. ERDs Defined, Extended and Translated into Relational Schemas

An ERD can be formally defined (but we will not here) as a certain type
of labeled, directed graph **EG = (N,E)**, where the nodes in **N** are boxes
(entities), diamonds **(relationships)** or circles **(attributes)** and the
edges in **E** are arrows from diamonds (or in the extended cases boxes) to
boxes, or else edges are connectors directed to circles.   See Figure 1.

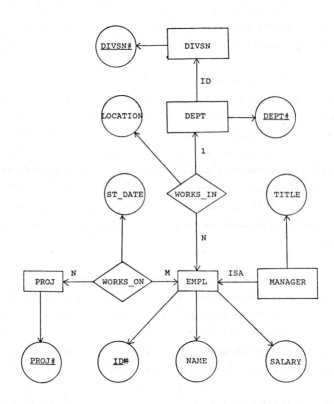

FIGURE 1. Entity-Relationship Diagram for Example 1

DEFINITION 1:   ERD edges in E are in one of these four forms:

(i) $E_i \rightarrow A_j$,   (ii) $R_i \rightarrow A_j$,

(iii) $E_i \rightarrow E_j$,   (iv) $R_i \rightarrow E_j$,

and may be labelled in exactly one of these four respective ways:

   (a) an edge of form (i) is not labelled, but A_j is underlined iff
A_j is an identifier for entity set E_i;

(b) an edge of form (ii), to a non-identifier attribute A $_j$ of a relationship set, is not labelled;

(c) **an edge of form (iii) represents either an "ISA" or an "ID" relationship, and is so labeled;**

(d) an edge of the form (iv) is labeled "1", whenever at most one entity from the entity set E $_j$ may be related to any combination of entities from the other entity sets of R $_i$; or else, an edge of form (iv) is labelled by "m" or "n" (many-labeled) when zero, one or more than one E $_j$ entity may be related to a combination of entities from the other entity sets of R $_i$.

EXAMPLE 1: The ERD represented by Figure 1 has five entity sets, two of which are **"weak entity sets"**, DEPT and MANAGER, and two relationships shown as diamonds, plus the "ISA" and "ID" relationships. DEPT can only be fully IDentified with DIVSN# plus DEPT# in its key; MANAGER has no self-identifier, but it is an **"ISA"** (<u>subset</u>) entity of EMPL, and uses ID#. EMPL has three attributes: identifier **ID#, plus NAME and SALARY.** LOCATION is the only attribute of the relationship WORKS_IN, which relates EMPL to DEPT is many-to-one; WORKS_ON is many-to-many between EMPL and PROJ. [Employees can work on several projects but only in one department.]

NOTE: A directed path from node X to node Y is denoted X ->-> Y. A maximal directed path in an ERD is called an **ISA-path** if all the edges on the path are ISA edges, or an **ID-path** if exactly one edge on it is an ID edge. For clarity, we only allow ID-paths with single ID edges as seen in practice. **Either ISA-paths or ID-paths can be denoted by X ->-> ENT.** In Figure 1, WORKS_IN ->-> DIVSN is an ID-path.

DEFINITION 2: An ERD as defined above is said to be **well-formed** if it has these further (semantically desirable) properties, for all i and j:

(0) **Each A-node has just one connector, from an E-node or R-node.**

(1) **An E-node cannot have both ISA and ID outgoing edges,** and it has an identifier Iden(E $_i$) if either E $_i$ has an ID edge or no edge to another entity, but not if E $_i$ has an outgoing ISA edge.

(2) **Every R-node has outdegree greater than one, with edges to at least two E-nodes.**

(3) **The ERD is connected as a directed graph.**

(4)   There are no parallel edges between two nodes unless they connect
a (reflexive) binary relationship with one E-node, nor are there any
unlabelled edges of the form $X_i \rightarrow E_j$, for any node X_i.

(5)   There are no two distinct ISA-paths nor two distinct ID-paths
from any node E_i, and   (6) the ID/ISA paths are acyclic.

Figure 1 is obviously a well-formed ERD. For any "real-world" ERD, we
feel these properties are reasonable to assume. When the attributes are
given prefixes to identify them globally,   (0) is no restriction. Note
that in any ERD without loops involving "diamond" relationships, a
directed cycle might consist of ISA or ID paths, but property (6) here
says that such cycles do not exist in well-formed ERDs. As noted in
[20], which uses most of these assumptions, the meaning of this
restriction is that an entity set will not "depend" (via ID or ISA) on
itself for identification, nor be defined as a subset of itself!

Property (4) prevents multiple participations of one entity in the same
relationship. All of these properties are checked for a proposed ERD, as
part of our ERD-design algorithm, with reasonable efficiency. The sample
[Turbo]PROLOG code below checks connectedness of the ERD.

A.   Translation of ERDs into Canonical Relational Schema

We sketch here the mapping of a well-formed ERD into its "canonical"
relational schema,   of the form (R,K,I), where K and I are the sets of
key and inclusion dependencies, respectively. Our map extends (in some
respects) the similar map of [20]. This mapping is based on the usual
translation of the E-R model into the relational model, with which the
reader can be presumed familiar [27].

SAMPLE PROLOG CODE IN WELL-FORMED-CHECK ALGORITHM:

```
/* Depth-First Search */
searchfrom(X) :- assertz(visited(X)), search(X).
search(X) :-
    edge(X,Y,_), not(visited(Y)), searchfrom(Y), fail, !.
search(X) :-
    edge(Y,X,_), not(visited(Y)), searchfrom(Y), fail, !.
search(_).

disconnected_or_not(_,[]) :- !.          /* verification */
disconnected_or_not([H1|_],[H2|_]) :-    /* diagnosis    */
    errmsg3A(H1,H2).
```

ALGORITHM I: MAPPING ERD EG = (N,E) TO RELATIONAL SCHEMA (R,K,I):
Where **EG = (N,E)** is the input ERD, for each E-node or R-node X_i in **N**,
  denote $Atr(X_i)$ = U { attributes A_j | X_i -> A_j is an edge in **E** }.
  begin
    1. **initialize R,K,I to be empty;**

    2. **//assure globally unique entity identifier labels//**
       for each A-node A_j in **N** such that A_j = $Iden(E_i)$:
         prefix the label of E_i to the label of A_j;

    //compute the following sets of attributes//

    3. **for each E-node in N:**
       $Key(E_i)$:= $Iden(E_i)$ U {$Key(E_j)$ | E_i->->E_j};
       $TotAtr(E_i)$:= $Atr(E_i)$ U $Key(E_i)$;
    //acyclicity of the ERD assures finiteness of this step//

    4. **for each R-node in N:**
       <u>if</u> all edges R_i -> E_j to E-nodes are 1-labeled
       <u>then</u> $Key(R_i)$:= $Key(E_j)$ for the first such E_j;
       <u>else</u> $Key(R_i)$:= U{$Key(E_j)$ | R_i -> E_j is m-labeled};
       $TotAtr(R_i)$:= U{$Key(E_j)$ | R_i -> E_j in E} U $Atr(R_i)$;

    5. **for** each E- or R-node X_i in N: let R_i be the label of X_i;
    //define its relation scheme and Key Dependency//
       S_i := $TotAtr(X_i)$; K_i := $Key(X_i)$;
       add $R_i(S_i)$ to the relation schemes in **R**;
       add the KD K_i -> S_i to the set **K**;

    6. **for** each edge X_i -> E_j in **E**, where X_i is an E- or R-node:
    //define an Inclusion Dependency on the entity relation//
       <u>if</u> R_i and R_j are the respective relation schemes
       <u>then</u> add the IND $R_i[K_j]$ ⊆ $R_j[K_j]$ to the set **I**;
    [7. eliminate 1-attribute schemes & their INDs as redundant.]
  end

NOTE: For an entity node E_i that is NOT a weak (ID dependent or ISA subset) entity set, step 3 forms its key as Key(E_i) = Iden(E_i), as usual. **If an ISA or ID edge starts at this node, then step 3 generates an expanded key for the weak entity set.** Note that the KDs defined in step 5 for a subset entity set E_i imply K_j -> Atr(E_i), for the (unique) ISA-path E_i ->-> E_j. In this case, K_j is the key of E_i: it is K_i, by step 3 above, because <u>an ISA relationship identifies the subset.</u>

DEFINITION 3:   The image **(R,K,I)** of the (well-formed) ERD **EG** via Algorithm I is called the **canonical relational schema** of the ERD.   Such a schema is considered to be "E-R consistent"; cf. [20, 2].

EXAMPLE 1A: For the ERD of Figure 1, by application of Algorithm I, the canonical relational   schema contains these relation schemes (with keys given by the underlined attributes); one-attribute schemes are dropped.

            MANAGER(<u>EMPL.ID#</u>, TITLE)
            EMPL(<u>EMPL.ID#</u>, NAME, SALARY)
            WORKS_IN(<u>EMPL.ID#</u>, LOCATION, DEPT#, DIVSN#)
            DEPT(<u>DEPT#, DIVSN#</u>)
            WORKS_ON(<u>EMPL.ID#, PROJ#,</u> ST_DATE)
and the inclusion dependencies (**INDs**):
            MANAGER[EMPL.ID#] ⊂ EMPL[EMPL.ID#]
            WORKS_IN[EMPL.ID#] ⊂   EMPL[EMPL.ID#]
            WORKS_IN[DEPT#, DIVSN#] ⊂   DEPT[DEPT#, DIVSN#]
            WORKS_ON[EMPL.ID#] ⊂ EMPL[EMPL.ID#]
ID#, the key of EMPL, functionally determines DEPT#.

B.   Definition of (Extended) Regularity

Many facts are known about the set I of INDs used in **(R,K,I)**.   We cite here some useful conclusions, most of which are shown in [20]:

FACTS: 1. There is an ERD-associated <u>IND graph</u> IG = (R,A), where
        R -> R' is an arc in **A** iff R[X] ⊂ R'[Y] is in I and R,R' in **R**;

        2. The associated IND graph IG and the corresponding reduced ERD (without attributes) are isomorphic (un)directed graphs, if we omit the optional step 7 of Algorithm I;

3. IG is a directed acyclic graph;

4. The INDs in I are typed and key-based [22];

5. Since I is a set of typed INDs, an IND $R_i[X] \subseteq R_j[Y]$ is implied by I iff it is trivial or X=Y and there is a path from R_i to R_j in IG corresponding to a sequence of INDs in I of the form $R_i[W] \subseteq ... \subseteq R_j[W]$ where $X \subseteq W$.

An important fact follows about any relational database schema (R,K,I) and its sets I and K of INDs and KDs, respectively; cf. [22]:

$$(I \cup K)+ = I+ \cup K+ \qquad \text{(Theorem 5.3 in [3].)}$$

This fact says that the logical closure of the unioned INDs and KDs, $(I \cup K)+$, can be found by unioning the closures of I and of K taken separately. **This means that implications from basic sets of INDs and KDs proceed independently.** We use this in the following:

DEFINITION 4: An ERD (with ISA and/or ID edges) is **(extended)** <u>regular</u> if all the FDs and INDs satisfied by its canonical relation schema follow from the KDs for its entity and relationship nodes, and from the basic INDs of its various relationship, ISA, and ID edges, as defined by Algorithm I. (If the ERD has no ISA or ID edges and we disregard INDs, we may [24] call it **"regular"** if the condition is satisfied for only the FDs.)

In **Example 1A,** if the KDs and INDs explicitly given imply (indepen-dently) all the functional and inclusion dependencies true in its canonical relational schema, then **the ERD of Figure 1 is extended regular. We assume this to be the case.** This means that no other such dependencies, not deducible from these, can later surprise us! We <u>need</u> to assume this is the case in general, so that the ERD actually is a **reliable, robust** database design methodology. Otherwise, it is not!

C.   **Regular ERDs are biased towards Boyce-Codd Normal Form**

Almost all relation schemes in R for regular ERDs are in BCNF [14]. To get ALL relation schemes in a regular ER-consistent (R,K,I) to be in

BCNF, a highly desirable but not always possible outcome, it seems that one needs an extra assumption: e.g., that there are no (non-reflexive) "loops" in the reduced ERD, even as an undirected graph. One result in [15] showed that if an ERD is regular and "loop-free" as defined, then its canonical relational schema R is in BCNF.

DEFINITION 5: An ERD EG is <u>loop-free</u> iff its reduced ERD is Berge-acyclic when considered as a hypergraph [10].

Considering the reduced ERD as a hypergraph (H,S), where H is the set of E-nodes and S is the set of relationships, simply means that we consider each R in S as a "hyperedge", i.e. as the set of E-nodes that R relates. Then the condition of **Berge acyclicity** on this hypergraph is **defined to mean that: there is no "path"of two or more distinct** hyperedges (R_1, R_2, ...) from an E-node E_1 through at least one other E-node and back to E_1. [This still allows (reflexive) self-loops.]

One situation which captures the loop-free condition on the ERD, of being quite acyclic, is the case when the reduced ERD EG' considered as an UNdirected graph (and ignoring self-loops) is acyclic, i.e. when its isomorphic form (via Fact 2), the IND graph IG, is viewable as an undirected tree, as in Figure 1. We state this equivalence; cf. Fig. 2.

Proposition 1: For a well-formed ERD EG, its IND graph IG is an undirected tree if and only if the ERD is loop-free.

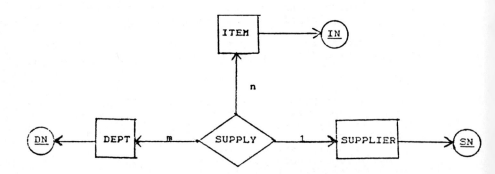

FIGURE 2. A ternary relationship's diagram

The PROLOG code below checks the loop-free condition, with sample outputs from it in Figure 10. While we will not formally prove Proposition 2 here, one can make an intuitive argument based on the difference between loop-free ERDs as in Figures 1 and 2, and the opposite case as in Figure 3: if there are no loops, there can be no embedded "extra" FDs, such as IN -> SN. While ISA and ID paths could possibly participate in ERD loops, they do not add to the FDs between keys of the entities that they relate. Hence, new FDs across the boundaries of entity relation schemes, the only type of FDs that could possibly violate BCNF, do not exist due to the addition of ISA or ID edges. Hence, we need only consider many and one-labeled edges. The full argument yields the following:

Proposition 2: For a regular ERD EG, if EG is loop-free, then all relation schemes in its (R,K,I) are in BCNF.

PART OF THE PROLOG CODE FOR THE LOOP-FREE TESTING OF AN ERD:

```
loopfree :-
    findall(Ent,entity(Ent),Le),
    findall(Rel,relationship(Rel),Lr),
    append(Le,Lr,L), loopfree1(L).

loopfree1([]) :- !.
loopfree1([H|T]) :-
    search_E_R_from(H),
    restore_edge, /* restore retracted edges */
    findall(Node,visited(Node),L),
    test_loop(H,L), loopfree1(T).

/* Depth-First Search from X:
     1) each edge passed by is retracted
     2) each node can be visited more than once
     3) any A-node is not visited, since it is never
        along any loop for any well-formed ERD       */

search_E_R_from(X) :-
    assertz(visited(X)), search_E_R(X), !.

search_E_R(X) :-
    edge(X,Y,Label),
    retract_edge(X,Y,Label), /*retract the edge passed by*/
    gettype(Y,Type), /* get type of Y--'E', 'R', or 'A' */
    not(Type = 'A'), search_E_R_from(Y), fail, !.
search_E_R(X) :-
    edge(Y,X,Label), retract_edge(Y,X,Label),
    gettype(Y,Type), not(Type = 'A'),
    search_E_R_from(Y), fail, !.
search_E_R(_).
```

```
/* test if H is visited more than once
   if so, H is along at least one loop                     */

test_loop(H,L) :-                   /* verification */
    renewvisited,
    minuslist(L,[H],[],L1),
    listlen(L,Len), listlen(L1,Len1), Len - Len1 = 1, !.
test_loop(H,[_|T]) :-           /* diagnosis    */
    errmsg_loop(H,T).

/*
errmsg_loop(H,T) :- issue the warning message and let user
    be able to choose to see the loop part graphically.
                                                            */
```

Of course not every Berge-cyclic ERD yields a non-BCNF R, as the reader can see from simple cases. The conditions of Proposition 2 are strictly sufficient, but not necessary, to yield BCNF. However, because the question of deciding BCNF-ness for a relation scheme is an NP-complete problem [27], we do not expect to find a fully equivalent condition that is efficiently decidable. Testing whether a regular ERD is loop-free can be done by cycle checking [10], in $O(|E|)$ time.

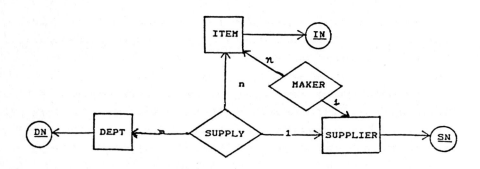

FIGURE 3. A regular ERD that is not in BCNF

The condition of Berge acyclicity is a stronger condition on the ERD's relational schema than "gamma acyclicity" [10]. These acyclic conditions relate to our work on lossless outer joins, which deals with gamma-acyclic relational schema [16, 17]. It is known that the latter schema, if in BCNF, have highly desirable query processing and update properties [4].

III. THE GRAPHICAL (E-R) DATA MODEL REPRESENTATION, IN PROLOG

Since the earlier data models - such as the hierarchical, network, or even the relational - are computer-oriented, they are found inadequate for expressing data semantics as understood by real-world designers. The newer graphical data model, the Entity-Relationship model, is preferred for easier designing, better understanding, and improved modeling. E-R designs can incorporate most of the important semantics information about real world scenarios (except domain constraints, which can be added as documentation), and they are much easier to learn to use.

Moreover, the graphically expressed E-R model can be more easily understood by non-technical people. Due to the many advantages of the visual __and__ semantic features of the E-R model, we chose it as the highly visible centerpiece of our visual database design system -- ERDDS.

A.   ERD Representation in PROLOG

To achieve our prototype's goals effectively, we chose the [Turbo] PROLOG compiler package. PROLOG is unique as a design/programming language in that it provides built-in "database" facilities in which to store information; it also provides access methods into this database. In such a structured environment, the ERD graph can be easily represented as well as stored and retrieved throughout the whole design process. That is, we don't worry about distracting details in deciding and declaring which data structures to use, as we do with most other programming languages.

In our system an ERD is represented in the **PROLOG** database in the form of logical assertions of **predicates** acting on **Objects** as follows:

```
entity("Entity")
relationship("Relationship")
iden("Entity","IdentifierList")
other_attributes("Entity/Relationship","AttributeList")
edge("StartNode","EndNode","Label").
```

David Maier wrote of PROLOG's database applicability:

   "Prolog has a good impedance match to relational databases... The language can be easily augmented, both in function and syntax. Special operations, new data structures...can be added readily, by defining new predicates. ... Virtual data definition is simple. Views can be readily added...and may reference other views" [19], pp.22-23. For example, the internal representation of the ERD of Figure 1 is shown below in Figure 7, which is the example's .DBA file, made by ERDDS.

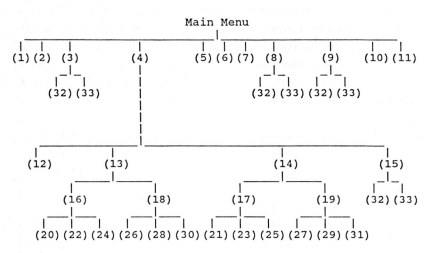

(1) Tutorial
(2) DOS Shell
(3) Initialize ERD
(4) Update ERD
(5) List nodes and edges of ERD
(6) Load ERD database file
(7) Save ERD database on file
(8) Test well-formedness of ERD
(9) Test loop-freeness of ERD
(10) View ERD
(11) View Canonical Relational Schema
(12) Change identifier of entity only
(13) Append part of ERD graph
(14) Retract part of ERD graph
(15) Update by editing database file
(16) Add (17) Delete nodes
(18) Add (19) Delete edges
(20) Add (21) Delete entity
(22) Add (23) Delete relationship
(24) Add (25) Delete attributes
(26) Add (27) Delete many- or one-labeled edges
(28) Add (29) Delete ISA edge
(30) Add (31) Delete ID edge
(32) Introduction
(33) Execution

Figure 4. ERDDS tree structure of menus

B.   Menu-driven Visual Database Designer Interface System

In developing a system, no matter how large and complex or how small and simple, good interfacing between users and computers should be one of the chief design aims. A programmer may develop a very useful and desirable system, but if it is difficult or confusing to use, it will not be used. Therefore, to avoid this disadvantage, we chose menu-driven interfacing for our inter-active system, to get users easily involved in the system by way of choosing the next operation from a menu, instead of memorizing a lot of operational steps.   **The menu of our system is tree-structured (see Figure 4).   With the menu driver, a user can do several operations:**

```
 _____ERD-BASED DEMONSTRATION DESIGN SYSTEM_____
|                                                         |
|                                                         |
|                                                         |
|                           ____Main menu____             |
|                          |Tutorial           |          |
|                          |DOS Shell          |          |
|                          |                   |          |
|                          |Initialize ERD     |          |
|                          |Update ERD         |          |
|                          |List nodes and edges of ERD|  |
|                          |                   |          |
|                          |Load ERD database file|       |
|                          |Save ERD database on file|     |
|                          |                   |          |
|                          |Test well-formedness of ERD|  |
|                          |Test loop-freeness of ERD|     |
|                          |View ERD           |          |
|                          |View Canonical Relational Schema|
|                          |_____|          |
|_____|
```

ESC: Quit this menu -- Use arrow keys to select, hit RETURN
or F10 to activate.

Figure 5. Main Menu of the System

1. Construct an ERD interactively:

  The user is given a menu of options, including:

  (a) initialize an ERD: upon choosing this item from

    the main menu (see Figure 5), the user is

    prompted to enter nodes and edges for the ERD.

  (b) update the ERD: choosing it from the main menu,

    the user can update the ERD by way of choosing

    "Change identifier of entity only," "Append part

    of ERD graph," or "Retract part of ERD graph" from

    the submenu (which looks like an Edit Mode).

    For a veteran user there is an alternative menu,

    "Update by editing database file", to use.

  (c) list nodes and edges of the ERD: with this menu choice

    the user can proof-read the input data and save the listing

    (see Figure 6, below) for future reference.

2. Load or Save the ERD database file:

  In Turbo Prolog, we can save the ERD database (see preceding section
  for its representation) into some .DBA disk file, so that the
  initialized or updated ERD can be saved and simply loaded next time
  when it is needed. **This can save much work;**cf. Figure 7.

3. Test well-formedness of the ERD:

  (a) first test if the user-input ERD is well-formed by

    invoking the well-formed-ERD check; ERDDS may issue an

    error message indicating for what reason the ERD

    fails to be well-formed, and finally it graphs

    the "ill-formed" part of the ERD, as an option.

```
NODES --
  ENTITIES --
    EMPL -- IDENTIFIER = ["ID"], OTHER ATTRIBUTES =
              ["NAME","SALARY"]
    DEPT -- IDENTIFIER = ["DEPT#"], OTHER ATTRIBUTES = []
    DIVSN -- IDENTIFIER = ["DIVSN#"], OTHER ATTRIBUTES = []
    MANAGER -- IDENTIFIER = [], OTHER ATTRIBUTES =
                ["TITLE"]
    PROJ -- IDENTIFIER = ["PROJ#"], OTHER ATTRIBUTES = []
    RELATIONSHIPS --
    WORKS_IN -- IDENTIFIER = [], OTHER ATTRIBUTES =
                ["LOCATION"]
    WORKS_ON -- IDENTIFIER = [], OTHER ATTRIBUTES =
                ["ST_DATE"]

EDGES --
  EMPL      --Iden-->   ID
  EMPL      ---->    NAME
  EMPL      ---->    SALARY
  DEPT      --Iden-->   DEPT#
  DIVSN     --Iden-->   DIVSN#
  MANAGER   ---->    TITLE
  PROJ      --Iden-->   PROJ#
  WORKS_IN    ---->    LOCATION
  WORKS_ON    ---->    ST_DATE
  WORKS_IN    --N-->     EMPL
  WORKS_IN    --1-->     DEPT
  WORKS_ON    --M-->     EMPL
  WORKS_ON    --N-->     PROJ
  MANAGER   --ISA-->     EMPL
  DEPT      --ID-->   DIVSN
```

Figure 6. List of Nodes and Edges of the example ERD

(b) The user receiving the error message is able

to return to 1(b) to update the ERD, and then

repeat testing and updating until it is well-formed.

4. **Test loop-freeness of the ERD:**

As described earlier, if a regular ERD is not loop-free,

then some relation schemes in its canonical relational

schema may not be in BCNF. So, in order to more securely

achieve the desired robust logical schema, the user is

given this opportunity to test if his or her ERD is

loop-free, even though not every "loopy" ERD yields a

non-BCNF relational schema.

If this test is positive, the system will issue a warning message
describing where the loop exists. The user then can optionally
remove the loop by updating the ERD. See Figure 9, below.

```
entity("EMPL")
entity("DEPT")
entity("DIVSN")
entity("MANAGER")
entity("PROJ")

relationship("WORKS_IN")
relationship("WORKS_ON")

iden("EMPL",["ID"])
iden("DEPT",["DEPT#"])
iden("DIVSN",["DIVSN#"])
iden("MANAGER",[])
iden("PROJ",["PROJ#"])
iden("WORKS_IN",[])
iden("WORKS_ON",[])

other_attributes("EMPL",["NAME","SALARY"])
other_attributes("DEPT",[])
other_attributes("DIVSN",[])
other_attributes("MANAGER",["TITLE"])
other_attributes("PROJ",[])
other_attributes("WORKS_IN",["LOCATION"])
other_attributes("WORKS_ON",["ST_DATE"])

edge("EMPL","ID","Iden")
edge("EMPL","NAME","")
edge("EMPL","SALARY","")
edge("DEPT","DEPT#","Iden")
edge("DIVSN","DIVSN#","Iden")
edge("MANAGER","TITLE","")
edge("PROJ","PROJ#","Iden")
edge("WORKS_IN","LOCATION","")
edge("WORKS_ON","ST_DATE","")
edge("WORKS_IN","EMPL","N")
edge("WORKS_IN","DEPT","1")
edge("WORKS_ON","EMPL","M")
edge("WORKS_ON","PROJ","N")
edge("MANAGER","EMPL","ISA")
edge("DEPT","DIVSN","ID")
```

Figure 7. Prolog Representation of the ERD in Figure 1

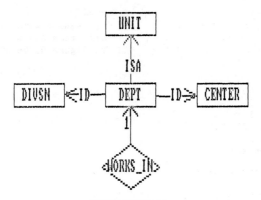

```
──────────────── ERROR MESSAGE ────────────────
Error 1: E-node DEPT has both ISA and ID outgoing edges.

Press any key to continue ...
```

Figure 8. An Example of testing for well-formedness

```
──────────────── ERROR MESSAGE ────────────────
Warning: The ERD has a loop--starting and ending in ITEM.
         --> Note: Both ITEM nodes on the screen are identical.
```

```
──────────────────────── HELP ────────────────────────
F1: HELP again    F2: Remove HELP    ARROW KEYS: View adjacent screens
NOTE: Duplicate nodes on the screen are identical!
ESC: Quit this reduced ERD demo
```

Figure 9. Detection of the loop of Figure 3

5. View the ERD (automatic layout of the ERD):

When the user chooses this option from the main menu,
the system invokes the well-formed and loop-free tests
on the ERD, then issues (with options) any required error
and/or warning messages, and draws the ERD on (up to nine)
multiple screens using the usual diagrammatic [27, Chap.1]
conventions of the ERD, if it is well-formed. The curious
user can view the well-formed ERD (even if it has some loops),
or its reduced (upper conceptual domain) representation,
and/or the (lower level) attributes of chosen entities or
relationships. For a full ERD layout grid, see Figure 10.

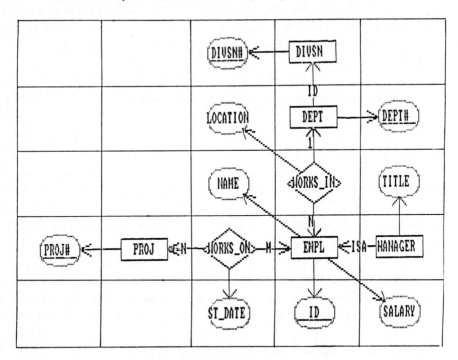

Figure10. Grid of one screen for the ERD layout

6. View the Canonical Relational Schema of the ERD:

After the well-formed and loop-free tests have been
executed, the system will list (Figure 11) the Canonical
Relational Schema of the ERD if it is well-formed, and ERDDS
advises the user if the schema satisfies the loop-free test.
**Taking its offerred advice, the user can re-design the current
relational schema, via the ERD, to get loop-freeness (=> BCNF).**

Other than the above six operations, the user can choose a "Tutorial"
menu to learn some general information about the system, or "DOS Shell"
to use DOS commands. Moreover, there is some introductory information
available for a few main menus upon the user's request, such as: the
**definition of the ERD, the ERD representation in the Prolog database,
the properties of the ERD, the error messages,** and so on - which can
also be viewed from each submenu before executing the related operation.

C. Explanation of the major ERDDS Heuristics

For a better understanding of ERDDS, it is necessary to be acquainted
with the algorithms it uses. In this subsection, we will present the
major ERDDS procedures and their heuristics, to help ensure clear
knowledge of the whole system, and of its new departures.

Automatic Layout of the ERD: In order to visualise clearly a large ERD
which cannot fit on one screen, ERDDS displays the diagram on several
(extensible) multiple screens. **Each screen is divided into regions: 5x5
cells. One cell represents one node. That means one node will have at
most eight neighbor nodes: boxes, circles or diamonds (see Figure 10).**
Then we utilise four steps for automatic layout of the ERD, as follows:

1) ask the user to choose a starting node some "central" object;

2) start traversing from the user's chosen node: visit nodes and store

their relative position using a Breadth-First-Search Technique:

(A) the priority sequence for visiting adjacent nodes:
   (i) entities or relationships;
   (ii) nodes with edges going to the node;
   (iii) identifiers;
   (iv) other attributes.

(B) the direction preferences to place adjacent nodes:
     West > North > East > South > NW > NE > SE > SW, circularly;

(C) store the calculated logical (relative) positions of
   nodes and edges in the database using internal coding;

3) centralize the ERD: translate the stored positions of the objects
as near to the center of (the nine) multiple screens as possible.

4) lay out (part of) the ERD on the screen, on the user's request,
using the stored position data to speed layout of:

(A) the whole ERD: first lay out the central screen.
   What to show next depends on the user's request. The
   other screens are shown by translating the stored logical
   coordinates to the sreen's physical coordinates.

(B) the reduced ERD: the same layout as that of the
   whole ERD, except that A-nodes are excluded.

(C) the lower level of any chosen node: for some of the
   entities or relationships, due to the limitation of
   only eight adjacent nodes allowed, some of their
   attributes cannot be shown on the whole ERD layout.
   By choosing this option, which allows ERDDS to lay out
   only the chosen node and its attributes, users are able
   to view the "hidden", pop-up, lower domain attributes.

Testing for Well-formedness of the ERD: The definition of well-formed
ERD, presented earlier, gives us seven properties (0 to 6) that any
well-formed ERD should have. In other words, **they are the rules** to
verify if an ERD is well-formed. For our system, we rewrote these

verification rules as Prolog logical clauses. **They are the kernel of its E-R semantics knowledge base.** ERDDS applies all the verification rules from the rule base to any given ERD stored in the Prolog graph database. To be well-formed, the ERD **must satisfy all** these rules. If not, the system will give a diagnosis and generate a description of the error. An example of one verification test is shown in Figure 7, with a graphic display of the "ill-formed" part, and an informative error message.

Testing for Loop-freeness of the ERD: To test if a well-formed ERD is loop-free, we do Depth-First Search for each E-node, after a node-degree check detects that it is a non-tree. **Certain points must be noted: for each edge passed by, we disconnect it temporarily; edges are considered undirected; we don't visit any A-nodes because they never exist on any loop in any well-formed ERD.** Once we finish a search, we test to see if the start node is on a loop by checking if it is visited more than once. If so, then the node exists along at least one loop in the ERD.

For the display of each loop on the screen, we choose to break the loop, let the "start/end node" of the loop be shown on the screen twice, and advise the user that duplicate nodes are identical. To display a whole ERD with more than one loop, we simply store an "extra" node for each loop in the database. When a display is requested, these nodes will be displayed multiply. This way we can lay out more than one loop on the screen without the confusion of crossed edges. The loop of the ERD shown in Figure 3 is detected in Figure 9.

Translation of ERD into CRS: To translate the ERD into its Canonical Relational Schema, we use the PROLOG version of ALGORITHM I, which includes all rules mapping the ERD EG = (N,E) into its CRS (R,K,I). **We coded these rules into a large Prolog knowledge base for our system, and the rule-based mapping applies these clauses to a given well-formed ERD, thereby generating its Canonical Relational Schema.** Figure 11 shows the output for the ERD in Figure 1. At the end of the output, ERDDS also advises the user if some relation in the CRS may not be in BCNF, when the ERD has loops. Figure 12 shows the corresponding SQL CREATE statements, which needs the user's further input of domain data types.

<<< RELATION SCHEMES >>>

-- WITH KEYS GIVEN BY BRACKETED ([]) ATTRIBUTES --
-- KD: KEY DEPENDENCY --

EMPL([EMPL.ID] NAME SALARY)
  KD [EMPL.ID] --> EMPL.ID NAME SALARY

DEPT([DEPT# DIVSN#])
  KD [DEPT# DIVSN#] --> DEPT# DIVSN#

MANAGER([EMPL.ID] TITLE)
  KD [EMPL.ID] --> EMPL.ID TITLE

WORKS_IN([EMPL.ID] DEPT# DIVSN# LOCATION)
  KD [EMPL.ID] --> EMPL.ID DEPT# DIVSN# LOCATION

WORKS_ON([EMPL.ID PROJ#] ST_DATE)
  KD [EMPL.ID PROJ#] --> EMPL.ID PROJ# ST_DATE

<<< INCLUSION DEPENDENCIES >>>

WORKS_ON[EMPL.ID] belongs to EMPL[EMPL.ID]
WORKS_IN[EMPL.ID] belongs to EMPL[EMPL.ID]
WORKS_IN[DEPT# DIVSN#] belongs to DEPT[DEPT# DIVSN#]

MANAGER[EMPL.ID] belongs to EMPL[EMPL.ID]

FOOTNOTE: If the well-formed ERD is regular (every
     functional dependency which is true for the
     canonical database scheme is a logical
     consequence of the KD's listed above), then
     each relation listed above is in BCNF.

Figure 11. Example output of Relational Schema of Figure 1

```
CREATE SCHEMA
AUTHORIZATION ALL

CREATE TABLE EMPL
         EMPL.ID  INTEGER   NOT NULL   UNIQUE
         NAME   CHARACTER
         SALARY   REAL

CREATE TABLE DEPT
         DEPT#   INTEGER   NOT NULL   UNIQUE
         DIVSN#   INTEGER   NOT NULL   UNIQUE



CREATE TABLE MANAGER
         EMPL.ID   INTEGER   NOT NULL   UNIQUE
         TITLE   CHARACTER



CREATE TABLE WORKS_IN
         EMPL.ID   INTEGER   NOT NULL   UNIQUE
         DEPT#   INTEGER
         DIVSN#   INTEGER
         LOCATION   CHARACTER

CREATE TABLE WORKS_ON
         EMPL.ID   INTEGER   NOT NULL   UNIQUE
         PROJ#   INTEGER   NOT NULL   UNIQUE
         ST_DATE   NUMERIC
```

Figure 12.   SQL output for the Example 1 ERD

IV.   TESTING AND EVALUATION OF ERDDS

ERDDS has E-R semantics built into its PROLOG knowledge base that favor
E-R diagrams with more robust relational schema; the latter are assured
by rigorous checks for desirable properties of regular, well-formed ERDs,
represented as PROLOG "databases" of facts, and loop-freeness of the ERD.

In general, we have accomplished our intended research objective: an
ERD-based Database Design System with a visual semantics knowledge base
that gives advice, much like an expert system. ERDDS has been developed
following an analysis of the use of well-behaved ERDs in the logical
design of relational database schemas.   To check how well our system
works we have done several tests, to be reported elsewhere, and find that
the ERDDS system is intelligent enough:

1. to detect the well-formed and loop-free properties of the ERD built by the system from the designer's description of a planned information system in terms of Entities, Attributes, and Relationships.

2. to lay out the ERD centrally on multiple screens, which is very useful for larger databases. (So far we set up our system with nine screens, and it would be trivial to extend that number.)

3. to save the .DBA file, which, when the enterprise environment changes, can be handily retrieved to edit the ERD and to get a new CRS, to fit better the changed environment. A novice user can use the menus for editing, while an expert user can access the .DBA file directly to edit the ERD.

4. to generate the CRS and advise the user by footnotes if the ERD is loop-free, so that the CRS is in BCNF. Receiving a "loop exists" note, the user can go back to Edit mode to remove the loop, optionally, to achieve a more robust CRS.

D.   Assessment of the ERDDS Strategy for Database Design

ERDDS has similarities, and differences, with several recent E-R-based tools for essentially the same end-goal: relational DB logical design. We shall focus on major tools presented at E-R Approach Conferences since 1983:

INCOD, INCOD-DTE, GDOC, GINCOD (1983-87) - these famous tools of the Universita' di Roma DB group, GESI, pioneered the min-grid E-R diagram technic, incorporated graphic editing & coherency checking, and stressed four system features: ease of use; self-documentation; adaptability to users; and compatibility with their other design/DB tools [Bati83, Bati85, Tama]. These systems have the advantage of mainframe power.

EASY ER (1985) - Another GESI product, made to run on a PC, it enforces structured methodology on the RDB design goal, using an extended E-R model (with hierarchic structures that we omit). EASY ER alone has a feature to integrate local schemata into one global schema [Ferr83, GESIa, GESIb]. See remarks below.

TSER (1987) - a LISP near-equivalent of our original idea, but it stressed "Two-Stage E-R" design, via (1) a Semantic E-R model user interface, (2) algorithmic mapping to other models, e.g. the RDB, and (3) a knowledge base of [parts of] the RDB design field [13].

CHRIS (1987) - this expert system tool for DB design, written in PROLOG, also queries the user in NL and has a 3-stage design process focusing on, besides the conceptual and logical stages, a shared goal: an SQL generator enforcing integrity constraints via rules.

Compared with some of these recently released major ER-based tools that have the same relational database logical design aim, such as INCOD, GINCOD, EASY ER, and TSER, our system is not yet so powerful in layout options [26, 13]. Nevertheless, being strongly positive of its potential, we plan to continue ERDDS development until our system becomes competitive with any of these university prototypes. Unlike some of these others, ERDDS outputs the logical schema with a set of relevant constraints plus SQL CREATEs output as declarations of the relations.

We plan to develop ERDDS, a normal-form-biased demonstration system, until it is a full-featured E-R layout system competitive with any of those above. The next phase towards that goal would be more full and extensive testing, beyond the first two hundred DBs so far designed.

Our further research shall focus on the following relative advantages: First, we shall improve the system so that one can edit the design ERD directly on its graphical (Object-Oriented) representation. Second, like the systems mentioned above, we could layout loopy ERDs as they actually are (even though we don't like them - ERDDS is biased towards BCNF), instead of using duplicate nodes. Third, users will be given a chance to test if the schema satisfies normal forms weaker than BCNF. Fourth, we look forward to the research and development of a reverse translator from relational schemas to ERDs, for cases when we need to change the relational schema directly, to fit better the users' changed environment (e.g., to normalize new schemes) so that the new relational schema can determine the new ERD. [This is a harder map, as the inverse of the "many ERDs to one CRS" map of Algorithm I.]

ERDDS assists database design in two stages: user objects to ERD, then from ERD to CRS and SQL. So far, our system allows users to edit their ERD only by way of menus and prompts. One possible improvement is to try to edit the ERD more directly, on the graphical representation. To achieve this goal, we plan to experiment more with object-oriented methods and messages, in redesigning the visual interface of Edit Mode.

The alleged advantage of object-oriented computing is: what the user sees on the screen at any moment is a direct and true representation of the state of the viewed object, the so-called "what you see is what you get" (WYSIWYG) principle. We respect this objective in that the ERD really reflects the DB schema, at any instant; ERDDS already displays all truly essential features of a disciplined, database-designer-oriented visual system. It is now and always will be based on the "WYDIWYG" principle: What You DIAGRAM is What You Get! We mainly need to distribute our E-R semantic knowledge to each object class, to let objects communicate by messages generated by their attached methods.

As a research tool, what our system shows is that the Graphical E-R Data Model is preferable for its universality and ease of understanding, with labels in any language. We have shown that Logic Programming (PROLOG) is compatible with the object-oriented design of relational DBs, and allows an elegant translation of input terms to visual objects which, after quality control, are mappable to SQL logical schema for the database, with full preservation of semantic information. In fact, ERDDS achieves semantic enhancement: theory adds its generic knowledge to the user's application-specific information.

- %#S -

ACKNOWLEDGEMENT: WE THANK THE USA NATIONAL SCIENCE FOUNDATION FOR GOOD SUPPORT OF THIS RESEARCH, INCLUDING A RECENT "RESEARCH EXPERIENCES FOR UNDERGRADUATES" SUPPLEMENT, WHICH WILL ALLOW FURTHER TESTING IN 1989.

WE ALSO MUST THANK THE TC-2/ WG 2.6 REFERREES FOR THEIR HELPFUL REMARKS AND ENCOURAGEMENT. THEIR ATTENTION TO DETAIL WAS SUPERIOR, AND WAS USED!

REFERENCES

[1] C. Batini, **"What is a good diagram? A pragmatic approach"**, in [7], pp. 312-319.

[2] M.A. Casanova and J.E. Amaral de Sa, "Mapping uninterpreted schemes into entity-relationship diagrams: two applications to conceptual schema design", **IBM J. Res. & Develpmt.** 28, 1 (Jan. 1984), 82-94.

[3] M.A. Casanova and V.M.P. Vidal, "Towards a sound view integration methodology", **Proc. 2nd ACM Symp. on Principles of Database Systems**, 1983, 36-47.

[4] E.P.F. Chan and H.J. Hernandez, "On the desirability of gamma-acyclic BCNF database schemes", **Proc. 1st Intl. Conf. on Database Theory**, Rome, Sept. 1986 (preprints), 18 ms.pp.

[5] **P.P. Chen, "The entity-relationship model: toward a unified view of data,"** ACM Trans. Database Sys. 1, 1 **(March 1976), 33-37.**

[6] **P.P. Chen, ed., Entity-Relationship Approach to Information Modeling and Analysis,** Proc. of the 2nd Intl. Conf. on the E-R **Approach,** E-R Institute (1981).

[7] P.P. Chen, ed., Entity-Relationship Approach: The Use of E-R Concept in Knowledge Representation, **Proc. of the 4th Intl. Conf. on E-R Approach,** IEEE CS Press/North-Holland (1985).

[8] I. Chung, F. Nakamura, and P.P. Chen, "A decomposition ofrelations using the entity-relationship approach", in: [6], pp. 151-173.

[9] C.G. is, et al., eds., Entity-Relationship Approach to Software Engineering, **Proc. of the 3rd Intl. Conf. on E-R Approach,** North-Holland, 1983.

[10] R. Fagin, "Hypergraphs and Relational Database Schemes," **J. ACM 30** (3), July 1983, 514-550.

[11] F.M. Ferrara, "GDOC, a tool for the computerized design and documentation of database systems", **ACM DataBase,** Smr. 1984.

[12] I.T. Hawryszkiewycz, "A computer aid for E-R modeling," in [7], pp. 64-69.

[13] C. Hsu, A. Perry & M.Bouziane, "TSER: a data modeling system using the Two-Stage E-R Approach," in [21].

[14] S. Jajodia, P.Nq, and F.N. Springsteel, "The problem of equivalence for entity-relationship diagrams", **IEEE Trans. Software Engr.** 5 (SE-9), 1983, 617-630.

[15] S. Jajodia, P.Nq, and F.N. Springsteel, "Entity-relationship diagrams which are in BCNF", **Intl. J. Comp. & Info.Sci.** 12(4), 1983, 269-283.

[16]   S.Jajodia and F.N. Springsteel, "Lossless outer joins of relations
       containing nulls", **Proc. 19th Hawaii Intl. Conf. on System
       Sciences,** 1986, 438-444.

[17]   S.Jajodia and   F.N. Springsteel,   "Construction of universal
       instances for loop-free network databases, using a join-like
       operation", **IEEE Trans. Software Engr.** SE-13 (1987), 811-819.

[18]   Y.E. Lien, "On the semantics of the Entity-Relationship data
       model", in **Entity-Relationship Approach to System Analysis and
       Design,** (P. Chen, ed.), North-holland (1980), 131-146.

[19]   D. Maier, **"Databases in the Fifth Generation Project: Is Prolog a
       database language?",** in: Ariav & Clifford, **New Directions for
       Database Systems,** 1986, Ablex, Norwood, NJ:

[20]   J.A. Makowsky, V.M. Markowitz and N. Rotics, "Entity-
       Relationship consistency for relational schemas", **Proc. 1st
       Intl. Conf. Database Theory,** Rome, Sept.86 (preprints) 18pp.

[21]   S. March, ed., **Proceedings of the Sixth Intl. Conf. on Entity-
       Relationship Approach,** E-R Institute, 1987.

[22]   J.C. Mitchell, "The implication problem for functional and
       inclusion dependencies", **Information and Control** 56, 3 (March
       1983) 154-173.

[23]   H. Sakai, "E-R Approach to Logical Database Design", in **[9], 155-
       187.**

[24]   F.N. Springsteel, **"Regular   E-R   Diagrams:** their normalized
       structures", **Proc. 17th Hawaii Intl. Conf. Sys. Sci.,** 433-443.

[25]   F.N. Springsteel and P-J. Chuang, "ERDDS: the _intelligent_   E-R-
       based Database Design System", Proc. 7th E-R Approach Conf.,
       (North Holland) Novem. 1988, Rome, Italy, in press.

[26]   R. Tamasia, "New layout techniques for large E-R diagrams", in
       [7], pp. 304-311.

[27]   J.D. Ullman, _Principles of Database Systems,_ 2nd edition, ex-
       Computer Science Press, 1982.

[28]   E. Wong and R.H. Katz, "Logical design and schema conversion for
       relational and DBTG databases", in **Entity-Relationship Approach to
       System Analysis and Design,** (P. Chen, ed.), North Holland (1980),
       131-146.

Session 4

USER INTERFACE

Visual Database Systems
T.L. Kunii (Editor)
Elsevier Science Publishers B.V. (North-Holland)
© IFIP, 1989

SOME PRINCIPLES OF ICON CONSTRUCTION *

Fang Sheng Liu, Ju Wei Tai

Institute of Automation
Academia Sinica
P.O.Box 2728, Beijing, China

Now visual computing has been a tendency in
computer science and are finding more and
more applications. But human computer communication by graphics sometimes causes ambiguity. So how to construct a good external
expression set, including menu and icon, is
an urgent problem to solve. This paper takes
an integrated viewpoint of menu and icon,
with both of them being wiewed as a dual
representation (meaning, image), and motivated by the ideas of Chinese character
category theory, called " 六书 ", puts up six
icon construction principles. It focuses on
the image part of a generalized icon in its
dual representation and discusses the method
of applying them to icon image construction
and the evaluation of the constructed icons.

Key Words and Phrases: generalized icon, menu, menu extraction, icon construction, meaning, Chinese character generation, interactive system, visual computing, iconic representation, attributed grammar.

1. INTRODUCTION

With the emergence of high-quality low-cost graphic
workstations, human computer interaction is given more and
more emphases. Visual and natural representations of data,
operations and processes now become the tendency in research
and market, which open a new field for visual human machine
communication in terms of various visual styles, such as

---

* The work is supported partially by the national grants of
high technology.

iconic languages and menus. People believe that visual
representations can help reduce complexity and especialy
mental memory workload [6]. S. K. Chang put up icon semantics
[5] which is based upon generalized icons of dual representation,

            a generalized icon = (meaning , image)

and an icon algebra. In the dual representation, "image" is
the external graphic representation of an icon, whereas
"meaning" is the internal representation of meaning (in
computer) of the icon image (short for image part of a
generalized icon). The icon algebra is used to construct
complex icons from other icons (elementary icons for example)
of simple meaning. So a complex icon has a more complex
meaning part [5] (complex semantics for short). According
to Chang, complex icons include composite icons composed
from sub-icons using operator and structural icons consisting
of other icons without composing mechanism specified.In fact,
when we communicate with computer,taking an icon as language
unit,we can only percept the image part of an icon on screen.
So in most cases,we can only know the meaning from the image.
But the meaning that we know from the image is not
necessarily what the "meaning" means in the dual representa-
tion.Generally, a set I of graphic representations corresponding to image part may be chosen for a given "meaning" m. So
we have a many-to-one mapping R,

                    R : I x { m }.

Elements in I may have shade of difference in conveying the
semantics of m, but they seem to be more appropriate to
different poeple for m. They even have different meaning to
different poeple. That is to say, due to the lack of conventions and standardizations , what "image" part means
("meaning") to computer may be quite different from what it
means ("mental-meaning") to human. Hence comes the problem.

    How do we construct an icon image to express the
    "meaning" more exactly to human, that is,to minimize
    the difference between "meaning" to computer and the
    "mental-meaning" to human.

One solution is to minimize set I and make it a convention
and/or standard so that people know the exact correspondence
between e ∈ I and m. This is too time and efforts-consuming
to be done. Another solution is to give a set of icon

construction principles so that poeple can understand the meaning of constructed icons more exactly. This will be discussed in the paper in details. From a unified viewpoint, the "image" part of a generalized icon (meaning, image) may be text and/or graphic. Therefore, we have three denotational combinations to represent the image part.They are as follows:

(meaning , text) ...... (1)
(meaning , graphics) ...... (2)
(meaning , graphics+text). ...... (3)

In (meaning, text), "text" may be verbal descriptions or function words.The latter is in fact the menu frequently used today.Suppose that the verbal descriptions and function words are both chosen comparatively well. We have the following table to compare verbal descriptions with function words menu.

TABLE 1
Comparision of Verbal Description with Function Words Menu

	physical space for representation	time to be understood	semantics	ambiguity
function words menu	less	less	concise	?
verbal descrip-tion	more	more	verbose	?

Verbal descriptions alone need more space for representation, more time to be understood, and more translation effort to the real manipulating action [6]. On the other hand, function words menu is recognized more friendly than verbal descriptions. Generally, function words menus are self-evident. User gets familiar with it (i.e. knows its meaning) quite fast. The representations of menus by function words are much easier than that of icons. So we focus on the last two expressions in (2) and (3) in the following sections. The icon, as a kind of ideograph, is simpler than and different from complex image (see TABLE 2).

TABLE 2
Comparision of Icon with Complex Image

	physical space for representation	time to be understood	semantics	ambiguity
icon	less	less	narrow	?
complex image	more	more	wide	?

Chinese characters are pictographs. They have been evolving from ancient forms that were small pictures each into the the modern forms, Chinese ideogram. They are the cream of the Chinese culture. Chinese character category theory called " 六书 " generates Chinese characters from small meaningful picture and combines them to form new ones. So its formation and interpretation have close relation with the Chinese culture. It says that there are six categories of Chinese characters [12].

Category1:(象形) pictographic characters or pictographs;
Category2:(指事) self-explanatory characters;
Category3:(会意) associative compounds, which are formed by combining two or more elements, each with a meaning of its own, to create a new meaning;
Category4:(形声) pictophonetic characters, with one element indicating meaning and the other sound;
Category5:(转注) mutually explanatory or synonymous characters;
Category6:(假借) phonetic loan characters, characters adopted to represent homophones.

From our knowledge, we think that the underlying corresponding generation rules are as follows.

Rule1: Shape-like Generation: a Chinese character looks like the external shape of an objective thing, called pictographic character;
Rule2: Symbolic Marking Generation: a Chinese character

is created by putting a symbolic mark onto a pictographic character;

Rule3: Generation by Understanding: a Chinese character is created by combining two or more pictographic characters;

Rule4: Generation by Image-and-Sound:a Chinese character is formed by two halves; one is often a pictographic character;the other gives the pronouciation;

Rule5: Characters with the Same Component Explaining Each Other;

Rule6: Generation by Borrowing: a Chinese character is used by borrowing from existing words that have the same name and pronouciation.

Motivated by the ideas of the generation rules we discuss icon image construction in the next sections.

2. SOME ICON CONSTRUCTION PRINCIPLES

The expression in (2), (meaning, graphics), we emphasize graphical representation of "meaning". This section pays attention to the way of expressing meaning with icon image more exactly to eliminate ambiguity (due to the difference between "meaning" and "mental-meaning") more efficiently, that is, the principles for icon image construction. So, we focus on what appearance an icon may have to express its meaning, and the organization of icons. It should be pointed out that the following principles are not completely parallel with the six categories of the Chinese character formation and interpretation theory. First, we discuss the principles for constructing icons.

2.1. Principle 1: Appearance Reference

No matter what objects or processes we are faced with, we have three classes of things:

natural things that may be found in nature,
artificial things made by man, and
abstract things.

For natural things, we may take their natural shape as the icon image. If a natural thing has not visual shape, we may take the graphic representation of its phenomena and/or behavior, etc as the icon image. Some examples is shown in FIGURE 1.

image	meaning
	mountain (山)
	electricity
	fire (火)
	sun (日)
	moon (月)
	bird (雀)

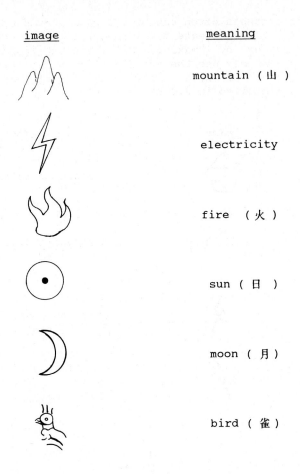

FIGURE 1
Examples of Icons for Natural Things

The icon image of the artificial things may also take their external appearance. FIGURE 2 gives one example.

image	meaning
	disk

FIGURE 2
An Example of Icons for Artificial Things

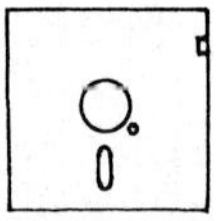

Abstract concepts often cannot be represented so directly as the above. So we create icon image by combination and/or similarity or by making the abstract the concrete. In addition, we may use the artificial symbols that have been standardized or have become conventions as icons. Four examples are given in FIGURE 3.

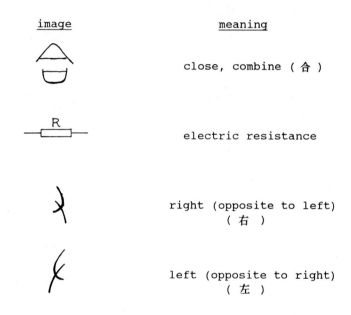

FIGURE 3
Examples of Icons for Abstract Concepts

Here, " △ " is a cover (for a pan); " ▽ " is cooking container that looks like a pan;so the top icon in FIGURE 3 means to put them together, i.e. "close or combine".The third icon in FIGURE 3 is a right hand drawn in a simplified style, so its meaning is "right", with the modern Chinese ideogram in the bracket next to the meaning.

2.2. Principle 2: Marking Emphases

    Mark a special position of an image or add special markers to an icon image to emphasize the "meaning", to make clear and evident the local semantics and its relation to other part of the icon image. Usually we use point marker,

arrow, circle, color, blinking, highlightening, etc to make
the "meaning" evident to user. Here are some examples (in
FIGURE 4).

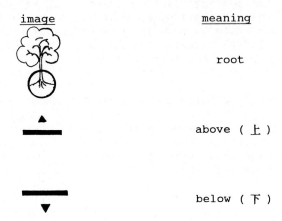

image   meaning

                                                    root

                                            above (上)

                                            below (下)

FIGURE 4
Examples of Icons by Emphasis-Making

2.3. Principle 3: Similarity-Abstraction Reference

By similarity, we create half of an icon image, which
shows the class to which what the icon denotes belongs or its
relation that the meaning of the icon has to a definite thing
type may be similiar in some sense. By   abstraction, we
construct the other half of the icon image, which shows its
peculiar or characteristic meaning or properties.In FIGURE 5,
the icons both consist of two parts.

image   meaning

                                    female animal (牝)

                                    male animal (牡)

FIGURE 5
Examples of Icons of Similiar Properties

In the upper icon in FIGURE 5,the left half of the icon is an
ox head, meaning the icon being for animal. The right half of
the icon is mark for ewe, sow, mare, etc. Hence,the interpretation of the meaning is "female animal". In the lower icon,
the right half of the icon is a mark for ram,boar,horse, etc.
Hence, the meaning is male "male animal". Another example is
shown in FIGURE 9 (a3)-(e3), in which the similar half is
"house", meaning the icon having relation with house or
building.

2.4. Principle 4: Borrowing from Other Representations

By borrowing, we express the icons that are not easily
expressed directly. The borrowed image may have a visible
external shape and take the "meaning" as its property,
function, behavior, etc.

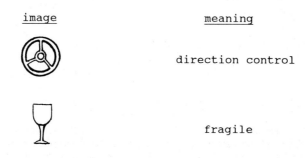

image   meaning

                                 direction control

                                 fragile

FIGURE 6
Examples of Icons Constructed by borrowing

Secondly, we discuss the organization of primitive icons
to form complex icons with icons created under the guidance
of the above principles and other rules.

2.5. Principle 5: Interpretation through Integration and Transformation

Combining two or more meaningful images or simple (primitive) icon images,transforming existing icons, or both transforming and combining other icons, may form a new icon image.
Like the Chinese character generation, we have also different
subrules to guide the formation of a new icon image [4]. Here
is one example.

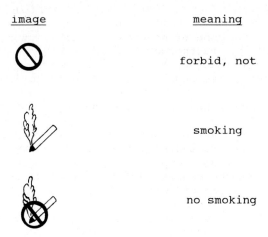

FIGURE 7
An Example of Complex Icon

Another two examples are shown in FIGURE 9 (a2)-(e2) and (a3) -(e3).

2.6. Principle 6: Combination of Graphics with Text

This concerns with the expression in (3),that is,(meaning, graphics+text)."text" here means function words or key words. In this way, the image part may be described vividly and more accurately. This principle may be nearer to Category 4 in some sense, for example,

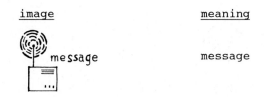

FIGURE 8
An Example of Icon with Text.

For more complex icon generation from simpler ones,attributed tree grammar may be used [4]. Hence more complex concepts may be formed (see the next section).

3. METHODOLOGY

We discuss some principles for constructing icons in the above section. Furthermore, these principles can be used in different combinations to construct icons of different semantics. We will give some examples in this section.

3.1. Tree Representation of Complex Icons

For a given set of primitive icons, we may construct new icons from them to satisfy the needs for new semantic structures. In creating complex icons, we observe the fact that they often can be represented by a tree, as shown in FIGURE 9 (a1) are a strand of silk and a hand. (b1) shows a hand combining two strands of silk, meaning take them together. Hence, the interpretation of the meaning is "connect" in (e1). (a2) are a tower over a city gate (the picture like a arrow),

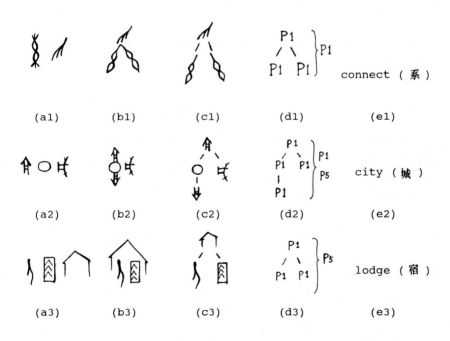

(a1)	(b1)	(c1)	(d1)	(e1)
(a2)	(b2)	(c2)	(d2)	(e2)
(a3)	(b3)	(c3)	(d3)	(e3)

FIGURE 9

3 examples of tree representation; (a),(b),(c),(d) and (e) are components, icon image, tree representation, principles used for components and the whole icon (on the right side of the bracket), and meaning respectively.

city wall or an area (the circle) and an axe-like ancient
weapon. The left half of (b2) shows two standing towers over
a city and the right half is meant to defence the city wall
with weapon. Hence, the interpretation of the meaning "city"
in (e2). (a3) gives a person, a mat and a house. (b3) shows a
person lying on a mat in a house. Hence, the meaning is
"lodge" in (e3).

Complex icons can be generated from the tree representation as well as the primitives in it [4].

3.2. Iconic Description of Meaning

Many concepts in computations such as what, what-to-do,
where, when, why, often give semantics that does not vary
with time and/or space. The visualization of the semantics
with such property generally does not has variant forms. For
example, for a given source program, its program structure is
definite. The iconic representation of such semantics for
the given definite structure is also time and space-invariant
[3] [11], as shown in FIGURE 10. Here the flow chart of a
given function is treated as a complex icon composed of a
complete set of primitive icons [4].

```
aa(b)
int b;
{ int i,j;
  i=0;
  if(i<b) j=0;
  else j=2;
  b=i*j*100;
}
```

(a)   (b)

FIGURE 10
An example of semantic structure(a)
and its visual form (b)

Icon-based human computer communication and many fields
of visual computing deal semantics with dynamic properties
(i.e. time- or space-invariant meaning) a lot, including
visual changes in man machine dialogue, dynamic processes and
animation [10]. In many cases, the visual representation of
semantics with dynamic property consists of iconic representation of semantics that is time and space-invariant and

dynamic marking. Principle 2 is often used there.For example, in an industrial process conrol flow chart, the semantic structure with dynamic properties is constructed through iconic representation of its time and space-invariant semantic structure and dynamic graphic marking (e.g. control position, local states, etc) by colors, markers, blinking, etc.

3.2.1. Visualization of Data

In many cases, objects have time and space-invariant semantics conceptually. As an example, "file" is visualized in FIGURE 11 (a) (b) as a static icon.

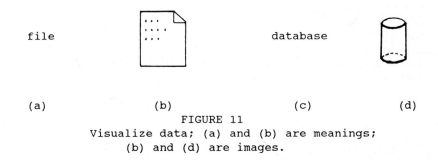

file   database

(a)   (b)   (c)   (d)
FIGURE 11
Visualize data; (a) and (b) are meanings;
(b) and (d) are images.

Even when data vary, its iconic representation, as shown in FIGURE 11 (c) (d), may be static externally. In some other cases, if we want to know the exact values of data or varia- bles, graphic representations only are not enough. Tools for visual organization of data should be provided [8].

3.2.2. Visualization of Operations

If we treat operations as nonprocedural actions, regard- less of thier implementation, operations themselves give the semantics of what-to-do. The semantics is in fact time and, space-invariant, although an icon sequence, in which such primitive icons as arrow exist, as a whole is used for the iconic representation of an operation, as shown in FIGURE 12.

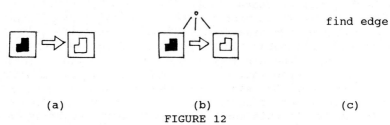

find edge

(a)   (b)   (c)

FIGURE 12
Visualize the meaning of an operation; (a) operation;
(b) tree representation; (c) meaning.

The principles in section 2 is usually used in an integrated, alternate way for constructing either primitive icons
or complex icons. Sometimes it is hard to tell only one of
the principles but not others is used. But the principles
really work. To construct icons of complex semantics, principles 5 is much more often used, which reflects the relation
between complex icons and interpretation.

4. CONCLUSIONS AND DISCUSSIONS

Visualization of information in human computer interaction help reduce difficulties for user to learn and use the
system. Because of the lack of conventions and standardization, human computer communication by graphics may cause
ambiguity in meaning. The same meaning may be depicted with
two or more different icon images. Ambiguity may be produced
for this reason and may be caused due to the lack of dynamic
behavior in an icon, i.e. the lack of additional information
to eliminate ambiguity in a picture. So we need principles to
guide the design and understanding of the image part of an
icon.
In fact, these principles are not only used for basic or
primitive icons but also for complex icons; not only for
describing simple semantics but also for describing complex
semantics; not only for concrete things but also for abstract
things;not only for semantics with static properties but also
for semantics with dynamic properties.
On the other hand,iconic communication has the properties
of universalness. Furthermore,for a set of basic icons,if you
grasp a typical example, you will grasp the whole category,
that is to say, comprehend by analogy. Icon image itself as
language unit needs evolution and stadardization to represent

its meaning accurately. Although there is ambiguity in icon image, iconic communication is more efficient and now is warmly recieved by users.

The principles mentioned in the paper are efficient. From our experience, the assessment of the construction of icons is more or less subjective. For a primitive icon,its assessment depends on whether it can reflect its semantic features and concept intension. For a complex icon, its assessment depends more upon the ease with which its semantics is interpreted.When it can be interpreted differently, the icon image has ambiguity. In this case "graphics+text" combination is very effective. Of course,there is always a user's subjective acceptability of the iconic representations for a given meaning.

REFERENCES

[1] Liu, F.S., An Approach to Interactive Human Computer Interface Design, Proc. of 2th China National Conference on CAD and Computer Graphics, Dalian, China, Aug., 1987

[2] Liu, F.S. and Fang, F., A General Purpose Interactive Environment Supporting Intelligent Decision Support Systems, China 6th National Conference on Pattern Recognition and Machine Intelligence, Beijing, China, Oct., 1987

[3] Wang, J., Liu, F.S. and Tai, J.W.,Technical Report on the Research of a Visual Debugger System "VisualBug", (Institute of Automation, Academia Sinica, Beijing, China, May, 1988)

[4] Liu, F.S. and Tai, J.W., Icon Generation Based on Attributed Tree Grammar, A Technical Report, (Institute of Automation, Academia Sinica,Beijing, China, May, 1988)

[5] Chang, S.K., Icon Semantics--a Formal Approach to Icon System Design, International Journal of Pattern Recognition and Artificial Intelligence, Vol. 1, No. 1 (1987)

[6] Rohr, G., Understanding Visual Symbols,1984 IEEE Computer Society Workshop on Visual Languages, Hiroshima, Japan, Dec. 1984

[7] Chen, Z.Y., Liu, F.S., and Fang, F.,Research and Practice of Intelligent Decision Support Systems, China 6th National Conference on Pattern Recognition and Machine Intelligence, Beijing, China, Oct. , 1987

[8] Liu, F.S. and Tai, J.W., A Constructive Window System with Descriptive Power. A Technical Report, (Institute of Automation, Academia Sinica,Beijing, China, April, 1988,)

[9] Yoshimoto, I., Monden, N., Hirakawa, M., Tanaka, M. and Ichikawa, T., Interactive Iconic Programming Facility in

HI-Visual, IEEE Workshop on Visual Languages'86, June 25-27, 1986, Dallas, Texas, U. S. A.

[10]Liu, F.S. and Tai, J.W., An Appraoch to Computer Animation, a Technical Reprot, (Institute of Automation, Academia Sinica, Beijing, China July, 1988)

[11]Liu, F.S., Wang, J. and Tai, J.W., About the Research of a Visual Debugging System: VisualBug, 1988 Flexible Technology Center Conference, Academia Sinica, Aug. 1988, Beidaihe, China

[12]Zuo, A.M., Explaining Chinese characters by Examples, (China Youth Press, 1984)

Visual Database Systems
T.L. Kunii (Editor)
Elsevier Science Publishers B.V. (North-Holland)
IFIP, 1989

IMPLEMENTATION OF VISUAL DATABASE INTERFACE USING AN OBJECT-ORIENTED LANGUAGE

C. Thomas WU and David K. HSIAO

Naval Postgraduate School
Department of Computer Science, Code 52
Monterey, CA 93943
U. S. A.

KEYWORDS:Object-oriented language, visual interface, prototyping.

Many different visual interfaces to database are proposed in recent years. One of them is GLAD (*G*raphics *LA*nguage for *D*atabase), which supports a high-level semantic data model. Our immediate research goal is to implement a prototype for GLAD interface and experiment with different interface styles within the GLAD framework. To accelerate the prototype development, we have adopted an object-oriented language as our implementation tool. The features such as inheritance, polymorphism, and message passing of object-oriented language have helped us enormously in reducing the development time. In this paper, we describe the current status of GLAD interface and the merits of using an object-oriented language in implementing GLAD.

1. INTRODUCTION

Relational systems are the prevalent database management systems being installed in recent years. They are based on a solid mathematical foundation and provide better query languages compared to those of network and hierarchical

This research is partially funded by Naval Data Automation Command and Naval Ocean Systems Command. Actor is a trademark of The Whitewater Group, Inc. Microsoft Windows is a trademark of Microsoft Corporation.

systems. Although relational query languages such as SQL and QUEL are much better languages than those for network and hierarchical systems, they are still not an ideal languages for end-users. For database systems to become truly useful as information managers, end-user participation is indispensable because otherwise we must rely on data processing professionals to develop an application software. Such arrangement is prohibitively expensive for the coming decades of information explosion. We believe a visual interface, which supports a high-level semantic data model, holds a best potential as a end-user interaction tool.

Many visual interfaces to database systems have been proposed [BRYC86, ELMA85, FOGG84, GOLD85, HEIL85, HERO80, LARS84, MCDO74, STON82, SUGI84, WONG82, WU86, WU87, ZHAN83, ZLOO77]. We believe the research of user interface in general and visual user interface in particular is not fully explored yet. We have just started with many new proposals, and the field is still in infancy. There is no firm understanding of what constitute a good user interface. At this stage of research, it is beneficial to experiment with as many different approaches as possible. In order to facilitate experimentation with different approaches, we need a software development tool which will allow us to produce a prototype rapidly. Utilizing a right rapid prototyping tool is critical to the success of experimentation, which leads to a eventual success of visual database interface research. In this paper, we discuss the merits of using object-oriented language as a prototyping tool for implementing GLAD [WU86, WU87].

GLAD (Graphics LAnguage for Database) provides a coherent interface methods for both data manipulation and program development interactions. By providing a coherent interface method, it achieves a high degree of ease of learning and using. The key to this coherent interface is a simple visual representation of database schema. Users can visually interact with the system for data manipulation and program development. Data manipulation aspect of GLAD has been designed and partially implemented. Program development aspect is in the design stage. GLAD interface is described in the next section.

Desirable characteristics for our development tool include the ability to conduct rapid prototyping, modifiability, and extensibility. The development language should be powerful enough to allow complex ideas and relationships to be expressed without awkward structures and lengthy segments or excessive repetition of code. An excellent choice which incorporates these strengths is an object-oriented language. Since GLAD provides an object-oriented data model, there is a close relationship between the structure of database to be modeled and the logical entities used within the object-oriented programming environment.

The specific object-oriented language chosen for the implementation of GLAD was the language Actor. Actor is designed to run within the Microsoft Windows environment on an IBM compatible personal computer with at least 640K memory and a hard disk. The language forms a sophisticated and powerful development environment for such application as GLAD. It is interactive in nature and features development tools such as a Browser for development of code, an Inspector for examination of objects, and a Debugger for correction of errors.

The paper is organized as follows. We describe the visual interface GLAD in the next section. In Section 3, we present the features of an object-oriented language which are relevant to our implementation efforts. We then show in Section 4 how the features such as inheritance, message passing, and polymorphism of object-oriented language have expedited our development effort. We conclude the paper in Section 5 with a brief description of our future work.

2. DESCRIPTION OF GLAD

We illustrate GLAD by going through a sample session. At appropriate points during the illustration, we describe our design philosophy and the core aspects of GLAD data model. The illustration given in this section is limited to those that have a direct relevance to our implementation efforts detailed in Section 4.

Figure 1 shows the top-level GLAD window. All these menu choices apply to the manipulation of database. The HELP option provides an assistance to the user by explaining the other menu choices. The context-sensitive help system supports our first design principle. ***Design Principle 1****: Be able to provide more information when asked.* This design principle covers much wider area than a simple help system. We will discuss more on this design principle later in the section. The QUIT option exits the application. If the user removes any database during the session, the dialog box requesting the confirmation of removal appears before exiting GLAD. This confirmation for removing the database before the termination of GLAD supports our second design principle. ***Design Principle 2****: Be able to recover from the unintended or erroneous operation.*

Instead of selecting the QUIT menu option, the user may select the CLOSE option under the system menu box, see Figure 1. The third way of quiting GLAD is double-clicking (click the mouse button twice in a quick succession) the system menu box. To let the user perform the same operation in more than one way is our third design principle. ***Design Principle 3****: Be able to perform the same operation in more than one way.* By allowing more than one way of

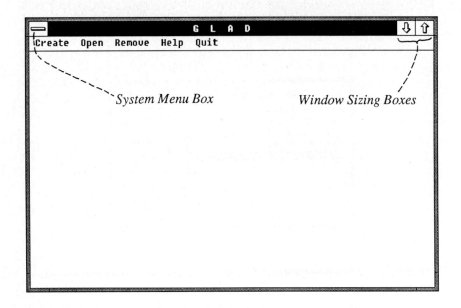

FIGURE 1

The top-level GLAD window. All figures in this paper are the actual screen dumps with minor adjustments. The text in italics and dotted lines are the captions added for the explanation. Since color images are reproduced in black and white, all coloring appear as black shading. Caption is added to tell the actual color.

carrying out the same operation, the user will be able to use the one he feels most comfortable with. This helps in supporting larger number of users. For example, the novice user may prefer using the QUIT menu at the beginning, but as he becomes more proficient in interacting with GLAD, he may prefer to close GLAD by double-clicking the system menu box.

The system menu box and the QUIT menu choice will appear in every GLAD window. Their style and function are consistent over all GLAD windows. If the user know how to use them in one window, then he also knows how to use them in any other GLAD window. This is our fourth design principle. *Design Principle 4: Be able to perform the logically equivalent operation in a consistent manner.*

Both the OPEN and REMOVE options cause a dialog box with a list of databases to appear on the screen. It allows the user to either open or remove any of the listed databases. Figure 2 shows that the database ''University Database'' is currently highlighted and readied to be OPENed. When the database is properly

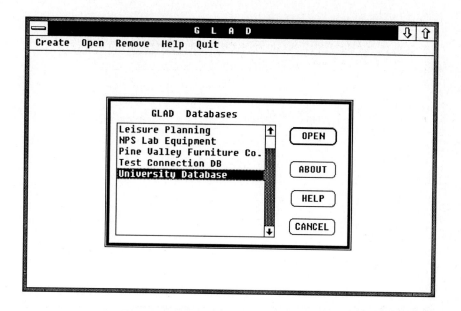

FIGURE 2

The state after the menu option Open is selected. A list of databases appears. The database "University Database" is currently selected and readied to be opened.

opened, the user is presented the Data Manipulation (DML) Window, see Figure 3. It shows three rectangles with captions DEPT, EMPLOYEE, and EQUIP-MENT. A rectangle represents both object type (i.e. database schema) and a set of objects (i.e. database instance) currently in the database. As such, there are two categories of operations: one that applies to a rectangle as an object type and another that applies to a rectangle as a set of instances. We call them *object type operation* and *object instance operation*, respectively. In the following discussion, we will use the terms object and rectangle synonymously. It should be clear from the context whether we are refering to an object type or a set of object instances.

Describe, Expand, and ShowConnectn are the three object type operations. To initiate menu options Describe and Expand, the user must first select one of the objects. When an object is selected by the user, the outer border line of the rectangle is thickened to reflect the most recently selected object. Operations will be applied to this rectangle. The color of selected rectangle will also change. We see in Figure 4 that the EMPLOYEE rectangle is selected. The selection is

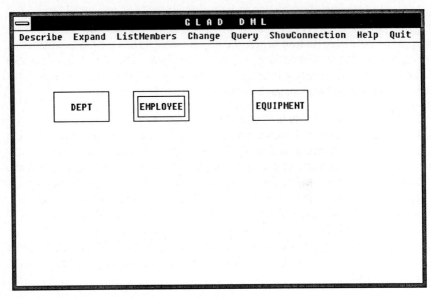

FIGURE 3

The University Database is opened. There are three objects DEPT, EMPLOYEE, and EQUIPMENT in this database.

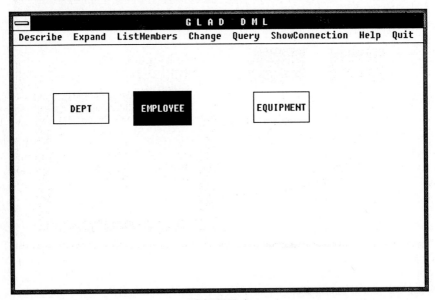

FIGURE 4

The EMPLOYEE object is selected. The menu choices Describe, Expand, ListMembers, Change, and Query apply to the selected object.

made by moving the cursor within the rectangle and clicking the left mouse button. De-selection is made by clicking the right mouse button. Whenever inappropriate mouse button is pressed or inapplicable menu option is selected, an error box with corresponding message will appear. The user will not be able to continue without acknowledging the error (by pressing the OK button). This interaction is based on Design Principle 2.

The Describe menu choice is for the user to see the relational information of the selected object. Figure 5 shows that the EMPLOYEE object has relationships Name, Age, Pay, Address, and WorksFor. GLAD data model supports basically two semantic contructs: object type and relationship. The object types are categorized into *user-defined* and *system-defined*. The system-defined object types are those predefined by the system. Two system-defined types currently supported by GLAD are INT for integers and STRING for strings. The user-defined types are the application specific types defined by the user. Only the user-defined object types are displayed on the DML window. The characteristics (or attributes) of the object is determined by the relationships it has to other

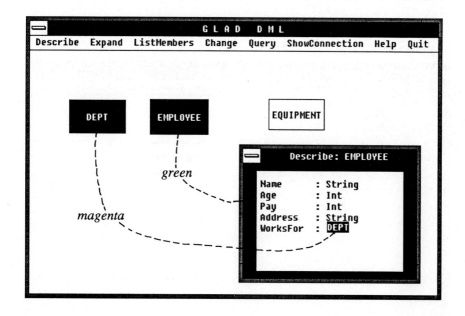

FIGURE 5

The Describe window appears after the menu option Describe is selected. Notice the use of coloring for showing the relatioship.

objects. For example, an age of employee is view as a relationship Age that relates an EMPLOYEE object to the INT object. In case the related object is also user-defined, then the object name and its corresponding rectangle in the DML window are shaded in the same color. We see in Figure 5 that the relationship WorksFor relates an employee object to another user-defined object DEPT. The object name DEPT in the Describe window and the DEPT rectangle in the DML window are shaded in the same color. This color referencing will provide a clear visual representation of object relationships.

In other proposed visual interfaces [BRYC86, ELMA85, FOGG84, GOLD85, MCDO74, WONG82, ZHAN83], the whole database schema is presented to the user. If we apply the same idea to GLAD, then we would be displaying every object type and relationship in the DML window. We believe it would be too overwhelming to many users, especially the novices. We therefore decided to provide a sort of summary information first (Figure 4) and display more information when the user requests it (Figure 5) via Describe and other commands. The idea of displaying more information when requested is based on our Design Principle 1.

The user is not limited to just one Describe window. He can request to open Describe windows for other objects. Figure 6 shows the state where multiple Describe windows are displayed. This displaying of multiple windows with each window conveying certain amount of information supports our fifth design principle. ***Design Principle 5: Be able to display multiple information at the same time.*** Having this capability of displaying multiple information will allow the user to see the varying degree of details. To the experienced user of the University Database, just having three rectangles on the DML window is enough, since he is fully aware of other details. To the first time users of the University Database, he may wish to open several Describe windows to constantly remind him the structures of those objects. The maximum number of Describe windows he can have on the screen corresponds to the number of objects present in the DML window. The user can move the objects and windows in any position he desires. Besides changing the position, the window size may also be adjusted -- expanded to show more of its content or shrunk to show previously hidden parts of other windows.

We notice in Figure 6 that there are three relationships between the objects. This is easily visible because the types of the characteristics and their related objects in the DML window are shown in the same colors. The user can also select ShowConnectn choice to globally display the relationships among the objects in a more concise form. In the ShowConnectn window, relationships are depicted by the directed lines drawn between the objects, see Figure 7. This feature is base on our sixth, and last, design principle. ***Design Principle 6: Be able to display***

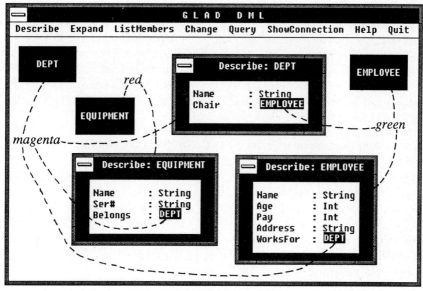

FIGURE 6

The Describe windows for all objects are displayed. The objects and the Describe windows are repositioned to avoid any overlapping.

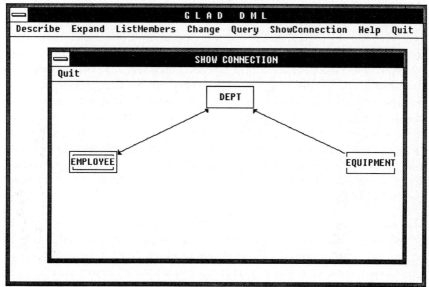

FIGURE 7

The ShowConnection window is displayed. It globally depicts the relationships that exist among the objects. The arrow shows the direction of reference.

multiple views of the same information. Multiple display of the same information provides a confidence to the user by allowing him to verify the information with another view of the information.

The Expand menu option may be applied to an object with a IS_A hierarchy. It is a special kind of relationship that exists between the two objects. An object with a IS_A hierarchy is drawn as a nested rectangle. To view this IS_A hierarchy, the user clicks the Expand menu option after the object is properly selected. Figure 8 shows the state after the EMPLOYEE object is expanded. A nested DML window appears on the screen. It has a title caption "SubClass of: <selected object's name>." Except for ShowConnectn, this window has all the menu options that the DML window has. Existence of nested DML window supports the Design Principles 5 and 6.

We now illustrate the object instance operations. There are two additional windows, which we shall call *ListMembers* and *OneMember* windows, to perform the object instance operations. These two windows allow the user to view and change data and formulate queries. Querying function is not yet fully implemented. Two menu options corresponding to these two windows appear in

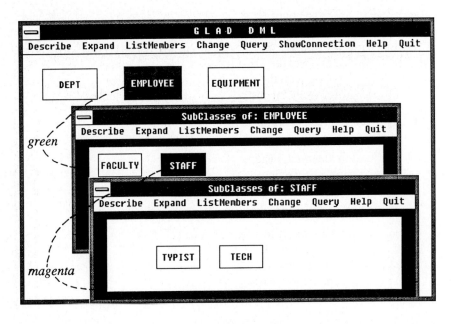

FIGURE 8

Two levels of IS-A hierarchy for the EMPLOYEE objects are shown.

the pull-down menu under ListMembers. They are "All at Once" for the ListMembers window and "One by one" for the OneMember window. The "All at Once" is for viewing all the instances of the selected object. The number of data items viewed by the user at any given time depends on the size of the opened window. The "One by one" is for viewing an instance of the selected object one at a time. We have provided users with two visual clues to maintain an easy and quick association between the object in the DML window and its ListMember and OneMember windows. The first clue is the object's name within the title caption. The second is the coloring of the window border with the same color of the object.

There are four menu options for the ListMember window. Menu options HELP and QUIT are already explained. All GLAD windows have HELP and QUIT, and they have the same funtionalities, supporting the Design Principle 4. We will not elaborate on the option MODIFY other than to say that this option allows the user to modify the highlighted data. Menu option MORE provides the user with an additional window for viewing a particular instance in more detail. This is especially useful when some values are too long to fit in the ListMember window. The maximum length we allow for any value to appear on a line is limited to 20 characters. So any value that is longer than 20 characters is cut off at the 16th character and concatenated with three dots and a space. Such a case is shown in Figure 9, where the address values are too long to fit in the allowed maximum of 20 characters. To see the complete address of an highlighted individual, the user chooses the MORE option. A OneMember window appears with full address (along with the rest of information) is shown, see Figure 10. This window is also used for modifying the data and specifying the search condition in a manner similar to QBE. This is the same window the user sees if he chooses "One by one" from the DML window's menu choice. If the OneMember window is created from the DML window and there is no ListMember window, then the first instance of the object will be displayed in the OneMember window. Opening the same window from two different places supports the Design Principle 3. Opening both the ListMembers and OneMember windows at the same time supports the Design Principle 5.

A simple, yet useful browsing feature is supported by the OneMember window. The user may browse through the instances of the selected object by selecting menu options Prev, Next, and GoTo. If selected choice cannot be carried out correctly, an appropriate error dialog box will appear on the screen (Design Principle 2). When the All menu choice is selected, a ListMember window will appear. This window is of course the same one that appears if the user selects the "All at once" choice from the DML window. If there was already a ListMember window, the All option causes that window to be brought to the top of other windows.

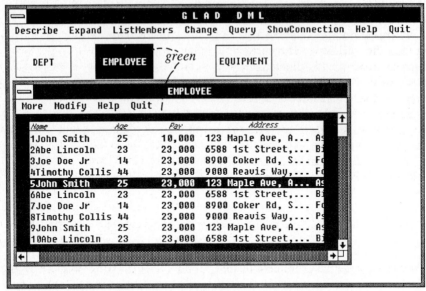

FIGURE 9

Instances of the EMPLOYEE object are displayed in the ListMembers window.
The display is in the summary format. Notice that the full address does not fit in
the allocated space.

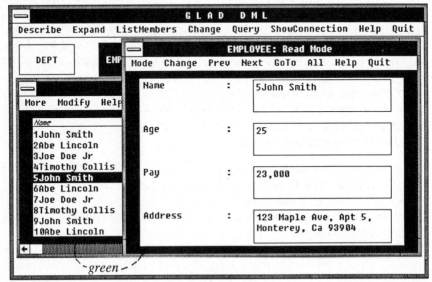

FIGURE 10

The highlighted instance of the EMPLOYEE object in the ListMembers window is
now also displayed in the OneMember window with all the values fully shown.

When the two windows are present, as in Figure 10, the user sees two views of same data. They can be opened in many different ways (Design Principle 3). They are connected in a sense that an operation in one window will be reflected in the other window. The current data element in the OneMember window corresponds to the highlighted one in the ListMember window. When the Prev, Next, or GoTo option is selected in the OneMember window, the new data is displayed in it and the corresponding one is highlighted in the ListMember window. When the user moves the cursor in the ListMember Window, the pointed row is highlighted and the corresponding data is displayed in the OneMember window. We feel that establishing this behavior between the two windows is beneficial to the user because it gives a confidence to the user that "what he is seeing is what he wants."

3. DESCRIPTION OF OBJECT-ORIENTED LANGUAGE ACTOR

We briefly describe prominent features of an object-oriented language in this section to provide necessary background in discussing implementation issues in the Section 4. Although the syntax of sample codes we provide here is specifically of ACTOR's, our description in this section applies to any object-oriented language. A fundamental concepts in a object-oriented program are objects, classes, and methods. A class is a grouping of similar objects, and an object is an instance of a class. Objects of a same class have an identical set of *instance variables*, which are used to hold values for these objects. For example, we could have a class **Person** with instance variables **name**, **age**, and **sex**. There may be an object X, who are an instance of **Person**, with **name** = 'Amadeus Mozart', **age** = 35, and **sex** = 'M'. A object-oriented program consists of interacting objects from various classes. These objects interact by sending messages to other objects. The object who is the receiver of a message responds to it by executing a corresponding method. A method is much like a procedure or function in conventional languages.

The message name is called the *selector*. The syntax used for ACTOR messages puts the selector first followed by parentheses containing the receiver and arguments (if any) to the message. So, for example, to start our GLAD application software, we would send a *start* message to the object G (an instance of the class GladApp) as

    start(G, FULL_SCREEN)

where the FULL_SCREEN tells G to use the full screen for displaying the window. (Examples used in this section are for illustration purpose only. Actual code for GLAD is different from those shown here.) Notice that the above looks much like a procedure call on surface, but it is completely different. We are not invoking a procedure; rather, we are sending a message to G with one argument. When an object of a class is sent a message to it, it responds to the message by executing a corresponding method. For every legal message that can be sent to an instance of a class, there must be a corresponding method defined in that class. In fact, the message name must be exactly same as the method name. So if we are allowed to send a message *start* to an instance of class GladApp, the method *start* must be defined in GladApp. In our GladApp class, it is defined as

```
Def start (self, screenUse)
{
    /* some initialization*/
    show(self, screenUse)
}
```

The keyword *self* serves as a placeholder for the receiver of a message and the variable *screenUse* is local to this method. The local variables cannot have the same name as instance variables. After the initialization, a *show* message is sent to itself, which is the actual message that displays the top-level GLAD window on the screen.

To be able to send a message to an object, this object must exist. The method to create a new instance of a class is called *new*. The *new* method is unique in that it is a message sent to a class itself, where most other methods are sent to instances of a class. The *new* method is referred as *class method* and other methods sent to instances as *object methods*. Since we cannot send messages to an object without creating it first by the *new* method. We must first create an object and then send the *start* message to it as

```
G := new(GladApp);
start(G, FULL_SCREEN)
```

in order to start the GLAD application. The variable G is global and thus visible to the whole application.

An object-oriented language exhibits three distinctive features -- classes, poly-morphism, and inheritance. A *class* defines the structure and behavior of its members. In other words, objects being members of a class have a well-defined set of data and operations associated to them. Objects of the same class have the same set of information and behave anlogously. So a class can be viewed as a grouping of similar objects which encapsulates both the structural and behavioral aspects of its members. This encapsulation of structure and behavior allows us to develop a highly structured, modular programs.

The word *polymorphism* is used in the object-oriented language to describe a situation where the same message causes different responses depending on who the receiver of message is. This is made possible by a technique known as *dynamic binding*. Polymorphism facilitates a rapid prototyping because when properly used, it requires less or no changes to the already written code at the software is extended or modified.

The third feature of object-oriented language, inheritance, results from the hierarchical arrangement of classes in the class tree. The most generic classes are located near the top of the tree while those with more detailed features and specialized functions are located further down the hierarchy. Each class in ACTOR has only one direct ancestor, an arrangement known as *single inheritance*. All objects inherit both methods and instance variables from their ancestors. If an object is sent a message invoking a method which it defines internally, this method is used just as expected. But if an object is sent a message which references a method not defined in the class of the object, a search is begun up the class's ancestral path looking for the method in question. In the above example, the *show* method is not defined in the GladApp class but in its ancestor class. The ACTOR system will search the immediate ancestor of the class and then the ancestor of that class and so on until either the method is found or the top of the class tree is reached. This inheritance mechanism facilitates a rapid prototyping by allowing programmers to reuse the existing codes.

4. BENEFITS OF IMPLEMENTING GLAD VIA ACTOR

An object-oriented language, especially ACTOR, is an excellent high-level language for developing our GLAD interface. We will discuss the benefits of using ACTOR as our implementation language. Specifically, we will elaborate on the benefits of inheritance, message passing, and polymorphism. Concept of program modularity is well supported by ACTOR. Each window functionality such as DML, ListMember, OneMember, Describe, and so forth are implemented by separate window classes. The DML window is implemented by DMWindow class, Describe window by DscrbWin class, and so forth. Each class has it own instance variables and methods. A clear division of labor by classes helped us develop a finely structured, modular application software which has an excellent flexibility for modification and extension in a continued development or future maintenance.

4.1 Benefit of Inheritance

A benefit of inheritance is most conspicuous in our development of the nested DML window for displaying a IS_A hierarchy. The availability of inheritance in an object-oriented language shortens the development time and increases the power of application without a major effort. In our design of nested DML window, we only need to modify the behavior of our DML window slightly to get the necessary results. Only few methods were needed to be written to create a new window class which has the same capability of the original DML window minus the menu option ShowConnectn. ShowConnectn menu choice is not included in the nested DML window since it only applies globally to the whole database.

We defined a new class NestDMWindow, which is a subclass of DMWindow. As such, all the instance variables and methods of DMWindow class is inherited by the new NestDMWindow class. We may view NestDMWindow as a specialized DMWindow where data manipulation functions are exactly same as DMWindow but it must have a colored window border and has no ShowConnectn menu choice. To achieve this behavior of NestDMWindow, we first made it a subclass of DMWindow so it will inherit all the methods of DMWindow. We then rewrote some of the inherited methods, so the functionalities special to NestDMWindow can be attained. To remove the Showconnectn menu choice from the menu bar, we modified the *start* method to dynamically eliminate this menu choice from the available list. Another function we rewrote is the *paint* method. The *paint* method of DMWindow draws the window content when it is first displayed or whenever the redrawing of the content is necessary. For the NestDMWindow class, whenever the window content is (re)drawn, its border must be colored in a proper color. The *paint* method of NestDMWindow is defined as

```
Def paint (self, hdc)
{
  shadeOuterRegion(self,hdc);
  paint(self:DMWindow,hdc)
}
```

The variable hdc stands for a *h*andle to *d*isplay *c*ontext. This is a data structure which holds all necessary information about the window so the system can properly draw the window content. The message *shadeOuterRegion* is sent to itself to color the border. The value for the color is stored in the class's instance variable. Then the message *paint* is sent to itself for drawing of the window content. Notice that the object class for is typed as *self:DMWindow*. It forces the receiver to be an instance of DMWindow class, and this is exactly what we want, because the drawing of NestDMWindow content is same as that of DMWindow except the coloring of border.

We also add a new method *expand* to the DMWindow class to handle a new menu option. This is a simple addition because we only have to provide a definition for *expand*. There would be no change to other parts of DMWindow class. There is no need for recompilation of them either. In a conventional language, such addition of a new function requires the recompilation of a whole module where the new function belongs to.

With these minor changes, we were able to add a new functionality to our GLAD interface. If we were using a conventional language such as C, we would be forced to rewrite a major portion of code and to recompile a large segment of code. Or worse, we would be writing a whole software in a completely different way since a conventional language does not encourage or support the concept of program development via inheritance. We feel the inheritance is a very powerful programming paradigm.

4.2 Benefits of Message Passing

We now discuss the benefits of message passing to program development. Message passing has also made the task of extending the program functionality easier. By adding a message passing protocol between two classes which we developed separately, we were able to improve the quality of GLAD interface dramatically. ListMember and OneMember classes for displaying data were developed separately without any prior consideration of cross referencing at the later stage. During the development we realized that a change in one window should be reflected in another window. The cross reflection of these two windows are described in the previous section. We were able to achieve this new functionality by again adding few methods to these classes. What we did was quite simple. Inside every method that changes the content of a window, such as displaying new data and highlighting a new row, we add a message that is sent to another window. For example, inside the Prev method of OneMember class, we add a message *hiLiteNewItem(aLMWin,idx)* that is sent to the instance *aLMWin* of ListMember class. A newly defined method *hiLiteNewItem* of

ListMember class simply highlights the *idx'th* data of Glad object. The same message is added to *next*, *first*, *last*, and *ith* methods of OneMember class. Analogously, a new method *displayNewMem* is added to OneMember class. Corresponding messages are included to the methods in ListMember class so the changes in ListMember window are reflected in OneMember window by sending a message *displayNewMem* to it.

4.3 Benefit of Polymorphism

Polymorphism in an object-oriented language means an ability to send the same message to instances of different classes. The proper use of it could lead a cleaner code with less awkward control structures. It also leads a easier extension of code. A good example of this occurred when we were developing the cross referencing capability between ListMember and OneMember classes.

When both the OneMember and ListMember windows are present, the messages *hiLiteNewItem* and *displayNewMem* are correctly sent to the intended receivers. However, when only one of them is present, we encountered an execution error. Let us take the case of *hiLiteNewItem* message. Suppose only OneMember window is present. Since there is no ListMember window, the message *hiLiteNewItem (aLMWin, idx)* inside one of the OneMember class will not be sent to an instance of ListMember class. In other words the variable *aLMWin* does not hold the instance of ListMember class because there is none. Instead the value for *aLMWin* is Nil, and this Nil will be the receiver of the message. The value Nil is system defined and belongs to the class called NilClass. To eliminate the execution error, we could replace every occurrence of

        hiLiteNewItem (aLMWin, idx)

to

        if aLMWin <> Nil then
            hiLiteNewItem (aLMWin, idx)
        else
            /*some error handling here*/
        endif

This will require a time-consuming task of finding all methods that contains the offending message and recompiling these methods. It also lengthens the code itself. A much better solution which we adopted is to add a new method *hiLiteNewItem* to NilClass. This method will contain the logic for the else part of the above. By this approach, no changes were necessary to the already defined methods and thus, no space-taking control structure is added. We only have to define and compile a single method in NilClass.

5. CONCLUSION

We described our current effort of implementing GLAD interface in this paper. To facilitate a rapid prototyping and experimentation of different interface styles, we have adopted an object-oriented language ACTOR as our primary implementation tool. To best of our knowledge, we are the only ones who used an object-oriented language in implementing a visual interface to databases. From our experience we conclude the following:

* The principles of information hiding and program modularity are fully supported by the concepts of class, instance variable, and message passing.

* The use of inheritance and polymorphism reduces the development time by avoiding the time-consuming rewriting and recompiling of code.

* The use of message passing facilitates ad hoc experimentation by easily allowing behavioral changes of interacting classes.

* The concepts of inheritance, polymorphism, and message passing are very powerful programming paradigms for developing application software.

The following relates specifically to ACTOR:

* The available predefined classes in ACTOR provide robust capacity to build rapid prototypes.

* The syntax of ACTOR is conducive to those who are accustomed to conventional languages.

Our immediate future tasks include the extended capability of already existing window classes, addition of full querying facility, and linking of GLAD interface to commercially available database management systems and to an experimental backend database machine. Some of our long-term goals are development of visual interface theory, data-oriented visual programming, and a unified GLAD interface to multiple, heterogeneous databases.

ACKNOWLEDGEMENT

We thank Michael Rowell and Robert Schuett for participating in our GLAD project.

REFERENCES

[BYRC86] Bryce, D. and Hull, R. SNAP: A graphics-based schema manager. In *Proceedings of 2nd IEEE International Conference on Data Engineering* (Los Angeles, 1986), 151-164.

[ELMA85] Elmasri, R. A. and Larson, J. A. A graphical query facility for ER databases. In *Proceedings of 1985 Conference on Entity-Relationship Approach* (Chicago, 1985), 236-245.

[FOGG84] Fogg, D. Lessons from "Living in a Database" graphical query interface. In *Proceedings of 1984 SIGMOD Conference* (Boston, 1984), 100-106.

[GOLD85] Goldman, K. J., Goldman, S. A., Kanellakis, P. C., and Zdonik, S. B. ISIS: Interface for a semantic information system. In *Proceedings of 1985 SIGMOD Conference* (Austin, 1985), 328-342.

[HEIL85] Heiler, S. and Rosenthal, A. G-WHIZ, a visual interface for the functional model with recursion. In *Proceedings of 11th Conference on Very Large Data Bases* (Stockholm, 1985), 209-218.

[HERO80] Herot, C. F. Spatial management of data. *ACM Transactions on Database Systems*, Vol 5, No 4 (Dec. 1980), 493-514.

[LARS84] Larson, J. A. The forms pattern language. In *Proceedings of IEEE International Conference on Data Engineering* (Los Angeles, 1984), 183-191.

[MCDO74] McDonald, N. and Stonebraker, M. CUPID - the friendly query language. Memo ERL-M487, ERL, University of California, Berkeley, October, 1974.

[STON82]   Stonebraker, M. and Kalash, J. TIMBER: A sophisticated relation browser. In *Proceedings of 8th Conference on Very Large Data Bases* (Mexico City, 1982), 1-10.

[SUGI84]   Sugihara, K., Miyao, J., Kikuno, T. and Yoshida, N. A semantic approach to usability in relational database systems. In *Proceedings of IEEE International Conference on Data Engineering* (Los Angeles, 1984), 203-210.

[WONG82] Wong, H. K. T. and Kuo, I. GUIDE: graphical user interface for database exploration. In *Proceedings of 8th Conference on Very Large Data Bases* (Mexico City, 1982), 22-32.

[WU86]   Wu, C. T. A new graphics user interface for accessing a database. In *Proceedings of Computer Graphics Tokyo '86* (Tokyo, 1986), 203-219.

[WU87]   Wu, C. T. GLAD: Graphics Language for Databases. In *Proceedings of 11th International Conference on Computer Software and Applications* (Tokyo, 1987).

[ZHAN83] Zhang, Z.-Q. and Mendlezon, A. O. A graphical query language for entity-relationship databases. In *Entity-Relationship Approach to Software Engineering*, Elservier Science Publishers, 1983, 441-448.

[ZLOO77] Zloof, M. M. Query-by-example: a data base language. *IBM Systems Journal*, 4 (Dec. 1977), 324-343.

Visual Database Systems
T.L. Kunii (Editor)
Elsevier Science Publishers B.V. (North-Holland)
© IFIP, 1989

Sophisticated Form-Oriented Database Interface for Non-Programmers

Yukari Shirota, Yasuto Shirai and Tosiyasu L. Kunii

Department of Information Science
Faculty of Science
The University of Tokyo

By focusing on interface productivity in situations involving users who are not computer specialists, this paper introduces the concept of **Enhanced Menu-Based Software (EMBS)** for human-computer interaction, and describes an automatic generator for such software. The EMBS is a *form-oriented* human-computer interface designed for specific applications, and uses a *link-oriented* data model for its data management. A screen image in the EMBS consists of two types of display elements: *buttons* and *cells*. Action invocation is triggered by a button selection or a cell value change. Following the initial action invocation, subsequent actions are executed in turn and the dependent cells are automatically reevaluated. The EMBS incorporates data manipulation facilities of a DBMS, and the users can perform database operations through cells. Moreover, from the users' view, these cells are treated in the same manner as other cells. An EMBS generator lets the users specify their own menu-based software without the aid of software specialists. This system employs a new design concept called **Program-Specification-by-Examples.** The users first specify screen layouts with example values in place of cell values. These examples are used as variable identifiers when specifying the actions corresponding to the screen. This approach offers greater understandability and helps the users shape their ideas into working software.

1. Introduction

In the current office automation research, *form-oriented* database interfaces

Authors' address: Department of Information Science, Faculty of Science, the University of Tokyo, 7-3-1 Hongo, Bunkyo-ku, Tokyo 113 JAPAN

are identified as one of the most important issues. The forms provide users with easy-to-use interfaces with data manipulation facilities. As surveyed in [3, 12, 16], a variety of *form-oriented* office automation systems have been developed and are available now; notable among them are STAR RP [7, 13], OBE [15, 18] and QBE [18, 19], OFS [14], OPAS [6] and FORMAL [10, 11], FORMDOQ [2, 3], and FORMANAGER [16, 17]. A form is character- ized as an extended type of user application views. And, these form- oriented systems are classified into several categories by the complexity of data structures supported within views. They range from flat tables to net- work structures. Table 1 compares major form-oriented systems with respect to their database facilities.

Now we summarize the problems confronted by the conventional form- oriented systems, and determine the requirements that are yet to be satisfied.

(1) Database Management System (DBMS)

Some form-oriented systems do not have underlying database management systems (DBMSs). One reason for not having a DBMS is to avoid the over- head caused by database accesses. For example, the Records of Processing (RP) component of STAR [7, 13], used a file system rather than a DBMS. File systems, however, are not powerful enough to support an application involving a large amount of data and complex transactions. Thus, it is essential for a form-oriented system to be provided with a DBMS or a data management facility with processing capability comparable to that of a DBMS.

(2) Data Structure in a View

Most form-oriented systems adopt the relational data model [1]. One prob- lem with the relational model is that a relationship represented in the form of a table is hard for the users to grasp. For novice users to take full advantage of a form-oriented system, it is desirable to offer an environment in which they can formulate their application domain in the manner similar to how they actually perceive it. A network structure is a convenient tool for representing association among objects. So the second requirement for form-oriented systems is that it support, preferably, a general network struc- ture. It is known that networks allow 1:n and m:n relationships among real world objects, thereby providing a high degree of flexibility in formulating an application domain.

(3) Triggers and Automatic Recalculation

Table 1. Comparison of Form-Oriented Systems

name	data structure	query language	model of the DBMS
STAR RP	nonflat table	CUSP	none DBMS
OBE	flat table	QBE	relational
OFS	flat table	SQL-like	relational
OPAS	general hierarchy	FORMAL	FORM (nested tables)
FORMDOQ	general hierarchy	NT operations	NTD (nested tables)
FORMANAGER	2-level hierarchy	SQL	relational
EMBS	general network	GDL	GDM (extended relational)

Cells are often inter-related; if one cell changes, cells that are dependent on that cell must also be modified to restore overall consistency. Spreadsheets such as MULTIPLAN and EXCEL[†] performs consistency restoration operation using automatic recalculation capability, i.e., changing one cell achieves automatic recalculation of dependent cells. When defining forms, details of automatic recalculation must be specified. Spreadsheets mentioned above offer only limited specification facilities, and as the complexity of applications increases the task of action specification can easily go beyond the capability of non-specialists. It is thus necessary to develop a method for action specification which resembles intuitive perception of the action.

(4) Types of Action Functions

Next, let us consider the types of action functions. Form-oriented systems are provided with the two type of functions:

    (a)   arithmetic expressions; and

    (b)   aggregate functions such as CNT(count), SUM(sum), and AVG(average).

OBE/QBE is exceptionally rich in its action functions. Beside the above two, the following actions are also included.

    (c)   **SEND(trigger).object**: Send the data from the relational tables to the given area within the objects such as business graphs, text, and menus ("trigger" here specifies when the data is to be transferred); and

    (d)   **EXECUTE(trigger).program**: Invoke the given program.

In OBE, however, a program is defined as a screen including the relational table(s), and is different from a program in a conventional sense. Therefore, the OBE users cannot invoke general functions written in a programming language such as C. Most form-oriented systems as well as the OBE/QBE system, do not have the capability to call general functions. Thus, it is required that a form-oriented system be capable of invoking general functions including database operations.

(5) Integrated system

The importance of an *integrated system* has long been recognized among the researchers of various fields such as office automation (OA) and computer-aided design (CAD). Several commercial systems support common data

---

[†] MULTIPLAN and EXCEL are trademarks of Microsoft Corp.

format, so as to facilitate information exchange between different applications, e.g., between a spreadsheet and a database. For example, Xerox's STAR and Lotus 1-2-3[†] [5] belong to this category. Whang and others [15] call this type of integration *surface integration*. Our last requirement is the integration of heterogeneous OA tools such as spreadsheets and two-dimensional CAD, through a DBMS. An integration with the DBMS at its kernel, facilitates more efficient handling of a large amount of data, compared with surface integration.

In the next chapter, we give an overview of Enhanced Menu-Based Software (EMBS) and its generation process. Chapter 3 describes the database management system used by EMBS and the data model used there. Then, the data manipulation facility of EMBS is discussed in Chapter 4. An example of EMBS is presented in Chapter 5. Chapter 6 summarizes the paper and briefly discusses the future prospects.

2. Overview of EMBS Generation

The Enhanced Menu-Bases Software (EMBS) is designed to meet the requirements identified in the previous chapter. It consists of *menu-screens* and the linkages between them. A *menu-screen* is an image displayed on a terminal screen, and consists of three types of image elements: cell image, button image and background image. An action (procedure) is invoked by a button selection or by a cell value change. After the initial invocation, subsequent actions are invoked one after another, and the dependent cells will be changed/recalculated automatically. The detailed explanation of EMBS is presented in [9]. Here we focus our attention on an automatic generator for EMBS and how the users specify their EMBS definitions in the specification language we have developed.

2.1. EMBS Generation Process

The purpose of the EMBS generator is to help the users design and create their own EMBS without the aid of the software specialists. Seven requirements relevant to the EMBS generation are:

- to facilitate the specification of actions on *menu-screens* and transitions between them;

[†] Lotus 1-2-3 is a trademark of Lotus Development Corp.

- separation of screen layout and action design;
- free-form and full screen layout;
- easy and quick regeneration;
- reusable application program modules;
- ease of learning; and
- integrated database management facilities.

The EMBS generation process proceeds, as can be seen in Figure 1. First, the users write a specification file consisting of the screen definition part and the action definition part. The automatic generator then processes the specification file to produce a program code that performs the desired function. The generator consults the action function library and extracts action functions necessary to compile the specification into a working program.

2.2. EMBS Specification Language

In this section, we shall describe the EMBS specification language by which users define their EMBS requirements.

2.2.1. Specification File Structure

As mentioned in Section 2.1, a specification file consists of two definition parts: (1) *screen definition part,* and (2) *action definition part.* When one specification file is used to define more than one *menu-screen,* definitions for each *menu-screen* are ordered within the file in the ascending order of the *menu-screen* number (see below).

An EMBS specification file structure
$$ 0 $$
screen definition for *menu-screen* 0
$$
action definition for *menu-screen* 0
$$ 1 $$
screen definition for *menu-screen* 1
$$
action definition for *menu-screen* 1
$$ 2 $$
:
:
$$ END $$

("$$" is a delimiter.)

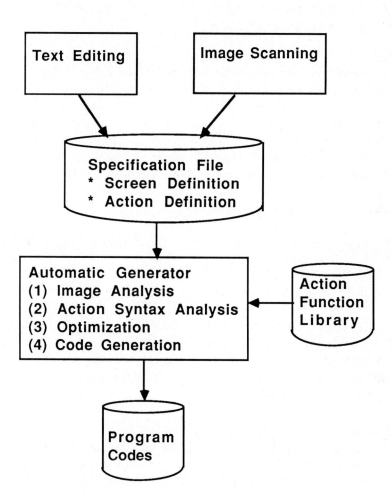

Figure 1. The EMBS generation process.

2.2.2. Screen Definition

The *menu-screen* image is composed of the following three elements: buttons, cells, and backgrounds (Figure 2).

a. <u>button</u>

A boxed area in a screen definition as shown below defines a button. The string enclosed in the box is registered as its identifier.

$$\boxed{\text{cancel}}$$

b. <u>cell</u>

An area enclosed in "[" and "]" defines a cell. The example value placed in the cell is registered as the cell identifier. The following four data types are allowed as the example values:

(1) **text**: A string of any printable characters, e.g., Japanese kanji characters, is permitted.

(2) **integer**.

(3) **float**: During execution, a cell value is formatted into the decimal notation of the example value. For example, if a float value "93.489" is given as an example value of a cell, the data to be displayed in that cell follows the format *mm.nnn* where the length of the string of *n*'s specifies the precision.

(4) **money**: A money-typed example value shall be specified with every three digits quoted by a comma, and its first character must be "$" (e.g., "$12,563,987.00").

c. <u>background</u>

All strings except buttons and cells are registered as the background of the *menu-screen*. The user may also superimpose images read in by an image scanner, upon the text image to create a more attractive background image.

The example values of buttons/cells must be unique within a *menu-screen,* because they will be used as the identifiers in the following action definition.

2.2.3. Action Definition

The users specify the action definition part using the button/cell identifiers. An action is specified by a triplet, called an *action tuple*:

Integrated Image

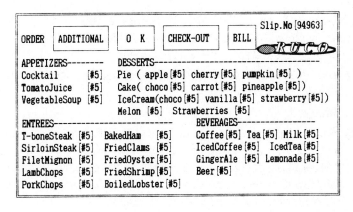

Figure 2. The lexical analyzer of the automatic EMBS generator separates the input screen definition into three image elements; *button image, cell image,* and *background image* that may further decomposed into *text representation image* and *scanned image.*

Button Image

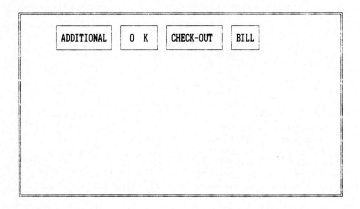

Cell Image

Figure 2. (continued)

Text Representation Background Image

```
                                        Slip.No
 ORDER

 APPETIZERS--------    DESSERTS----------------------------------
 Cocktail             Pie ( apple     cherry     pumpkin     )
 TomatoJuice          Cake( choco     carrot     pineapple   )
 VegetableSoup        IceCream(choco    vanilla     strawberry   )
                      Melon       Strawberries
 ENTREES------------------------    BEVERAGES----------------
 T-boneSteak      BakedHam          Coffee     Tea     Milk
 SirloinSteak     FriedClams        IcedCoffee      IcedTea
 FiletMignon      FriedOyster       GingerAle    Lemonade
 LambChops        FriedShrimp       Beer
 PorkChops        BoiledLobster
```

Scanner Background Image

Figure 2. (continued)

<trigger_list> <action> <object_list>

a. trigger

Either a button selection by the user or a cell value change can be a trigger. During the execution of the EMBS, the end-user can directly manipulate the cell values. If any trigger is activated, the action tuple including that trigger will be executed. If an activated trigger is common to several action tuples, those tuples will be executed one by one in the order defined in the specification file.

b. action

An action identifier in a tuple is converted by the generator to the function identifier registered in the action function library. If the action has any arguments, a parenthesized list of arguments separated by commas will follow the identifier. The system also provides an aliasing facility for action names, and the users may use aliases of their own choice to define actions.

c. object

The cells are the only objects. An object in one action tuple may also be a trigger in another tuple.

As a result of the action execution, the object cells in the corresponding tuple will be recalculated. If a recalculated cell is also a trigger in another tuple, that tuple will be subsequently activated. When a user directly manipulates a cell value, we call it *direct cell change;* and the subsequent cell value changes following the direct cell change is referred to as *indirect cell change.*

Generally, the cell changes cascade through several *menu-screens,* and such a propagation is described by the *action propagation graph* (APG) model [9]. The APG is basically a directed acyclic graph, and the action propagation through it is checked for acyclicity by the parser of the automatic EMBS generator. If the APG has any cycle, the action propagation may fall into an endless loop.

In an action definition, the user can also refer to the button/cell on another *menu-screen*; it is represented by the identifier and its *menu-screen* number separated by "@", e.g., "coffee@3" for the cell "coffee" on the *menu-screen* 3.

In the specification language, there are three types of action tuples. Here "t" implies a trigger, "o" an object, and "f" an action function.

(1) Action statement with objects:
    t1 t8 --<f1()>--> o3 o4

(2) Action statement with an empty object list:
    t9 t10 --<f4()>--

(3) Arithmetic expression:
    t1 + t2 × t3 --> o4

In addition to the action function modules written in a conventional programming language (these modules are stored in the action function library), arithmetic operators such as "+" and "−" are also available as the action functions. In an arithmetic expression, we represent a substitution into a cell by a right arrow "-->".

During an EMBS session, a cell value change, direct or indirect, is always followed by a cell value display function so that a change is immediately reflected in the screen image for the users to confirm. The invocation of a cell value display function is fully controlled by the generator, and the users need not specify it explicitly in the action definition.

2.2.4. Features of EMBS Specification Language

The EMBS specification language has two distinguished features.

(1) Program-Specification-by-Examples

The EMBS specification language employs a new concept which we refer to as *Program-Specification-by-Examples*. Query-by-Example (QBE) [18, 19] was a forerunner of the example-oriented paradigm. In QBE, the example elements are used for cross-referencing between fields by entering identical values in several fields within the database tables displayed on the screen. EMBS uses example values in a wider sense as variable identifiers in *visual programming* and *example-oriented programming* involving database operations. Moreover, the example values can be placed anywhere on a two-dimensional screen as compared with the restricted tabular form of QBE. Use of example values improves understandability and helps the users shape their ideas. Our EMBS embodying the concept of *Program-Specification-by-Examples* can serve as an easy-to-use prototyping tool that greatly reduces the initial learning barrier for users who are not familiar with computers.

(2) Aliasing Facilities for Action Names

The language construct of our specification language has only limited number of reserved words. Moreover, all reserved words are given as strings of symbols, rather than alphabetical characters. So, unlike usual programming languages, the learning of our specification language is not dependent upon the understanding of a certain language. Since the cell names serve as variable identifiers, users may use, say, their mother tongue for these identifiers. Moreover, with the aliasing facilities for action names, action definition can also be done in their mother tongue. So the entire specification process may be carried out in the environment familiar to the users in the linguistic sense. If the users' mother tongue is Japanese, it is far easier for them to construct the specification file using Japanese than using English. Moreover, using a scanned image instead of a text image, it is possible to construct a *menu-screen* with icons or actual figures, instead of character strings, to represent real world objects.

3. Graph Data Model and G-BASE

The database management facilities of EMBS are performed by a database called G-BASE[†] [8]. It is based on Graph Data Model (GDM) [4] which belongs to a family of extended relational data models. Its main departure from the relational model consists in the introduction of link types, thereby making it a *link-oriented* model.

In this Chapter, we will give a brief description of GDM and G-BASE, and demonstrate its feasibility as an underlying DBMS for a menu-oriented system.

3.1. Features of GDM and G-BASE

GDM consists of two kinds of objects: *records* and *links*. A record type in GDM corresponds to a relation in the relation model. A link type in GDM represents a binary association between two record types. The network-structured views of GDM are realized by the link types. In GDM, a

---

[†] G-BASE is a trademark of Ricoh Co., Ltd.

database schema **S** is defined as a pair (**R**, **L**), where **R** is a set of record types and **L** is a set of link types. Each record type $R_i \in$ **R** is as a list of fields: $R_i(A_1, A_2, ..., A_n)$. Associated with each A_i is a domain of values *Domain*(A_i). Let X be a list of fields (A_1, A_2, ..., A_n), then *Domain*(X) is defined as the Cartesian product of *Domain*(A_i), i = 1, ..., n. A link type $L_j \in$ **L** is defined as a pair of record types: $L_j = (R_1, R_m)$, where R_1, $R_m \in$ **R**. GDM permits a *recursive* link type (a self loop), i.e., $L_{rec} = (R_1, R_1)$, and *parallel* link types L_{par1} and L_{par2} such that $L_{par1} = L_{par2}$ and par1 $\neq$ par2.

A state, \$S, of **S** is the set of all occurrences stored in the database at a given time. \$S is determined by the states of **R** and **L**, \$R and \$L, respectively. \$R is in turn determined by the state of each record type, thus \$R = $\{\$R_i\}_i$. Similarly \$L = $\{\$L_j\}_j$. Furthermore, the state of a record (link) type is defined by the set of its occurrences, i.e., \$R = $\{r_i\}_i$ (\$L = $\{l_j\}_j$). Note that a link occurrence l is defined as a pair of record occurrences.

Every record occurrence r of type R has the unique identifier r[ID_R]. ID_R is a subset of the fields of R which is defined as R's primary key by the users. In GDM, the unique identifier is called *Unique Record Identifier* (URI).

Link types in GDM are defined either *real* and *virtual*. Real link types is used to represent m:n relationships between two record types. In G-BASE, a real link type is realized in the form of a *link file*. A link file stores the pairs of URIs of the two record linked together. The file is modified through *connect* and *disconnect* operations. On the other hand, a virtual link type has neither a physical representation nor manipulative operations associated with it. When defining a virtual link type between two record types, the same number of fields in the two records are designated as "linking fields". A virtual link is established between records of the two types, if their linking fields contain the same values. A virtual link type is used to represent 1:n relationships between record types. In *Graph Data Language* (GDL) of GDM, the real and virtual link types are defined in the following manner:

real link R_i ../ L_{real} /.. R_j;

virtual link $R_i(X_i)$ ../ L_{vir} /.. $R_j(X_j)$;

Here X_i and X_j are lists of fields of R_i and R_j, respectively, and they are of the same length.

In GDM, a data structure called *record list type* RL is used to store the intermediate result of an operation. It is an ordered set of record types: RL= $(E_1, E_2, ..., E_k)$ where $E_i \in R$ (i = 1, ..., k). E_l and E_m where $l \neq m$ may be identical for any pair of l and m.

In processing a query, the record list type associated with it is equivalent to the set of access paths for that query. Usually this path set is created temporarily and thrown away after the query evaluation is completed. G-BASE offers a construct called a *target* for users' further manipulation on this intermediate result. In the DML of G-BASE, a target is defined as a list of record types. Adjacent record types in the list may be connected by a link type; if no link type is specified, the Cartesian product is assumed. It is also possible to add a qualification to the target definition.

A target, which is a set of paths, is stored in a target file, and there is a *cursor* pointing to an element, i.e., path, in the target file. (The path pointed to by the cursor is referred to as the *current path*.) The cursor may be moved up and down over the entire range of the target file and facilitates the *recored-at-a-time* operations. Figure 3 illustrates the organization of a target file and the data structure for storing a path. Note that only the upper layer consisting of URIs is stored in the target file.

Figure 4 shows a simple database schema modeling employees and departments in a company. Two record types **employee** and **dept** are linked by two link types **manages** and **belongs_to**. On this schema, a query to find all manager-subordinate pairs can be formulated as follows:

    alias manager employee;
    target t manager, dept, employee;
    find t = manager ../manages/.. dept ../inverse belongs_to/.. employee
            [manager.pno != employee.pno];
    for t print manager.name, employee.name;

3.2. Advantages of GDM and G-BASE

It is for the following two reasons that G-BASE is suitable for the use with a form-oriented system:

(1) G-BASE is capable of representing general network-structured views.

    A network structure often arises in the application domains of a form-oriented system. Also, the cardinality of an association in such domains are not limited to 1:1 or 1:n; an m:n association is frequently

Target File Structure

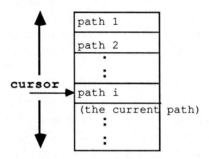

Path Data Structure

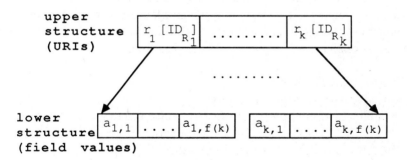

Figure 3. The target file structure and the path data structure.

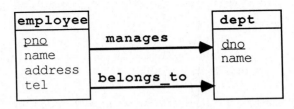

Figure 4. A GDM database schema modeling employees and departments in a company.

encountered. Since G-BASE is capable of handling these two issues, the complexity of application software is greatly reduced.

(2) G-BASE allows *record-at-a-time* operations on a target file.

In a form, each cell is allowed to contain only one atomic value. The result of a relational operation is in general a set, but a set cannot be displayed in a cell; for a form-oriented system, it is essential to have a facility for accessing the query result record-at-a-time rather than set-at-a-time. In G-BASE, this facility is provided by the cursor pointing to a path stored in a target file. Paths stored in a target file are the intermediate result of a query evaluation. Since the cursor operation accesses a database through this intermediate result, efficient access is made possible.

4. EMBS Data Manipulation Facilities

In EMBS, all database manipulation is performed through the use of the target function of G-BASE. In this chapter, we shall describe how the end-users define a target, and how the target operations are handled in EMBS.

4.1. Target Definition

In the action definition stage, users first define targets to be used in the subsequent action definition. A target is defined using a path expression.

In our specification language, a target definition is specified in the following manner:

```
target_def -->  target_id : path_expr ;
                       /* define the access path of the target file */
path_expr -->  path_term
          -->  path_expr [ qualification ]
          -->  path_expr ../ link_id /.. path_term
          -->  path_expr .. path_term
                       /* ".." denotes a Cartesian product */
path_term -->  record_id ( field_id { , field_id } )
          -->  target_id
          --> ( path_expr )
field_id -->  cell_id    /* example values in the screen definition */
         -->             /* null */
```

It is assumed that users are aware of the following information on the database being used: the name of the database, the names of record types and link types, and the fields of each record type. For the database of Figure 4, a target containing information on manager-subordinate relationships can be defined as shown below:

> database : company ;
> alias   manager employee ;
> manager-sub : manager(, Brown, ,)../manages/..
>   dept(, Personnel)../inverse belongs_to/.. employee(, Smith, ,)
>   [manager.pno != employee.pno] ;

"Brown", "Personnel" and "Smith" are the example values which have already been specified as the cell identifiers in the screen definition part. The fields where example values are inserted are used in the action definition. The fields that are left blank in the target definition are not used.

4.2. Data Manipulation Action

Action funstions used in the action definition are all stored in the action function library (see Figure 1). For database manipulation, six primitive functions are provided. They can be combined to define complicated actions. After any of these six operations, the cells are refreshed with the values taken from the current path so that any change is immediately reflected in the screen image. At the beginning of the EMBS execution, all cells are initialized to null. When its value is null, a question mark ("?") is displayed in the cell. It is also possible to set a cell value to null by inputing "?" into that cell.

(1) *find*(target_id)

The *find* function evaluates the path expression of a given target. Let X_i $(A_1, A_2, ..., A_k)$ be a list of fields of the record type R_i which have been declared with example values in the target definition. Also, let $(C_1, C_2, ..., C_k)$ be a list of cells corresponding to X_i. If every C_i has a null value, i.e., "?", the access path will be evaluated as it was defined without any further qualification. If any cell C_i is set to some value V_i, then the qualification in the path expression is temporarily modified to combine a new factor "$A_i = V_i$" or "V_i match V_i" into the qualification part. Note that *and* is used here as the connective. Then this temporary path expression is evaluated to obtain a target file.

After this operation, the cursor points to the first path in the target file.

(2) *delete*(record_id1, record_id2, ...)

The *delete* function is used to delete the record occurrence specified by record_id. The URI of the record to be deleted must be in the current path. Deleting a record occurrence causes the deletion of all links incident to that record occurrence.

If any part of a path in the target file is deleted by the *delete* function, that path is automatically deleted from the target file.

(3) *insert*(record_id1, record_id2, ...)

The *insert* function is used to insert a new record occurrence(s) in the record type(s) specified by record_id(s). The record_id specified here must appear in the target definition. The current cell values are used as the field values of the new record(s). For the fields that are left blank in the target definition, the system substitutes the default values specified in the database definition.

(4) *update*(target_id)

The *update* function modifies the field value(s) of the records along the current path. The fields are updates with the current cell values. Note that URIs cannot be modified with this function. This function updates both the target file and the original database.

(5) *disconnect*(link_id [, target_id])

The *disconnect* function is used to disconnect a real link of the type link_id whose endpoints are the record occurrences r_i and r_{i+1} in the current path. If the same link_id is used more than once in the target definition, the user must specify the target_id to remove ambiguity. After this operation, the current path is deleted from the target file and the cursor points to the next path.

(6) *connect*(link_id [, target_id])

The *connect* function is used to create a real link occurrence of the type link_id between the URIs currently displayed.

In addition to the above six functions, three action functions are provided for the record-at-a-time operations: *current*(target_id), *next*(target_id) and *previous*(target_id). The screen image does not always reflect the current path. The *current* operation is used to update the displayed image to the state corresponding to the current path. The other two operations are used to move the cursor over a given target; *next* and *previous* imply a step forward and a step backward, respectively.

5. An EMBS Example

This chapter presents an exmaple EMBS to demonstrate how easy it is to create EMBS using our specification language. Here we consider a system for order input and check-out in a restaurant. Figure 5(a) shows a *menu-screen* for the order input process. Additional order is accepted through another order input *menu-screen* (Figure 5(b)). The *menu-screen* "ADDI-TIONAL ORDER" can be called from "ORDER" by pressing the button "ADDITIONAL". Another *menu-screen* is provided for "CHECK OUT" (Figure 5(c)). The customers make the payment either in cash or by a credit card. If a payment is charged on a card, the necessary information is entered using the buttons displayed on the *menu-screen* or by passing the card through the card ready attached to the terminal. The *menu-screen* of Figure 5(d) is used for checking the accumulated orders.

This restaurant system is based on a database with the following schema:

```
ACCOUNT(ACC-NO, MEMBER-NAME, MEMBER-ADDR,
                        CREDIT-CO, EXPIRE);
SLIP(SLIP-NO, ACC-NO, DATE, CLERK, APPR, CASH, CREDIT);
ORDER(ORDER-NO, SLIP-NO, ITEM, QUANTITY);
MENU-ITEM (ITEM, PRICE);
virtual link ACCOUNT(ACC-NO) ../PAYS/.. SLIP(ACC-NO);
virtual link SLIP(SLIP-NO) ../CONTAINS/.. ORDER(SLIP-NO);
virtual link ORDER(ITEM) ../UNIT-PRICE/.. MENU-ITEM(ITEM);
```

Figures 6 through 8 present the screen definitions and the action definitions of this EMBS.

6. Conclusions

We described the EMBS for human-computer interaction, and an automatic generator for such software. The data manipulation facilities of EMBS are performed by a DBMS based on a link-oriented data model. The following two features of this DBMS make it a suitable choice for the DBMS underlying a form-oriented system: (1) capability of representing general network-structured views, and (2) record-at-a-time operations on a target.

EMBS and its generation system can be applied to a variety of fields. In fact, prospective application areas span all situations involving users not familiar with computers. The EMBS can easily be tailored to suit the users'

(a)

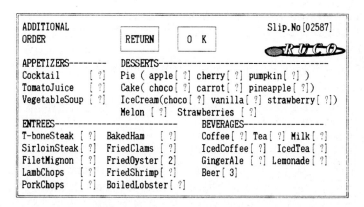

(b)

Figure 5. *Menu-screens* for a restaurant order entry and check-out system.

(c)

```
CHECK
OUT    [ ORDER ]   [ CARD-READ ]    [ APPROVE ]   [ CHECKOUT ]   [ BILL ]

Acc.No. [3849-0300-6976-3212]                                    Slip.No
Expire(M/Y) [10/89]              [ VISA ]  [ AMEX ]  [ MC ]      [02587]
CardHolder [George Brown ]
                                 Credit Co. [AMEX        ]
#Guests [ 3]
Date(Y/M/D) [88/12/11]           Amount  [      $156.00]
Clerk   [Smith      ]            Tax     [       $16.00]
Approval No. [0283713 ]          Total   [      $172.00]

Tea Lounge RUCO                  Cash    [        $0.00]
  Tel(03)812-2111                Credit  [      $172.00]
```

(d)

```
                                                      Slip.No [02587]
   BILL                         [ ORDER ]  [ CHECKOUT ]


[Toma.Juice] [ $3.00] [ 2] [  $6.00]  [Beer       ] [ $4.00] [ 3] [ $12.00]
[Vege.Soup ] [ $4.50] [ 1] [  $4.50]  [           ] [      ] [  ] [        ]
[Sirloin   ] [$24.00] [ 2] [ $48.00]  [           ] [      ] [  ] [        ]
[B.Lobster ] [$30.00] [ 1] [ $30.00]  [           ] [      ] [  ] [        ]
[Cake.cho  ] [ $3.00] [ 1] [  $3.00]  [           ] [      ] [  ] [        ]
[Ice.vani  ] [ $2.00] [ 2] [  $4.00]  [           ] [      ] [  ] [        ]
[Coffee    ] [ $1.50] [ 2] [  $3.00]  [           ] [      ] [  ] [        ]
[IcedCoffee] [ $1.50] [ 1] [  $1.50]  [           ] [      ] [  ] [        ]
[Beer      ] [ $4.00] [ 3] [ $12.00]  [           ] [      ] [  ] [        ]
[F.Oyster  ] [$16.00] [ 2] [ $32.00]            Total      [$156.00]
```

Figure 5. (continued)

$$ 0 $$

```
CHECK
OUT    ┌───────┐ ┌───────────┐ ┌─────────┐ ┌──────────┐ ┌────────┐
       │ ORDER │ │ CARD-READ │ │ APPROVE │ │ CHECKOUT │ │  BILL  │
       └───────┘ └───────────┘ └─────────┘ └──────────┘ └────────┘
Acc.No. [4980-0300-8203-0186]                              Slip.No
Expire(M/Y) [10/89]         ┌──────┐ ┌──────┐ ┌──────┐   [94963]
CardHolder [John-Smith  ]   │ VISA │ │ AMEX │ │  MC  │
                            └──────┘ └──────┘ └──────┘
                            Credit Co.[DINERS     ]
#Guests [ 5]
Date(Y/M/D) [88/12/24]      Amount   [      $150.00]
Clerk    [Brown      ]      Tax      [       $15.00]
Approval No.[652349  ]      Total    [      $165.00]

Tea Lounge RUCO             Cash     [      $100.00]
  Tel(03)812-2111           Credit   [       $65.00]
```

$$
database : restaurant ;
a : ACCOUNT(4980-0300-8203-0186, John-Smith, , DINERS, 10/89) ;
m : MENU-ITEM(#coffee@1, #$1.50@1) ;
s : a../PAYS/..
    SLIP(94963,4980-0300-8203-0186,88/12/24, Brown,652349, $100.00, $65.00)
    ../CONTAINS/..ORDER(, 94963, #coffee@1, #5@1) ../UNIT-PRICE/.. m ;
BILL   --< jump(1) >--
ORDER --< jump(2) >--
CARD-READ --< CR()>--> 4980-0300-8203-0186 DINERS
4980-0300-8203-0186 DINERS --< find(a)>--> John-Smith 10/89
$150.00   5   --< cal_tax($150.00, 5)>--> $15.00
$150.00 + $15.00 --> $165.00
$165.00 - $100.00 --> $65.00
APPROVE --< approve(4980-0300-8203-0186, DINERS, $65.00) >--> 652349
VISA AMEX MC --< select() >--> DINERS
CHECKOUT --< insert(SLIP) >--

Figure 6. The screen definition and the action definition.
The example values such as "VISA" and "$150.00" are
used in the action definition as the cell identifiers.

$$ 1 $$

```
                                                     ┌──────── Slip.No [94963]
                                ┌───────┐  ┌─────────┐
   BILL                         │ ORDER │  │CHECKOUT │
                                └───────┘  └─────────┘


[#coffee    ] [#$1.50] [#5] [ #$7.50]   [#coffee    ] [#$1.50] [#5] [ #$7.50]
[#coffee    ] [#$1.50] [#5] [ #$7.50]   [#coffee    ] [#$1.50] [#5] [ #$7.50]
[#coffee    ] [#$1.50] [#5] [ #$7.50]   [#coffee    ] [#$1.50] [#5] [ #$7.50]
[#coffee    ] [#$1.50] [#5] [ #$7.50]   [#coffee    ] [#$1.50] [#5] [ #$7.50]
[#coffee    ] [#$1.50] [#5] [ #$7.50]   [#coffee    ] [#$1.50] [#5] [ #$7.50]
[#coffee    ] [#$1.50] [#5] [ #$7.50]   [#coffee    ] [#$1.50] [#5] [ #$7.50]
[#coffee    ] [#$1.50] [#5] [ #$7.50]   [#coffee    ] [#$1.50] [#5] [ #$7.50]
[#coffee    ] [#$1.50] [#5] [ #$7.50]   [#coffee    ] [#$1.50] [#5] [ #$7.50]
[#coffee    ] [#$1.50] [#5] [ #$7.50]   [#coffee    ] [#$1.50] [#5] [ #$7.50]
[#coffee    ] [#$1.50] [#5] [ #$7.50]                 Total        [$142.50]
```

$$
94963   --> 94963@0
EACH #coffee --< find(m) >--> #$1.50
EACH #$1.50 X #5 --> #$7.50
#$7.5 --< total() >--> $142.50
$142.50   --> $150.00@0
ORDER   --< jump(2) >--
CHECKOUT --< jump(0) >--

Figure 7. The definition for the "BILL" *menu-screen.*
The "#" in an example value implies that it is an element
of an array.

```
$$ 2 $$
```

```
┌─────────────────────────────────────────────────────────────────────┐
│                  ┌──────────┐ ┌─────┐ ┌───────────┐ ┌──────┐ Slip.No[94963] │
│  ORDER │ ADDITIONAL │   O  K │ CHECK-OUT │   BILL    │                │
│                                                                       │
│  APPETIZERS--------    DESSERTS-------------------------------------   │
│  Cocktail       [#5]   Pie ( apple[#5]  cherry[#5]  pumpkin[#5] )      │
│  TomatoJuice    [#5]   Cake( choco[#5]  carrot[#5]  pineapple[#5])     │
│  VegetableSoup  [#5]   IceCream(choco[#5] vanilla[#5] strawberry[#5])  │
│                        Melon [#5]  Strawberries [#5]                   │
│  ENTREES------------------------    BEVERAGES----------------         │
│  T-boneSteak [#5]  BakedHam    [#5]    Coffee[#5] Tea[#5] Milk[#5]     │
│  SirloinSteak[#5]  FriedClams  [#5]    IcedCoffee[#5]  IcedTea[#5]     │
│  FiletMignon [#5]  FriedOyster [#5]    GingerAle [#5] Lemonade [#5]    │
│  LambChops   [#5]  FriedShrimp [#5]    Beer[#5]                        │
│  PorkChops   [#5]  BoiledLobster[#5]                                   │
└─────────────────────────────────────────────────────────────────────┘
```

```
$$
ADDITIONAL   --< jump(3) >--
CHECK-OUT    --< jump(0) >--
BILL         --< jump(1) >--
94963  --> 94963@1
EACH  #5     --> #5@1
EACH  #5     --< what_is( #5 )>--> #coffee@1
OK           --< insert( ORDER ) >--
```

Figure 8. The definition for the order input
menu-screen.

requirements, and the users can specify their own EMBS without the aids of software specialists.

ACKNOWLEDGEMENT

This research is partially supported by Software Research Center (SRC) of Ricoh Co., Ltd. Dr. Hideko S. Kunii, Director of SRC, has been especially helpful to the authors. Mr. Katsumi Kanasaki of SRC and Dr. Issei Fujishiro of the University of Tsukuba offered many helpful comments through the course of this work. The authors' gratitude also extends to Mr. Kihachiro Masumoto, President of Central Development, Inc., who gave them a motivation for the research in automatic software generation.

REFERENCES

[1] Codd, E.F., "A Relational Model of Data for Large Shared Data Banks," *CACM,* Vol.13, No.6, pp.377-387, June 1970.

[2] Kitagawa, H., Kunii, T.L., et al., "Formgraphics : A Form-Based Graphics Architecture Providing a Database Workbench," *IEEE CGA,* Vol.4, No.6, June 1984, pp.38-56.

[3] Kitagawa, H., *Structured Forms Handling By Nested Table Data Model,* D.Sc. Thesis, Department of Information Science, Faculty of Science, the University of Tokyo, Japan, Jan. 1987.

[4] Kunii, H.S., *Graph Data Language: A High Level Access-Path Oriented Language,* Ph.D. Dissertation, the University of Texas at Austin, 1983.

[5] Lotus Development Corp., *Lotus 1-2-3 User manual,* Combridge Mass., 1983.

[6] Lum, V.Y., Choy, D.M., and Shu, N.C., "OPAS: An office procedure automation system," *IBM Syst. J.,* Vol.21, No.3, 1982, pp.327-350.

[7] Purvy, R., Farrell, J., and Klose, P., "The design of STAR's records processing: Data processing for the noncomputer professional," *ACM Trans. on Office Inf. Syst.,* Vol.1, No.1, Jan. 1983, pp.3-24.

[8] Ricoh, Co. Ltd., *G-BASE manuals* (in Japanese), 1988.

[9] Shirota, Y. and Kunii, T.L., "Automatic Generator for Enhanced Menu Based Software -- Program-Specification-by-Examples --," to appear in *Proc. HCI International '89, the third International Conference on Human-Computer Interaction,* Boston, Sept. 18-22, 1989.

[10] Shu, N.C., "FORMAL: A Forms-Oriented, Visual-Directed Application Development System," *IEEE Computer,* Vol.18, No.8, Aug. 1985, pp.38-49.

[11] Shu, N.C., "FORMAL: A Forms-Oriented, Visual-Directed Application Development System," in Kunii, T.L.(ed), *Application Development Systems,* Springer, Tokyo and Berlin, 1986, pp.2-26.

[12] Shu, N.C., *Visual Programming,* Van Nostrand Reinhold Company Inc., N.Y., 1988.

[13] Smith, D.C. et al., "Designing the Star User Interface," *BYTE,* Vol.7, No.4, July 1982, pp.242-282.

[14] Tsichritzis, D.C., "Form Management," *CACM,* Vol.25, No.7, July 1982, pp.453-478.

[15] Whang, K.Y. et al, "Office-by-Example: An Integrated Office System and Database Manager," *ACM Trans. on Office Inf. Syst.,* Vol.5, No.4, Oct. 1987, pp.393-427.

[16] Yao, S.B., Hevner, A.R., Shi, Z., and Luo, D., "FORMANAGER: An office forms management system," *ACM Trans. on Office Inf. Syst.,* Vol.2, No.3, July 1984, pp.235-262.

[17] Yao, S.B. and Kitagawa, H., "Structured Application Generation Using XDB," *Proc. AFIPS National Computer Conference,* Chicago, July 1985.

[18] Zloof, M.M., "Query-by-example: A data base language," *IBM Syst. J.,* Vol.16, No.4, 1982, pp.324-343.

[19] Zloof, M.M., "QBE/OBE: A language for office and business automation," *IEEE Computer,* Vol.14, No.5, May 1981, pp.13-22.

[20] Zloof, M.M., "Office-by-example: A business language that unifies data and word processing and electronic mail," *IBM Syst. J.,* Vol.21, No.3, 1982, pp.272-304.

Session 5

MODEL-DRIVEN APPROACH

Visual Database Systems
T.L. Kunii (Editor)
Elsevier Science Publishers B.V. (North-Holland)
© IFIP, 1989

Model-Driven Image Analysis to Augment Databases

Gio Wiederhold, Jim Brinkley*, Ramin Samadani, and C. Robert Clauer

Stanford University
Departments of Computer Science, Medicine, and Electrical Engineering
Stanford CA, USA

Abstract   In this paper we consider how information may be obtained from images. To search large image collections we need to search on secondary parameters. We may look for images containing certain types of objects, for images where the objects are of a certain size or shape, or for images having certain features. Since we now have techniques to rapidly acquire and store many images, we need techniques for automatic image analysis to generate such parameters. This paper describes a promising category of image analysis, namely model-driven methods. Two examples, operating in very different domains, are presented.

1. Introduction

To be able to retrieve images stored in databases we must associate identifying parameters with each of the images. It is through these parameters that we can select stored images for display, comparison, and further analysis. Primary parameters are produced when the images are obtained, and describe the imaging event and its process. For satellite images of earth we would have the time of observation, the setting of the scanner and the satellite, and, immediately derived from those data, we can determine the satellite's path and the portion of the earth seen. For medical images the primary parameters are the name of the patient, the date, and the operator of the scanner, positioning information, and the purpose of the scan.

Any each of those technologies can generate thousands of images. For systematic analysis we need to retrieve images based upon their contents. The pixels which make the images themselves are rarely suitable for direct search. If we can provide secondary parameters indicating the type of objects seen on the earth or the type of abnormality seen in a body, then database searches could be enabled that directly serve the end-users' objectives. Large scale on-line image storage without such a retrieval capability will not be justifiable [Arvidson 1986]. This need for image-oriented search is well recognized, for instance [Chang 1988] presents a suitable iconic query language and shows examples, but does not explain how the icons are being generated from the images.

Today, the majority of secondary parameters, when available at all, are entered by humans after visually scanning an image. There are some exceptions, generally based on a bottom-up analysis of image contents. By bottom-up we mean pixel-based inductive processing, in order to find pixel agglomerations as lines, intersections of lines, or bounded

* now at the Department of Biomedical Structures, Univ. of Washington, Seattle WA.

areas. If the pictures are well-behaved, like the maps presented to PSQL queries, then direct manipulation may be feasible [Roussopoulos 1988]. Analysis of structured images is also feasible [Kasturi 1988].

1.1   Model-based Image Analysis

The alternative, top-down image analysis, starts with a general expectation of what is to be found. The expectation is represented by a model, and if the model cannot be matched, then the object or feature is assumed not to be present. For instance, in high-energy physics, programs will scan automatically for *interesting* events, which generate images that are easily described, as the track angles after an impact. Quality control imaging applications compare images versus a model image of a correct part.

Often the objective of image analysis is to look for variations in objects. The two basic approaches for representing variation are:

  1 placing the variation in the matching function
  2 placing the variation in the model

The first approach, which is more common, is to devise prototypical instances of a particular shape, then develop a metric for comparing a new shape with a library of prototypical instances. This approach can be very successful and is widely used for image analysis. However, since the metric is usually only computed after all the features have been observed in the image to be classified, the variations found cannot be used to aid the search for image features.

We deal here with images which are variable, so that we adopt the alternative where the model is adapted as features are located. The variation is now represented in the model itself, thus defining a generic model which describes all expected instances of a particular shape class. If a particular object reconstruction can be described by this model then the object is an instance of the shape class. Several computer vision systems attempt to provide model knowledge in order to guide the analysis.

An example of this approach for machine vision is ACRONYM, a model-driven system developed by Brooks for finding airplanes in satellite images [Brooks 1981]. This system used generic models defined by structured assemblies of generalized cylinders as described by [Binford 1971]. By placing ranges on the parameters describing the generalized cylinders it was possible to describe the expected range of variation for various classes of airplanes, thereby building up a classification tree which at the root described all airplanes, and which became progressively more specific as the tree was traversed towards the leaves. The advantage of this approach is that the system could initially be told it was looking for some kind of airplane. Once it had found a few parts of an actual airplane on the image, it could use the dimensions of these parts to specialize the generic model to only those airplanes that were consistent with the image. The cylinders were generalized to cones for organ desciptions [Soroka 1981]. The specialized model generates expectations about where to search for additional parts of the airplane on the image, thereby providing a top-down approach to searching the image based on a-priori knowledge about the contents of the image.

1.2   Obtaining Secondary Parameters

Image analysis based on parameterized models can be expanded to cover a wide variety of objects and features by defining more general models, and appropriate adaptation schemes. The operations needed for matching form the basis for descriptive parameters to augment the database.

To enable subsequent search, at a useful level of abstraction, requires further processing. The findings must be aggregated to form meaningful secondary parameters. Detected features can be used to classify objects found into types and subtypes. For three-dimensional objects volume and aspect ratios can be produced which may be more significant than their lengths, widths, and heights. These secondary parameters become candidates for indexing the database, so that images containing certain object types can be rapidly retrieved [Wiederhold 1987].

In this paper we present two application, from quite different domains, which use abstract models for image analysis. Parameters derived from adapting the model to the image become the indexable attributes to be placed into the database. We believe that such techniques have great promise, and that their application will broaden the usefulness of image databases.

1.3 Problems with Image Analysis.

Images obtained from scanning devices are rarely complete, and also have artifacts. In the work described in this paper we have images of objects, but because of physical constraints the observations on an image are incomplete. Having a model helps to ignore artifacts, but we still must obtain information about the object proper.

If parts of the border of an object are missing or obscure, edge-following algorithms can easily get lost, and reconstruction must use images obtained in a later scan with different viewing angles and illumination. The models we use are intended to overcome this problem in two application domains. In the first, a medical application, the shape model is constrained only by geometric first and second-order continuity. Multiple images, taken at different angles, reduce the uncertainty. In the second, a space sciences application, we use a physical analogy to constrain the model transformations.

Ultrasound Images   One of the two applications presented in this paper deals with images obtained in pre-natal medical care, using ultrasound. Ultrasound is one of the least invasive of imaging techniques. It is hence appropriate for delicate tasks, as the imaging of a human fetus, so that abnormalities, typically slow growth, can be diagnosed early. Each ultrasound scan produces a two-dimensional image plane; many such images must be combined to obtain an adequate three-dimensional view of the fetus. The successive images are not evenly spaced, nor all at the same angle, since the scanning head must follow the contour of the maternal body. The components of the scans are also incomplete; in particular, surfaces which are not close to perpendicular to a beam will not be recorded. Also, ultrasound does not pass through bone or air, obscuring portions of the image. Similar limitations exist for the imaging of other organs.

For analysis of medical images this model-based approach is very appealing because it is already known what to expect in the images, and there are only a finite (albeit large) number of useful abnormal shape categories representing known pathologies. The major problem is how to capture the essential shape and range of variation in the model. Relatively simple geometric models such as generalized cylinders are unlikely to accomplish this.

Satellite Images   The aurora borealis is one of the most spectacular phenomena of nature. It occurs in a roughly circular or oval region around the magnetic poles of the earth. Auroral displays are the result of processes which transfer energy from the solar wind to the Earth's magnetosphere and ionosphere. Many of these processes cause the energization and scattering of charged particles which precipitate along magnetic field lines into the high latitude upper atmosphere. There they ionize atmospheric constituents to produce visible and UV emissions. Auroral phenomena are present most of the time, though they vary greatly in dynamic behavior and intensity.

In earth surface scanning by satellites in visible wave lengths cloud cover can obscure views of the earth. This is not a problem for our auroral images, but here solar illumination obscures the dayside portion of the auroral oval. The auroral images gathered by the DE-1 satellite are simpler to model than the medical images presented above. To a first-order approximation, the auroral emissions form an oval or an elliptical region in the images. Even for this simple representation, there are practical problems to be solved in finding the oval. One of the difficulties is that the auroral region does not always appear continuous. The images sometimes show gaps in the auroral oval. The physical processes associated with the formation of the auroral oval, however, suggest that one should interpolate across gaps to define a continuous model for the oval.

1.4   Object Parameterization

Humans seem to utilize a mental model to compensate for incomplete or obscured data in the image. The parameterized geometric shape models presented earlier seem too rigid for our task. Biologic and other natural objects are not easily captured by this representation. Objects such as the kidney or heart are not describable by analytic formulas that maintain accuracy while capturing essential shape parameters and range of variation. Still, for breadth of application it is wise to use general models; for the experiments directed towards fetal imaging we used balloons of various shapes in a water bath.

2.   Model-based Medical Image Analysis

In recent years there has been a proliferation of medical imaging techniques. There is also a trend towards generating digital (as opposed to analog) images, both as two-dimensional slices and as complete three-dimensional reconstructions. With the proliferation of digital images has come the development of picture archiving and communications systems (PACS) in radiology departments, which are being built to allow efficient storage, retrieval, and display of these images. With the development of PACS and the ever-increasing number of digital images there is a growing need for efficient and useful indexing schemes.

2.1   Indexing of Images

As in other imaging fields, the prime methods for indexing are manual input of primary parameters such as patient name, type of exam, etc. Diagnosis codes are also often included, following interpretation by the radiologist. Even with these relatively simple indexes, use of a PACS greatly increases the accessibility and usefulness of medical images. Without PACS the filmed images are placed into manila-paper jackets, identified with a sequence number, and shelved. A PACS can retrieve in one request all images of a specific patient and can also cross-reference images by patient diagnosis. Rapid availability of multiple images via a computer network increases the physicians' expectations for new retrieval options.

This setting motivates use of the computer for automatic or semi-automatic interpretation and classification of images. Although a completely automated analysis is a very distant and questionable goal, semi-automatic analysis and classification will be useful to reduce the tedium of scanning the ever-increasing number of images that are being produced. Such systems will allow improved quantification of organ parameters such as shape and volume, which are useful as subtle indicators of disease and response to therapy, and will be useful secondary parameters. Quantification in particular is very tedious and error-prone when performed manually, since it usually requires many detailed measurements on the images.

2.2 Current Medical Image Analysis Techniques

Image enhancement techniques are based on work done in other areas, such as analysis of satellite images. The next phase is the application of image analysis techniques for classifying images. For medical imaging it is not sufficient to simply match a complete image against a set of stored templates because the number of possible variations is too great. First the image must be segmented into meaningful regions corresponding to anatomic structures, then parameters of these regions (such as area, average grey level, etc.), can be measured. Measurements are used to establish features, and these features are used to classify the individual biologic structures.

Most methods utilize low-level image processing techniques such as region-growing, and edge-detection [Yachida 1980] to separate the regions of interest. There is continuing development of techniques for image understanding using such concepts as mathematical morphology [Brady 1982].

In several cases these simple low-level techniques perform well, as long as there is an unambiguous means for separating regions or edges based on a statistical classifier such as a discriminant function. A particularly simple and useful example is the segmentation of bone from the other parts of the images in 3D reconstructions from computed tomography (CT) scans. In this case the CT number stored in each 3D pixel or *voxel* of the 3D image representing bone differs from the CT numbers representing soft tissues so that a simple thresholding technique may be used, and this is the basis for several commercial systems. However, for separating soft tissues in CT or magnetic resonance imaging (MRI) scans no simple thresholding technique is adequate.

2.3 Model-based Image Segmentation of Ultrasound Images

An example of a medical imaging modality where simple thresholding of regions is grossly inadequate is ultrasound. Ultrasound instruments produce two-dimensional real-time slices by transmitting pulses of high-frequency sound waves into the tissues, and then creating an image from the returned echoes. Brightness discontinuities occur where impedance mismatches between adjacent tissues produce returned echoes. However, ultrasound does not pass through bone or air, and the ultrasound beam must be more or less at right angles to tissue interfaces, so edges at other angles representing organs are often not continuous.

Although the images from ultrasound do not have the resolution of X-ray images, ultrasound has the advantage that it uses no ionizing radiation, is painless, low-cost, and produces images in real-time. Thus, it is useful for fetal imaging, where it is not appropriate to use ionizing radiation, and for heart imaging, where motion is a problem for slower imaging methods, such as X-ray tomography.

Because of the difficulty of using thresholding techniques in processing ultrasound images, segmentation is done by hand tracing of the borders. However, since organs are three-dimensional, three-dimensional reconstructions are needed to give accurate volume and shape estimates. In these cases hand tracing of all the borders would be hopelessly inefficient and error-prone.

A radiologist is able to segment ultrasound images because knowledge of anatomy compensates for missing or ambiguous edge data. This is evidenced by noting that a novice looking at an ultrasound image can usually make nothing out of it, while after training in anatomy and experience with ultrasound images, the novice is able to see things not seen before. Thus, one of the main goals of this work is to give the computer knowledge of anatomy that mimics the radiologist's knowledge.

This knowledge is in the form of a general model of both normal and abnormal anatomy, and forms the basis both for aiding the analysis and segmentation of images. Parameters describing the specific model adaptation are then used for indexing these images in a visual database. The model should eventually include many different features and would form the basis for a knowledge base of human anatomy, but current work concentrates on the representation of shape.

2.4   Representing Anatomic Shape

The difficulty with developing a shape model of anatomy is that it is very difficult to represent the essential shape of an organ as well as the range of variation. This problem is not as acute in machine vision for man-made objects, since these objects are often describable by geometric shapes used during the design of these objects. For a biologic object such as a kidney, no combination of simple shapes is able to capture the essential shape as well as the range of variation.

In our experiments with ultrasound we attempted to develop a generic model for anatomical objects. This model is only applicable to objects which could be described as distortions of a sphere, which includes, for example, the left ventricle of the heart or the kidney. The model was tested on three-dimensional ultrasound reconstructions of two balloon shape classes (round and long-thin) ultrasonically imaged in a water bath. Several reconstructions from each shape class were used as a training set to establish the generic models for round and long-thin balloons. These models were then used to aid the analysis of images from new round or long-thin balloons that the computer had not seen before. The use of the model allowed fewer images of one object to be examined while still maintaining accuracy of volume and shape. It also showed the feasibility of model guided search for edges in the images. The following summarizes our issues based on results reported in [Brinkley 1985].

2.5   Model Representation

Figure 1 shows the basic model structure, which consisted of a set of fixed radials emanating from the origin of an object-based coordinate system. Three variable vertices along each radial, when connected via triangular surface patches to nearest neighbors, defined an inner and outer uncertainty surface, and a middle *bestguess* surface which was halfway between the inner and outer uncertainty surfaces. The inner and outer uncertainty surfaces defined the uncertainty volume within which the organ was expected to lie, while the bestguess surface was the computer's best guess, at any particular time in the processing, as to where the actual surface was, consistent with the data it had seen so far. Initially, the inner and outer vertices were set to small and large values respectively, thus ensuring that the initial model enclosed any possible organ instance.

2.6   Interaction of the Shape Knowledge with the Data

This initial model was superimposed on actual 3D image data by manual input of the 3D coordinates of the two balloon endpoints, thus bypassing the very difficult problem of aligning the model with the data. This approach was considered reasonable in an interactive system because it is relatively simple for a human operator to indicate a few landmarks in the data. For large volume processing it will be desirable to automate this step as well.

Given the two endpoints for a new balloon the program superimposed the initial model on the data, then generated a smaller uncertainty volume by moving the inner and outer vertices closer together. The smaller uncertainty volume was generated via interaction of learned shape knowledge contained in the generic model with the two endpoints representing the initial data from the image. The shape knowledge was represented as constraints on the range of possible slopes of each of the edges connecting adjacent radii. The ranges were obtained from the training set of similarly-shaped balloons. The constraints on edges, together with the model vertices, formed a constraint network [Brinkley 1987]. The hypothesis was that the collection of local constraints when interacting together in a relaxation process, were enough to generate the global shape and range of variation for the object.

The two endpoints of the balloon each defined the best guess and uncertainty vertices for the two radii at the poles of the model. This information was then propagated throughout the network of radial vertices by utilizing the learned slope constraints. Thus, for the radials adjacent to the pole vertices the slope constraints allowed the uncertainty to be reduced from the initial large value, even though no direct data was obtained at these radials. The reduced uncertainty at these radials in turn reduced the uncertainty at their neighbors, and so on throughout the network. The process was similar to the progress of a wave traveling over a globe covered with water. Waves of information began at the poles where data was obtained, and traveled outward towards the equator. The further the wave traveled away from the data, the more it became attenuated, so less information was known at the equator than at the poles.

Figure 2 shows the uncertainty volume for the generic model of long-thin balloons, after it had been superimposed on the 3D ultrasound data by indicating the two balloon endpoints manually. The uncertainty surfaces are those generated by interaction of the generic slope constraints with the two endpoints. The fact that the data was acquired at the poles is indicated by a narrow uncertainty volume in these regions. Figure 3 shows the initial bestguess model superimposed on the actual data, which in this case consisted of 3D coordinates of balloon edges manually input with a light pen. Note that the generated model is a reasonable depiction of what might be considered the *essential* shape of a long-thin balloon, even though no prototype was ever created.

Figure 2 also shows the intersection between an ultrasound slice and the uncertainty model. The ultrasound data for a balloon was obtained from a series of 2D slices related to each other by a position locating device. Given the position information and the superposition of the model on the data it was not difficult to determine the relationship of each slice to the model. The intersection of the model with each slice then produced a 2D tolerance region on each slice which provided a region within which to search for edges in the ultrasound image. These edges could then be used to update the model in the same manner as the initial balloon endpoints updated the model.

Thus, Figure 4 shows the result of updating the uncertainty volume after taking into account edge information from the first selected ultrasound slice, and Figure 5 shows the resulting bestguess surface. Note that now the uncertainty in the model is much narrower, and the bestguess surface is a much better fit to the data.

The model-fitting process was allowed to continue in this fashion. A particular ultrasound slice was selected for examination, the edges on that slice were used to update the model, and the process was repeated. Since numeric uncertainty and bestguess volumes were always available the procedure could terminate when uncertainty volume did not change much between successive scans. Thus, the computer *knew* when it had seen enough data. For the balloons this usually occurred after about one-third of the scans had been examined. We demonstrated that volume accuracy was the same at early termination as if all the scans were examined.

2.7   Feature Extraction

The generality of the model causes that many parameters, among others measures along all the radials, are generated. These are not useful for indexing. although they do define the actual shape much more precisely than would be possible by relying only on measurements from selected two-dimensional observations. However, now the volumes of the shapes and subshapes can be computed. Volume is a useful secondary parameter for indexing the database. Since volume is a direct corollary of fetal weight an eventual operational system will be able to collect in the database the most critical parameters of fetal growth.

3.   Modeling Satellite Images of the Aurora

In this section, we present a model used in ongoing scientific investigations of the aurora. The model is based on assumptions regarding the representation of the aurora in images obtained by high altitude polar satellites. One current assumption, still to be validated, is that the aurora is at a constant altitude above the poles. This permits us to work with a 2-D model. Assumptions about the physics of the aurora provide techniques for finding features in the images. We show the results of preliminary demonstrations of the techniques using auroral images obtained from the Dynamics Explorer 1 (DE-1) satellite.

Investigations of auroral phenomena during the 1960's and 1970's utilized arrays of all-sky cameras to study the development of auroras all around the polar cap throughout the night- and day-side portions of the earth. Polar-based global imaging of the aurora utilizing satellites was initiated over 7 years ago with the Dynamics Explorer-1 (DE-1) auroral imaging photometers at visible and UV wavelengths. More than 500,000 images have been acquired to date by DE-1 and upcoming satellites having higher temporal and spatial resolutions will produce over 600 images per day.

3.1   Information Content of Auroral Images

Images of the aurora contain significant information pertinent to many scientific investigations of magnetospheric and auroral physics. This information ranges from the location of the aurora (latitudinal boundaries as a function of position around the earth) to the intensity of the aurora at different wavelength emissions, to structural features within the aurora and the time evolution of auroral disturbances. A number of important classification parameters for auroral images can be computed once the auroral boundaries are determined. Such secondary parameters include the total integrated intensity of the auroral oval, width of the auroral oval as a function of position around the earth, intensity of the aurora as a function of position around the earth, and the area of the dark region inside the auroral oval.

3.2   Modeling Auroral Images

As indicated in the introduction, auroral images are incomplete. There is a need, therefore, to model the oval region using closed, continuous curves which fill the gaps in the visible portions of the aurora. The set of techniques which we are using for identifying the auroral oval are based on recent computer vision work by Kass [Kass 1988]. Their method is related to fitting spline curves under tension to the image data.

Before trying to identify the auroral oval, one must eliminate the effect of dayside illumination which causes problems for the intensity-based modeling algorithms. The technique used for removing the dayside illumination involves a *shaded sphere* calculation, a technique used in the computer graphics community to render realistic images. The sun is assumed to be an infinitely distant point source of illumination. The reflectance from the atmospheric surface at ultraviolet wavelengths is approximated to follow a Lambertian law. These two approximations, together with information about location and position of the earth and sun provided by the DE-1 satellite ephemeris data, allows the calculation of the vector dot product between the sun's position vector and the local surface normal vector. With the additional assumption that the satellite is far from the earth, the illumination under the Lambertian law is proportional to the cosine of the incident angle between the sun vector and the surface normal. The dayside illumination is removed by subtracting from each pixel in the original image a value proportional to the cosine of the incident angle. Once the dayside illumination is removed, the curves describing the auroral oval may be found. The results shown below for finding the oval ignore the illumination compensation step since the auroral oval for the images shown are in the winter hemisphere and therefore appear in the dark portion of the earth.

The technique for finding the auroral oval is based on curve fitting with splines. For standard, one dimensional splines, there is a relationship between the fitting of the splines to the data and the bending energy of small deflections of a rod. The curves used here, developed first by Kass, are analogous to splines with an additional tension term used to fit two-dimensional data. That is, the curves are analogous to elastic materials which resist both bending and stretching.

3.3   The Basis for the Model

In this section, we discuss the model used for finding various features in the auroral images. Formally, the model simulates the statics of an elastic curve which is constrained to lie in the plane of the image [Kass 1988, Samadani 1989]. The image exerts forces on the elastic curve. Strings, thin lengths of rubber or thin metallic rod are examples of the materials which are simulated. The feature detection process starts by positioning the elastic curve on the image in some initial configuration. Starting from the initial configuration, a local minimum of the energy of the elastic curve is found. The configuration of the elastic curve at equilibrium provides the geometric description of the feature.

The total energy, E, of the elastic curve is given by [Terzopoulos 1988] as

$$E = \int_\Omega \alpha(s - s^0)^2 + \beta(k - k^0)^2 + P(x,y)da$$

where the integral is over the curve coordinate a. The natural arc length and the natural curvature of the elastic curve, given by s^0 and k^0, respectively, determine the preferred shape for the material. The actual arc length and the actual curvature of the elastic curve are given by s and k. The first term of the integral, therefore, describes the energy added to the system by perturbing the length of the material and the second term of the integral describes the energy added to the system by perturbing the curvature of the material. The constants α and β determine the characteristics of the material. For example, materials with large α will not stretch or shrink easily and materials with large β will not bend easily.

A potential, $P(x, y)$, derived from the image, applies external forces to the elastic curve. This potential can be modified to allow the tracking of various features. Feature extraction is defined as finding an extremum of the integral equation for the energy. An iterative method is used to step from an initial configuration of the elastic curve to an equilibrium configuration by choosing new configurations of the curve which lowers its energy. At the equilibrium, the shape and location of the elastic curve describes the feature. This equilibrium results in a smooth fit to the image data since the elastic components of the energy are lower for smooth functions.

3.4 Implementation

We have developed an interactive software system to allow experimentation with the use of elastic curves to find auroral oval features. The software was developed using the Sun 3/260 computer and the SunView* windowing system. The software system was developed to allow users to gain experience with the elastic materials. Preliminary results show that the techniques used in the system are successful in finding the curves passing through the most intense locations of the oval and in outlining the inner and outer boundaries of the oval. The system may also be used to track the changes of the auroral oval through time.

The system assumes default values for various of its parameters. While the system is running, it allows the user to interactively modify the default parameters by using a graphical interface of software-simulated sliders and buttons. The parameters under user control include the elastic constants which control the material's resistance to bending, resistance to stretching and the preferred rest length of the material. The user may also modify the step size of the gradient descent iteration and the boundary conditions which determine whether the elastic material forms a closed loop or is open at the ends. The user can select new images and also control the elastic material's positions. The elastic material may either be input from a file or the user may use a mouse to draw the initial configuration of the elastic material.

3.5 Interactive Image Analysis

By choosing different functions of image intensities, one may find various features. The first, simplest application is finding a curve which goes through the most intense parts of the oval. To do this, one chooses a potential field directly proportional to the image intensities. Then, one first draws the elastic curve outside of the actual oval.

The initial configuration of the elastic curve is currently input manually, but this step may be automated by using latitude and longitude information from the satellite to define an ellipse which is certain to enclose the actual auroral oval. The length at rest of the elastic material is chosen to correspond to a natural perimeter which is smaller than the perimeter of the actual oval. After setting of the initial parameters, the iteration process is started.

The technique for finding the curve through the maximum intensity areas of the oval was applied to a section of a DE-1 image containing the auroral oval. This image is shown in grayscale in Figure 6. The initial and final configurations of the curve are shown in Figure 7, superimposed on the auroral intensities. In this figure, the initial, irregular hand-drawn elastic curve is found outside of the oval. Also shown is the final location of the elastic curve at equilibrium. The auroral intensities shown in Figure 7 have been decreased to make the curves more visible. The curve at equilibrium fits smoothly the

---

* SunView is a trademark of Sun Microsystems, Inc., Palo Alto CA

maximum intensity points of the oval. Figure 8 shows the intermediate results of the iterative algorithm. Appearing in the figure from left to right, and top to bottom are the various images which depict snapshots of the configuration of the elastic curve as it proceeds from its initial configuration to its equilibrium configuration.

The equilibrium configuration of the elastic curve through the most intense points could be used to study bright spots in the aurora. An example of the secondary parameters that could be obtained here are the image intensities along the elastic curve. As an alternative, one could store the average intensity in small neighborhoods of pixels along the curve. This information could be used to search for bright spots above some threshold.

Another application of the system is finding the inner and outer boundaries of the oval. This is done by using two independent elastic curves, one for each boundary. The potential field used in this case is directly proportional to the negative values of the image intensities. To find the outer boundary, one draws an elastic curve outside of the actual oval and sets its rest length to correspond to a natural perimeter for the curve which is smaller than the perimeter of the oval. During the iterative process, this elastic curve shrinks to fit the outer boundary of the oval. It stops at the outer boundary since further shrinking would result in a higher energy due to the potential field term derived from the negative intensities of the image. To find the inner boundary, one draws an elastic curve inside oval and sets its rest length to correspond to a natural perimeter which is larger than the perimeter for the actual oval. During the iteration process, this elastic curve will grow to fit the inner boundary of the oval.

The technique for finding the inner and outer boundaries of the oval was applied to the image in Figure 6. Figure 9a shows the initial configurations of the two elastic curves which are used to find the boundaries, superimposed on the auroral intensities. The auroral intensities have been decreased in the image to make the curves more visible. Figure 9b shows the equilibrium configurations of the two elastic curves, which are found to fit the inner and outer boundary of the superimposed aurora. Figure 10a shows the intensity values of the image before processing. Figure 10b shows the intensity values of the image, but only at those locations that correspond to auroral features between the inner and outer elastic curves. Thus, a comparison of Figures 10a and 10b demonstrates that the preceding steps are successful in extracting meaningful information from the original image data.

The configurations of the inner and outer curves at their equilibrium could be used as the basis for secondary parameters. One can compute from these inner and outer boundaries the area enclosed between the inner and outer boundaries, which reflects the extent of the aurora. The area inside the inner boundary is also a useful parameter. Other secondary parameters, such as the average integrated auroral intensity between the boundaries could be obtained. The equilibrium configurations of the inner and outer curves allows the extraction of each of the parameters mentioned.

3.6 Tracking of Changes through Time

In addition to finding features, one may use the elastic curves for tracking features through time. This can be done by applying the elastic curves to a time sequence of images. For example, consider the tracking of the brighter areas of the oval. Start with the first image in the sequence and find the bright regions of the oval in this image by using the technique described above. Now, use the equilibrium configuration of the elastic curve in the first image as the initial configuration of a second curve applied to the second image in the sequence. Solving, as in the first image, the equilibrium configuration is found for this, second image. This procedure is repeated for each image in the sequence, resulting in a sequence of curves whose equilibrium configuration changes with time. The parameters obtained from one image can be used to initialize the model for the next image.

The motion tracking technique was applied to the image sequence shown in the top row of Figure 11. Because of satellite scanning speed, there is roughly a 25 minute interval between consecutive images in the sequence. The bottom row of the figure shows the sequence of equilibrium configurations of the elastic curves corresponding to the images above them. The changes in the configurations of the elastic curves tracks the changes of the bright areas of the oval through time. The same technique could be used to track inner and outer boundaries or other features.

3.7 Feature Extraction

The techniques described above can be used to find various features in the images. The examples shown have used the configurations of elastic curves to find the positions of the highest intensity regions of the oval, the positions of the inner and outer boundaries of the oval, and to track the changes in the oval through time. Other applications may be developed by changing the definition of the potential field derived from the image intensities.

For all applications, the results of the feature extraction is a description of the two dimensional coordinates of discrete points along the curves. These parameters are suitable for indexing an image database. They provide a compact description of the interesting features in the images. Also, the data structure is one-dimensional, simplifying its storage. Even though the data structure is one dimensional, useful two-dimensional geometrical parameters can be derived from this information, with far less effort than analysis of the original images. For example, perimeter and centroid are readily calculated in a time linear with respect to the number of points on the curve. The changes in perimeter and centroid may also be easily followed through time. Other parameters, such as local motion of a segment of a curve, requires further processing, but methods for such calculations are known [Hildreth 84]. The curves can be used to derive the geometrical quantities to be stored in the database, or the curve parameters themselves could be stored and queries made directly on them. The choice between the two will be easier to make once we have more experience with the processing speed requirements of the application.

4. Summary

We have shown that similar principles can be applied to widely differing applications of image analysis. By using a high-level adaptive model and establishing parameters which describe the adaptation of the model we obtain information of a type which low-level image analyses, characterized by image-enhancement techniques, cannot provide. Adaptive-model-based image analysis extracts image features to augment the database and index the images for query and further selection.

The features extracted require much less storage than the original images. The database system may be designed to use different media and access capabilities for the image storage and the searchable portion of the database.

Medical Image Information   The representation used here to describe general non-structured biologic objects is a set of geometric distortions of a sphere. The system uses this model to extract three-dimensional organ reconstructions from a series of arbitrarily-oriented ultrasound slices. A training set of ultrasonic reconstructions of similarly-shaped objects is used to give the computer generic knowledge of a given shape class.

An hypothesize-verify paradigm is employed to alternately request new data and to update the tolerance region and bestguess surface. This enabled the analysis program to build an accurate three-dimensional representation from a series of arbitrarily-oriented ultrasound image slices of the object.

Auroral Image Information   The model used to describe the auroral shape is based on an analogy with elastic material. The properties of the material are parameterized. The system allows a user to interactively choose parameters which vary the material's rest length and its resistance to either stretching or bending. For example, to find the outer boundary of the aurora oval, elastic material is placed in a circle of arbitrary size which encloses the aurora. The initial rest length of the elastic material is chosen to guarantee that it is less than the perimeter of the outer boundary. The equilibrium configuration of the elastic material then describes the outer boundary. The inner boundary is found symmetrically.

4.1   Indexing Parameters

Parameters for database obtained for the medical shapes are volume measures. Such a secondary parameter is useful to indicate growth, where it desirable, as in a fetus, or not desirable, as in cancers and some cardiac conditions. For the aurora borealis the model provides the perimeter, centroid, and area enclosed within the boundary. These parameters are made available for querying by the scientist, who can now conveniently track series of images. The environment planned for by [Crehange et al 1984] has that flavor.

Once an object has been recognized and measured, then further parameters, indicating normality or abnormality, might be useful. Abnormalities might be unexpected length-to-width ratios, or large local variations in a surface. Analysis of multiple objects in an image can provide measures of relative size, placement, and orientation.

4.2   Limitations and Extensions

The models we used will also have to be extended to allow more complex structured objects. A larger class of objects is possible if the vertices are allowed to move in arbitrary directions rather than only along their radials. A development of this approach showed partial success in the representation of proteins by constraint networks [Brinkley 1987].

Due to the large number of images which are becoming available, it is best to develop feature extraction methods which will involve little or no human interaction. The techniques we show are currently used, at least partially, interactively, but full automation of the processing is the eventual goal. There are two aspects where interaction is currently important:

1 Defining some initial fiducial points so that the program does not have to search for an anchorpoint for the model. This is difficult if the image can contain multiple candidate objects.

2 Guiding the program if an incorrect object boundary is accepted early on. Such an error will unfairly bias the resulting model.

The problem of guidance occurs in most areas of science, where partial data may suggest an incorrect hypothesis, which then must be corrected to account for new data.

Approaches to be considered for dealing with this problem are to use more knowledge, such as probabilistic descriptions of the constraints, allowing backtracking, and to use least-commitment concepts by allowing a set of possible edges in defining each boundary, rather than just one.

4.3 Parallel Image Analysis

The heavy computing demands engendered by image processing drive us to consider parallel processing. Most considerations of parallelism to date have focused on pixel-oriented, synchronous, analysis of images, and that will remain an important preliminary phase for many images [Yamaguchi 1982].

Model-based interpretation of images presents an opportunity for extending asynchronous parallel processing. Currently some projects exploit parallelism to deal with multiple objects in a scene. We think that multiple candidate objects and models can be investigated in parallel, adding one more dimension of parallelism. An independent demon may abort some of the model processes which have located the same object. A measure of matching success attained by these independently operating processes can be the criterion for letting them continue. Even left alone, successful processes would tend to terminate earlier than problematical ones. The final collection of objects and models matched may be pruned, or we might populate the database with multiple *maybe* candidates.

4.4 Incomplete Processing

In any case, if we avoid manual interaction and refinement, we may not be able to resolve the image contents determination to a single, highly probable set of objects. But we can permit having multiple indices to one image. Some false images will be retrieved in response to queries on secondary parameters. We then must leave the final selection of relevant images to the eventual user of the image information. In this approach the secondary parameters provide a relatively coarser filter than we now seek to obtain with our interactive analyses. However, the real objective of having secondary parameters would *not* be violated by this approach, since the concept of using secondary parameters to aid the user by providing a manageable set of images is still being achieved.

5. Finale

We have used adaptive model-based techniques to obtain secondary parameters for indexing images stored in databases. While these applications differed greatly they also show important commonalities. The top-down approach employed permits the use of generic shape knowledge to compensate for limitations of the imaging modality, and can reduce the analysis time by requiring less data to be acquired.

This techniques are not adequate for full automation of real-world image processing. It appears, however, that they are sufficiently effective to be used as an augmentation for manual indexing. If employed in that manner, the experience gained will help us in developing the technology for more complete automation.

If model-based image processing develops as we would hope then we can envisage specialized image knowledge-bases. For instance, a knowledge-base of human anatomy would represent both normal and pathologic shape variation in different shape classes. When classifying a new set of three-dimensional image data defining a likely object one or a set of ranked hypotheses could be suggested by the matching parameters vis-a-vis the database.

Not being able to reduce, during analysis, the findings to a single object hypothesis need not discourage work in automated image analysis. Any significant reduction in search space will be helpful to the users of large image databases.

Acknowledgements

Knowledge-acquisition research was partially supported through the RX project, funded by the National Center for Health Services Research (HS-3650 and HS-4389) and the National Library of Medicine (LM-4334). Research towards fetal imaging was supported by NIH under grants HD-12327, RR-0785, and by a fellowship (F32 GM08092) to J. Brinkley. The scans were made in the department of Gynecology and Obstetrics of Stanford University, and we thank the chairman, faculty — especially Desmond McCallum, and staff for their assistance. Figures 1–5 came from [Brinkley 1984].

The work on auroral images has been supported by the Center for Aeronautics and Space Information Systems (CASIS) under NASA grant NAGW419. We thank Domingo Mihovilovic for providing most of the code for the interactive elastic curve system on the Sun. We thank Drs. L.A. Frank and J.D. Craven at the University of Iowa for use of the DE-1 auroral images examined in this research. Michael Walker participated in the conceptualization of the work on auroral feature extraction and measurement; this research is continuing through a grant from the NASA Center for Excellence in Space Data and Information Systems (CESDIS), further focusing on interaction with large scale data management.

Basic research on the interaction of knowledge and data is supported by the Defense Advanced Research Projects Agency under DARPA N39-84-C-211.

References

Arvidson, Raymond, Gio Wiederhold, et al: *Issues and Recommendations Associated with Distributed Computation and Data Management Systems for the Space Sciences*, volume 2; Committee on Data Management and Computation, Space Sciences Board, National Academy of Sciences, National Academy Press, 1986.

Binford, T.O.: "Visual Perception by Computer"; Invited talk at the IEEE Conference on Systems, Science and Cybernetics, Miami, 1971.

Brady, M.; "Computational Approaches to Image Understanding"; *ACM Computing Surveys*, Vol. 14 No. 1, pp. 3–71, 1982.

Brinkley, J.F., W.E. Moritz, and D.W. Baker: "Ultrasonic Three-dimensional Imaging and Volume from a Series of Arbitrary Sector Scans"; *Ultrasound Med. Biol.*, Vol. 4, pp. 317–327, 1978.

Brinkley, James F.: Ultrasonic Three-Dimensional Organ Modelling; PhD thesis, Committee on Graduate Studies, Stanford Unversity 1984.

Brinkley, J.F.: "Knowledge-driven Ultrasonic Three-Dimensional Organ Modelling"; *IEEE Transactions on Pattern Analysis and Machine Intelligence*; Vol. PAMI-7 No. 4, pp. 431–441, 1985.

Brinkley, J.F., B.G. Buchanan, R.B. Altman, B.S. Duncan, and C.W. Cornelius: "A Heuristic Refinement Method for Spatial Constraint Satisfaction Problems"; Stanford University, STAN-CS-87-1142, KSL-87-05, Jan. 1987.

Brooks, R.A. and T.O. Binford: "Geometric Modeling in Vision for Manufacturing"; *SPIE Proceedings* 281, 1981.

Chang, S.K., C.W. Yan, D.C. Dimitroff, and T. Arndt: "An Intelligent Image Database System"; *IEEE Transactions on Software Engineering*, Vol.14 No.5, May 1988, pp. 681-688.

Crehange, M., A. AitHaddou, M. Boukaiou, J.M. David, O. Foucaut, and J. Maroldt: "EXPRIM, an Expert System to Aid in Progressive Retrieval from a Pictorial and Descriptive Analysis"; in *New Applications of Databases*, Gardarin and Gelenbe(eds), Academic Press, 1984.

Hildreth, Ellen C.: *The Measurement of Visual Motion*; MIT Press, Cambridge MA, 1987.

Kass, M.A., A. Witkin and D. Terzopoulos: "Snakes: Active Contour Models"; *International Journal of Computer Vision*, Vol. 1, pp. 321–331, 1988.

Kasturi, R. and J. Alemany: "Information Extraction from Images of Paper-Based Maps"; *IEEE Transactions on Software Engineering*, Vol.14 No.5, May 1988, pp.671-675.

Roussopoulos, N., C. Faloutsos, and T. Sellis: "An Efficient Pictorial Database System for PSQL"; *IEEE Transactions on Software Engineering*, Vol.14 No.5, May 1988, pp. 639-650.

Samadani, Ramin: "Changes in Connectivity in Active Contour Models"; to appear in IEEE Workshop on Visual Motion, March 1989, Irvine, CA.

Soroka, B.I.: "Generalized Cones From Serial Sections"; *Computer Graphics and Image Processing*, Vol. 15, pp. 154–166, 1981.

Terzopoulos, Demetri, John Platt, Alan Barr and Kurt Fleischer: "Elastically Deformable Models"; *ACM Transactions on Computer Graphics*, Vol. 21, No. 4, July 1987, pp. 205–214.

Wiederhold, Gio: *File Organization for Database Design*; McGraw-Hill Book Company, New York, NY, March 1987.

Yachida, M., M. Ikeda, and S. Tsuji: "A Plan-guided Analysis of Cineangiograms for Measurement of Dynamic Behavior of Heart Wall"; *IEEE Transactions on Pattern Recognition and Machine Intelligence*; Vol. PAMI-2 No. 6, pp. 537, 1980.

Yamaguchi, K. and T.L. Kunii: "PICCOLO, Logic for a Picture Database Computer and Its Implementation"; *IEEE Trans. Computers*, Vol.C-31 No.10, Oct.1982, pp.983–996.

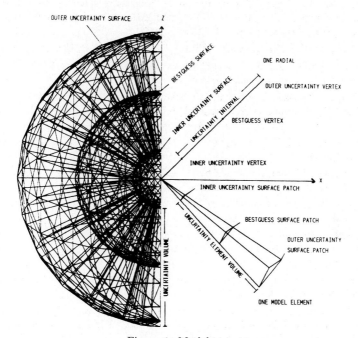

Figure 1: Model structure.

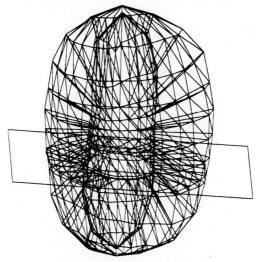

Figure 2: Initital uncertainty volume and first selected slice, long-thin ballon.

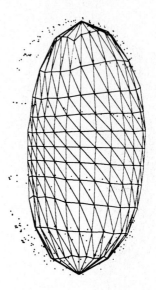

Figure 3: Initital bestguess surface superimposed on data, long-thin ballon.

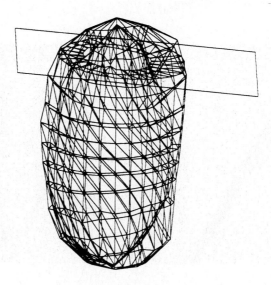

Figure 4: Uncertainty volume after global updating by first
selected slice, second selected slice, long-thin ballon.

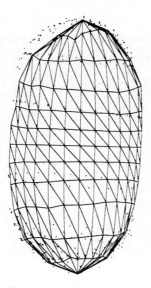

Figure 5. Bestguess surface after first selected slice, superimposed on data, long-thin ballon.

Figure 6. Graylevel coded intensity values for the portion of a DE-1 satellite image containing a winter hemisphere auroral oval.

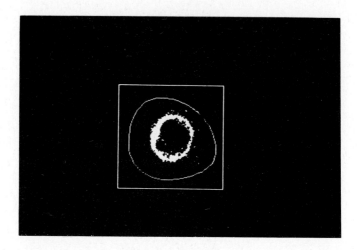

Figure 7.   The initial and equilibrium configuration of an
elastic curve superimposed on a darker grayscale representation
of the auroral oval of Figure 6.   The curve is used to find
the most intense boundary of the oval.

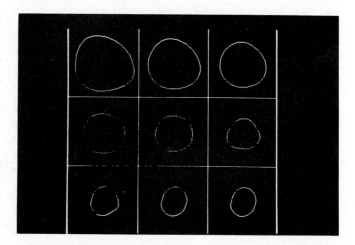

Figure 8.   Intermediate steps of the iterative solution, beginning
with the initial configuration and continuing to the equilibrium
configuration of the elastic curve used for finding the brightest
region of the oval.

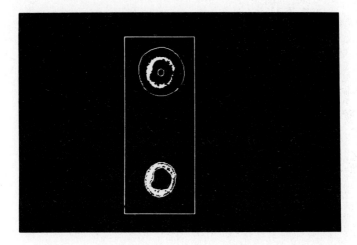

Figure 10. Graylevel coded intensity values of the DE-1 image shown in Figure 7, but only for the region between the inner and outer boundaries found by the elastic curves in Figure 9b.

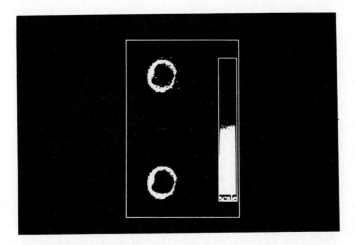

Figure 9. a) Initial configurations of the elastic curves used to find the inner and outer boundaries of the auroral oval. The elastic **curve** inside tends to grows and the elastic curve outside tends to shrink. b) The equilibrium configurations of the elastic curves which fit the boundaries of the aurora.

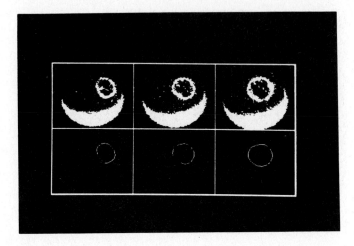

Figure 11. a) The three images in the top row show a sequence of DE-1
satellite images taken within one hour. b) The three images in the
bottom row show the configurations of the elastic curves as they
follow the motion of the maximum intensity areas of the auroral oval.

Session 6

SOLID DATABASE

Visual Database Systems
T.L. Kunii (Editor)
Elsevier Science Publishers B.V. (North-Holland)
© IFIP, 1989

Representing CSG Solids Using a Logic-Based Object Data Model

T. Lougenia Anderson***   Hitomi Ohkawa**
Jack Gjovaag*   David Maier**†   Sheryl Shulman*,**

*Tektronix Laboratories

**Oregon Graduate Center

***Servio Logic Development Corp.

ABSTRACT: Constructive Solid Geometry (CSG) is a widely-used method of describing three-dimensional solids. This paper reports on our experiences in applying TEDM, an object-oriented logic-based data model, to the problem of modeling CSG solids. In addition, we report on a new representation for the spatial relationships between CSG primitives based on constraints. These constraints are modeled as first-class objects in TEDM, and hence are available explicitly to programs for reasoning about properties of the resulting CSG representation. Further, the constraint mechanism supports information hiding, provides support for capturing tolerencing information for a CSG solid, allows partially-specified solids, and appears appropriate for the design system user interface.

KEYWORDS: Constructive Solid Geometry, object-oriented data models, logic-based data models, constraints, inferencing techniques

1. INTRODUCTION

There is a growing perception in the CAD community that Object-Oriented Database Management Systems (OO-DBMSs) provide the best modeling paradigm for handling the complex, interrelated data structures found in CAD applications. In a joint research project between Tektronix, Inc. and the Oregon Graduate Center we have developed the Tektronix Engineering Data Model (TEDM), a logic-based object model for such an OO-DBMS [8,2]. This paper reports on our experiences in applying TEDM to the problem of modeling Constructive Solid Geometry (CSG) solids, and on a new representation for the

† D. Maier's work was partially supported by a contract from Tektronix Computer Research Laboratory and NSF grant IST 83 51730, co-sponsored by Tektronix Foundation, Intel, Digital Equipment, Servio Logic, Mentor Graphics and Xerox.

spatial relationships between CSG primitives that exhibits some distinct advantages over the commonly used transformational matrix approach.

The joint work on TEDM grew out of a requirements analysis which indicated that traditional database systems are no longer sufficient for engineering design applications [9]. TEDM shares with other object-oriented data models the capability of constructing complex data objects that accommodate hierarchical structures with shared subparts or even cyclic data, a major departure from the relational data model. In addition to handling complex objects, TEDM also supports object identity, a type hierarchy, deductive elements for virtual data definition, and a rule-like data language.

One of the most important requirements for our CSG data model is that it be possible to treat constraints as objects. The ultimate goal is to be able to reason about various characteristics of a particular CSG solid, such as part rigidity, manufacturability, or whether the part is over- or underconstrained. The reasoning process requires examining and manipulating constraints on the relationships between CSG primitives as data. Since everything is an object in an object-oriented data model, such constraints are no different from the more conventional data objects stored in the database and can be manipulated in a similar fashion.

Primitive shapes, such as spheres, cones, and cylinders, form the basis for a CSG representation of a three dimensional solid. Each complex solid is defined by specifying a Boolean combination of such primitive shapes and other similarly defined complex shapes, where constraints may be placed on the relative position of the two shapes being combined. This Boolean combination process is continued recursively until the desired solid is completely specified. Note that such a recursive definition is easily translated into a binary-tree form where the interior nodes correspond to operations such as binary Boolean operations (union, intersection or difference), and the leaf nodes correspond to primitive shapes such as sphere, cylinder, or plane. The specification of rigid translation/rotation is usually accomplished by adding additional interior node types. Also, the translation/rotation specification may be pushed down to the leaves of the tree and thus can occur only in the leaf nodes.

Past CSG models have used a Transformation-matrix (T-matrix) approach to specify rigid motion/relative position between the two shapes being combined in a CSG representation [6,7,17]. In our work we have developed a second approach to specifying relative position based on *reference features*. Each of the primitive shapes has a set of attached reference features (basically some set of points and lines). For example, an infinite cylinder can be defined in terms of a central axis and a radius. Correspondingly, a complex shape has as its reference features some subset of the reference features of its components. Relative position of two shapes is specified in terms of the corresponding reference features. What is novel about our approach is that we have examined a number of the possible relationships between various pairs of reference features and have defined equivalence classes based on relative spatial topology (i.e., all pairs of reference features in a particular equivalence class are obtainable from each other by some combination of translations and rotations). We then use these equivalence classes for reference features pairs as the basis for modeling rigid motion in the TEDM data model for CSG.

The reference feature approach seems to have several advantages over the conventional T-matrix approach to specifying rigid motion/relative position. First, it has more promise in being able to capture tolerancing information than does the T-matrix. Second, it seems more appropriate as the model for rigid motion that should be used in the user interface (it appears that few CSG modelers actually think in terms of T-matrices, for example). Third, it appears to be good abstraction mechanism which supports information hiding, since it is possible to use a subset of the reference features of the components of a complex object as the reference features for the complex object. Finally, the reference features approach offers more versatility in specifying degrees of freedom in the rigid motion/relative position between two shapes than does the T-matrix approach. For example, one might want to specify only that two spheres are a certain distance apart rather than totally specifying their relative position and rotation with respect to some coordinate system. This partial specification of relative position is not as easy using the T-matrix approach, since the only option is to leave elements of the matrix undefined. Problems arise when such a partially specified T-matrix is combined with another matrix (e.g., what is the meaning of matrix multiplication when some of the elements of one or both of the operands are undefined).

The remainder of the paper is organized as follows. Section 2 covers previous work in CSG data modeling. Section 3 discusses the salient features of the TEDM data model and Section 4 outlines CSG modeling for those not familiar with the technique. In Section 5 we present the TEDM data model for CSG, including reference features, and then use the data model in a simple example in Section 6. Section 7 critiques the model presented with respect to applying inferencing techniques to answer questions about a particular CSG solid, and discusses future work.

2. PREVIOUS WORK

Lee and Fu use a design methodology based on a semantic data model to derive a relational schema for CSG [6]. The paper defines a grammar structure for representing CSG trees in which the primitive solids are bounded shapes rather than the more general half-spaces we use. Relative spatial relationships between the CSG solids (whether primitives shapes or complex structures) are defined using the T-matrix approach. The resulting relational schema is based on the assumption that the first primitive shape in the CSG tree defines a world coordinate system and that all other rotations and translations are given with respect to this world coordinate system. (This approach raises problems when one attempts to combine two complex CSG solids, both of which have different coordinate schemes.)

Finally, the paper defines three extensions to the SEQUEL language to support the CSG schema. First, a data definition statement is added that will automatically define the underlying base relations necessary to support the aggregation and generalization abstractions in the semantic data model. The second extension is a set of integrity assertions that maintain the required

referential constraints between relations representing the CSG tree. In the last
extension the authors use the SEQUEL trigger facility to define a procedure for
updating all the base relations to represent the addition of one level in a CSG
tree.

The work by Spooner, et al. is similar to our work in that it takes an
object-oriented approach to defining the CSG model [17]. It, however, does not
rigourously define an underlying DBMS data model but rather draws on elements from the programming language SmallTalk, and further shows that the
generalization and aggregration abstractions from semantic data models have
direct correlates in the language. This approach is in harmony with the main
point of the paper, which is to show that the object-oriented approach provides
a flexible and responsive data model that will accommodate the diverse types of
data present in mechanical CAD.

The paper includes the outline of a data model for both boundary representations and CSG representations for three-dimensional solids. In their model it
is possible to combine objects specified using either representation in a Boolean
tree. This flexibility is a good demonstration of the power of the abstractions in
an object-oriented approach, which enable different data structures to be
integrated and treated in a uniform fashion. However, the combining operators,
with the exception of the T-matrix, are not discussed in the paper. (NB: Combining operators appear as interior nodes in the Boolean tree.) The data model
interpretation of the T-matrix is also rather sketchy (e.g., with respect to what
coordinate system is the translation given?).

The important aspects of the Spooner paper is that it is the first attempt
at modeling CSG using an object-oriented approach, and that it demonstrates
the feasibility of integrating the different data representations found in CAD
applications.

3. TEDM OVERVIEW

Databases under TEDM are collections of objects, the basic building blocks
provided by the model. Objects in TEDM are either *simple* or *complex*. Simple
objects are non-decomposable atomic values and are taken from a fixed set of
base types, which for our examples will be String, Integer and Boolean.
(String literals appear in single quotes; integers are prefixed with #.) Complex
objects are collections of *fields*, each of which has the form

        fieldname -> value

where the value is a simple object or another complex object (thus arbitrary
nested data objects can be constructed). These complex objects are similar to
the ψ-terms of Ait-Kaci [1]. The following object describes a department.

```
(deptName -> 'Research',
 budget -> #1253500,
 manager ->
   (name -> (first -> 'William',
             last -> 'Porter')),
 building -> 'C51',
 building -> 'C52').
```

Note that we may have multiple occurrences of a fieldname in an object.

Each object has a unique identity that is represented by an internal *object identifier* (OBID). The OBID of an object is unique with respect to the entire database, and it will not change during the lifetime of the object. The OBID of an object and the state of the object are orthogonal — while the state may change as the database evolves, the OBID always stays the same. With this notion of object identity, each object is distinguishable and therefore the system can discriminate any two objects without depending on their states. Also, two or more fields can have the same object as their value.

To capture multiple references to the same object in a linear syntax, TEDM uses *object tags* prefixing objects. For example, if we want the department manager to reference the department in which he works, we can use a tag D:

```
:D(deptName -> 'Research',
   budget -> #1253500,
   manager ->
     (name -> (first -> 'William',
               last -> 'Porter'),
      worksIn -> :D),
   building -> 'C51',
   building -> 'C52').
```

TEDM supports types for objects. A type definition looks much like an object description, but with type names for values.

```
PersonName = (first -> String:,
              last -> String:).

Person = (name -> PersonName:).

Department = (deptName -> String:,
              manager -> Person:,
              building => String:).
```

The type that is the value of a field in a type definition is called the *range type* of the field. For example, `Person` is the range type of the `manager` field. The double arrow indicates a field that may have multiple occurrences. We will usually write object descriptions with type names inserted, except for simple values.

```
Department:D
   (deptName -> 'Research',
    budget -> #1253500,
    manager ->
      Person:(name ->
                 PersonName:
                    (first -> 'William',
                     last -> 'Porter'),
              worksIn -> Department:D),
```

```
building -> 'C51',
building -> 'C52').
```

TEDM support several syntactic conventions that facilitate readability. In a type definition if two or more fields have the same range type, this is indicated by listing the fields separated by commas on the left-hand side as in

```
name1, name2 -> String:.
```

Also, if a field has multiple range types, these may be listed on the right-hand side separated by |'s as in

```
value -> PosNum: | NegNum:.
```

Each type has a corresponding *type set* of objects that conform to the type description. An object may belong to several type sets, and need not belong to every typeset to which it conforms. Furthermore, types in TEDM are *prescriptive*, not *proscriptive*: an object may have more fields than required by a type. In the example above, there is a `budget` field that is not required by the `Department` type. Types are organized into a hierarchy, where a subtype inherits all the fields and restrictions of the supertype, but can add other fields and restrictions. Thus, we could define

```
Employee = (name -> PersonName:,
            age -> Integer:,
            salary -> Integer:).
```

```
Person > Employee:.
```

as a subtype of `Person`. The top of the hierarchy is the type `All`, whose typeset contains all objects known to the system.

TEDM also supports two special kinds of fields, *abstract* fields and *virtual* fields. Abstract fields are prefixed with `@` as in `@listElement`. Types with abstract fields cannot be directly instantiated. Rather, they serve to define type structure and generic field specifications shared by subclasses. When an abstract field is inherited by a subtype, it is always specialized (as in `name@listElement`). Once specialized in a type definition, a field may be referred to by its specialized name without the `@` suffix. If, for example, a specialized abstract field such as `name@listElement` is used in a rule following a type definition or is inherited by a subtype, it may be referred to as `name`.

Virtual fields contain computed or derived values and are indicated by the `*` prefix as in `*distance`. Their derivation is given by a rule that follows the type definition. If a virtual field is defined for a type, then it is inherited by all subtypes of the type. Also, a non-virtual field of a type may be redefined as a virtual field in a subtype.

The data language for TEDM is influenced by logic languages, and consists of *commands*, which handle update and I/O, and *rules*, which define virtual fields and objects. Both constructs have the basic form

```
<head> <arrow> <pattern>
```

where <arrow> is <= for a command and <- for a rule. The <pattern> is a sequence of *terms*, which are templates for matching objects in the database, and look like partial object descriptions. However, what were tags before are now *object variables*. The <head> for a command is a term indicating an update operation, such as changing a field value, adding an object to a type set, or creating an object. The head for a rule looks like the term for an update operation, but denotes demand, rather than immediate, evaluation.

Variables are shared between the <head> and <pattern> parts. The semantics of a command is that for every binding of the variables to database objects that fulfills the <pattern>, perform the update (or other operation) given in the <head>.

Examples: Add a salary field to the person named William Porter.

```
:P(salary -> #63000) <=
    Person:P
        (name -> PersonName:
                        (first -> 'William',
                         last -> 'Porter')).
```

Add that person to the `Employee` typeset.

```
Employee:P <=
    Person:P
        (name -> PersonName:
                        (first -> 'William',
                         last -> 'Porter')).
```

Change that person's name.

```
:P(name ->
    PersonName:*
        (first -> 'O',
         last -> 'Henry')) <=
    Person:P
        (name ->
            PersonName:(first -> 'William',
                        last -> 'Porter')).
```

The `*` in the head term indicates the creation of a new object. Rules look much the same as commands. The rule

```
:M(manages -> :D) <-
        Department:D(manager -> Person:M).
```

defines a virtual field `manages` for persons who manage departments.

Few joins are necessary in TEDM queries, as they are not needed to overcome the decomposition of objects forced by normalization in the relational model. Most semantic connections can be made by following paths. When a join is necessary, it can be on object identity, rather than just on simple values.

```
SameManager:*
    (dept1 -> :D1, dept2 -> :D2) <=
        Department:D1(manager -> Person:M),
        Department:D2(manager -> :M).
```

A more detailed description of this data model is given in [8]. Its formal logic is presented in [10], where *O-Logic* is developed to provide formal semantics for the data model. The TEDM command language has been prototyped in Prolog using a storage structure based on binary and ternary relations [20]. Finally, [2] reports on applying TEDM to the problem of modeling the DBMS user interface, and [18] reports on adding features to the model to provide a uniform framework for making the query language entities persistent.

4. CSG OVERVIEW

Solids are represented in conventional CSG systems as Boolean combinations of solid components, where a solid component is either a primitive shape defining a half-space, (such as a plane, sphere, cylinder, etc.) or another composite CSG solid. The combining operators are set operators such as union, intersection, and difference. As shown in [6], and [12], the following grammar describes the tree structures that result from using the Boolean combining operators recursively.

<CSG tree> ::== <primitive leaf> |
           <CSG tree> <set operator> <CSG tree> |
           <CSG tree> <motion operator> <motion arguments>

Note that this is not the only possible grammar for a CSG representation. For example there are a variety of grammar forms in use in commercial systems [13]. An example of a typical CSG tree structure and corresponding rigid solid are shown in Figure 1 (the solid, our "two-tooth comb" example, is shown in orthographic projection). The CSG tree for the comb example assumes the existence of two box composite solids, Box B1 and Box B2. Box B1 has dimensions of 1 x 3 x 1 (along the x, y, and z axes) and Box B2 has dimensions of 3 x 1 x 1, as shown in Figure 1. Note that boxes are not primitives in our system, but are constructed from planar half-spaces. A complete TEDM description of the generic box solid will be given in Section 6.

Our grammar for the CSG trees is similar to the grammar defined above. However, we have eliminated the last term, involving the <motion operator>, from the right hand side of the <CSG tree> production rule. Instead, constraints between pairs of nodes in the CSG tree are used to specify relative position.

Each node in the CSG tree has a set of associated *reference features*. Reference features are usually points and lines, but may be arbitrarily complex shapes. A constraint between a pair of nodes places conditions on the reference features of the two nodes that must be met. Reference features will be defined more formally in the next section, but a brief explanation is included here. Each primitive shape has default reference features. For example, the default reference features for a plane are a pair of directed infinite lines, where the first line is perpendicular to the plane and points in the direction of the positive half-space for the plane and the second line intersects the first and lies in the plane. Each composite shape (formed by constructing a CSG tree) has a set of reference features that is either a subset of the features of its components or is derived from those features. Note that an arbitrary number of reference

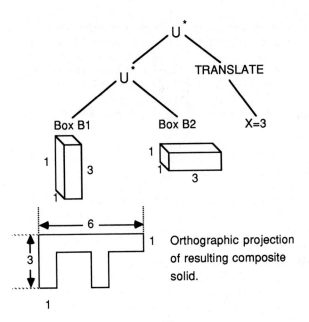

Figure 1. CSG Tree Example

features may be added to both primitive shapes and composite shapes at the designer's discretion. For example, the two boxes used in the comb example in Figure 1 are both instances of a generic box composite shape. The generic box, shown in Figure 2, is formed by taking the intersection of six planar half-spaces. The reference features of the generic box composite are defined, as will be shown formally in Section 6, to be three orthogonal planes from the six used to construct the box. In order to instantiate a specific box composite solid, the three edge dimensions should be specified. Thus to instantiate Box B1 and Box B2 used in the comb example above, the following TEDM statements would be necessary.

```
Box: (name -> 'B1',
      edge1 -> 1.,
      edge2 -> 3.,
      edge3 -> 1.)

Box: (name -> 'B2',
      edge1 -> 3.,
      edge2 -> 1.,
      edge3 -> 1.)
```

Constraints relate pairs of reference features from nodes in the CSG tree, and are of the form:

```
<constraint> :==
     <reference feature> <constraint specification> <reference feature>
```

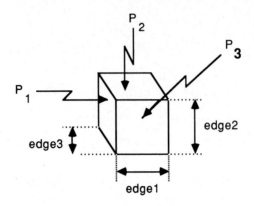

Figure 2.   The Generic Box Solid

For example, Figure 3 shows the CSG tree for the comb example using constraints to specify relative positions in three-space (constraint arcs between
pairs of nodes are shown as dashed lines). The example assumes that the reference features for Box B1 are the planes P_1^{B1}, P_2^{B1}, and P_3^{B1}, and that the
reference features for Box B2 are the planes P_1^{B2}, P_2^{B2}, and P_3^{B2}. Thus the
constraints between Box B1 and Box B2 are that the planes P_1^{B1} and P_1^{B2} are
coincident, and that the planes P_2^{B1} and P_2^{B2} are coincident, as shown on the
dashed arc connecting the two nodes.

Box B1 and Box B2 are composed to form two composite solids, rooted at
the two nodes with names of C1 and C2 respectively. C1 and C2 are each a
"tooth" in the comb example as shown in the orthographic project of the entire
solid in Figure 3. The reference features for C1 are the planes P_1^{C1}, P_2^{C1}, and
P_3^{C1}, and for C2 are the planes P_1^{C2}, P_2^{C2}, and P_3^{C2}. Note that constraints are
also used to specify the relationship between reference features for C1 and C2
and their components, as shown by the dashed arcs between the nodes
corresponding to these two composite solids and the node labeled Box B1.

The model includes a set of predefined primitive reference feature types
and a corresponding set of primitive constraint types. Primitive reference
feature types include points, infinite lines, directed lines, and crossed directed
lines. Primitive constraints specify such things as distance between two points,
distance between a point and a line, and relative positions of two lines in three
space. More complex reference feature types (such as planes) and constraint
types (such as coincidence) may be defined in terms of the corresponding primitives.

5. A DESCRIPTION OF CSG IN TEDM

This section discusses the elements of our CSG model in detail, gives their
definition in TEDM, and develops the corresponding type hierarchies. Section
5.1 defines the basic reference features in the model, points and infinite lines,
and the predefined constraints types for these basic primitives. Section 5.2

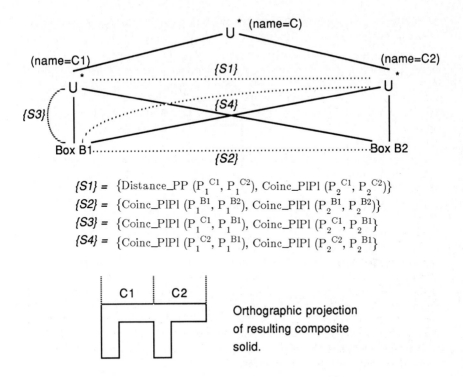

$\{S1\} = \{\text{Distance\_PP } (P_1{}^{C1}, P_1{}^{C2}), \text{Coinc\_PlPl } (P_2{}^{C1}, P_2{}^{C2})\}$

$\{S2\} = \{\text{Coinc\_PlPl } (P_1{}^{B1}, P_1{}^{B2}), \text{Coinc\_PlPl } (P_2{}^{B1}, P_2{}^{B2})\}$

$\{S3\} = \{\text{Coinc\_PlPl } (P_1{}^{C1}, P_1{}^{B1}), \text{Coinc\_PlPl } (P_2{}^{C1}, P_2{}^{B1}\}$

$\{S4\} = \{\text{Coinc\_PlPl } (P_1{}^{C2}, P_1{}^{B1}), \text{Coinc\_PlPl } (P_2{}^{C2}, P_2{}^{B1}\}$

Figure 3.   CSG Tree Example With Constraints

defines the more complex reference features, directed lines and pairs of directed lines, in terms of the basic reference features and gives the predefined constraint types for them. In Section 5.3 we use these reference features to define the basic shapes, such as planes, spheres, etc., that appear as terminals in a CSG tree. Finally, Section 5.4 gives the type hierarchies for all of these reference features, shapes, and constraint types.

5.1. The Basic Reference Features

The most basic units of data in the model are points and infinite lines, since they are at the right level to be considered as components of the basic shapes, and also to be perceived as conceptual units in their own right. The TEDM type specifications of points and infinite lines have no internal structure (as shown below) since their geometric properties are identical for all instances (no parameterization is necessary in order to specify an individual point or line uniquely). We will use the term line to refer to infinite line in future discussion, unless some ambiguity would result.

```
InfLine.
Point.
```

The identity or uniqueness of a particular point or line object (i.e., an instance of the type InfLine or Point) is of interest only with respect to the constraints that are placed on its spatial relationship to other objects.

Now we turn to the specific constraint types for these primitives. As mentioned in Section 4, each constraint type involves a pair of reference features. Thus in the remainder of this section, we will define constraint types for pairs of points, a point and a line, and a pair of lines. All constraint types are subtypes of StructConst, which has two abstract fields, @comp and @rel. Thus all constraint types specialize these abstract fields as in line@comp and distance@rel.

In considering all possible spatial relationships between points and lines, an equivalence class is formed for all topologies that are obtainable from each other by an arbitrary combination of translations and rotations. Such equivalence classes determine a constraint type, and the parameters for the constraint type are those that uniquely determine the relative spatial relationship between any pair of reference feature instances to which the constraint type applies.

(A) Pairs of Points

The constraint type for two points is the simplest of all cases. Distance between two point instances uniquely determines relative position, and a unique distance can be obtained from any pair of points. The constraint type Distance_PP below represents this relative spatial relationship between any two point objects.

```
Distance_PP = StructConst:
                (pt1@comp, pt2@comp -> Point:,
                 distance@rel -> NonNegFloat:).
```

The two fields, pt1 and pt2, contain the two reference feature objects (in this case, instances of the Point object type for which the constraint is specified). The distance@rel field contains the obvious distance parameter. The @rel suffix indicates that the field is a specialization of the abstract field defined by superclass StructConst. As such, it contains a constraint to be satisfied by the components.

The Distance_PP constraint type can be specialized if the two point objects are coincident. In the CoincP constraint type given below, the distance field (a specialization of the distance@rel field inherited from Distance_PP) is defined to be a virtual field (as indicated by the * prefix) whose value is given by the rule that follows the constraint type definition. This rule is read "If CP is a CoincP object, then the distance field contains the value #0.0."

```
CoincP = Distance_PP:(*distance -> NonNegFloat:).

:CP(distance -> #0.0) <- CoincP:CP.
```

(B) A Point and a Line

The constraint types between a point and an infinite line are also relatively simple. Distance between a point object and a line object is defined to be the length of a line segment perpendicular to the line. Thus the constraint type is defined as follows.

```
Distance_PL = StructConst:
                  (pt@comp -> Point:,
                   line@comp -> InfLine:,
                   distance@rel -> NonNegFloat:).
```

Again, the `Distance_PL` constraint type is refined in the `On` constraint type in a fashion similar to the `CoincP` constraint type.

(C) Pairs of Lines

Constraints between two infinite lines are divided into three separate cases. First, if two lines intersect each other then an angle between them is adequate to uniquely specify the relative spatial relationship if the angle is restricted to being between zero and ninety degrees. The `2D_Angle` constraint type captures the relative spatial relationship between two intersecting line objects.

```
2D_Angle = StructConst:(line1@comp, line2@comp
                            -> InfLine:,
                         intPt@comp -> Point:,
                         angle@rel -> NonNegFloat:,
                         *on1@rel, *on2@rel -> On:).
```

```
:A (on1 -> On[:IP, :L1],
    on2 -> On[:IP, :L2])
    <- 2D_Angle:A[:L1, :L2, :IP].
```

The syntax `On[:IP,:L1]` is a shorthand for specifying an instance of type `On` in which the order of the field specifications is the same as in the `On` type definition. The `intPt@comp` field in the `2D_Angle` constraint type definition contains the intersection point of the two lines. Note that `on1@rel` and `on2@rel` are virtual fields whose rule definition requires that the intersection point be on both lines.

The constraint type `RightAngle_LL` refines the `2D_Angle` type by defining a value for the `angle@rel` field of ninety degrees (using TEDM rules as was done in this section for the `CoincP` and `On` constraint types).

When two lines do not intersect, they are either parallel or skewed. For the skewed case, the two lines lie on two planes that are themselves parallel to each other. Further, there exists a line perpendicular to the two lines, which defines a common normal to the two parallel planes on which the two lines lie (see Figure 4.1). We define the distance between the two skewed lines to be the distance between the two parallel planes along the common normal.

For two skewed lines, four things are necessary to specify the relative spatial relationship: (1) an angle between one line and a projection of the other line on the plane containing the first line, (2) how the angle is measured, (3) the distance between the two lines along the common normal, and (4) the direction of view in order to differentiate mirror images. The example shown in Figure 4 illustrates the requirement for direction of view. Suppose one views the relative topology from the direction of view shown in Figure 4.1. It is easy to see that the relative spatial relationship of the two lines is specified by giving an angle α and distance d, where the angle is measured from line1 to line2. However, it is also possible to construct a mirror image of the original topology with the same angle α and distance d by reversing the direction of view, as shown in Figure 4.2. In order for the mirror image to yield the same angle, the direction of view must be opposite. These two mirror images cannot be obtained from each other by rotations and/or translations.

The `3D_Angle` constraint type captures the four necessary pieces of information to represent relative spatial relationships for skewed infinite lines. The angle is given by the `angle_measure@rel` field. We assume the convention that the angle is measured counterclockwise. The angle is measured starting at the line given in the `angle_from@rel` field and ending at the line given in the `angle_to@rel`. The `distance@rel` field gives the distance between the two lines, measured along the common normal given by the `intLine@comp` field, which intersects the two skewed lines at the points `closestPt_1f@comp` and `closestPt_1b@comp`. The direction of view is given by the order of the lines, where the `line_front@comp` and `line_back@comp` fields contain the line in front and the line in back, respectively. Note that all information is necessary to distinguish mirror images. For example, with `line_front@comp` and `line_back@comp` only, mirror images may result from the same data, depending on whether the angle is measured from the line in front or in back. The convention of allowing only acute angles would not solve this problem. The + notation on the `distPt@rel` field indicates that the constraint depends on a user-supplied value, in this case the `distance@rel` field. This is called a *parameterized constraint*.

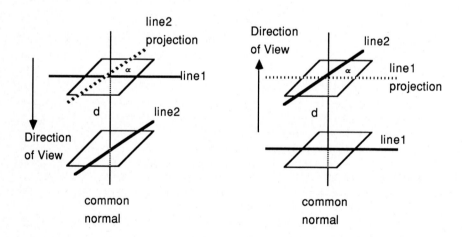

Figure 4. Original Topology and Mirror Image

Note also that it follows from the semantics of the fields that either

```
( line_front@comp = angle_from@comp
    and
  line_back@comp = angle_to@comp )
            or
( line_front@comp = angle_to@comp
    and
  line_back@comp = angle_from@comp ) .
```

Such alternative constraints are represented in TEDM by having multiple type definitions for each alternative. The following type definition represents the case where `line_front` is equal to `angle_from` and `line_back` is equal to `angle_to` (see the rule following the type definition where object tags are used to constrain the identities). The type definition for the second case would be identical except for the definition of the rule in which the object tags would be rearranged to constrain the second set of identities.

```
3D_Angle = StructConst:
            (line_front@comp, line_back@comp,
             angle_from@comp, angle_to@comp
                -> InfLine:,
             closestPt_lf@comp, closestPt_lb@comp
                -> Point:,
             intLine@comp -> InfLine:,
             distance@rel, angle_measure@rel
                -> NonNegFloat:,
             *rightAg1@rel, *rightAg2@rel
                -> RightAngle_LL:,
             +*distPt@rel -> Distance_PP:) .


:A (rightAg1 ->
      RightAngle_LL[:L1, :L3, :P1],
    rightAg2 ->
      RightAngle_LL[:L2, :L3, :P2],
    distPt ->
      Distance_PP[:P1, :P2, :D])
        <- 3D_Angle:A(line_front -> :L1,
                      line_back -> :L2,
                      angle_from -> :L1,
                      angle_to -> :L2,
                      closestPt_lf -> :P1,
                      closestPt_lb -> :P2,
                      intLine -> :L3,
                      distance -> :D) .
```

Two parallel lines occupy three space, where the angle between one line and a projection of the other is zero degrees (or one hundred and eighty degrees). In this case, however, both lines lie on the same plane (i.e., the system becomes two dimensional) and it is not necessary to differentiate mirror images. Therefore, specifying distance alone is sufficient for the definition of the relative spatial relationship of two parallel lines. The `ParaL` constraint type requires that the common normal be perpendicular to both lines. The constraint type `CoincL` refines `ParaL` simply by requiring that the distance between the two parallel lines be zero.

5.2. Directed Reference Features

Directed reference features are of two types, directed lines and crossed directed lines. As will be seen in Section 5.3, a directed line is used for indicating the positive half-space for a plane, and crossed directed lines are used for indicating rotation and translation for the symmetrical half-spaces such as spheres and cones, or for any composite shape.

A directed line is build from an infinite line and two reference points on the line, as shown in Figure 5.1. It is assumed that the direction of the line is always from the `origin@comp` to `posRefPt@comp`. Therefore, those two points must be distinct. The TEDM type definition for a directed line `RefDirLine` specifies that these two points are distinct objects and lie on the line.

Figure 5.2 shows the salient features of crossed directed lines. The TEDM type `RefCrossDirLns` for this reference feature includes fields that contain the two lines as well as their intersection point. The constraints specified for the type are that the two lines be at right angles and that the intersection point be the origin of both lines. We say that the `refLine1@comp` field is the *primary axis* of the crossed directed lines, and that the `refLine2@comp` field is the *secondary axis*.

(A) Pairs of Directed Lines

Constraint types for pairs of directed reference lines are similar to those for pairs of lines. The differences are due to dealing with the directionality of the lines involved, and to dealing with the interaction between origin points for the lines. For example, each topology for two undirected lines yields two separate topologies when the lines are given direction, as shown in Figure 6. The two separate topologies for directed lines have identical specifications except for the

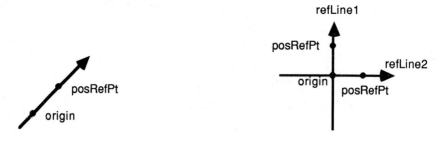

Figure 5.   A Directed Line and Directed Line Pair

angle values for all three kinds of line interactions (intersecting lines, skewed lines, and parallel lines). The angles describing the two topologies are, of course, complementary as shown in the figure. In particular, two parallel directed lines can have either the same or the opposite direction as shown in Figure 6(c). To accommodate the two cases, we have adopted the convention that the angle is always measured between the two positive ends of the directed lines, and can take on a value between zero and one hundred eighty degrees.

The `2D_Angle_RefDirLns` constraint type is a refinement of that for undirected lines, as shown below in the TEDM specification. The additional fields `dist_intPt_origin1@rel` and `dist_intPt_origin2@rel` contain the distance from the origins of the directed lines `line1` and `line2`, respectively, to the intersection point of the two lines given by the `intPt@comp` field. Note that the distance from the origin of a line may be negative if the

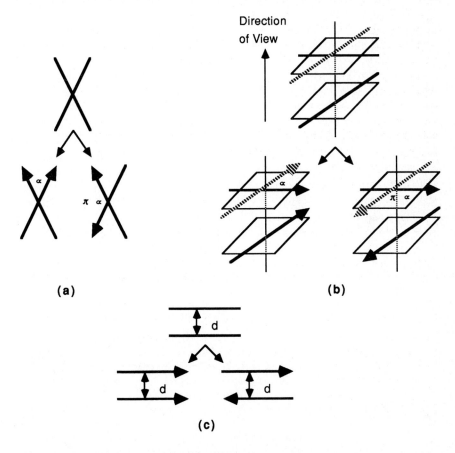

(a)   **(b)**

(c)

Figure 6.   Adding Direction to Lines

intersection point is on the negative side of the origin.

```
2D_Angle_RefDirLns = 2D_Angle:
                    (line1, line2 -> RefDirLine:
                    dist_intPt_origin1@rel,
                    dist_intPt_origin2@rel
                    -> Float:).
```

The `RightAngle_RefDirLns` constraint type is a refinement of the `2D_Angle_RefDirLns` type with the added requirement that the measured angle be 90 degrees.

The `ParaRefDirLns` constraint refines the `ParaL` constraint for undirected lines. The additional fields required for the constraint type are `same_dir@rel`, indicating whether or not two lines have the same direction, and `dist_twoOrigins@rel`, which specifies the distance between the origin for `line1` and a projection of the origin of `line2` onto `line1`. The `CoincRefDirLns` constraint type is also a refinement of `ParaRefDirLns` with the added requirement that the distance between the two parallel directed lines be zero.

The `3D_Angle_RefDirLns` constraint type refines the `3D_Angle` type for undirected lines in a manner similar to the `2D_Angle_RefDirLns`.

(B) Pairs of Crossed Directed Lines

The constraint type `Pair_RefCrossDirLns` defines the relative spatial relationships for two `RefCrossDirLns` reference features. (It may help the reader to imagine two crosses floating in three space, with the requirement that one would like to give some (possibly partial) specification of their relative locations with respect to one another. The two crosses correspond to the values contained in the `cross1@comp` and the `cross2@comp` fields of the constraint type.)

```
Pair_RefCrossDirLns = (cross1@comp, cross2@comp
                    -> RefCrossDirLns:,
                    primaryTransform@rel
                    -> 2D_Angle_RefDirLns: |
                       3D_Angle_RefDirLns: |
                       Para_RefDirLns:,
                    rotate@rel -> NonNegFloat:).
```

In order to specify the relative spatial relationship between cross1 and cross2, first the two primary axes of each crossed line must be compared. This comparison is given by constraining their relative spatial relationship using either `2D_Angle_RefDirLns`, `3D_Angle_RefDirLns`, or `Para_RefDirLns` depending on whether the two lines intersect, are skewed, or are parallel. The `primaryTransform@rel` field contains this relative spatial relationship between the two primary axes. (Note that the | notation indicates a union type — the value of the field may be either of type `2D_Angle_RefDirLns`, of type `3D_Angle_RefDirLns`, or of type `Para_RefDirLns`.) Assuming that the primary axis of the first cross has been projected onto the primary axis of the second cross, the remaining item of information is the relative relationship between the two secondary axes, or angle of rotation required to move one into the other; this is contained in the `rotate@rel` field of the constraint type.

5.3. The Primitive Shapes

Our CSG model relies on five primitive shapes: plane, sphere, cylinder, double-cone, and torus. Each of these shapes divides three space into two parts, what we intuitively think of as an inside and an outside. (For a plane, the inside and outside must be designated explicitly. We will use a normal to accomplish this, as will be seen shortly.) Each of the primitive shapes has a mathematical description in the form of a polynomial equation of low degree. However, there are abstractions commonly used to describe these primitive shapes that are more intuitive than the equation descriptions. These abstractions appear as parameters in the TEDM type definitions for the shapes, as shown in Figure 7 and outlined below. A TEDM type definition for each shape is also given.

(1) Plane: normal.

(2) Sphere: center point and a radius.

(3) Cylinder: center axis and radius.

(4) Double-cone: center point, center axis and angle.

(5) Torus: center point, center axis and two radii, one for the size of a ring and the other for its thickness.

```
Plane = BasicShape:(normal@comp -> RefDirLine:,
                    inSide@rel -> Boolean:,
                    *on@rel -> On_PtPl:).

:PL(on -> On_PtPl[:O, :PL])
    <- Plane:PL(normal -> (origin -> :O)).

Sphere = BasicShape:(center@comp -> Point:,
                     rad@rel -> NonNegFloat:,
                     inSide@rel -> Boolean:).

Cylinder = BasicShape:(centerAxis@comp -> Infline:,
                       rad@rel -> NonNegFloat:,
                       inSide@rel -> Boolean:).

ConicShape = BasicShape:(centerPt@comp -> Point:,
                         centerAxis@comp -> InfLine:,
                         angle@rel -> NonNegFloat:,
                         inSide@rel -> Boolean:,
                         *on@rel -> On:).

:CS(on -> On[:CP, :CA])
    <- ConicShape:CS(centerPt -> :CP,
                     centerAxis -> :CA).
```

```
Torus = BasicShape:(centerPt@comp -> Point:,
                    centerAxis@comp -> InfLine:,
                    rad1@rel -> NonNegFloat:,
                    rad2@rel -> NonNegFloat:,
                    inSide@rel -> Boolean:,
                    *on@rel -> On:).

  :T(on -> On[:CP, :CA])
      <- Torus:T(centerPt -> :CP,
                 centerAxis -> :CA).
```

Note that for the `ConicShape` type the center point is required to be on the infinite line that defines its axis. There is a similar requirement for the `Torus` type. Half spaces are designated by boolean fields. For the `Plane` type, it is assumed that the positive side of the normal designates a halfspace on the inside and the negative side designates a halfspace on the outside.

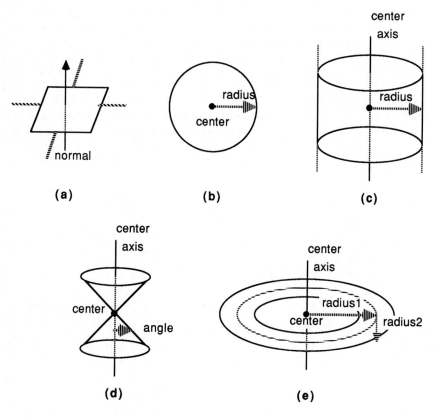

Figure 7. The Primitive Shapes

Each of the primitive shape types also has a subtype defined that specifies a default reference feature for it. For all five shapes, the default reference feature is a crossed directed line (i.e., an instance of type `RefCrossDirLns`). By comparing this default reference feature to reference features of other basic primitive instances or to other composite object instances, its relative spatial relationship may be determined. Figure 8 shows two of the basic shapes, a plane and a cylinder, with their added default reference features (the remaining three are similar to the cylinder example). For the plane, the primary reference line of the `RefCrossDirLns` type is coincident to its normal. For the other four basic shapes, which are all rotationally symmetric about some axis, the primary reference line of the `RefCrossDirLns` type coincides with this symmetric axis. Furthermore, the intersection point of the `RefCrossDirLns` type is assumed to be the center point for the sphere, torus, and double cone.

5.4. The Type Hierarchy for CSG Solids and Constraint Types

The last three sections have developed and defined the primitive shapes, reference features, and constraint types used in our CSG model. There are three type hierarchies defined that relate subsets of these types via generalization. This section describes each of these type hierarchies briefly.

Figure 9 shows the type hierarchy for reference features. There are two types, `BasicFt` and `DirectedFs`, that have yet to be defined. The `BasicFt` type is a generalization of the basic feature types `InfLine` and `Point`, and hence has no internal structure. The `DirectedFs` type is a generalization of `RefDirLine` and `RefCrossDirLns`, and defines the abstract `@comp` field containing objects of type `BasicFt` and the `@rel` field containing objects of type `StructConst` (the root type for all constraint types, to be defined in the third type hierarchy). Note also that the `RefDirLine` type is a

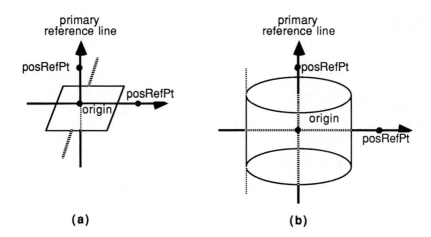

Figure 8. Primitive Shapes with Default Reference Features

subtype of `InfLine` as well as a subtype of `DirectedFs`. Thus it inherits the field definitions and constraints of both types.

The root of the second hierarchy is the `Region` type. This type hierarchy describes the CSG solids, which include both the primitive and composite shapes as shown in Figure 10. The `BasicShape` type is the generalization of all the primitive shapes defined in the last section. The `CompositeShape` type includes all non-primitive shapes that are described by CSG tree structures. We will examine in detail the type definition of the `CompositeShape` type, since this is where the tree structure appears.

```
CompositeShape = Region:(name -> String:,
                         @comp =>
                           BasicFt: | Region: |
                           DirectedFs:,
                         @rel =>
                           Boolean: | Float: |
                           PairComp: | StructConst:).
```

Each `CompositeShape` has a name, as seen in the TEDM type definition above. This name field can be thought of as a basic pointing device (similar in function to a mouse for a graphics display). For each subtype of `CompositeShape` the abstract `@comp` field may be specialized to contain objects of type `BasicFt`, `Region`, or `DirectedFs`. (Examples of this will be seen in Section 6 where the generic box is defined as a composite shape.) The abstract `@rel` field may be specialized to contain objects of type `Boolean`, `Float`, `PairComp`, or `StructConst`. The `PairComp` range type of the `@rel` field is of interest, as this is where the conventional CSG tree structure is specified, as shown below.

```
PairComp = StructConst:(c1@comp -> Region:,
                        c2@comp -> Region:,
                        mode@rel -> CompMode:).

CompMode = {intersection, union, difference}.
```

The `CompMode` type is an *enumerated* type, since all of its instances are specified in the type definition. The `c1@comp` and `c2@comp` fields contain the left and right subtree components for the CSG tree.

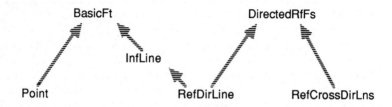

Figure 9. The Reference Feature Type Hierarchy

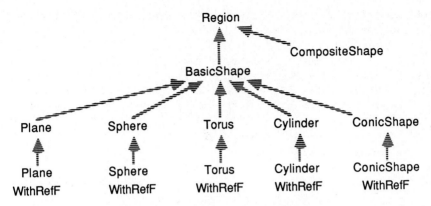

Figure10. The Shape Type Hierarchy

The third generalization hierarchy relates all the constraint types covered in Sections 5.1 and 5.2, as shown in Figure 11. The root of the hierarchy is the StructConst type (short for structured constraint). The TEDM definition for the root type specifies that @comp fields of the type may contain objects of type BasicFt, Region, or DirectedFs. Further, the @rel fields of the root type are permitted to range over the types Float and StructConst. Thus a constraint type may use other constraints in its definition (see the 2D_Angle type definition, which uses the On constraint).

6. THE GENERIC BOX EXAMPLE

In Section 4 we used a generic box composite shape to construct the two-tooth-comb example. In this section, we will give a complete TEDM description of the generic box by combining primitive shapes in a CSG tree and then inter-relating the nodes with constraints.

The generic box is constructed from six planar half-spaces, where each plane has as its default reference feature a crossed directed line. The pair-wise intersection of the six planes forms the box. The box is generic since it is underconstrained — no specific dimensions are given. Rather, the dimensions of the box are left as parameters to be specified for each instance of its use. These parameters are passed on to the underlying constraints used to define the box. We call these *parameterized constraints*, since their complete definition depends on parameters given at the time of instantiation.

Since planes play an important role in defining the box, we will also define some complex constraint types that relate pairs of planes in terms of the con-straints defined in Section 5. It also seems obvious that these constraints between pairs of planes are interesting in their own right, since planar surfaces play an important role in the design process as well as in manufacturing. In any case, this exercise serves to illustrate complex constraint definition for pairs of basic shapes.

The first constraint for a pair of planes is the RightAngle_P1P1, which defines two planes perpendicular to each other by specifying the relationship of

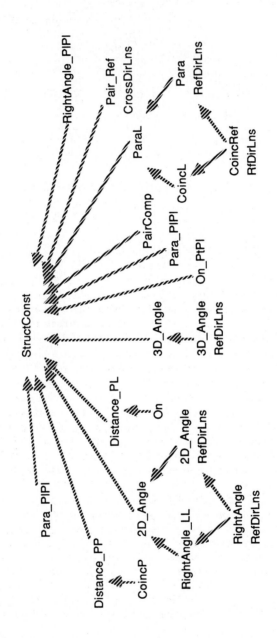

Figure 11.   The Structured Constraint Type Hierarchy

their normals as shown below.

```
RightAngle_PlPl = StructConst:
                     (pl1@comp, pl2@comp -> Plane:,
                      *normal1_normal2_ra@rel
                         -> 3D_RightAngle_RefDirLns:).

  :RAPP(normal1_normal2_ra ->
        3D_RightAngle_RefDirLns:(line_front -> :N1,
                                 line_back -> :N2))
      <- RightAngle_PlPl:RAPP(pl1 ->
                              (normal -> :N1),
                              pl2 ->
                              (normal -> :N2)).


3D_RightAngle_RefDirLns = 3D_Angle_RefDirLns:
                            (*angle_measure ->
                             NonNegFloat:).

  :RARDL(angle_measure -> #90.0)
      <- 3D_RightAngle_RefDirLns:RARDL.
```

The second constraint type for pairs of planes is `Para_PlPl`, which requires that two planes be parallel to each other. Its TEDM definition is constructed using two parallel normals (i.e., with the `PararRefDirLns` constraint). Note that the `Coinc_PlPl` used to construct the two-tooth-comb example in Section 4 can be defined as a refinement of `Para_PlPl`.

The `Box` type has nine component fields, six fields (`side1@comp` through `side6@comp`) to contain six planar half spaces, PL1 through PL6. There are also three fields to contain the default reference features for the box (`refF1@comp` through `refF3@comp`). The three reference features are three orthogonal planes from the six specified by the `side1@comp` through `side6@comp` fields. In addition there are three constraint parameter fields, `edge1@rel` through `edge3@rel`, that specify the dimensions of the box in the x, y, and z directions. The CSG tree structure is created recursively by the five fields, `comp1@rel` through `comp5@rel`, where each field constructs one node in the tree and relies on the node constructed by the previous field. The resulting tree structure is shown in Figure 12.

There are two sets of constraints on the nodes in the tree structure. The first set, contained in fields `para1@rel` through `para3@rel`, requires that the following pairs of planes be parallel: PL1 and PL4, PL2 and PL5, PL3 and PL6. The second set of constraints, contained in fields `rightAg1@rel` through `rightAg3@rel`, requires that the following pairs of planes be at right angles: PL1 and PL2, PL2 and PL3, PL1 and PL3. All of these constraints are shown as dashed lines connecting node pairs in Figure 12. The following is the complete TEDM specification for this tree structure and its attached constraints.

T.L. Anderson et al.

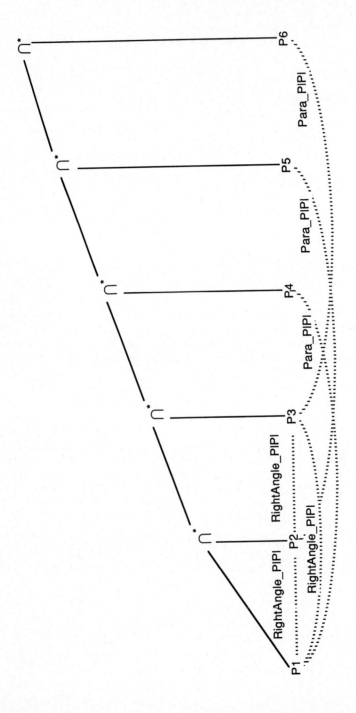

Figure 12. The CSG Tree for the Generic Box

```
Box = (name -> String:,
        side1@comp, side2@comp, side3@comp,
        side4@comp, side5@comp, side6@comp
             -> PlaneWithRefF:,
        *refF1@comp, *refF2@comp, *refF3@comp
             -> PlaneWithRefF:,
        edge1@rel, edge2@rel, edge3@rel
             -> NonNegFloat:,
        *rightAg1@rel, *rigthAg2@rel, *rightAg3@rel
             -> RightAngle_PlPl:,
        +*para1@rel, +*para2@rel, +*para3@rel
             -> Para_PlPl:,
        *comp1@rel, *comp2@rel, *comp3@rel,
        *comp4@rel, *comp5@rel
             -> PairComp:).

:B(rightAg1 ->
     RightAngle_PlPl[:PL1, :PL2],
   rightAg2 ->
     RightAngle_PlPl[:PL2, :PL3],
   rightAg3 ->
     RightAngle_PlPl[:PL1, :PL3],
   para1 ->
     Para_PlPl[:PL1, :PL4, :E1],
   para2 ->
     Para_PlPl[:PL2, :PL5, :E2],
   para3 ->
     Para_PlPl[:PL3, :PL6, :E3],
   comp1 ->
     PairComp:IS1[:PL1, :PL2, intersection],
   comp2 ->
     PairComp:IS2[:IS1, :PL3, intersection],
   comp3 ->
     PairComp:IS3[:IS2, :PL4, intersection],
   comp4 ->
     PairComp:IS4[:IS3, :PL5, intersection],
   comp5 ->
     PairComp:[:IS4, :PL6, intersection])
      <- Box:B(side1 -> :PL1(inSide -> true),
               side2 -> :PL2(inSide -> true),
               side3 -> :PL3(inSide -> true),
               side4 -> :PL4(inSide -> true),
               side5 -> :PL5(inSide -> true),
               side6 -> :PL6(inSide -> true),
               refF1 -> :PL1,
               refF2 -> :PL2,
               refF3 -> :PL3,
```

```
edge1 -> :E1,
edge2 -> :E2,
edge3 -> :E3).
```

Note that there are other ways to construct a box. One may, for example, start by defining a `slab` composite shape to be the intersection of two parallel planes (the normals of each plane would point in opposite directions). The `box` type could then be defined as the intersection of three slabs (with appropriate constraints between them). The use of the slab shape to define the box is preferable only if the slab shape is generic and can be used in other situations.

7. CONCLUSIONS AND FUTURE WORK

The preceding sections detail our experience using an object-oriented CSG model to describe shapes. However, what we really want to do is to describe and then reason about the properties of different shapes and relationships among different shapes. This section discusses what things we want to reason about and discusses some of the ways that our particular model affects the way we do inferencing.

Up to this point, our discussion has covered a description data model in that the purpose of the model is to facilitate description of complex objects. A related goal worth considering is how to facilitate the design of a complex object. This second goal requires different features and has different tradeoffs of efficiency and expressivity. This section will cover the inferencing issues of both data model goals. As such, it represents an alternative evaluation of the CSG data modeling exercise.

7.1. Inferencing With Respect to a Complete Description

There may be many characteristics by which one may want to judge a CSG description. Among those we have identified are:

(1) If a description is over or under constrained (e.g., the rigidity of the solid).

(2) If two or more CSG descriptions refer to the same object.

(3) Ease of manufacturability.

Currently, none of these are characteristics that may be simply evaluated and stored in the database. In general, these judgements are extrinsic to the database and the database objects.[1] In this section we will discuss additional modeling requirements necessary to support these judgements.

(1) Over or under constraint, rigidity

Currently the CSG type hierarchy contains basic shapes, which by definition are neither under- or over-constrained. Under composition, however, this situation can change. The question here is what information (in the description) is necessary to determine over-constraint and what inferences can

---

[1]With more flexible virtual fields (higher order functions) some of these judgements could however be moved to the database.

be made given this information. A description is over-constrained if a component becomes derivable in more than one way, such as from both internal defining constraints, and external constraints introduced via composition. In general, for manufacturing purposes, an object should be constructible in only one way. A description which contains redundant (but consistent) constraints is a special case of over-constraint. In this case, the description is consistent but can be manufactured from only a subset of the specifications. Which subset is chosen may depend on the context in which the shape is manufactured.

A related judgement that can be made is, given an over-constrained description, which feature should be eliminated, and what information is necessary to determine this?

A CSG shape is under-constrained if it does not contain enough information to denote a unique 3-D solid. Again, a basic shape cannot be under-constrained, but an arbitrary composition of shapes might be. For instance, composing two thin slices/fat planes at right angles requires that the common edge be coincident. But while this information is necessary, it is not sufficient. Two shapes may be constrained by requiring that they share a common face. However, there may be more than one way to share the face with the resulting shapes being rigid but not identical. The rigidity of the resulting structure is not sufficient to form a unique shape.

(2) Multiple descriptions for the same object

There are three approaches, if a particular CSG description fails to be manufacturable for any of the reasons above:

(a) Use a different mapping of CSG description to manufacturing steps.

(b) Use a different CSG description for the same solid.

(c) The solid may be non-manufacturable — start again.

The first two solutions are inverses of each other. Given a large base of manufacturing "macros" (methods for manufacturing relatively complex objects), the first solution might be viewed as a pattern matching problem: find another manufacturing sequence that constructs the same (sub-)parts. However, the second solution appears more direct: alter the description to match the manufacturing reality. This alteration requires that the manufacturing primitives and constraints be explicit and that some notion of equality-preserving transformations exists, with the failure points of manufacturability used to direct the transformations. So if a description fails because of a problem in the order of steps, such as those mentioned above, that fault can be directly corrected by changing the order.

(3) Manufacturability

Given a CSG description of an object, it is necessary to determine the steps required to manufacture the object. This is an important area of research by others (see [15], for example), and one that we would like to pursue.

7.2. Design of Complex Objects

As mentioned before, TEDM was developed to support engineering design [10]. In the preceding portions of the paper, we have emphasized the nature of the target domain: i.e. the characteristics of geometric solids and the facets of the CSG data model that facilitate descriptions and reasoning about existing objects. However, the domain of the design of geometric solids has somewhat different criteria. Design may refer to either of two activities:

(1) Design of a CSG description for a previously conceptualized geometric solid.

(2) Design of a geometric solid and from that a CSG description.

The first problem is obviously the simpler of the two and is actually a generalization of the domain discussed in the previous section. The difference is that in this section the focus is on support for creating CSG descriptions.

(1) Design of a CSG description for an object

A solid can be described in a variety of ways and each description may have different characteristics of rigidity, ease of manufacturability, and so on. Support for designing a particular description for a solid that conforms to some specification entails:

(a) Shape preserving transformations and the ability to determine solid equality.

(b) Ability to determine when a CSG description (or the resulting solid) meets the specification goals (such as size, weight bearing needs, etc.).

(c) Generalizing over a class of solids.

Given a set of CSG descriptions, all describing a particular solid Sol_i it may be desirable to generalize to a new type. This new type can then be used for reasoning about the entire class.

(d) A manufacturing type hierarchy, incorporated the manufacturing primitives, procedural information, composition semantics, etc.

(e) Support in going from one type hierarchy to another perhaps via virtual fields and higher order functions (e.g. from an object description to relevant portions of the manufacturing type hierarchy).

(f) A *better than* ordering on manufacturing sequences.

(g) Support for partial objects whose status can be directly queried. (Is O_i manufacturable under the correct manufacturing assumptions, the correct specification goals, and any correct object designs that affect O_i?)

One of the goals here might be, given a base of initial CSG objects, to use the results of the above inferencing stage to direct the transformation of one description into another with the required characteristics.

(2) Designing a solid and CSG description

Designing a complex solid may involve the construction of new types and constraints. For instance, if the ultimate goal is to construct a ladder, some of the initial constraints (goals) might be *width*: $n \leq w \leq m$, *height*: $j \leq h \leq k$, and *weight_bearing*: $g \leq wb \leq i$. These constraints differ from object defining constraints in that they specify what the object must conform to rather than what the object is. The process of designing the target solid may involve refining the constraints (such as selecting what the width will be) in a top-down manner and constructing partial objects or types that reflect these design decisions.

This contrasts to the process of describing a solid, which takes existing basic objects and composes them in a bottom up construction. The top down refinement commits to design decisions that may be incorrect. Because it is advantageous to identify non-optimal decisions as early as possible, the partial objects must be first class values: one should be able to query their attributes, how they relate to the constraints, and to other (potentially partial) objects. Figure 13 shows the multiple possible paths from partial object description to the final goal of a fully instantiated database that result from refining the object descriptions, constraints, and manufacturing technology.

The process of designing a solid requires everything that is present in designing a CSG description plus some added generalizations.

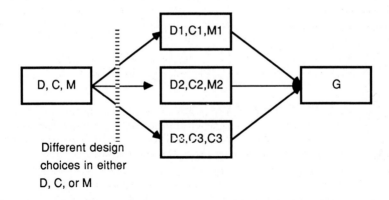

D: Primitive building blocks of the CSG description
C: Initial constraints/goals
M: Manufacturing technology
(Di, Ci, Mi): Refinement into more specific partial objects, constraints, and manufacturing technology
G: A fully instantiated database for a collection of objects, which fulfills the goal constraints and the manufacturing technology

Figure 13. Refining Partial Descriptions to Satisfy Goals

(1) Parameterization to allow a class of constraints to be constructed uniformly.

(2) Incremental analysis on partial objects to allow them to be queried and analyzed, and to keep this partial information as a design aid for future design decisions.

(3) Higher order functions allowing more flexible virtual fields (thus allowing values which are not fully ground terms).

In general, support for design requires that we reason about many different aspects of a design and thus all information, including constraints, must be explicit [3].

7.3. Conclusions

Our experiences in the CSG modeling exercise reported in this paper have provided us with insights in two areas. First, there are aspects of the TEDM data model that need to be improved in order to fully support the inferencing requirements outlined in the last section. For example, there is a need to support partially instantiated objects (objects with unknown or partially known data values), and a need to support more flexible virtual fields and higher order functions in the data model. Also, support for inheriting properties across composition modes (e.g., intersection, union, and difference) should be investigated. Finally, some of the constraints one might want to support are expressible in TEDM but would be prohibitive for performance reasons. For example, requiring that the reference features of a composite object be a subset of those for its components is expressible in TEDM, but is stated here only implicitly due to performance considerations.

The second insight gained in the modeling exercise was the power of constraints and the underlying reference feature mechanism in expressing spatial relationships between CSG objects. We need to explore their use further to determine to what extent changes will be required to support tolerancing information. Further, we would like to investigate their impact on the design of the user interface for a CSG application. Finally, using the constraint objects in one of the complex inferencing tasks outlined in the last section is a challenging problem for future research.

Acknowledgements

We wish to thank the referees for their valuable comments. They pointed out several conceptual errors in our understanding of CSG modeling and are responsible for significant improvements in the paper.

References

1. H. Ait-Kaci and R. Nasr, *LOGIN: A Logic Programming Language With Built-In Inheritance,* MCC Technical Report, AI-068-85, Austin, Texas (1985).

2. T.L. Anderson, E.F. Ecklund, and D. Maier, "PROTEUS: Objectifying the DBMS User Interface," in *Proceedings of the International Workshop on Object-Oriented Database Systems,* , Pacific Grove, California (September 1986).

3. G.F. Bruns and S.L. Gerhart, *Theories of Design: An Introduction to the Literature,* MCC Technical Report, STP-068-86, Austin, Texas (March 20, 1986).

4. R. Davis and B.G. Buchanan, "Meta-Level Knowledge: Overview and Applications," in *Fifth International Joint Conference on Artificial Intelligence,* (1977).

5. R. Davis, B.G. Buchanan, and E.H. Shortliffe, "Production Rules as a Representation for a Knowledge-Based Consultation System," in *Artificial Intelligence,* (1977).

6. K.S. Fu and Y.C. Lee, "A CSG Based DBMS for CAD/CAM and its Supporting Query Language," in *Proceedings of the ACM SIGMOD Internation Conference on the Management of Data - Database Week,* , San Jose, California (May 1983).

7. Alfons Kemper and Mechtild Wallrath, "An Analysis of Geometric Modelling in Database Systems," *ACM Computing Surveys* **19**(1)(March 1987).

8. D. Maier, *The TEDM Data Model,* Working Paper, Oregon Graduate Center, Beaverton, Oregon (1985).

9. D. Maier, "A Logic for Objects," in *OGC Technical Report CS/E-86-012,* , Oregon Graduate Center, Beaverton, Oregon (November 1986).

10. D. Maier and D. Price, "Data Model Requirements for Engineering Applications," in *IEEE First International Workshop on Expert Database Systems,* , Kiawah Island, South Carolina (October 1984).

11. H. Ohkawa, *Mapping an Engineering Data Model to a Distributed Storage System,* Ph.D. Research Proficiency Paper, Oregon Graduate Center (May 1987).

12. A.A.G. Requicha, "Representation for Rigid Solids: Theory, Methods, and Systems," *ACM Computing Surveys* **12**(4)(December 1980).

13. A.A.G. Requicha and H.B. Voelcker, "Solid Modeling: A Historical Summary and Contemporary Assesment," *IEEE Computer Graphics and Applications* **2**(2)(March 1982).

14. A.A.G. Requicha and H.B. Voelcker, "Solid Modeling: Current Status and Research Directions," *IEEE Computer Graphics and Applications* **3**(7)(October 1983).

15. A.A.G. Requicha and H.B. Voelcker, "Research on NC Machining: Simulation, Planning, Systems and Sensors," in *Proceedings of the Fifteenth NSF Grantees Conference on Production Research and Technology,* , Berkeley,

California (January 1989).

16. D.L. Spooner, "Towards an Object-Oriented Data Model for a Mechanical CAD Database System," in *Proceedings of the International Workshop on Object-Oriented Database Systems*, , Pacific Grove, California (September 1986).

17. D.L. Spooner, M.A. Milicia, and D.B. Faatz, "Modeling Mechanical CAD Data With Data Abstractions and Object-Oriented Techniques," in *Proceedings of the Second International Conference on Data Engineering*, , Los Angeles, California (February 1986).

18. J. Zhu, *Prototype Implementation and Storage Design for An Engineering Data Model*, Ph.D. Research Proficiency Paper, Oregon Graduate Center, Beaverton, Oregon (May 1986).

19. J. Zhu, *The Notion of Abstract Object in an Engineering Data Model*, Ph.D. Thesis Proposal, Oregon Graduate Center, Beaverton, Oregon (January 1987).

20. J. Zhu and D. Maier, "Abstract Objects in An Object-Oriented Data Model," in *Proceedings of the Second International Conference on Expert Database Systems*, , Tysons Corner, Virginia (April 1988).

Visual Database Systems
T.L. Kunii (Editor)
Elsevier Science Publishers B.V. (North-Holland)
© IFIP, 1989

Integration of Functional Data Model into Programming Environment: Application to Solid Database

Xu Yu*, Nobuo Ohbo**
Hiroyuki Kitagawa** and Yuzuru Fujiwara**

*Program in Engineering Sciences
**Institute of Information Sciences and Electronics
University of Tsukuba
Tennohdai, Tsukuba, Ibaraki 305, Japan

Abstract

This paper presents a new scheme for design and implementation of an integrated database management system, and its application to 3D-solid modeling system. It provides a high-level user interface integrated into the programming language LISP. The notion of functional data model is extended to allow users to define functions which calculate computationally complex procedural semantics associated with application objects. Rich data modeling facilities embedded in LISP make an object-oriented database based on the new scheme of functional data model easy to understand and highly expressive. LISP is used to implement solid applications as well as retrieve solid data in the TIME2 database. TIME2 has been developed on the commercial database system G-BASE[1].

1   Introduction

This paper discusses the design and implementation of a new object-oriented database system TIME2[Yu87] and its application to 3D-solid database in the CAD environment. It draws upon ideas from functional data model[Shi81], object-oriented database[Con84,Ban87] and the concept of integration of database language and programming language[And87,Blo87,Kan87,Pur87].

Many attempts have been made to design and implement concise, highly descriptive, easy-to-manipulate solid models[Bae79,Kem87]. The CSG(Constructive Solid Geometry)[Req82] and the boundary representation[Bra75] are widely approved of their accuracy, simplicity and convenience. Relatively fewer attempts have been made to design and implement a general and efficient solid database which deals with a large collection of solids. Most of them have adopted the approach either of

---

[1]G-BASE is a trademark of RICOH Co.,Ltd.

designing a system tailored to solid application or of connecting existing solid models with conventional DBMSs. Although the first one is surely efficient, sharing data between an application program using these solid models and other application programs in a CAD environment is difficult. On the other hand, the second approach is general enough. However, conventional DBMSs are not so powerful and sufficient as to support complex data semantics associated with solid models. An integrated database system with capabilities of managing engineering applications such as solid modeling as well as business applications is highly desirable.

Fortunately, however, object-oriented database systems proposed recently by many authors as a new concept for supporting engineering applications offer very promising prospects for modeling and handling a collection of solids. The notion of "complex object"[Lor82] or of "molecular object"[Bat85] reflects the fact that objects in the engineering world are composed of parts that may among themselves undergo a variety of other relationships. It gives a foundation of treating a complex solid description such as a CSG-tree and an octree as a whole database entity. The notion of "abstract data type"[Jam83,Osb86,Sto83] in the context of object-oriented databases facilitates to deal with procedural semantics associated with solid manipulation operations, such as "or" and "rotate" operations defined on octrees.

TIME2 is designed and implemented as an integrated database system with capabilities of object-oriented access and manipulation of data. The approach differs from others in the following points.

- The notion of functional data model is extended to allow users to define computationally complex functions to deal with procedural semantics of application objects.

- Rich data modeling facilities to specify an object-oriented database based on the notion of functional data model are introduced into LISP.

- It provides a high-level user interface integrated into the programming language LISP. LISP is used to implement solid modeling applications as well as to manipulate solid data in TIME2 databases.

The prototype solid database has been implemented on top of the commercial database system G-BASE[Kan87,Kun83]. It opens up the world of solid database to novice users by eliminating the burden of writing complex programs to use solid database systems. The system handles most of the details by actually managing complex semantics of solids.

2   Requirements for the integrated database system

A successful integrated database system must support data semantics and flexible application development in a general purpose programming language. The former requires powerful data modeling facilities, and the latter a high level user interface.

2.1   Integration of database language and programming language

Applications in the CAD environment require not only that database systems should have capabilities of describing and manipulating complex semantics of application objects but also that rich modeling facilities should be freely available from programming languages. Incompatible modeling constructs between database languages and programming languages severely limit the scope of application development. Therefore, an embedded language is a cumbersome way to implement a successful user interface.

Many attempts to integrate a database language into a programming language have been proposed[Atk87,Fis87]. Since many programs are dynamically generated and executed in the CAD environment, languages which need compilers are not adequate. We chose LISP as a programming language both for writing a CAD application and for interfacing between applications and a database. Facilities for constructing an object-oriented database and for manipulating the database have been designed and implemented on top of LISP.

2.2   Rich modeling facilities of database system

The notion of object-oriented database is very promising. But it has not yet been clear how to design and implement a successful database which satisfies both structural requirements and operational requirements imposed on object-oriented databases.

- **Structural Requirements:** A database system should support the notion of "complex object" and/or "molecular object". In other words a database system has to provide facilities for mapping complex objects onto database strucutres and for retrieving these objects as entities.

- **Operational Requirements:** A database system should provide constructs to define manipulation of application objects in a manner that is familiar to designers. In other words, a system should allow users to convey meanings associated with application-specific operators such as boolean operations and geometrical operations in the CSG scheme.

Typical approaches to satisfying the structural requirements are based on hierarchical extensions to the relational model, but they do not usually fulfill the operational requirements. Introduction of ADTs (Abstract Data Types) [Jam83][Osb86] [Sto83] into the relational context is a well-known attempt to satisfy the latter requirements. But the scheme necessitates sophisticated representation of objects in order to fulfill the former requirements. On the other hand, the functional data model represented by language DAPLEX[Shi81] is a very promising candidate for the development of object-oriented databases. The basic constructs of DAPLEX are the entity and the function. Entities are intended to model real-world objects, whereas functions define their properties. It also allows the representation of generalization hierarchies[Smi77]. Derived functions which are used to derive properties of one object from those of others allow users to express conceptual abstractions such as aggregation hierarchies[Smi77]. Functions, together with derived functions, support the semantic modeling based on the abstraction such as complex object[Lor82] and molecular object[Bat85]. Since DAPLEX does not have programming language interface integrating the database language, it provides no facilities to specify application on specific manipulation of objects.

Programming in terms of functions in DAPLEX is very similar to programming in LISP. If we can provide a way to produce LISP functions each of which corresponds to either an entity or a (derived) function in DAPLEX, then database manipulation of an object-oriented database based on functional data model is attained in a more integrated form in the LISP environment. TIME2 provides, in the LISP environment, constructs for defining LISP functions representing entities, LISP functions describing their properties, and LISP functions corresponding to DAPLEX derived functions. We call these LISP functions and constructors for generating them *functional data descriptors* and *database modelers*, respectively. Functional data descriptors together with user-defined LISP functions representing procedural semantics associated with entities, are chosen as fundamental constructs for modeling object-oriented database in TIME2. User-defined LISP functions are powerful enough for the system to satisfy the operational requirements, and functional data descriptors support abstractions necessary for fulfilling the structural requirements. This methodology is similar to but different from IRIS[Fis87] which embeds an extension of SQL, called OSQL, into LISP programming on which a lexical style of interface was provided. ADAPLEX[Smi83] is an extension of ADA to incorporate new data types and control structures corresponding to the functional model DAPLEX. However, ADAPLEX limits the use of entities. Derived functions in ADAPLEX are not allowed.

3   Object-oriented database

In this section we discuss data modeling concepts of TIME2. First we present solid models used in our example database. Then, database modelers are presented, and how to specify a schema of an object-oriented database is discussed. Finally, we present examples of database manipulation.

3.1   Solid models

Usefulness of combining several alternative solid representations in a solid modeler has been well recognized. We adopt a dual representation scheme for solid modeling of mechanical parts. The CSG representation is used for solid definition in a database[Har87,Kcm87,Lcc83], while the octree representation[Jac80,Fuj83] is used for manipulation and visualization. In order to define a collection of closely interrelated solids, the CSG representation is slightly modified to allow sharing of subtrees. Its syntax is defined as follows.

solid ::= primitive | combined

combined ::= instance boolean-op instance
instance ::= geometric-op solid
geometric-op ::= translate | rotate | scale
boolean-op ::= or | and | diff
primitive ::= box | cylinder | ...

An example of a solid and its CSG representation is shown in Fig. 1.

3.2   Database modelers

Database modelers, each of which is a LISP function, are used to define and generate functional data descriptors. A functional data descriptor is a LISP special form which accesses to database objects. A set of functional data descriptors specifies a schema of an object-oriented database. Database modelers and outline of their syntax are listed below (Detailed syntax appears in Appendix.)

1) (create-entity-func entity-descriptor entity)
2) (create-property-func property-descriptor data-type-name)
3) (create-derived-func derived-descriptor construction-specification)
4) (create-semantic-func semantic-descriptor abstract-data-type lisp-function)

The modeler *create-entity-func* generates an *entity-descriptor* modeling a type of real world entities. A generalization abstraction between two entity-descriptors is assumed, if an entity-descriptor defined elsewhere appears at the place of entity.

The modeler *create-property-func* generates a *property-descriptor* corresponding to a function in DAPLEX. An entity-descriptor defined elsewhere can be specified at the place of data-type-name.

The modeler *create-derived-func* generates a *derived-function-descriptor* which derives a property of an entity from properties of other entities. LISP facilitates more flexible definitions of functional compositions. However, derived-function-descriptors generated by this modeler are expected to manipulate a database more efficiently than similar functions dynamically defined in the LISP environment, because optimal access methods can be selected at the compilation of these descriptors.

The modeler *create-semantic-func* generates a *semantic-descriptor* which represents procedural meanings associated with the entity type defined by the corresponding modeler. For example, a predicate, "overlap", which decides whether two solids are overlapped or not, will be modeled on semantic-descriptors. Semantic-descriptors are defined by LISP functions each of which is so designed as to manipulate instances of an abstract data type(ADT) defined in an application domain. For example, the predicate "make-oct" defined on solids will be implemented by a LISP function "oct-rep", which is defined as a procedural meaning of an ADT "octree".

An example of a schema of a solid database defined by a set of functional data descriptors is shown in Fig. 2.

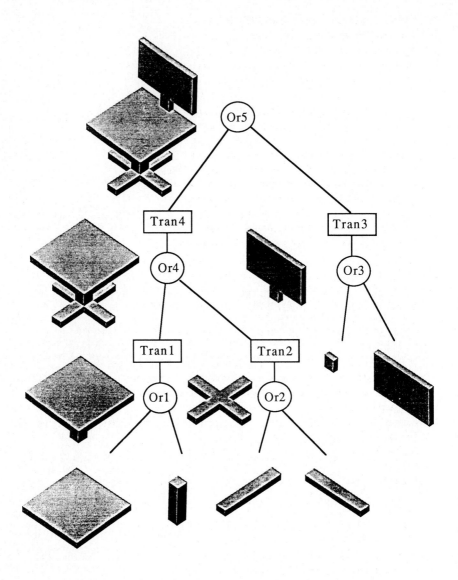

Fig. 1. An example of CSG representation.

```
(create-entity-func    solid() entity)
(create-property-func id(solid) integer)
(create-entity-func    comb()   solid)
(create-property-func id(comb) integer)
(create-property-func op(comb) string)
(create-property-func left(comb) instance)
(create-property-func right(comb) instance)
(create-entity-func    instance() entity)
(create-property-func id(instance) integer)
(create-property-func op(instance) string)
(create-property-func arg(instance) solid)
(create-property-func x(instance) float)
(create-property-func y(instance) float)
(create-property-func z(instance) float)
(create-entity-func    prim() solid)
(create-property-func id(prim) integer)
(create-entity-func    cylinder() prim)
(create-property-func id(cylinder) integer)
(create-property-func radius(cylinder) float)
(create-property-func height(cylinder) float)
(create-entity-func    box() prim)
(create-property-func id(box) integer)
        ......
(create-semantic-func make-prim(prim) octree oct-prim)
(create-semantic-func make-comb(comb) octree oct-comb)
(create-semantic-func make-oct(solid) octree oct-rep)
(create-semantic-func make-instant(instance)   octree oct-inst)
(create-semantic-func make-cylinder(cylinder) octree oct-cylinder)
(create-semantic-func be-prim(solid) bool  is-prim)
(create-semantic-func be-comb(solid) bool  is-comb)
(create-semantic-func be-inst(solid) bool  is-inst)
(create-semantic-func volume(prim)    float prim-volume)
        ......
```

Fig. 2. Data Description of Solid Model.

Each entity descriptor corresponds exactly to the non-terminal symbol appearing in the syntax description of our CSG scheme. Let us consider a number of statements in this example. *(create-entity-func cylinder() primitive)* This statement defines LISP function "cylinder" as an entity descriptor. Here the function "cylinder" evaluates to a set of entities of type "cylinder", which is a subtype of "primitive". The statement *(create-property-func radius(cylinder) float)* states that "radius" is a function descriptor which maps entities of type "cylinder" to entities of type "float". "Float" is one of a number of fundamental entity types. The function applied to a "cylinder" entity returns a float value. The statement *(create-semantic-func make-cylinder(cylinder) octree oct-cylinder)* states that "make-cylinder" is a function which is applied to a "cylinder" entity and returns an "octree". The function "make-cylinder" is implemented by a LISP function "oct-cylinder". The LISP function "oct-cylinder" treats an entity of type "cylinder" as a record having a form of (radius(cylinder) height(cylinder)), where "radius" and "height" are property-descriptors.

3.3   Database manipulation construct

As we have described in the previous sections, TIME2 compiles functional data descriptors into internal forms of LISP functions accessing the physical database. Therefore, a flexible and powerful database manipulation is possible in the LISP environment. However the access of database is specified in an uncontrolled way, thus the management of database will become very annoying. TIME2 provides a simple but powerful database manipulation construct[Bac78,Bun82]. The outlined syntax of the construct is shown below (Detailed syntax appears in Appendix.). In the followings, functional data descriptors are treated as special LISP forms. We use capital letters to denote functional data descriptors. It is noteworthy that entity-descriptors represent abstract types of entities, and concrete data manipulation with respect to the entities should be specified through either property-descriptors or semantic-descriptors.

(db-get set-form predicate-form value-form)

where the *set-form* is a form which returns a list of entities, and the *predicate-form* is a form representing a predicate which is applied to each entity and returns a boolean value. The *value-form* is an arbitrary LISP form which is applied to entities satisfying the qualification specified by the predicate-form and returns a list of data of either a fundamental type or a user-defined ADT.

A simple example of the use of db-get and the corresponding DAPLEX query is shown below.

Query1: Retrieve the id of the cylinder with radius 0.5.

```
(db-get CYLINDER
        (= RADIUS(CYLINDER) 0.5)
        ID(CYLINDER))

    FOR EACH x IN cylinder
    SUCH THAT
          radius(x) = 0.5
    PRINT  id(x)
```

Here, CYLINDER is an entity-descriptor, and RADIUS and ID are property descriptors.

The next example shows a simple use of a semantic-descriptor in db-get.

Query2: Display the cylinder which satisfies the condition that the ratio of its height to its radius is less than 0.2.

```
(display
    (db-get CYLINDER
            (< (/ HEIGHT(CYLINDER) RADIUS(CYLINDER))
               0.2)
            MAKE-OCT(CYLINDER)))
```

Here, MAKE-OCT is a semantic-descriptor which generates an octree representation of a solid. "Display" is a LISP function defined as a procedural meaning of the ADT "octree". Arbitrary LISP functions, i.e., "/" in the above example, can be used in db-get.

LISP functions that manipulate user-defined ADTs can also be used in db-get.

Query3: Retrieve a set of boxes which overlap with a given octree

```
(db-get BOX
        (oct-overlap MAKE-OCT(BOX)
                     (oct-constant))
        ID(BOX))
```

Here, "oct-overlap" and "oct-constant" are LISP functions associated with ADT "octree". Especially "oct-constant" represents a constant octree whose specification is implementation dependent.

Examples of queries listed above relate only one type of entities. The next example shows how to formulate a query navigating between two types of entities.

Query4: Find pairs of cylinders and boxes having nearly equal volumes.

```
(db-get (CYLINDER BOX)
        (< (- VOLUME(CYLINDER)
              VOLUME(BOX))
           0.1)
        (list ID(CYLINDER) ID(BOX)))
```

So far we have explained the main construct of database manipulation in our scheme. Usually, manipulation is formulated in the form of db-get. However, it is often the case that db-get is not sufficient to succinctly specify manipulation. Our scheme provides users with the construct create-derived-func to define derived-function-descriptors which nearly correspond to derived functions in the DAPLEX scheme. A derived-function-descriptor models a collection of entities satisfying specified qualifications. First, we show a simple example of the use of it.

```
(create-derived-func SUBCYLINDER()
    (Select CYLINDER
            (<= RADIUS(CYLINDER) 0.2)
            CYLINDER))
```

Derived-function-descriptor "SUBCYLINDER" evaluates to a subset of "cylinder", each element of it satisfies the qualification specified by the "Select" clause. It is noteworthy that "Select" clause has a very similar syntax to that of the construct "db-get". The main difference is that the "Select" clause returns a set of entities, and can neither return data of fundamental types nor ADTs.

We can formulate a derived-function-descriptor which represents an aggregation of two types of entities with the use of the "Select" clause.

```
(create-derived-func AGGCOMB()
   (Select COMB
          (= OP(COMB) "or")
          (Cartesian LEFT(COMB) RIGHT(COMB))))
```

Thus, derived-function-descriptor can create a new aggregation entity. If users want to associate new properties or to calculate properties from properties of other entities, the construct "create-semantic-func" is available for defining semantic descriptors for this purpose. Here, "Cartesian" is a special operator which is defined on entities. As stated previously, the system does not allow users to deal with entities directly. No LISP functions are provided which accept entities as their arguments. The system provides users with limited set of special operators such as Cartesian, Union, Intersection and Set for manipulation of entities and AS for formulating a qualification on entities.

Two examples listed above show the way of formulating derived-function-descriptors representing entity types. On the other hand, it is possible to formulate derived-function-descriptors representing properties of entities in a similar way. An example is shown below.

```
(create-derived-func AGGCOM1(COMB)
   (Select COMB
          (= OP(COMB) "or")
          (Set LEFT(COMB) RIGHT(COMB))))
```

where the special operator "Set" is used to construct a set by enumerating its elements.

In order to compute complex objects, it is required to support traversing property-descriptors recursively. It is , of course, possible to realize such recursion by using LISP constructs if we encode relationships represented by property-descriptors, in term of LISP data, such as integer and real. However, it is more natural and convenient to provide users with the recursive operation defined on entities. The TIME2 has "Transitive" similar to the concept appearing in the DAPLEX scheme. In order to exemplify the use of "Transitive" in our scheme, we define first a derived-function-descriptor which retrieves those solids referred to "ARG(LEFT(SOLID))" or "ARG(RIGHT(SOLID))" for a given "SOLID".

```
(create-derived-func GET-SOLID(SOLID)
    (Set ARG(LEFT(AS SOLID COMB))
         ARG(RIGHT(AS SOLID COMB)))))
```

Then we give an example of a derived-function-descriptor which retrieves objects belonging to the complex object illustrated in Fig. 3. A special operator "AS" is a predicate for type checking.

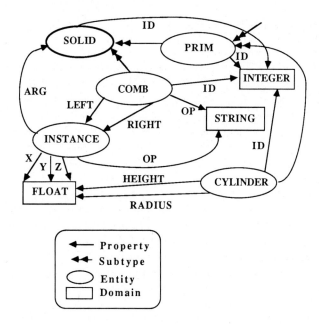

Fig. 3. An Example of retrieving a complex object.

```
(create-derived-func GET-ALL-SOLID(SOLID)
    (Transitive GET-SOLID(SOLID)))
```

Furthermore, using the function "GET-ALL-SOLID" in the db-get clause, octree representations of all solids participating in a complex object can be retrieved. An example is shown below.

```
(db-get (Select SOLID
                (= ID(SOLID) 1)
                (GET-ALL-SOLID(SOLID)))
        TRUE
        (cond (BE-PRIM(SOLID)
                   MAKE-PRIM(SOLID))
              (t   MAKE-COMB(SOLID))))
```

The set-form of db-get returns a set of solid entities, all of them are in the transitive closure of the specified solid having identification number 1, and the semantic-descriptors "MAKE-PRIM" and "MAKE-COMB" generate octrees of each type.

There is also a basic construct "db-new" for creating a new entity. The "setf" can be used within the scope of "db-get" to update properties, whereas the "exclude" within the "db-get" scope deletes entities. Referential integrity associated with the deletion is maintained.

4   Implementation

To implement the above mentioned scheme, first we have to develop an integrated LISP environment provided with database handling facilities. TIME2 is implemented on a relational database. Our implementation is based on a relational DBMS G-BASE, which has a well devised LISP programming interface. In subsection 4.1, we give an overview of G-BASE. In subsection 4.2, we outline our implementation scheme of TIME2 on top of G-BASE.

4.1   G-BASE

G-BASE database management system is described briefly. G-BASE is an extended relational database based on a graph data model[Kun83] and is implemented on top of UNIX[2] operating system. G-BASE features its LISP interface, called *dblisp*[Kan87], which has a set of functions for directly accessing data in the database.

For accessing data stored in the database, dblisp has four layers, which are internal interface, procedural system interface, algebraic system interface and end-user interface. Each layer is composed of a set of functions for getting information from the database dictionary and for accessing the database. In procedural system interface, for example, function "open-database" opens the specified database and return a database identifier, and "fetch-record" fetches a record of a specified record identifier returned by function "find-rtype". In algebraic system interface, functions for executing relational algebra are provided. All of them are based on the concept of path set representing the result of a relational algebra operation in the LISP environment. In end-user interface, a special function named "eval-dml" is provided. This function compiles its argument, an S-expression into a form and evaluates it by eval. Any form of expressions for data definition, data manipulation and user application specification can be processed easily as follows:

- First, translate each statement in the expressions into the corresponding S-expression acceptable to "eval-dml",

- Second, send the S-expression to data manager of G-BASE by calling "eval-dml", and

---

[2]UNIX is a trademark of AT&T Bell Laboratories.

- Finally, get the necessary information from the data manager. Database management system with LISP interface, is generally very beneficial for developing CAD applications.

4.2   Implementation of TIME2

The database described in Fig. 2 has been implemented by a set of relations in G-BASE as shown in Fig. 4. Functions provided in G-BASE are powerful enough. TIME2 encapsulate those functions into abstract statements hiding the detailed information such as database identifier, record identifier from end users[Fig. 5]. To execute the expression of our data manipulating scheme, we have implemented a function called "eval-xdml" taking the place of "eval-dml" originally provided in G-BASE. "eval-xdml" is in charge of translation of expressions represented in section 3 into database accessing functions. Expressions accepted by "eval-xdml" are further divided into three types. Expressions of the first type are to insert data definitions to and retrieve these appropriate tuples from the data dictionary of G-BASE. The effects of "create-entity-func" and "create-property-func" are really to insert information into the data dictionary for creating a relation and an attribute, respectively. "Create-derived-func" and "create-semantic-func" register the definition information into a special relation. The second type deals with retrieval of data stored in the database following all of the necessary information in the data dictionary. There are five basic set-forms mentioned in the db-get clause and these are also the basis for constructing derived functions. The detailed syntax for set-forms appears in Appendix.

set-form ::= derived-func | relational-func
         | selection-func | transitive-func | entity-func

"Entity-func" stands for a function generated by "create-entity-func". "Selection-func" and "relational-func" represent relational algebra. In addition to these, "transitive-func" and "derived-func" are provided. The former is to calculate the transitive closure, whereas the latter stands for a derived-function. The third type is to convert internal representations of entities into those manipulatable in the LISP environment. The entity is an abstract object in the database and has no way to be accessed in the LISP environment directly. So it is necessary to provide the facilities to map entities to corresponding LISP representations and vice versa. Note that semantic-descriptors are different from user-defined LISP functions. The semantic-descriptors have roles to represent procedural meanings of entities in the database system, even if their bodies are expressed as LISP function. In contrast to this, user-defined LISP functions cannot directly be applied to entities. In TIME2, we emphasize the difference by using distinct forms evaluation. The form semantic(entity) denotes evaluation of a semantic-descriptor for an entity, and the form (func entity) denotes evaluation of a user-defined LISP function.

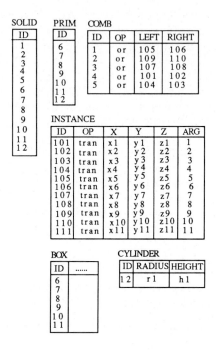

Fig. 4. Solid database.

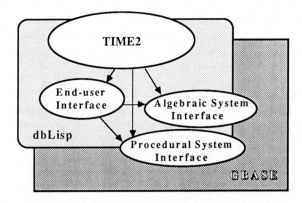

Fig. 5. Architecture of TIME2.

5 Conclusion

This paper has proposed a scheme for design and implementation of the new object-oriented database system. The study is motivated by the need for improving tools and techniques for the specification, design and implementation of 3D-solid databases in the CAD environment. Key constructs of our scheme are integration of user interface into the programming language LISP and the extension of the functional data model. The proposed scheme has capabilities of supporting both structural semantics such as complex object and procedural semantics associated with application objects. Our scheme has the following advantages.

1. The scheme has rich modeling constructs to describe real world naturally.

2. The scheme makes it easy to manipulate solid databases. Novice users can manipulate databases with little burden of writing complex programs.

3. The scheme has powerful manipulation constructs. Advanced users can formulate highly powerful manipulation directly in the LISP environment.

Future works remaining are

1. to manage correctly integrity and consistency problems occurring in update, insertion and deletion operations, and

2. to devise a sophisticated optimization scheme for database manipulation constructs.

Acknowledgements

The authors wish to thank many members of database division of Ricoh Software Lab. for their helpful discussion on TIME2 design. Special thanks are due to Mr. A. Iizawa for helping us to solve implementation problems. This work is partially supported by grants from University of Tsukuba Project Research.

Appendix

The meta language is described as the same of DAPLEX. The upper literal and "..." stands for terminal symbol. The optionality is expressed by square brackets, i.e., [a] stands for a or ϵ. The grouping is served by using parenthesses, e.g., (a|b)c stands for ac or bc. The repetition is expressed by curly brackets, i.e., {a|b} denotes a random sequence constituted by a, b, aabb,aaaaa, bbba, etc.

Statements ::= declarative
    | imperative

imperative ::= set-operation
    | insertion

declarative ::= "(" CREATE-ENTITY-FUNC func-name "(" ")" dec-form ")"
    | "(" CREATE-PROPERTY-FUNC
    func-name "(" func-name ")" dec-domain ")"
    | "(" CREATE-SEMANTICS-FUNC func-name "(" func-name ")"
        lisp-func-name ")"
    | "(" CREATE-DERIVED-FUNC func-name "(" func-vars ")"
        set-form ")"
dec-form ::= ENTITY | func-name
dec-domain ::= INTEGER | FLOAT | CHAR
    | STRING | BOOL | func-name
set-form ::= entity-func
    | derived-func
    | selection-func
    | relational-func
    | transitive-func
selection-func ::= (SELECT set-form predicate-form value-form)
relational-func ::= "(" relational-op set-form set-from ")"
relational-op ::= CARTESIAN | INTERSECTION
    | UNION | DIFFERENCE
    | SET | "(" func-name {, func-name } ")"
transitive-func ::= "(" TRANSITIVE set-form ")"
derived-func ::= func-name "(" [fun-vars] ")"
entity-func ::= func-name
set-operation ::= "(" DB-GET set-form predicate-form value-forms ")"
predicate-form ::= bool-term
    | "(" OR predicate-form bool-term ")"
bool-term ::= bool-fact
    | "(" AND bool-term bool-fact ")"
bool-fact ::= bool-prim
    | "(" NOT bool-prim ")"
bool-prim ::= TRUE | FALSE
    | "(" comparison-pred ")"
    | user-defined
comparison-pred ::= expr comp-op expr
comp-op ::= "=" | ">" | "<" | ">="
    | "<=" | "<>" | user-defined
expr ::= expr-term
    | "(" "+" expr expr-term ")"
    | "(" "-" expr expr-term ")"
expr-term ::= expr-fact
    | "(" "/" expr-term expr-fact ")"
    | "(" "*" expr-term expr-fact ")"
expr-fact ::= ["+" | "-"] expr-prim
expr-prim ::= constant-value
    | "(" expr ")"
    | property-func

```
        | aggregation-func
        | user-defined
        | semantic-func "(" property ")"
property-func ::= func-name
        | func-name "(" property-func ")"
        | "(" AS property-func func-name ")"
aggregation-set ::= "(" aggregation ")"
        | user-defined
aggregation ::= { COUNT | AVG | MAX | MIN | SUM } expr
insertion ::= "(" DB-NEW func-name
              "(" LET "(" { "(" func-name ( value-forms | set-form ) ")" } ")" ")" ")"
value-forms ::= lisp-form
```

The non-terminal symbols having no further explanation are described below briefly. The func-name is a function name of either entity function or property function and the func-vars is a set of func-names. The user-defined is a user defined function for defining a new aggregation, comparison operator or expression. The general-form is a form which generates a new set-form as its return-value. Basically, the set-form is a lisp-form.

References

[And87] Andrews, T. and Harris,C.: Combining Language and Database Advances in an Object-Oriented Development Environment,*ACM OOPSLA'87 Proceedings*, pp.430-440, (1987).

[Atk87] Atkinson, M.P. and Buneman, O.P.: Types and Persistence in Database Programming Languages, *ACM Computing Surveys,* Vol.19, No.2, pp.105-190, (1987).

[Bae79] Baer,A, Eastman, C. and Henrion,M.: Geometric modeling: a survey, *CAD,* Vol.11, No.5, pp.253-272, (1979).

[Bac78] Backus,J.: Can Programming Be Liberated from the von Neumann Style? A Functional Style and Its Algebra of Programs, *Commun. ACM*, Vol.21, No.8, pp.613-641, (1978).

[Ban87] Banerjee,J., Chou,H.T., Garza,J.F., Kim,W., Woelk,D. and Ballou,N.: Data Model Issues for Object-Oriented Applications, *ACM Trans. Office Information Syst.*, Vol.5, No.1, pp.3-26, (1987).

[Bat85] Batory, D.S. and Won Kim: Modeling Concepts for VLSI CAD Objects, *ACM Trans. Database Syst.*, Vol.10, No.3, pp.322-346, (1985).

[Blo87] Bloom,T. and Zdonik,S.B: Issues in the Design of Object-Oriented Database Programming Languages, *ACM OOPSLA'87 Proceedings*, pp.441-451, (1987).

[Bra75] Braid,I.C.: Teh Synthesis of Solids Bounded by Many Faces, *Comm. of ACM*, Vol.18, No.4, pp.209-216, (1975).

[Bun82] Buneman,P., Frankel, R.E. and Nikhil R.: An Implementation Technique for Database Query Languages, *ACM Trans. Database Syst.*, Vol.7, No.2, pp.164-186, (1982).

[Con84] Conpeland,G. and Maier,D.: Making Smalltalk a Database System, *ACM SIGMOD'84*, pp.316-325, (1984).

[Fis87] Fishman, D. H., et al: Iris: An Object-Oriented Database Management System, *ACM Trans. Office Information Syst.*, Vol.5, No.1, pp.48-69, (1987).

[Fuj83] Fujimura,K., Toriya,H., Yamaguchi,K. and Kunii,T.L.: Octree Algorithms for Solid Modeling, *Proceedings of Inter. Graphics'83*, Vol. B2-1, pp.1-15, (1983).

[Jac80] Jackins,C.L. and Tanimoto,S.L.: Octrees and their Use in Representing Three-Dimensional Objects, *Computer Graphics and Image Processing*, Vol.14, pp.249-270, (1980).

[Jam83] James,J., Fogg,D. and Stonebraker,M.: Implementation of data abstraction in the relational database system INGRES, *ACM SIGMOD-RECORD*, pp.1-14, (Apr.1983).

[Har87] Hardwick,M. and Spooner,D.L.: Comparison of Some Data Models for Engineering Objects, *IEEE Computer Graphics and applications*, Vol.7, No.3, March 1987, pp.56-66.

[Kem87] Kemper,A. and Wallrath,M.: An Analysis of Geometric Modeling in Database Systems, *ACM Computing Surveys*, Vol.19, No.1, pp.46-91, (1987).

[Kan87] Kanasaki,K.: A Query Evaluation Model and Its Implementation in Lisp, Tech. Report of Ricoh Software Lab., SRC-TR-87-01, (1987).

[Kun83] Kunii,H.: Graph Data Language: A High Levewl Access-Path Oriented Language, Ph.D. Dissertation, Univ. of Texas at Austin, (1983).

[Lee83] Lee, Y.C. and Fu, K.S.: Integration of Solid Modeling and Database Management for CAD/CAM, *20th Design Automation Conf.*, pp.367-373,(1983).

[Lor82] Lorie, R.: Issues in Databases for Design Application, Encarnacao,J. and Krause, F.L.(ed.), *File Strucutres and Data Bases for CAD*, pp.213-222, Holland, Amsterdam, (1982).

[Pur87] Purdy,A. and Schuchardt,B: Integrating an Object Server with Other Worlds, *ACM Trans. Office Information Syst.*, Vol.5, No.1, pp.27-47, (1987).

[Osb86] Osborn,S. and Heaven,T.E.: The Design of a Relational Database System with Abstract Data Types for Domains,*ACM Trans. Database Syst.*, Vol.11, No.3, pp.357-373, (1986).

[Req82] Requicha,A.A.G.: Representations for Rigid Solids, Theory, Methods and Systems, *ACM Computing Surveys*, Vol.12, No.4, pp.437-464, (1980).

[Shi81] Shipman,D.: The Functional Data Model and the Data Language DAPLEX, *ACM Trans. Database Syst.*, Vol.6, No.1, pp.140-173, (1981)

[Smi77] Smith,J.M. and Smith, D.C.P.: Database Abstraction: Aggregation and Generalization, *ACM Trans. Database Syst.*, Vol.20, No.2, pp.405-413, (1977).

[Smi83] Smith, J.M., Fox, S. and Landers, T.: ADAPLEX: Relationale and Reference Manual, 2d ed., Computer Corporation of America, Cambridge, Mass, (1983).

[Sto83] Stonebraker,M., Rubenstein,B. and Guttman,A.: Application of Abstract Data Types and Abstract Indices to CAD Data, In *Proc. of the Engineering Design Applications of ACM-IEEE Database Week*, San Jose, CA, pp.107-114, (1983).

[Yu87] Yu,X., Ohbo,N., Masuda,T. and Fujiwara,Y.: Database Support for Solid Modeling, *The Visual Computer*, Vol.2, No.6, pp.358-366, (1987).

Session 7

DATA MODELS

Visual Database Systems
T.L. Kunii (Editor)
Elsevier Science Publishers B.V. (North-Holland)
© IFIP, 1989

Abstract Data Types in Graphics Databases

Shi-Jie Jiang*, Hiroyuki Kitagawa**, Nobuo Ohbo**
Isao Suzuki**, and Yuzuru Fujiwara**

* Program in Engineering Sciences
** Institute of Information Sciences and Electronics
University of Tsukuba
Tennohdai, Tsukuba, Ibaraki 305, Japan

This paper presents a new scheme for integrated use of ADTs(Abstract Data Types) in the framework of the relational model. Motivation comes from object-oriented and flexible manipulation of graphics databases. The scheme makes relational database systems substantially more expressive and powerful, especially in handling semantics of graphical objects. As key constructs, relations on ADT domains, ADT aggregation, ADT hierarchy, and ADT function composition are supported in the scheme. They provide several levels of abstraction for mapping naturally the real world problems to the relational scheme. Implementation of some features has been completed on UNIX environments and they are put into experimental evaluation.

1   Introduction

This paper presents a new scheme for the specification, design, and implementation of graphic databases. The fundamental ideas are from abstract data type[4,10,17], functional programming language[1], relational database[5], and semantic modeling[6].

In recent years computer graphics is emerging as one of the more interesting areas of application for database technology[2,11,15,16,18]. Most of the works are based on the relational model, because of its data-independent representation, and high-level information access facility. However, it has been pointed out that conventional relational database management systems do not allow the modeling of graphical objects in a natural way or at least they do not support the retrieval and manipulation of such objects in a way that is familiar to engineers[7,9]. When data structures in a database system will not support the actural structure of information in the real world as in the case of graphics databases implemented on the standard relational model, then the form of the real world information gets over-simplified in the database scheme or it must be encoded into available data structures.

Fortunately, however, developments in programming language and artificial intelligence areas offer very promising prospects for modeling data accompanied by complicated graphical semantics[3,4]. Abstract data type (ADT) in the programming language area facilitates uniform description of graphical data and non-graphical data[10]. An ADT is an encapsulation of a data structure along with a collection of operations for manipulating the data structure. Semantic data modeling in the artificial intelligence area gives a clue for solving problems of complicated type hierarchy naturally appearing in graphical applications. Our scheme is intended to support data abstractions such as ADTs and data type hierarchy in a relational context. In many approaches employing ADTs in a relational context, a relation is considered as an ADT[14]. Instead of treating an entire relation as an ADT, Stonebraker, Osborn and others suggested that individual columns of a relation can be ADTs[8,13]. By adding ADTs for encapsulating graphical objects to the standard types, sophisticated data structures can be more directly described in the relational framework. For our purpose of graphics database definition and manipulation, use of one of the above schemes, namely "relation as an ADT" and "column as an ADT", is beneficial by self. However, they are only special cases of ADT utilization. If ADTs are used in more and more integrated manner, graphics data handling capability of the database system is greatly enhanced.

The scheme proposed in the paper provides a sound basis for integrated use of ADTs in the framework of the relational model. Key constructs of our schemes are as follows:

1. Relations on ADT Domains: As in the scheme of "column as an ADT", relations may be defined on ADT domains as well as primitive domains.

2. ADT Aggregation: Aggregations of attribute values in tuples can be interpreted as representing application specific ADT instances. Then, data in the database can be manipulated by operations and/or predicates applicable to the ADT instances. The scheme of "relation as an ADT" expresses a special case of ADT aggregation.

3. ADT Hierarchy: ADTs involved in relation definitions and ADT aggregations are organized into a type hierarchy. The hierarchy represents supertype/subtype relationships. It is used for managing various ADT definitions, and its property inheritance feature fairly reduces redundant ADT definitions.

4. ADT Function Composition: Basic operations for handling ADTs are provided in ADT definitions. Function composition facilities enable the user to build application specific operations from the basic ones in a controlled way.

Although the construct (1) is based on the proposals of Stonebraker, Osborn, and others, constructs (2) through (4) are unique features of our scheme. Our scheme has been implemented on UNIX environments as a part of the TIME project. Implementation of some features has been completed, and they are put into experimental evaluation.

The remainder of this paper is organized as follows. Section 2 describes our motivations for this study in more details with a graphics database example. In Section 3 we define concepts of ADT, ADT functions, ADT aggregation, and ADT hierarchy in our scheme. In Section 4 we describe the ADT function composition facilities. In Section 5 we apply our scheme to an example graphics database to exemplify its applicability. Section 6 describes the prototype implementation of our scheme. Section 7 is devoted to conclusion and discussion of the future research topics.

2 Motivations

In this section, we describe our motivations for developing the scheme based on the four key constructs: relations on ADT domains, ADT aggregation, ADT hierarchy, and ADT function composition. We use a simple graphics database example for illustration.

2.1 Relations on ADT Domains

As mentioned in Section 1 and elaborated in Section 3, an ADT is a user-defined data type specified by the encapsulated data structure and externally visible operations for its manipulation. Use of ADTs in individual attributes of relations is the starting basis for our study. In graphics databases, new data types such as point, edge, and polygon have to be supported. Without attributes of ADT domains, those graphics objects have to be encoded in flat tabular structures only consisting of primitive data items such as integers, reals, and character strings. However, this restriction sometimes brings about awkward representations of graphical objects and makes database manipulation very irritating.

Figure 1 shows sample relations defined on an ADT domain. Relation "triangle" has attributes "id", "color", "v1", "v2", and "v3". Attributes "v1", "v2", and "v3" represent three vertexes of a triangle and have ADT "POINT" [1] as their domains. Relation "rectangle" has attributes "id", "color", "v1", "v2", "v3", and "v4", and the last four attributes also have "POINT" domain. Since attributes representing vertexes have ADT domains, operations and/or predicates defined for the ADT instances are applicable to the attribute values. For example, if "distance" operation is defined to derive the distance between two "POINT" instances, it is directly applicable to vertex attribute values in queries.

---

[1] In this paper, we use capital letters to denote ADT type names.

triangle

id	color	v1	v2	v3
t1	red	(0.0 1.0)	(1.0 2.0)	(1.0 0.0)
t2	green	(2.0 2.0)	(0.0 1.0)	(5.0 0.0)
t3	blue	(1.0 2.0)	(5.0 0.0)	(2.0 2.0)
t4	white	(1.0 0.0)	(0.0 1.0)	(2.0 1.0)
:	:	:	:	:

(a)

rectangle

id	color	v1	v2	v3	v4
r1	grown	(0.0 0.0)	(2.0 0.0)	(2.0 2.0)	(0.0 2.0)
r2	yellow	(1.0 4.0)	(-1.0 4.0)	(-1.0 -4.0)	(1.0 -4.0)
r3	green	(3.0 1.0)	(3.0 0.0)	(-3.0 0.0)	(-3.0 -0.0)
r4	black	(2.0 0.0)	(0.0 2.0)	(2.0 4.0)	(4.0 2.0)
:	:	:	:	:	:

(b)

Fig. 1. Sample Relations in Graphics Database

2.2   ADT Aggregation

Although ADTs in individual attributes indeed facilitates graphics database handling, they are not enough. Let us consider relation "triangle" for example. Each tuple in "triangle" semantically represents an instance of triangle, and values of attributes "v1", "v2", and "v3" determine its geometrical position and shape. Let us assume we want to retrieve all isosceles triangles registered in the relation. We can formulate this query using "distance" operation applicable to two vertex attributes. However, this query expression becomes a little complicated. If we want to formulate queries concerning the area each triangle covers, query formulas become more complicated and hard to understand at a glance.

This problem can be solved if DBMS can interpret the aggregation of the three vertex attributes as vertex coordinates of the abstract triangle, and internally map the attribute values into an ADT "TRIANGLE" instance. Then, we can formulate queries directly in terms of operations and/or predicates on ADT "TRIANGLE". We have deviced a mechanism named ADT aggregation, which defines interpretation of an aggregation of attribute values as an ADT instance.

An alternative to solve this problem is to directly define an attribute whose domain is "TRIANGLE". However, it is an issue of database design. If the relational schema including the three vertex attributes is resulted from analysis of the whole application requirements, we cannot always resort to construction of huge ADTs complying with a specific application.

2.3   ADT Hierarchy

Owing to the ADT aggregation, we can associate an instance of ADT "TRIANGLE" with each tuple in relation "triangle". Similarly, we can associate ADT "RECT-ANGLE" instances with tuples in relation "rectangle". Then queries on geometrical properties of triangles and rectangles can be formulated straightforwardly. However, a problem arises when we want to formulate queries joining both relations. For example, suppose we want to retrieve pairs of a triangle and a rectangle which intersect with each other. One way is to specify the intersection condition in terms of vertex attribute values in both relations. Queries formulated in this way, however, become very complicated. The other way is to map tuples in both relations into instances of higher level ADT "CLOSED-POLYLINE" and specify queries using predicate "inter-section" presumably defined on ADT "CLOSED-POLYLINE". This solution can be naturally derived if we can define "CLOSED-POLYLINE" as a common supertype of "TRIANGLE" and "RECTANGLE".

We have put the concept of ADT hierarchy to handle supertype/subtype rela-tionships among ADTs. Figure 2 shows a part of the ADT hierarchy defined for the example graphics database.

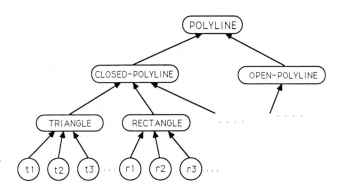

Fig. 2. A Part of Example ADT Hierarchy

2.4   ADT Function Composition

By means of ADTs, we can directly bring domain specific operations in the database manipulation. However, it is rather difficult to predict all operations required for applications in advance. When new operations are required by the user, the database

administrator can additionally define new ones. If the addition of new operations
is performed in an uncontrolled way, however, management and use of ADTs will
become very annoying. As a means of getting rid of this danger, we have decided
to include facilities for constructing application specific operations in a disciplined
manner.

Suppose an application need to calculate the distance between the origin and the
inner center of a triangle. It may be reasonable to associate a function with ADT
"TRIANGLE" which returns the inner center. Usually, however, it will be too biased
to the specific application requirement to define a function which directly performs
the above calculation. In such cases, our function composition facility can be utilized
by the application to customize original ADT functions. As described in Section 4,
five kinds of structures are provided for function composition.

3   ADT and ADT Functions

3.1   ADT

An ADT in our scheme is defined along the line in programming language theory.
An *abstract data type (ADT)* A is modeled as the following triplet:

$$A = (N, S, F),$$

where N is the type name of A, S is specification of data structures implementing
instances of type A, and F is a set of ADT functions. Only type name and *ADT
functions* are externally visible properties of type A, and data structures constrained
by S are accessed and updated only through ADT functions. ADT functions of type
A are classified into the following three types.

1. B-function f: $A \times A_1 \times ... \times A_m \times P_1 \times ... \times P_n \rightarrow$ boolean

2. P-function f: $A \times A_1 \times ... \times A_m \times P_1 \times ... \times P_n \rightarrow P'$

3. A-function f: $A \times A_1 \times ... \times A_m \times P_1 \times ... \times P_n \rightarrow A'$

Here, $m \geq 0$, $n \geq 0$, A_i (i = 1, ..., m) and A' are ADTs which are not necessarily
distinct from A. P_j (j = 1, ..., n) denotes a primitive data type. We designate integer,
real, character string, boolean as primitive data types. P' denotes a primitive data
type other than boolean. *B-function* is a function which returns a value of boolean
type. It can be used as a predicate in the conditional statement of a query. *P-function*
has a primitive data type other than boolean as its codomain, and can appear where
values of primitive data type can occur in an arithmetic or logic formula. *A-function*
stands for an operation between ADTs.

For example, the following expression gives definition of an ADT "POINT" in our
prototype implementation:

ADT-definition(
    ADT name = POINT,
    parent = null,
    B-function is-unit
        is POINT → boolean,
    P-function distance
        is POINT × POINT → real,
    A-function transpose
        is POINT → POINT,
    ......
    ......
    filename = "/usr2/kyo/adt/POINT")

ADT "POINT" has no ADT as its parent. ADT function "is-unit" is a B-function which checks whether the vector from the origin to the point is a unit or not. Function "distance" is a P-function which calculates the distance between two points. Function "transpose" is an A-function which returns a point having x and y coordinates exchanged. The keyword "parent" is specification of inheritance of the ADT. This information is used to organize ADT hierarchy as explained later. "Filename" is the name of the file that contains the definitions of ADT functions, which are written by the user.

We define another ADT "TRIANGLE" as follows:

ADT-definition(
    ADT name = TRIANGLE,
    parent = CLOSED-POLYLINE,
    B-function isosceles
        is TRIANGLE → boolean,
    B-function enclose-origin
        is TRIANGLE → boolean,
    A-function inner-center
        is TRIANGLE → POINT,
    A-function outer-center
        is TRIANGLE → POINT,
    A-function inscribed-circle
        is TRIANGLE → CIRCLE,
    ......
    ......
    filename = "/usr2/kyo/adt/triangle")

In this definition, "TRIANGLE" is defined as subtype of "CLOSED-POLYLINE" and has its ADT functions declared as above.

3.2   Relations on ADT

Columns of a relation can be declared to contain ADT values. Therefore, in our scheme a *relation* is defined as follows:

$R \subseteq D_1 \times \ldots \times D_n,$
where D_i (i = 1, ..., n) stands for a primitive domain or an ADT domain. An example of such a relation has been given in Figure 1. All the ADTs involved in relation definitions have to be defined as explained in the previous subsection.

Once a relation is defined over an ADT, its ADT functions can be used in any place of a query where an attribute specification for the relation may appear. Therefore, domain specific data operations can be directly specified in queries. Examples are given in Section 5.

3.3   ADT Aggregation

As exemplified in Section 2, in order to represent the semantics of graphical objects, it is sometimes useful to interpret attribute values as information designating ADT instances. For representing this graphical data semantics, our scheme provides ADT aggregation which maps aggregation of attribute values into ADT instances. ADT aggregation can be specified by the following form:

$G: D_1 \times \ldots \times D_n \rightarrow A$

where D_i (i = 1, ..., n) stands for a primitive domain or an ADT domain, and A stands for an ADT.

For example, we can declare two ADT aggregations as follows:

Aggregation-definition(
    name AS-TRIANGLE
    type POINT × POINT × POINT → TRIANGLE
    filename "/usr2/kyo/adt/aggregation/triangle")

Aggregation-definition(
    name AS-RECTANGLE
    type POINT × POINT × POINT × POINT → RECTANGLE
    filename "/usr2/kyo/adt/aggregation/rectangle")

Here the ADT domain appearing in such a definition must be defined beforehand. If we define an ADT aggregation from all attributes of a relation to an ADT, this ADT aggregation just realizes the scheme of "relation as an ADT" as a special case. In this sense, our scheme naturally integrates schemes of "column as an ADT" and "relation as an ADT" into one uniform framework.

By introducing this ADT aggregation mechanism, we can have a view of relation "triangle" shown in Figure 1(a) as Figure 3.

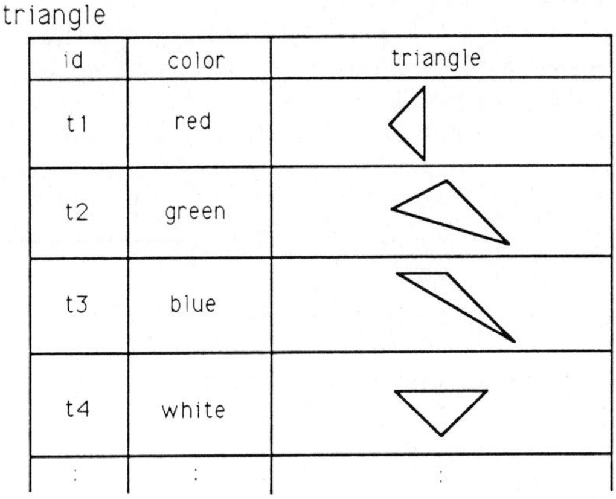

triangle

id	color	triangle
t1	red	
t2	green	
t3	blue	
t4	white	
:	:	:

Fig. 3. A View of Relation "triangle"

3.4 ADT Hierarchy

ADT hierarchy enables the user to specify that a subtype ADT inherits the function definitions of its supertype. The primary advantage of ADT hierarchy is that it is an efficient method of representation. Generally, this mechanism enables the ADT subtype referring to the functions associated with its supertype. Then there is no need to redefine the same ADT function for the subtype. Moreover, it can reduce the possibility of specifying contradicting ADT definitions. In our scheme, a multiple inheritance hierarchy is supported, which enables an ADT to have more than one parent.

In Subsection 3.1, we have mentioned that the specification of inheritance must be given when an ADT is defined. It also presented an example of defining ADT "TRIANGLE", which has been defined to be a subtype of "CLOSED-POLYLINE". An ADT function such as "enclosure", originally defined upon ADT "CLOSED-POLYLINE", would then be applicable to values of the type "TRIANGLE".

4 Composition of ADT Functions

So far we have explained the first three key constructs of our scheme. Operations and predicates basically required for manipulating ADT instances are usually given in the definition of the ADT as ADT functions. However, it is often the case that ADT functions are not sufficient to directly specify the application requirements. For example, we may have a natural demand to apply a function to the argument if the specified predicate is satisfied and to apply another function otherwise.

Our scheme provides the user with function composition facilities to define more application specific operations and predicates combining the basic ones. ADT functions directly specified in ADT definitions are called primitive ADT functions, and those defined with the function composition facilities are called composite ADT functions. We use the term ADT functions to generally refer to functions of both types. First of all, we give some examples. We consider the relation "triangle" shown in Figure 1(a). In this relation, attributes "id" and "color" have a built-in primitive domain of character string. Attributes "v1", "v2", and "v3" have ADT domain of "POINT" defined in Subsection 3.1.

A simple query example may look as follows:

    range of t is triangle
    retrieve (distance <inner-center outer-center>
                        (AS-TRIANGLE[t.v1 t.v2 t.v3]))
    where t.color = "red"

This query using ADT aggregation "AS-TRIANGLE", A-functions "inner-center" and "outer-center" derives the distance between the inner center and the outer center of the triangle. There is a function composition case of "distance" and "<inner-center outer-center>" in this example. The expression "<inner-center outer-center>" stands for an example of function construction.

Another example can be given in the following form:

    range of t is triangle
    retrieve (distance ((enclose-origin → inner-center outer-center)
                        (AS-TRIANGLE[t.v1 t.v2 t.v3]))
             "(3.0 -2.0)")
    where (distance t.v1 t.v2) < 5

This query has a case of conditional function composition with form (enclose-origin → inner-center outer-center). For the triangle in which the distance between the first point and the second point is smaller than 5, this query finds out the distance between the point "(3.0 -2.0)" and the inner center of the triangle if the triangle encloses the origin, and the distance between the point and the outer center otherwise. Here it is worthy of note that this query can be specified in only one query formulation. Without our function composition facility, it must be split into the following two query statements, whose total effect is equal to the above query.

    range of t is triangle
    retrieve (distance (inner-center (AS-TRIANGLE[t.v1 t.v2 t.v3]))
                        "(3.0 -2.0)")
    where (enclose-origin (AS-TRIANGLE[t.v1 t.v2 t.v3]))
        and ((distance t.v1 t.v2) < 5)

    range of t is triangle
    retrieve (distance (outer-center (AS-TRIANGLE[t.v1 t.v2 t.v3]))
                        "(3.0 -2.0)")
    where not(enclose-origin (AS-TRIANGLE[t.v1 t.v2 t.v3]))

and $((\text{distance t.v1 t.v2}) < 5)$

Now we introduce function composition facility in detail. There are five ways of combining functions in our scheme.

1. *Composition*
   Given ADT functions f_i ($i = 1, 2, ..., n$), $[f_1 \, f_2 \, ... \, f_n](x)$ is obtained by successively applying f_i to $[f_{i+1} \, ... \, f_n](x)$, that is, $[f_1 \, f_2 \, ... \, f_n](x) = f_1(f_2(\, ... \, (f_n(x)) \, ... \,))$.

2. *Construction*
   Given functions f_i ($i = 1, 2, ..., n$), $<f_1 \, f_2 \, ... \, f_n>(x)$ is a list of n elements whose ith element is obtained by applying f_i to the argument x, that is, $<f_1 \, f_2 \, ... \, f_n>(x) = (f_1(x) \, f_2(x) \, ... \, f_n(x))$. If one specifies an ADT function returning a list value in the query, it is interpreted as a tuple of values.

3. *Conditional* $(p \rightarrow f \, g)(x)$
   Here, p stands for a P-function. If the P-function returns truth $(p \rightarrow f \, g)(x) = f(x)$, and if P-function returns false $(p \rightarrow f \, g)(x) = g(x)$, that is, $(p \rightarrow f \, g)(x)$ = IF $p(x)$ THEN $f(x)$ ELSE $g(x)$.

4. *Insert Left* $/f(x_1 \, x_2 \, ... \, x_n)$
   $/f(x_1 \, x_2 \, ... \, x_n)$ is the result of applying ADT function f to the list consisting of x_1 and the result of $/f$ applied to the rest of the argument list, that is, $/f(x_1 \, x_2 \, ... \, x_n) = f(x_1 \, /f(x_2 \, ... \, x_n))$.

5. *Insert Right* $f/(x_1 \, x_2 \, ... \, x_n)$
   $f/(x_1 \, x_2 \, ... \, x_n)$ is the result of applying f to the list consisting of the result of $f/$ applied to the argument list except the last element x_n and x_n, that is, $f/(x_1 \, x_2 \, ... \, x_n) = f(f/(x_1 \, ... \, x_{n-1}) \, x_n)$.

6. *Apply to All* $@f(x_1 \, x_2 \, ... \, x_n)$
   $@f(x_1 \, x_2 \, ... \, x_n)$ is the results of a list of f applied to each element of the argument list, that is, $@f(x_1 \, x_2 \, ... \, x_n) = (f(x_1) \, f(x_2) \, ... \, f(x_n))$.

Using the above composition facility, we can build complicated composite ADT functions which are expressed in terms of the primitive ADT functions.

5 Examples of Graphics Database Manipulation

As we have claimed in the previous sections, our scheme indeed meets our requirements for flexibly manipulating graphics data in the relational database environments. In this section we demonstrate the power of our scheme in the context of sample graphics data handling. The example database includes two relations shown in Figure 1.

Each tuple in the relations semantically represents an instance of two-dimensional figure, that is, a triangle or a rectangle. Therefore, if we can associate abstract instances of ADTs "TRIANGLE" or "RECTANGLE" with tuples, specification of data manipulation and query formulation becomes straightforward. For this purpose, we can use the ADT aggregations "AS-TRIANGLE" and "AS-RECTANGLE" defined in Subsection 3.3.

We have already defined the ADT "TRIANGLE" in Subsection 3.1. Definition of ADT "RECTANGLE" is given as follows:

```
ADT-definition(
      ADT name = RECTANGLE,
      parent = "CLOSED-POLYLINE"
      ......
      ......)
```

As explained in Section 2, we need to handle triangles and rectangles as subtypes of closed polylines. For this purpose, we define ADT "CLOSED-POLYLINE" as a parent of ADTs "TRIANGLE" and "RECTANGLE".

```
ADT-definition(
      ADT name = CLOSED-POLYLINE,
      parent = POLYLINE,
      B-function intersection
            is CLOSED-POLYLINE × CLOSED-POLYLINE → boolean,
      A-function enclosure
            is CLOSED-POLYLINE × CLOSED-POLYLINE → CLOSED-POLYLINE,

      A-function intersection-part
            is CLOSED-POLYLINE × CLOSED-POLYLINE → CLOSED-POLYLINE,

      ......
      filename = "/usr2/kyo/adt/closed")
```

Now we illustrate query examples.

Query 1. Retrieval of the id and color of isosceles triangles can be expressed as follows:

```
      range of t is triangle
      retrieve (t.id t.color)
      where (isosceles(AS-TRIANGLE[t.v1 t.v2 t.v3]))
```

In this example, ADT aggregation AS-TRIANGLE interprets the three vertex attributes as designating an instance of ADT "TRIANGLE". Then ADT function "isosceles" can be used to check whether it is an isosceles triangle or not.

Query 2. Query which displays the inscribed circle of the triangle of blue color can be formulated in the following form:

```
      range of t is triangle
      retrieve (inscribed-circle (AS-TRIANGLE[t.v1 t.v2 t.v3]))
      where t.color = "blue"
```

In evaluation of ADT function "inscribed-circle", data structures representing "CIR-

CLE" instances are returned, and then they are used to generate a graphics display as shown in Figure 4(a).

Query 3. The following query displays closed polylines defined as enclosures of pairs of a triangle and a rectangle, if they have intersections:

```
range of t1 is rectangle
range of t2 is triangle
retrieve (enclosure(AS-RECTANGLE[t1.v1 t1.v2 t1.v3 t1.v4])
               (AS-TRIANGLE[t2.v1 t2.v2 t2.v3]))
where (intersection(AS-RECTANGLE[t1.v1 t1.v2 t1.v3 t1.v4])
               (AS-TRIANGLE[t2.v1 t2.v2 t2.v3]))
```

Data structures returned by this query can be used to display the figure as shown in Figure 4(b).

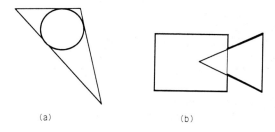

(a)   (b)

Fig. 4. Example Graphics Displays

6   Implementation

Our scheme is being implemented on an extended relational DBMS G-BASE.[2] G-BASE runs on UNIX.[3] G-BASE is distinguishable from other commercially available relational DBMSs by its Lisp-based program interface. The interface is called DM-Lisp, and it intends to provide a more powerful and flexible environments for database application development. DM-Lisp consists of usual lisp functions and database handling functions. "LRT(Lisp Run Time)" is a set of functions, which accepts S-expressions of queries and translates them into DM-Lisp forms. Then, by evaluating those forms, database accesses are carried out.

Our prototype implementation scheme is shown in Figure 5.

---

[2]G-BASE is a trademark of RICOH Co., Ltd.
[3]UNIX is a trademark of AT&T Bell Laboratories.

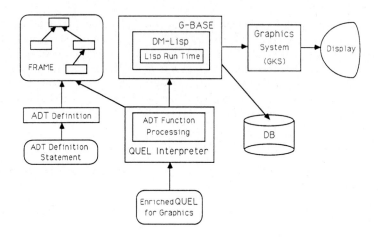

Fig. 5. Implementation of the Prototype

We have selected QUEL as a basis of our query language because it has a comparatively simple syntax and is widely used. Needless to say, some extensions have been done in order to handle embedded ADT functions and associated composition facilities. We have developed a module called "QUEL Interpreter" which translates the extended QUEL statements into Lisp S-expressions. The S-expressions are further translated into DM-Lisp forms by LRT as mentioned above. For this purpose, LRT is also modified to accept ADT function calls appearing in places field specifications can be used. "ADT Function Processing Module" is a submodule of "QUEL Interpreter" and in charge of analysis of ADT function calls. It looks up the ADT definition to perform function type checking. It also handles function compositions used in the queries.

Management of ADT definitions and implementation of ADT hierarchy are based on a frame system[12]. A frame is allocated for each ADT. It contains a system slot denoting the characteristic values of the ADT such as inheritance information, and a set of general slots representing ADT functions associated with the ADT. Values for these slots are either explicitly given in the frame or inherited from higher-level frames via an 'ako' facet in the system slot. Inheritance role can be specified in three ways, that is, S means simple inheritance, U means multiple inheritance, and I means no inheritance.

Currently our efforts are devoted to implement the scheme on top of SUN3 workstation. In the first stage of our project, we are developing a prototype of a graphics database system capable of drawing 2-dimensional pictures. This prototype will serve as a test vehicle for a detailed study of the important ADT issues in the context of a general purpose graphics system for CAD application.

7   Conclusion

This paper has proposed a scheme for integrated use of ADTs in the relational model framework. Basic motivations of this study have been to object-oriented and flexible manipulation of graphics databases. Key constructs of our scheme are relations on ADT domains, ADT aggregation, ADT hierarchy, and ADT function composition facility. The scheme makes relational database systems substantially more useful, especially in handling semantics of graphical objects. Our approach has a number of advantages. They include the following points:

1. The scheme is intuitive, easy to use, and easy to understand.

2. It is expressive. It provides a rich set of constructs for modeling and manipulating graphics data.

3. It provides a useful level of abstraction. The real world problems can be abstracted and mapped naturally to the relational scheme.

There remain a number of future research issues. Our efforts are exerted to reach the following subgoals along the line of our project objectives.

1. Completion of the query processing implementation including updates to ADTs. At the same time we are also trying to find out efficient ways to do query optimization, especially, methods of smart use of indexes to ADTs.

2. Development of a three-dimensional graphics system which enables the user to formulate ADT queries concerning solid objects. For this purpose, we also have to devise a input method of three-dimensional object data which can be put into real use.

Acknowledgements

The authors wish to thank many members of database division of Ricoh Software Lab. for their helpful discussion on our project. This work is partially supported by grants from University of Tsukuba Project Research.

References

[1] Backus, J., Can Programming be Liberated from the Von Neumann Style? A Functional Style and Its Algebra of Programs, *ACM Turing Lecture, CACM,* Vol. 21, No. 8, Aug. 1978, pp. 613-641.

[2] Becerril, J. L., Casajuana, R. and Lorie, R. A., GSYSR: A Relational Database Interface for Graphics, in Data Base Techniques for Pictorial Applications, Blaser, A., Ed., *Springer-Verlag,* New York, 1980, pp. 459-474.

[3] Bloom, T. and Zdonik, S. B., Issues in the Design of Object-Oriented Database Programming Languages, *ACM OOPSLA'87 Proceedings,* 1987, pp. 441-451.

[4] Cardelli, L. and Wegner, P., On Understanding Types, Data Abstraction, and Polymorphism, *ACM Computing Surveys,* Vol. 17, No. 4, Dec. 1985, pp. 471-522.

[5] Codd, E. F., A Relational Model of Data for Large Shared Data Banks, *CACM,* Vol. 13, No. 6, Jun. 1970, pp. 377-387.

[6] Codd, E. F., Extending the Database Relational Model to Capture More Meaning, *ACM Trans. Database Syst.,* Vol. 4, No. 4, Dec. 1979, pp. 397-434.

[7] Hardwick, M. and Spooner, D. L., Comparison of Some Data Models for Engineering Objects, *IEEE Computer Graphics and Applications,* Mar. 1987, pp. 56-66.

[8] James, J., Fogg, D. and Stonebraker, M., Implementation of Data Abstraction in the Relational Database System INGRES, *ACM SIGMOD Record,* Apr. 1983, pp. 1-14.

[9] Kemper, A. and Wallrath, M., An Analysis of Geometric Modeling in Database Systems, *ACM Computing Surveys,* Vol. 19, No. 1, Mar. 1987, pp. 47-91.

[10] Liskov, B. and Zilles, S., Programming with Abstract Data Types, *ACM SIGPLAN Notices,* Apr. 1974.

[11] Lorie, R. and Plouffe, W., Complex Objects and Their Use in Design Transactions, *Proceedings of ACM SIGMOD Conference on Engineering Design Applications,* San Jose, May 1983, pp. 115-121.

[12] Minsky, M. A., A Framework for Representing Knowledge, *in The Psychology of Computer Vision, Winston, P., Ed., McGrow Hill,* 1975, pp. 211-277.

[13] Osborn, S. L. and Heaven, T. E., The Design of a Relational Database System with Abstract Data Types for Domains, *ACM Trans. Database Syst.* Vol. 11, No. 3, Sept. 1986, pp. 357-373.

[14] Rowe, L. and Shoens, K., Data Abstraction, Views and Updates in RIGEL, *Proceedings of ACM SIGMOD Conference on the Management of Data,* Boston, June 1979.

[15] Sharman, G., A Picture Drawing System Using a Binary Relational Data Base, *in Data Base Techniques for Pictorial Applications, Blaser, A., Ed., Springer-Verlag,* New York, pp. 495-508.

[16] Soop, K., Data Aspects of Graphical Applications - Experience from an Engineering Joint Study, *in Data Base Techniques for Pictorial Applications, Blaser, A., Ed., Springer-Verlag,* New York, pp. 509-526.

[17] Stonebraker, M., Rubenstein, B. and Guttman, A., Application of Abstract Data Types and Abstract Indices to CAD Data, *Proceedings of the Annual Meeting Database Week,* San Jose, May 1983, pp. 107-115.

[18] Yamaguchi, K., Ohbo, N., Kunii, T. L., Kitagawa, H. and Harada, M., ELF: Extended Relational Model for Large, Flexible Picture Databases, *Proceedings of the Workshop on Picture Data Description and Management,* Aug. 1980, pp. 95-100.

Visual Database Systems
T.L. Kunii (Editor)
Elsevier Science Publishers B.V. (North-Holland)
© IFIP, 1989

A GRAPHICAL INTERFACE FORMALISM :
SPECIFYING NESTED RELATIONAL DATABASES

Geert-Jan HOUBEN
Eindhoven University of Technology
the Netherlands

Jan PAREDAENS
University of Antwerp
Belgium

An interface is considered as an automaton, for which the dynamics are represented by transitions on a set of states. Part of the actual state is currently represented by the screen. As such a program in R^1 represents the possible dialogue between the user and the system. An overview of R^1, a language for specifying interfaces, is given. R^1 is illustrated by specifying the R^2-interface, which is a graphical interface for handling nested relational data. The definition of the R^2-interface is such that queries on a database can be expressed in a way that suits the nested relational model, which means that objects at arbitrary levels can be specified directly, i.e. without referring to objects at other levels. Keywords : graphical interfaces; menus; icons; nested relational data; query languages; complex objects.

1. Introduction

In current database research there is a trend towards easier use of database systems. In the field of relational databases there has recently been a lot of attention to *nested* structures [1-8]. From this the Nested Relational Database Model (NRDM) has evolved, in which the constraint that databases have to be in First-Normal-Form has been relaxed. The basic difference between the classical Relational Database Model (RDM) and the NRDM is that, whereas in both models relations are sets of tuples, in the RDM the components of tuples have atomic values and in the NRDM the components may have structured values, which means that they may be relations themselves.

For the flat relations from the RDM there are a number of well-known formalisms for expressing *queries*. The move towards nested structures has led to the introduction of new formalisms suitable for expressing queries in a nested structure. An example of such a formalism is the *nested algebra* [9-13], which is an extension of the relational algebra. In [14,15] the authors studied the expressibility of the nested algebra.

The Verso model [16] has many of the features essential to handle nested relations. This model is a good step in the direction of the model of complex objects. In [17] a model was defined with a query formalism, the R^2-*algebra*, that not only has many of the features that make the other models useful. It also has operations to handle computable information with operations like aggregation and computation, and with a more general notion of selection. Also recursion is embedded in the model.

The main characteristic of the R^2-algebra however is the fact that the query formalism has been designed having in mind that queries on the database should be specified through a *graphical interface*. Recently, graphical query languages and graphical interfaces [18-20] are often suggested as an easy-to-use means of communicating with a database system.

The big advantage of a graphical interface is the intuitive way of specifying queries. This implies that systems offering such interfaces are *easier-to-use* by inexperienced users. Without a lot of training they are able to express queries themselves, since they do not need to learn languages that, because of their mathematical origin, are difficult to use for the average database user.

Using the advantages of the recent graphical techniques, like multiple windows, icons, pointing devices and several kinds of menus, operations can be specified directly without referring explicitly to the access path or the environment of the required values.

The R^2-algebra is designed with a graphical interface in mind. It is based on the nested algebra, which means that we want to define operations that have at least the power of the nested algebra. Besides giving the possibility of specifying operations at deeply *nested levels* in a direct way, this interface also has operations to compute *aggregates* and to apply *sequences* of operations recursively. Further there is an extension such that the *functions* used within operations like selection and aggregation (in order to compute the selection condition or the aggregation result) can be chosen not only from a set (menu) of standard functions, but also from a set of functions specified by the user himself. These latter functions are specified to the system by entering a program that the system is able to run whenever the function has to be applied.

Since operations in the R^2-algebra mainly are manipulations of schemes and since schemes are represented in the interface by *trees*, the operations in the interface are specified by means of clicking nodes in trees and of choosing options from menus. This implies that in order to express queries the user must manipulate trees such that trees are obtained that represent the resulting relations.

In this paper we use the language R^1 to define the manipulations in the interface needed to specify operations in the R^2-algebra. In R^1 it is described for each algebraic operation which menu *options* have to be chosen and which *nodes* have to be clicked, and how this affects the system's *state*. The system's state contains information about the relations known to the system. Furthermore it contains information on issues like which of the relations are represented on the screen.

The language R^1 can also be used to specify other interfaces. The strategy that we use with R^1 can easily be used for specifying other graphical interfaces. The big advantage of this language is the ease with which the usage of an interface can be described. Usually the formal definition of the system's operations is hard to understand. The task of the interface is to *abstract* from these difficult operations. This also implies that the definition of the use of the interface must be easy to understand.

Another advantage of the interface specification is the *independence* from the implementation of (in our case) the query formalism. In the specification of the R^2-interface we use very often strings. After we have defined how the two-dimensional figures (trees) are translated in (one-dimensional) strings, the manipulations of the trees are defined by the manipulations of the corresponding trees. This implies that we can easily choose other two-dimensional figures as representation of the relations without bothering about the specification of the operations.

As will become clear during the presentation of the R^2-algebra this algebra is likely to be extended to cover items like *complex objects*. Whenever attributes start living their own live, using user-defined operations (as with the selection and the aggregation), then they can be viewed as representations of complex objects. The hierarchical approach used within the NRDM is just a good point to start from. The specification of an interface for such a model for complex objects can be very much the same as for the R^2-interface, when R^1 is used to specify the interface.

In this paper the language R^1 for specifying graphical interfaces is described. The R^2-interface is described in section 2. In section 3 we introduce the language R^1 as necessary to understand the specification of the R^2-interface. There we also sketch the general idea of an R^1-specification. The basic operations of the R^2-interface are specified in section 4. The aggregation and the computation are covered in section 5, whereas the definition of sequences of operations and the (recursive) execution of sequences are subject of section 6.

2. R^2-interface

The purpose of this paper is to demonstrate R^1 by describing the R^2-interface in R^1. This interface is defined in [17].

The basic concepts of the R^2-algebra are analogous to those used in the Nested Algebra (NA). Both are related to the NRDM, where *relations* are viewed as sets of tuples that have as components either atomic data values or sets of tuples. The *structure* of a relation is defined by its scheme. A scheme is a list of attributes, where attributes are associated with a set of atomic data values (domain) or they are schemes themselves. Just like in the NA the operations in the R^2-algebra mainly use structural information, i.e. they mainly depend on the scheme. This is also the reason why we choose to represent relations by the representation of their scheme and to hold the corresponding instance in the background.

Now we will consider the concepts of the R^2-algebra. and their representation in R^1, in more detail.

A *scheme* of a relation is an identifier followed by a list of attributes enclosed within brackets, where an attribute is either *atomic* or *structured*. An atomic attribute is an identifier, called the name of that attribute. A structured attribute is a scheme, where the name of that scheme is called the name of the structured attribute. All identifiers (names) in a scheme must be different.

With every atomic attribute α a set, called its domain, $\text{dom}(\alpha)$ is associated, for instance the set of natural numbers. If $n(\alpha_1, .., \alpha_n)$ is a scheme λ with name n where

α_i is an attribute, then the domain of this scheme dom(λ) is equal to the Cartesian product of the attributes dom(α_1) $\bowtie$ .. $\bowtie$ dom(α_n). The set of *instances* of scheme λ, denoted by Inst(λ), is the set of finite subsets of dom(λ). The elements of an instance of scheme λ are called *tuples* over λ.

An example of a scheme with name *students* and with four attributes, two of which are structured (*addresses* and *exams*), is

$$students(name, addresses(street, nr, city), year, exams(subject, date, result)).$$

In the interface a scheme is represented by a *tree*, for which the nodes correspond to the attributes of the scheme. A directed edge of the tree from node x to node y denotes that the attribute corresponding to x is structured and that the attribute corresponding to y is an attribute of its list. A node will be labeled with the name of the corresponding attribute.

The above mentioned scheme would be represented like :

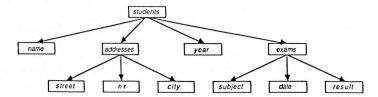

The representation of an instance could be arranged in the same tree-like manner. However, since the operations of the algebra mainly concern the schemes, we will not bother about the instances in this paper. An additional operation in the interface will be used to get the instance corresponding to a tree.

A possible R^2-representation of an instance of the above scheme could be :

students							
name	addresses			year	exams		
	street	nr	city		subject	date	result
John	Road	10	Town	1	Math	060888	8
	Avenue	7	Village				
Jim	Street	66	City	0			

The main advantage of the use of trees is the two-dimensional (graphical) nature of the objects that have to be manipulated. Attributes (at any nested level) can be specified in a *direct* way, which means that not, as in the NA, a path from the root has to specified. This makes it possible to reason about nested attributes, partial objects, rather independent of their environment, which makes the reasoning more intuitive.

In our model we have chosen to represent a *database* as a set of relations. We could have modeled a database as one nested relation (universal nested relation). By choosing for a set of relations we leave the user the freedom to specify what he wants. An additional advantage is the ease of defining different *defaults*, such as the representation of values, the operations allowed on the values and the user-defined functions and operations.

When formulating *queries* the starting point is a set of relations represented by a screen of trees (plus corresponding instances in background). From the menu of available operations the user chooses a sequence of operations in order to obtain a screen of trees that represent relations that contain the answer of the query. Every operation requires a number of arguments, among which the relation(s) on which the operation should be applied. This means that after choosing an operation, depending on the arity of the operation, one or two trees have to be pointed out. Depending on the operation, nodes in such a tree have to be clicked in order to specify attributes that play a role in the operation.

As an example we consider the query on the above relation where we want for every student his name and his addresses. Starting with the *students* tree on the screen the user first chooses the projection option from the menu containing all the possible operations. Then he clicks the *name* and *addresses* nodes and the system computes the new instance and shows the corresponding tree on the screen. After the user has entered a name for the new relation, *result* say, the relation with that name is represented on the screen and its instance contains the answer to the user's query.

3. Using R^1 for the Specification of the R^2-interface

Since we want to use R^1 for the specification of the R^2-interface we first have to pay attention to the different parts of that interface. Basicly there are four different aspects of the use of the R^2-interface.

1. The users must be able to apply the *operations* of the underlying R^2-algebra. This means that they have to specify which operation they want the system to apply and on which relation. The possibility to execute algebraic operations is the most important one, in the sense that nothing goes without it.

2. Except applying single algebraic operations it also has to be possible to define *sequences* of algebraic operations that can be applied as one operation. It is obvious that for expressing queries it has advantages to have powerful, predefined operations available to compose a query. With such a mechanism complex queries can be build from less complex queries in an easy way.

3. Another issue is the use of *windows* to hold the relations. When there are a lot of relations known in the system, it is obviously not sensible to just have them stored in one big pool of relations. This could mean for instance that they are all stored in one menu and that there is one screen with representations for those relations that are relevant for some query. If one uses multiple windows to arrange the (representations of) relations in small meaningful units, it is much easier to retrieve a relation while composing a query. For the specification of a query it is then possible to work on one window with all the relations that are relevant.

4. In order to make it possible for users to style the interface in the way that they think is preferable for their situation, they must have the means to style the *menus* as they like. This implies that they must be able to create new options in menus or to change them. When creating some new option they have to specify to the underlying system what to do when that option is chosen. This means that they have to tell the system what program to execute in that case.

We will now look at these four aspects and we will see in which way R^1 is helpful in the specification. This implies that we first introduce the relevant elements of the language. After that we will present the items of the *global system state* that we use to define the semantics of the expressions in R^1. For expressions related to the first two of the above aspects we describe the semantics in more detail than for the other two aspects, for which we only sketch how meaningful expressions (with straightforward semantics) can be constructed.

For the specification of the application of algebraic operations we basicly need three kinds of manipulations and therefore three kinds of expressions in R^1.

- The first kind of manipulation specifies the picking of an option from some menu. The R^1 expression [*Menu* ▷ *Option*] denotes the choice of the option *Option* from the menu *Menu*. This should imply that the system executes the task that corresponds to *Option*.

- In order to denote the clicking of a node in a tree visible on the screen, we use [*Tree!Node*]. This expression will mean that in the tree with name *Tree*, the name of a tree being the label of the root, the node labeled *Node* is clicked. This is necessary for the specification of the attributes of some relation that have to serve as parameters of an operation.

- The third kind of manipulation is the entering of a new label for a node in a tree computed by the system, but for which the label is not yet specified. For this we use the expression [*Tree*; *Node?Label*], where *Node* denotes the node of the tree *Tree* that will get *Label* as its label. This is important when new trees or attributes are created that will have to get a unique user-defined name.

As far as *sequences* are concerned two aspects seem relevant. Since we want the use of a (predefined) sequence of operations to be similar to that of a single operation we do not need additional expressions in R^1 for this aspect.

For the definition of a sequence the user has to specify all the operations in the right sequence on some *dummy* relations. The major difference with the application of single operations is that the system must know that of those dummy relations only the structure is important. This means that when the sequence is applied on some relation this relation must have a scheme with the same structure as the dummy relation, i.e. the names of the attributes can be different and the instance is completely irrelevant. So, for the definition of sequences we only have to define proper semantics for expressions using only the three elements of R^1 described above.

In the interface there are two things important about handling *windows*. First the user has to be able to group a number of (representations of) relations into one window and give it some unique window name. The second thing is that one has to be able to choose some window and make it the *active* window, i.e. the window that is visible on the screen. For the first issue we need the following expression in R^1 :

- For denoting the simultaneous clicking of a set of trees visible on the screen and creating a new window with exactly those trees, we use [*Setoftrees* $\Diamond$ *Window*]. This means that the trees that are elements of the set of trees *Setoftrees* become the trees of the window with name *Window*.

How the simultaneous clicking of a set of trees is implemented is not important here, as long as it stays within the rules that the semantics describe for the management of all the relations.

Now we consider the *menu* structure. For the creation of an option in some menu we use an expression in R^1 that makes the system know what to do when this specific option is chosen.

- The adding to the menu *Menu* of the option *Option*, where the choice of *Option* should lead to the execution of the program *Program*, is denoted by [*Menu* $\triangleleft$ *Program*; *Option*]. We assume that outside the interface a number of programs is available for the system to include within the interface if specified by the user.

In general we use (pull-down) menus that are available to the users (to choose options from) at any time. However sometimes we want to build in some restrictive use of a menu. For instance in the specification of a selection it is necessary to specify some selection function. This selection function has to be chosen from some menu of selection functions. It is feasible to restrict the possibility to choose options from that menu to the situation where a selection is being specified. We call these menus *temporary* menus, where temporary relates to the availability and not to the existence of the menu.

The *semantics* of the R^1-expressions are defined using a global system state in which we hold all the information that is important for the interface. The parts of the system state relate to those aspects that are considered important for the use of the interface (described above).

- MENU will be a function that assigns to each menu name the set of options that can be chosen from that menu. The domain of MENU will contain for example Operations and Windows. In MENU(Operations) we will have options like Union, Selection and Projection. TEMPORARY will be a subset of the domain of MENU denoting the menus that are temporary menus. AVAILABLE will be a subset of the domain of MENU denoting the menus that are available for the user to choose from : at least all the menus that are not temporary are available.

- RELATION will be a function that assigns to each scheme the instance corresponding to that scheme. The domain of RELATION will contain all those schemes that are known to the system and which can be shown on the screen. The range of RELATION holds all the instances that in general are held in the memory, but which can be represented on the screen.

- WINDOW will be a function that assigns to each window name the set of relations (schemes) that belong to that window. Every relation belongs to at most one window. ACTIVE will be a subset of the domain of WINDOW, such that ACTIVE holds those windows that are currently shown on the screen. SCREEN will be the set of all schemes that are in the WINDOW value of an element of ACTIVE.

- PROGRAM will be a function that assigns to each option in each menu a piece of program that the system can execute. The range of PROGRAM consists of all the pieces of program that the system can execute. This pool of programs is available outside the interface.

In the next three sections we consider the semantics of the application of algebraic operations and the definition and application (possibly recursive) of sequences of operations.

Here we will shortly go into the issues concerned with the use of windows and menus.

Since in this paper we do not consider the aspect of the creation of relations, i.e. we start from existing relations, we use *windows* to manage the available relations. It means that we have partitioned the relations across several windows and we have some windows that are currently *active*, i.e. together they build the screen. The list of available windows is held in the menu Windows.

In the Main menu a user can choose the option Create Window. Subsequently he has to click simultaneously a set of schemes shown on the screen, such that they can build a new window. The unique name of the window is specified by the user and the system then adds the window to the Windows menu and represents the window on the screen.

We will now specify this in R^1 using a small example. Conditions on (parts of) the global system state are stated between —— and ——. Such conditions are supposed to hold for the entire expression as long as they are not contradicted in new conditions. Note that ; denotes composition in R^1.

—— Main $\in$ AVAILABLE, Create Window $\in$ MENU(Main) ——
[Main $\triangleright$ Create Window];
—— $males(l_1) \in$ WINDOW(M), $females(l_2) \in$ WINDOW(F) ——
—— $\{M, F\} \subseteq$ SCREEN ——
—— $Persons \notin$ MENU(Windows) ——
[{ $males(l_1), females(l_2)$ } $\diamondsuit$ $Persons$]
—— $Persons \in$ MENU(Windows) ——
—— WINDOW($Persons$) = { $males(l_1), females(l_2)$ } ——
—— $males(l_1) \notin$ WINDOW(M), $females(l_2) \notin$ WINDOW(F) ——
—— $Persons \in$ SCREEN ——

The deletion of a window is performed by choosing the Delete Window option in the Main menu and subsequently choosing the desired window from the Windows menu.

By choosing the Active Window option from the Main menu the user is able to make a window appear on the screen by choosing the desired window from the Windows menu.

The specification in R^1 of these two interface operations is straightforward.

As far as *menus* are concerned we are only interested in the creation of a new option in a menu. We illustrate this with an example in which a new selection function has to be added to the (temporary) menu Selection Functions. A selection function is a small algorithm (*program*) that the system uses as one of the parameters in order to execute some selection. We assume that LT is a program that verifies the "less than" relationship and that *LT* is known to the system.

—— Main ∈ AVAILABLE, Create Option ∈ MENU(Main) ——
[Main ▷ Create Option];
—— Selection Functions ∈ MENU(Windows) ——
[Windows ▷ Selection Functions];
—— Selection Functions ∈ AVAILABLE ——
[Selection Functions ◁ *LT* ; *Less Than*]
—— *Less Than* ∈ MENU(Selection Functions) ——
—— PROGRAM(*Less Than*, Selection Functions) = *LT* ——

The modification of an option, i.e. specifying a new underlying program, is done in a similar way. The deletion of an option is performed by simply choosing the Delete Option option from the Main menu and then clicking the desired option.

4. Basic R^2-operations

In this section we will specify in R^1 the basic R^2 operations, by which we mean those operations that come from the nested algebra : union, difference, join, projection, selection, renaming, nest and unnest. The formal definition of the operators of the R^2-algebra is given in [17].

First the binary operations which are the *union*, the *difference* and the *join*. The definition of these operators is a straightforward generalization of the nested algebra [14], which implies that the operation can be applied at *any level*, not just at the first level.

In order to specify such a binary operation (on the screen) the user first has to specify which kind of *operation* he is interested in. This implies that in the Operations menu the operation is chosen. After the system knows that the operation is a union, say, the user has to specify the *arguments*. For specifying an entire relation the user has to click the root of the tree representing the relation. If the user wants to specify some structured attribute as argument of the operation then the node representing that attribute has to be clicked. Note that the order in which these two arguments are specified is important. The system now knows that a new relation has to be computed, which is either the union of two given relations or a relation with a new attribute that is the union of two given attributes. Therefore it computes the scheme and the instance of this new relation and it represents the scheme on the screen, i.e. a new tree appears. Note that at this stage the scheme is not yet complete since the unique name for the relation (the root of the tree) is not yet specified. This implies that the user's last activity is to enter that *name*. If the union is nested, i.e. a new attribute is constructed, then the name for that new attribute has to be specified also.

We assume here that the user has indicated to the system that an algebraic operation is going to be specified by choosing the right option from the Main menu. The system will then make the Operations menu available. A second assumption is that the argument relations are held in a window that is visible on the screen and that the resulting relation becomes visible within that window. In the specification we omit the conditions related to those assumptions.

We will now specify a *union* in R^1, again stating conditions on the values of the components of the system state between —— and ——.

Consider two relations r_1 and r_2 with scheme $n_1(l)$ and $n_2(l)$ resp. and with instance v_1 and v_2 resp.. Suppose we want to express $UNI[n_1(l); n_2(l); n_3]\,(r_1, r_2)$, which denotes the union such that the result has scheme $n_3(l)$ and value v_3 (equal to $v_1 \cup v_2$). We use $\square$ as a special label for a node for which a new name has to be specified.

—— Union $\in$ MENU(Operations) ——
—— $\{n_1(l), n_2(l)\} \subseteq$ SCREEN ——
—— RELATION$(n_1(l)) = v_1$, RELATION$(n_2(l)) = v_2$ ——
[Operations $\triangleright$ Union];
$[n_1!n_1]$; $[n_2!n_2]$;
—— $\square(l) \in$ SCREEN, RELATION$(\square(l)) = v_3$ ——
$[\square; \square?n_3]$
—— $\square(l) \notin$ dom(RELATION) ——
—— $n_3(l) \in$ SCREEN, RELATION$(n_3(l)) = v_3$ ——

For this union it is required that both the argument relations are represented at the screen at the start of the operation. The result of the first three manipulations is that dom(RELATION) and SCREEN are augmented with $\square(l)$ and that RELATION$(\square(l))$ equals the instance of the union of the relations with schemes $n_1(l)$ and $n_2(l)$. The fourth manipulation replaces in the scheme with name $\square$ the label $\square$ by n_3, such that $n_3(l)$ is the scheme of $UNI[n_1(l); n_2(l); n_3](r_1, r_2)$ and that RELATION$(n_3(l))$ is its instance.

Note that again the conditions on MENU, RELATION and SCREEN that hold at the start are supposed to hold as long as they do not contradict the new conditions. For instance, $n_1(l)$ stays in SCREEN during the entire operation.

In [17] the exact definition of the binary operations at a *nested level* is not given, but with [15] it is easy to define $UNI[n(l); n_1; n_2; n_3; n']$ to denote the nested union of the attributes n_1 and n_2 within scheme $n(l)$, such that a new relation is computed with scheme $n'(l')$, where in l' n_3 is the new attribute that contains the union of n_1 and n_2.

Suppose r is a relation with scheme $n(l)$ and instance v, where r' equal to $UNI[n(l); n_1; n_2; n_3; n'](r)$ is to be computed. Let the scheme of r' be $n'(l')$ and its instance v'. Suppose l'' is l' with n_3 replaced by $\square_2$. Then the specification of the union is defined by :

—— Union $\in$ MENU(Operations) ——
—— $n(l) \in$ SCREEN, RELATION$(n(l)) = v$ ——
[Operations $\triangleright$ Union];
$[n!n_1]$; $[n!n_2]$;
—— $\square_1(l'') \in$ SCREEN, RELATION$(\square_1(l'')) = v'$ ——
$[\square_1; \square_2?n_3]$
—— $\square_1(l'') \notin$ dom(RELATION) ——
—— $\square_1(l') \in$ SCREEN, RELATION$(\square_1(l')) = v'$ ——
$[\square_1; \square_1?n']$
—— $\square_1(l') \notin$ dom(RELATION) ——

— $n'(l') \in$ SCREEN, RELATION$(n'(l')) = v'$ —

So the difference with the first union is that, since in the second and third manipulation nodes in the same tree are clicked, the nested union is computed and a new name for the new attribute is required.

As an illustration of the nested union we consider in the next figure the application of the union

$$UNI[parents(sons(child), daughters(child));$$

$$sons; daughters; children; persons]$$

on a relation represented by the tree with name *parents*. Its result would be a relation represented by the tree with name *persons*.

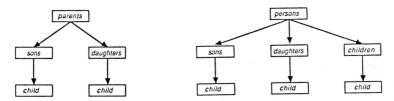

The specification for the difference and the join are basicly the same, however for the join the R^2-algebra specifies other conditions for the schemes of the arguments, i.e. they may not contain attributes with the same name.

For the *projection* a similar strategy is followed. A projection is such that one specifies a number of nodes in the tree of a relation, where the nodes represent the attributes that one wants to have in the scheme of the new relation. These nodes need not to be all at the first level, as in the nested algebra. However there is a *constraint* on which nodes can be specified [17]. It is not allowed to project out nodes without projecting out all their descendants.

The definition can be such that the number of nodes to be specified is minimized. Here we will use, as in [17], the rule that for every node clicked the corresponding attribute, its predecessor and its descendants are specified to occur in the new scheme.

Since the number of nodes to specify is not fixed the end of the specification has to be specified (using the EOL option in the Specification menu, say).

Let us consider the projection $PRO[n(l); lan; n']$ on the relation r with scheme $n(l)$ and instance v, where the result is r' with scheme $n'(l')$ and instance v'. Suppose $lan = n_1, .., n_k$.

— Projection $\in$ MENU(Operations), EOL $\in$ MENU(Specification) —
— $n(l) \in$ SCREEN, RELATION$(n(l)) = v$ —
[Operations $\triangleright$ Projection];
$[n!n_1]; .. [n!n_k]$;
[Specification $\triangleright$ EOL];
— $\Box(l') \in$ SCREEN, RELATION$(\Box(l')) = v'$ —
$[\Box; \Box?n']$

—— $\Box(l') \notin$ dom(RELATION) ——
—— $n'(l') \in$ SCREEN, RELATION$(n'(l')) = v'$ ——

As an illustration of a projection we consider applying

$$PRO[studs\text{-}scheme; name, city; citizens]$$

on the *students* relation of section 2, where we use *studs-scheme* as a shorthand for the scheme of *students*. The next figure shows the tree of the resulting relation.

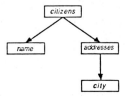

The main characteristic of the *selection* results from the possibility in the R^2-algebra of choosing the selection function from a set of *user-defined* functions. This implies a (temporary) menu of selection functions. For every option in that menu the system has an algorithm that, given some attributes for the function's parameters, serves as a selection criterion.

Let us consider the selection $SEL[n(l); f; lan; n']$ on the relation r with scheme $n(l)$ and instance v, where the result r' has scheme $n'(l)$ and instance v'. Suppose $lan = n_1, .., n_k$ and f a function with k parameters, such that with $n_1, .., n_k$ for these parameters a selection function is specified.

—— Selection $\in$ MENU(Operations), $f \in$ MENU(Selection Functions) ——
—— $n(l) \in$ SCREEN, RELATION$(n(l)) = v$ ——
[Operations $\triangleright$ Selection];
[Selection Functions $\triangleright f$];$[n!n_1]; ..[n!n_k]$;
—— $\Box(l) \in$ SCREEN, RELATION$(\Box(l)) = v'$ ——
$[\Box; \Box?n']$
—— $\Box(l) \notin$ dom(RELATION) ——
—— $n'(l) \in$ SCREEN, RELATION$(n'(l)) = v'$ ——

Note that we suppose that the system is able to deduce from the selection function the number of nodes to be clicked, so that it is not required to choose EOL to specify the end of the list.

If f is a function that checks whether a value is equal to 1, then the application of $SEL[studs\text{-}scheme; f; year; first\text{-}year\text{-}students]$ would result in a relation with exactly the same tree as the *students* tree, except for the root which is now labeled *first-year-students*.

An other operation is the *renaming*. It is used to substitute given attribute names by new names. This is achieved by clicking some nodes and by then entering new names for those nodes. We choose to do this for several nodes at a time.

Consider $REN[n(l); lan; lan'; n']$ on the relation r with scheme $n(l)$ and instance v, resulting in r' with scheme $n'(l')$, where l' equals l with the attributes from $lan =$

$n_1, .., n_k$ replaced by the corresponding ones from $lan' = n'_1, .., n'_k$.

— Renaming $\in$ MENU(Operations), EOL $\in$ MENU(Specification) —
— $n(l) \in$ SCREEN, RELATION($n(l)$) = v —
[Operations $\triangleright$ Renaming];
$[n!n_1]; ..[n!n_k];$[Specification $\triangleright$ EOL];
— $\square(l'') \in$ SCREEN, RELATION($\square(l'')$) = v' —
$[\square; \square_1?n'_1]; ..[\square; \square_k?n'_k];$
— $\square(l'') \notin$ dom(RELATION) —
— $\square(l') \in$ SCREEN, RELATION($\square(l')$) = v' —
$[\square; \square?n']$
— $\square(l') \notin$ dom(RELATION) —
— $n'(l') \in$ SCREEN, RELATION($n'(l')$) = v' —

The application of

$$REN[studs\text{-}scheme; year, subject; period, task; task\text{-}students]$$

on the *students* relation would lead to a relation with the following tree.

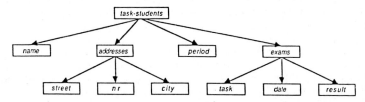

Two operations typical for the nested algebra are the nest and the unnest. With the *nest* it is possible to construct, given a number of attributes from one list of attributes, a new structured attribute with those attributes as its attributes.

Consider the nest $NES[n(l); lan; an; n']$ on relation r with scheme $n(l)$ and instance v. The result r' will have scheme $n'(l')$ and instance v'. Suppose $lan = n_1, .., n_k$ and l'' is l' with an (the new attribute's name) replaced by $\square_2$.

— Nest $\in$ MENU(Operations), EOL $\in$ MENU(Specification) —
— $n(l) \in$ SCREEN, RELATION($n(l)$) = v —
[Operations $\triangleright$ Nest];
$[n!n_1]; ..[n!n_k];$[Specification $\triangleright$ EOL];
— $\square_1(l'') \in$ SCREEN, RELATION($\square_1(l'')$) = v' —
$[\square_1; \square_2?an];$
— $\square_1(l'') \notin$ dom(RELATION) —
— $\square_1(l') \in$ SCREEN, RELATION($\square_1(l')$) = v' —
$[\square_1; \square_1?n']$
— $\square_1(l') \notin$ dom(RELATION) —
— $n'(l') \in$ SCREEN, RELATION($n'(l')$) = v' —

Consider the application of

$$NES[studs\text{-}scheme; year, exams; education; persons]$$

on the *students* relation. The resulting tree is shown in the next figure.

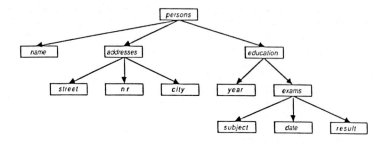

Using the *unnest* it is possible to substitute for a structured attribute the list of its attributes. So, consider $UNN[n(l); u; n']$.

—— Unnest ∈ MENU(Operations) ——
—— $n(l)$ ∈ SCREEN, RELATION$(n(l))$ = v ——
[Operations ▷ Unnest]; $[n!u]$;
—— $\square(l')$ ∈ SCREEN, RELATION$(\square(l'))$ = v' ——
$[\square; \square?n']$;
—— $\square(l')$ ∉ dom(RELATION) ——
—— $n'(l')$ ∈ SCREEN, RELATION$(n'(l'))$ = v' ——

The application of $UNN[studs\text{-}scheme; addresses; persons]$ would lead to a relation with the next tree.

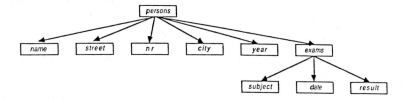

5. Aggregation and Computation

Two operations in the R^2-algebra that do not originate from the nested algebra are the aggregation and the computation. These are operations that do not handle structural information as in the nested algebra, but they concern *computable* information [14]. The aggregation computes new values based on values of a structured attribute, whereas the new values of the computation are based on values of a tuple.

An *aggregation* is defined by giving a number of attributes from the list of some structured attribute α. For every value of α, which is a set of tuples, the multiset of subtuples over these attributes is computed. Using some aggregation function a new value is created from this multiset. Typical aggregation functions would be functions that compute the sum or the average of a set of numbers. The new values become values of a new attribute, for which the node is a sibling of that of α.

Consider the aggregation $AGG[n(l); f; lan; an; n']$ on relation r with scheme $n(l)$ and instance v. Let f be an aggregation function, which can have the attributes from $lan = n_1, .., n_k$ as parameters and which produces values of the new attribute an. The result r' will have scheme $n'(l')$ and instance v'. Let l'' be l' with an replaced by $\square_2$.

—— Aggregation $\in$ MENU(Operations) ——
—— $f \in$ MENU(Aggregation Functions) ——
—— $n(l) \in$ SCREEN, RELATION$(n(l)) = v$ ——
[Operations $\triangleright$ Aggregation];
[Aggregation Functions $\triangleright f$]; $[n!n_1]; ..[n!n_k]$;
—— $\square_1(l'') \in$ SCREEN, RELATION$(\square_1(l'')) = v'$ ——
$[\square_1; \square_2? an]$;
—— $\square_1(l'') \notin$ dom(RELATION) ——
—— $\square_1(l') \in$ SCREEN, RELATION$(\square_1(l')) = v'$ ——
$[\square_1; \square_1? n']$;
—— $\square_1(l') \notin$ dom(RELATION) ——
—— $n'(l') \in$ SCREEN, RELATION$(n'(l')) = v'$ ——

If *sum* is a function that computes for a set of numbers the sum of those numbers, then the result of $AGG[studs\text{-}scheme; sum; result; total; student\text{-}results]$ would be a tree like:

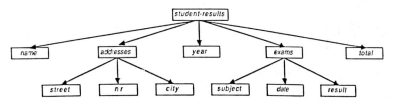

As in the R^2-algebra we require that the parameter attributes of the aggregation and its result attribute are atomic. The system should be able to interpret a choice from the Aggregation Functions menu in such a way that a user-defined algorithm is used to compute new values with the specific attributes as parameters to the algorithm.

The *computation* operation is a variant of the aggregation where a new value is computed based on one tuple rather than on a set of tuples. This implies that the new attribute becomes a sibling attribute of the attributes, that are specified as the parameters of the computation function, instead of a sibling of their parent.

The specification is analogous to that of the aggregation using the Computation option in the Operations menu and using the Computation Functions menu.

6. Recursion

With the previously introduced operations the user is able to specify single algebraic operations. The interface must supply the user with the possibility to specify *sequences* of operations that can be applied *recursively*, thus specifying recursive expressions. This implies the ability to specify sequences of operations and to specify that sequences are applied recursively.

For the recursion a *stop* criterion is required. As in [17] we define that a sequence of operations is executed again and again as long as the instances do not stay unchanged. In our interface this means that the recursion is stopped, whenever an execution of the sequence does not change SCREEN and RELATION any more. We could have defined other stop criteria and a menu from which the desired criterion could be picked, but we will use only the above criterion.

Applying a sequence of operations recursively is a special case of applying a sequence of operations. A sequence can have relations (i.e. schemes) as parameters in order to be able to apply sequences to relations, that are different but that have schemes on which the same operations can be applied, i.e. relations with the same structure.

In order to *define* a sequence one must switch from normal mode to the mode in which sequences can be defined, by choosing the Define Sequence option from the Main menu. Subsequently operations are specified, just as described before. The system knows that it only has to deal with the schemes, since the instances play a role only at the time of the actual application. The sequence definition is ended by choosing EOL from the Specification menu. The system then asks for a name of the sequence and stores the sequence (or rather the corresponding program) such that if that name is chosen from the Sequences menu the system knows what to do.

In [17] it was defined that sequences started with sets of relations and ended with sets of relations, thus being able to consider only relevant relations, not intermediate results. In the interface this is specified by the state of SCREEN at the beginning and at the end of the program definition, where the manipulation of windows is used to erase trees from the screen. This implies during the definition phase that for the elements of SCREEN the RELATION value is not defined (i.e. they have the value $\perp$, say).

For the *execution* of a sequence (not recursively) the Execute Sequence option from the Main menu has to be chosen and then the desired sequence has to be specified in Sequences. Note that the state of SCREEN must be such that the relations represented on the screen correspond to the schemes that were in SCREEN at the beginning of the definition of that sequence.

Now the system is able to compute new relations according to the sequence, thus altering SCREEN and RELATION. The new trees should then represent the relations in which the user was interested.

For the *recursive* execution the specification is the same, except for the choice of Recursive Sequence from the Main menu. With the recursion the state of SCREEN at the end of one execution of the sequence must be such that for another execution SCREEN has the proper starting value. Usually this requires some renaming of relations, i.e. replacing old trees by new trees with old names.

Let us consider the sequence s that starts from two relations with schemes $n_1(l_1)$ and $n_2(l_2)$ and that produces a new relation with scheme $n_3(l_3)$, that is renamed to $n_2(l_2)$, whereas the original $n_2(l_2)$ is renamed to $n_1(l_1)$. Suppose v_1 and v_2 are the instances corresponding to $n_1(l_1)$ and $n_2(l_2)$ at the start and suppose v_3 corresponds to $n_3(l_3)$.

Executing this sequence once is specified as :

— Execute Sequence $\in$ MENU(Main), $s \in$ MENU(Sequences) —
— $\{n_1(l_1), n_2(l_2)\}$ = SCREEN —
— RELATION$(n_1(l_1))$ = v_1, RELATION$(n_2(l_2))$ = v_2 —
[Main $\triangleright$ Execute Sequence];
[Sequences $\triangleright$ s]
— $\{n_1(l_1), n_2(l_2)\}$ = SCREEN —
— RELATION$(n_1(l_1))$ = v_2, RELATION$(n_2(l_2))$ = v_3 —

If we suppose that s could be applied to two relations with the trees shown in the next figure, then the application of s would not change anything on the screen, however the corresponding instances have probably changed.

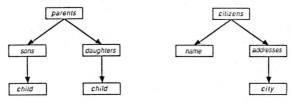

The only difference of recursive execution is the choice of Recursive Sequence. The resulting state of SCREEN and RELATION is such that another application of s would not change anything.

At the moment the interface does not supply the user with the possibility of applying sequences to *parts* of relations. The idea of that generalization is that if a sequence requires a scheme with a specific structure, then the sequence can also be applied to relations with that scheme as subscheme. At instance level this implies that the system has to compute a resulting instance starting from the instance with every value of that subscheme considered separately.

7. Conclusions

The language R^1 for the specification of *graphical interfaces* is introduced. Any interface is considered as an automaton, for which the dynamics are represented by transitions on a set of states. Part of the actual state is currently represented by the screen. As such a specification in R^1 represents the possible dialogue between the user and the system.

Using R^1 a graphical interface for *nested relational databases* is described. The organization of the information within the system is specified (MENU, RELATION, WINDOW, PROGRAM). The usage of the interface is described by defining the semantics of several kinds of manipulations, like clicking on the screen, choosing from menus and entering data from the keyboard. All in all we have specified a uniform way of communicating with the database system. This uniform way of handling the data within the system makes it easy for non-experienced users to work with the system through this interface.

Many of the *essential* features for graphical interfaces of database systems [18] are integrated within the R^2-interface. Queries are specified by the user in a *piecemeal* manner. With the information concerning the structure of the database always on the *screen*, the user formulates queries by constructing new relations using basic operations from the underlying formalism. In this way the user is able to express *complex* queries from the R^2-algebra in an intuitive and uniform way.

The strategy that we have followed with R^1 was to first define one-dimensional representations for the two-dimensional figures that are shown on the screen and that give the user insight into the information currently held in the system. Then the manipulations that the user is able to execute are defined by specifying their implications for the system's state. The basic purpose of R^1 is to specify the interface's *functionality*. An additional advantage of the use of the one-dimensional formalism is the possibility of telling in an unambiguous way what the interface must do without already designing the lay-out of screens and other non-functional features.

When specifying graphical interfaces (for database systems) the need for a language like R^1 is very obvious. In the design phase of such an interface one first of all wants to specify the *functionality* of the system. At that moment one does not want to bother very much about the figures on the screen but one wants to specify which information is represented on the screen. Furthermore it is important to specify which manipulations are possible and the effects that they cause.

Doing this in this uniform way makes it much easier for the designer to test the functionality by building *prototypes* and ask future user's to try to use this prototype for the work that they want to be able to do with the real system. Also specifications like these are much better to use when the actual implementation has to be made and this job has to be done by several people. With this formalism the specifications for the different tasks of the implementors can be stated in a more *intuitive* but *precise* way. Discussing an interface design is always easier using specification in a rather formal language. However the language is intuitive enough to be able to use it with future users that do not have any formal mathematical background.

Currently, one of the authors is engaged in a project to extend the database model used here to incorporate *complex objects*. The new model should not only allow for formulating queries but also for formulating updates in a uniform way. By viewing the nested attributes as complex objects, each with their own operations, the modeling power increases. Note that many existing implementations of *object-oriented* databases map the object-oriented systems to relational databases. Since however in the NRDM sets are a key issue, it is much cleaner to map complex objects to nested relational databases than to flat relations.

The big advantage is the increased embedding of *dynamics* within the database, thus being able to model the behaviour of real-world objects. One of the main items will be the integration of data manipulation and programming. This idea is in the R^2-interface already illustrated by the aggregation. When we have a language in which data definition, data manipulation and general computation are integrated in a uniform way, then the applications are much easier to design and to use. If we also have incorporated complex objects, then we are able to work at a higher level of abstraction, which also benefits a rapid design of database systems. Because of this approach prototyping will not cause the implementation to change completely.

For this model we can use an interface which is very similar to the R^2-interface. The specification in R^1 will therefore be very analogous to the one in this paper.

An important extension will be that MENU will be structured in the same way as the information is structured. Every attribute will get its own menu's with possible operations. Whereas in the R^2-interface the selection functions are held centrally, they can be made dependent on the attributes in the extended approach. Giving each attribute its own set of operations it is much easier to model the behaviour of complex real-world objects.

Also the introduction of operations for the modeling of updates will not cause any problems. We only have to add these operations to MENU and to make sure that the system knows how to interpret such operations. Using R^1 this can be solved in the same way as with the query formalism. One can define exactly how the system's state changes.

It must be clear that a language like R^1 can serve as a clean formalism for the *specification* of (graphical) interfaces. A *system independent* formalism like this can also help to make an integration between the system and its interfaces. During the design of the system a specification in R^1 of the necessary interfaces can help to *guide* the designers towards a completely integrated, though efficient system. Furthermore the design of an interface can benefit from a formalism like this because of the future user's ability to evaluate the specification (or the prototype) and to suggest improvements.

References

[1] Thomas, S.J. and Fisher, P.C., Nested Relational Structures, in : Kanellakis, P.C., (ed.), Advances in Computing Research III, The Theory of Databases, (JAI Press, 1986) pp. 269-307.

[2] Schek, H.J. and Scholl, M.H., The Relational Model with Relation-Valued Attributes, (Information Systems, Vol. 11, No. 2, 1986) pp. 137-147.

[3] Scholl, M.H., Theoretical Foundation of Algebraic Optimization Utilizing Unnormalized Relations, in : Ausiello, G. and Atzeni, P., (eds.), Proc. 1st ICDT, (Lecture Notes in Computer Science, Vol. 243, Springer Verlag, 1987) pp. 380-396.

[4] Scholl, M.H., Paul, H.B. and Schek, H.J., Supporting Flat Relations by a Nested Relational Kernel, in : Proc. 13th VLDB, (1987) pp. 137-146.

[5] Roth, M.A., Korth, H.F. and Silberschatz, A., Theory of Non-First-Normal-Form Relational Databases, (Tech. Rep. TR-84-36 (Revised January 1986), University of Texas, Austin, 1986).

[6] Pistor, P. and Andersen, F., Designing a Generalized NF^2 Model with an SQL-Type Language Interface, in : Proc. 12th VLDB, (1986) pp. 278-288.

[7] Kitagawa, H. and Kunii, T.L., Form Transformer - Formal Aspects of Table Nests Manipulation -, in : Proc. 15th Hawaii Int. Conference on System Sciences (Vol.2), (1982) pp. 132-141.

[8] Arisawa, H., Moriya, K. and Miura, T., Operations and the Properties on Non-First-Normal Form Relational Databases, in : Proc. 9th VLDB, (1983) pp. 197-204.

[9] Van Gucht, D., On the Expressive Power of the Extended Relational Algebra for the Unnormalized Relational Model, in : Proc. ACM SIGACT-SIGMOD-SIGART Symposium on Principles of Database Systems, (1987) pp. 302-312.

[10] Paredaens, J. and Van Gucht, D., Possibilities and Limitations of Using Flat Operators in Nested Algebra Expressions, in : Proc. ACM SIGACT-SIGMOD-SIGART Symposium on Principles of Database Systems, (1988) pp. 29-38.

[11] Ozsoyoglu, G., Ozsoyoglu, Z.M. and Matos, V., Extending Relational Algebra and Relational Calculus with Set-Valued Attributes and Aggregate Functions, (ACM TODS, Vol. 12, No. 4, 1987) pp. 566-592.

[12] Gyssens, M. and Van Gucht, D., The Powerset Operator as an Algebraic Tool for Understanding Least Fixpoint Semantics in the Context of Nested Relations, (Tech. Rep. 233, Indiana University, Bloomington, 1987).

[12] Gyssens, M. and Van Gucht, D., The Powerset Algebra as a Result of Adding Programming Constructions to the Nested Relational Algebra, in : Proc. SIGMOD Conference on Management of Data, (1988) pp. 225-232.

[14] Houben, G.J., Paredaens, J. and Tahon, D., Expressing Structured Information using the Nested Relational Algebra : An Overview, in : Casas, I., (ed.), Proc. 8th SCCC Int. Conference on Computer Science, Santiago, (1988) pp. 291-303.

[15] Houben, G.J., Paredaens, J. and Tahon, D., The Nested Relational Algebra : A Tool to Handle Structured Information, (Tech. Rep. CSN 88/04, University of Technology, Eindhoven, 1987).

[16] Abiteboul, S. and Bidoit, N., Non First Normal Form Relations : An Algebra Allowing Data Restructuring, (Journal of Computer and System Sciences, Vol. 33, 1986) pp. 361-393.

[17] Houben, G.J. and Paredaens, J., The R^2-Algebra : An Extension of an Algebra for Nested Relations, (Tech. Rep. CSN 87/20, University of Technology, Eindhoven, 1988).

[18] Kim, H.J., Graphical Interfaces for Database Systems : A Survey, in : Proc. 1986 Mountain Regional ACM Conference, (1986).

[19] Kim, H.J. Korth, H.F. and Silberschatz, A., Picasso : A Graphical Query Language, (Tech. Rep. TR-85-30 (Revised October 1986), University of Texas, Austin, 1986).

[20] Kim, H.J. and Korth, H.F., Psycho : A Graphical Language for Supporting Schema Evolution in Object-Oriented Databases, in : Proc. 3th Annual User System Interface Conference (USICON88), (1988).

Visual Database Systems
T.L. Kunii (Editor)
Elsevier Science Publishers B.V. (North-Holland)
© IFIP, 1989

ESCHER - Interactive, Visual Handling of Complex Objects in the Extended NF^2-Database Model

Lutz M. Wegner

FG Informatik, FB Mathematik
Gh - Universität Kassel
D-3500 Kassel, West Germany

Abstract. The extended NF^2 data model permits structured values (sub-tables, lists, tuples) to be included in relations. It is thus well suited to represent complex objects for non-standard applications. To ease the handling of these objects for simple tasks, an interactive interface is under development which uses a visual representation of NF^2 tables. This paper discusses the principal design issues and experiences with the working prototype.

Key words. non first normal form relations, complex objects, graphical interface, prototyping, recursive structures

1. Introduction

The *extended NF^2 data model* [4, 5, 6, 12] permits four basic types of attribute values: *(multi)sets*, *lists*, *tuples* and *atomic* values in arbitrary depth of nesting. The resulting tables are thus not in 1. Normal Form (NF^2: *N*on *F*irst *N*ormal *F*orm). Structured values are called *complex objects* as opposed to *atomic objects* which are formed from the usual types like *integer, real, string*, etc. and user defined unstructured types like *date* or *time*.

It is called the *extended* NF^2 data model in contrast to the 'pure' NF^2 data model [1, 9, 13, 18] which only permits nested tables (relations with relation valued attributes). Here, we only consider the extended NF^2 data model.

The following example shows a table MeetingsW48 (meetings in the 48th week) with the corresponding schema Meetings. The participants of the individual meetings form a sub-table with attributes NAME (string) and TEL (here declared as integer).

Departing from the "flat" tables of the classical relational database systems thus permits the aggregation of objects according to their contextual relation. This applies to view, query, manipulation and storage, provided the internal model supports this aggregation as well. For non-standard applications, e.g. in a CAD/CAM environment where geometrical data are to be manipulated (cf. [5]), the approach is expected to yield increases in productivity on the user side and performance gains in the execution. Office automation is seen as another application where structured forms may be mapped into corresponding tables.

Research supported by IBM Heidelberg Scientific Center
Author's address: Gesamthochschule Kassel - Universität, FB 17, AVZ, Postfach 10 13 80, D3500 Kassel, FRG

A disadvantage of the extended NF^2 data model are the increased demands on the user in formulating nested SQL-queries. This is an initial experience with the *AIM-P* (*A*dvanced *I*nformation *M*anagement - *P*rototyp) and its query language *HDBL* under development at the IBM Heidelberg Scientific Center. In many situations, however, a visual interface with a restricted set of operations would suffice. A typical example might be a plant floor where naive users (workers) visually review and adjust robot movements.

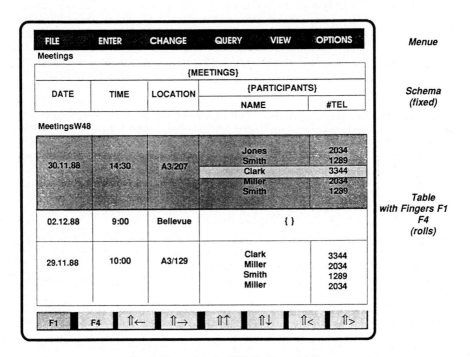

Fig.1: Example of a NF2 Table and Schema

The system presented here introduces such a visual, graphics-based interface. In general, graphical interfaces to database systems are quite common these days (cf. [2, 3, 8, 10, 11, 14, 16, 19, 20, 21, 22]). At present, design evaluations for visual database systems are being undertaken (cf. [17]). To our knowledge, however, no other prototype has been developed for the extended NF^2 data model. The closest similar approaches are the *FORMAL* development at IBM's Los Angeles Scientific Center [19] and the work by Kitagawa, Kunii and others on the form-based user interface of NF^2 relations and its prototype development [10, 11]. Since implementing a full relational DBMS would clearly surpass our resources, the system here is to provide a restricted set of options. Thus, it resembles in many ways more a spread sheet than a database system. Supplemented with a suitable exchange protocol, however, it could act as an off-line front-end to a full NF^2 DBMS.

Historically speaking, the system was born out of the need to provide a test environment for a duplicates elimination algorithm for AIM-P. The latter DBMS runs on a mainframe to which no access existed within the author's university. Thus it was decided to create a small rudimentary system on a workstation. To permit porting of the basic algorithm to AIM-P at a later time, the system was written in PASCAL which is the implementation language of AIM-P. Given the fact that most modern PASCAL dialects provide powerful graphics packages, the decision to "go graphics" was obvious.

By restricting the functionality and with the freedom (the duty) of writing the system from scratch, the intention was to make the system a test vehicle for new ideas. One idea was to use self-referencing (recursive) methods to implement parts of the system. The principle is not entirely new [15] and is used e.g. to bootstrap compilers written in a subset of their own source language. Fairly trivial uses of this technique are in treating schemas as tuples of a schema table and in storing all system parameters and messages (error windows, drop-down menues, etc.) as NF^2 tables which faciliates porting the system to a foreign language environment.

More demanding uses are in mapping internal data structures into NF^2 tables. Examples are fingers (structured cursors), window contents, and index structures. In particular, a bootstrap method which possibly uses interpretable operation scripts (procedures) as attri-bute values of a bootstrap table is a challanging perspective. Because of these intensions, the system was named after the famous Dutch graphical artist *M.C. Escher* (1898-1972), whose work depicts these self-reflecting, "impossible" worlds [7].

2. User Interface and Functions

ESCHER is to provide visual presentation and interactive manipulation of objects within the extended NF^2 model. It relies on *colors* to guide the user. Bit mapped graphics are not needed *per se*, but are introduced through user demands in comfort which ask for zooming in order to have a condensed, full view of the tables which tend to become quite large ho-rizontally.

Colors are used to underlay objects. Colored objects are said to have a *finger* pointing to them. Basically, a finger is the analogon to a cursor in a text editor. The idea is then to use fingers to browse and edit NF^2 tables in the same way a user would operate with a cursor in a text. Note, however, that a finger always encompasses an objekt as a whole, i.e. an atomic value, a set, a list, or a tuple.

Several fingers can coexist in a table or schema. However, only one finger can be *active* at any one time. Identification of the active finger is possible through blinking, intense video, or similar features. Each finger has a different color and *finger key* assigned. The function keys F1, F2, ... available on most computer keyboards provide a handy association for using them as finger keys. The so called *finger line* at the bottom of the screen lists all exi-sting fingers using the Fi, Fj, ... abbreviation and the assigned colors. Figure 1 above and the following next two figures show two fingers (F1 and F4).

Each table has by default a "colorless" finger F0 assigned. This finger becomes active as the table is loaded. Additional fingers are created through a key combination or from a drop-down menue. They are forked off from the active finger and thus point to the same object initially. An object with two or more fingers on it is shown in white. The correspon-ding fingers in the finger line alternate from white to their associated color and back. If

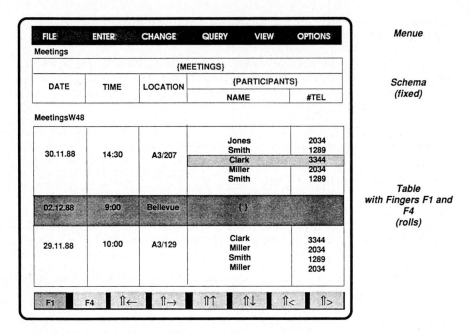

Menue

Schema
(fixed)

Table
with Fingers F1 and
F4
(rolls)

Fig. 2: Result of Moving F1 Down

Menue

Schema
(fest)

Table
(rolls)
with Fingers F1 and
F4
expecting
input for DATE

Fig. 3: Result of Insertion

one of the two or more fingers on the object is the active finger, then its token in the finger line blinks.

Pressing a finger key activates the corresponding finger. Coloring of the deactivated fingers remains untouched. The active finger may be moved using cursor keys. The movement is context dependent. At first glance one seems to recognize 3 dimensions:

- up or down in a list or set
- left or right in a tuple
- into an object to its first element or out to the surrounding object.

Accordingly there are 6 key combinations. What would constitute a suitable choice for IN and OUT is still open; Figures 1 - 3 use Shift+>, resp. Shift+<. Semantically speaking, the first two dimensions are identical: the finger is moved to the successor, resp. to the predecessor. In Figure 1, the finger on the tuple [clark, 3344] can only be moved up or down. A direct change to the location attribute A3/207 is not possible. To move to A3/207, the user first has to go "outwards" to the surrounding set of participants and then left to location.

Erroneous finger movements, like "into" an atomic object, "out" of the global set or list, "left" of the first attribute, etc., would cause the bell to ring, which can be switched off. Similarly, finger movement can be directed by a mouse or through a touch screen. Furthermore, the table window can roll using the usual cursor keys, i.e. page up, page down, one column left or right, Home, End. Jumping back to any finger, including the active one, is by pressing the corresponding finger key F_i.

Insertions and deletions are relative to the active finger. Insertion creates an "undefined" object with undefined values (shown as ?? for atomic values, {?} for sets, <?> for lists, and [?] for tuples). The new object is placed immediately behind the current finger on the same level. Figure 3 depicts a tuple for MEETINGS with finger F1 on the first attribute. Simultaneously the attribute in the schema above is highlighted. In addition, a seperate window might be opened to indicate the expected types and other restrictions.

Deletion uses both the common "DEL" and "Backspace" keys known from editors. Thus either the active finger moves to the next object or the preceeding object is removed and the active finger stays stationary. Since fingers can be nested, we require that any object which is removed does not contain another finger within. Thus, tuple [clark, 3344] with the active finger F4 may be removed in Figure 1, even though F1 points to the surrounding object [30.11.88, 14:30, A3/207, {[Jones, 2034], ..., [Smith, 1289]}]. Doing it the other way around would not be possible.

All other operations are initiated by means of drop-down menues from the menue line. In particular, projection requires clicking the corresponding attribute(s) in the schema and selection offers a choice of conditional operators like "<", "=", ">" and requires entry of a value.

To illustrate the potential of this approach, we give another simple example from a banking environment. Suppose a clerk has to validate the signature on a presented check withdrawing a large amount from an account. Provided with a terminal with modest graphics - a PC with EGA graphics would actually suffice - he/she might do a 'finger-based'

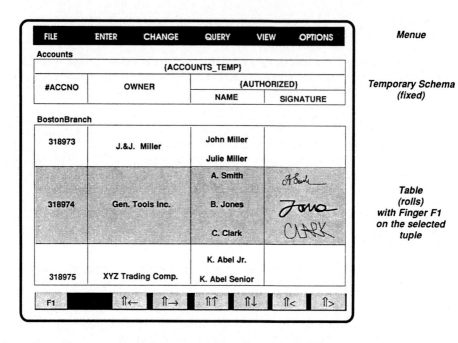

Fig. 4: Selecting a Tuple with a Bit-mapped Image

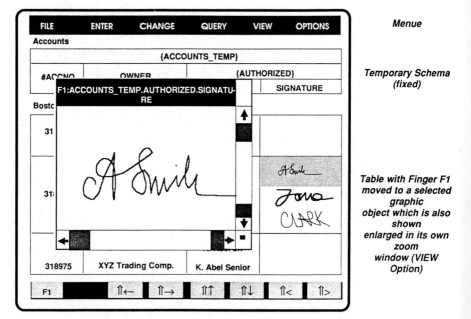

Fig. 5: Moving F1 to a Bit-mapped Image and Zooming

query to have the signature(s) for the drawn account displayed. Clicking QUERY in the menue line, he/she picks SELECT from a drop-down menue. Assuming that Accounts is the current schema and BostonBranch the current table, a 'SELECT-Finger' could be used to project the query result to, say, ACCNO (Account Number), OWNER, NAME and SIGNATURE of registered persons with signatory power, ignoring other attributes like BALANCE, ADDRESS, CREDITLINE, etc.

Next the system would drop a menue with possible selection criteria, say ACCNO and OWNER. Clicking ACCNO and entering the desired number would complete the formulation of the query (corresponding to a SELECT [ACCNO, OWNER, <AUTHORIZED>] FROM BostonBranch WHERE ACCNO = 318974 in a modified SQL). Fig. 4 shows the output with a finger F1 on the selected tuple. Seeing that three persons have signatory power for account 318974, the clerk might move F1 into the selected tuple, then right to the list valued attribute AUTHORIZED, then into the list to the first element (a tuple), again into the tuple and finally right to the second attribute SIGNATURE. There he/she might call a VIEW-option to zoom the signature until sufficient resolution allows validation of the check (Fig. 5).

Note that we implicitly assumed that bit-mapped images are integral part of the visual interface. While the extended NF^2 data model does not provide for generic types 'picture' and 'graphics', they can be handled via user defined abstact data types [12]. Still, it would be a desirable featue of a DBMS for non-standard applications (e.g. in engineering) to provide manipulation methods for objects with a visual representation. The claim is then that the finger concept introduced here is such a manipulation method.

Displaying and manipulating complex objects of the extended NF^2 data model in the tabular way shown above is not without problems. On the input side, preformulated queries in a SQL-like language often would be more convenient. On the output side, interesting (and difficult) questions arise in displaying extended objects, e.g. a meetings-tuple with a

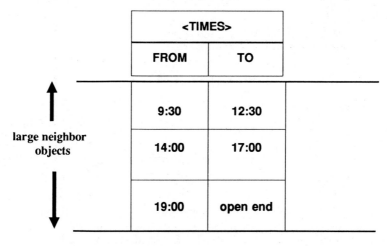

Fig. 6: Displaying Repeating Objects

few hundred participants. Where, resp. when, should the atomic values for DATE, TIME and LOCATION appear? Do they roll as well? Do the values appear once in the very beginning, in the middle, at the end? What if TIME is a list of tuples of the type shown in Figure 6: do we see all three times together or drawn appart?

In summary, we see the proposed interface to an extended NF^2 DBMS not as a cure-all for the old (and hard) problem of integrating text and graphics in a database. Rather we belief that the extremely powerful extended NF^2 data model with its sound set of semantic rules would benefit from a user-friendly visual interface with intuitive syntax. In combination they could handle the majority of spontaneous queries from non-standard applications in engineering, office automation, and science.

3. Storage Structures and Finger Implementation

The implementation of ESCHER in its present form may be described by three catch words:

- Internal memory model
- Index orientation
- Use of Fingers

The implications are that ESCHER expects to hold its objects in memory as it is typical for spread sheet programs. ESCHER relies on the underlying heap management of the PASCAL compiler but tries to faciliate the task by allocating objects in fixed sizes, preferably in powers of 2. Particular attention is paid to space saving techniques, i.e. small objects should occupy little space. The following limits per object follow from the sizes reserved for length indicators:

- degree of tuples is max. 255
- cardinality of sets and lists is max. 65.535

At present, *empty* (multi)sets and lists occupy 16 bytes for size, sortindex, lines to represent object, element type and some reserved space. These 16 bytes form the so-called *head* of an object. *Nonempty* sets or lists occupy at least another 24 bytes - the body - which contains either data elements or 4 so-called reference pointers which, through indirection, lead to practically any number of data blocks (256 bytes each). Note that sets and lists require exactly one element-type indicator per object.

Tuples occupy 40+k*256 bytes where the 40 bytes divide into degree, sortindex, lines to represent object, some reserved space, 6 type indicators and either 6 data elements or 4 reference pointer. This preliminary design was choosen to encourage aggregation of data within the NF^2 model, i.e. by combining up to 6 attributes to form a complex object, the user has the chance not only to improve legibility but also efficiency. Nesting of objects is practically unlimited (see implementation of the finger concept below).

Any object has exactly one physical representation. All objects together form a tree with the POOL-Table as root. This POOL-Table holds both schemas (the catalog) and tables. Chaining is my means of 4-Byte pointers at present but tuple identifiers are possible to map objects to pages of any underlying memory management system. To store objects between sessions and for temporary swapping in and out of objects, a simple sequential interchange format was devised. It basically seperates atomic values through a distinguished

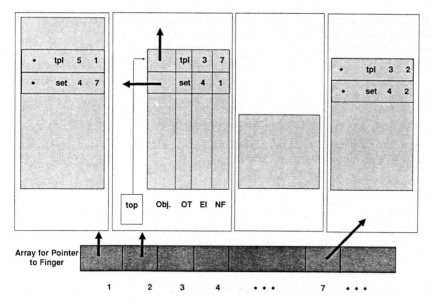

Fig. 7: Implementation of Fingers as Stacks

symbol (e.g. BLANK), and denotes the end of a complex object through a second symbol (e.g. New Line). This format is not structure preserving on its own but needs the previous output schema to reconstruct the input.

The second aspect concerns the way objects are referenced. Internally, an object is identified by its index in the surrounding object, i.e. the i'th entry within a list, set or tuple yields the address of the i'th sub-object. As an example consider the tuple [Clark, 3344] from Figure 1. Given the base address of the table as a whole, its location in memory can be calculated by following the index path (1, 4, 3). This is also the basic idea for implementing fingers, i.e. a finger is an index path augmented by other information and implemented as a stack. Therefore nesting of objects is only limited by the space assigned to finger paths which are implemented as stacks. Insertions and deletions change the index of all objects following the inserted or deleted sub-object but only within the object in which the change occurred.

Apart from the problem of having to create/close a gap to insert/delete an address, which is a data structure problem, this does not touch the object tree at all. What might need to be changed are all fingers which contain this object on their index path. This, however, is efficiently solved by chaining all finger pointers to identical objects. Objects are easily added/dropped from chains when a finger movement occurs by looking through the chains of their surrounding objects which are one below in the stack.

Fig. 7 gives an example with three fingers shown in more detail. Their index in the finger array is 1, 2, 7 respectively. Finger #2 presently 'sits' on a tuple (Object Type OT = tpl) whose physical address is indicated by an array. It is the third element in the surrounding set (EI = 3). Since Finger #7 sits on the same object, the NF (Next Finger) field points to 2.

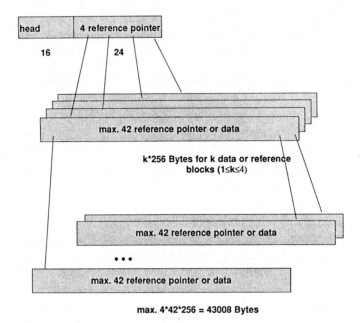

E.g. set or list of Integers (2 Bytes each)

- **up to 12 values directly in the objectbody**
- **up to 512 values with one level of indirection**
- **up to 21.504 values with two levels of indirection**
- **up to 903.168 values with three levels of indirection**

Fig. 8: Use of Indirection for Large Objects

The NF field there points back to 2, i.e. there are exactly two fingers on this object. The surrounding object is below. It occurs three times in a finger path as indicated by the chain $1 \rightarrow 7 \rightarrow 2 \rightarrow 1$. The finger on the very left (#1) shows a tuple (OT = tpl) which is the 5th element in the surrounding set. It occurs exactly once on a finger path because the NF field points back to itself.

Addressing objects through the index in the surrounding object has its counterpart in the physical storage structure. The 'fat arrows' in the field Obj of the finger stacks (Fig. 7) are physical pointers to the head of an object. Its subobjects have their addresses stored sequentially in the body of this object. If the object is large, the i'th subobject (either the datum itself, if atomic, or its physical address, if complex) is within a data block of size

256 Byte. These blocks may be partially filled and are merged, resp. split on underflow, resp. overflow. This results in a semi-direct access which requires following a chain of so called reference pointers, each 6 bytes long. A reference pointer contains the size of the subtree and the address of the root block of the subtree. Given an index, we have to search sequentially through the reference pointers within a reference block adding up the sizes until the given index is less or equal the sum of sizes. The search may then continue on the sublevel until we reach a data block.

The idea of using blocks which contain addresses of further blocks was borrowed from the original file scheme in UNIX. As can be seen from Figure 8, the longest search path possible in theory for three levels of indirection requires at most 88 additions and comparisons and references the last element in a set of 903,168 integers which is well above our limit of 65,536 elements. On the average, we may expect 2 additions and comparisons for sets or lists of size at most 500, given random access. Similarly, 23 additions and comparisons are needed, on the average, for sets/lists of size about 20,000.

The index path to an object cannot be used as address in tables for secondary key search because their update following insertion/deletion would require too much work. Here, a TID is needed which would point to the corresponding data block. If the user selects an object via a secondary key and then decides to have a finger point to it, its index path is unknown. The solution here is backward chaining of the data and reference blocks.

The finger concept is also used for internal operations. One example is the display of tables which can become quite complex. Following manipulations of the window or finger movements, the table display should be refreshed instantly. Because each column may contain an object which requires more "lines" than the current window can show, a preorder traversal of the object tree is not good enough: we have to jump quickly from column to column and back. At present we assign a finger to each column (attribute with atomic value) and scan them from left to right.

In summary, this unusual storage concept is an attempt to marry the features of index oriented spread sheet programs with the tree oriented NF^2 data model. Needless to say that most of the physical layout decisions will undergo changes as the implementation progresses. However, as more and more features are being added, a final decision must soon be made on whether this index concept is a sound basis for storing and displaying complex objects in acceptable time.

4. Modular Design

At present, ESCHER is divided into six Pascal Units, called *Managers* (cf. Fig. 9). On the top level is the MAIN MANAGER (MainMngr) which initializes the system by calling OpenShop(Status) in the BOOT MANAGER (BootMngr). This loads system tables of available schemes and NF^2 tables, initializes the system to the last recorded settings (fonts, windows, macros, etc.) and performs other bookkeeping tasks.

MainMngr then continues with a loop which is terminated only by a user 'quit', a fatal error or a suspend command to exit to the operating system temporarily. Each pass through the loop constitutes one user action, initiated through a call NextAction(Status) to the

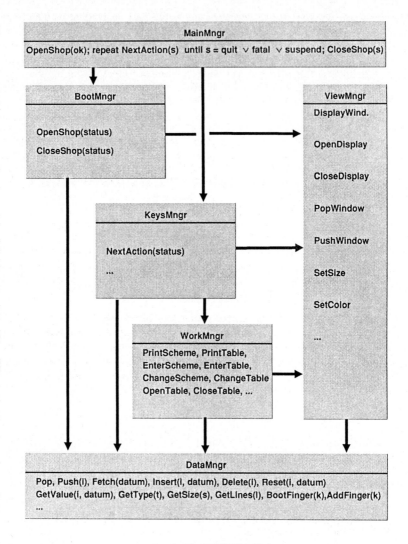

Fig. 9: The ESCHER Units

KEYS MANAGER (KeysMngr). MainMngr is also responsible for bringing the system down by calling CloseShop(Status) in BootMngr.

KeysMngr handles the dialog with the user. It reads input from the user and interprets it relative to the current system state, e.g. a Backspace in edit mode for input of an atomic value has a different meaning than a Backspace in edit mode with the active finger on the atomic value. When KeysMngr knows what needs to be done, it delegates the task to the specific function in the WORK MANAGER (WorkMngr).

UNIT DataMngr (DM.pas)

Function	Comment
(Remark:	all functions return an error code and operate relative to the active finger)
Pop	go to surrounding object
Push(i)	go into i'th subobject
AFetch(datum)	pass to datum the value of the active atomic object
AInsert(i, datum)	insert atomic value datum after i'th subobject
CInsert(i, finger)	insert complex object pointed to by finger after i'th subobject
Delete(i)	remove i'th subobject (atomic or complex)
AReset(i, datum)	change i'th atomic subobject to datum
CReset(i, finger)	change i'th complex subobject to object pointed to by finger
SyncValue	update copies of pointers to current object
GetValue(i, datum)	pass to datum atomic value of i'th subobject in current object
GetType(t)	determine typ t of active object
GetSize(s)	determine number s of elements of the active object
GetLines(l)	determine number l of lines needed to display the active object
AddFinger(fn, fo)	add finger fn to object pointed to by existing finger fo
DropFinger(fd, fa)	delete finger fd, make fa the active finger
MakeActive(f)	make f the active finger
...	...

Fig. 10: Available Functions of the DATA MANAGER

WorkMngr contains a set of routines for performing logical operations on the database, like displaying a schema, displaying a table, creating a new schema, loading a file for a table, doing a projection, etc. It knows nothing about physical addresses but manages its own set of fingers and moves them through the tables to initiate the more elementary operations like *fetch*, *insert*, *delete*, etc. It also receives specific error codes from the basic functions in the DATA MANAGER (DataMngr) and acts upon them (open an error window, read the reply, decide what can be repaired, etc.). It returns a more global status which is either one of 'ok', 'fatal', 'quit' or 'suspend'.

`BootMngr`, `KeysMngr`, `WorkMngr` may use basic functions from the VIEW MANAGER (not to be confused with 'views' in database terminology) which handles all aspects related to the display of system information and user data. `ViewMngr` knows about windows, their location, sizes, colors but does not interpret their contents. To perform its task it may use its own set of fingers and call upon basic routines in `DataMngr`. It is planned to 'buy' most of the windowing services from a suitable package, like X WINDOWS for a UNIX-based solution.

Finally, the DATA MANAGER (`DataMngr`) is a unit which shields all data-specific aspects from the other units. It can be asked to manipulate the i'th subobject in an object on which the active finger rests. In answering this request, it translates indices to physical addresses and may move the finger to the subobject. Since fingers are stacks, `Push(i)` and `Pop` are two frequent operations for moving a finger into an object, resp. moving out to the surrounding object. Fig. 10 gives an abreviated list of presently available functions of the DATA MANAGER.

As a prototype for testing ideas, ESCHER is a single-user, single-task system. Multi-tasking would be added to the `WorkMngr` Unit using a message passing mechanism. As an example, calls to the DATA MANAGER would instruct the called functions to send fetched items directly to the VIEW MANAGER, freeing `WorkMngr` from the duty of having to wait for returned values.

Similarly, multi-user functionality would be added to the KEYS MANAGER. `NextAction` would then poll the user community for pending requests and would decide which requests could be served based on the usual conflict resolution rules of DBMSs. In summary, our present experience with this rather simple modular design has been quite satisfactory and we believe that it can serve as basis for further refinements.

5. Self-referencing Structure

The use of self-describing methods in the design of a DBMS is a well-known principle and may find its way even into an ISO standard [15]. However, the emphasis there is on describing the intension-extension dimension and deals with conceptual schemas and data model standardization. Our approach is more concerned with the internal model, i.e. our initial goal is to alleviate the task of having to implement the basic object storage and manipulation management. Thus we try to map internal structures, needed for the management of objects, into NF^2 objects.

Unfortunately, using this kind of bootstrap mechanism proved to be less fruitful than thought. The following reasons were identified:

- Even today it is not quite clear which basic operations are both necessary and sufficient.
- Any comfortable management of the internal data base would have to be high level, possibly based on a SQL-type interface. This requires a long bootstrap phase which makes the effort less worth while.
- The use of index paths to access an object (which translates largely to the common retrieval by address) makes self-modification harder than associative access (content addressing); the latter is only achieved through secondary keys which again require a large initial phase.

- Intuition tells us that performance problems might be expected in the display.
- The approach is basically bottom-up and thus stands in contrast to main software engineering principles which favor top-down design.
- The user can take on the role of the system designer because there are no differences between user and system tables in principle. This is a fascinating perspective which, however, must find its limit somewhere unless the system becomes corrupted.
- Presumably, a system bootstrap requires operation scripts (shell scripts), i.e. procedures as attribute values. This implies writing an interpreter to call the operations (easy part) once it is known which operations are needed (hard part).
- Tools like menue generators and windowing systems can speed up the implementation yet are in conflict with self-referencing principles, e.g. most menue generators produce

BUCHER

{Books}			
<Authors>		Title	#Year
First_Name	Last_Name		

(a) A schema for a table to hold descriptions of books

BOOT_SCHEME

{s0}								
Name	Type	#Degree	#Width	{s1}				
				Name	Type	#Degree	#Width	{s2}
								...

(b) The abreviated boot schema

Books	set	3	73	Auth	list	2	22	First	..	{}
								Last	..	{}
				Titl	text	0	46	{}		
				Year	int	0	6	{}		

(c) The "books" schema as tuple of the scheme table

Fig. 11: Schemes as Tuples of a Scheme Table

source code which stores layout, headers, items, help lines, etc. as part of the code. In a self-referencing design these data would be stored in NF^2 tables to be querried at runtime.

- Last but not least our tradition in implementing large scale software systems together with the use of an imperative programming language creates a mental barrier which is hard to overcome.

The list above should not lead to wrong conclusions. Some steps into the right direction have been taken, e.g. storing and treating schemas as tuples of the catalog table. Furthermore, the DATA MANAGER has become quite stable and our understanding of which basic operations are most likely needed has improved. Large tasks still await completion, e.g. the display management, management of external storage, the interface design (menues, keys management, error handling). These are all areas asking for the use of NF^2 structures.

Even in our rudimentary system we can already test the power of the self-referencing methods. As an example we include in the Appendix the entry of the scheme for a table to hold fingers. Note how easy it is to store the stack as a list! Thinking about a possible definition and entering this definition into ESCHER took no longer than three minutes! Deeper thought was required for the definition of a boot schema as can be seen in Fig. 11. We note that this schema is actually infinite. To implement it properly, the NF^2 data model should allow recursion and some kind of variant record to end the recursion. The same holds if we plan to store catalog and tables in a common POOL-Table.

We leave it to the reader to define the fairly obvious schemas for NF^2 tables which implement B- or B*-trees for secondary key indexes. Note that the user might ask for secondary indexes on complex objects!

6. State-Oriented Systems

In most interactive graphical systems, such as text processors, DTP, spread sheets, windowing systems and database systems with a visual interface, the user moves in a *state-oriented environment* with *operational semantics*.

In ESCHER-terms, state-oriented means that the user sees the active schema and table window, the active finger is highlighted, the status line indicates the available options, etc. By opening or closing windows, moving fingers, select and project operations, the system is moving to a new state which is again depicted through the graphical interface. The common question "where am I?" can be answered by escaping from the present state back to a more global state with which the user is familiar. From there one navigates back to that state which the mental picture suggests as being most appropriate for the task which the user wants to perform. Thus, the user has a mental picture of the system state and transforms it into a new state through his/her actions.

Operational semantics, as opposed to denotational or propositional (axiomatic) semantics, means that the DBMS acts as an abstract machine which explains the meaning of relational operations by a sequence of state transformations and output actions. The new state can again be inspected but there are no state-independent specifications to guide the user. To paraphrase a catchword from DTP: What You Got Is What You See.

If the system is well designed and fault tolerant, i.e. uses confirmation and warning windows, undo and shadow back-up operations, etc., an insufficiently clear state representation is annoying to the user but not directly dangerous as long as all state-action pairs are defined in the domain of the state transition function. However, if the implemeter works with operational semantics as well, i.e. if programming steps are based on a mental picture of the program state, represented by the program counter, assignments to variables and parameters, contents of system tables, etc., this is bound to fail past a certain size of the software system. The "limits of sanity" can be raised by specifying pre- and postconditions on all invoked procedures but they cannot be trusted once the state space becomes too large.

This can already be observed in ESCHER. Most operations require that the active finger be in a well defined state. However, it is often not immediately clear whether an object which we want to deal with is already on the stack or whether the operation is expected to push it onto the stack as its first task. Trivial operations, like moving an atomic value to a display window, can turn into disaster if the top element is in reality still the surrounding complex object. Where the user can *see* the state of affairs, the implementer drives blindfolded, must rely on assertions and must possibly confirm them through a series of control questions.

It is our hope that the use of self-referencing methods can lead the implementer out of the dark. Quite clearly the availability of a display routine for NF^2 structures can be used during debugging by giving a visual representation of the program state as documented in the internal tables. But this is not enough. Better than debugging faulty code is to prevent it by enforcing integrity constraints on the internal structures in exactly the same way we build integrity checks into the DBMS for, say, an accounting application.

As an example, consider displaying a complex object. It is implemented by assigning a finger to the object and moving it through the object, say depth-first, transfering a value whenever the finger rests on an atomic value. Thus we already use our own finger concept to implement finger related display features. The first subtask would then be to find a free system finger and to assign it to the complex object. In a traditional implementation, a procedure would run through the finger array searching for the first pointer-to-finger with nil-value. It thus must know the location of the array and its internal record structure. Moreover, race conditions must be avoided if multiple tasks search for free fingers.

A self-referencing approach, on the other hand, would issue a SELECT FingerIndex FROM FingerTable WHERE Status = free. The request is thus independent of the data representation and the usual lock-unlock database mechanisms would handle concurrent access. But now the problems start. What if the SELECT-implementation is again via assigning a free finger to FingerTable and then moving the finger through the table? While this example of an infinite recursion is easily repaired by having a permanent finger on FingerTable, other more subtle problems abound.

Despite many open questions, it nevertheless has become obvious in the process of our implementation that the extended NF^2 data model is the ideal tool for mapping traditional data structures like lists (queues), stacks and trees into tables. The same holds for storing the visual attributes of the system like size, colors and locations of windows. More research seems to be needed on a 'data manipulation language for database implementations', in particular, a bootstrap DML suited to the NF^2 data model.

7. Summary

The present system is the result of a two year study of the NF^2 data model and about a year of intense design and implementation. At its present state (Sept. 1st, 1988), it comprises about 6000 lines of PASCAL-code and compiles into a modest 120 KB run time modul. By the end of 1988, the system is expected to reach the 10,000 lines barrier at which time a public domain window interface is to be added. How much of the full relational operations will then be available is open and depends on the user acceptance. Most likely its strength lies in its simplicity which makes it suitable as a front-end to a full NF^2 DBMS like IBM's *AIM-P* for simple editing tasks by the naive casual user.

The current execution task on a 10 MHz work station is very encouraging. Computing the layout of a schema took 375 ms on a PC with EGA graphics and 130 ms on a PS/2 Model 60 with VGA graphics, where the schema had the shape of a complete binary tree with 8 leaves and alternating set-list inner nodes of degree 2. This time includes the actual display of the schema with line drawing and centering of text. Still this time is not good enough for recalculating a table layout and displaying the table window as the result of, say, a cursor movement. Much more work seems needed here to make complex objects look simple in a visual database system.

References

[1]   S. Abiteboul, N. Bidoit: Non First Normal Form Relations: An Algebra Allowing Data Restructuring, Rapport de Recherche No 347, Institut de Recherche en Informatique et en Automatique, Rocquencourt, France, Nov. 1984

[2]   S. Bing Yao, A.R. Hevner, Z. Shi, and D. Luo: FORMANAGER: An Office Forms Management System, ACM TOIS, Vol. 2, No. 3, July 1984, pp. 235-262

[3]   D. Bryce, R. Hull: SNAP: A Graphics-based Schema Manager, Proc. IEEE Intl. Conf. on Data Engineering, Feb. 1986, pp. 151-164

[4]   P. Dadam, K. Küspert, F. Andersen, H. Blanken, R. Erbe, J. Günauer, V. Lum, P. Pistor, G. Walch: A DBMS Prototype to Support Extended NF2 Relations: An Integrated View on Flat Tables and Hierarchies, Proc. ACM SIGMOD Conf., Washington D.C., May 1986, pp. 356-367

[5]   P. Dadam, K. Küspert, N. Südkamp, R. Erbe, V. Linnemann, P. Pistor, G. Walch: Managing Complex Objects in R^2D^2, IBM Heidelberg Scientific Center, TR 88.03.004 (March 1988)

[6]   U. Deppisch, J. Günauer, G. Walch: Storage Structures and Addressing Concepts for Complex Objects of the NF^2 Relational Model (in German), Proc. GI Conference on "Datenbanksysteme für Büro, Technik und Wissenschaft", Karlsruhe, March 1985, pp. 441-459

[7]   B. Ernst: Der Zauberspiegel des Maurits Cornelis Escher, TACO Verlagsgesellschaft und Agentur mbH, 112 pp., Berlin, 1986

[8] D. Fogg: Lessons from a "Living in a Database" graphical query interface, Proc. ACM SIGMOD Int. Conf. on the Management of Data, 1984, pp. 100-106

[9] G. Jaeschke, H.J. Schek: Remarks on the Algebra of Non First Normal Form Relations, Proc. ACM SIGACT-SIGMOD Symp. on Principle of Data Base Systems, Los Angeles, Cal., March 1982, pp. 124-138

[10] Kitagawa, et al: Form Document Management System SPECDOQ, Proc. ACM SIGOA Conf. on Office Information Systems, Toronto, Ont., Canada, June 25-27, 1984 (published as SIGOA Newsletter, Vol. 5, Nos. 1-2), 1984, pp. 132-142

[11] Kitagawa, et al.: Formgraphics: A Form-Based Architecture Providing a Database Workbench, IEEE Computer Graphics and Applications, Vol. 4, No. 6, 1984, pp. 38-56

[12] V. Linnemann, K. Küspert, P. Dadam, P. Pistor, R. Erbe, A. Kemper, N. Südkamp, G. Walch and M. Wallrath: Design and Implementation of an Extensible Database Management System Supporting User Defined Data Types and Functions, Technical Report TR 87.12.011, IBM Heidelberg Scientific Center, Dec. 1987

[13] R.A. Lorie, W.Plouffe: Complex Objects and Their Use in Design Transactions, Proc. Annual Meeting - Database Week: Engineering Design Applikations (IEEE), San Jose, Cal., May 1983, pp. 115-121

[14] D. Luo and S. Bing Yao: FORM Operation by Example - a Language for Information Processing, Proc. SIGMOD Conf., June 1981, pp. 213-223

[15] L.Mark and N. Roussopoulos: Metadata Management, IEEE Computer, Vol. 19, No. 12, Dec. 1986, pp. 26-36

[16] R. Purvy, J. Farrel, and P. Klose: The Design of Star's Record Processing: Data Processing for the Noncomputer Professional, ACM TOIS, Vol. 1, No. 1, Jan. 1983, pp. 3-24

[17] G. Rohr: Graphical User Languages for Querying Information: Where to Look for Criteria, Proc. IEEE Workshop on Visual Languages, Pittsburgh, PA, Oct. 10-12, 1988

[18] H.J. Schek, M.Scholl: The Relational Model with Relation-Valued Attributes, Information Systems, Vol. 11, No. 2, 1986, pp. 137-147

[19] N. Shu: FORMAL: A Forms-Oriented, Visual-Directed Application Development System, IEEE Computer, Vol. 18, No. 8, Aug. 1985, pp. 38-49

[20] M. Stonebraker, J.Kalash: TIMBER: A sophisticated relation browser, Proc. 8th Int. Conf. Very Large Databases, 1982, pp. 1-10

[21] M. Stonebraker, H. Stettner, N. Lynn, J. Kalash, and A. Guttman: Document Processing in a Relational Database System, ACM TOIS, Vol. 1, No. 2, April 1983, pp. 143-158

[22] M. Zloof: Query-by-Example: A data base language, IBM Systems Journal 6 (1977), 324-343

Appendix

Defining the Finger Stack as NF^2 Object

(Printscreen output of the actual entry in the current version of ESCHER)

```
Enter top level attribute name!: Fingers
Complex Type - are the elements tuples? Y/N:  y
Enter degree (no. of columns); min 2 max 255:  3
```

(a) Root attribute has type set

```
FINGERSCHEME
```

{Fingers}		
??	??	??

```
Enter attribute name:
```

(b) Default column width is 10 (can be changed by the user)

```
FINGERSCHEME
```

{Fingers}		
??	??	??

```
Enter attribute name: FID
Enter Attribute Type: One of
  1Set 2List 3Integer 4Text :?  3
```

(c) FingerID is declared as integer

```
FINGERSCHEME
```

{Fingers}		
#FID	??	??

```
Back in Fingers
Next Attribute - going down one level
Enter attribute name:
```

(d) ESCHER reports the current depth (to be shown through color later)

Appendix

FINGERSCHEME

{Fingers}		
#FID	#Top	??

```
Back in Fingers
Next Attribute - going down one level
Enter attribute name: Stack
Enter Attribute Type: One of
  1Set 2List 3Integer 4Text :?   2
```

(e) Stack declared as list

FINGERSCHEME

{Fingers}					
#FID	#Top	⟨Stack⟩			
		??	??	??	??

```
Enter attribute name:
```

(f) Default undefined tuple of degree 4

FINGERSCHEME

{Fingers}					
#FID	#Top	⟨Stack⟩			
		#Obj_Addr	Obj_Type	#El_Index	#Next_Finger

```
Do you want to enter another scheme? Y/N :
```

(g) Schema completed

Session 8

PICTORIAL
DATA PROCESSING

Visual Database Systems
T.L. Kunii (Editor)
Elsevier Science Publishers B.V. (North-Holland)
© IFIP, 1989

AN ALGEBRA FOR SYMBOLIC IMAGE MANIPULATION
AND TRANSFORMATION

Erland JUNGERT

FOA (Swedish Defence Research Establishment)
Box 1165, S-58111 Linkoping, Sweden

and

S. K. CHANG

Department of Computer Science
University of Pittsburgh
Pittsburgh, PA, USA

Manipulation and transformation of symbolic images requires, in order to become efficient, various high-level data structures and procedures. This is especially true for applications of heuristic type. This work introduces an image algebra which is based on symbolic projections and includes three fundamental aspects, i.e. a set of powerful relational operators, a generalized representation of "empty space" objects and multilevel data representation for hierarchical data.

1. Introduction

The requirements for abstract or high level data structures for manipulation and transformation of symbolic images normally involve applications of both algorithmic and heuristic types. Especially, there is an obvious interest for integration of such data structures in both image data base systems and in data base systems of visual type. This work describes an algebra which is based on symbolic projections [4] including a limited set of relational operators. The algebra also includes a generalized "empty space" object, which supports general descriptions and manipulations of the images. Multi-level data structures can also be described, as well as the generation of graph structures. These results show that this algebraic approach to image manipulation and transformation constitutes a powerful means for many different applications.

Many alternative approaches of pictorial data structures have been developed. Among them are hierarchical structure of various kinds such as the quad-tree [1]. However, all these approaches demonstrate a lack of generality, since in order to manipulate or transform images based upon these structures, complicated functions must be developed. These functions are usually highly application dependent, and inefficient in either execution time or storage requirement. Winston [2] describes a different approach called "natural constraints" intended mainly for description of the contours of objects in an image. Winston's method requires much pre-processing which again is a drawback. Picture grammars [3] can also be employed in certain applications advantageously. Recently, Kundu [10] has developed another hierarchical structure for the description of 2D planes where the tree is of irregular type. However, there is often the need to transform different representations, so that the algorithms and the representations can have a good match. The new approach proposed in this paper, avoids many of the drawbacks of other approaches.

2. Basic Global Operators and the Partition Technique

In the original work on symbolic projections by Chang [4], only two relational operators were introduced. These two operators were <(less than) and =(equal to). Later, Jungert [5] introduced a number of relational operators corresponding to local and global relationships. Among these operators the | (edge-to-edge) operator has the status of being both local and global, just like the two introduced by Chang. The | operator is a powerful operator which completes the original set such that no other global operator is needed. Hence, for the algebra proposed, the following set of global relational operators is defined:

G-op = { =, <, | }

The semantic meaning of the first two corresponds to their general logical definitions. The third one, i.e. the edge-to-edge operator has the following definition:

Two objects are edge-to-edge if the objects are in direct contact with each other either in east-west or north-south direction.

Obviously, this definition is also true for segments of objects that are partitioned parallel to either the y- or the x- coordinate axes.

Figure 1 illustrates the edge-to-edge relationship and the corresponding projected string.

U: A | B

Figure 1. An example of the edge-to-edge operator.

Along with this set of relational operators, a method to partition the image into smaller sections is suggested. The image is partitioned according to the following rules.

Rule 1: The image is partitioned both parallel to the y- and the x- coordinate axes.

Rule 2: The partitions are performed at all the extreme points of all the present objects.

An extreme point of an object is either a concave or a convex object-point. A line corresponding to a cut, partitions all objects that are crossed by the line. The number of cuts parallel to each coordinate axis might not be the same, since a cut is only made orthogonal to the coordinate axis to which the extreme point can be directly projected. The partitioning technique is illustrated in Figure 2.

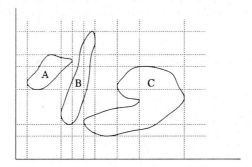

Figure 2. Illustrations of the partitioning technique.

The 2D-strings corresponding to the partitions made in Figure 2 is then generated in accordance with the principles outlined in [4] using the operator set defined above. Thus, from Figure 2 we obtain

U: A I B=A I B I C=B I C I C=C I C

V: C I B=C I A=B=C I A=B I B

or more concisely

U: A I BA I B I CB I C I CC I C

V: C I BC I ABC I AB I B

since the '=' operator can be left out without any semantical loss. In the second pair of 2D-strings, AB is equivalent to A=B. All segments of the same objects must be included in the 2D-strings, otherwise there will be a loss of information.

One important observation is that the two orthogonal sets of lines corresponding to the cuts are totally independent of each other.

There might occur ambiguities when it comes to 2D-string representations of the objects. Figure 3 shows an example of such a case.

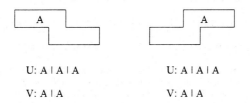

U: A I A I A   U: A I A I A

V: A I A   V: A I A

Figure 3. Example of two ambiguous 2D-String representations.

The solution to this problem, which is suggested here, is segmentation of the objects in accordance with the above proposed rules, as shown in Figure 4.

U: A2 | A1 A2 | A1   U: A1 | A1 A2 | A2

V: A1 | A2   V: A1 | A2

Figure 4. Segmentation of objects to resolve ambiguities in 2D-string representations.

Another solution which seems to fit better with the approach described here, would be to use the technique to be described in Section 3. In other words, by using the generalized empty space as part of the strings, all objects can be described uniquely.

The basic data structure for object descriptions, recommended in this approach, is the run-length-code (RLC). RLC is chosen, because in [6] and [7] it has been shown that the RLC used as an object-oriented structure is very powerful for object manipulation.

3. The Empty Space Object

The concept of "empty space" is introduced here to describe not only the whole image but also to make it possible to describe the space outside the objects of interest. The term "empty space" was first used by Lozano-Perez in [8] partly for the same purpose as given here, i.e. to build up a structure which can be used to describe the space of an image. Lozano-Perez used a Quad-tree related structure for this purpose. In his paper, Lozano-Perez introduced FULL, MIXED and EMPTY spaces. The empty space outside the objects are solid rectangles representing the free space outside so-called MIXED cells. Here the empty space is divided into smaller areas as well, but not necessarily into rectangles. The shape of the empty space blocks are the result of the partition of the image. Hence, they are linear along the two cutting lines and along any of the coordinate axis. But when touching an object the empty space has the shape corresponding to that object. However, when used as a knowledge structure the useful heuristic approach is to regard the empty space objects as rectangles. This is done by Jungert and Holmes [9] in a somewhat different approach that will be discussed later.

An empty space area is defined as:

$$e_{i,j}^{s} = [T_{i-1}^{s}, T_{i}^{s}]$$

for i = 1, ... , n   and j = 1, ... , m

where $T_{i}^{s} = x_{i}$ for s = u

$T_{i}^{s} = y_{i}$ for s = v

and n is the number of cutting lines and m the number of e-objects in the corresponding interval.

$T_{o}^{u} = x_{o}$ corresponds to the y-axis, and

$T_{o}^{v} = y_{o}$ corresponds to the x-axis.

Hence, an empty space object is defined as the interval between two consecutive partition-lines along any of the coordinate axis. The two other sides could be either the coordinate axis and an object or two objects. Figure 5 shows three objects A, B and C and the partition of the area between the objects. Each empty space area is considered an object of its own.

The partition in Figure 5 gives the following 2D-string along the y- axis.

$$V: e_{1,1}^{v} \ | e_{2,1}^{v}Ce_{2,2}^{v} \ | e_{3,1}^{v}Ae_{3,2}^{v}Ce_{3,3}^{v} \ | \ e_{4,1}^{v}Ae_{4,2}^{v} \ | e_{5,1}^{v}Ae_{5,2}^{v}Be_{5,3}^{v} \ | e_{6,1}^{v}Be_{6,2}^{v} \ | e_{7,1}^{v}$$

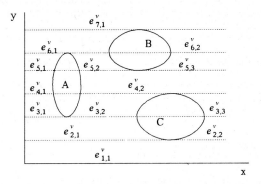

Figure 5. The empty space areas corresponding to the projections along the y- axis.

The situation that occur for the U-string projections is analogous and corresponds to Figure 6, from which we get the following string.

$$U: e_{1,1}^{u} \ | e_{2,1}^{u}Ae_{2,2}^{u} \ | e_{3,1}^{u} \ | e_{4,1}^{u}Be_{4,2}^{u} \ | \ e_{5,1}^{u}Ce_{5,2}^{u}Be_{5,3}^{u} \ | e_{6,1}^{u}Ce_{6,2}^{u} \ | e_{7,1}^{u}$$

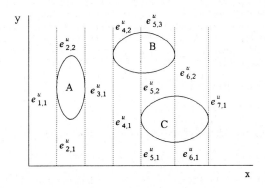

Figure 6. The U-string partition of the empty space for Figure 5.

Any portion of the free space can be identified by means of set theoretical expressions. This is demonstrated in Figure 7a and 7b. The shaded area 'a' in Figure 7a is calculated from

$$a = e_{2,2}^{u} \bigcap e_{6,1}^{v}$$

The area 'b' in Figure 7b corresponds to:

$$b = e_{2,2}^u \bigcap ((e_{4,1}^v \mid e_{5,1}^v \mid e_{6,1}^v) \bigcup (e_{4,2}^v \mid e_{5,2}^v))$$

Hence, almost any empty area can be described.

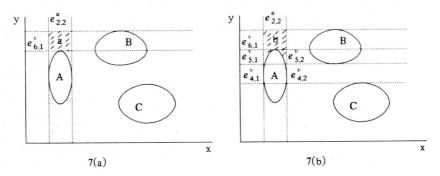

7(a)   7(b)

Figure 7. Two examples illustrating arbitrary sub-areas of empty space.

The example from Figure 7b shows also that the shape of the identified area does not necessarily have to be rectangular.

The strings can also be stripped with respect to the empty areas, e.g.

U: A < B | CB | C

V: C | AC | A | AB | B

Hence, the following law is applicable,

S: < unstripped string > => S: < stripped string >

The inverse cannot be performed directly without first defining the empty space.

The empty space is defined as:

$$E = (e^u, e^v)$$

The union of E and the stripped representation gives the unstripped string.

S: < unstripped string > <= U (E^s , S: < stripped string >)

The operator U is, however, different from the ordinary set theoretical operators since it assumes that the union of an object and a part of the empty space is equal to the object, provided the two areas coincide. Hence

U(E^u , U: A < B | C B | C) =>

$$e_{1,1}^u \mid e_{2,1}^u Ae_{2,2}^u \mid e_{3,1}^u \mid e_{4,1}^u Be_{4,2}^u \mid e_{5,1}^u Ce_{5,2}^u Be_{5,3}^u \mid e_{6,1}^u Ce_{6,2}^u \mid e_{7,1}^u$$

Empty space objects $e_{i,j}^{u}$ can also be generalized such that no differentiation is made between them. Hence, the expressions from Figure 5 and 6 can be transformed into

U: e | eAe | e | eBe | eCeBe | eCe | e

V: e | eCe | eAeCe | eAe | eAeBe | eBe | e

where e is the generalized empty space object. Hence, e indicates empty space between either two objects or between one object and the edge of the image, without considering the size, the shape or the position of the empty space. These 2D-strings can of course also be stripped, and as will be demonstrated below, the empty space object is an important aspect of the algebra on image manipulation. The empty space object e is therefore a natural extension of the language that is based on the global operator set defined in Section 2.

The ambiguous example given in Figure 3 and Figure 4 of Section 2, can now be solved by enclosing the objects in their least square and use the generalized empty space to describe the full object inside the minimal enclosing rectangle. Thus, the objects can be described uniquely by:

U: eA | A | Ae
V: eA | Ae

and

U: Ae | A | eA
V: Ae | eA

As can be seen, these strings correspond to the As can be seen, the strings now describe all the objects inside the minimal enclosing rectangle.

4. Laws of the Generalized Empty Space

Several laws apply to 2D-strings that contains the e-object. The most basic ones are four, which emphasize mostly on the effects of stripping. These work only in one direction and are analogous to what was shown about stripping above.

The laws of stripping

(i) s: e a => s: a $\quad\quad \boxed{\begin{array}{c} a \\ \hline e \end{array}} \;\Rightarrow\; \boxed{a}$

(ii) s: e | a => s: a $\quad\quad \boxed{e\;|\;a} \;\Rightarrow\; \boxed{a}$

(iii) s: a | e => s: a $\quad\quad \boxed{a\;|\;e} \;\Rightarrow\; \boxed{a}$

(iv) s: a e => s: a $\quad\quad \boxed{\begin{array}{c} e \\ \hline a \end{array}} \;\Rightarrow\; \boxed{a}$

In these rules 'a' is an arbitrary object.

Since e is a generalized expandable empty space object, expressions of the following type will never be permitted

e < a or a < e.

One further consequence of the e-object is the law

(v) a l e l b <=> a < b

which works in both directions and does not violate what was said about the < relations above.

Since the e-objects do not correspond to any particular size or shape they can be split or merged in any arbitrary direction. Hence, four further laws that reshape e-objects can be identified.

The laws of reshaping

(vi) s: e a l e <=> s: e (a l e)

(vii) s: a e l e <=> s: (a l e) e

(viii) s: e <=> s: e e

(ix) s: e <=> s: e l e

Some other transformations exist but they are derivable from the above, e.g.:

s: e e <=> s: e l e

5. Object Manipulation Laws

The laws on the generalized e-object can partly be modified and applied to objects of any kind. The two most basic ones are

$$(x) \qquad s: \qquad a_1 a_2 \cdots a_n \, | \, a_1 a_{n+1} \cdots a_m \, | \, \cdots \, | \, a_1 a_{m+1} \cdots a_k \qquad <=>$$
$$a_1(a_2 \cdots a_n \, | \, a_{n+1} \cdots a_m \, | \, \cdots \, | \, a_{m+1} \cdots a_k)$$

(xi)   s: $a_1 a_2 \cdots a_{n-1} a_n \mid a_{n+1} \cdots a_m a_n \mid \cdots \mid a_{m+1} \cdots a_k a_n$ <=>
$(a_2 \cdots a_{n-1} \mid a_{n+1} \cdots a_m \mid \cdots \mid a_{m+1} \cdots a_k) a_n$

In both laws the expressions within the parentheses are considered *compound objects*, which are objects composed from other objects. This assumption is made throughout this paper.

The laws (x) and (xi) seem to be true from an inductive viewpoint, but there is also a visual interpretation which shows the validity of these rules. For example, according to law (x):

(1) U: ab ⎮ ac ⎮ ad <=> U: a(b ⎮ c ⎮ d)

The visualization of this example is then in accordance with Figure 8.

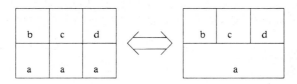

Figure 8. Visualization of the transformation in (1).

(2) U: ba ⎮ ca ⎮ da <=> U: (b ⎮ c ⎮ d) a

This is a transformation according to the law (xi). The visual interpretation of this example is similar to the one in Figure 8, although in (2) the object a is on top of b, c and d, instead of being below them as in Figure 8.

Implicitly in both (x) and (xi) it is assumed that

(3) $(a_1 \mid \cdots \mid a_1) => a_1$

Since both laws are bidirectional this will not cause any harm, but taken from a broader perspective (3) could imply loss of information, as will be illustrated below.

Another law that in some ways is a generalization of (x) and (xi) is:

(xii) s: $a_1 \cdots a_{i-1} a_i a_{i+1} \cdots a_m \mid a_{m+1} \cdots a_{i-1+m} a_i a_{i+1+m} \cdots a_{2m} \mid \cdots$
$\mid a_{nm+1} \cdots a_{i-1+nm} a_i a_{i+1+nm} \cdots a_{(n+1)m}$
<=>
$(a_1 \cdots a_{i-1} \mid a_{m+1} \cdots a_{i-1+m} \mid \cdots \mid a_{n,m+1} \cdots a_{i-1+nm}) a_i$
$(a_{i+1} \cdots a_m \mid a_{i+1+m} \cdots a_{2m} \mid \cdots \mid a_{i+1+nm} \cdots a_{(n+1)m})$

An example of this law is:

(4) U: AaC ⎮ BaC ⎮ BaD <=> U: (A ⎮ B ⎮ B)a(C ⎮ C ⎮ D)

Here (A⎮B⎮B) can be transformed into (A⎮B) and (C⎮C⎮D) into (C⎮D) but in both these cases information is lost, since

(5) U: (A ⎮ B ⎮ B)a(C ⎮ C ⎮ D) => U: (A ⎮ B)a(C ⎮ D) => U: AaC ⎮ BaD
       $\neq$ AaC ⎮ BaC ⎮ BaD.

This is a result that obviously does not correspond to the original expression in (4). Hence (3) is dangerous due to the risk of losing information. This is especially apparent in (xii). The obvious and visual transformation of the expression in (4) can be seen in Figure 9.

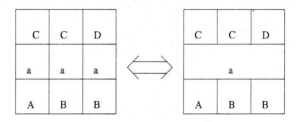

Figure 9. Visual interpretation of the transformation in (4).

However, neither of the images in Figure 9 correspond to the original. The original which easily can be obtained by

(6) $(B \mid B) \Rightarrow B$

(7) $(C \mid C) \Rightarrow C$

is left to the reader to create.

Next we want to describe law (xiii), which is a simplification of law (xii).

(xiii) $(a_1 \mid \cdots \mid a_i \mid \cdots \mid a_n)(b_1 \mid \cdots \mid b_i \mid \cdots \mid b_n) <=> a_1 b_1 \mid \cdots \mid a_i b_i \mid \cdots \mid a_n b_n$

This law can simply be illustrated with the following example

(8) U: $(A \mid A \mid C)(D \mid B \mid B) <=> U$: $AD \mid AB \mid CB$

Obviously, there is also here a risk to go to far in simplification since here too there could be a loss of information if some of the edge-to-edge-relations are dropped.

The example in (9) below shows a special case of law (xiii), where the risk of losing information is also apparent.

(9) U: $(A \mid A \mid B \mid B \mid C)(F \mid G \mid G \mid H \mid H) <=> AF \mid AG \mid BG \mid BH \mid CH$

In the above only the U-strings have been considered. It is, however, clear from the general representation of the laws that projections along all axes are applicable. Furthermore, in the examples and in the laws the assumptions have been made that the transformation can be done without considering information available in the orthogonal object string. This is, however, not always the case. Assume the following:

(10) U: $AB \mid A$

    V: $A \mid BA$

According to law (x) the U-string can be rewritten as

(11) U: A(B l)

But this does not look appropriate, because the meaning of (Bl) is unclear and by investigating the V-string it is more likely that

(12) U: A(B l A)

because it can easily be shown that A has the shape of a twisted capital 'L'. This can be verified by looking at the 2D-strings from the following view:

(13) U: U1 l U2 = U: AB l A
　　 V: V1 l V2 = V: A l BA

where U1 = AB, U2 = A, V1 = A and V2 = BA. The object part that we are talking about is

(14) $U: U_2 \bigcap V_2 = A \bigcap BA = A$

and

(15) $(U_1 l U_2) \bigcap V_1 = (AB \, l A) \bigcap A = A \, l A = A$

Hence, it is possible to expand the definitions of the laws (x) through (xiii) by using the technique from (14) and (15).

Thus far

$s': s'_1 l \cdots l s'_i l \cdots l s'_n$

$s'': s''_1 l \cdots l s''_i l \cdots l s''_m$ where s' is not equal to s''

and for all i, $s'_i = s'_{1i} as'_{2i}$ such that $s' \bigcap s''_j = a$ for some j then

$s': (s'_{11} l \cdots l s'_{1n}) a (s'_{21} l \cdots l s'_{2n})$.

This corresponds to law (x) if $(s'_{11} l \cdots l s'_{1n})$ is empty and to law (xi) if $(s'_{21} l \cdots l si_{2n})$ is empty. Otherwise we can apply either law (xii) or law (xiii).

If $s'_i \bigcap s''_{i-1} = a$ for any i=2,...,n then $s'_i = s'_{1i} aas'_{2i}$.

and

If $s'_i \bigcap s''_{i+1} = a$ for any i=1,...,n-1 then $s'_i = s'_{1i} aas'_{2i}$.

By using this extension to the laws of this section all cases can be handled correctly. However, there are also two further laws that have been mentioned during the above discussion but have not explicitly been pointed out. These are related to the reshaping laws among the empty space laws

(xiv) s: a l ... l a => s: a

(xv) s: a ... a => s: a

As pointed out earlier the elimination of the l operator might lead to loss of information, therefore the law (xiv) has to be handled with care. The inverse of both laws is not completely clear since they will require creation of new partition lines.

Finally, there is also the law of substitution

(xvi) Any portion of either one or both 2D-strings can be substituted.

An illustration of this is, for instance, the expression in (9)

(16) U: (A l A l B l B l C)(F l G l G l H l H) substitute (A l A l B l B l C) with M

(17) U: M (F l G l G l H l H)

The substitution has changed the application of the laws. Hence it is not correct to distribute M inside the parentheses according to law (x).

(18) U: MF l MG l MG l MH l MH

If we now try to insert the old expression for M it is easy to see that this doesn't work. However, it would be possible to solve this problem by changing the '=' operator into, say '-', thus indicating that a substitution has been performed and that some operations corresponding to the laws are prohibited.

6. Compound Objects and Multilevel Structures

Consider the symbolic image in Figure 10, from which the following 2D-string along the x-axis can be obtained.

(1) U: AF l BGH l CGI l DK

This string can then according to law (xii) be transformed into

(2) U: AF l (B l C) G (H l I) l DK

and finally through law (xiii) into

(3) U: (A l (B l C) l D)(F l G (H l I) l K)

In this example it is easy to see that in the final expression a more or less hierarchical structure is obtained, this is also illustrated in Figure 10.

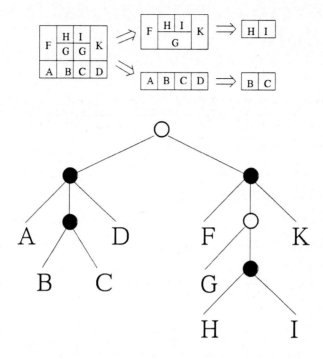

Figure 10. Example of algebraic compound object degeneration.

Using this technique for determining compound objects and their hierarchical structures any multi-level structure can be obtained. This also completes the features of the algebraic language which is described in this paper.

To demonstrate the multi-level approach, the image in Figure 11 is transformed into a structure analogous to a quad-tree.

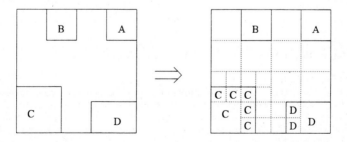

Figure 11. An illustration of an image and its corresponding quad-tree structure.

The view of the quad-tree itself can easily be obtained from the figure to the right in Figure

11. However, the 2D-string of the image is in the basic representation:

U: Ce | CeB | eB | e | De | DeA
V: CeD | Ce | e | eBeA

which does not represent any sub-object levels.

In accordance with the usual technique for quad-tree development the image is divided first into four parts of equal size and then into sixteen parts and so on. The procedure when transforming the 2D-strings, is similar except that at each division new compound objects are created on lower levels in the multi-level structure.

1st division step

U: $(U1 | U2) = U$: $(Ce | CeB | eB) | (e | De | DeA)$
V: $(V1 | V2 = V$: $(CeD | Ce | e) | (e | eBeA)$

where $U1 = (Ce | CeB | eB)$
$U2 = (e | De | DeA)$
$V1 = (CeD | Ce | e)$
$V2 = (e | eBeA)$.

This first step is fairly straight forward, although it is obvious that the generation of this multi-level-structure requires some kind of low level search while the program is performing the transformation.

2nd division step

$(U1 | U2) = ((U11 | U12) | (U21 | U22)) = (((Ce) | (CeB | eB)) | ((e | De) | (DeA)))$

$(V1 | V2) = ((V11 | V12) | (V21 | V22)) = (((CeD) | (Ce | e)) | ((e) | eBeA)))$

3rd division step

$((U11 | U12) | (U21 | U22)) = (((U111 | U112) | (U121 | U122)) | ((U211 | U212) | U22))$
$= (((((Ce) | (Ce)) | ((CeB) | eB))) | (((e) | (De)) | (DeA)))$
$= ((V11 | V12) | V21 | V22)) = ((V11 | V121 | V122)) | (V21 | V22))$
$= (((CeD) | ((Ce) | (e))) | ((e) | (eBeA)))$

Note that U22, V11, V21 and V22 need not be divided further after the 2nd step.

7. Tile Graph Generation

In [9], it was shown that it is possible to generate a graph made up by nodes of empty space and create a graph structure from them. The nodes in this graph are called tiles. The graph itself is part of a knowledge structure, which can be used for hierarchic navigation or planning of the shortest path between two arbitrary points in a map of free-space and obstacles. Figure 12 illustrates the tiles.

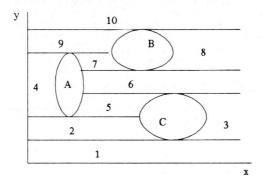

Figure 12. The tile structure of an image with three obstacles and free-space.

The objects A, B and C correspond to obstacles while the areas with the numbers 1 through 10 correspond to the tiles. As can be seen the lines that correspond to the horizontal edges of the tiles are a subset of the lines in figure 5, which creates the $e^v_{i,j}$ objects. We can conclude that, since a tile graph can be generated from Figure 12, a tile-graph can also be generated from the type of structure such as shown in Figure 5. However, the general structure of the tile graph is such that a node has at most four neighbors which are connected by arcs. The image in Figure 12 corresponds to the tile-graph in Figure 13.

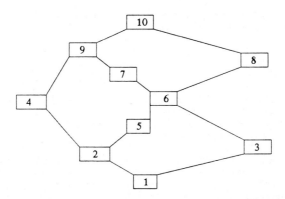

Figure 13. Tile-graph corresponding to the tile structure in Figure 12.

A closer look at the Figures 5 and 12 shows that, for instance, tile 4 corresponds to $e^v_{3,1} \mid e^v_{4,1} \mid e^v_{5,1}$, tile 7 corresponds to $e^v_{5,2}$, and so on. It is easy to see that there exist three classes of tiles, i.e. tiles between:

1) the edge of the image and an object

2) two objects

3) the left and right edge of the image.

For class 1 more than one empty space object is needed for the creation of the tile, see e.g. tile 4. The second and the third class are more trivial because one tile corresponds to only one empty space object. Hence, the rules for tile generation can be defined.

For k= 1,...,n, the tiles t_k are generated according to the following rules:

(1) $e^s_{i,j}$ | or
     | $e^s_{i,j}$ | or   => $t_k = e^s_{i,j}$
     | $e^s_{i,j}$

(2) $e^s_{i,j} a \cdots | e^s_{i+1,j'} a ... | \cdots => t_k = e^s_{i,j} | e^s_{i+1,j'} | \cdots$

(3) $\cdots a e^s_{i,j} | \cdots a e^s_{i+1,j'} | \cdots => t_k = e^s_{i,j} | e^s_{i+1,j'} | \cdots$

(4) $a_1 e^s_{i,j} a_2 => t_k = e^s_{i,j}$

where a, $a_1 a_2$ are obstacles.

The first rule corresponds to the third class of tiles. The second and the third rule belong both to the first class, while finally the fourth rule corresponds to the second class of tiles.

In rules 2 and 3, the 2D strings can be transformed in accordance with law (xii).

(1) $(e^s_{i,j} | e^s_{i+1,j'} | \cdots) a (....)$

(2) $(....) a (e^s_{i,j} | e^s_{i+1,j'} | \cdots)$

In (1) the first sub-object corresponds directly to the tile and the last in (2) similarly to the tile of the rule.

8. Conclusions

This paper describes an algebra for symbolic image manipulation and transformation. The algebra is based on symbolic projections and contains: 1) A set of three elementary and powerful relational operators, 2) generalized empty space objects (e), and 3) means for description of multi-level data structures.

From these fundamental aspects, a number of algebraic laws have been defined, which make it possible to manipulate and transform symbolic images in arbitrary ways. The technique can be used as a knowledge structure and also for the development of graph structures, which can be applied to heuristic navigation. Hence, this algebra forms a structure that can be used for symbolic image processing.

Applications of interest for the algebra are, for instance, visual data base systems and image data base systems. Since this algebra can be used to describe shapes, it is applicable to the description and parsing of visual sentences. Other types of applications of which many might be of heuristic type exist as well, e.g. in the areas of navigation, and temporal graph description.

Finally, the discussion in this paper was confined to two dimensions. However, it is our belief that the algebra can be generalized into three dimensions as well.

References:

[1] H. Samet, "The Quad-Tree and Related Hierarchical Data Structures", ACM Computing Survey, Vol 26, 1984, pp. 187-260.

[2] P. H. Winston, "Artificial Intelligence", Addison-Wesley, Reading, Mass., 1977.

[3] K. S. Fu, *Syntactic Methods in Pattern Recognition*, Academic Press, 1974.

[4] S. K. Chang, Q. Y. Shi and C. W. Yan, "Iconic Indexing by 2-D Strings", IEEE Trans. on Pattern Analysis and Machine Intelligence, Vol PAMI-9, No 3., pp. 413-428, 1987.

[5] E. Jungert, "Extended Symbolic Projections Used as a Knowledge Structure for Spatial Reasoning", In Pattern Recognition, Springer Verlay, proc. of the 4th BPRA Conference on Pattern Recognition, March 28-30, 1988, Cambridge.

[6] E. Jungert, "Run-Length-Code as an Object-Oriented Spatial Data Structure", Proceedings of the IEEE Workshop on Languages for Automation, Singapore, August 27-29, 1986.

[7] S. K. Chang and E. Jungert, "A spatial Knowledge Structure for Image Information Systems Using Orthogonal Symbolic Projections", Proceedings of the Fall Joint Computer Conference, Dallas, TX, November 2-6, 1986.

[8] Tomas Lozano-Perez, "Automatic Planning of Manipulator Transfer Movements", IEEE Trans. on Systems, Man and Cybernetics, Vol SMC-11, No. 10, October 1981, pp. 681-698.

[9] E. Jungert and P. Holmes, "A Knowledge-based Approach to the Shortest Path Problem in a Digitized Map", Proceedings of 1988 Workshop on Visual Languages, Oct. 1988, Pittsburgh.

[10] S. Kundu, "The Equivalence of the Subregion Representation and the Wall Representation for a Certain Class of Rectangular Dissections", Communications of the ACM, Vol. 31, No. 6, June 1988, 752-763.

Visual Database Systems
T.L. Kunii (Editor)
Elsevier Science Publishers B.V. (North-Holland)
© IFIP, 1989

Unified Data Structures for Mixed 3D Scene Management

Jean-Luc CORRE and Gérard HEGRON

IRISA */INRIA* [†]
Campus de beaulieu
35042 Rennes Cedex
France

With the advent of simulation and animation of highly complex 3D environments, we have to deal with the unification of different computer graphics methodologies. In other words, "mixed scenes" whose data structure must face creation, animation, visualization and on-line user interaction constraints and must incorporate different object geometric models simultaneously. The data structure must be described and managed in a coherent way. In this paper, our methodology and development of unified data structures which allow dynamic management and visualization of 3D mixed scenes is presented. The scene description includes both topological and morphological levels, and hierarchical and relational structures. The object geometric modelling and visualization take into account variable-resolution representation and different levels of realism. An object-oriented implementation whose class hierarchy includes both modelling classes and display classes, provides flexibility and efficient handling of the scene database. Our results are illustrated by two applications: a computer animation system including mechanical laws and the design of graphics system devoted to submarine intervention.

Key words : mixed scene, hierarchical and relational data structures, geometric modelling, visualization, variable-resolution representation, object-oriented implementation, animation, interactivity.

---

[*]Institut de Recherche en Informatique et Systèmes Aléatoires.
[†]Institut National de Recherche en Informatique et Automatique.

1 Introduction

Traditionally data structures and models used for scene description are different from which used for scene visualization. For example, in a flight simulator, a graphic data structure, suitable for fast rendering, is extracted from the scene model used to describe the environment. Both data structures have their own hierarchy and geometric models adapted either to interaction or to visualization. With the advent of very powerful workstations and the new requirements of applications, like simulation and animation of highly complex environments, we have to deal with the unification of the different computer graphics concepts. For instance in a Computer Aided Teleoperation System [1], not only synthetic visual feedback is required on-line but also environment changing and interaction like identification of an object, attaching several objects together (grasping), modifying geometrical aspects, and so on. Therefore informations and data stemmed from scene creation and graphic structures have to be shared. In other words, "mixed scenes" have to be created and managed in a coherent way. "Mixed scene" means that scene data structure has to face creation, animation and user interaction constraints and has to incorporate different object geometric models. The synthetic image of the scene may also present different levels of realism, from wireframe presentation to realistic image, in order to render the pertinent information according to the application.

In this paper we present our methodology and development of unified data structures which allow dynamic management and visualization of 3D mixed scenes. First, we describe the scene description which includes both topological and morphological levels and hierarchical and relational structures. Thereafter the object geometric modelling and visualization are developed taking into account variable-resolution representation. Then, the object-oriented implementation of this approach is discussed. Our results are illustrated by two applications : a computer animation system including mechanical laws, and the design of a graphics system devoted to submarine intervention.

2 3D Scene data structure

The description of a 3D universe is achieved by defining objects and their relationships. The scene and object data structures have to facilitate creating, editing, animating and accessing objects and their relationships. Two description levels of a scene can be distinguished :

- the *topology* which describes the logical connections between the parts of the scene without any assumption on its geometric modelling. At this level the scene structure is a semantic network containing propositional representations.

- the *morphology* which defines the scene *style* by specifying its object and connection attributes (geometric models, texture and photometry information, mechanical properties, etc.). To one morphology corresponds an infinity of scene instances.

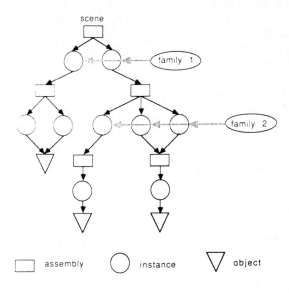

Figure 1: Hierarchical scene data structure

In this way the designer defines the structural architecture of the scene in a first step. Then he chooses any style he wants to get. For example a chair can be made of four legs and of a back of seat connected to the seat, but its style may be a draft (wireframe representation), or modern, or ancient (Louis the 14th, Louis the 15th, etc.) and the legs may be embedded anywhere in the seat.

In order to manage complex environments the database employs both hierarchical and relational structures [9] [23]. The hierarchical construction forms a directed acyclic graph with assemblies at the non-terminal nodes, components (objects) at the leaves, and instances in the links between the nodes (figure 1). Position and orientation are given relative to that of the assembly owning the instance. "Super-instances" might be introduced to model a set of the same assembly or of the same component which occurs several times in the space at regular relative positions; for example like the small balls in a ball-bearing. The directed graph represents a vertical hierarchy which organized the whole scene in sub-scenes and so on. To be able to treat not only elements one by one, an horizontal hierarchy which constitutes a one-level hierarchy, is created by means of instance families (figure 1).

If we build multibody mechanical systems containing open and/or closed chains, a relational structure is used to specify object adjacencies. It is a general graph where the elementary bodies (nodes) are linked together by mechanical joints (arcs). For example a car is broadly a set of an instance of a car body and of four instances of a wheel (vertical hierarchy). But the car mechanical system is obtained by linking (adjacencies) the four wheels one by one to the car body. This adjacency graph is used to compute the motion of the car induced by the mechanical laws. At each joint between two bodies, a body moves relative to the other one, via one to six translational or rotational degrees of freedom (d.o.f.). A joint links two static frames of reference associated to the two respective bodies. The classification of the geometrical types of joints is showed in the following table :

Number	Joint	Rot	Trans	d.o.f. nb
1	Embedding	0	0	0
2	Pin	1	0	1
3	Sliding	0	1	1
4	Twist sliding	1	1	1
5	Cylindrical	1	1	2
6	Plane on plane	1	2	3
7	Ball and socket	3	0	3
8	Cylinder on plane	2	2	4
9	Ball in a cylinder	3	1	4
10	Ball on plane	3	2	5
11	Flying object	3	3	6

These hierarchical and relational data structures allow the user to build the scene by descendant and ascendant ways :

- the descendant technique is suitable for ordering the data base into sets and sub-sets and into families.

- to assemble a complex mechanism, the user makes it up by linking the elementary objects (bodies) in an ascendant way.

During the utilization of the scene data base, we have to deal with three main functions. The first one is the object displacements according to relative coordinate systems and mechanical constraints. The second one is the dynamic management of the body adjacencies. For instance, if a robot arm picks up an object lying on a table, the link between the object and the table is removed and a new link is created between the object and the manipulator hand. The third function is the designation of a scene part either by picking it on the screen or by typing its name. To acheive these functions, ad hoc procedures access and update the data structures.

3   Variable-resolution scene representation

In a mixed scene several geometric models may cohabit : wireframe objects, polygonal and free form surfaces, solids (CSG model, boundary representation, octree, etc.), and fractals. Why is it so ? Because a geometric model is suitable either for object creation (CSG model, generalized cynlinder, free form surface), or for object treatments like boolean operation or physical property computation (octree), or for object

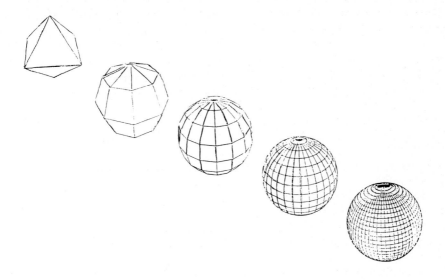

Figure 2: Five uniform polygonal decomposition levels of a sphere

visualization (boundary representation). In order to manage these various models simultaneously two solutions can be used either by converting the different models to a single one [26] [18] [5], or by using ad hoc algorithms for each model. Both approaches are complementary and useful : to display the scene the polygonal representation is now the most efficient, but to keep the exact description of an object, for instance a sphere, an algebraic form is required.

From exact representation to polygonal approximation an adaptive decomposition of the geometric model can be achieved during the vizualisation process according to the distance between the object and the observer [10]. This treatment decreases the polygon number to display and increases the efficiency of the hidden-surface removal algorithm without degrading the image rendering. But the ratio between the decomposition time and the visualization gain must be large. So to minimize this pretreatment, the decomposition is done off line and ordered in a few levels. Quadrics, for example a sphere, are uniformly subdivided (figure 2). With each increasing level a closer approximation to the primitive boundary is achieved.

For free form surfaces the subdivision must be flexible to take into account the irregularities [4]. As shown in figure 3, the node sampling of the surface is more dense where the curvature is important. This adaptive sampling produces a fewer polygons and a better approximation of the surface [3].

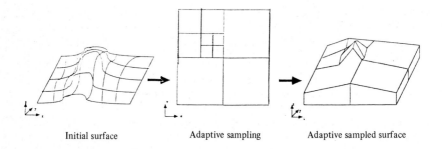

Initial surface   Adaptive sampling   Adaptive sampled surface

Figure 3: Non uniform sampling of a free form surface

For boundary representation of a solid, a variable-resolution model provides strictly object-dependant polyhedral descriptions of the surfaces enclosing an object and allows both a fast surface rendering [24] and an efficient detection of object intersection [13]. A variable-resolution boundary representation can be regarded as a tree structure in which the root is the highest level of abstraction of a polyhedral description, and where the nodes describe a segmentation of the parent face in the tree [15]. An approximation error is usually associated with any face further refined into a connected set of faces [14].

Jointly these variable-resolution model representations, an adaptive detail computation can be added according suitable priority metric [7]. If this approach is a priori attractive, its implementation is not obvious :

- the hierarchy of levels of detail is done by hand. For example, for the hierarchical representation of a human stick figure [19] [8], at the coarsest resolution the human body can be represented by a single upright cylinder; at the next level of resolution we have a collection of attached cylinders representing the torso, head, arms and legs, and so on. Each level geometric representation has to be specified by the designer.

- the detail hierarchy is always descendant [10], that is to say the objects are modelled in greater and greater details. What's happened if the previous human stick figure carries a big suitcase ? The descendant hierarchy is not respected any more.

- levels of detail are predefined off-line, but their geometric specifications might change during an animation : for instance, at the coarsest resolution, the cylinder size is not the same if the human body is standing or crouching.

- in the relevant literature, only the geometric aspect is taking into account but not the rendering. What is the colour of the body cylinder at the lowest resolution if at the next level the colours of torso, head, arms and legs are different ?

In the brute-force approach, in our implementation each object primitive is by default and individually displayed or not according its size and a simple metric. But the user can a priori enforce its visualization if the detail is pertinent for the scene understanding or rendering.

4   Toward an object-oriented implementation

The object-oriented approach encapsulates the representations of database entities and relationships with the procedures that manipulate them [21]. The two qualities that are most directly addressed by object-oriented techniques are *extensibility* and *reusability* [20].

The extensibility may be defined as the flexibility of software products with respect to specification changes. For example, in the encapsulation of the class framework, not only different geometric models may coexist [6], but the class framework makes manageable the multi-representation of a particular geometric model. In this way, the class of the solid primitive *sphere* contains a solid geometric model and boundary representations (Brep). The Brep includes precomputed polygonal decompositions of the unity sphere boundary (figure 2). Besides the computation of the decomposition level of a given sphere, according to its size in the scene and to its projection size in the image, no overheads are induced by the conversion of the given sphere from its solid model to its polygonal decomposition. Since the precomputed polygonal decompositions belong to the class of the solid primitive sphere, they are shared by the instances of the class. The Brep includes multiple structures according to the adjacency relationships needed [28] [29]. The visualization in real time uses the relationship *face-vertex*. The identification task of an object on the screen needs a more hierarchical structure *surface-face-edge-vertex*. An adjacency relationship is constructed at the initialisation of the system by a method of the class if the relationship is a default one, else the relationship is constructed only if it is required. The different geometric models and the multiple structures are oriented to a specific application [25]. Furthermore, the efficiency of specialized methods attached to a particular representation need not be diluted by further extensions of the class framework [12].

The reusability is the ability of software products to be reused, in whole or in part, for new applications. By code sharing and by exploiting the commonality in the software encountered before development, effort can be reduced.
Futhermore the static managment of the class framework is enhanced in the object-oriented programming because the software manipulations are localized to the scope of the changing class. However the dynamic management of the evolving class framework

remains a major problem. The behavior of an object is modified on-line overtime by stepwise refinement. The desired behavior changes induce structural changes in the class, manipulation of executable programmes and modification of parameters.

In object-oriented languages, classes are defined by a set of instance-variable declarations an a collection of methods. In our 3D scene, many elements follow common patterns (windows, doors). In our system, instance variables common to the scene belong to a class. The choice of a class for a given pattern is still let to the operator but the manipulations of the instance variable are restricted to the methods of the class providing a tool for integrity management and avoiding any inconsistent pattern manipulations [30]. These methods include both direct manipulations of the specific parameters of the class and forward manipulations of the subclass.

In our system the description of an instance includes an identifier attribute, a geometric description in multiple models, a set of non-geometric attributes, a network representing the decomposition of the domain object into subobjects, a network representing the mechanical links, and a set of specific operators used to manipulate permanent data of the instance [12].

By integrating the concept of abstract data types into both the data definition and data manipulation, the system user can define efficient data types and methods that correspond to application-specific objects.

With the object-oriented approach, the operator can use the system in two ways: the structural (data driven) and the behavioral (model driven) object orientation [17].

The structural approach reflects the bottom-up creation of an object morphology in the engineering world, that is composed of parts that may among themselves undergo a variety of other relationships. This typical approach is based on hierarchical models that are used in the geometric modeling systems [25].

Structurally object-oriented models "provide facilities for mapping complex objects onto structures and for retrieving these objects as entities" [17] and this kind of organization is imposed on the information about the environment at the macroscopic level [11]. Object decomposition and hierarchical representation require the decomposition of the object into parts and the construction of relational links between decomposed parts [6]. The hierarchical structures stress the design and the knowledge of the system user, the locality of access in our hierachical models ensures that the system runs quickly.

The behavioral approach reflects the top-down manipulations of an object topology. At an instant the user of our system can see or remind only a small part of the large-scale structures in the scene database. To overcome the local "observation" of the objets during their creations and the undersea navigation in the preexisting database, our system offers the user a concise precomputed representation of the objets that can be created and manipulated as a whole. The individual data item of the entity hidden to the user, are initialized by default. Either input facilities provide access to the arguments that have default values or the missing values are supplied by the system like a compiler of the C++ language does [27].

In order to implement the concepts for strutural, as well as relational, object orientation, the architecture underlying the scene model is a network-based multi-layered representation. In this architecture the class framework manages the top-down (model driven or behavioral) and the bottom-up (data driven or structural) approach. A node in the network can be either:

- Primitive object which is an undecomposable physical entity

- Object which represents aggregated objects and which can be recursively decomposed into networks of subobjects: either objects or primitive objects.

The desciption of a primitive object includes:

- a geometric description: type of the geometric model with subdivision levels, position, bounding-box,

- a set of non-geometric attributes (color, texture),

- a set of inter-objects connections (physical, logical),

- a set of operators for manipulating the object (subdivision methods, visualization methods, picking techniques) [22].

If restricting the manipulation of abstract data type provides a tool for integrity management of one object (it avoids any inconsistent manipulations), problems occur when a subobject is added or deleted, the network containing the object should be tagged as invalid and new links should be recomputed if needed. A similar action must be taken when the location of an object changes. When a mecanism object is added to the network and connected to another mecanism object, it may be possible to merge the two objects into a single one.

Another problem seems to be that the representation is split up into very small partitions (for example the geometric class *vertex*). This might lead to inherently inefficient data manipulation processes, unless we can manage to cluster data appropriately (for example the class *vertices_array*).

5   Applications

At IRISA we are implementing these data structure concepts in a few computer graphics applications. In particular we are working on the design of a general animation system including motion generation defined by use of mechanical laws [16] [2]. The system is built around a structured graph which includes hierarchical and relational structures. A link between two instances may represent various properties like propositional relations or analogical relations. For example in figure 4, the connection between car.1 and road.1 is a contact (propositional relation), the joints between the

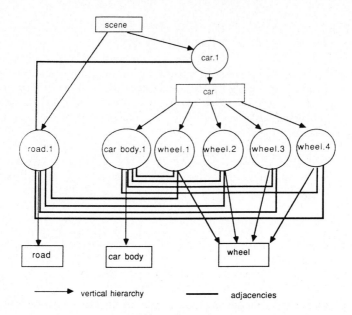

Figure 4: Scene example: a car on a road

structures. A link between two instances may represent various properties like propositional relations or analogical relations. For example in figure 4, the connection between car.1 and road.1 is a contact (propositional relation), the joints between the car body and the four wheels are pins, and between the road and the four wheels are rolling without sliding (analogical relations). The propositional relation "contact" is valid if and only if at least one part of the car is connected to the road with analogical relation (joints).

This graph structure allows the generation of general multibody systems including open and closed chains where rigid bodies are linked together by mechanical joints which may have a dynamic behavior like springs and dashpots. From this static description of the mechanism including the computation of the body dynamic properties (inertia center, inertia matrice, weight), and from the specification of actuator forces and torques the differential motion equations are automatically built by performing symbolic derivations. Then a finite difference method for time derivatives and a Newton-Raphson algorithm for solving nonlinearities are used.

Another application field we are working on, is the development of a graphics system intended for the assistance of submarine pilotage and intervening. As the submarine environment is turbid, the system helps the pilot to see it, to situate himself in the context and to locate objects. As the scene is well known, the graphics system provides the operator a synthetic image of the modelled environment from any virtual or real point of view. Robotic tasks could be incorporated which involve off-line modelling of manipulators, programming of trajectory, inteference checking and defining functional regions and artificial constraints, and on-line providing real-time

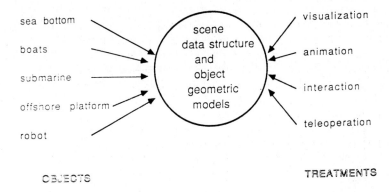

Figure 5: Submarine environment and treatment constraints

information feedbacks to the operator during the task performance by synthetic visual feedback.

For the implementation of this system we have to face all the relevant constraints of mixed scenes (figure 5). The object types are various : the sea bottom is a surface got from bathymetry; boats, submarines, offshore platform and robots are described from plans and have different shapes (free form surfaces, primitive solids like cylinders and blocks) and different structures (articulated chains, complex rigid structures). In the same way during the online utilization of the system we have to manage the scene vizualisation, the animation of objects (camera, submarine) and multibody mechanisms (robot arm), interactive functions (object picking, point acquisition, modifying geometrical aspects), and the dynamic updating of links (attaching several objects together: grasping).

To illustrate some of our implementations of these techniques, let us look at picture 1 and picture 2. Picture 1 shows a hulk on the beach. Picture 1-a is a hidden line view of the scene which is the less time consuming ; and picture 1-b is a shaded hidden surface view which is more time consuming than the previous one. In order to do a compromise between line-drawing and realistic image a mixing of different image presentation can be achieved according to user's wishes. Picture 1-c renders this idea where drawing (beach) and image (hulk) coexist. Picture 2 represents an offshore platform lying on the sea bottom. Picture 2.a is a hidden line view of the whole structure. Picture 2.b is a nearer view of the same scene on which the shaded tube has been picked up. The next closer view (picture 2.c) presents the same polygonal subdivision level of object primitives (here cylinders) as the previous one. The closest view (picture 2.d) shows the highest subdivision level and gives a good 3D perception of the pointed out element thanks to shading.

6 Conclusion

For the dynamic management of mixed 3D scenes, we propose a unified data structure where hierarchical and adjacency (relational) structures are embedded and where topological and morphological levels are distinguished. This data structure allows description the whole scene in both ascendant and descendant ways, and design of an animation of complex multibody systems. As mixed scene includes various geometric models and can be displayed with different levels of realism, we propose some variable resolution representations of the object models and object rendering. We have shown why and how object-oriented implementation is suitable for such a unified approach and we underlined the relevant problems.

Most of these concepts have been implemented into a computer animation system and into a graphics system devoted to underwater navigation and intervention. Future work leads us to integrate our whole unification methodology in an on-line interactive system.

Acknowledgements
This research was partially supported by IFREMER (Institut Francais pour l'Exploitatio de la Mer) under grant no 86/2.350.522.

References

[1] G. André and A. Fournier. The generalized information feedback concept in computer-aided teleoperation. In *Proc. 6th Symposium on Theory and Pratice of Robots and Manipulators*, ROMANSY 86, September 1986.

[2] B. Arnaldi. *Conception du Noyau d'un Système d'Animation de Scènes Tridimensionnelles intégrant les Lois de la Mécanique*. PhD thesis, Université de RENNES 1, Juillet 1988.

[3] A.H. Barr B. Von Herzen. Accurate triangulations of deformed, intersecting surfaces. *Computer Graphics*, 21(4):103–110, July 1987.

[4] M.D. Dippe B.A. Barsky, T.D. DeRose. *An Adaptive Subdivision Method With Crak Prevention for Rendering Beta-spline Objets*. Technical Report, Berkeley University, March 1987.

[5] D. Badouel and G. Hégron. Set operation evaluation using boolean octree. In Springer-Verlag, editor, *New Trends in Computer Graphics*, pages 275–287, CGI'88, May 1988.

[6] B. Bhanu and C.C. Ho. Cad-based 3D object representation for robot vision. *Computer*, 20(8):19–35, August 1987.

[7] E. Blake and S. Cook. A metric for computing adaptive detail in animated scenes. In G. Maréchal, editor, *Proceedings of the EUROGRAPHICS*, pages 295–307, EUROGRAPHICS'87, August 1987.

[8] E. Blake and S. Cook. On including part hierarchies in object-oriented langages. In *Proceedings of the European Conference on Object-Oriented Programming*, pages 41–50, ECOOP'87, June 1987.

[9] I.C. Braid. *Notes on a geometric modeller*. CAD Group Document 101, University of Cambridge, Juin 1980.

[10] J.H. Clark. Hierarchical geometric models for visible surface algorithms. *ACM Graphics and Image Processing*, 19(10):547–554, October 1976.

[11] E. Triendl D.J. Kriegman and T. Binford. A mobil robot: sensing, planning and locomotion. In *Proceedings 1987 IEEE International Conference on Robotics and Automation*, pages 402–408, IEEE Council on Robotics and Automation, March 1987.

[12] P. Amburn E. Grant and T. Whitted. Exploiting classes in modeling and display software. *IEEE Computer Graphics and Applications*, 6(11):13–20, November 1986.

[13] O.D. Faugeras and J. Ponce. Prism trees: a hierarchical representation for 3D objects. In *Proceedings of the IJCAI 83*, pages 982–988, IJCAI'83, August 1983.

[14] L. De Floriani. Adjacency finding algorithms in a variable-resolution boundary model. In Springer-Verlag, editor, *New Trends in Computer Graphics*, pages 298–307, CGI'88, May 1988.

[15] L. De Floriani and B. Falcidieno. A hierarchical boundary model for solid object representation. *ACM Transactions on Graphics*, 7(1):42–60, January 1988.

[16] B. Arnaldi G. Hégron and G. Dumont. Toward general animation control. In Springer-Verlag, editor, *New Trends in Computer Graphics*, pages 54–63, CGI'88, May 1988.

[17] A. Kemper and M. Wallrath. An analysis of geometric modeling in database systems. *ACM Computing Surveys*, 19(1):47–91, March 1987.

[18] M. Mantyla and R. Sulonen. Gwb: a solid modeler with euler operator. *IEEE Computer Graphics and Applications*, 2(7):17–31, September 1982.

[19] D. Marr. Visual information processing: the structure and creation of visual representations. In *Proceedings of the IJCAI 79*, pages 1108–1126, IJCAI'79, August 1979.

[20] B. Meyer. Genericity, inheritance and type checking. In *Tutorial 3 of The 1st European Software Engineering Conference*, pages 54–75, ESEC'87, September 87.

[21] B. Meyer. Object-oriented design and programming. In *Tutorial 3 of The 1st European Software Engineering Conference*, pages 1–33, ESEC'87, September 87.

[22] E. Grant P. Amburn and T. Whitted. Managing geometric complexity with enhanced procedural models. In *Proceedings of the SIGGRAPH'86*, pages 189–195, Computer Graphics, August 1986.

[23] A. J. Polinsky and P. Brock. *A Unified Interactive Geometric Modeling System for Simulating Highly Complex Environments*. Thesis for the Degree of Master of Science, Cornell University, August 1986.

[24] J. Ponce and O. Faugeras. An object centered hierarchical representation for 3D objects: the prism tree. *Computer Vision, Graphics and Image Processing*, 38(1):1–28, April 1987.

[25] A.A.G. Requicha. Representation for rigid solids : theory, methods, and systems. *ACM Computing Surveys*, 12(4):437–464, December 1980.

[26] A.A.G. Requicha and H.B. Voelcker. Boolean operations in solid modeling: boundary evaluation and merging algorithms. In *Proceedings of the IEEE*, pages 30–44, IEEE'85, January 1985.

[27] B. Stroustrup. *The C++ Programming Language*. Addison-Wesley, Reading, Massachusetts, 1986.

[28] K. Weiler. Edge-based data structures for solid modeling in curved-surface environments. *IEEE Computer Graphics and Applications*, 5(1):21–40, January 1985.

[29] T.C. Woo. A combinatorial analysis of boundary data structure schemata. *IEEE Computer Graphics and Applications*, 5(3):19–27, March 1985.

[30] D.R. Rehak W.T. Keirouz and I.J. Oppenheim. *Development of an Object Oriented Domain Model for Constructed Facilities*. Research Report, Carnegie Mellon University, October 1987.

Figure 6: Picture 1.a

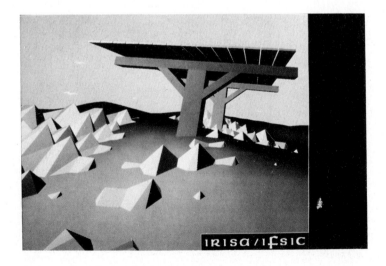

Figure 7: Picture 1.b

Figure 8: Picture 1.c

Figure 9: Picture 2.a

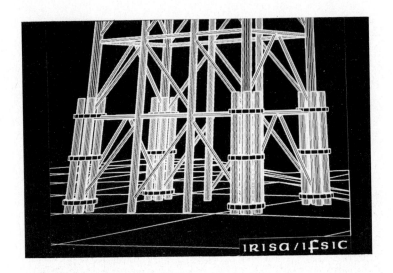

Figure 10: Picture 2.b

Figure 11: Picture 2.c

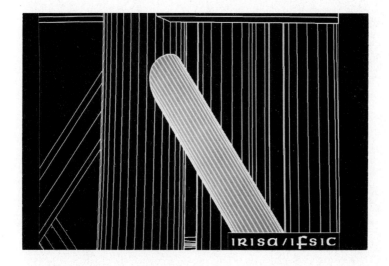

Figure 12: Picture 2.d

Visual Database Systems
T.L. Kunii (Editor)
Elsevier Science Publishers B.V. (North-Holland)
© IFIP, 1989

A Diagrammatic Interface
to a Database of Thangka Imagery

Ranjit Makkuni

System Sciences Laboratory
Xerox Palo Alto Research Center
Palo Alto, CA 94304

*ABSTRACT. The Electronic Sketch Book of Tibetan Thangka Painting is
a craft medium that uses video and computing representations to preserve
and disseminate the vanishing practice of Tibetan Thangka painting.
Though visually expressive, Thangka painting is governed by precise rules
of composition that have been passed down, master to pupil through
proportioning diagrams, canonical treatises and verse. This paper illustrates
the construction of a prototype electronic Thangka sketch book. The sketch
book consists of an audio-visual database of Thangka imagery that includes
diverse views of the compositional process, and a user interface for
navigating the database. The student painter interacts with the Thangka
sketch book by means of a diagrammatic language, which supports indexing
and retrieval of elements in the database. It furnishes the painter with
mechanisms to experience the content of the database, and provides a simple
point of entry into a complex web of process representations. The
diagrammatic language is calligraphic and provides continuity, bridging
between static Thangka representations in traditional media and process
oriented representations in electronic media.
Key words: Hyper-media, Visual Databases, Gestural Interface,
Representations of Design Process, Design Craft, Craft Preservation, Craft
Renewal, Craft Dissemination, Tibetan Thangka Painting.*

1. INTRODUCTION

Tibetan paintings or Thangka [1-2] (the word literally means "something that is rolled
up," hence, a rolled-up image or a painting scroll) are expressive images based on a
complex visual language. The focal point of a Thangka painting is usually the image
of a central deity *(Figure 1)*. Associated with each deity in the pantheon is a visual
language, or a collection of composition rules, that prescribe how the deity may be
depicted. This language is the accepted means of communication between the artist
and the viewer. Some of the rules in the language dictate bodily proportions in

Figure 1. Thangka painting of Shakyamuni Buddha, sixth century BC founder of Buddhist teachings.

accordance with the iconometric classification. Other rules regulate the portrayal of particular meditative postures, gestures, symbolic offerings, garments, ornamentation, and landscapes. The central deity is typically surrounded by schematically placed lesser deities, or scenes narrating incidents in the life of the central deity. All of these figures are tied together by background elements of landscape--clouds, canyons, trees, flowers, and bodies of water. The rendering of landscape is also governed by rules that amplify or complement the glory of the central deity. Passed down from master to pupil, these rules have been transmitted by proportioning diagrams, example sketches, and verses in Tibetan canonical literature for over two thousand years.

Today a variety of forces threaten the practice of Thangka painting, moving the craft towards irrevocable simplification. As a part of a monumental task to preserve the artistic heritage of Tibet, the remaining Thangka painters, at the request of the Dalai Lama, have become wanderers, traveling the world as a living archive, and carrying with them the knowledge of the ways of Thangka painting. The Electronic Sketch Book of Tibetan Thangka Painting project [3] is conceived as a way of using computing and video representations to preserve Thangka imagery and the cultural context in which it is created, and as a way to use these representations to reveal the process of composing Thangkas. The project is a collaborative effort between Senge Lama, one of the last two living artists of the "Karma Gadri" tradition of Thangka painting, Xerox researchers, the curators of the Asian Art Museum of San Francisco, and the Tibetan community.

The project is situated in a research environment which studies the relationship of electronic technologies and the practice of design [4-6]. Concentrating on the process of design as craft, rather than just the final design artifact, prior research has explored the representation of successful design processes using electronic media. The "process of formation" of the artifact is captured in computational form, and the outward appearance of the process is represented by video records. These electronic process records serve as a diary of design experience. When reviewed or re-enacted across situations, these representations can connect members in a design group across time, communicate experience within the group and across projects, and provide a basis for formalized design craft. In addition, representations of design experience serve an educational purpose, providing beginning designers with a rich library of previously preserved scenes of process, which, in turn can be assimilated into future design practice.

The Electronic Sketch Book is seen as having two roles or functions: first, preservation role, and second, dissemination role. In the preservation role the sketch book takes form as a chronicle, an audio-visual diary of Thangka imagery similar to traditional manuscript illuminations and narrative paintings. In the dissemination role, the sketch book serves as a medium of transmission, one that can connect Thangka master with beginning painters, or in museum settings serve as an interpretive guide to both the context and process of Thangka painting.

This paper discusses preliminary research into the construction of a prototype sketch book for instructional use within the craft environment for Thangka painting. The sketch book contains a database of sounds and images of the process of Thangka composition including: audio recordings of conversations, computational graphic representations, video based re-enactments of compositions and sketches, and video stills. The sketch book's user interface models the content of the diverse elements in the database and provides navigational mechanisms.

Contemporary hyper-media systems [7-8] provide powerful tools for authors and designers to structure multi-media records, and create trails through related records. Nevertheless, the presentation of the records to the designer, and the designer's subsequent interaction with the database is textually-oriented. There is a discontinuity in the designer's experience with the records in the database, between textual means to summon records from the database and the visual images that are summoned. While recognizing that this textual-orientation is acceptable to many hyper-media systems, and in many domains, this paper explores a visual means to interact with visual databases. This provides a uniform and consistent mode of interaction. Especially given the visual nature of the records in the Thangka database, we believe that the presentation of the records and a designer's interaction process with the records make up integral parts of the design experience with electronic media.

The student painter interacts with the Thangka sketch book calligraphically using a diagrammatic language. The diagrammatic language provides a means for presenting the content of the database, as well as a means for indexing and retrieving categories of elements in the database. In doing so, it permits the student to control access to the database in a manner that is consistent with the content of the database. This furnishes the beginning painter with a powerful point of entry into a complex web of process representations. The interaction language bridges between Thangka representations in traditional media and process-oriented representations in electronic media.

The rest of this paper is organized into three main sections: (1) traditional media of transmission; (2) recording Thangka imagery; and (3) user interface. The first two sections progressively reveal the complex practice of Thangka painting, especially emphasizing the relationship of traditional representations and Thangka practice. These two sections set the stage for the discussions on user interface so that the various tools may be understood in terms of the appropriate cultural context of Thangka painting. The first section begins with an introduction to the traditional media of Thangka transmission. The second section surveys the electronic records making up the Thangka database, and describes how they are organized. Thirdly, the paper describes the sketch book's user interface, providing an example of how the intimacy between interaction techniques and the database content enhances the sketch book's pedagogical value.

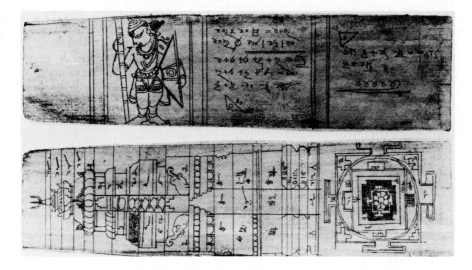

Figure 2. Palm-leaf manuscript of a temple diagram showing: architect with surveyor's rod and triangle, calculations of proportions, vertical section of a temple tower with indications of heights, and the mandala, on the basis of which the architect composes the ground-plan.

2. TRADITIONAL MEDIA OF TRANSMISSION

The artistic pantheon of Tibet is populated by various divinities of the Vajarayana Buddhist faith, nature spirits who reside in the mountains, passes and rivers of Tibet, and various mystics and saints who have attained Enlightenment. The different members of the pantheon have different functions, and in general, personify knowledge, insight, or compassion [9-10]. Many of them also serve as protectors or act as spiritual guides.

The representation of the various members of the artistic pantheon, and narrative biographies of the members, were the favorite themes of Thangka painters. Current practice indicates that images on the paintings were dedicated in an attempt to secure both material and spiritual well-being for the donor, the donor's family, and the greater community [11]. In accordance with the donor's needs, the painter would compose a Thangka featuring a particular deity or combination of deities from the pantheon that guarantee the required spiritual or material benefits.

Thangka painters have long been required to learn precise rules of composition which were documented in iconographic manuals. These manuals are interpretations of the *Shilpasasthras*, (the term meaning the "theory and practice of the visual arts"), the book of rules containing the compositional theories of divinities in painting and sculpture, and the design of temple architecture *(Figure 2)*.

The iconographical manuals provided the painters with both visual and verbal models: The visual models [12-13] prescribed proportioning relationships between the parts to the whole of various divinities, and example sketches of rendering the divinities. The verbal models [14-15] are the descriptive invocations of the different deities in the artistic pantheon, and as such, provide the infrastructure for the visual models. Together, the descriptive guidelines in Tibetan verse (verbal models) and proportioning diagrams (visual models) have served as the medium of transmission of the craft of Thangka painting across time.

The verbal models are commited to memory by the masters and recited to the students. The visual models have been represented in sketch books which were guarded by various painting work-shops. In addition to these process records, countless images of Thangka were expressed in a variety of media, such as stone, metal, or wood sculptures, ink manuscript illustrations painted on paper and cloth, acrylic or water color paintings on cotton and silk banners, and mural paintings or inscriptions on the walls of monasteries.

3. RECORDING THANGKA IMAGERY

Like the verses in canonical treatises, or the prototypical sketches and proportioning diagrams of the Thangka masters, the electronic sketch book records the verbal and visual models, but does so using video media. This section reviews the different audio-visual records that make up the source material for the database: the instructional ingredients of Thangka painting.

3.1 Verbal Models

Verbal models provide the Thangka painter with a description of the basic iconography of the deities. Verbal models are the descriptive invocations, known in Sanskrit as *Dhyana*, of a deity [14-15]. They are vivid, graphic, precise, detailed, and evoke more fantasy than the paintings. For example, consider the following Dhyana, which instructs the painter on the rendering of eyes [14]:

> *"Their eyes, bespeaking of equanimity, should be made to resemble a bow made of bamboo. . . . In the case of women and lovers, should be made eyes that resemble the belly of a fish. . . . It is laid down that to express fright and crying, eyes resembling thepetal of a padma (lotus) should be used. The eyes of those troubled by anger and grief should be presented resembling a cowrie shell. . . . "*

Dhyana records consist of the master's recitation of the verses describing the ways to render the various deities. For the database, these were recorded in conversations with the master in a "question and answer" style. Dhyanas provide the beginning painter with descriptions of expressions on the various divinities' faces, metrics and nuances of rage or tranquility in their appearance, the attire of deities, the settings in which they are to be depicted, their residences, vehicles, thrones, weapons and other possessions.

3.2 Visual Models

The visual models consist of both prototypical sketches, and proportioning diagrams of the various deities *(Figures 3 a, b, c)*. Thangka masters use these models as aids to instruction so that, their pupils, in faithfully redrawing and rendering the diagrams and sketches, acquire proportioning, compositional, and coloring skills.

The proportioning diagrams of the Thangka masters are set forth on iconometric theory, i.e. *"the grammar of drawing, the science of mathematical proportions which imparts harmony to an image"* [12-13]. The Thangka iconometry is based on the study of the proportions of the human body. Hence, the measures of man -- face, palms and fingers -- were its units of measurement.

Although the deities of the pantheon are classified semantically as various emanations of the Buddhist essence, compositionally, they are divided into three basic classes: peaceful divinities, wrathful divinities, and ordinary human beings. The Thangka iconometry relates the appropriate proportioning of the figures in accordance with this classification. For the electronic sketch book, proportioning diagrams for important deities were recorded as video still frame to serve as reference material. Next, catalogues of various gestures, offerings, landscape elements, and example sketches of deities were recorded.

The example sketches preserved rendering sequences, for example: generating a proportioning grid, outlining within the proportioning grid the form of a naked deity, clothing the deity with robes, seating the deity on a throne, rendering the throne and garments, drawing the nimbuses or halo around the deity, and placing symbolic offerings before the deity. The preservation of painting sequence is most important for the student painter, because the sequence is related to mythological beliefs, and the process of drawing is considered an inviolable ritual. For example, the last strokes in the depiction of Buddha's head are the outlining and rendering of the eyes. Just as the masters describe, the final strokes of outlining Buddha's eyes, indeed, brings the deity to life.

Other electronic records of visual models include images of Tibetan cultural life, landscapes, people, sounds, ceremonies, example paintings of Thangkas in museums, and curatorial analyses of museum Thangkas. Scenes of cultural imagery and Tibetan landscape aid as visual references in the recordings of Dhyanas. Museum Thangkas, and curatorial analyses were selected to provide examples of artistic exploration and improvisation: the rules for breaking the rules. Though all artists obey the rules of

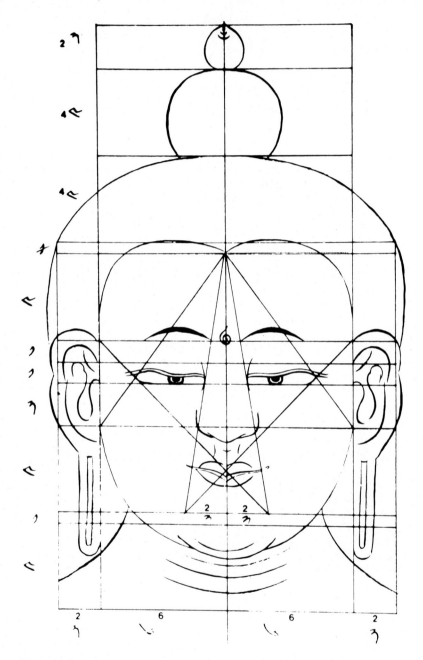

Figure 3a. Proportioning diagram of Buddha's face.

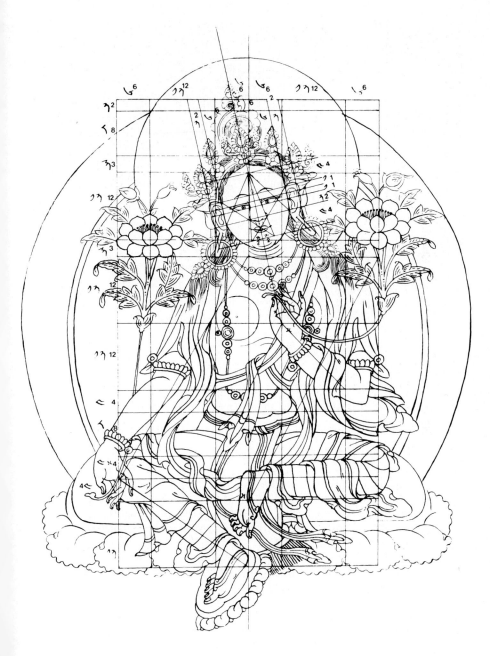

Figure 3b. Proportioning diagram of Green Tara.

Figure 3c. Catalogue of hand gestures.

composition, no two paintings are alike. Each illustrates not only the technical prowess, but also illustrate the artists' imaginative power of visualization.

3.3 Video Recording of the Compositional Process

Video records can be played back under computer contol. Hence, unlike static sketches and diagrams in traditional media, video representations introduce into the craft environment a medium that is fundamentally about process, and hence about the sense of time. Along with static diagrams and sketches, the sketch book collected action sequences in which craftsmen create Thangkas. Through these scenes, each action, however large or small, whether it is the shading of a deity's eyes, or examining the different compositional schemes for a whole painting, can be re-played. Beginning painters or spectators can replay scenes, experience them, almost as if they were actually present with the master, and thus learn the craft by re-enacting process.

The video records were created to capture the presence of the master. In scenes containing the recitations of verbal models, and discussions about theology, the records capture the master's simple presentation style, countenance, and demeanor.

The medium provides the ability to connect process-related records such as proportioning details, iconographic descriptions, to the master's personality. This differs from traditional forms of representing process which separates a technical description of the master's action from the action as the master performed it.

As a meta-medium, video allows us to inter-mix and uniformly present representations originally in diverse media. Combined in this way, visual models, verbal models, still images of catalogues, sketches, and curatorial analyses provide beginning Thangka pupils with a rich compositional schema.

3.4 Computational Model of the Video Scenes

The recordings of the master were condensed and edited into discrete video segments. Each video segment corresponds to a computational record in a relational database. Fields in the record characterize the segment's content, and its visual format. The content of the video segment includes a painting's name, historical information such as date, stylistic period, the deity depicted on the Thangka, etc.. In the case of verbal models, key words identify deities, deities' compositional details, the embodiments of theological concepts, etc. Included with each recorded segment is information about the visual format of the segment, whther the camera-shot is a close up of a painting, wide shot, detail of a deity's part, or close up of the master, etc.

The database records for the segments were created by transcribing the conversations to text, an then by defining or extracting key words from the transcript. The creation of the records was supported by an editor, and additional tools for the computer control of the video-disk players. Computer-control of the video-disk provides for previewing segments on video-disk, searching for and replaying particular segments. The creation and modification of the records was supported by an editor. The video-disk control, and transcript editing functions were combined into the *Transcription Editor (Figure 4).* As shown in the figure, it consists of three windows: the top window contains the title of the record in the database; the middle window provides an interface to the video disk player functionalities; the bottom window is a text editing workspace. Key words are indicated by different font styles in the text portion of the editor. The textual transcription of video segments, and the subsequent specification and extraction of key words provide simple means for authors such as museum curators, and Thangka painters, to transcribe the video segments.

This transcription editor is a standard textually-oriented solution. In the introduction of the paper, we stated that this research would explore diagrammatical means to interact with the database. To clarify, the focus of this paper is on the diagrammatic interaction of the student painter, and not on the authoring of the database by the master. While the focus is on the presentation of the database, we acknowledge that the construction of the database is also important. We still continue to grapple with the issues of non-textual means for the authoring of the database.

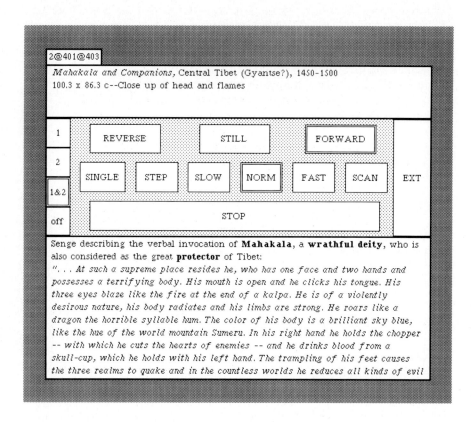

Figure 4. Transcription Editor consists of three windows: the top window contains the title of the record in the database; the middle window provides an interface to the video disk player functionalities; the bottom window is a text editing workspace.

In the future we would like to make the tools for authoring and the tools for presentation closely alligned to each other.

Parsing the video record into discrete segments works well for the cataloguing the still images of proportioning diagrams, Thangka compositional elements, museum paintings, and other reference material. However, this tactic flounders in organizing the conversations with the master painter. In the course of conversations, he made diverse associations, ranging from aspects of Thangka composition to discussions on theology. Also, in the process of discussing a particular deity, he alluded to other deities, or digressed into other topics.

Thus, the conversations cannot be adequately represented as a series of segments. Instead, we view the conversations as a continuous performance whose content can be examined by a system of overlapping entry and exit points.

The selection of entry and exit points will be influenced by the subsequent presentation and structuring of the database. Based on this we recognize that, in the future we will have to balance the pre-scripted production of the video scenes, especially in "question and answer" form, with presentation of segments of spontaneous conversation.

For the prototype sketch book, we have deferred issues arising from the use of the database by multiple audiences. For example, in the section of video that shows drawing an eye, one index might point to the master just marking on the paper (for the art student), another might show a longer version that begins with the master picking up the pencil (for the audience in an art gallery), and another might begin with the master talking about the signifigance of eyes and end with him just starting to draw (for those interested in the details of Tibetan Buddhism). In this important way, parsing of the video records should be "soft." Looking in on any one point of view loses too much of the interest value for another perspective.

4. USER INTERFACE

The previous section described the diverse process representations that make up the database of Thangka imagery. This section will discuss the computational mechanisms that allow a master painter to present the records, and a beginning painter to access and navigate the database.

Tibetan painting can be appreciated on one level for its form alone, but more deeply based on its content. At a purely compositional level Thangka painting is accessible to all, pleasing the viewer's eye with its vividness, and decorative charm. Deeper appreciation is usually reserved for the student of Buddhism, who has the ability to translate the symbols into the religious experiences whose spiritual fire the paintings seek to express. The approach from both composition and religious experience informs the student, on the one hand, of the Tibetan's pre-occupation with ornamentation, and on the other hand, of the inner spiritual life of the Tibetan people. The initial approach to Thangkas may be made from either perspective. Starting from composition, the student might discover the expression of the doctrinal principle in symbols. Starting from theology, the student might discover the visual representations of its religious ideals.

Both composition and theology are united in their expression of the deitys' essence. The Thangka painter paints with infinite patience, identifying with the deity to be represented. The painting strokes are considered sacrificial rites invoking the deity's presence. The action may be the interpretation and realization of the verbal models in form. Thus, the different video representations illustrate different views of the same Thangka process. Traditionally, the records exist in different media, offering to the painter different perspectives of the same compositional process, and different experiences of the process. The experience of these media occur in various settings, such as, circambulating around temple walls frescoed with murals, or reciting verbal models, or painting while chanting verbal incantations. These different representations of Thangka process are like transparent overlays, elucidating inter-relatedness of expressions in diverse media. Thangka painters carry with them as implicit knowledge of the relationships among the representations in the different media.

The purpose in the structuring of the representations is to make explicit the relationships between the overlays, illustrating the inter-relatedness of the representations. In a basic sense, this involves filtering of rich inter-connections between proportioning grids for any deity in the pantheon, re-playable compositional sketches, catalogues for rendering garments and landscapes, previously executed Thangkas, discussions on mythology, verbal models of iconongraphy, etc.

4.1. Classification Of Deities

The basic unit of organization is the deity. Following traditional classification of the artistic pantheon, the deity serves as the basis for assembling diverse representations. Deities are classified by religious content into five Buddha families, or by composition into seven iconometric classes. Since the classification schemes are straight-forward and complete, representations for them can be easily expressed in the Smalltalk programming environment [16]. The Smalltalk class heirarchy enables easy definition of classified objects according to shared and differing properties.

The iconometric classification of deities into peaceful deities, wrathful deities and ordinary human beings comprises the uppermost layer of classes, each with its own sub-heirarchy. For example, under the Peaceful deities are the different types of Buddhas, and Boddhisattvas. Smalltalk provides a framework in which deities can be represented in terms of their differences from other deities. The classification allows for the inheritance of all the video representations related to a deity's class. At the upper layers of the heirarchy, the associated video segment give overviews; at the lower layers they convey focussed treatments of specific topics.

4.2. Computational Models of Video Segments that Link Diverse Representations

In art historical analyses of Thangka paintings, and in traditional educational settings of Thangka painting, curators and teachers employ sequential methods to describe and analyse the visual language. The methods identify a deity, and reveal its emblematic characteristics.

Let us revisit a desciption of a Thangka shown in *Figure 1*. In this painting, the Buddha, dressed in a monk's robes, is shown meditating in still repose, and turning away from all attachments to seek a cure for the world's sorrow. His yogic posture is called, "Vajra-asana," the diamond pose, diamond connoting that his concentration is indestructable. A lotus supports his body for, indeed, his feet cannot rest on the physical earth. His right hand touches the cushion upon which he meditates, calling the earth to witness the occasion of his enlightenment. This expression is called the gesture of "earth witnessing" or "earth pressing." Similarly, his left hand, expressing the gesture of "meditative equipoise," accepts in its palms a begging bowl. Positioned around the perimeter of the throne, although greatly reduced in scale, are acolytes and attendants, goddesses and demons, leaves and flowers, dragons and deers, whose purpose is to emphasize the majesty of the central personage. Various offerings -- the symbolic wheel, conch shell, bowls, jewels, auspicious birds -- are laid before the Buddha. Motifs of landscape, evoking mystery -- steep mountains and canyons, turbulent lakes with dancing waves, and whirling clouds -- form the background of the painting.

Implicit in the above description of the deity is a sequence of steps by which the master explains the visual language. The master leads the student's eye across the painting, from one point to the other, progressively revealing the deity's emblamatic characteristics -- meditative postures, hand gestures, objects that the hands clasp, lotus thrones, clothing, landscape elements, and surrounding characters. Deities are identified by postures (called "asana"), hand gestures (called "mudra"), thrones or mounts (called "vahana"), differences in ornaments and garments, and the various symbols that they hold.

4.2.1. The Layout Editor
The *Layout Editor* uses the visual presentation language as a frame organizing and presenting video records. It consists of a display window containing a line drawing image of a deity. The deity's image provides a graphic a basis for organizing and laying out the video representations related to that deity. The Editor decomposes the deity's image by regions, such as the region of the face, halo, nimbus clothing, jewelry, offerings, hand gestures, thrones, and landscape elements. It arranges and distributes related video representations across the graphic regions of the deity's image. *Figure 5* illustrates the different regions of a deity.

The regions of the deity's image are mouse-sensitive for a painter's interactive query. For example the student painter, by clicking at the region of the hands of a deity,

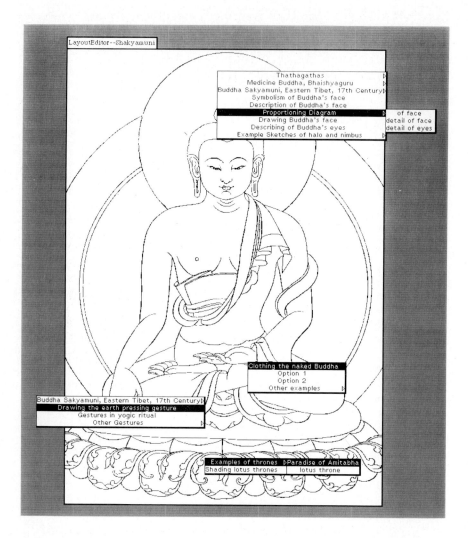

Figure 5. Layout Editor illustrating mouse sensitive regions of the Shakyamuni's face, clothing, left gesture, and lotus throne.

obtains a menu of the titles of video records associated with that region. Video segments for the region of a deity's hand include, depiction of that hand gesture, similar hand gestures of other deities, drawing exersices of that gesture, symbolism of the gesture, stories, etc. Similarly, clicking at the region of the face reveals the titles of the video records describing the deity's face: the proportioning diagram for the face, verbal models for the eyes, stories, etc.

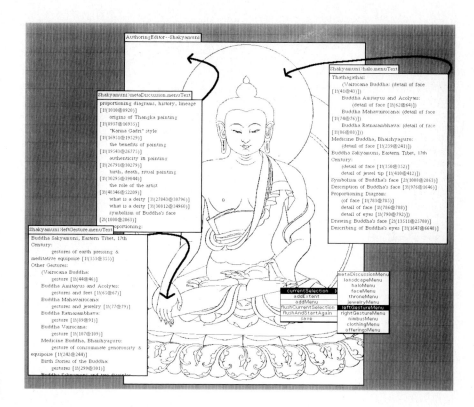

Figure 6. Assigning menus of titles to regions.

Virtually every line on the deity's image is available for questioning. Selection from the menu list of video segment titles executes the playback of the corresponding segment.

The Layout Editor transparently provides for the accretion of new items into the database. It periodically reviews the records in the database to find new entries. For any particular deity, it retrieves all the video segments that are relevant to that deity, distributes the segments across the different regions, and constructs a pop-up menu of the scene titles.

4.2.2. Clustering Video Segments

The *Authoring Editor* allows the master to cluster video records relevant to the deity onto the deity's image, for use in the Layout Editor. It allows the master to perform various operations. First, the master prepares line drawings for the various deities in the database. Next, the master interactively specifies regions on the line drawings. To re-capitualte, regions are specified for a deities's face, halo, nimbus clothing, jewelry, offerings, hand gestures, thrones, and landscape elements. Even individual lines such as within the regions of the eyes or neck can be rendered mouse-sensitive.

After the regions are specified, the master creates the different lists containing titles of video representations for the different regions. Finally, the master assigns these lists to various regions. *Figure 6* illustrates the basic regions of the deity, and the assigned lists to these different regions.

4.2.3.Scripting

A selection from the menu of titles in the Layout Editor plays back the corresponding scene. Or the selection may be temporarily stored in a script. This permits the definition of a series of video segments that might, for example, show related compositional steps for a number of deities, or show several discrete steps in a single compositional process. For example, a script might be constructed for the compositional process of an entire group of wrathful deities, or for a specific compositional step, such as, rendering of the offerings to Avlokiteswara, the deity of compassion. Scripts are made by selecting menu items from the Layout editor, and creating a list of titles in sequential order in a script. The script can include the co-ordinated replay of video segments across multiple players. For example, the student can combine the audio segments of verbal models, with other visual images of that deity.

4.3. Diagrammatic Language

Now that we have a means of assembling video representations, and relating diverse representations of video in terms of an organizational unit, i.e., the deity, let us examine how a student navigates, and how this process of navigation contributes to the student's appreciation of the content of the database.

Deities are specified by means of a diagrammatic language: a collection of diagrams that represent various deitys' essential graphic characteristics. A deity's diagram is a pictorial representation *(Figures 7a-b)* which includes the dimensions of body parts, and proportioning relationships among parts. Based on the positioning reltionships of body parts, a deity's yogic posture and gesture may be extracted from the diagram. Proportioning relationships also identify the deity's iconometric class. Hence, a diagram is a concise representation that not only serves as a graphic index to an image of a particular deity, but also provides clues about a deity's iconometric class. It provides the means to interact as well as index and retreieve elements from the database.

Figure 7a. Diagrams for Sukhasiddhi and Vajravarahi.

4.3.1. Representation of Deities' Diagrams

Figures 7a-b illustrate some graphical indices (diagrams) for various deities. Deities are modeled after ritual yogic postures. *Figure 8* illustrates how the deities' yogic pose contributes to the construction of the diagram. In this figure, the spinal column is formed by joining various points of energy on a yogi's body. These points in spinal column serve as points for the construction of the center of axis of a deity's digaram. A deity's spinal column might be vertical as in the case of Buddha, or may lean to the right or left as in the case of Goddesses. The spinal column is joined to the deity's arms and legs. Similarly, the arms and legs have varying positions. Arms may be raised, may stretch outward, or may relax in the lap, etc.. Legs may be in locked, standing, or dancing positions, etc.. Gestures, the varying positions of deity's hands are identified by the direction they point to, and based on the position of its connecting arm.

Figure 7b. Diagrams for Milarepa and Saraswati.

In the electronic sketch book, such a diagram is computationally represented as a collection of splines. These splines represent various parts of a deity's skeletal structure, such as the spinal column, the upper arms, lower arms, hand gestures, legs, and feet. A spline is represented as a collection of knot-points which will be useful in re-constructing it. Consider the posture, "Dhyana-asana," which is a common meditative pose for all the Buddhas. In this pose the legs are loosely locked, and hands are making the gesture of equipoise. Or consider the pose "Lalit-asana" in which one leg is pendant, usually supported by a lotus flower, while the other is in a squatting pose.

The different splines preserve connectivity of the deity's skeletal structure, mirroring the connectivity of a human skeleton. For example, hand gestures rotate about the lower arm, the lower arm rotates about the elbow, and the upper arm rotates about the shoulder. Angular ranges for the rotation of body parts with respect to each other have to be preserved without fracturing the deity's skeleton. For example the range of

Figure 8. Extraction of points from a Yogic pose.

rotation for lower arm with respect to the upper arm is 67 degrees, or the range of rotation for upper arm with respect to the shoulder is 123 degrees. Related work on notational systems for dance, stick figure representations, and criteria for the selection of representations are available in the references [17-21].

Figure 9 illustrates deity diagram parsed by direction. This provides a table of angles that the different body parts make with respect to some fixed origin, and in turn, a table of angles that the different body parts make with each other. These angles are useful in determining, for example, whether a deity's lower arm is pointing towards the heart, pointing towards the lap, or pointing towards the knees, etc.. Various angles of the upper and lower legs identify whether the deity is squatting in still repose, or in dynamic poses, etc.. Together, the different angles of all the body parts, and the relationships of parts between each other, uniquely identify a deity's yogic posture.

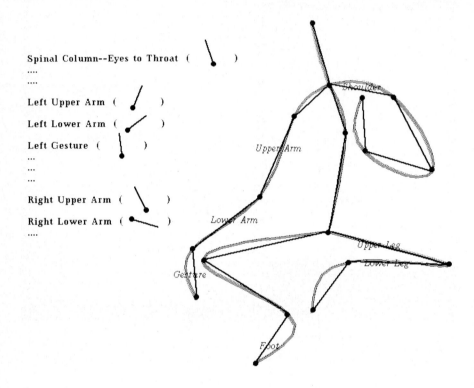

Figure 9. Directional Representation of a deity.

Posture diagrams for dieties may be computed from proportioning diagrams, or they may be digitized. A proportioning diagram is constructed from a collection of numbers that can construct a grid of horizontal and vertical lines. From these collections, a grid of horizontal, vertical, and diagonal lines is constructed. A diety's diagram is extracted from this grid. Using the grid as a reference, various points are extracted. For example, the operation sequence, "compute the mid point between the line joining the deity's eyes, link this point to the point below the deity's neck" defines the first segment of the deity's vertical axis. *Figure 10* illustrates the relationship of the posture diagram to the proportioning diagram.

Posture diagrams for various deities were defined, and from these diagrams angular ranges and directional topologies were extracted. This allowed the construction of a table of deities, and their identifying posture diagrams (which, in turn is defined in terms of directional topologies, and angular ranges). Characterised this way, the diagrams can be used for recognition or pattern matching.

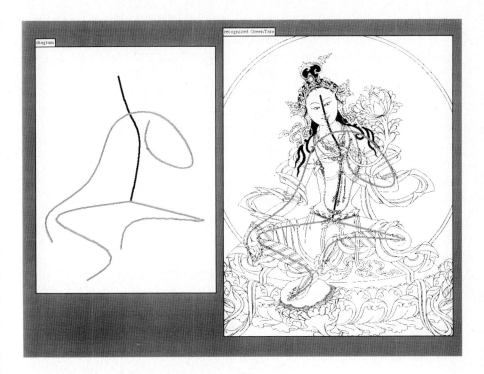

Figure 10. A direction diagram and a layout diagram.

4.4. Interaction by Creating Diagrams of Deities

The *Diagram Editor* allows the Thangka painter to define and manipulate posture diagrams. Since all deities share a common representation, any diagram can be transformed into other through a sequence of manipulations. The Diagram Editor consists of a window upon which the Thangka painter may sketch or manipulate a posture diagram *(Figure 11)*.

A Thangka painter manipulates the diagram by rotating the parts to change the positions of the diety's parts, or by changing the dimensions of the parts. Changes to the positions of parts are constrained by the acceptable ranges of relative rotation (between that body part, and the body part about which it can rotate). Changing the dimensions of body parts allows the student painter to specify the iconometric class of a deity. In Thangka iconometry, face and palms are termed the "great" or "large" measures; they in turn contain 12 or 12.5 "small" measures. Classification is based on the relationship between the overall length of a body of a portrayed divinity and the large measures. For example, in the class of peaceful deities such as the Buddha, the

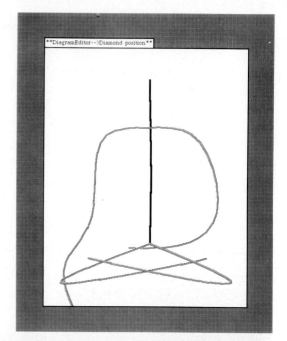

Figure 11. The Diagram
Editor.
Figure 12. Gesturing over a
prototype diagram, progressively
varying the positions of
a deity's parts

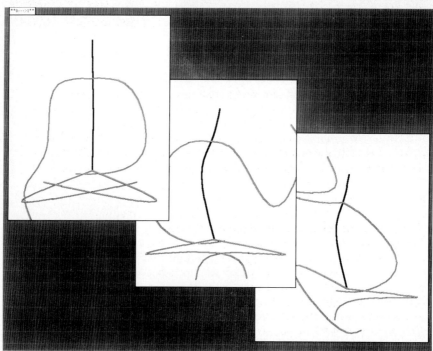

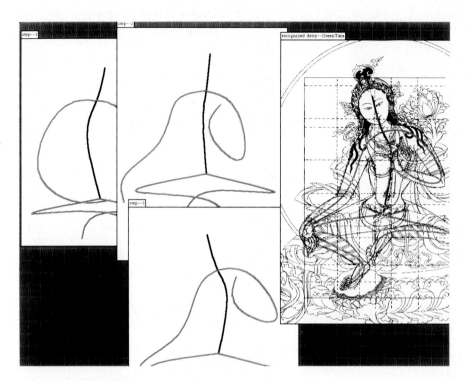

Figure 13. Diagrammatic editing, and deity identification.

body is equal to 10 large measures, and a large measure is equal to 12.5 small measures (length of a hand, or face). Or in the class of wrathful deities, the body is equal to 8 large measures, and a large measure is equal to 12 small measures. Therefore, shortening the distance between the first two segments of the spinal column, i.e., the distance between the eye and the neck, is a step towards making a deity with peaceful proportions to one with wrathful proportions.

A painter might begin with the lotus position ("Dhyana-asana"), subsequently select the deity's left arm and gesture, re-position the left arm to point towards the knee, and change the left gesture from the gesture of equipoise (pointing to the right) to the gesture of earth pressing (pointing vertically down). In doing so, the painter transforms the lotus posture into the diamond posture ("Vajra-asana"). Positions of body parts can be changed either by gesturing, or sketching. In the first case, a painter selects the part and gestures with a mouse. Selcting the first point of the spinal column and sweeping to the right indicates to the Diagram Editor that the spinal column is to be tilted to the right. Upon interpreting the gesture, the Diagram Editor re-draws an appropriately re-positioned diagram. To modify by sketching, the painter sketches a change over the existing diagram. The Diagram Editor extracts the sketched changes and re-draws the diagram. In either case the painter is gesturing over a prototype diagram, progressively varying the positions of a deity's parts *(Figure 12)*.

The modified posture diagram is matched against the dictionary of pre-defined diagrams by comparing its body parts with those of the diagrams in the dictionary. The closest match identifies the deity, and a Layout Editor providing access to the video records for that deity is invoked. Thus through gesturing the designer is enraptured into the various representations of the deity *(Figure 13)*.

The cyclic process of manipulating diagrams, matching against deities, retrieving and viewing video segments, and manipulating diagrams once again, is how the Thangka student navigates and browses through the Thangka database. Interacting through diagrams has pedagogical value as a way of discovering the compositional essence [22] of deities. The diagrammatic language provides the student with a taste of the compositional flavour, as well as glimpses of the content. It aids in the understanding of the visual language of the varying hand gestures and postures. The student's diagrammatic strokes also can be recorded over time, and this historical sketch reveals the process of discovering the deitys' characteristic postures.

Argueably, proportioning diagrams in static media also suggest a deity's graphic form. In building an interface for the sketch book, we could, of course, transfer these representations into electronic media. But instead, we used the previous representations to re-invent a representation capturing the dynamic possibilities of the computing media, thus revealing the animating form of deities. The computing representations come full circle, back to ritual yogic dance, which, the static diagrams of Thangka tradition aimed to represent in the first place.

Besides serving as graphical survey of the deity, the diagram provides the beginning painter with sensation of anticipation, and the sense of time. The diagram serves as a door into the reservoir of process representations. The actions of gesturing and manipulation of diagrams preserve the rites of entrance. In doing so, it is a pre-figuration, not in the sense of a pattern of actions that is to be followed, but in the sense of anticipating the future [23]. The gesturing is a step towards the student's participation in the unfolding of the future records into the student's conscious present.

The presentation of Thangka Imagery was biased from a fixed and particular point of view. Because of the disciplined appearance of Thangka visual language, and of Thangka painting, we postponed issues of the presentation of multiple points of view. Future work involves embedding the system in a museum setting, and examining uses by variety of audiences, such as student painters, curators, docents, and museum goers.

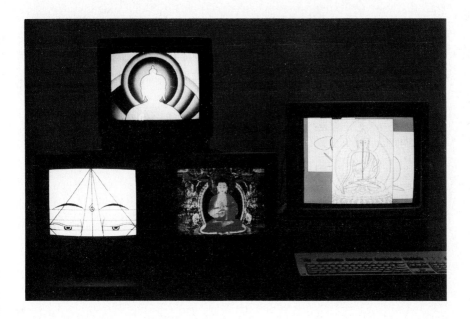

Figure 14. The electronic sketch book.

4.5. Implementation

Figure 14 illustrates the outward appearance of the electronic sketch book. The hardware consists of three video monitors, three video disk players, a switcher to control video output, and a computer. *Figure 15* illustrates that the electronic sketch book is used in close relation with a composition system, whether the composition system is based in traditional media, or based in an electronic setting.

Figure 16 illustrates the sketch book in two modes: authoring of the database and the instructional use of the database. The various authoring activities of the Thangka master are: recording and editing video segments, transcribing conversations and defining key words from the transcripts, constructing a computational model of the video records, clustering and connecting records for use by the Layout Editor, and constructing a dictionary of deity diagrams. The student painter manipulates the diagrams by gesturing. The resulting diagram is recognized by pattern matching with a dictionary of diagrams. A Layout Editor containing video records of deities for the identified deity is created, from which, the student selects and reviews video segments, or scripts video segments for replay.

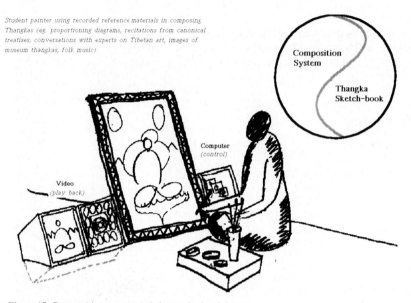

*Student painter using recorded reference materials in composing
Thangkas (eg. proportioning diagrams, recitations from canonical
treatises, conversations with experts on Tibetan art, images of
museum thangkas, folk music)*

Figure 15. Composition system and electronic sketch book.

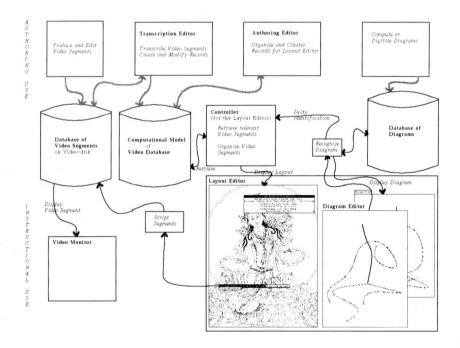

Figure 16. Sketch Book in authoring and instructional use.

Clearly, the two modes of authoring and instruction have different means of interaction -- one textual, and the other diagrammatic. In the future, we wish to narrow the differences between the authoring and instruction modes, and provide common visual means for both authoring and instruction.

5. CONCLUSION

We took a first step towards an expressive craft medium for Tibetan Thangka painting. The diverse elements of the database preserve process representations of Thangkas, not only of the technical records, but of the master's presence as well. The sketch book's user interface provides intimate connection to the database, softening the boundaries between "interface" and the underlying "database." The interface derives its character from the content of the database.

The diagrammatic language establishes threads of continuity between previous Thangka representations, and representations appropriate to new media -- representations suitable for indexing, recognition and retrieval. In interacting with the sketch book, the language preserves the immediacy of experience, obviating the need to switch between visual and textual thinking. The diagrammatic language is not a luxurious ornamentation over contemporary textual means. It is utilitarian in providing the means to interact as well as be communicative of the domain of Thangka painting. It is necessary for the efficacy of the sketch book.

The painter's hands and eyes work together. In our contemporary pre-occupation with the display of images, and with the speed at which they are presented, we have neglected and subtracted the communicative content of interaction techniques. Electronic media are powerful in engaging the painter's eyes. This research is a step towards engaging the painter's hands.

>**"Waga kokoro waga te wo yaku;**
>**Waga te waga kokoro ni ozuru.**
>
>*Our spirit must make our hands its servitor;*
>*Our hand must respond to each behest of our spirit."*

ACKNOWLEDGEMENTS

*The author wishes to thank Robert Stults & David Robson of Xerox PARC, and Terese
Bartholomew & Rand Castile of the Asian Art Museum of San Francisco for supporting
the project. Senge Lama provided the instructional materials for the Thangka database.
In conceptualizing and developing the technology, the project benefited from discussions
with Enrique Godreau, Steve Harrison, David Liebs, Randy Smith, Bob Stults, and
Frank Zdybel. Karon Weber contributed her video production expertise. Frank Zdybel,
Bob Stults, Dave Robson, and Sara Bly were critics of the paper.*

*Figure 1 was drawn by Jamyang, and is provided by Wisdom publications, London. The
diagrams in figure 3 were drawn by Wandrak, and are reproduced from Jackson, D.,
Jackson, J., "Tibetan Thangka Painting: Methods and Materials," (Copyright 1988,
Snow Lion Publications, Ithaca). The rest of the Thangka illustrations in the paper
were drawn by Senge Lama and his teacher, Gega Lama; they are provided courtesy of
the Karma Sonam Gyamtso Ling, Belgium.*

REFERENCES

[1]   Tucci, G., *Tibet: The Land of the Snows* (Stein & Ray, New York, 1967), chapter
      on art.
[2]   Pal, P., *Tibetan Paintings: A Study of Thankas Eleventh to Nineteenth Centuries*
      (Ravi Kumar and Sotheby Publications, Basel, 1984).
[3]   Makkuni, R., *The Electronic Sketch Book of Tibetan Thangka Painting: Project
      Description and Motivations* (Xerox PARC, 1987).
[4]   Harrison, S., *Design and Media Spaces*, Video (Xerox PARC, 1986).
[5]   Stults, R., *Media Space*, Technical Report (Xerox PARC , 1986).
[6]   Makkuni, R., *"Gestural Representation of the Process of Composing Chinese
      Temples,"* IEEE Computer Graphics & Applications Vol. 6 No. 12 (1987).
[7]   Morrell, K., Trigg, R., *"From Books to Work Stations: Problems in Developing
      Computer-based Curriculum in the Humanities,"* Proceedings of the International
      Conference on Databases in the Humanities and Social Sciences, Montgomery,
      Alabama (July 1987), in print.
[8]   Yankelovich, N., Haan, B. J., Meyrowitz, N. K., Drucker, S. M., *"Intermedia:
      The Concept and Construction of a Seamless Information Environment,"* IEEE
      Computer Vol. 15 No. 11 (1988), pp. 81-96.
[9]   Coomaraswamy, A. K., *The Elements of Buddhist Iconography* (Munshiram
      Manoharlal, New Delhi, 1972).
[10] Bhattacharyya, B., *The Indian Buddhist Iconography* (Firma K. L.
      Mukhopadhyay, Calcutta, 1968).
[11] Pal, P., *The Light of Asia* (Los Angeles County Museum of Art, Los Angeles,
      1984).
[12] Gega Lama, *Principles of Tibetan Art* (Karma Sonam Gyamtso Ling, Belgium,

1981).

[13] Jackson, D., Jackson, J., *Tibetan Thangka Painting: Methods and Materials* (Snow Lion Publications, Ithaca, 1988).

[14] Goswamy, B. N., Dahman-Dallapicola, A. L., *An Early Document of Indian Art* (Manohar Publications, New Delhi, 1976).

[15] Nebesky-Wojkowitz, R., *Oracles and Demons of Tibet* (Moutin Press, The Hague,1956).

[16] Goldberg, A., Robson, D., *Smalltalk-80: The Language and its Implementation* (Addison-Wesley Publishing Company, Reading, 1983).

[17] Marr, D., Nishhara, H. K., *"Representation and Recognition of Spatial Organization of 3D shapes,"* in: Proceedings Royal Society of London Series B. Vol. 200 (Royal Society of London, London, 1978) pp. 269-294.

[18] Hutchinston, A. G, *Dance Notation: The Process of Recording Movement On Paper* (Dance Horizons, New York, 1984).

[19] Landsdown, J., *"Computer Choreography and Video,"* in: Lusignan, S., North, J., (eds.), Proceedings of the Third International Conference on Computing in the Humanities (University of Waterloo Press, Waterloo, 1977), pp. 244-252.

[20] Zeltzer, D., *"Motor Control Techniques for Figure Animation,"* IEEE Computer Graphics and Applications Vol. 2 No. 9 (1982), pp. 53-59.

[21] Larkin, J. H., Simon, H. A., *"Why a Diagram is (Sometimes) Worth Ten Thousand Words,"* Cognitive Science Vol. 11 No. 1 (1987) pp. 65-99.

[22] Yanagi, S., *The Unknown Craftsman,* Adapted by Leach, B., (Kodansha International, Tokyo, 1972), see chapter on Pattern.

[23] Coomaraswamy, A. K., *Traditional Art and Symbolism,* edited by Lispey, R., (Princeton University Press, Princeton, 1977), see chapter on primitive mentality.

Visual Database Systems
T.L. Kunii (Editor)
Elsevier Science Publishers B.V. (North-Holland)
© IFIP, 1989

PROCESSING GRAPHIC INFORMATION IN Sv-PARAMETERS

Vadim P. CHIZHEVICH

Institute for Automation and Control Processes
Vladivostok, USSR

The paper outlines a new, highly discriminative system for describing, inputting, manipulating and out-
putting graphic information. A graphic object (GO) B
is specified as a set of its discriminative fragments
presented in terms of coordinates (x_j, y_j) and Sv-
parameters of their vertices b_j. The classification
and terminology of Sv-parameters are proposed and
descriptions of various objects are given. The input
of graphic information may be executed in one of three
modes: manual, semiautomatic, and automatic. The application of the Sv-parameter system permitted implementing basic set operations and various "composite"
operations on GO of arbitrary connectivity. A significant aspect in using the Sv-parametrization system
is that the checking of object descriptions is possible at any processing stage. The paper discusses a
checking technique for a basic description format.
Several methods are proposed for forming representations of objects described in Sv-parameters on vector
and raster output devices. The last part of the paper
concerns the application of the Sv-parametrization
system to the description and some operations on 3-D
objects.

1. PROBLEM STATEMENT

The aim of this paper is to present a system for describing
and processing 2-D graphic objects (GO) whose every line
segment is parallel to rectangular axes XOY. The system is
intended to describe the geometry of objects in rather

simple fashion and to allow them to be further transformed
according to specified requirements.

2.   DEFINITION OF Sv-PARAMETER

Despite the fact that there are various techniques for para-
metrizing GO [1], building and processing numeric models of
sufficiently complex objects is a time-consuming and ill-
defined process.

In order to overcome the difficulty in building numeric
models of the said kind of GO we introduce a parameter CBЮ3
(Север, Восток, Юг, Запад), which is assigned to each vertex
of GO to specify its relation to neighboring vertices.
Parameter CBЮ3 considers a vertex as a point from which line
segments may exit in four directions parallel to axes of
reference +x, -x, +y, -y. It is evident that any type of
intersection can now be determined by a point with known coordinates and a set of the above directions.

By convention, directions in parameter CBЮ3 will be listed
in the following sequence: +x, -x, +y, -y. The content of
CBЮ3 can then be described by a four-bit code $\alpha_1\alpha_2\alpha_3\alpha_4$ where
α_i = 1 stands for an existent line segment leaving a given
vertex in the corresponding direction and α_i = 0 stands for
an absent line segment in the direction. In the following
we will callthis binary number a CBЮ3 code or simply a CBЮ3
of vertex and will denote it by Sv for brevity. For example,
  - CBЮ3 a = Sva = 0111, that is, three rays emanate from
    point a in directions -x, +y and -y;
  - CBЮ3 b = Svb = 1010, two rays emanate from point b in
    directions +x and +y.

Any graphic object B of the above kind then may be described
as a set of its vertices b_0, b_1,..., b_j,.... in terms of
their coordinates (x_j, y_j) and Sv-parameters, i.e., B =
$\{b_j(x_j, y_j), Svb_j /j = \overline{1,k}\}$. A more compact description
$\{\langle b_j, Svb_j\rangle\}$ or simply $\{b_j, Svb_j\}$ is equivalent to the above
description. The set $\{b_j, Svb_j\}$ may then have an arbitrary
sequence of b_j. It is evident that $\{Svb_j\}$ is, essentially,

a set of relations between vertices b_j. Fig. 1 depicts
examples of GO, their interpretations with Sv-parameters,
and their formal descriptions.

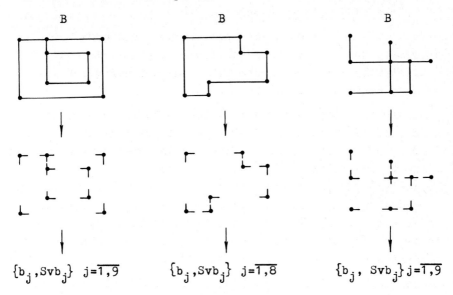

$\{b_j, Svb_j\}\ j=\overline{1,9}$ $\{b_j, Svb_j\}\ j=\overline{1,8}$ $\{b_j, Svb_j\}\ j=\overline{1,9}$

FIGURE 1

Graphic interpretation and description of contours of a GO.

A branch is a ray of Sv emanating in one direction +x, -x,
+y or -y.

Table 1 contains all types of Sv-parameters together with
their graphic representations, codes and names which will be
used in the following.

Let Sva_i denote Sv for a vertex a_i. In accordance with
Table 1 Sva_i may be zero, blind, simple, complex or complete,
which is written as $SvNa_i$, $SvTa_i$, $SvEa_i$, $SvSa_i$, $SvPa_i$, respectively. In the case where a vertex is already known a_i
is omitted. The same is true when characteristic features
of Sv are discussed which is independent of its assignment
to some vertex. For example, isolate a subset $\{h_n\}$ in a vertex set $\{h_i\}$, in which each vertex would have SvS (or SvP,
and so on).

Table 1. Classification of Sv-parameters.

Graphic Representation	Sv α_1 α_2 α_3 α_4	Conventions	Name
•	0 0 0 0	SvN	Zero
•—	1 0 0 0	SvT1 ⎫	
↓	0 0 1 0	SvT2 ⎬ SvT	Blind
—•	0 1 0 0	SvT3	
↑	0 0 0 1	SvT4 ⎭	
∟	1 0 1 0	SvE1 ⎫	
⊥	0 1 1 0	SvE2 ⎬ SvE	Simple
⊤	0 1 0 1	SvE3	
⌐	1 0 0 1	SvE4 ⎭	
—•—	1 1 0 0	SvX	
⇕	0 0 1 1	SvY ⎭	
⊢	1 0 1 1	SvS1 ⎫	
⊥	1 1 1 0	SvS2 ⎬ SvS	Complex
⊣	0 1 1 1	SvS3	
⊤	1 1 0 1	SvS4 ⎭	
✛	1 1 1 1	SvP	Complete

During various types of object transformation, the necessity arises to perform algebraic and logic operations +, -, U, ∧, ⌐ on Sv. In the operations, Sv-parameters are regarded as usual binary codes, with graphic interpretation of results taken into account.

Branches of Sv for two vertices are referred to as adjacent, if the branches lie along the line segment connected these vertices. It is evident that their directions differ only in signs. Two vertices are referred to as neighboring or adjacent, if they have adjacent branches of their Sv-parameters. When graphic information in terms of Sv-parameters is processed we frequently use notions of entry and exit branches of Sv. Either of adjacent branches is called an entry one and another branch is called an exit one, depending on a tracing sequence of two neighboring vertices.

A branch of Sv that shows a direction to search a neigh
boring vertex is called an exit branch and denoted by SvW.
For example, $SvWb_j$ is an exit branch of vertex b_j. Similarly, a branch of Sv (adjacent to $SvWb_j$) for the neighboring
vertex is an entry branch of Sv and denoted by SvV.

In some object transformations, it is useful to apply the
Sv-parameters for which a branch sequence is (+x, +y, -x, -y)
or (-y, -x, +y, +x), with the sequence being obtained by
clockwise (or counterclockwise) listing branches of Sv. The
Sv-parameters are referred to as cyclic and denoted by Sv°.
Conversion of Sv into Sv° and vice versa is done by rear-
ranging bits in the code Sv or Sv°.

That there are various graphic objects requires to distinguish between polygonal lines which are a boundary of an
area and those which are not a boundary and form certain
"wired" or "skeleton" objects. To distinguish between such
cases we introduce an asterisk (*) as a mark for those
branches of Sv that belong to some area. This is accomplished by introducing additional bits in binary codes $\langle b_j,$
$Sv*b_j\rangle$. The mark itself may have its own parameters which
characterize the area to which it belongs.

3. Sv-MODELS OF GRAPHIC OBJECTS

Any object made up of line segments parallel to axes x and y
may be described by a set of its vertices in terms of their
coordinates (x, y) and Sv-parameters. The vertex sequence
plays no part, and depending on object types and other conditions, we may accept a lexicographic or different, but
convenient for processing, sequence.

With B to denote an object, we may write

$$B = \{B^k\} = \{b_j^k(x_j^k, y_j^k), Svb_j^k\}$$

where B^k is a connected component in B,
$\qquad b_j^k$ a vertex of B,
$\qquad k = \overline{1,t}$, t is the number of connected components in B,
$\qquad j = \overline{1,\tau}$, τ is the number of vertices in each of compo-

nents.

To describe graphic compositions similar to one shown in Fig. 2 a necessity arises to determine relations between unconnected components of an object.

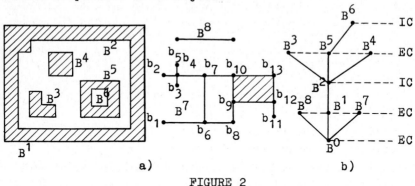

FIGURE 2

A graphic composition and its occurrence tree.

We present some relation between unconnected components with the help of an oriented graph whose vertices are components themselves and whose edges specify the occurrence of one component in another. It is evident that the term "occurrence" can only be applied to closed contours. We will use the method of building occurrence trees D for multiply connected and unconnected compositions, regardless of the fact if their boundaries are closed contours or not [2]. For example, Fig. 2b shows an occurrence tree D_B of B (Fig. 2a). Here B_o is the root vertex.

If an object or a certain its separate component is a multiply connected area, its occurrence tree allows an attribute IC or EC to be assigned to each contour in accordance with the level to which the associated contour vertex belongs. Here IC stands for an inner contour and EC for an external contour.

It is evident that after determining attributes IC and EC we can isolate areas in the object and then label branches of Sv that belong to the boundaries of the areas.

Fig. 2a shows an object which is a composition of eight

separate fragments B^1, B^2,..., B^8:

$$B = \{B^k\}, \quad k = \overline{1,8}; \quad B = \{b_j{}^k(x_j{}^k, y_j{}^k), Svb_j{}^k\}, \quad j=1,2,...$$

Fragments B_1 - B_6 should first be described as a multiply connected area. To build D_B we should execute the following steps:

- isolating connected fragments in the set $\{b_j, Svb_j\}$, i.e., finding $\{B^k\}$;
- finding a subset of such B^k that are boundary contours of the multiply connected area found above;
- building an occurrence tree for the subset B^1 - B^6;
- building an occurrence tree for the subset B^1, B^7, B^8;
- labelling branches of Sv for those vertices which belong to boundary contours.

As a result, we obtain a description $B = \{b_j(x_j, y_j), Svb_j\}$, D_B of object B. An object described in this way is ready for various transformations and set operations to be performed on it.

An alternative version of the description of B is a specification $B = \{b_j(x_j, y_j), Svb_j\}$ plus a list of vertices (in terms of their coordinates x, y) which, as known, belong to areas. An uncomplicated algorithm (see Section 5) isolates contours for the areas.

In both cases we obtain a set $\{b_j(x_j, y_j), Sv*b_j\}$ with labelled branches of Sv. This set is usually divided into a number of subsets, with each of them describing one connected object fragment. This is useful for further processing. Each connected fragment has, so-called, a beginning vertex b_o which differs in that it is the leftmost vertex and among several vertices it is the very bottom vertex for the fragment under discussion or for the GO as a whole. We give a description of B shown in Fig. 2a.

$$B = \{b_j, Svb_j\}, \quad j = 1, 2,...$$
$$B = \{B^k, k = \overline{1,6}\}, \quad D_B$$
$$B^1 = \{b_j{}^1, Sv*b_j{}^1\}, \quad j = \overline{1,4}$$

$$B^2 = \{b_j{}^2, \; Sv*b_j{}^2\}, \quad j = \overline{1,6}$$

$$\cdot \; \cdot \; \cdot \; \cdot \; \cdot \; \cdot \; \cdot \; \cdot \; \cdot \; \cdot \; \cdot \; \cdot \; \cdot \; \cdot$$

$$B^7 = \{b_j{}^7, \; Svb_j{}^7\}, \quad j = \overline{1,13}$$

$$B^8 = \{b_j{}^8, \; Svb_j{}^8\}, \quad j = \overline{1,2}$$

4. Sv-ALGEBRA

To present composite objects we extend set operations to include Sv-parameters, with the set operations graphically interpreted. Toformalize the set operations we introduce algebra over Sv. It is evident that we have to examine set
operations on Sv only when vertex coordinates for branches
of the same name coincide. To preserve generality we denote
any of branches as α_i = +x, -x, +y, -y. Table 2 illustrates
all possible branches of the same name for coincident vertices a and b. Set operations have the following form:

$$\alpha_i \cup \alpha_i = \alpha_i \qquad \alpha_i \cap \alpha_i = \alpha_i \qquad \alpha_i \setminus \alpha_i = \overline{\alpha}_i$$

$$\alpha_i \cup \overline{\alpha}_i = \alpha_i \qquad \alpha_i \cap \overline{\alpha}_i = \overline{\alpha}_i \qquad \alpha_i \setminus \overline{\alpha}_i = \alpha_i$$

$$\overline{\alpha}_i \cup \overline{\alpha}_i = \overline{\alpha}_i \qquad \overline{\alpha}_i \cap \overline{\alpha}_i = \overline{\alpha}_i \qquad \overline{\alpha}_i \setminus \alpha_i = \overline{\alpha}_i$$

$$\overline{\alpha}_i \setminus \overline{\alpha}_i = \overline{\alpha}_i$$

Using the algebra we are able to perform set operations on
arbitrary Sv-parameters of coincident vertices. For example,
if $Sva = \alpha_1\alpha_2\overline{\alpha}_3\overline{\alpha}_4$ and $Svb = \overline{\alpha}_1\alpha_2\alpha_3\alpha_4$, then

$$Sva \cup Svb = \alpha_1\alpha_2\alpha_3\alpha_4$$

$$Sva \cap Svb = \overline{\alpha}_1\alpha_2\overline{\alpha}_3\overline{\alpha}_4$$

$$Sva \setminus Svb = \alpha_1\overline{\alpha}_2\overline{\alpha}_3\overline{\alpha}_4$$

$$Svb \setminus Sva = \overline{\alpha}_1\overline{\alpha}_2\alpha_3\alpha_4$$

Fig. 3 graphically interprets the above examples.

5. ISOLATING CONNECTED FRAGMENTS

To perform various operations on GO, as well as set opera-

Table 2. Sv-parameter algebra.

Union	Intersection	Subtraction
$\text{Sva} = \alpha_i$ $\cup$ $\text{Svb} = \alpha_i$ $=$	$\text{Sva} = \alpha_i$ $\cap$ $\text{Svb} = \alpha_i$ $=$	$\text{Sva} = \alpha_i$ $\setminus$ $\text{Svb} = \alpha_i$ $= 0$
$\text{Sva} = \alpha_i$ $\cup$ $\text{Svb} = \bar{\alpha}_i$ $=$	$\text{Sva} = \alpha_i$ $\cap$ $\text{Svb} = \bar{\alpha}_i$ $= 0$	$\text{Sva} = \alpha_i$ $\setminus$ $\text{Svb} = \bar{\alpha}_i$ $=$
$\text{Sva} = \bar{\alpha}_i$ $\cup$ $\text{Svb} = \alpha_i$ $=$	$\text{Sva} = \bar{\alpha}_i$ $\cap$ $\text{Svb} = \alpha_i$ $= 0$	$\text{Sva} = \bar{\alpha}_i$ $\setminus$ $\text{Svb} = \alpha_i$ $= 0$
$\alpha_i \cup \alpha_i = \alpha_i$ $\alpha_i \cup \bar{\alpha}_i = \alpha_i$ $\bar{\alpha}_i \cup \alpha_i = \alpha_i$ $\bar{\alpha}_i \cup \bar{\alpha}_i = 0$	$\alpha_i \cap \alpha_i = \alpha_i$ $\alpha_i \cap \bar{\alpha}_i = 0$ $\bar{\alpha}_i \cap \alpha_i = 0$ $\bar{\alpha}_i \cap \bar{\alpha}_i = 0$	$\alpha_i \setminus \alpha_i = 0$ $\alpha_i \setminus \bar{\alpha}_i = \alpha_i$ $\bar{\alpha}_i \setminus \alpha_i = 0$ $\bar{\alpha}_i \setminus \bar{\alpha}_i = 0$

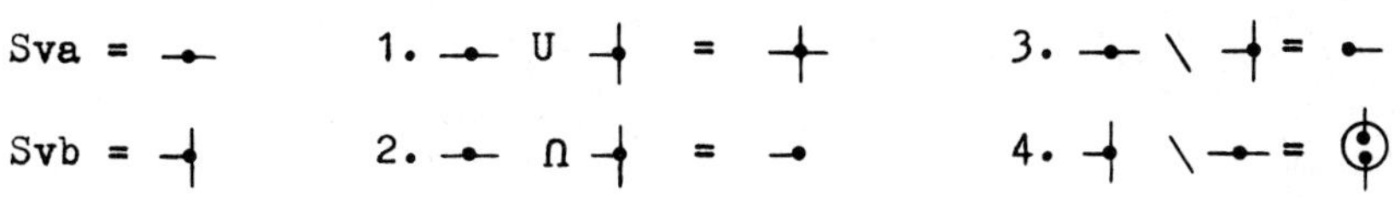

Sva =   1. $\cup$ $=$ 3. $\setminus$ $=$

Svb =   2. $\cap$ $=$ 4. $\setminus$ $=$

FIGURE 3

Operations on Sv-parameters.

tions, a procedure for isolating connected fragments of a given GO is rather frequently used. The algorithm of this procedure can be built in two ways: (1) for objects which are areas (in general, separate multiply connected areas) and (2) for objects which are compositions of areas and line segments. It is evident that the algorithm for arbitrary GO is unified, but more complicated and leads to much computing expenses. The algorithm for isolating contours in separate multiply connected areas is more simple.

5.1. Finding Area Contours

If a set $B = \{b_j, Svb_j\}$ defines a separate multiply connected area, then the following operations must be performed
to isolate connected subsets which graphically correspond to
area contours:

1. Are there any vertices in the set $\{b_j\}$?
    If yes, go to Step 2.
    If no, go to Step 10 (the end).

2. $n = n+1$ (enumerate contours)

3. Sort members of $\{b_j\}$ to find a vertex b_o^n which cor-
    responds to the beginning vertex b_o of the contour n,
    and place it into an output set $\{b_j\}^n$ to be formed.
    For the first contour $n = 1$, for the second one $n = 2$, and so on.

4. Take the clockwise direction to trace contours. In
    this case $SvVb_o = SvT1$ because $Svb_o = SvE1$. Find an
    exit branch of Sv: $SvWb_o = Svb_o - SvVb_o$.

5. Find a neighboring vertex b_{k+1} in $\{b_j\}$ in the direc-
    tion $SvWb_o$ (in general, b_k).

6. Test for the contour end: $b_{k+1} = b_o$.
    If yes, remove b_{k+1} from $\{b_j\}$ and go to Step 1.
    If no, go to Step 7.

7. Find an entry branch of Svb_{k+1}.
    If $SvWb_k = SvT1$ or $SvT3$, then $SvVb_{k+1} = SvX - SvWb_k$
    and go to Step 8.
    If $SvWb_k = SvT2$ or $SvT4$, then $SvVb_{k+1} = SvY - SvWb_k$
    and go to Step 8.

8. Find an exit branch of Svb_{k+1}: $SvWb_{k+1} = Svb_{k+1} - SvVb_{k+1}$.

9. Place b_{k+1} into $\{b_j\}^n$ and remove it from $\{b_j\}$. Go to
    Step 5.

10. The end.

This rather simple algorithm combines the isolation of connected subsets $\{b_j\}^n$ in $\{b_j\}$ and the listing of vertices b_j
in the subsets $\{b_j\}^n$. The listing of b_o^n in Step 3 is
carried out in a lexicographic order.

5.2. Finding Connected Fragments in a Composite Object

An object which is made up of areas, line segments and separate vertices is called a composite object.

We must isolate connected fragments in the set $B = \{b_j, Svb_j\}$. An example of a similar GO is shown in Fig. 4. An algorithm to be built will find an ordered set $B = \{B^p\}$ in which each member is a connected subset of the set B. $\{b_i\}*$ stands for a buffer set. Data in the buffer are organized in such a way that all the vertices form a que the beginning of which is a member b_i*. After examining and "serving" it b_i* is removed from the que and the que is advanced one step further. The second vertex in the que becomes the first one and the vertex to be placed into $\{b_i\}*$ is put in the end of the que.

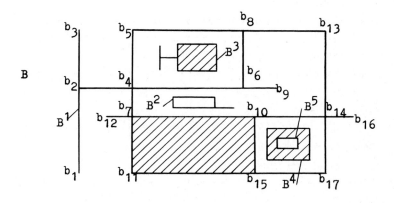

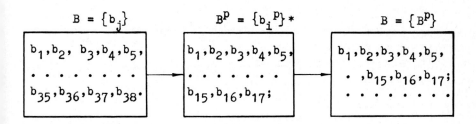

FIGURE 4

Isolating connected fragments.

The general-purpose algorithm prposed allows us to isolate
connected fragments or subsets in any GO. The main point of
the algorithm is to find a beginning vertex in $\{b_j\}$ and further "pull" all vertices connected with b_o out of $\{b_j\}$.

1. Find b_o in $\{b_j\}$.
2. If Svb_o = SvE1 or SvT2, label $SvT2b_o$.
    If Svb_o = SvT1, label $SvT1b_o$.
    Denote the labelled branch by $SvWb_k$.
    b_k := b_o; put b_k on the que in $\{b_j\}$*.
3. Find a neighboring vertex b_n in $\{b_j\}$ in the direction
    $SvWb_k$.
4. Find and label $SvVb_n$.
5. Check to see if b_i* = b_n.
    If yes, go to Step 8.
    If no, go to Step 6.
6. Put b_n on the que in $\{b_j\}$*.
7. Go to Step 9.
8. Unite Svb_i* and Svb_n together with their labels and
    assign the obtained Sv-parameter to vertex b_i* in
    $\{b_j\}$*, i.e., Svb_i* = Svb_i* U Svb_n.
9. Read b_i* out of $\{b_j\}$*.
10. Is there any unlabelled branch in Svb_1*?
    If yes, go to Step 11.
    If no, go to Step 13.
11. Find the first unlabelled branch in Svb_i*. Label and
    denote it by $SvWb_i$*. Rewrite the labelled branch
    into $\{b_j\}$*.
12. b_k := b_i*; go to Step 3.
13. Remove b_i* from $\{b_j\}$* and place b_i* into B^p which is
    a connected subset of B. Build a counter p=1,2,...
14. Remove b_i* from $\{b_j\}$*.
15. Is there any member in $\{b_j\}$*?
    If yes, go to Step 16.
    If no, go to Step 17.
16. Call the next member in $\{b_j\}$* the first one b_1*.
    Go to Step 9.
17. The end.

Using this algorithm, we found the first connected fragment or subset B^1 (Fig. 4). The numeration of vertices in $\{b_i\}$* was defined by the algorithm run.

6. SET OPERATIONS ON WIRED OBJECTS

The section describes how the above operations are performed on graphic objects which do not include plane areas. The basic operations are union, intersection and subtraction. The slight modification of the operations permits to implement a number of different, more complicated set operations. Given objects $B = \{b_j, Svb_j / j = \overline{1,k}\}$ and $R = \{r_n, Svr_n / n = \overline{1,m}\}$. On superimposing B on R a "graphical grid" (GG) H is formed. Here $H = \{h_i, Svh_i / i = \overline{1,t}\}$, t is the number of grid vertices. The grid H contains intersection points, vertices of coincident segments of B and R, and "stand-alone" vertices belonging only to B or R. On the other hand, the entire vertex set $\{h_i\}$ of H is the union of several subsets:
- $\{b_j, Svb_j\}$, the vertices belonging to B;
- $\{r_n, Svr_n\}$, the vertices belonging to R;
- $\{c_1, Svc_1\}$, the intersection points of X- and Y-edges of B with Y- and X-edges of R, respectively;
- $\{d_m, Svd_m\}$, the vertices of coincident edges of B and R.

By using uncomplicated algorithms to find intersection points from the descriptions of X- and Y-edges of B and R, we form sets of vertices $\{c_1\}$ and $\{d_m\}$ and their Sv-parameters. All the vertices in sets $\{b_j\}$, $\{r_k\}$, $\{c_1\}$, $\{d_m\}$ are sequentially compared to each other and in case their coordinates coinside, the vertices and their Sv-parameters are united. We obtain a desired set:

$$H = \{h_i, Svh_i\} = \{b_j\} \cup \{r_k\} \cup \{c_1\} \cup \{d_m\}$$

The vertices with SvX or SvY which contain no information about the topology of H are redundant, but they are required for the following set operations. Fig. 5 illustrates a GG formed from objects B and R.

6.1. Union of Graphic Objects (R $\cup$ B)

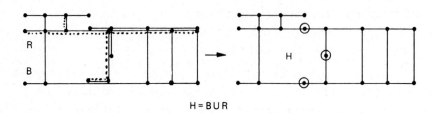

H = B U R

FIGURE 5*

Union of wired objects.

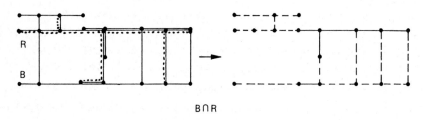

B ∩ R

FIGURE 6*

Intersection of wired objects.

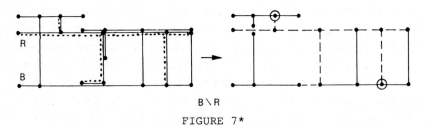

B \ R

FIGURE 7*

Subtraction of wired objects.

---

*In the original manuscript submitted for publication, the dotted lines (....) in the left-hand parts of Figures 5, 6, and 7 were represented by unbroken red lines.

The graphical grid is, essentially, the union of objects, except for vertices eith SvX and SvY which are redundant. In other words, to obtain the object which is the union of B and R we should remove redundant vertices from H:

$$R \cup B = H - \{h_s, Svh_s\} \text{ where } Svh_s = \begin{cases} SvX \\ SvY \end{cases}$$

The GG H (Fig. 5) may serve as an example of the union operation if we remove vertices labelled by circles.

6.2. Intersection of Graphic Objects (B ∩ R)

The operation B   R is replaced by operation $((B \cup R) \cap B) \cap R$, i.e., by the intersection of one of the objects and grid H and the successive intersection of another object and the obtained one. To do this, we successively compare coordinates of vertices $\{h_i\}$ and $\{b_j\}$ and, in case they equal, execute operation $Svh_i \cap Svb_j$ to form Sv-parameters for the vertices. We again perform the same operations on the obtained vertex set $\{r_k, Svr_k\}$, which leads to a desired set B ∩ R. The illustration of the operation B ∩ R is shown in Fig. 6.

6.3. Subtraction of Graphic Objects (B \ R, R \ B)

The operations B \ R and R \ B are replaced by equivalent operations (B ∪ R) \ R and (B ∪ R) \ B, respectively. After comparing coordinates of vertices in grid H and subtrahend, we perform the subtraction operation on Sv-parameters of the vertices with equal coordinates. Here we distinguished between two cases: (1) Sv of the minuend contains SvY, and Sv of the subtrahend is equal to SvX, and (2) Sv of the minuend contains SvX, and Sv of the subtrahend is equal to SvY. Therefore, the subtraction results in "two" vertices with equal coordinates and opposite Sv-parameters. The graphic interpretation of this situation will be the "cut" of a line at the point of intersection with an orthogonal line.

An example of the intersection of B and R is illustrated in Fig. 7.

7. SET OPERATIONS ON AREAS

A graphic object which is a separate, multiply connected
area may be described by a set of disjoint contours $\{B^k\}$,
$k = \overline{1,t}$. Each contour is described in the Sv-parameter system as $B^k = \{b_j{}^k(x_j{}^k, y_j{}^k), Svb_j{}^k\}$ and the relationship between contours is specified by an occurrence tree D_B. A
graphic object made up of bounded areas will be denoted by
Ω_B. Then $\Omega_B = \{B^k\}$, D_B (as distinct from $B = \{B^k\}$, D_B
which may be a wired object or a composition of areas and
polygonal lines). Then, as follows from tree D_B, the vertices of Ω_B which belong to odd levels are associated with
external contours (EC), and the vertices of even levels are
associated with inner contours (IC) of bounded areas.

7.1. Union of Areas (Fig. 8)

Consider a case where bounded areas Ω_B and Ω_R are superimposed on each other, with their boundary contours intersecting in an arbitrary fashion. As a result, a graphical grid
H is formed which is described as $\{h_i, Svh_i\}$. Building the
grid is outlined in the previous section.

By using branches of Sv to choose the counterclockwise direction we successively trace vertices of a contour R^n on
the grid $\{h_i, Svh_i\}$ starting from a beginning vertex r_0. We
then label every left (in terms of the tracing direction)
branch of SvS and SvP of encountered vertices h_i, if the
contour R^n has a mark IC. If the contour R^n has a mark EC,
then we must label right branches of SvS and SvP of encountered vertices. As a result, all the branches of Sv will be
labelled that will define a bounded area which is enclosed
between the external (EC) and inner (IC) contours of Ω_R.
A similar procedure is then used to trace contours of $\{B^k\}$,
with chosen branches of SvS and SvP of verices being
labelled.

To find a right or left branch of Sv (in terms of SvV) we
use cyclic Sv°-parameters. Because exit branches in Sv° are
enumerated successively it is not difficult to determine a
right or left branch (in terms of the tracing direction), if

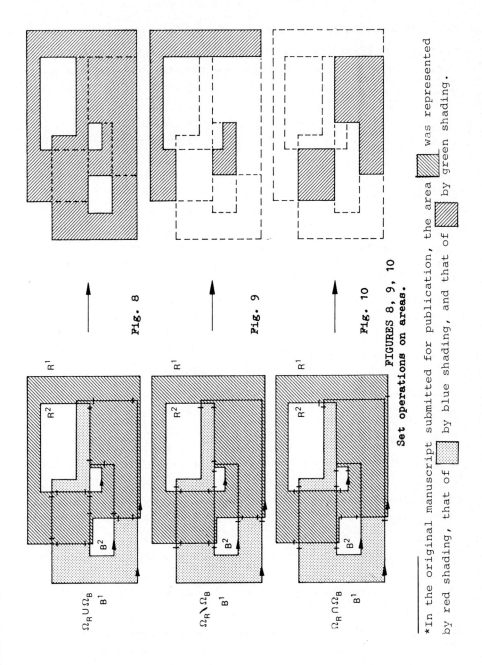

FIGURES 8, 9, 10

Set operations on areas.

*In the original manuscript submitted for publication, the area ▨ was represented by red shading, that of ▨ by blue shading, and that of ▨ by green shading.

we know SvV and SvW.

If we visually isolate labelled branches of Sv in the representation of GG H (Fig. 8), we come to the conclusion
that the following steps should be carried out to obtain a
union area of Ω_R and Ω_B:

- remove every $h_p \in \{h_i\}$ if it belongs to a vertex chain
  "coupling" the labelled branches of Sv;
- remove every h_k belonging to the vertex chain in which
  at least one branch of Sv at the chain end is blind
  (SvT);
- remove all the labelled branches of Sv from $\{Svh_i\}$.

It is evident that as the result of fully removing all the
above branches and vertices the set $\{h_i, Svh_i\}$ becomes its
own subset $\{h_i, Svh_i\}'$, with every vertex having a special
feature $Svh_i = SvE$. The set is a desired result of the operation $\Omega_R \cup \Omega_B$.

It is not difficult to isolate, if necessary, contours M^t in
$\{h_i, Svh_i\}'$ by using a successive search starting, for
example, from a vertex b_o. The contours are to comprise a
set $\{M^t\}$ which in conjunction with D_M will define a desired
function $\{M^t\}$, $D_M = \{R^n\}$, $D_R \cup \{B^k\}$, D_B.

7.2. Subtraction of Areas (Fig. 9)

Implementing the operation $\Omega_R \setminus \Omega_B$ also begins with forming
a grid H on which vertices of contours R^n and B^k are traced
in the counterclockwise direction. The procedure of labelling branches of SvS and SvP of encountered vertices h_i is
then used in accordance with the following rules:

- in tracing contours R^n (of the minuend) with mark EC,
  label right branches of all SvS and SvP;
- in tracing contours R^n with mark IC, label left branches
  of encountered SvS and SvP;
- in tracing contours B^k with mark EC, label left
  branches of SvP and SvS;
- in tracing contours B^k with mark IC, label right
  branches of SvS and SvP.

As is the case with union operations, we remove necessary vertices and branches in $\{h_i\}$ in the above consequence and isolate in the remainder vertex subset $\{h_i\}'$, a number of contours $\{F^l\}$ which form a desired difference:

$$\{F^l\}, \ D_F = \{R^n\}, \ D_R \setminus \{B^k\}, \ D_B$$

7.3. Intersection of Areas (Fig. 10)

Implementing the intersection operation $\Omega_R \cap \Omega_B$ is similar to implementing union and subtraction operations with the only difference that branches of SvS and SvP are labelled according to the following rule:

- in tracing contours R^n and B^k with mark EC, label right branches of SvS and SvP;
- in tracing contours R^n and B^k with mark IC, label left branches of SvS and SvP.

The above procedure will result in a desired intersection area:

$$\{C^m\}, \ D_C = \{R^n\}, \ D_R \cap \{B^k\}, \ D_B$$

In some cases, the intersection or subtraction operation results in polygonal lines which join areas obtained. Certain previous conditions are then specified, whether the lines will be included in an operation result or not.

As follows from the above description of introduced operations, the procedure is independent of the type of operation and only a particular operation defines a step combination.

8. COMPOSITE OPERATIONS

The system of Sv-parameters permits a relatively simple implementation of graphic operations described in [3]. Adhering to the author's designations we will consider how the operations are to be performed. We make a convention that areas are colored using algorithms of isolating contours, as described in Section 5.

The operations are all performed on two multiply connected objects B and R.

Independent of a performed operation, it is necessary for each of the two objects to build their occurrence tree D_B and D_R and take the following steps:

- building GG H = $\{B^k\}$ U $\{R^n\}$;
- performing a number of steps to implement a given operation itself;
- isolating areas which are painted in colors R and B;
- painting the isolated areas in specified colors.

8.1   Operation R over B (Fig. 11a)

When counterclockwise tracing vertices of a contour R^n (starting from r_o) in the grid H, label left branches of SvS and SvP for vertices h_i, if the contour R^n has a mark EC. If a contour R^n has a mark IC, label right branches of SvS and SvP.

Remove the labelled branches and the vertices that "connect" these branches. As a result, we have a desired GG H*. Build an area $\Omega_B \setminus \Omega_R$ to paint it in colour B. The whole area R will be painted in color R.

Thus, we have obtained a GO which is depicted at the right of Fig. 11a. Here and further dotted lines are used to denote removed vertices, branches and edges.

8.2.   Operation R in B (Fig. 11b)

The operation R in B includes an intersection operation R ∩ B (see Section 7) and an operation of painting the area R ∩ B in color R.

8.3.   Operation R out B (Fig. 11c)

The operation R out B includes a subtraction operation $\Omega_R \setminus \Omega_B$ and an operation of painting the area $\Omega_R \setminus \Omega_B$ in color R.

8.4.   Operation R atop B (Fig. 11d)

The operation R atop B can be performed in two ways. In the first case, in GG, right branches of SvS and SvP for ver-

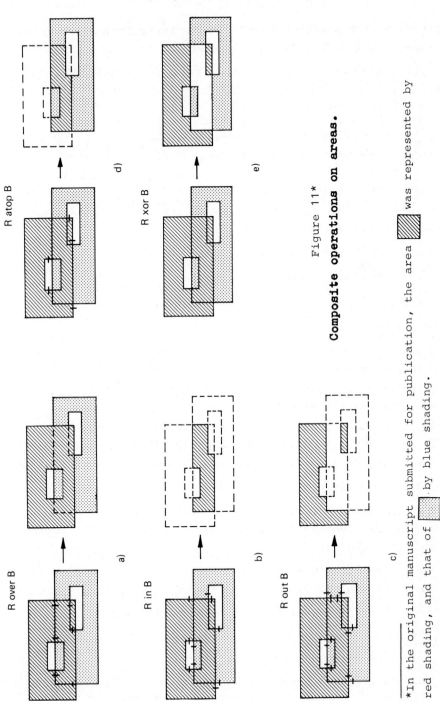

Figure 11*

Composite operations on areas.

*In the original manuscript submitted for publication, the area ▨ was represented by red shading, and that of ▦ by blue shading.

tices h_i are labelled when contours B^k with mark EC are traced, and left branches are labelled when contours with mark IC are traced. Further, labelled branches and the associated vertices are, as usual, removed. The grid H* obtained is a desired GO in which certain areas should be isolated and painted. To do this, we perform operation $\Omega_R \cap \Omega_B$ and paint the obtained area in color R. To paint a certain area in color B we first perform operation $\Omega_B \setminus \Omega_R$ and then paint the area obtained in color B. For another way of implementing the operation R atop B, it is represented as a sequence of two known operations together with the associated area painting:

R in B = C; C over B

8.5. Operation R xor B (Fig. 11e)

The operation R xor B is a "superposition" of two objects, with their intersection area being removed. However, it may be necessary that the intersection area will not be removed, but painted in the third color. One of the obvious variants of the operation is to build GG to paint an area $\Omega_R \setminus \Omega_B$ in color R and an area $\Omega_B \setminus \Omega_R$ in color B. In the case where the intersection area is painted we must perform operation $\Omega_{R.} \cap \Omega_B$ and paint the obtained area in the third color. If the known operations are used as basic ones, R xor B may be represented as a sequence of two following operations:

$$\Omega_R \text{ out } \Omega_B, \ \Omega_B \text{ out } \Omega_R.$$

9. CHECKING GRAPHIC INFORMATION

When a graphic object is described in the Sv-parameter system and various processing operations are performed on it, the necessity for checking the validity of graphic information can arise at any stage. To check graphic information we make use of some capabilities inherent to the Sv-parametrization system.

As follows from the description of GO B in the form $\{b_j, Svb_j\}$, every edge of B is described via the coordinates of

two end vertices and branches of Sv which leave the vertices
and are conjugate to each other. Thus, if the description
of an edge does not contain only one of edge vertices or
branches, the edge is not considered to be defined completely. This is an error symptom. In other words, the absence
of only one of description parameters results in the uncertainty of the description. This allows one to isolate errors by means of examination of every vertex. The same is
true for the isolation of redundant vertices when the vertices have Sv $\neq$ 0. This kind of check fails only for some
stand-alone vertices with Sv = 0. But these objects are
rather rare and may be checked with additional means.

The essence of the checking of GO B is to find a beginning
vertex b_o and successively search and examine vertices connected with b_o, depending on the type of their Sv-parameters:

- if b_o is a stand-alone vertex (Svb_o = SvN), remove b_o
  from B and proceed to search the next beginning vertex;
- if b_o is a vertex with a blind Sv-parameter, remove b_o
  from B and search for an adjacent vertex b_k in B in the
  direction Svb_o;
- if b_o is a vertex with a simple Sv (Svb_o = SvE), specify
  a search direction $SvWb_o$ to find an adjacent vertex b_k,
  and subtract $SvWb_o$ from Svb_o to place b_o with a new
  Svb_o into B;
- find a vertex b_k in B that is adjacent to b_o; if there
  is no vertex of the kind or if Svb_k has no branch conjugate to $SvWb_o$, this shows that the description of B
  has an error; if there is a vertex b_k and its Sv-parameter has a branch conjugate to $SvWb_o$, remove the found
  branch $SvVb_k$ from Svb_k, specify $SvWb_k$ and continue the
  search in a described manner.

A multiple repetition of the described procedure will lead
to the exhaustive search of all vertices and their successive removal from B. The existence of vertices which have no
conjugate branches of Sv is an error symptom.

Fig. 12 illustrates the checking of GO B in the form of

fragments I-V. Here the arrows indicate a sequence of
examining vertices, and vertices and branches to be removed
are crossed. A description error was intentionally introduced in the specification of Svb_n in vertex b_n: there was
no branch of Sv in the direction of +y, which was discovered
at Step V of the algorithm run.

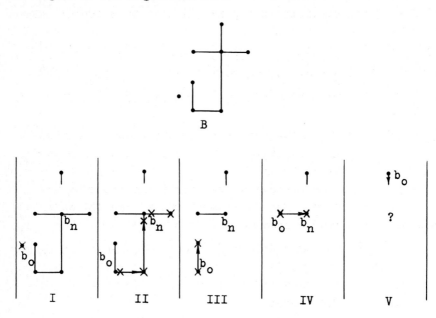

FIGURE 12

Checking graphic information.

10. INPUTTING GRAPHIC OBJECTS

Procedures for inputting graphic objects can be divided into
three categories:

- a manual input;
- a semiautomatic input;
- an automatic input.

As for a manual input, a rather simple object is directly
described via the coordinates and Sv-parameters of its vertices. Objects of more complex geometry are described by
successively listing all edges beginning from a vertex whose

coordinates are known. It is then supposed that the lengths
of edges connecting the vertices are known. A tracing path
is of no importance, and some of the edges can be listed
several times. If the lengths of the edges and the coordinates of the beginning vertex are known, it is not difficult
to build an algorithm to compute coordinates and Sv-parameters of all vertices, i.e., to describe GO B in the basic
format.

In the case where GO is a composite object, fix a point, as
well as its coordinates, in each plane area. The only requirement is that the point should not belong to a boundary
contour.

The semiautomatic input can be implemented with a digitizer
which reads off coordinates of its cursor which is placed on
a read-in vertex of GO on the plot. After reading the coordinates (x, y), an Sv-code of the vertex is typed on the
digitizer keyboard. For convience's sake, the following two
read-in modes can be used:

- Reading "contour" objects, i.e., such objects whose
  vertices have no SvS and SvP. Contour vertices are
  successively read off, when the contours themselves are
  successively listed.

- Reading arbitrary objects when an ordered vertex input,
  as well as the generation of (x, y) and Sv, is possible.
  In the operation mode, a lexicographic listing of vertices along x- and y-axes is usually taken as an ordering sequence. Information about the availability or
  absence of plane areas within the contours is entered
  by reading the coordinates of one point within each of
  the contours together with a certain area sign.

The automatic input is based on the use of television technique and equipment to read off graphic objects which are
ususally represented on paper medium. These may be drawings
or other contour representations of objects. Several techniques and devices which use various scanning paths are proposed in [4]. A main aim of these techniques is to increase

the validity of read-in information. This has resulted in
the representation of GO as a set of vertices with codes
similar to Sv-parameters. By converting read-in codes and
further processing vertex sets obtained we may build the
description of GO in the form $\{\langle b_j(x_j, y_j), Svb_j\rangle\}$.

11. FORMING OBJECT REPRESENTATIONS

This section deals with techniques for forming object representations on vector and raster output devices.

11.1. Forming Object Representations on a Vector Device

The description itself of GO B as a set of vertices together
with specification of relations between vertices ($\{b_j, Svb_j\}$)
is naturally bound up with the formation of its vector representation.

It is evident that if edges between vertices are all "drawn"
in a certain sequence according to Svb_j, then a desired object representation will be built as a whole.

In an ideal case, each GO requires its own sequence of listing segments or edges, which provides a minimum path or time
of its drawing. However, because of computational difficulties and long computation time, the following variants of
the representation formation technique is possible:

  - drawing all X- and Y-edges (i.e., edges which are parallel to axes x and y, respectively) in some specified order,
for example, in a lexicographic order according to the
values of coordinates x and y;

  - successively drawing all connected fragments or subsets
of GO (the fragments themselves are built by listing neighboring or adjacent vertices). The method is preferable for
drawing contours of multiply connected areas (see Section 5);

  - successively drawing line segments or edges which leave
b_j in the direction +x and/or +y up to neighboring vertices
belonging to $\{b_j, Svb_j\}$.

A choice of a particular variant is dependent on the structure of the obtained object and the technical characteristic

the graphic output device used.

Let us consider, in more detail, the last variant when a X-Y plotter is used to reduce drawing time to a considerable extent. Drawing line segments in the directions +x and/or +y from a vertex b_j of GO B to adjacent vertices is carried out for vertices where Svb_j = SvE1, SvT1, SvT2. A drawing sequence is of no significance and only effects on the duration of the entire drawing process. The whole procedure can be presented as follows:

- find and remove a vertex b_n in $\{\langle b_j, Svb_j \rangle\}$ where Svb_n = SvT1, SvT2, SvE1;
- find adjacent vertices b_α and b_y in $\{\langle b_j, Svb_j \rangle\}$ in the directions SvT1b_n and SvT2b_n, respectively;
- draw the fragment obtained.

The drawing process terminates after a last member b_n in $\{b_j\}$ is found.

Another important pint in building object representations is to minimize time taken for listing all fragments, which is basically dependent on a sequence of their vertices b_n or the length of a tracing path.

Several variants of the technique for minimizing the path and various algorithms are available.

11.2. Forming Object Representations on a Raster Device

The representation of GO B can be built as a union of all line segments parallel to axis x and all line segment parallel to axis y. In other words, for raster scanning, a desired representation is a union of "line" X-decomposition and "column" Y-decomposition. Since the "column" decomposition cannot be obtained for the horizontal raster scanning, use of line X-decomposition is made together with isolating elements containing Y-decomposition (SvT2, SvT4) and further using them to represent each raster element.

To this end, by using sorting methods, we make up B = $\{\langle b_j,$ $Svb_j \rangle\}$ in the form B = U B^k where B^k = $\{\langle b_j^k, Svb_j \rangle\}$ is the subset in which y_j^k = const for every member b_j^k. In other words, the subset B^k describes the content of single raster line provided $B^k \neq 0$. By introducing a concept of binary X- and Y-decomposition ([X], [Y]) we obtain, from B^k, two binary series which define the X- and Y-decomposition of a given subset.

A procedure to form the representation of GO B can be described as follows:

- successively read members $\langle b_j^k, \text{Svb}_j^k \rangle$ of a subset B^k out of the display storage;
- examine branches Svb_j^k in each b_j^k.

The existence of SvT1, SvT3 in some raster element corresponds to "1" in an X-decomposition line. Similarly, SvT2 corresponds to "1" of N-decomposition. Finally, SvT4 corresponds to "1" of Z-decomposition. The N- and Z-decompositions are components of the Y-decomposition.

The algorithm requires a memory of capacity to store the Y-decompostion of one raster line. The complete or P-decomposition of each element of a raster line is then made up as $[P] = [X] \cup [Y]$ where $[Y] = ([\hat{Y}] \setminus [N]) \setminus [Z]$. Here the square brackets stand for binary decomposition, $[\hat{Y}]$ is the decomposition of the previous raster line.

The discussed principles of forming object representations allow us to introduce various marks in object descriptions to characterize color of selected areas. Of course, the marks are then used to form color representations. The study conducted allows us to hope that color systems will be developed, which will make use of the capabilities of the Sv-parametrization.

12. TRANSMITTING GRAPHIC INFORMATION

One of the most attractive features of the Sv-parametrization system is a reduction of information volume which is required to describe a graphic object as compared to approaches under usage. In our estimation, a significunt reduction in information volume is possible. Certain features of the Sv-parametrization allow us to eliminate the redun-

dancy in GO description and to compress graphic information
by using well-known approaches.

Equipment can be developed to transform the raster representation of GO in its Sv-description, to compress the Sv-description, and to transmit it via a communication channel.
After receiving the information its reverse transformation -
from the compressed form into the basic format of Sv-description - takes place in order to obtain a usual raster
representation on a display.

13. Sv-DESCRIPTION OF THREE-DIMENSIONAL GRAPHIC OBJECTS

Describing and processing three-dimensional (3-D) objects is
a significantly more complex problem. Thus, some simple
problems become bulky in the 3-D case.

The present paper does not fully study the usage of Sv-parameters in 3-D graphics. However, some results obtained
allows us to hope that the proposed system can be applied in
a rather effective way. Alike the two-dimensional case, the
information about GO B is specified as a set of its discriminative fragments (DF): (x_j, y_j, z_j) and Svb_j of its vertices, i.e.,

$$B = \left\{ \langle b_j(x_j, y_j, z_j), Svb_j \rangle \right\}$$

An Sv-parameter system has been introduced which uses and
extends the classification of Sv-parameters on a plane. To
distinguish between constructions described, the same vertex
set, additional marks for vertices and branches of Sv have
been introduced which allow us to describe a construction in
a unique manner. 3-D objects made up of solids, plane surfaces and line segments may be described. To describe multiply connected 3-D objects a well-known technique is used in
which a solid is represented as a set of boundary contours
of its sections parallel to one of the coordinate planes.
The description and operations on the section contours are
performed in the Sv-parameter system and a desired result is
a set of DF, as stated above. For multiply connected solids,
algorithms which implement set operations of union, inter-

section, subtraction have been developed, which permits building fairly complex constructions from standard objects.

The Sv-parameter system will further be studied and algorithms which are to implement operations on arbitrary object compositions and to form volumetric representations on display screens, will be developed.

14. CONCLUSIONS

The application of the Sv-parametrization system to the processing of graphic information allows one to greatly simplify and unify various operations on GO. The development of a system for matching S-parameter descriptions and available graphics languages excludes the inconvenience in the description of GO, with a number of new capabilities simulataneously provided in the languages.

As our study shows, a main procedure in graphics algorithms is a procedure of comparing vertex coordinates and Sv-parameters of object descriptions. It is evident that this procedure effects a substantial saving in computer time as compared with well-known processing methods.

That the description of a GO can practically be checked at any stage provides new capabilities for transmitting graphic information via communication channel. On the other hand, the redundancy in any Sv-description allows one to further compress information.

It is very useful to apply the Sv-parametrization together with available raster scanning methods to process color object representations.

The present paper does not practically concern the description and processing of 3-D objects, although it is evident that a 2-D parameter is a component of a certain 3-D Sv-parameter. A number of our investigations allows us to wait interesting results in the application of the Sv-parametrization to the processing of 3-D objects.

REFERENCES

[1] Pratt, W.K., Digital Image Processing (New York, 1978)
[2] Feinberg, V.Z., Sverdlov, A.G., Rabinovich, E.V.
     Electronics 11 (1978) 48-52 (in Russian).
[3] Porter, T. and Duff, T., Computer Graphics 18 (1984)
     253-259.
[4] Chizhevich, V.P. and Samoshkin, M.A., A System for
     Inputting and Processing Graphic Data, in: CAD Software
     and Hardware (Minsk, 1986) pp. 120-124 (in Russian).

Session 9

PICTORIAL DATABASE

Visual Database Systems
T.L. Kunii (Editor)
Elsevier Science Publishers B.V. (North-Holland)
    IFIP, 1989

SYMMETRY BASED APPROACH TO MECHANICAL DRAWINGS RETRIEVAL, AN A.I. APPLICATION

Eugenio CASTELLI

Associate Professor

Dipartimento di Meccanica
Politecnico di Milano

Abstract
To value the problem of satisfying some functional requirements using mechanical drawings which have already been memorized, the hypotesis is made that there is a correlation between the functional requirements and the symmetries which are necessarily present in the piece which satisfies these requirements.
Then the most suitable code for the subsequent identification of these symmetries is identified and this proves to be the chain-code. The extraction algorithms are also described.

1. INTRODUCTION:

1.1 Intelligent use of databases

In 1970 Codd [1] listed the problems of databases, proposing a relational structure for them, since then many authors have thought to find solutions for CAD databases, finally suggesting an abstraction hierarchy." When an user adds information to a part, he is eleborating the data describing a subsystem previously defined more grossly. The gross description defines the assumed performances and resources that the subsystem is to achieve". Eastman [2].
This process involves the action of the user, just as the introduction of the logical picture (Chang-Lin) [3] or a hierachical system of images presupposes labelling, as the most recent works confirm [4] [5].
Therefore, the intelligence involved is mainly human and not artificial.

1.2 Scope

This paper studies the possibility of carrying out a search for an appropriate mechanical design, already contained in a visual database, the only input required being the mechanical task to be performed.
The search is effected with reference to the inherent mechanical qualities of the single shapes rather than to the qualities attributed to it at the moment of filing.

2. THEORETICAL FOUNDATIONS

2.1 Congruences

If we wish to discover whether an object belongs to a class of objects which satisfy certain requisites, we must either check this directly which is only possible when there is a congruence between object and requisite, or we must make the passage from some property which is uniquely linked to both the category of objects and that of the requisites. For example, an incubator as an object is certainly not congruent with the needs of hens' eggs but it can, however, have the property of generating a temperature which is within the range of temperatures linked with the development of the eggs.

In our case, there is generally a congruence between form and mechanical force.

2.2 Principle of zero work done

An active mechanical part moves, rotating around an axis and when it is working the forces applied to it perform work done zero.
The principle of zero work done constitutes the law of motion in a force field of the forms of active mechanical parts, and the forces which are considered to be applied can be measured by this principle. Therefore, this principle constitutes the link between form and force.

2.3 The principle of work done zero and its practical application

The principle of work done zero can be practically applied by utilising, case by case, the laws of symmetry, which are nothing more than an organisation of the movements, manipulating the concepts of line and angle.
For example, the symmetry of translation organises movement without rotation. If we examine parts which have a form which is the same as this symmetry we see immediately that the summarised concept of parallelism is expressed in their form.

3. STATEMENT OF PRINCIPLE

Many mechanical functions which make a given object suitable for a given use can be associated to geometrical properties.
If the symmetrical properties can be extracted from the code of a drawing than mechanical and design functions can be associated with them.

4. EXAMINATION OF THE MOST COMMON MECHANICAL FUNCTIONS

4.1 Thrust components (rods)

The function of a rod is to transmit forces or movements along the axis. This function creates great instability since an infinitesimal disalignment causes complete turn-over of the rod. Therefore it must be sufficiently long for the guide shoes to be able to act as guides; in other words the length must be geometrically twice that of the stroke and the linear sections parallel to the axis.(Rule A1)

In addition, when there is dissymetry, the function provokes and unsupportable bending moment (the so-called point load), which makes axial symmetry a necessity.

Adequate identical normal surfaces at the extremity collect the forces. Therefore, the ideal theoretical shape is one with double symmetry.(Rule A2)

4.2 Components designed to transmit tractive forces (or equivalent movements) (tie-rods).

Since mechanical components can transmit force only through thrust, surfaces are required whose normal is opposed to the local direction of the desired force at the extreme, equal to two extremes. Thus there are concavities. (Rule A3)

It is also wise to have axial symmetry in order to avoid damaging overstresses.(Rule A4)

4.3 Components designed to transmit forces to other components of whatever orientation (connecting rods).

The comments made with regard to rods also apply here since the basic form is the same.

The indetermination of the sign of the force and its direction imposes the need for the simultaneous presence of surfaces orientated in opposite directions at each extremity thus providing local symmetries in several directions.(RuleA5). If there must be all directions (turn angle) then the thrust surfaces must be arranged in a circle, that is to say a self-closing shape. Since this shape conflicts with the basic rod form, it must develop in a negative form (a hole) or in another plane. Two of these elements are required, one per extremity.(Rule A6)

4.4 Components for amplifying and/or redirecting forces (levers).

We introduce the concept of the INVARIANT with respect to a form of symmetry for which a symmetry can be freely applied without having effect on the invariant.

The bending moment at the fixed end of a cantilevered beam loaded at the free end in a direction normal to the axis is an invariant with respect to the symmetry of rotation.(Rule A7)

Let us now consider a fixed beam of an unit length. If we extend it up to length "e" we can consider this to be a symmetrical operation, in effect a rescaling. The bending moment at the support produced by a normal end load equal to 1/e is an invariant in this operation. So a fixed beam can be "normalized" by an opportune rescaling (Rule A8)

As regards the transmission of forces, the situation is similar to that of the connecting rod, and if we also consider the force in play at the fulcrum, the leverage can be interpreted as the combination of two connecting rods, affected at the level of the right-hand circular element (hole) for one and the left-hand circular element (hole) for the other, which merge into a single whole in corrispondence of the remaining holes.(3 holes in all)

Regarding to the moments the two merged connecting rods act as two fixed beams and equilibrium requests normalization. So a lever is characterized by a combination of holes (3) and rotational symmetry after rescaling (rule A9)

4.5 Components for oblique thrust

The ratio between vertical and horizontal forces is the same as the symmetrical shearing action. (Rule A10)

4.6 Fixed parts

4.6.1 Mating components

Two different parts often have to mate perfectly for construction or inspection reasons. These parts which are intended to mate also have a symmetrical relationship (a turned over relationship).(Rule A11)

4.6.2 Fixed mating components

Like the tie-rods, there must be surfaces with the normal inverted with respect to the principal.(concavity)(Rule A 12). Pieces fixed into one another have a turned over symmetrical relationship.

5. CODING OF DRAWINGS AND THEIR COMPATIBILITY WITH A SEARCH FOR SYMMETRY

The properties of the code can be expressed as intersection of the manipulative capacity of the code itself and the properties of the object to be coded.
Since symmetry is one of the inherent properties of the object a code must be found which has symmetry as one of its manupulation capacities, thus maintaining the two basic concepts of the symmetry of line and angle.

5.1 Summary examination of the most widely-used methods of encoding.
(Fuller explanation can be found in the general texts [6] [7] [8] [9] [10] [11])

There are three basic three-dimensional approaches: primitive instancing, constructive solid geometry (CSG) and boundary 8representation (B.R.)

The first approach can be defined as a fixed, correlated sequence of descriptions of parts of the configuration; for example, a drilled angle iron with four holes is described in the record as "drilled angle iron (holes: 4) correlated with an array with the positions of the holes.

Each object is defined by name on the assumption that it is highly structured and well-known.

Therefore, this approach is not suitable for the study of objects which have not been predefined.

In the second approach, constructive solid geometry, the object is described as a composition of a small number of primitive geometrical forms, parallelepipeds, cylinders, cones, spheres, pyramids.

Composition is effected by means of certain combining operators (union, intersection, difference) and movement operators (rotation, translation, changes of scale).

The composition of an object is then expressed by a tree whose depth depends on the complexity of the object itself.

This approach is easy to understand and, therefore, data input is easy but the computer has difficulty in handling the data since it prefers data which are less symbolic.

Therefore, the data suppplied in C.S.G. are normally transformed in the third approach, boundary representation.

With B.R., the coordinates of the vertices of a polygonal object, the relationships between these and the edges and the relationships between the edges and the faces are supplied.

Thus this is a tree whose depth is always equal to three.

With this approach, it is easy to draw the input object and it is also easy to draw it from different points of view with different perspectives, including the classic orthographic projection and section views. In fact, if the coordinates of the vertices are multiplied by simple displacement and transformation matrices, the new apparent coordinates are obtained while the relationships with the edges and the faces remain unchanged.

It is also possible to calculate the general properties of the object such as volume, moment of inertia, surfaces without excessive difficulty.

The Euler operator method is based on the possibility of simplifying a polyhedron processing it by reductions which leave the Euler number unchanged. The form is then identified from the final form and the sequence of these operations.

Another interesting approach is to convert flat drawings (the regular six orthogonal views) to three dimensions by associating faces and lines and giving them a three-dimensional value, defining the concavity or convexity of each edge by heuristic rules of the admissible compositions associated with Euler's rule or the concept of a plane of gradients in which each plane is represented by a point. The final result of the operation in all cases is to obtain a B.R. type code.

5.1.1 Comment

The main problem of three-dimensional systems is that filing and reading of the codes is always one-dimensional and that while this flattening does not damage the final result of a reconstruction on the screen of an image built up piece by piece in the order of the file (for example, one on the right before one above, followed by one at the centre) it doesn't maintain anygeometrical order

5.1.2 Field of action of the two-dimensional approaches

Let us consider the active mechanical parts. If the forces in play can be expressed in terms of a drawing, the mechanical parts in play can be expressed in terms of flat drawings since they can have a constant thickness or the silhouette of a cylinder or can be superimpositions of parts which are functionally flat.

The active mechanical parts which cannot be expressed as flat drawings are those which have spherical joints, but all mechanical engineers know that these cases are quite rare.

Thus if we pay greater attention to active mechanical parts than to supporting or containing parts, the two-dimensional approach would appear to be sufficiently exhaustive.

5.2 Two dimensional approaches

Different two-dimensional approaches are used to code filled figures and boundary lines. In the first case there are run-length-code and quadtree and in the second, a system using primitives and the chain code.

5.2.1 In the first approach the figure is examined, one television line after another (raster), indicating the abscissa of the first pixel which is alight and that of the last, obtaining a string of numbers.

5.2.2 The quadtree is a tree description in which the image is divided into four fields and these are coded as white, black or mixed. The mixed portions are divided into four once again and recoded. The operation is repeated until there are no more mixed fields, obtaining a tree.

5.2.3 Primitive approach decomposes the shapes into primitive parts-line, arc segment, convex part (Pavlidis) [9], T-shaped etc. or obtaineu by mathematical morphology (Shapino, Mac Donald, Stenberg) [15] and extracts the properties of and relationships among these primitives. The resultants structural descriptions are matched to structural models.

5.2.4 The chain code is obtained tracking a contour superimposed to a discrete square grid, choosing in time the next best approaching node between teh 8 neighboring nodes (Freeman) [16] [17].

5.2.5 The chain-difference code is carried out by following the polygonal outline in an anticlockwise direction, indicating at each vertex the angle with which it continues and the length of the next segment, thus obtaining a single string of numbers (Freeman). [17]
It is important to note that the final string in chain difference code is not affected by the orientation.

6. RECONSTRUCTION POSSIBILITIES

The listed relationships between mechanical functions and symmetries are sufficiently unique to constitute the key for the extraction of the encoded forms on the basis of the expressed requests.

6.1 Choice of the most suitable encoding system

The choice must fall on the encoding system which best conserves the evidence of symmetry. Thus, equal details must have identical fragments of encoding so that the symmetrical correspondances can be easily checked. The only code in which this occurs is the chain difference code and, therefore, this is the method utilised.

6.2 Extraction of the chain code

The extraction of the relative chain code of a drawing shown on the video screen is automatically carried out by a procedure of boundary tracking in a fixed direction (clockwise or anticlockwise) pixel after pixel, noting the direction and the number of pixels which are found and thus obtaining the absolute chain code. A fast generation of chain-code is possible. (Batchelor, Marlow) [19].
A chain-code encoding can also be obtained from a run-code encoding. (Kim, Lee, Kim) [18]. The chain difference code is extracted from chain-code by means of simple mathematical operations and the angles of this chain code are intended as relative to the preceding direction and not affected by the orientation.

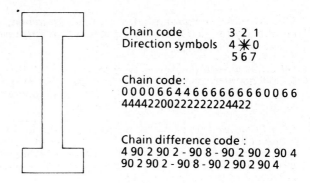

Chain code   3 2 1
Direction symbols   4 ✳ 0
                    5 6 7

Chain code:
0 0 0 0 6 6 4 4 6 6 6 6 6 6 6 6 6 0 0 6 6
4 4 4 4 2 2 0 0 2 2 2 2 2 2 2 2 2 4 4 2 2

Chain difference code :
4 90 2 90 2 - 90 8 - 90 2 90 2 90 4
90 2 90 2 - 90 8 - 90 2 90 2 90 4

6.3 Extraction of symmetries from the chain difference code.

The chain difference code encoding is presented as a string of numbers (alternatively an angle and a segment).

The following are the characteristics which can be extracted and the procedures for extraction:

6.3.1 Check of general symmetry:

Rule B1-there is double symmetry when all the elements are comparable with a string taken from the preceding one, inverting the sequence.

Rule B2-there is single symmetry when at least half of the elements are comparable in this operation. The first and last element successfully compared determine the axis of symmetry.

6.3.2 Check of local symmetry:

RuleB3- is the equivalent of single symmetry, for only a part of the coding.
Check of mating:

Rule B4- for a section of the string, must be successfully compared with the string of the second object altered by inverting both the sequence and the signs of the angles.

6.3.3 Check of parallel sections (guides) or perpendicular sections (opposing):

Rule B5- starting from the vertices/axes of symmetry, a count is made until the initial angle (parallel to the axis) is annulled or up to 90° (perpendicular sections).

6.3.4 Check of concavity

Rule B6- Concavity corresponds to sections between negative sign angles.

6.3.5 Check of rotational symmetry

Rule B7- effective if two consecutive sections of code are similar

6.3.6 Rescaling

Simple mathematical operation

6.3.7 Holes:

These must be found with other methods.
Their description on the symmetrical components can be linked to the chain code
as an attachment to the pair of nearest vertices.

7. CONCLUSIONS

(A) rules link requested mechanical functions to symmetries;
(B) rules found drawings with requested symmetries;

the entire set is able to found drawings witch satisfy the mechanical requests and
his hierarchical structure allows an easy use as set of rules for a convenient expert
system.

8. WORKED EXAMPLE

Hypothesis: the figure matches the request of transmission of traction forces.

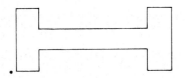

Chain difference code :
4 90 2 90 2 - 90 8 - 90 2 90 2 90 4
90 2 90 2 - 90 8 - 90 2 90 2 90 4

Bisymmetric?
Yes: inverted code is the same.

Where are axes?
They are where half code is the same: in correspondence to two 4 and two 8.

Are there parallel to axis concavities?
Yes: 2 - 90 8 - 90 2 centrated to second axis.
Answer: yes, the figure matches the request of transmission of traction forces.

REFERENCES

1) Codd: 1970 . A Relational Model of Data for Large Shared Data Banks. Commun. ACM Vol 13 n.6

2) Eastman: 1981.Database Facilities for Engineering Design. Proc.IEEE vol. 69 n.10

3) Chang, Liu: 1984. Picture Indexing and Abstraction Tecniques for Pictorial Databases IEEE Tr. PAMI 6 n.4

4) Kemper, Wallrath: 1987. An Analysis of Geometric Modeling in Database Systems. ACM Computing Surveys Vol. 19. No1

5) Ketabchi, Berzin: 1988. Mathematical Model of Composite Objects and Its Application for Organizing Engineering Databases. IEEE Trans. on Software Engineering Vol. 14 No1

6) Ballard, Brown: 1982. Computer Vision; Prentice-Hall. Englewood Cliff. USA

7) Gonzalez, Wintz: 1977. Digital Image Processing. Addison- Wesley. Reading. USA

8)Batchelor: 1985. Principles of Digital Image Processing in: Batchelor, Hill, Hodgson: Automated Visual Inspection. IFS- North Holland

9) Pavlidis: 1982. Algorithms for Graphics and Image Processing, Springer-Verlag. Berlin

10) Rosenfeld, Kak: 1976. Digital Picture Processing. Academic Press. N.Y. USA

11) Shirai: 1987. Three-Dimensional Computer Vision. Springer- Verlag. Berlin

12) Mortenson: 1985. Geometric Modeling. Wiley. N.Y. USA

13) Preparata, Shamos: 1985. Computational Geometry: An Introduction. Springer-Verlag. N.Y. USA

14) Serra: 1982. Image Analysis and Mathematical Morphology. Academic Press. N.Y. USA

15) Shapiro,MacDonald,Sternberg: 1987. Ordered Structural Shape Matching with Primitive Estraction by Mathematical Morphology. Pattern Recogn. Vol. 20 n.1

16) Freeman: 1961. On the Encoding of Arbitrary Geometric Configurations. IRE Trans. on Electronic Computers Vol. EC.10

17) Freeman: 1974. Computer Processing of Line-drawing Image. Comput. Surveys. No6

18) Kim, Lee, Kim: 1988 A New Chain Coding Algorithm for Binary Images Using Run-Lenght Code. Comp.Vis.,Graph. and Image Proc.41

19) Batchelor Marlow: 1980. Fast generation of chain code. IEE proc. vol. 127E n.4

20) Brady, Agre: 1985. The Mechanic's Mate in: Advances in Artificial Intelligence. Tim O'Shea Editor. North-Holland.

Visual Database Systems
T.L. Kunii (Editor)
Elsevier Science Publishers B.V. (North-Holland)
IFIP, 1989

GRIM_DBMS:
a GRaphical IMage DataBase
Management System

Fausto RABITTI (*) and Peter STANCHEV (**)

(*) Istituto di Elaborazione della Informazione
National Research Council
Via Santa Maria 46
56100 Pisa, Italy

(**) Institute of Mathematics
Bulgarian Academy of Sciences
G. Bonchev Str., 8
1113 Sofia, Bulgaria

Because of the diffusion of graphical editors in different application areas (e.g. business graphics, CAD, multimedia documents, etc.), graphical images are nowadays produced in large amounts. In this paper we address the problem of building a database system for graphical images (GRIM_DBMS), in which the images can be accessed by a partial description of the image content. The approach is based on a limited automatic analysis for images belonging to a domain described in advance to the system. The semantic objects, recognized in the graphical images during the analysis process, are interpreted according to the theory of evidence. The image query processing is based on special access structures generated from the image analysis process. An example demonstrates the main functions of the GRIM_DBMS in a specific application domain.

1. INTRODUCTION

When large amounts of images have to be managed in a computer system, the need to apply the database technology naturally arises. In the last decade, much of the work in the field of "image databases" appeared in the proceedings of the "IEEE Workshops on Pictorial Data Description and Management", starting from 1977, and in some other series such as "Computer Graphics and Image Processing", "Computer Vision, Graphics, and Image Processing", "Image and Vision Computing", etc.

Other sources are the work edited by Chang and Kunii [Chan81a] and the collections of papers on pictorial applications and information systems in [Blas80], [Chan80b], [Goos80]. The valuable survey of Tamura and Yokoya [Tamu84] includes insights into many actual approaches, as well as descriptions of several systems, such as the Graphics–oriented Relational Algebraic Interpreter (GRAIN), the Relational Database system for Images (REDI), the Database system of Microscopic Cell Images (IDB), etc. Another work [Chan85] presents a survey of seven commercial systems, currently available and their software capabilities: Xerox's 8010 Information System, TERA's Automated Records Management Systems, Teknotron's Systems, Scitex's Response 250, Toshiba's Document Image Filing System DF2100, CCA's Spatial Data Management System, IIS's System 600 series of software products. Different query approaches are described in works such as [Choc84], for low level image retrieval, [Rose84], for image retrieval in CAD/CAM systems, [Tang81], for alphanumeric and image data retrieval. Image query languages are described in [Chan80a], [Chan81b]. A review of approaches to machine interpretation of remotely sensed images is presented in [Tail86].

However, most of the systems appearing under the heading of image databases are often image systems without full database functionalities or database systems not directly dealing with images [Nagy85]. In fact, most of the existing systems are application specific, that is, the way in which images are stored, organized and retrieved is specific of a certain application and cannot be generalized to different applications.

The main conceptual problem in dealing with images derives from the difficulty to exactly define and interpret the content of images. Images can be very rich in semantics, but are subject to different interpretations according to the human perception of the application domain. On one hand, it is difficult to recognize the objects (with the associated interpretation) contained in an image, on the other hand is difficult to determine and represent the mutual relationships among these objects, since they form structures which vary greatly from image to image.

For the problem of image retrieval by content, one could think to apply Data Base Management System (DBMS) or Information Retrieval System (IRS) techniques. However, with respect to DBMS's, it is difficult to recognize regular structures of objects contained in images, and then organize image instances into a limited number of types, to which the interpretation is associated. This is the approach required by the strictly typed data models adopted in database systems [Tsic82]. In IRS, instead, a free formatting of text is allowed, usually respecting some loose hierarchical structuring in sections, sub-sections, paragraphs and sentences. These systems do not attempt to understand the text (unless some expert system approach is adopted), but still allow an effective retrieval on text. In fact, as opposed to image objects, they can exactly recognize words (as ASCII patterns), on which they base their retrieval capabilities with the possible help of a thesaurus to support synonyms [Salt83]. This is possible, in case of text, because a common semantic is associated to the words used in the natural language. Hence, both DBMS and IRS approaches cannot be directly applied to image retrieval.

In addressing the problem of image retrieval of stored images, if we want to think of a system trying to do for images what DBMS and IRS do for formatted data and text, we must accept some indeterminantness, characteristic of images, and then deal with the inaccuracy introduced by this fact. In [Rabi87a] an approach based on fuzzy set theory has been applied to the analysis and description of pictorial images. Certainty factors for the recognition of objects inside the images are computed using fuzzy logic rules.

A major practical problem for pictorial images is **element recognition.** The first step in the image analysis and recognition process is the decomposition of the images into relevant and identifiable elements, which are the basic components which will constitute the building blocks of the image structure.

In this step, often called segmentation in pictorial image processing [Ball82], the image space is partitioned into meaningful regions, corresponding to image elements. After the segmentation, the system must recognize the tentative elements in the image, matching them with the pictorial representation of the elements to be searched. In this process, different variations as changes in size, rotation, translation (eg. using discrete Fourier transforms), can be attempted. An additional problem arises when partial element overlapping occurs in the image.

The result of this process should be the set of basic elements recognized and their relative positions. However, this is a highly computing intensive process which often requires special hardware, such as array processors, exploiting the inherent parallelism of the algorithms in order to have acceptable response times. In the end, the system might even not be able to exactly identify the single elements.

Instead, in dealing with graphical images we have the advantage that the images are not entered into the system through a scanning device but are generated by some interactive graphical editor. Therefore, the segmentation process is not necessary. Basic elements are recognized without uncertainty since they can be described in terms of the graphical primitives of the graphical editors.

In this paper, a database system for graphical images, GRIM_DBMS, is presented. This system supports the analysis and retrieval of graphical images. It is required that the images belong to a specific domain which must be described in advance to the system. A limited automatic analysis of the images is performed before storing the images in the database. This process is accomplished using a rule-based system. The interpretation of the content of the images is based on the Dempster-Shafer theory of evidence [Gord84]. An example for implementation of the GRIM_DBMS to the area of House – furnising design is also presented.

2. THE GRIM_DBMS SYSTEM

The main functions and the correspondent tools of GRIM_DBMS are illustrated in Fig. 1.

Domain Description	Image Creation, Analysis & Storage	Image Retrieval
a) Multi–functional graphical editor /function "elements & relation definition"/ b) Dialog system for filling in rules for object definition c) Multi–functional graphical editor /function "definition of class representative images"/	a) General purpose graphical editor b) Image analyzer	Query processor

Fig. 1. *Main Phases and Correspondent Tools in GRIM_DBMS*

2.1. Domain Description in GRIM_DBMS

The purpose of this phase is to describe the characteristics of the application domain of the images to be classified and retrieved. The domain description function supplies the initial information necessary for the various phases of the image analysis. It comprises: a) definition of basic elements, relations and corresponding attributes (this information will be used in the ARG-based element recognition); b) definition of production rules (this information will be used in the semantic object recognition and image interpretation); c) definition of class representation images (this information will be used in image clustering).

2.2. Image Creation, Analysis and Storage in GRIM_DBMS

A) Image Creation

For image creation, it is possible to use any graphical editor producing a representation of the image in terms of graphic primitives according to a chosen standard (ACM-CORE, in the actual implementation). After the desired image is developed, it is stored as a file specified by the name of the image and containing the correspondent editor primitives for the graphical image. In this way, the following phase of Image Analysis is independent from the editors used in the image creation.

The system also provides a multi–functional graphical image editor, which is specialized for the specific application domain. From a table containing all the basic elements of the GRIM_DBMS application domain it is possible to select basic graphical elements and to transfer them to the drawing area of the editor using a "mouse" as pointing device. After an element is moved to the right place, the user can apply some functions allowing modifications on the element as scaling, rotation, translation and deletion. These operations can be repeated as many times as necessary for all the elements of the image. This specialized editor generates also an ARG representation of the image (see following section) and so the first phase of the Image Analysis process (i.e. Image Element Recognition) is not necessary.

B) Image Analysis

The image analysis includes four steps:

* Element Recognition. Since the number of the basic graphical elements (eg. polilines, curves, etc.) can be very large in a single image (in the order, of thousands) a very efficient approach is required for recognizing the basic elements which are meaningful in the application domain. They constitutes the basic symbols which compose the semantic objects in the image. In this phase, it is not possible to adopt a rule system, based on a generalized inference mechanism with back-tracking, because of its computational complexity. We need instead more efficient and specialized algorithms (with polynomial computation complexity) even if we have to pay this with a description system less rich in semantic content. For this reason we have adopted an approach based on the Attributed Relational Graphs [Eshe86].

The ARG graph is a relational structure which consists of a set of nodes and a set of branches representing the relations between the nodes, as both nodes and branches may have some attributes assigned to them.

During the Image Element Analysis, an ARG representation of the image (in terms of basic elements of the application domain, thier relationships and attributes) is obtained and stored in the same image description file.

* Object Recognition. The purpose of this phase is to recognize more semantically meaningful objects from the basic elements derived and organized in the previous phase. This task is accomplished by recursively applying the production rules defined for the chosen application domain. An inference mechanism based on backward chaining tries to derive from the basic elements more general objects and to give a recognition degree to the object recognized. In this phase a generalized inference mechanism is used. Its computational complexity is acceptable now, since fewer objects (in the order of hundreds) are present in the image.

The inference process starts from production rules obtained from the ARG image representation. After this step, a sequence in the form (1) is obtained:

$$(1) \qquad \{O_{1\ 1}(\mu_{1\ 1}, l_{1\ 1}), \ldots, O_{1\ s_1}(\mu_{1\ s_1}, l_{1\ s_1})\}, \ldots,$$

$$\{O_{n\ 1}(\mu_{n\ 1}, l_{n\ 1}), \ldots, O_{n\ s_n}(\mu_{n\ s_n}, l_{n\ s_n})\}$$

Such a sequence describes an image with n distinct physical objects. The unit $O_{i\ j}(\mu_{i\ j}, l_{i\ j})$ is a semantical representation of the physical object $i(i = 1, 2, \ldots, n)$ in the image in the j−th $(j = 1, 2, \ldots, s_j)$ recognition (i.e. a semantic object). $\mu_{i\ j}$ and $l_{i\ j}$ are respectively the recognition degre (RD) and the list of attributes of the i−th physical object in the j−th recognition.

* Image Interpretation. Using a procedure similar to Barnett's scheme [Barn81], based on the Dempster–Shafer theory of evidence [Gord84], and fully described in [Rabi87b], we convert the results obtained from the previous phase into a list of new structures containing information for each object:

$$(2) \qquad \{O_{1\ 1}([Bel(O_{1\ 1}), 1 - Bel(\overline{O}_{1\ 1})], l_{1\ 1}), \ldots,$$

$$O_{1\ q_1}([Bel(O_{1\ q_1}), 1 - Bel(\overline{O}_{1\ q_1})], l_{1\ q_1})\}, \ldots,$$

$$\{O_{n\ 1}([Bel(O_{n\ 1}), 1 - Bel(\overline{O}_{n\ 1})], l_{n\ 1}), \ldots,$$

$$O_{n\ q_n}([Bel(O_{n\ q_n}), 1 - Bel(\overline{O}_{n\ q_n})], l_{n\ q_n})\}$$

Here $q_i \leq s_i (i = 1, 2, \ldots, n)$. The function $Bel(O_{i\ j})$ $(i = 1, 2, \ldots, n,\ j = 1, 2, \ldots, q_i)$ is a belief function.

The belief function $Bel(O_{i\ j})$ gives the total amount of belief committed to the object $O_{i\ j}$ after all evidence bearing on $O_{i\ j}$ has been pooled. The function Bel provides additional information about $O_{i\ j}$, namely $Bel(\overline{O}_{i\ j})$, the extent to which the evidence supports the negation of

$O_{i\ j}$, *i.e.* $\overline{O}_{i\ j}$. *The quantity* $1 - Bel(\overline{O}_{i\ j})$ *expresses the plausibility of* $O_{i\ j}$, *i.e., the extent to which the evidence allows one to fail to doubt* $O_{i\ j}$. *The interval* $[Bel(O_{i\ j}), 1 - Bel(\overline{O}_{i\ j})]$ *is called belief interval.*

In the expression (2), object interpretations with "low" belief (e.g., in the sense of interval mean value less than a chosen one) could be omitted.

* Image Clustering.   The image clustering process is in principle similar to the document clustering of text documents used in Information Retrieval Systems [Salt83]. The most significant classes of images in the application domain are defined in terms of representative images, one for each class. The image interpretations are clustered by comparing them with the class representative images. After this computation, the clustering description of the image is expressed as a sequence:

$$(3) \qquad\qquad \mu_1, \mu_2, \ldots, \mu_p,$$

where μ_i is the membership degree of the image to the i-th class. .

C) Image Storage and Indexing

The image representation is stored in a file containing the graphical image as the sequence of the graphical primitives used for the composition by the graphical editor.

The derived image information, resulting from the analysis phase (expressed in terms of the probabilistic model as composition of objects, at different level of complexity, with the associated interval of belief) is stored in an "image header", associated to the image file. In this header, it is stored:

– A sequence, containing the image clustering description. Each term of these sequence contains the membership degree of the complete image to one of the image classes of the application. This kind of information is more synthetical, since it refers to the image as a whole.

– A sequence, containig the objects description. One and the same object may appear more times in the sequence, one for each appearance of that object in the image interpretation. This kind of information is more analytical, since it refers to the composition of the image.

Access structures (that is, the image indices) can be built for a fast access to image headers. Two type of indices are constructed:

– **Object index.**   Each entry of the index is associated to a distinct object. For each object, a list is maintained. Each element of the list is constituted by a list of elements (BI, IMH), where IMH is a pointer to an image header, meaning that the object is present in that image, BI is the associated belief interval. For query processing, it is very important to maintain the list in decreasing order of BI. The order is computed using the mean values of the belief intervals.

– **Cluster index.** Each entry of the index is associated to a distinct image cluster. For each class defined in the application, a list of elements (MD, IMH) is maintained. IMH is a pointer to an image header, corresponding to an image with a non-null degree of membership to this cluster, and MD is the value of the membership degree. For query processing, it is very important to maintain the list in decreasing order of MD.

2.3.   Query Processing in GRIM_DBMS

According to our query language, the user specifies a query statement of the form: **RETRIEVE IMAGES** <image_clause> .

The <image_clause> contains a <cluster_clause> and/or an <object_clause>.

The <cluster_clause> is a boolean combination of <cluster_-predicate>s, each of the form: <class_name> <cluster_degree> .

The <cluster_predecate> indicates that the images in the database with a similarity to the named class higher than the <membership_value> should be retrieved (as requested in the boolean expression). The <cluster_clause> may be missing if the <object_clause> is present.

The <object_clause> is a boolean combination of <object_-predicate>s, each of the form: <object_name> <degree_of_-recognition>.

The <object_clause> must be evaluated, according to the boolean expression, taking into account only the images in the database containing those objects, named as <object_name>, with the left value of the belief interval higher than the <degree_of_recognition>. In the <object_predicate> WITH operator is envisaged, which serves the purpose of adding conditions to the attributes associated to the object.

All the stored images "not very distant" from the query statement (in a chosen sense) constitute the query answer set. With this approach, the query answers can be ordered by decreasing similarity to the query specification, so a user may limit the size of the answer and can receive a ranked output of the retrieved images. (These advantages are typical for the information retrieval techniques [Salt83]).

Since the image retrieval is not an exact process (there is no exact way of defining the image content) and even the user may forget essential characteristics of the sought images, not one, but several non pertinent images are usually retrieved as a result of a query. The existance of relevance feed-back and query reformulation [Salt83] become essential since at any moment the user can go back to the query formulation step, if dissatisfied by the results which he is getting, and change some aspects of the query specification (usually, the values of the belief intervals).

3. GRIM_DBMS APPLIED IN A SPECIFIC APPLICATION DOMAIN

As an example of application, we choose the area of House–furnishing design. We now briefly explain the main functions of GRIM_DBMS, as applied in this field of application.

3.1. Domain Description

a) We limit the demonstration to the basic elements shown in Fig.2, with the associated attributes, and the relations shown in Fig. 3.

union (none)

intersection (none)

Fig. 3. *Relations*

b) Now, we must define the rules for object recognition. We want to make provision for the recognition of the following objects : **dou-ble_bed, table, chair, window, door, wall, room, sitting_room, bedroom, double_bedroom, livingroom, bathroom, kitchen**. We must define production rules for each of these objects. The production rules for image **room**, using Prolog syntax, are expressed in Fig. 4. The last six objects are the most complex ones to recognize. Cross, wall_inside and codify are productions which calculate the cross point of two lines, existance of a wall inside the room and the number of objects (rooms) in the image.

c) Suppose that the following images are chosen as class representative images: **block_of_flats, commercial_house, hospital_building, concert_hall**. For all these images, correspondent representations are to be obtained.

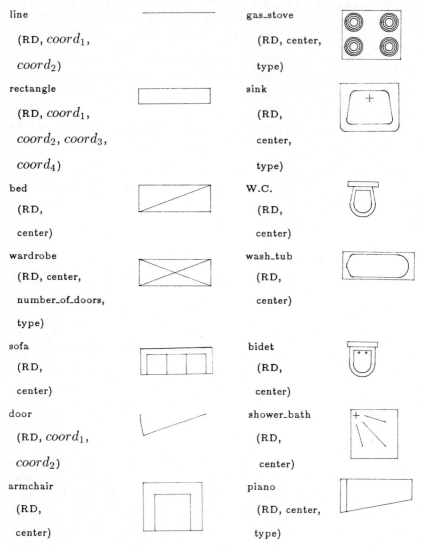

line

(RD, $coord_1$,

$coord_2$)

rectangle

(RD, $coord_1$,

$coord_2$, $coord_3$,

$coord_4$)

bed

(RD,

center)

wardrobe

(RD, center,

number_of_doors,

type)

sofa

(RD,

center)

door

(RD, $coord_1$,

$coord_2$)

armchair

(RD,

center)

gas_stove

(RD, center,

type)

sink

(RD,

center,

type)

W.C.

(RD,

center)

wash_tub

(RD,

center)

bidet

(RD,

center)

shower_bath

(RD,

center)

piano

(RD, center,

type)

Fig. 2. *Basic Elements*

3.2. Image Creation and Storage

A) Image Creation

Let the graphical image shown in Fig. 5 be designed using the multi–functional graphical editor (specific of this application domain).

```
room (RD, V1, V2, V3, V4, N) :-
     wall (RD1, P1, P2, N1),
     wall (RD2, P3, P4, N2),
     N1 < N2,
     cross (P1, P2, P3, P4, V1),
     wall (RD3, P5, P6, N3),
     N3 > N1, N1 <> N2,
     cross (P3, P4, P5, P6, V2),
     wall (RD4, P7, P8, N4),
     N4 > N1, N4 > N2, N4 <> N3,
     cross (P5, P6, P7, P8, V3),
     cross (P1, P2, P7, P8, V4),
     not (wall_inside (V1, V2, V3, V4, N1, N2, N3, N4)),
     RD = (RD1 + RD2 + RD3 + RD4) / 4,
     codify (N1, N2, N3, N4, N).
```

Fig. 4. *Prolog rules for "room"*

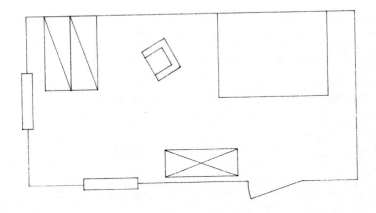

Fig. 5. *Example Image*

The corresponding ARG representation of the image, is expressed in Fig. 6.

B) Image Analysis

N (node set)$= \{n_1, n_2, \ldots, n_{15}\}$;

B (branch set)$= \{b_1, b_2, b_3, b_4\}$;

A (node attribute alphabet):

element	attributes
line	R.D, $coord_1$, $coord_2$
rectangle	R.D, $coord_1$, $coord_2$, $coord_3$, $coord_4$
bed	R.D, center
wardrobe	R.D, center, number_of_doors, type
sofa	R.D, center
door	R.D, $coord_1$, $coord_2$
armchair	R.D, center
gas_stove	R.D, center, type
sink	R.D, center, type
W.C.	R.D, center
wash_tub	R.D, center
bidet	R.D, center
shower_both	R.D, center
piano	R.D, center, type

E (branch attribute alphabet):

relation	attributes
union	none
intersection	none

$G_N : n_1 \rightarrow$ line (1, [0.0, 0.0], [2.0, 0.0])
$n_2 \rightarrow$ line (1, [0.0, 0.0], [0.0, 2.0])
$n_3 \rightarrow$ line (1, [0.0, 6.0], [12.0, 6.0])
$n_4 \rightarrow$ line (1, [4.0, 0.0], [8.0, 0.0])
$n_5 \rightarrow$ line (1, [0.0, 4.0], [0.0, 6.0])
$n_6 \rightarrow$ line (1, [12.0, 0.0], [12.0, 6.0])
$n_7 \rightarrow$ line (1, [10.0, 0.0], [12.0, 0.0])
$n_8 \rightarrow$ rectangle (1, [7.0, 6.0], [11.0, 6.0] , [11.0, 3.0], [7.0, 3.0])
$n_9 \rightarrow$ rectangle (1, [-0.2, 4.0], [0.2, 4.0], [0.2, 2.0], [-0.2, 2.0])
$n_{10} \rightarrow$ rectangle (1, [2.0, 0.2], [4.0, 0.2], [4.0, -0.2], [2.0, -0.2])
$n_{11} \rightarrow$ door (1, [8.0, 0.0], [10.0, 0.0])
$n_{12} \rightarrow$ bed (1, [1.2, 4.6])
$n_{13} \rightarrow$ bed (1, [2.1, 4.6])
$n_{14} \rightarrow$ wardrobe (1, [6.3, 0.7], 2, wood)
$n_{15} \rightarrow$ armchair (1, [4.9, 4.3])

$G_B : b_1 \rightarrow (n_{12}, n_{13}), b_2 \rightarrow (n_{12}, n_3), b_3 \rightarrow (n_{13}, n_3), b_4 \rightarrow (n_8, n_3), -$
union

Fig.6. *The ARG representation of the example image*

* Object Recognition

Using the production rule base, the following sequence is obtained: sequence(1): { double_bedroom (RD = 0.9, window(RD = 1), window(RD = 1), double_bed(RD = 1), wardrobe(RD = 1, number_of_doors = 2, type = wood), armchair(RD = 1), (table(RD = 0.9), sofa(RD = 0.5)), door(RD = 1)), living_room (RD = 0.7, window(RD = 1), window(RD = 1), double_bed(RD = 1), wardrobe(RD = 1, number_of_ doors =2, type = wood), armchair(RD = 1), (table(RD = 0.9), sofa(RD = 0.5)), door(RD = 1)) }.

* Image Interpretation

After the object interpretation phase, the following sequence is obtained: sequence(2): { double_bedroom (BI = [0.73, 0.81], double_bed(BI = [1, 1]), wardrobe(BI = [1, 1], number_of_doors = 2, type = wood), armchair(BI = [1, 1]), table(BI =[0.81 0.91]), window(BI = [1, 1]), window(BI = [1, 1]), door(BI = [1, 1])), living_room (BI = [0.19 0.27], double_bed(BI = [1,1]), wardrobe(BI = [1, 1], number_of_doors = 2, type = wood), armchair(BI = [1, 1]), table(BI =[0.81 0.91]), window(BI = [1, 1]), window(BI = [1, 1]), door(BI = [1, 1])) }.

* Image Clustering

By comparing the image interpretation (sequence(2)) with all class representative descriptions, the membership degrees of the image to each class are obtained. The clustering description of the image is the followinge:

sequence(3): { block_of_flats(0.9), commercial_house(0.0), hospital_building(0.5), concert_hall(0.0) }.

C) Image Storage and Indexing

From the sequences (2) and (3), we obtain the new information to enter in the object and cluster indexes.

3.3. Query Processing

The query: "find the draughts for a room in a block_of_flats or in hospital_building, which present double_bedroom with a table and at least one wordrobe (with at least two doors, and of type "wood")", could be expressed in our query language as follows:

```
RETRIVE IMAGES (block_of_flats/0.9) OR
(hospital_building/0.7)
CONTAINING
double_bedroom/1.0 AND
(AT LEAST 1 wordrobe 0.8 WITH
```

(number_of_doors $\geq$ 2 AND type MATCH "wood"))

Then the query processing is very fast since only indices are used and no information is to be extraced, in this phase, from the images.

4. CONCLUSION AND FUTURE WORK

GRIM_DBMS runs on SUN/3 workstations, under Unix 4.2. It is written in C and Quintus Prolog and uses the SUNCORE graphical package [SunC86].

The design of GRIM_DBMS is based on the experiences of a previuos prototype, described in [Rabi87b], which was based on fuzzy set techniques. This prototype was implemented on an IBM PC/AT computer and was intended for the management of business graphical images, generated by a commercial business graphical editor (IBM Graph Assistant).

We plan to apply the results obtained with GRIM_DBMS in the project MULTOS, which is part of the ESPRIT (European Strategic PRogramme for Information Technology) [Bert85]. In this project, a first prototype for the storage (based on optical media) and retrieval of multimedia office documents has already been implemented. However, in this prototype images are treated as passive components in the multimedia documents, that is, components which are retrieved as part of the document but cannot actively contribute in the retrieval process (no condition on images can be part of the query, only conditions on attributes, text and the document structure) [Bert88]. In the second MULTOS prototype, we plan to build a specialized subsystem, functionally similar to GRIM_DBMS, which will allow a higher integration of images in the document retrieval process.

REFERENCES

[**Ball82**] Ballard D., Brown C.,*"Computer Vision"*, Prentice Hall (1982)

[**Barn81**] Barnett J.,*"Computational Methods for a Mathematical Theory of Evidence"*, in Proc. 7-th Inter. Joint Conf. on Artificial Intelligence , Vancouver, B.C., pp.868-875 (1981)

[**Bert85**] Bertino E., Gibbs S., Rabitti F., Thanos C., Tsichritzis D.,*"Architecture of a Multimedia Document Server"*, Proc. 2nd ESPRIT Technical Week, Brussels (Sept. 1985)

[**Bert88**] Bertino E., Rabitti F., Gibbs S., *"Query Processing in a Multimedia Document System"*, ACM Trans. on Office Information Systems,

Vol.6, N.1, pp.1-41 (1988).

[Blas80] Blaser A., (edt.) *"Database Techniques for Pictorial Applications"*, Springer Verlag, Berlin (1980)

[Chan80a] Chang N., Fu K.,*"Query-by-Pictorial-Example"*, IEEE Transactions on Software Engineering, Vol. SE-6, No. 6, pp.519-524 (Nov. 1980)

[Chan80b] Chang S., Fu K., (eds.) *"Pictorial Information Systems"*, Springer Verlag (1980)

[Chan81a] Chang S., Kunii T.,*"Pictorial Data-Base Systems"*, IEEE Computer Vol.14 (Nov. 1981)

[Chan81b] Chang N., Fu K.,*"Picture Query Languages for Pictorial Data-Base System"*, IEEE Computer Vol.14 (Nov. 1981)

[Chan85] Chang S.,*"Image Information Systems"*, Proc. of the IEEE, Vol. 73, No. 4, pp.754-764 (Apr. 1985)

[Choc84] Chock M., Cardenas A., Klinger A.,*"Database Structure and Manipulation Capabilities of a Picture Database Management System"*, IEEE Transactions on Pattern Analysis and Machine Intelligence, Vol. PAMI-6, No. 4, pp. 484-492 (Jul. 1984)

[Eshe86] Eshera M., Fu K., *"An Image Understanding Systems Using Attributed Symbolic Representation and Inexact Graph-Matching"*, IEEE Trans. Pattern Anal. Macth. Intell., Vol. PAMI-8, No.5, pp.604-618 (Sept. 1986)

[Goos80] Goos G., Hartmanis J., (edt.),*"Pictorial Information System"*, Springer Verlag (1980)

[Gord84] Gordon J., Shortliffe E.,*"The Dempster-Shafer Theory of Evidence in Rule-Based Expert Systems"*, in *"Mycin Experiments of the Stanford Heuristic Programming Project"*, Buchanan B., Shortliffe E., (edt.), Addison - Wesley Publishing Company, pp.272-292 (1984)

[Nagy85] Nagy G.,*"Image Database"*, Image and Vision Computing, Vol. 3, No. 3, pp. 111-117, (Aug. 1985)

[Rabi87a] Rabitti F., Stanchev P.,*"An Approach to Image Retrieval from Large Image Databases"*, Proc. ACM-SIGIR Conf., New Orleans, pp.284-295 (1987)

[**Rabi87b**] Rabitti F., Stanchev P.,*"Graphical Image Retrieval from Large Image Databases"* , Proc. AICA Conf., Vol. 2, Trento, pp.69-89 (1987)

[**Rose84**] Rosenthal A., Heiler S., Manola F.,*"An Example of Knowledge - Based Query Processing in a CAD/CAM DBMS"*, Proc. Tenth Int. Conf. on VLDB, Singapore, pp. 363-370 (1984)

[**Salt83**] Salton G., McGill M.,*"Introduction to Modern Information Retrieval"*, McGraw-Hill (1983)

[**SunC86**] *"SunCore graphical package"*, SUN 3 Reference Manuale (1986)

[**Tail86**] Tailor A., Cross A., Hogg D., Mason D.,*"Knowledge – based interpretation of remotely sensed images"*, Image and Vision Computing, Vol. 4, No. 2, pp. 67-83 (May 1986)

[**Tamu84**] Tamura H., Yokoya N., *"Image Database Systems: A Survey"* , Pattern Recognition, Vol.17, No.1, pp. 29-43 (1984)

[**Tang81**] Tang G.,*"A Management System for an Integrated Database of Pictures and Alphanumerical Data"*, Computer Graphics and Image Processing 16, pp. 270-286 (1981)

[**Tsic82**] Tsichritzis D., Lochovsky F.,*"Data Models"*, Prentice-Hall, Englewood Cliffs, N.J. (1982)

Session 10

MULTIMEDIA DATABASE I

Visual Database Systems
T.L. Kunii (Editor)
Elsevier Science Publishers B.V. (North-Holland)
   IFIP, 1989

Visual Databases need Data Models for Multimedia Data

Wolfgang Klas, Erich J. Neuhold, and Michael Schrefl[*]

GMD-IPSI
Integrated Publication and Information Systems Institute
Dolivostr. 15
D-6100 Darmstadt, FRG

[*] Technical University of Vienna
Department of Applied Computer Science
Paniglg. 16   ·
A-1040 Vienna, Austria

This paper describes the special requirements that arise in the handling of multimedia data, e.g., the handling of incomplete information, the distinction between the (internal) modelling of information and its (external) multimedia presentation, the management of context-free and context-sensitive references between pieces of data, sharing of data among multiple objects, and versioning. In particular, the paper discusses how these requirements differ from or go beyond those met by traditional database systems. We then propose appropriate modelling concepts which meet these requirements better than traditional approaches. Based on object-oriented concepts and on concepts from semantic data models we introduce a data model that meets the requirements mentioned above. Thereby we clearly distinguish between concepts which belong to the modelling level and concepts which belong to the presentation level. The contribution of this paper is the identification of requirements for the management of multimedia information and the development of a set of modelling primitives to handle these requirements in an object-oriented environment. We show that object-oriented database systems offer a promising approach for the management of large amounts of complex multimedia data.

1. Introduction

   This paper identifies the requirements for the modelling of multimedia data and develops concepts which meet these requirements. At first, we discuss the problems independently from any special data model. The requirements are elaborated by using a trip report example, a multimedia document as it might be found in most organizations. Then, we propose modelling concepts based on object-oriented and semantic data model concepts which meet the requirements better than those found in traditional data models like the relational model.

Multimedia systems [IEEE84] have the capability to store and retrieve documents composed of text, images, and audio. After initial experiments with the management of multimedia data in projects like *Diamond* [FORS84], *MINOS* [CHRI84, CHRI86], *CCWS* [POGG85], *ORION* [WK87], and other experimental systems including hypermedia systems like *Neptun* [DEL86], *Intermedia* [GAR86, MEY86], *KMS* [AKS88] and *NoteCards* [HAL88, HAL87] the limitations of traditional database modelling concepts used by these systems have become increasingly apparent. The relational data model as well as the simple node and link model in hypermedia systems are not rich and complete enough to support the storage and information management as well as the presentation tasks required by multimedia applications [HAL88]. File system-based storage as in HAM [CAMP88] also falls short of what is needed.

In order to explain the concepts which will be introduced in this paper let us give a few definitions:

Multimedia data are data represented as text, sound and images (digitized images and complex drawings of vector graphics). The logical and physical characteristics of multimedia data and their usage in various application areas has been studied in [WL85, WLK87].

Multimedia documents are presentations of information by means of multimedia data. In classifying documents there are two extremes:

(a)   completely predefined documents and

(b)   non-predefined, free form documents.

Examples of completely predefined documents are "fill-in-the-blank" office forms or any document type defined by a formal grammer. Such forms do not allow for individual non-formatted entries; their layout and the types of their entries are known in advance. A filled-in form constitutes an individual document, e.g., an airplane ticket.

On the other hand, the layout of entries and the types of data that can be entered in non-predefined documents are not known in advance. Each such document is unique in its structure, i.e., a system does not know or maintain the structure of such existing documents. An example thereof is a personal notebook which might be composed of regular text, complex graphics and colored images.

Most documents do not fall into those two extreme cases, but somewhere in between. Some of the structure and some types of entries are known in advance, some are not. Typically examples are conference papers, office letters, or annotated bibliographies.

The term *complex object* stands for an abstract representation of a real world object, e.g., a person, a car, a document (including multimedia constituents), a video, etc., . A complex object consists of an aggregation of *structural* and *behavioral* properties. The structural properties consist of attributes and relationships. Attributes model the real world properties of an object. Relationships model the relationships between objects within a complex real world object, e.g., the part-of relationship. The value of an attribute cannot be interpreted as a reference, the value of a relationship has to be interpreted as a reference to an object. The object's behavioral properties are determined by a set of operations.

This definition of the term complex object extends the one used in data models of other approaches (e.g., *DAMOKLES* [GOT86], *DASDBM* [PSSW87], *IRIS* [FI87]) as it refers not merely to the object's structure but also to the object's operations. Looking at these aspects in more detail, we can distinguish three levels of object-oriented data models (OODM) [DIT86].

(1) A *structural* model allows to define data types of any complexity to represent structurally complex objects.

(2) An *operational* model as an extension of the structural model allows the definition of generic operators to handle the complex data types.

(3) A *behavioral* model allows to define object types together with the specification of specific operators for these types. Instances of an object type can only be used by calling these operators. Features like property and method inheritance are included in the data model (compare the object-oriented programming paradigm and abstract data types in [BOB86, GR83, COX86, STR86]).

Our investigation focuses on the second and third aspect of these levels. In particular, since we are concerned with the modelling of multimedia objects, it does not seem appropriate to consider their structure and representation decoupled from the operations one may want to use on them. It is obvious that an operational OODM may serve as a basis for a behavioral OODM.

The advantage of our approach is that - contrary to others - we support a general concept of object specialization. This gives us the opportunity to treat special issues, such as roles and categories of objects, under a uniform framework. We can handle different requirements by this uniform concept which may be interpreted in different ways, depending on the application requirements. This makes our model *general* and *easy* to understand, and it is a step along the road to an *open* and *adaptable* database model.

The rest of this paper is organized as follows: Section 2 deals with the fundamental requirements which have to be met by multi-media data model concepts. Section 3 proposes an architectural structure for visual database systems with respect to the distinction between the modelling and the presentation of objects. Section 4 introduces the modelling primitives which we believe to meet our requirements. Section 5 discusses briefly how the conceptual modelling layer and the presentation layer proposed in section 3 can be linked to each other, and it indicates how our modelling concepts fit into an overall environment for visual databases. Section 6 summarizes our approach.

2. Requirements

In this chapter we analyze the database requirements that arise for the handling of multimedia documents. In particular, we indicate how these requirements differ from or go beyond those met by traditional database systems. We discuss them independently from any special data model concepts and demonstrate them by an example.

2.1. Description of a representative multimedia document

Let us give an example of a multimedia document which will be managed (processed, stored, retrieved) in a multimedia database environment. It will have voice annotation, e.g., an oral report of the significant events as well as annotated images, e.g., the original receipts and tickets of the reported trip.

Our example document contains three parts: (a) a form "Travel Expense Voucher" which holds the information about the travel expenses, the traveller, approvals by superiors, and accounting information; (b) an appendix which holds all the original receipts and vouchers as evidence of the expenses; (c) a trip report which is a document consisting of regular text, a video clip concerning a demonstration of a software system, a voice annotation which comments a very expensive dinner, and an audial component which holds the discussion that followed the demonstration lecture.

Our sample document is processed as follows: Before travelling one has to get an approval by filling out (a part of) the travel expense voucher and getting all the necessary signatures. After the trip the remainder of the document has to be supplied and signed by the traveller and his/her superior.

Figure 1 presents parts of our sample document: the 'Travel Expense Voucher' which is in fact a fill-in-the-blank office form. Actually the form consists of a section which holds

Institute of Technology	Travel Expense Voucher Dept. CIS	FORM-x5749
DocNo.: A- *120662/88*	Purpose of Trip	
Name: *Jerry Simple*	*Workshop OODB, talk,*	
Address: *Dept. CIT /CD-576*	*Discussion with colleagues*	
Home: *1947 Spyll Road,*	Purchase Order No.:	
Berkeley, CA	Date from: to:	
Phone: x7299	Trip Report:	Reference:

P.O.No.	Issued	Account	Amount	Approvals	Name	Date
			$	Dean		
			$	Vice Pres.		
			$	Pres.		

I certify that the expenses		Budget	
were actually incurred		Controller	
Traveller Date			
Authorization:		Account. State Amount	

| 2-1050-5010   CA   1176.30 |

Disposition: ..... Mail to Above	......Send to Orig. Dept.	.... Hold for Pick-up

Date	9/7	9/8			TOTAL
Dinner		86.00			86.00

in other projects at GMD/IPSI

4. Plan for further work

Further work will concentrate interfaces of the POSTGRES with the transformation of req or access methods, and specia base groups at UCB, IPSI an each of these groups and to ev

5. References

[Klas88]   Klas, W., E.J.Neu
              Proc. of the Europ

[Klas88a]   Klas, W.: On the

DELTA AIR LINES
DU82P
VALID ONLY ON FLIGH
AND DATES SHOWN
KLAS MR

VOID   VOID   VOID
VOID   VOID   VOID
FRANKFURT
SAN FRANCISCO
FRANKFURT
DLK 1738.00 RA DL S

Figure 1. Parts of the example document - expense form, receipts, trip report

information about the traveller and the purpose of the trip, followed by a section which holds accounting and approval information, and a table which reflects the amount paid for a specific service. In addition Figure 1 shows parts of a scanned flight ticket (used as an original receipt) and parts of the trip report.

2.2. Requirements of multimedia data modelling

(1) There is a need to specify incomplete information.

Documents may be incomplete. Especially, during the phase of writing a document particular parts are not yet known in detail and are left open. In the database field incomplete information has been handled by null values [ZAN84, COD79, GZ88]. In hypertext [CON87, GAR88] a particular property that is not yet known may be given the range-class of the property as value. For example, a constraint for our example document might be that a travel report must be written not later than one month after the end of the trip. Therefore it should be possible to express that a travel report exists on 'DATE < (Start-Travel + 1 month)' where 'DATE' stands for the range of possible values to be filled in, and 'Start-Travel' evaluates to the date when the travel begins.

Usually, *defaults* are assumed when office forms are filled out. For example, the traveller may skip the field 'account number' to which expenses are transferred, if he wants the expenses transferred to his standard account given in the personal files.

(2) There is a need to extend the definition of some individual document beyond the definitions of its type.

Individual documents may have properties in addition to those specified in their type-definition. To contrast, in the database area a type definition is usually a sufficient and necessary condition. An instance of a data type may have no other properties as described in the type definition. However, this is different for documents. For example, an individual expense voucher may go beyond its type-definition, the standard expense voucher form. But in such a case, one does not introduce a separate expense voucher type for every single travel expense voucher (as would be required according to the axiom that types constitute a sufficient and necessary condition). The need to extend the definition of a particular document instance dynamically has been recognized in several systems [HAL88]. This leads us to look at types only as necessary conditions for their instances but not as sufficient ones.

In our example the standard travel expense voucher does not allow to describe the travel schedule in detail. Therefore it should be possible that the object modelling an individual trip can be extended by a property 'Schedule' which references a description of the schedule. In some situations forcing the user to alter the type definition could be appropriate. But this sort of extension should also be allowed to be done (dynamically) on demand.

(3) There is a need to integrate data from different databases and to handle them uniformly.

Multimedia documents contain information coming from several data sources, e.g., CAD-CAM databases, text databases, etc., [SVE87].

The object-oriented approach is particularly well suited to handle data from different sources uniformly. It follows the abstract data type concept in the sense that only the interfaces of types are made public, their implementations are hidden. Furthermore the same kind of operation may have a different implementation for different objects. This feature is called polymorphism. For example, the operation 'display' may be applied on a text object, on a graphics object, and on a sound object. Polymorphism means that each of these objects will use its own method to react to the 'display' message. The text object will print itself, the graphics object will display an image of itself, and the sound object will play itself.

In our example the fill-in form and the receipts might be stored in a database reserved for the administration, and the travel report in a database available for all the scientific staff. If the travel report contains confidential material, such parts of the report may be stored in a separate database. The multimedia data of a single document may be dispersed over several databases, as the different media may need special hardware and software. Digitized copies of the receipts might be stored in an image database. The video clip of the demonstration software and the voice annotation might be kept in the video and sound database, respectively. But, the object-oriented interface hides the actually different handling of the different media-parts of the trip report.

(4) There is a need to describe structured information.

The management of large amount of data requires adequate instruments for the organization of pieces of information. The data models of conventional database systems mostly provide modelling primitives which lead to flat database schemata, e.g., the relational database systems. Flat data models do not support a convenient and natural mapping of information, nor a modular organization of information pieces which belong together in respect of their logical context; object-oriented approaches consider these aspects.

A powerful data model should provide concepts for

- the modular organization of information *types* as well as mechanisms which define types as reusable units that can be imported by other types. One of these mechanisms is well known as *inheritance* of information.

- an adequate interpretation of data, i.e., information can be interpreted in different contexts dependent on the point of view. For most database systems the user can specify views, but those views are not inherent in the data model. We need primitives which allow a context-dependent interpretation and manipulation of information. And those primitives should be part of the data model, because they should be applied as early as possible in the process of mapping real world situations to a model.

(5) There is a need for distinguish between internal modelling and external presentation of objects.

Our example consists of text, tables, images, and has associated spoken information. In addition to modelling the multimedia contents and the structure of the document, we also have to model its presentation.

A presentation of a document is usually achieved by some combination of application of specified formatting and composition rules possibly with some interaction with a skilled layout artist (or producer in the case of multimedia works).

The outcome of this is then a rendered layout, a "physical" object - a book for example, or a finished electronic presentation, like a Hypercard stack. Components of these objects are pages, gutters, etc. or cards, backgrounds, etc. In so far as rendered layouts are to be stored, these are typical components that have to modelled. Their relationships to the internal information structures are often not only hard to model but even the subject of disagreement.

The ODA standard [ODA86] refers to both logical and layout structures of documents, but the relationship between the two is problematic in spite of the restriction of ODA to only a limited set of content architectures.

In publication systems, support for diverse crafts and expertise demands that a multiplicity of interrelated representations of a document be present in the system simultaneously. The VorTeX project [CHHA88] provides some insights in this respect. More powerful document models are needed, however, to provide the degree of integration required.

Alternatively, instead of denoting the outcome, "presentation" can refer to a functional description of the formatting and composition rules that are to be applied to the data.

In addition, the presentation involves the selection of the "view" of the data: which properties are to be used to represent the information that's to be communicated.

Here we model documents not as finished rendered layouts, but as structured multimedia objects together with rules and methods for producing presentations. (In another paper, we plan to attend in more detail to the issues of modelling presentations themselves).

A multimedia object can of course have several presentations. For instance, a bunch of numeric data may be presented either as a histogram or as a table, and the histogram or table may be stored as an object. The other one is to model the rules which allow to derive the presentations, e.g., the rules which defines how data has to be formatted to be presented as a histogram.

Thus we have to separate the modelling task into

(a) modelling the rules and methods for producing presentations

(b) modelling the structure and behavior of a multimedia object, especially adequate composition mechanisms for objects, i.e., inter- and intraobject relationships.

Presenting multimedia data.

Concerning the presentation of a document, i.e., its layout (or tone, etc.), we should make a distinction between two orthogonal aspects:

- static or dynamic presentation:

(i) the presentation of an object is modelled and stored as an object, e.g., the presentation of a person by a short description consisting of his name, his office number, his telephone number, and a photograph.

(ii) the presentation is determined dynamically on demand, where the layout (or tone, etc.) can be controlled by the user and may be specified by rules which define how to construct the presentation. E.g., if the user wants to see more personal data he should be able to request dynamically another presentation of the person, e.g., a curriculum vitae or a short description in prose, together with a digitized picture.

• linear or nonlinear presentation:

(i) a "linear" presentation, e.g., a printed book, (this might correspond to the default format for a presentation). A trivial example might be "Mr. Simple, born on Dec 6 1962" as a default presentation of the person mentioned in the expense voucher form.

(ii) a "nonlinear" presentation format, e.g., a hypertext presentation of a document which allows to navigate through the content of a document much easier than a linear presentation.

Modelling multimedia data.

The modelling of the structure of the document must be done independently of a particular presentation, say in terms of 'abstract objects'. The corresponding identification is supported by 'internal, non-printable object-identifiers' (e.g., 'authorized by: <obj-id#342>', 'approved by: <obj-id#654>', where <obj-id#342> and <obj-id#654> are the object identifiers of the appropriate persons).

Note, every object that is mentioned implicitly in the presentation (e.g., persons, who have to approve the expenses, mentioned by their name) should have a counterpart 'internal object identifier' in the logical structure of the document object. This has the advantage that only 'internal object identifiers' and no intrinsic data (e.g., text or pixels of images) must be handled at the logical level, and leads to a uniform treatment of object-oriented concepts (compare also [MAS87]).

But, what to do if one starts with a given document and some mentioned object is not uniquely identified, e.g., an author by its name? Then a data model should provide the following mechanisms:

(i)   Create a new internal object identifier for the mentioned author.

(ii) Treat internal object identifiers as referring to different real world objects, as long as the opposite has not been asserted.

(iii) The user or database administrator may assert that two database objects refer to the same real world object, e.g., somebody has realized that 'Klas, UC-Berkeley' = 'Klas, IPSI-Darmstadt'.

Adequate composition mechanisms.

Similar to hypermedia systems, where more advanced concepts (e.g., fileboxes, browsers) are built up from only two primitive constructs, nodes and links, the current generation of (experimental) multimedia data processing systems lack a powerful composition mechanisms. Although this simple strategy has been surprisingly successful, experience suggests that it is insufficient. Rich composition techniques are required to deal with groups of objects, to handle references between objects, and to treat references as unique objects separately from their components. These requirements influence mechanisms to define a well-suited conceptual schema of the database system which contains information about the objects mentioned in the document. Appropriate composition techniques are also necessary to cover the problem of inter- and intra object relationships.

All these aspects lead to the basic requirement that a data model is needed, which

(i)   clearly distinguishes between the modelling and the presentation of objects, and

(ii)   combines both aspects *homogeneously.*

(6) There is a need for context-free and context-sensitive references.

Objects mentioned in some multimedia document may refer to some other objects. In this respect we distinguish between references where the properties of a referenced object are considered independently of the referring object, and references where the properties of the referenced object have to be considered within the context of the referring object. In the first case we speak of *context-free* references, in the second one of *context-sensitive* references.

Let us explain the difference with an example. Assume we have modelled various flight descriptions, general descriptions of airplanes and special descriptions of the airplanes in the case that they are associated with a specific flight. In the flight description one can read "This flight always uses plane *'FRG-4711'* which is an Airbus-210.", where the string enclosed in single quotes refer to an object stored in the document database.

Suppose now, somebody is interested in a description of the general capacity of the plane *FRG-4711*. The system will respond with a description of the capacity, e.g., "This airplane has 268 seats, ..." This information can be interpreted independently of any properties of a specific flight description. The reference established from the flight description to the general description of the airplane is a *context-free* reference.

Someone else is interested in a description of the current load of the plane. He will be informed that "178 seats are taken, ...". This information depends on the flight description, i.e., it may differ if another flight description using the same plane is read. The reference established from the flight description to the description of the used airplane is context sensitive with respect to the flight description.

To summarize, a *context-free* reference is simply a reference from one object to another object. Its characteristic feature is that properties of the second object which are independent from the first one are retrieved, i.e., in the example the general description of the airplane's capacity.

In contrast, a *context-sensitive* reference describes the interdependence between several objects, e.g., in our example, the description of the number of taken seats depends on a specific flight description.

(7) There is a need to share data among multiple documents.

In the database area the notion of database views has been introduced to show users only the portions of the conceptual schema that they need to fulfill their tasks. Furthermore database views allow data to be customized to particular user needs.

Similarly, different people are interested in different presentations of the *same* document. Consider the travel document example again. The accountant is interested merely in travel expenses and dates, but not in technical matters. In contrast, the co-workers of the traveller are interested in technical matters discussed and in arrangements made in the business meetings. The traveler's manager, however, is to see the whole report.

In our example the accountant will be shown all the details concerning the expenses and receipts, but a colleague will not be offered accounting data, but all the technical aspects, i.e., the trip report.

In addition two *different* trip reports may refer to the same research lab, so the lab description will be shared among multiple documents.

As the reference of an object is concerned, it is appropriate to distinguish between a reference to a *copy* of an object and the *sharing* of an object [WKL86]. Logical copies of objects may be realized by deferred copies; a change of the referred object does not change the (logical) copy, i.e., the reference is to the object's current version at that time the reference has been established. In contrast, sharing an object by reference means that the reference is always to the most recent version of the object.

(8) There is a need to create and control versions.

Documents may exist in different versions. We can distinguish between alternative versions and historical versions.

As an example of alternative versions take different travel report forms which may be used for employees in different positions.

As an example of historical versions take the different historical stages of a travel form. The first stage, i.e., the first version is the travel application; the last state, i.e., the last version is the final travel document.

It has already been discussed earlier that individual documents may extend the definitions of its type. The same holds for versioning. Different versions of some document may be predefined at the type level, others may be dynamically introduced at the instance level, i.e., for a particular travel form.

In [WKL86, GAR88] powerful concepts are discussed. The experience with revision control systems like RCS [TICH82] in the area of software engineering may influence the development of appropriate versioning mechanisms for a data model.

Actually, a model should provide a solution for the following subtle issues:

(a) time-independent references to a particular object, meaning that if object O_1 references object O_2, always the *current version* of O_2 has to be referenced by O_1.

(b) time-dependent references, i.e., object O_1 references a particular version O_2' of object O_2.

(9) There is a need to include operations.

Documents need to have associated information on how they can be processed (manipulated, printed, edited, etc.). This sort of functionality always exists, either as separate programs or as something like methods (as in the object-oriented paradigm). An adequate modelling tool should provide a set of predefined operations that support the mapping of the operational information given with an application to the data model. The system should allow the extension of these operations and the definition of new operations by the user in order to meet generic or application and user specific requirements. E.g., a user should be able to adapt and redefine operations which create and delete objects, or to write an operation which controls the assignments of values to properties which correspond to special fields in a fill-in-the-blank form.

The following kinds of operations should be provided by a system, for definition as well as for instantiation.

(a) Predefined operations:

All generic information how to process documents should be provided as predefined operations by the system. We could enumerate a large set of operations which a system should support. Let us give just a few examples:

- create a multi-media object or a new version;
- define the logical structure of a multi-media object;
- define the layout, i.e., presentation;
- include a context-free reference to a current version of an object;
- include a context-sensitive reference to a specific version of an object;
- display (some parts of) a multi-media object;
- follow a context-free or context-sensitive reference.

(b) Application and user specific operations

Modelling a complex application which may include complex images, graphics or voice can be done much easier if we have the computational power of a programming language available at the modelling level. Assume we have a set of scanned images and a sequence of oral comments about them, we could now write an operation which processes the images in some specific order to show them on a screen and synchronizes the oral comments with the sequence of images.

In traditional approaches such algorithmic power was provided by the programming language in which the application program has been coded. The procedures have been separated from the model itself and this caused a lot of difficulties, e.g., inconsistent interpretation and manipulation of the data stored in conventional DBMS's. Current research in the database field starts dealing with that problem, either by extending the conventional DBMS techniques by introducing new concepts like user defined functions (e.g., [STONE86]) or investigating the object-oriented approach where operations are integrated with the data model (e.g., [KNS88, WKL86, COPE84, AHLS84]).

If a data model is to support 'natural' modelling it has to provide user-supplied operations. The best solution would be if the predefined operations mentioned above and user-supplied operations were integrated homogeneously.

(10) There is a need for concurrent access control.

Concurrent access control became important when databases allow several users to access and modify the same set of data. Similarly, if several users have access to and the right to modify the same multimedia document, whose structure may be of any complexity, concurrency is an important issue. It becomes even more complex when concepts are introduced that meet the requirements above.

Long lasting operations on multimedia objects which should be treated as atomic actions require that inconsistent database states caused by the execution of such an operation are visible. Some parts of a complex object should be accessible by other operations even though the entire object is in an inconsistent state. E.g., if the expense voucher form has been completed by the traveller, this part of the document should be accessible for the administration for further processing. However, the entire document may be inconsistent, because the trip report is still in progress.

New approaches to handle such transactions will be needed, but maybe even the semantics of the term *consistent data* as it is defined in the area of conventional database systems must be redefined in the context of large amount of complex structured data and associated operations.

3. Proposed Architecture

In this chapter we give a short description of the overall architecture of a visual database system. The different levels of the architecture are given in Figure 2.

Level A is the bottom layer. It consists of the conceptual schemata of several databases which support an integrated multimedia database system. According to the object-oriented paradigm these schemata are given in terms of classes, properties of classes and their associated operations (methods). However, data about some real world object, e.g., Mr. Simple, may be dispersed over several databases. For example, a digitized picture of Mr. Simple may be stored in the image database, his curriculum vitae in the full-text database, and his travel records in a relational database. In this case, the data about Mr. Simple would be described by three different object classes, one for each database, and stored as three different database objects, again, one for each database.

Level B describes the conceptual structure of real world objects, i.e., it *models* the real world. It consists of a set of *conceptual objects*, e.g., the "model of a document". The description of a *conceptual object* is given independent of any issues concerning the representation of the object itself. For example, the conceptual structure of a travel document consists of structures which model the traveller, the authorizing-person, the purpose of the trip, an expense statement, a trip report, etc.. But these conceptual structures can be seen in the environment of travelling for the company. That is, not all aspects of them are relevant for the travel document described by the conceptual model. The model however is independent from the fact, whether the traveller is represented in the travel document by his name, his social security number, or his portrait.

A *model object*, e.g., a document, may mention objects from several databases. For example, a person is described by his curriculum vitae, his portrait, and his travel records.

A *view* at this level has to be defined according to the information given by the conceptual schemata of several databases. The problem of view integration is described in [NS88, SN88].

Level C concerns the *presentation of objects*. Therefore, we speak also of the *presentation* layer and of *presentation objects*. Presentation objects are multimedia presentations of conceptual objects.

A presentation object may belong to more than one conceptual object, i.e., the presentation object may present more than one conceptual object together in a specific multimedia form. A presentation object must not reference conceptual objects from different views. For every conceptual object several presentation objects may exist, i.e., the same conceptual object may be presented differently to different users.

In the following chapter we discuss the data model issues relevant for the modelling layer. It constitutes the main part of this paper. In the subsequent chapter we discuss shortly issues concerning the presentation layer, and we discuss how the modelling layer can be linked to the presentation layer.

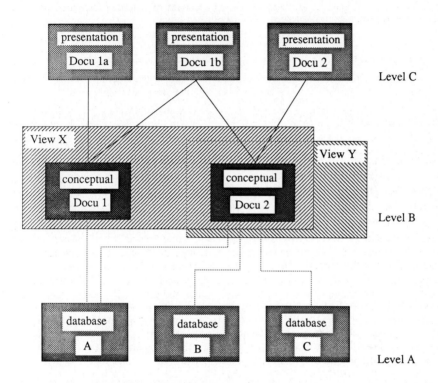

presentation ... specification of the presentation (layout)
conceptual   ... specification of the conceptual structure, the content (model)

Figure 2. Layers in an architecture of a visual database system

4. Modelling concepts

Based on object-oriented concepts and on modelling concepts of semantic data models we introduce a data model that meets the requirements set out above. It is currently developed at GMD-IPSI for a distributed multi-media object-oriented database system. For every concept introduced we show how it meets one (or more) of the requirements above. We argue why the followed approach is more appropriate than earlier approaches from the hypertext and from the database areas. More details about the data model and its implementation are described in [KNS88, FKRST88]. For a formal description see [DKT88].

4.1. Objects

Definitional properties versus factual properties.

Every object O has

(a) a set of *definitional* properties, that is,

$P^d(O) = \{(n, d) \mid n$ is a property name, d is a domain definition$\}$, and

(b) a set of *factual* properties, that is,

$P^f(O) = \{(n, v) \mid n$ is a property name, v the value of the property$\}$.

Definitional properties describe the structure and define the behavior of an object. As an example of a definitional property consider the attribute *Authorization* with the domain *SIGNATURE*. Definitional properties can be used to define a *type*, or in other words, a *type* is a collection of definitional properties.

A factual property gives the current value for some definitional property of the object. As an example consider the attribute *Authorization* with the appropriate value, which is the pattern of a signature of an individual person.

Clearly, for every factual property there must exist a corresponding definitional property. But, for some definitional property no factual property may have been given yet. Thus, the requirement No. 1 to specify incomplete information can be met partially.

The relationship between objects and types is defined as follows: For a given object O and a given type T the predicate

is-of-type(O, T) is true if O has all properties defined by type T.

We allow that definitional properties may be added at the instance level. That is, we can define properties for an object O in addition to the definitional properties of O defined by a type T. In this case the set of all definitional properties of O consists of the definitional properties defined by type T and the definitional properties defined at the object O itself. The predicate **is-of-type**(O, T) holds, but the definitions for the object O have been extended by the additional definitional properties. This meets requirement No. 2, that individual documents go beyond their standard predefined form.

Note: The definitional properties of a presentation object are defined upon the definitional properties of the corresponding conceptual objects. The factual properties of a presentation object are derived from the factual properties of the corresponding conceptual objects. E.g., a *traveller* is represented by *firstName*, and *secondName*, and maybe a *visitedCountry* is represented by *countryName* and *countryCode*.

4.2. Classification

Objects O_i with the same definitional properties are collected into *object classes*. These definitional properties form a type T associated with an object class, such that **is-of-type**(O_i, T) holds. An object O can be defined as an *instance of* some object class C, if O satisfies the type implied by that object class. That is, the predicate

instance-of(O, C) is true if $O \in C$,

and

if **instance-of**(*O*, *C*) holds, and **t**(*C*) is the type given by the object class *C*, then **is-of-type**(*O*, **t**(*C*)) holds.

Note, that a class is not a type, but introducing a class implies the definition of the type of all the instances of the class. A class serves as an object which (a) collects all its instances, and (b) provides the type definition *T*, such that **is-of-type**(O_i , *T*) holds for all instances O_i. The type definition determines the template used by the object class for the creation of an instance.

Furthermore, a *default factual property* may be given for a definitional property at the class level. This default factual property is inherited by an instance of the class, unless another factual property is given explicitly for the instance.

4.3. Properties of objects

We can distinguish the properties of an object by the general type of their values:

- **Attributes**

  Properties are called *attributes* if their values do not refer to other objects in the database, e.g., properties like an ASCII text or numerical values. An attribute value cannot be interpreted as a reference to another object, it has to be processed as the value of the property. As an example, consider the pixels of a picture or words in some text. But, the value itself can be built up by other values which can refer to other objects. E.g., words in a text may well refer to other objects in the database. Consider the example, "'I' met 'Mr. Wang'" from above. The string 'Mr. Wang' is used to represent the unprintable internal object-identifier for Mr. Wang externally. Be aware of the difference to the word "*met*" which does not serve as a representation of any internal object-identifier in this case.

  Example:
  DEFINE Class: Form
  ...
      memberProperties:
        name : String
        authorization-signature: BitMap
  ...

  The example above defines *name* and *authorization-signature* as attributes, i.e., the value of *authorization-signature* is a bit pattern of a signature, the value of *name* is a string. We also allow multi-valued attributes, for more details about those features of the model see [FKRST88].

- **Relationships**

  Properties are called *relationships* if their values refer to other objects. An object at which the reference is defined is called *owner* of the relationship. The properties of the object identified by the reference are *independent* of the owner of the relationship. *Relationships* are used to model *context-free* properties, and this meets the requirement No. 6, context-free references.

  In the following example the symbol ↑ is used to define such a reference.

Example:
DEFINE Class: Form

   ...

  memberProperties:
     authorizing-person: ↑ Person

   ...

The property *authorizing-person* is defined as an independent reference to an object of type *Person*, i.e., the value of the factual property is an object identifier, and the properties of the referenced objects are independent of an instance of class *Form*.

The system provides an option to control the automatic generation of the inverse relationship which is set up at the other object participating in the relationship. That is, we can specify an inverse relationship *authorizes* as an option of the definition of *authorizing-person*, which automatically causes the definition of the property *authorizes* as independent reference to *Form* in the definition of *Person*. For more details see [FKRST88].

- **Components**

  Properties are called *components* if their values refer to other objects, and the properties of the object identified by the reference are *dependent* on the superordinate object (i.e., the object to which the component belongs). *Components* are used to model *context-sensitive* properties, and this meets requirement No. 6, context-sensitive references (see also *role-specialization* below). In the following example the brackets '{', '}' define a set, the symbol '*' is used to define a property as a component.

  Example:
  DEFINE Class: ExpenseForm

     ...

    memberProperties:
       dinner-expense: Real
       dinner-comment: * Voice
       receipts: {* ReceiptCopy}

     ...

  In this example the attribute *dinner-expense* models the amount which had been paid for a dinner, *dinner-comment* is defined as a component, i.e., the value of this property is an object identifier which models digitized voice annotations. The property *receipts* models the copies of the original receipts approving the expense. The objects modelling the comments on the dinner and the receipt copies exist in the database *dependent* on the existence of an instance of class *ExpenseForm*. That is, if a special expense form is deleted, the attached copies of the receipts have to be deleted too, but not vice versa. For more details see [FKRST88].

  Note, the interdependence between two (or more) objects may be viewed conceptually in several ways: (a) as *a property* of one of these objects that is dependent on the other object(s), and (b) as *an object* of its own that describes the relationship between the interdependent objects. Alternative (a) is realized by components. The interdependence is asymmetric, because there is an object which is dependent on another one, but not the opposite. Alternative (b) is realized by the *aggregation* principle described later. In this case the interdependence between the objects is symmetric, because both objects depend on the other one.

- **Methods**

  Methods and message-passing as they are provided in object-oriented systems allow us to introduce both predefined and application- or user-specific operations described as requirement No. 9. In our data model the class definition contains the declaration of the method's signature (interface) and the class implementation section contains the body of the method.

  The example below shows the definition of the signature of a method and its implementation.

  Example:
  DEFINE Class: Form

  ...

  memberProperties:
      purpose-of-trip: String

  ...

  memberMethods:
      setPurposeOfTrip [purpose: String] **returns**: Object

  ...

  IMPLEMENTATION Class: Form
      setPurposeOfTrip [purpose: String] **returns**: Object
          {body of the operation which assigns a value to the property *purpose-of-trip*}

  ...

4.4. Specialization

In our data model, types are derived from other types by applying the concept of *type specialization*, called *typeOf*. The modelling language (VML) supports also the concept of *object specialization*, which allows the modelling of a real world object in several contexts. An object is described more detailed in a special context than by its general representation. VML supports two different primitives for object specialization, called *roleSpecialization* and *categorySpecialization*. The following subsections will explain the difference between these concepts.

4.4.1. Type specialization

In VML the principle of *type specialization* allows to build more specialized types by specifying how the new ones differ in their property and method definitions from already defined more general ones, called supertypes.

As defined above, the definition of a class C implies the definition of the type $t(C) = C^T$ of all instances of C. This type C^T can be derived from another type C_I^T by specifying the **typeOf** clause in the definition of class C. Of course, type C_I^T is implied by the definition of another class C_I, such that $C_I^T = t(C_I)$.

We call type C^T a subtype of type C_I^T, i.e., the predicate **subtype-of**(C^T, C_I^T) holds. And we call class C a subclass of class C_I, i.e., the predicate **subclass-of**(C, C_I) holds. The relationship between types and classes are defined as follows:

If **subtype-of(t(C), t(C_1))** holds for two classes C and C_1,
then **subclass-of(C, C_1)** holds.

A type C^T which is defined as subtype of another type C_1^T by means of the *typeOf* clause "imports" the complete property specification given by the supertype. That is, the set of definitional properties represented by type C_1^T is merged with the other specifications given for type C^T. If a property is defined twice, i.e., it is defined by type C_1^T and by another specification for type C^T, the specification of type C^T overrides the one of type C_1^T. This mechanism allows a refinement of definitional properties.

If a type is defined as a subtype of several other types, a special algorithm has to be applied to resolve possible conflicts which arise, when properties are defined by more than one type. For more details see [FKRST88].

An instance of a class C reflects then a structure and a behavior which is based on the specifications of type C_1^T and the additional definitional properties specified for type C^T. The *typeOf* relationship does not specify any relationship between the instances of the class C_1 and the instances of the class C. But according to the definition of **is-of-type** given above the following holds:

For all the instances O_i and the classes C and C_1,
such that **instance-of(O_i , C)** and **subtype-of(t(C), t(C_1))**,
is-of-type(O_i , t(C)) and **is-of-type(O_i , t(C_1))** hold.

> *Example:*
> **DEFINE Class: ExpenseForm with:**
>   **typeOf: Form**
>   ...
>   **memberProperties:**
>   authorizing-person: ↑ Chairman
>   traveller: ↑ Employee
>   **memberMethods:**
>   ...

In this example all the definitional properties given by the type *Form*, which is implied by the class definition of *Form*, are merged with the definitions specified in type *ExpenseForm* implied by the class definition of *ExpenseForm*, e.g., the properties *authorizing-person* and *traveller*. As the example shows the property *authorizing-person* has been redefined. It has been defined in the type definition for the instances of class *Form* as a reference to *Person*, but it is redefined in the type definition for the instances of class *ExpenseForm* as a reference to *Chairman*. This applies for *all* kinds of properties.

The *typeOf* clause does not specify any relationship between the instances of the class which implied type *Form* and the instances of the class *ExpenseForm*. But for an individual instance O the predicates

is-of-type(O, t(*ExpenseForm*)) and **is-of-type(O, t(*Form*))**

hold.

This concept makes a contribution to meet requirement No. 4, the need of structuring information types, because types can be composed of other types.

4.4.2. Object specialization

In order to understand the more advanced primitives *roleSpecialization* and *categorySpecialization* we want to explain the general principle which serves as a base for these concepts. In addition we can show that other useful mechanisms (e.g., versioning) can be built on top of this common concept:

The object specialization principle:

Let us remember the following postulate:

if **instance-of**(O, C), then **is-of-type**$(O, t(C))$,

which means that O has the properties specified in type $t(C)$. The set of the definitional properties of an object O, $P^d(O)$, consists of the definitional properties specified in $t(C)$ and the one defined at the object O itself.

Suppose we want to define a more specialized instance O' with respect to an object O, i.e., O will be conceptually the same real world object as O', but O' is a more detailed model of O. We then define the object O' to be a *specialization of* the object O. Let **specialization-of**(O', O) be the predicate which is true if O' is defined to be a *specialization of O*. The semantics of **specialization-of** is defined as follows:

If **specialization-of**(O', O), and

$P^d(O)$ and $P^d(O')$ are the sets of definitional properties, and

$P^f(O)$ and $P^f(O')$ are the sets of factual properties of O and O' respectively,
then

(1) for every definitional property $p = (n, d)$, $p' = (n, d')$, $p \in P^d(O)$, $p' \in P^d(O')$,

there is a factual property (n, v') for p' in $P^f(O')$ and

a factual property (n, v) for p in $P^f(O)$,

such that value v' may differ from value v,

i.e., a property can be redefined; and

(2) for every definitional property $p = (n, d)$, $p' = (n, d')$, $p \in P^d(O)$, $p' \notin P^d(O')$,

there is a factual property for p in $P^f(O')$ which is the *same* as in $P^f(O)$.

That is, the value for property p is *inherited* from $P^f(O)$. We call such a property p a virtual property of O'; and

(3) for every definitional property $p = (n, d)$, $p' = (n, d')$, $p \notin P^d(O)$, $p' \in P^d(O')$,

there is a factual property for p' in $P^f(O')$, but

no factual property for p' in $P^f(O)$.

Note:

This definition does not require that the set $P^d(O')$ is defined as a type T, such that **is-of-type**(O', T) holds.

This general principle serves as a base for both object specialization concepts, *Role-Specialization* and *Category-specialization*. In addition it can be employed to realize versioning.

Role-Specialization

The instances of some class may appear in different contexts which can be defined by specifying different role-specialization classes of that class. The instances of a role-specialization class are object specializations of the instances of the class that model the same real world object.

Let **RoleSpecializationOf**(C', C) be the predicate which is true if a class C' is defined as a role of class C, and let **roleSpec**(O', O) be the predicate which is true if an instance O' is defined as a role specialization of another instance O;

If **RoleSpecializationOf**(C_j, C), and **instance-of**(O_i, C_j) hold

then there exists an object O, such that

instance-of(O, C) and **roleSpec**(O_i, O) hold[1].

The semantics of the 'role-of' property at the instance level is defined as follows:

If **roleSpec**(O', O) holds, then
(1) **specialization-of**(O', O), and
(2) there is a class C', such that **RoleSpecializationOf**(C', C),
    where **instance-of**(O',C') and **instance-of**(O,C) hold,
    i.e., O' has the **instance-of** property explicitly defined,
    and the class of O' is defined as role-specialization of the
    class of C.

Note:

(a) **instance-of**(O', C) implies that at least a subset of $P^d(O')$ is specified in $t(C')$;

(b) the fact that a definitional property specified in $P^d(O')$ can override a definitional property specified in $P^d(O)$ ensures that if a definitional property $P = (n, d)$ is defined in $P^d(O)$, and a definitional property $P' = (n', d')$ is defined in $P^d(O')$, such that $n' = n$ (i.e., the properties P and P' have the same name), object O' has only the factual property for P'.

If two classes C' and C are related by the **roleSpecialization** relationship than every instance of the role specialized class C' models a real world object which is also modelled by an instance of the class C. But the instance of the role specialized class models the real world object in a specific situation or context which has not been explicitly considered in the class C. Of course, specializations into roles do not have to be disjoint, because real world objects can be considered in several different roles.

This concept meets the requirement of structuring and organizing information with respect to different viewpoints (requirement No. 4). In addition it provides a solution for requirement No. 6, different contexts for an object. Let us consider an example:

Let us assume we want to define a context-sensitive reference: type *ExpenseForm* defines a component *receipts* of type *ReceiptCopy* (compare section 4.3.). The corresponding class *ReceiptCopy* is defined as a role specialization of class *OriginalReceipt*. It declares the additional information about the copy of an original receipt, e.g., who has approved the copy, the signature of this approval, and the scanned image itself.

---

[1] Note, that it must not exist for every instance O of class C an O_i as instance of a class C_j.

Example:

DEFINE Class: OriginalReceipt ...
  memberProperties:
      subject: String
      bought-by: ↑ Person
      amount: Real
      id: Integer
   ...

DEFINE Class: ReceiptCopy **with:**
  roleOf: OriginalReceipt
  ...

  memberProperties:
      approved-on: Date
      approved-by: ↑ Person
      signature: BitMap
      image: BitMap
   ...

Assume, an instance A of *ExpenseForm* has the component *receipts* with object B', which is an instance of class *ReceiptCopy*, as its value. Object B' is a **roleSpecialization** of object B which is the general description of the (original) receipt. Then

B' ... models the context sensitive properties of the receipt with respect to A, and

B ... models the context-free properties of the receipt with respect to A.

In addition, it is possible to share the object B (i.e., the context-free properties) by several documents without running into any conflict with the context represented by A.

Note, that this meets also requirement No. 7, sharing data among multiple documents.

Category-Specialization:

The instances of a class may be categorized into disjoint sets with respect to a special aspect, e.g., documents may be categorized into forms, newspapers, books, etc., with respect to the style they satisfy. Classes like *form* can be defined by specifying appropriate category-specialization classes of the general class *document*. In addition to the general representation of an individual document it can be interpreted in one of these categories. They reflect a more specialized description of an object, i.e., they model some properties of the real world object which have been neglected in the general representation as a document.

Let **CategorySpecializationOf**(C', C, A) be the predicate which is true if class C' is defined as a categorization of class C with respect to an aspect A, and let **categorySpec**(O', O, A) be the predicate which is true if an instance O' is defined as a categorization of instance O with respect to a given aspect A;

  If **CategorySpecializationOf**(C_j, C, A) and **instance-of**(O_i, C_j)

then there exists an object O, such that

    instance-of(O, C) and **categorySpec**(O_i, O, A) hold[2].

The semantics of the 'category-of' property at the instance level is defined as follows:

if **categorySpec**(O', O, A) holds, then
  (1) **specialization-of**(O', O);
  (2) there is a class C', such that
    CategorySpecializationOf(C', C, A),
    where **instance-of**(O',C') and **instance-of**(O,C) hold,
    i.e., O' has the instance-of property explicitly defined
    and the class of O' is a category specialization of the
    class of C;
  (3) there does not exist any object $O'' \neq O'$, such that
    categorySpec(O'', O, A) holds (disjoint categorization).

It is important that the specialization into categories is *disjoint*. If the subcategories were not disjoint, we would miss some semantics. We then actually regard the same real world object in a different situation or context (i.e., different roles) if categories overlap. If the categories were not exhaustive the classification of real world objects into subcategories would remain incomplete, but the model allows that, however.

Of course, we can build more than one categorization hierarchy for a concept considering different aspects.

This concept does not meet only the requirement of structuring information types, it also supports the notion of context-sensitive interpretation and manipulation of information (compare requirement No. 4).

4.5. Versioning

What are reasons for keeping versions of an object? The result of manipulating an object may not replace the original object but may be valid in parallel to the original one. Actually, the following fundamental actions can be responsible for that:

(a) *Changing the values of properties*: Some properties of an object O may be changed, i.e., the version O' differs from the object O that O' has different values for properties given with O.

(b) *Changing the definition of properties*: Some property definitions of an object O may be changed, i.e., the version O' differs from the object O that O' has different definitional properties and corresponding factual properties.

(c) *Adding properties*: Object O' may have some additional properties.

(d) *Deleting properties*: A definitional property $p = (n, d)$ which is specified by an object O itself, i.e., $p \notin t(C)$, where **instance-of**(O, C), may be defined to be deleted for a version O'.

The versions of an object O form a tree with O as its root. Some versions serve as objects which can be interpreted as the final versions at a specific time. We identify by default as *current* versions all the leafs of the tree. The function $c(O)$ returns a set of object identifiers of current versions for a given object O. That is, it returns by default all the leafs in that subtree of which O is the root.

---

[2] Note, that it must not exist for every instance O of class C an O_i as instance of a class C_j.

Let us consider the following two aspects on versioning:

- *References to a particular version*: It should not be necessary to alter a particular version any more, e.g., O', if another version, e.g., O'', is introduced and made the final version of O. The reason is that other objects may still refer to the older version O' and it is expected that this version is not changed. For example, consider somebody lost one sheet of a trip report and orders another copy of this sheet. If the trip report has been written in several versions, the spare copy must be printed according to his version in order to fit into his document.

- *References to a current version*: In contrast, during the development of a travel report one will always expect references to a current version of the individual documents. In this case an object '*travel-report*' would reference not a particular version of an individual object O, e.g., O' or O'', but it would reference $c(O)$.

Assume that a version O_2 has to be created from an object O_1.

Let **version-of**(O_2, O_1) be the predicate which is true if object O_2 is defined as a version of O_1. The semantics of versioning is defined as followed:

If **version-of**(O_2 , O_1) and **is-type-of**$(O_1 , t(C))$, and

$P^d(O_1)$ and $P^d(O_2)$ are the sets of definitional properties, and

$P^f(O_1)$ and $P^f(O_2)$ are the sets of factual properties of O_1 and O_2 respectively,

then
(1) **is-type-of**$(O_2 , t(C))$, and
(2) for the definitional properties $(n, d') \in P^d(O_2)$ and

the factual properties $(n, v') \in P^f(O_2)$ holds either

(2a) $p^d = (n, d') \in P^d(O_1)$ and $p^f = (n, v') \in P^f(O_1)$,
i.e., version O_2 is a copy of object O_1;

(2b) $p^d = (n, d') \in P^d(O_1)$ and $p^f = (n, v) \in P^f(O_1)$,
i.e., the value of a property has been changed;

(2c) $p^d = (n, d) \in P^d(O_1)$ and $d \neq d'$,
i.e., the definition of a property has been changed;

(2d) $p^d = (n, d) \notin P^d(O_1)$, i.e., a property has been added to version O_2.

The method *create-version* which creates a new version O' for an object O takes one optional parameter: A set of definitional properties which specify the alterations of any definitions given for O, i.e., in the cases (b), (c) and (d) described above these definitional properties are the ones which are changed, added or deleted with respect to version O'. It creates a a new object according to the specifications passed as argument and defines the object as a current version.

We have to distinguish between the following two cases:

- *Historical versions*: If the method is applied on a leaf O_i of the version tree, the new version O_i' is called a *historical version*, i.e., there exists O_i' as the only version for the object O_i.

- *Alternative versions*: If the method is applied on an object O_i which is not a leaf of the version tree, i.e., there exists already at least one version O_i' of O_i, the new version is an alternative to all the versions of O_i and called an *alternative version*. In the case that there exists only one version O_i' of O_i, i.e., O_i' is a historical version, O_i' becomes also an alternative version.

Both kinds of versioning meet the requirement No. 8, the need to create and control versions.

4.6. Aggregation of independent objects

The current generation of hypermedia and conventional database systems generally lacks adequate and powerful composition mechanisms (compare [HAL88]). Questions raised by this problem concern sharing of data, referencing objects as well as components of objects, handling versions of composite objects, etc. Our model provides primitives described above which allow to share data, to refer to other objects and to manage versions. However, there arises the question how powerful should those primitives be? In the case of composite objects our model so far provides the mechanisms described in section 4.3. where the interdependence between two (or more) objects can be viewed conceptually as *a property* of one of the objects that is dependent on the other object(s). But, often one wants to model such an interdependence as an object of its own. It semantically represents a relationship between two or more independent objects and the properties of this relationship.

Example:
DEFINE Class: TravelExpenseForm **with:**
    aggregateProperties: (traveller-info, accounting-info, expense-info)
    ...

    memberProperties: {the properties of the relationship}
        created : Date
        traveller-info: ↑ TravellerForm {the properties which are the
        accounting-info: ↑ AccountingForm constituents of the entire
        expense-info: ↑ ExpenseForm   aggregate object}
    ...

The semantics is defined as follows: An instance of TravelExpenseForm can only exist, if the instances of all constituents - the traveller-info, accounting-info and expense-info - exist. The properties which serve as constituents of the aggregation are defined by *aggregateProperties*. This aggregation concept is used in the conceptual schemata of database systems as a composition mechanism for objects (compare requirement No. 5, distinction between internal modelling and external presentation of objects).

5. Multimedia presentation of objects

It is not the purpose of this paper to introduce a multimedia-document layout specification language, although the presentation of objects is the topic of another research project of our institute and it is subject of another paper. The point we want to make here is, that there should be a clear distinction between the description of the presentation and the conceptual structure of multimedia-objects.

The modelling layer, which we have described so far, is only concerned with the description of the conceptual structure of objects, e.g., the structure of documents. How a conceptual object is presented to the user is dealt with at the presentation layer where the layout of conceptual objects is defined.

The presentation of an object can only be defined according to the definition of a view. The same document may appear in different layouts, but the accounting department may not see confidential agreements mentioned in the travel report; the research department may not see the travel expenses. Similarly, accounting, sales and manufacturing may get a different transcript of a sales contract.

The presentation of objects could be modelled with the same basic concepts used at the conceptual layer. Classes can be defined for specific layouts, where basic presentation types like rows, columns, tables, histograms or regular text can be predefined in the system. The operations defined by these types implement appropriate formatting and composition rules which are needed to achieve a presentation of a document. A user can build more complex descriptions of a presentation using these predefined presentation types. In our example, different cell types for the columns and rows may be used for the description of the presentation of the expense form, e.g., cells for numeric data, cells with oral annotations, dynamic cells like the ones used in spread sheets, etc..

To complete our discussions let us indicate shortly how the conceptual layer and the presentation layer could be linked to each other.

Consider the Travel Expense Voucher Form of Figure 1. Its layout is defined upon the conceptual class *ExpenseForm* by means of the presentation class *TravelExpenseVoucher-Formx5749*, see Figure 3. The class *TravelExpenseVoucherFormx5749* defines how the columns and rows have to be combined, which cell types have to be used at specific locations within the columns and rows, etc.. In addition, the class specifies how the values for these cells are determined. That is, it defines operations which dynamically calculate the values or specifies paths where the values can be found. The problems which arise if the presentation layer is linked to the conceptual layer by path descriptions may be similar to the problems related to the dynamic view integration ([SN88]), where structural differences have to be resolved.

In our example shown in Figure 3 the class *TravelExpenseVoucherFormx5749* defines a property *applicant-box* which corresponds to the box with the name of the applicant, his

DEFINE Class TravelExpenseVoucherFormx5749
    typeOf: GeneralFormPresentation
    ...
    memberProperties:
      presents-object: ↑ ExpenseForm {refers to the conceptual object to be presented}
      header-box: ↑ HeaderBox   {a predefined layout for the haeder}
      applicant-box: [style: RegularTable;   {a predefined table layout}
                  nameField: String;
                  nameCell: PathDescription;
                  ...]
    ...

Figure 3. The definition of a class which defines a presentation of an expense form

DEFINE Class: Person   ...
   memberProperties:
      firstName: String
      lastName: Sting
    ...
   memberMethods:
      firstAndLastName[] **returns** String

DEFINE Class: Employee **with:**
   roleOf: Person
   ...
   memberProperties:
      department: String
      socSecNo: Integer
   ...

Figure 4. The definitions for class *Person* and class *Employee* as used in Figure 3.

office and home address, his phone number and the document number (compare Figure 1). The style of this box is the one of a *RegularTable*. It defines e.g., the size of the table, the number of rows and columns, the location of this table within the entire form and all the operations to manipulate the table. Some values for the property *nameField* may be "Name:" or "Nombre:" or "Nom:" according to the language in which the form has to be presented. Other values for the cells in this table may be determined by path descriptions, e.g., the value of the applicant's name, which is modeled by the property *nameCell* (see Fig. 3), may be determined according to the following path description:

presents-object ExpenseForm . traveller Employee . firstAndLastName String.

This path starts at the object which is presented by the presentation object, i.e., it starts at an instance of *ExpenseForm*. It then follows the property *traveller* to the object which represents the applicant (it is of type *Employee* which is defined as a role specialization of *Person*, see Figure 4). The last component in this path is the property *firstAndLast-Name* which is a method and determines the value. The method can be found at the general description of the applicant as a *Person*.

This subtle problem of linking the presentation layer to the conceptual layer is investigated in another project at our institute and it is subject of another paper.

6. Summary

In this paper we have presented an approach to meet a lot of requirements that arise in the handling of multimedia information. First we described the requirements, which were elaborated by a sample travel document consisting of a fill-in-the-blank form, a set of receipts, and a trip report. We then have introduced modelling primitives which meet these requirements: The concept of *objects* as it has been proposed supports the handling of incomplete information and allows the extension of the definitions for an object. The different kinds of *properties*, e.g., relationships, components, facilitate the modelling of context-sensitive and context-free references, and the definition of *methods* allows the encapsulation of operational and structural information of an object. *Type specialization* is a basic mechanism which can be used to compose complex structured information types. *Object specialization* is a basic mechanism for modelling objects in different situations. It contributes to a more adequate mapping of a real world situation to the data model. The *versioning* mechanism satisfies the requirement of managing historical and alternative versions homogeneously, and it provides a solution for the subtle problem of referencing always a particular version or a current version of an object. In addition we proposed an architecture for a visual database system that supports the distinction between the modelling and the presentation of information. We did not consider the problem of integrating and handling data from different databases in this paper, but this specific problem is investigated by another project [SN88, NS88].

Further work concentrates on the problem how the presentation and the conceptual layer can be linked together. This is investigated in another project of our institute and it is subject of another paper.

Acknowledgement

The authors wish to thank R.Minio and P.Fankhauser for helpful comments on an earlier version of this paper.

References

[AHLS84]   Ahlsen M., A.Bjornerstedt, S.Britts, C.Hulten, and L.Soderlund, "An Architecture for Object Management in OIS", ACM Transactions on Office information Systems, Vol. 2, No. 3, July 1984.

[AKS88]   Akscyn, R., D.L. McCracken and E.Yoder, "A distributed hypertext for sharing knowledge in organizations", Communications ACM 31, 7 (July 1988), pp. 820-835.

[BOB86]   Bobrow, D.G. and et. al., "CommonLoops: Merging Common Lisp and Object-oriented programming," ACM-SIGPLAN Notices, Vol. 21, No. 1, pp. 17-29, 1986.

[CAMP88]   Campbell, B., J.M.Goodman, "HAM: A General Purpose Hypertext Abstract Machine", Communications ACM 31, 7 (July 1988), pp. 856-861.

[CHHA88]   Chen, Pehong and Michael A. Harrison, "Multiple Representation Document Development", IEEE Computer, Vol 21, January 1988. pp 15-31

[CHRI84]   Christodoulakis, S., Vanderbroek, J., Li, J., Li, t., Wan, S., Wang., Y., Papa M., and Bertino, E., "Development of a Multimedia Information System for an Office Environment", Proceedings of the 10th International Conference on Very Large Databases, 1984, pp. 261-271.

[CHRI86]   Christodoulakis, S., F.Ho, and M.Theodovidou, "The Multimedia Object Presentation Manager of MINOS: A Symmetric approach", ACM SIGMOD 15(2), 1986.

[COD79]   Codd, E.F.: "Extending the database relational model to capture more meaning", in: ACM Transactions on Database Systems, Vol. 4., No. 4, 1979.

[CON87]   Conklin, J.: "Hypertext: An Introduction and Survey", in: IEEE-Computer, Vol. 10., No. 9., 1987, pp. 17-42.

[COPE84]   Copeland G. and D.Maier, "Making Smalltalk a Database System", ACM SIGMOD, June 1984.

[COX86]   Cox, B., "Object-oriented Programming: An evolutionary Approach", Addison Wesley, Reading Massachusetts, 1986.

[DEL86]   Delisle, N. and M.Schwartz, "Neptune: A hypertext system for CAD applications", in Proceedings of ACM SIGMOD '86 (Washington D.C., May 28-30). ACM, New York, 1986, pp. 132-142

[DIT86]   Dittrich, K.R., "Object-oriented Database systems: the Notion and the Issues", Proc. Int. Workshop on Object-Oriented Database Systems, 1986.

[DKT88]   Duchene H., M.Kaul, V.Turau, "Vodak Kernel Data Model", in K.R.Dittrich (Edt.), "Advances in Object-Oriented Database Systems", Lecture Notes in Computer Science, No. 334, 1988.

[FI87]   Fishman, D. et al., "IRIS: An Object-Oriented DBMS", ACM Transactions on Office Information Systems, 4(2), April 1987.

[FKRST88]   Fischer D., W.Klas, L.Rostek, U.Schiel, V.Turau, "VML - The VODAk Data Modelling Language", GMD-IPSI, to appear as technical report, Dec. 1988.

[GAR86]   Garret, L.N., K.E.Smith, and N.Meyrowitz, "Intermedia: Issues, strategies, and tactics in the design of a hypermedia document system", in Proceedings of the Conference on Computer-Supported Cooperative Work (Austin, Texas, Dec 3-5). 1986, pp. 163-174

[GAR88]   Garg, R., "Abstraction Mechanisms in Hypertext", in: Communications of the ACM, Vol 31, No. 7, 1888, pp. 862-870.

[GOT86]   Gotthard, W., "DAMOKLES: Das Datenmodell des UNIBASE- Entwicklungsdatenbanksystems", Verbundprojekt UNIBASE, Report, Forschungszentrum f. Informatik, Karlsruhe, March 1986.

[GR83]   Goldberg, A. and D.Robson, "Smalltalk-80: The Language and its Implementation", Addison-Wesley, Reading Massachusetts, 1983.

[GZ88]   Gottlob, G. and R. Zicari, "Closed World Databases Opened Through Null Values", in: Proceedings of the 14th VLDB Conference, 1988.

[HAL87]   Halasz, F.G., T.P.Moran, and R.H.Trigg, "NoteCards in a Nutshell", in Proceedings of the 1987 ACM Conference of Human Factors in Computer Systems (CHI +GI '87), (Toronto, Ontario, Apr 5-9). 1987, pp. 45-52.

[HAL88]   Halasz, F.G., "Reflections on NoteCards: Seven Issues for the Next Generation of Hypermedia Systems", Communications of the ACM, Vol. 31, No. 7, July 1988.

[IEEE84]   IEEE-Database Engineering Vol. 7., No. 3., 1984, Special Issue on Multimedia Data Management IEEE Computer Society.

[KNS88]   Klas W., E.J.Neuhold, M.Schrefl, "On an Object-oriented Data Model for a Knowledge Base", in: R.Speth (Edt.), Research into Networks and Distributed Applications - EUTECO 88, North-Holland, 1988.

[MAS87]   Masunaga, Y., "Multimedia databases: A formal framework", in: Proceedings IEEE-Office Automation Symposium, Gaithersburg, MD, 1987, pp. 36-45

[MBW80]   Mylopoulos J., P.A.Bernstein, H.K.T.Wong, "A Language Facility for Designing Database-Intensive Applications", ACM Transactions on Database Systems, Vol. 5, No. 2, 1980, pp. 185-207.

[MEY86]   Meyrowitz, N: Intermedia, "The architecture and construction of an object-oriented hypermedia system and applications framework", in Proceedings of the Conference on Object-oriented Programming Systems, Languages, and Applications (OOPSLA '86) (Portland , Oregon, Sept. 29 - Oct 2) ACM SIGPLAN Not. 21, 11 (1986).

[NS88]   Neuhold, E.J and M.Schrefl, "Dynamic derivation of personalized views", Proceedings of the 14th International Conference on Very Large Data Bases, Long Beach, Ca., 1988

[ODA86]   ISO/DIS 8613/1-8: Information Processing - Text and Office Systems - Office Document Architecture (ODA) and Interchange Format. International Organization for Standardization. 1986.

[POGG85]   Poggio, A., J.Garcia Luna Aceves, E.J. Craighill, D.Moran, L.Aguilar, D.Worthington, and J.Hight, "CCWS: A Computer-Based Multimedia Information System", IEEE Computer, Vol. 18, No. 10, Oct 1985, pp. 92-103.

[PSSW87]   Paul, H.-B., Schek, H.-J., Scholl, M., Weikum, G., Deppisch, U., "Architecture and implementation of the Darmstadt database kernel system", in Proceedings of the ACM SIGMOD Conference on Management of Data, San Francisco, May 27-29, 1987

[SN88]   Schrefl, M. and E.J.Neuhold, "A Knowledge-Based Approach to Overcome Structural Differences in Object Oriented Database Integration", in: "The Role of Artificial Intelligence in Database & Information Systems", IFIP Working Conference, Canton, China, July 88

[STONE86]   Stonebraker M. and L.Rowe, "The Design of POSTGRES", in Proc. of ACM SIGMOD Conference on Management of Data, Washington, D.C., May 1986.

[STR86]   Stroustrup, B., "An Overview of C++", SIGPLAN Notices, Vol. 21, No. 10, October 1986, pp. 7-18.

[SVE87]   Sventek, J., "An Architecture supporting Multi-Media Integration", in: Proceedings IEEE-Office Automation Symposium, Gaithersburg, MD, 1987, pp. 46-56

[TICH82]   Tichy, W., "Design, implementation, and evaluation of a revision control system", in 6th International Conference on Software Engineering, IEEE Computer Society, 58-67.

[WK87]   Woelk, D. and W. Kim, "Multimedia Information Mangement in an
            Object-Oriented Database System", in: Proceedings of the 13th VLDB
            Conference, Brighton, 1987, pp. 319-329.

[WKL86]   Woelk, D., W. Kim and W.Luther, "An Object-oriented Approach to Mul-
            timedia Databases", ACM SIGMOD, May 1986

[WL85]   Woelk, D. and W.Luther, "Multimedia Database requirements", MCC
            Technical Report DB-042-85, July 1985

[WLK87]   Woelk, D., W.Luther and W. Kim, "Multimedia Applications and Database
            Requirements", Proc. IEEE Computer Society Symposium on Office Auto-
            mation, April 1987.

[ZAN84]   Zaniolo, C., "Database Relations with Null Values", Journal of Computer
            and Systems Sciences, Vol. 28, 1984.

Session 11

MULTIMEDIA DATABASE II

Visual Database Systems
T.L. Kunii (Editor)
Elsevier Science Publishers B.V. (North-Holland)
© IFIP, 1989

Towards a Visual Language for an Object-Oriented Multi-Media Database System

Mun-Kew Leong, Shawn Sam, and Desai Narasimhalu

Institute of Systems Science
National University of Singapore
Heng Mui Keng Terrace, Singapore 0511

Abstract:
In this paper we describe **VILD** (*VI*sual *L*anguage for *D*atabase), a graphics based, visually oriented language for an object-oriented multi-media database system. We propose a set of desirable features for object-oriented visual languages, then compare **VILD** with other systems based on these features. We then describe the four parts of the **VILD** language set – a visual editor for defining a database, a browser for looking around in the structure and contents of a defined database, an object-oriented editor for creating and updating data, and an intuitive visual query language. We end by giving details of the current implementation of **VILD**, and possible future directions for it.

Key words and phrases:
object-oriented, multimedia, visual database language, user-friendly interface

1   Introduction

Recent trends for database systems have included the incorporation of multi-media facilities, object-oriented approaches, and temporal handling both within the database and in the query language [KKS87,OMA*87,Hir88,SS87,Sno87,WKL86,NKO*88]. Another focus of research has been in user-interface issues especially in making database systems more accessible to naive users, and more easily accessible to expert ones [KKS88,CEC87,Lar86,Her80]. In **VILD**, we see where these two areas meet to form an intuitive, user-friendly environment to interact with an object-oriented multi-media database system.

1.1   Features of a Visual Language

We accept the work of previous researchers and their justification of the need for graphical interfaces [JD86,KK86], and concentrate on the essential features for such interfaces. From Kim, et.al [KKS88], we have the following (paraphrased) list:

1. The interface should provide information to the user about the underlying database schema.

2. The user should be able to formulate queries incrementally.

3. There should be a browse facility.

4. There should be graphical feedback during query processing to guide the user.

At this point, we take the liberty of amending this list to reflect an object-oriented perspective. We believe that the logical schema of the database contains valuable semantic information. This is especially evident in a data model like MOTAR [Nar88], upon which **VILD** is based. For example, class-subclass relationships with its attendant inheritance properties is clearly seen only if the multiple object classes involved as well as the links between them are all displayed together. The entire schema should therefore always be presented to the user; thus the first point, as stated, becomes redundant. We amend it as follows:

1. The semantics of a database schema should always be available to the user. This requires that a user be acquainted with the symbols that define the schema, but once that is done, the naturalness of an object oriented system will readily make the semantics visible. Even a naive user can easily relate the schema to his concept of the real world.

However, since we are now talking of a complete language interface, we add the following points:

5. There should be consistency between different parts of a language that deal with the same type of information. This is just a primary tenet of good user interface design. Since the definition language, the browser, and the query language all work with the database schema (or a subset of it), the interface should be consistent between the three. Since the manipulation language is object-specific, it must necessarily be different.

6. The amount of information eg, the level of detail at any particular point should be user selectable. This, again, is a direct consequence of the object-oriented approach we have adopted.

With these six points in mind, we will explore further the visual interface **VILD**, and the infrastructure that supports it.

1.2   A Comparative Tour

To understand the strengths of **VILD**, we must first see where it stands in relation to other visual (graphic-based) systems. In the following list, we discuss the systems that share with **VILD** the qualities mentioned above.

1.2.1   Object-oriented and Multimedia

VILD is a language for an object-oriented multi-media database system (based on MOTAR). While there are some systems which share these properties [WKL86,Hir88], we have not come across any with a visual front end. The ISIS system [GGKZ85] is a graphical interface to the object-oriented Semantic Data Model (SDM) [Ham81]. The system designed by Larson [Lar86] is also object-oriented. But neither is multimedia. In contrast, MODES-2 [KKS87] handles multimedia but only in a relational data model.

1.2.2 Schema Presentation

ISIS makes the database schema available to the user, but the use of shaded patterns, and the lack of visual differentation between object classes presents the information poorly to the user. BAROQUE [Mot86] presents a very limited network view of a relational model. The graphical schema in Larson's system, however, reflects the conceptual schema in an obvious and natural way – the same way that **VILD** uses. Most other systems do not present the schema at all.

1.2.3 Incremental Query

This ability to construct new queries based on the results of existing ones is explicitly present only in PICASSO [KKS88]. It is also possible in ISIS as queries can be used to define new sub-classes which may then be used in further queries, though this roundabout method implies amending the database schema each time. Both these systems, however, have interfaces that are just grapic input systems to the query language (eg, in ISIS, instead of typing the word *"and"*, you click on the equivalent icon; in PICASSO the structure of an SQL query is translated into a visual equivalent using different mouse buttons for *select*, *where*, etc, and the mouse to select the required data fields).

1.2.4 Browsers

Almost every system mentioned so far has some form of a browser. This is probably the common starting point for many of these systems. The browsers vary in interface design (from text driven (BAROQUE) to templates (Larson) to graphics (PICASSO)) and in the display of data (using menus (BAROQUE), lists (ISIS), card-decks (MODES-2), etc).

1.2.5 Graphic Feedback

This is present to some degree or other in all the systems which have a graphic query language especially those capable of incremental query (see above). For simple queries, the feedback is rarely necessary.

1.2.6 Consistency

ISIS is the only system that shares this attribute with **VILD**. The question does not arise for some (eg, Campbell [CEC87]) as they have only a single function. In others, there is considerable variation. Larson, for example, uses a graphical representation of the schema to select objects of interest, uses a nested window system to display data, and a QBE style template for querying.

1.2.7 Selectable Levels of Detail

This is available only in **VILD**. Of course, this is really a valid question only for object oriented systems. Larson's system can constrain the objects of interest, but not the attributes or relationships of that object. In ISIS, you can not even do that – everything is shown to you and you either look at it or you don't. Incidently, Herot's Spatial DBMS [Her80] has levels of detail but these are built into the database – the more detail you want, the closer you zoom in – ie, the available level of detail has been previously decided by the database administrator.

1.3 Summary

We see that very few systems satisfy a majority of the desired features mentioned above. **VILD**, of course, was designed to satisfy them. This niche that **VILD** occupies is further isolated when we remember that MOTAR handles temporal attributes as well.

2 Infrastructure

VILD was designed as a visual interface to the Multimedia Database Management System (MDBMS) [PLKN88] developed at the Institute of Systems Science (ISS) for the Intelligent Public Information System (IPIS) [IoSS].

2.1 IPIS

IPIS was developed to demonstrate the essential capabilities and functions of presenting multimedia and multilingual information through a friendly and consistent interface. The first prototype was completed at ISS in June 1988. It demonstrates an intelligent tourism-oriented information system comprising an expert system restaurant guide, a knowledge based system for local history and a hotel information retrieval system. The first two systems explore different technologies, but the IPIS Hotel Information System integrates graphics, images, and text, in English and in Chinese, on top of the object oriented MDBMS.

2.2 MDBMS

The MDBMS system is best described in layers. At the theoretical level, we have MOTAR [Nar88], a data model that handles classes, composite objects, and temporal attributes and relations. MOTAR is mapped onto a frame-based structure (see Section 2.5) that constitutes the object-oriented interface to MDBMS. MDBMS currently supports object definition and object manipulation through batch input, and queries through an extensive range of object-based functions available through a programmatic interface with 'C'. MDBMS is implemented on top of a host relational DBMS. The defined objects are described in a *data dictionary* which is implemented as a set of relational tables. This dictionary is used to generate a further set of tables (called the *data tables*) which will store the attributes and relationships of the object instances. At the lowest level, data is stored on either magnetic media or optical disk [ONWC86], whichever is more appropriate (eg, the large amount of static data for an image would be perfect for optical storage). We can see this multi-layer structure of MDBMS in Figure 1. Figure 1 also shows that **VILD** fits into the heirachy as an interactive interface between the user and the database.

2.3 VILD: The Structure

VILD is a complete visual interface to MDBMS. Thus, it has four parts (as shown in Figure 2): object definition (corresponding to a DDL), object manipulation (DML), browser, and query interface. As you can see, there are two levels in **VILD**. At one level, the data model diagram (DMD) defined in MOTAR (for example, see Figure 3) is used as the visual format for the Object Definition Language (ODL), the Browser, and the Query Language. This is the schema of the database which is presented to the users of these three parts of **VILD**. Since the visual format and the DMD (data model diagram) are identical (within the limitations of screen display), any user who is familiar with MOTAR will immediately recognize the objects in the schema, and the attendant relationships between them. At the lower level, an object is mapped onto

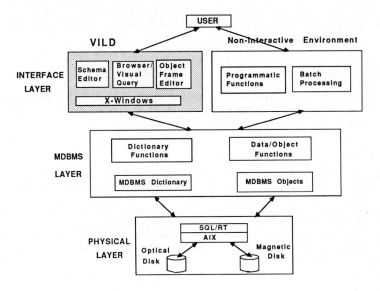

Figure 1: The Layout of MDBMS with VILD

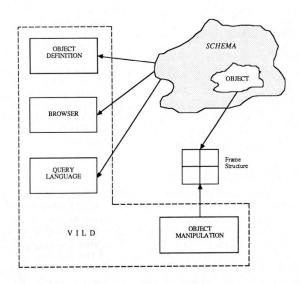

Figure 2: The Structure of VILD

the frame data structure of MDBMS. The Object Manipulation Language (OML) is the interface that handles a user's interaction with instances of the object.

2.4 The System Environment[1]

The IPIS prototype was developed on IBM RT/PC workstations linked by a Token Ring network. Each workstation has a high-resolution graphic display and a two-button mouse as an auxiliary input device. The workstations run the AIX 2.1.2 operating system with X-Windows Version 10.4 as the windowing environment. MDBMS is written in 'C' on top of a host database system – SQL/RT. **VILD** is also written in 'C' and uses X-Windows, X-Tookit, and the IUI-Toolkit [Kan88] developed by the IPIS user-interface group at ISS.

2.5 The Frame Structure of MDBMS

Before we get into **VILD** proper, we would like to describe the representation of a MOTAR object in MDBMS. That representation is called a *frame structure* and the representation of an instance of an object is called a *frame data structure*. The term was taken from the AI frame concept as the organization of the two are similar. The frame structure has slots which correspond to the attributes and relationships of an object, and each slot may optionally have facets which further describe the slot. These are attributes of attributes. We have also taken the artificial step of classifying the slots into four kinds:

OWN SLOTS These hold the attributes that we normally associate with the object. These will be the attributes defined in the database schema.

MEMBER SLOTS These hold the various inter-object links. There are three kinds:

- *Composite-component* relationships.
- *Class-subclass* relationships.
- *Generic relationships* which are user defined.

All the relationships are directed. Composite-component and class-subclass directions are obvious. For generic relationships, MOTAR requires that one of the objects involved be designated as the reference object. The direction of the relationship is from the reference object to the referred object. For example, in a family database, a relationship *is-the-father-of* has the parent as the reference object and the direction is from the parent to the child. Conversely, if the relationship is *-is-the-child-of* then the child is the reference object and the direction is consequently from the child to the father. Relationship data will be associated with the reference object of the relationship.

METHOD SLOTS One of the features of object-oriented systems is the inclusion of the methods which operate on an object. The capability to store canonical functions is provided in MDBMS but since we are running in a non-interpreted environment (using the 'C' language), this capability is not being utilized.

SPECIAL SLOTS This classification is designed for any attributes that do not fall into one of the types above. It may include such information as access control, security passwords, screen management information, and administrative trivia. Normally, information in the this category will not be available to a user browsing or querying the data in the system. The attribute descriptions will consequently not be reflected in the database schema available to that user.

---

[1]RT/PC, AIX, and SQL/RT are trademarks of International Business Machines Corporation.

Attributes of an object in a schema (see the following section) will be stored in the OWN SLOTs and the respective kinds of relationships in the appropriate MEMBER SLOTs.

2.6   The Example Schema and Database

For simplicity, we will be using the same example database to illustrate **VILD** throughout the paper. The schema is given in Figure 3. Objects are represented by circles,

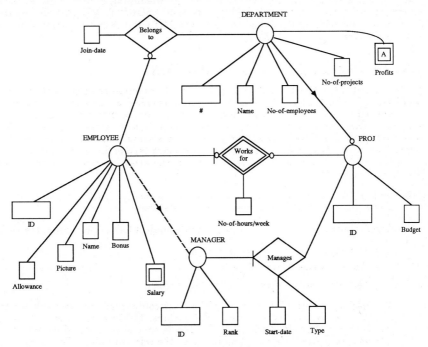

Figure 3: The Complete Schema of the example database

generic relationships by diamonds, attributes by squares, and keys by rectangles. A line with an arrow shows the direction of a composite-to-component relationship. A dotted line with an arrow shows the direction of a class-to-subclass relationship. Double borders denote a temporal attribute or relationship. Small circles at the ends of links show that the object or attribute which they abut may occur multiple times. A straight line at one corner of a diamond shows the reference object of that relationship. We can see that this database illustrates most of the features of the MOTAR data model. The figure looks very crowded, but notice that if we hide all the attributes of the various objects (as described in Section 1.2.7), the schema becomes quite simple (see Figure 4) and easy to understand.

3   The Object Manipulation Language

Finally we get to **VILD** itself. The logical place to start describing **VILD** would be the Object Definition Language (ODL) as that is where the physical process of

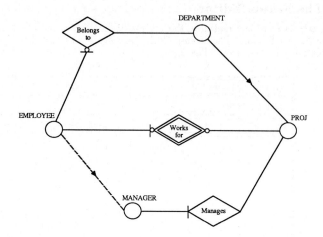

Figure 4: The Schema of the Database with All Attributes Hidden

database definition and creation begins. However, as we saw in Figure 2, the Object Manipulation Language (OML) is at a different level from the rest and may be treated separately.

At this point, also notice that there is no access to the frame structure of MDBMS except through the OML. This is no accident. There are deliberately no data manipulation functions within either the Browser or the Query Language. The example in ISIS where a user browses the database, spots an error, and corrects it on the spot may be good to illustrate the capabilities of ISIS, but does not truly reflect how the browsing functions and data manipulation functions are normally segregated at the user level ie, most users browsing the database should not have the authority to modify the data within it. In **VILD**, because the OML is a separate language sub-system, it is easy to build a security level to control access to it. Once security is built into its front end, the OML may be called from within the Browser or Query Language, but in these cases, control is being passed to the OML, and it is not the case that data manipulation is being done by the other two language parts.

3.1   The OML Interface

The OML is not meant to be used by the naive user, nor by someone unfamiliar with the schema of the database. An OML user wishing to enter data would already know the object[2] name and a user wishing to modify data would already know the object name and the specific instance of the object to be modified. The OML is therefore designed to facilitate getting to the required object or object instance. The user on starting the OML will see a list of defined objects and a prompt for the object of interest. He may type in the name of the required object or use a mouse to point and select it. If the number of choices is large, or the choices very similar, then it would be easier to type in the name. Otherwise, with a bit of practice, using the mouse is faster and less prone to errors. Having selected the object, a list consisting of the primary key of its instances is presented. The user may use either of the same two methods, typing or mouse-pointing, to select an instance, or may choose to create a new instance.

---

[2] All subsequent use of the term *object* is as an object-type or object class. Objects as instances of an object-type will be refered to as *instances*.

3.2   The Frame Editor

If a user selects an object instance, the OML assumes that it is to be modified and will start the Frame Editor. The Frame Editor presents the frame based representation of the instance to the user. The layout of the editor is shown in Figure 5. It has

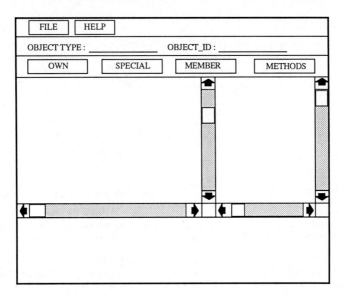

Figure 5: The major divisions of the Frame Editor

four regions: the command and information region across the top of the window, two vertical subwindows to display slot and facet information, and a horizontal window at the bottom for a media specific editor.

3.2.1   The Command Area

The command area lists the current object and object instance being edited, and displays the available commands that operate on the instance as a whole eg, the *quit* button. These commands are available as pull down menus, and include all the normal editing commands such as *save-and-quit*, *abandon-and-quit*, *reload-the-instance*, *help*, etc. The most interesting command, however, is the *compose* command. This is intended for 2-dimensional spatially oriented component data. For example, an animation sequence might consist of a background scene and a number of figures stored separately. The compose command would put the whole lot together in a new window.[3] Alternatively, a multi-media multi-lingual advertisment could be decomposed into different data types – image, Chinese text, English text, graphics, etc – and stored separately, then put together with the *compose* command for viewing.

3.2.2   Information Display

You will recall from Section 2.5 that the frame structure has four quadrants. There is a row of buttons at the top of the sub-windows to select among the four quadrants.

---

[3]The spatial formatting data required for this operation is an example of the information stored in the SPECIAL quadrant

The slot information is displayed in the left window, and any facets corresponding to a selected slot is displayed in the right window. The default display is the OWN quadrant. All four quadrants are edited in a buffer; switching from one to another does not imply an automatic commitment of the amendments made. On a colour display, the fields which have been changed are highlighted using a different colour.

The OWN[4] Quadrant

The specific presentation of the OWN slots in the left subwindow is given in Figure 6. Descriptions of the slots are listed in the window. The window may be scrolled (note

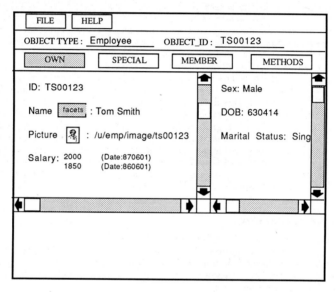

Figure 6: The Own Slots in the Frame Editor

the scrollbars at the sides of each of the windows) if all the slots cannot be displayed at one time. The values of the slots are given next to their descriptions up to the extent of the window. If the values are wider than the available space, the window may be scrolled sideways to show the data or the appropriate editor can be invoked to display them. Slots which are further described by facets have a button on the description line which, when clicked, will display these facets in the right subwindow. Text and numeric data are displayed in the slot or facet windows directly. Graphic and image data, which are captured as files, have their name and path displayed instead. There is also a corresponding icon displayed for each such slot or facet description eg, for an image datatype, a picture icon is used. Double-clicking with the mouse on that icon will pop up a new window displaying the image (see section 3.2.3 for more details). The MDBMS is a multi-lingual system as well, and all the slot (and facet) descriptions and values may be in an ideographic language with no difference to the layout or commands. The editor, of course, will be appropriate to the language, or data-type, concerned.

---

[4]The presentation for the SPECIAL and METHODS quadrants are similar to that of the OWN quadrant

The MEMBER Quadrant

The MEMBER Quadrant had 3 types of relationships. Consequently, when the MEM-
BER quadrant is selected, a menu is presented in which one of these three types of
relationships is chosen to be displayed in the left subwindow. As for the OWN slots,
facets describing a particular relationship slot are displayed in the right subwindow.
Class-subclass and composite-component relationships may have facets but normally
the subclass or component object will be defined separately.

3.2.3 The Editor Area

The last subwindow on the screen is the editor window. If a slot or facet is clicked
with the mouse, the appropriate editor (depending on the data type) will be invoked.
For romanized text, an ordinary text editor is used. For ideographic languages, an
editor designed for the language is used, eg, for Chinese[5] the CACIS editor developed
at ISS [CLN87,NLH*87] is used. There is no limit to the size of text entered. The
MDBMS mechanism for handling large amounts of data is transparent to the user.
For non-text data which is not stored directly in the database, a filename editor is
invoked. This allows the name of a file containing the data to be entered into the
database. Where relevant, this data can also be edited through an editor appropriate
to the medium involved eg, a graphic editor can be invoked from the OML to modify
the data file associated with a graphic-type slot or facet. Data that is retrieved from
the system is assumed to be consistent. Data that has been amended goes through as
thorough a validation as possible, and if any inconsistencies are found, an appropriate
error message is displayed and the offending field is highlighted. Such checks include
inconsistent field and data types (eg, text in an integer field), unfilled mandatory
fields, undefined objects specified as subclasses, etc.

3.3 Data Creation

If the user wishes to create a new instance of an object, then after selecting the object,
the user selects the *create* option. Alternatively, the user may type in the unique id
of the new instance. Since this does not exist in the database, the OML prompts the
user to either confirm the creation of a new object instance with this id, or to reenter
the name of an existing instance.

Having selected the input mode, the user is now presented with a screen identical
to the Frame Editor, except that all the data values are blank. The exception is
if the user had entered the unique id of the instance, which will be reflected in the
appropriate field. The user enters data using precisely the same mechanisms as are
available in the Frame editor. The data entered goes through the same validation
checks as in the editor, but additionally, the data is checked for consistency between
instances (eg, for duplicate values in key fields). Again, if any errors are encountered,
they are immediately flagged to the user. The user may not save an instance unless it
has no errors. Once saved, the data is written into the database but not yet committed.
The new data is committed only if the user explicitly issues a commit command, or
the user exits deliberately without abandoning the OML session.

4 The Object Definition Language

We now come to the schema of the database. There are three parts of **VILD** that
deal with the schema. The first is the definition. This is done by the Object Definition
Language (ODL).

---

[5]Currently, Chinese is the only ideographic language supported by the MDBMS.

4.1   The ODL Interface

The ODL takes the form of a window with three regions (see Figure 7): the command and information area at the top of the screen, a vertical list of definition icons on the left, and graphic definition area taking the rest of the window.

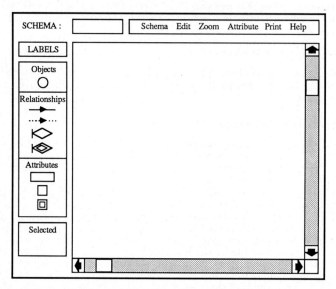

Figure 7: The Layout of the Object Definition Screen

4.1.1   The Command and Information Area

This area displays the name of the schema being defined (which may be blank if the schema has not yet been saved), and contains a horizontal row of pull-down menus. The menus and their various options are as follows:

Schema These are the commands that deal with the schema as a whole, including *load*-ing a schema (either to browse it, or to continue defining a saved but incomplete schema), *save*-ing a schema to continue later, *define*-ing a schema (by issuing the necessary calls to MDBMS to define the database), *validate*-ing a schema (to check for consistency), and *quit*-ing the ODL.

Edit These commands work on the various definable schema items[6] in the systems such as objects, relationships, and attributes. The ODL commands are also item-oriented. Commands which end with ellipsis take an item as an argument. This item is specified using the mouse as a pointer. The editing commands are *Undo*, *Cut...*, *Copy...*, *Paste*, and *delete....* Their functions are self-explanatory.

Zoom These commands allow for easier management of the schema, especially on displays where the resolution is low and only a small part of the schema can be clearly visible at one time. The *Zoom in* and *Zoom out* commands changes the

---

[6]The more appropriate word would have been *object* but we use *schema item* or just *item* instead to avoid confusion.

schema representation size using the center of the definition window as the focus of the enlargement or contraction, respectively. The *Zoom in on...* and *Zoom out on...* command uses the specified item as the focus instead.

Attribute From Section 1.2.7, recall that the level of detail in the schema should always be user controllable. The *Hide Attributes of...* and *Show Attributes of...* commands allows the user this flexibility. The *Hide All Attributes* command reduces a schema into its most compact yet complete form (compare Figures 3 and 4).

Print Just produces a hardcopy of the schema being defined.

Help Pops up a help window. The help information is variable, depending on the current or last command selected. If there is none, then general help information is given.

4.1.2 The Definition Icons

The definition icons are exactly the symbols defined in the MOTAR data model, and explained in Section 2.6. Thus a MOTAR data model has an exact representation in the schema of the defined database. The icons are used as menu buttons to specify what kind of a schema item is to be created – an object, one of several kinds of attributes, or one of several possible relationships. For attributes and relationships, the menus are cascading in that a second level of choice is presented. This is because each attribute has an additional icon to specify a multiply-occuring attribute, and each type of generic relationship has four additional icons to specify the *order* of the relationship ie, one-to-one, one-to-many, many-to-one, or many-to-many. There is another button at the top of the list called *Labels*. This is to allow the user to rename any of the schema items. Renaming is mandatory after any copy operation, for example. And lastly, there is a small window at the bottom of the list entitled *Selected*. This shows the icon that has been selected and consequently, what item is to be defined.

4.1.3 The Definition Area

This occupies the rest of the window. There are scroll bars at the bottom and to the right of the screen that allows the window to be scrolled if there is anything defined outside the visible area. Scrolling will normally be used only if a very large database schema is being defined, or a *Zoom in* command has been used.

4.2 The Specification Process

We use *specify* to mean the process of creating the various schema items in the database. This is different from *defining* a database which is possible only after all the items in the schema have been specified. There are a few rules that govern the specification process. In what follows, we use *existing* to describe an item that is present and named in the definition area.

- Attributes can only be added to an existing object, or to an existing relationship.

- Relationships can only be specified between existing objects.

- All objects and relationships must be given unique names. All attributes must have unique names within an object or a relationship. The possible exceptions are given in [Nar88].

- Every object must have a primary key. This key will uniquely identify an instance of the object.

In addition, there is one other condition. This condition need not be true during the specification process, but must be satisfied before the database can be defined.

- All objects in the schema must be joined together by one relationship or another. Two unrelated databases may not be defined in the same schema.

Given these rules, we will describe how a user will specify the following schema items:

Object The mouse is clicked on the object icon, then moved onto the definition area and clicked on an empty region. A circle representing the object is drawn, and a window pops up to ask for the name of the object, and its data type. An object data type is either *composite* or one of the supported media: image, graphic, alphanumeric, etc. If an object is *composite* then its attributes may be of any medium; otherwise, its attributes may only be of the same medium as the object data type (See [PLKN88] for more details).

Attribute An attribute must belong to an object or a relationship. So an object or a relationship must first be selected with the mouse (it is highlighted) then the appropriate attribute is selected from the icon menu. Wherever the mouse is clicked in the definition area, the appropriate icon and a line from the selected object to that icon are drawn, and a window is displayed to enter the name and data type of the attribute. Again, the data type of an attribute is one of the supported media (image, graphic, etc) and may be constrained by the data type of the object it describes, as mentioned above.

Relationship Recall from Section 2.5 that all relationships are directed between exactly two objects. So the order in which the objects are specified is important – the relationship goes from the first object specified (the reference) to the second (target) object. The user will click the mouse on the reference object (which will then be highlighted) then use the mouse to select the required relationship from the menu then click the mouse on the target object. A diamond representing the relationship is drawn joined to both objects by lines. The point of the diamond joined to the reference object will have a short straight line perpendicular to the joining line. As usual, a window is displayed to name the relationship.

The various items may also be specified using the *copy* and *paste* commands. Schema items that are copied must be renamed to remain unique at the appropriate level ie, attributes must be unique within an object or relationship, which in turn must be unique within the schema.

The specification process need not be completed at one sitting. The current state may be saved to be continued later, or may be saved periodically as a backup. At any point in the process, the user may select the *validate* command, and the schema so far defined is checked for consistency. As usual, if any errors are found, the appropriate message is issued and the offending section of the schema is highlighted.

4.3   The Definition Process

Once the schema has been specified, the *define* command may be selected. If the *validate* command was not the last command executed, then a validation is done. If the schema is valid, then the user is prompted for a name for the database – by default it is the schema file name – and its directory path. Under MDBMS, each database must occupy its own directory. If the path is an existing directory, then the directory is checked for an existing database (and rejected if one is found). Otherwise, the required directory is created. The appropriate MDBMS functions are called to create the necessary *dictionary* tables, then the valid schema is given to another function which will describe it into the dictionary and also create all the necessary *data tables* to store instances of the defined objects and the relationships between them. All these created tables, along with the directory path and the database name constitutes the defined database.

4.4   Defining the Example Database

We illustrate the process by defining a small part of the example database described in Section 2.6.

1. The user selects the *object* icon and clicks a spot in the definition area. A window pops up for him to enter the object name "Employee" (Figure 8). By default,

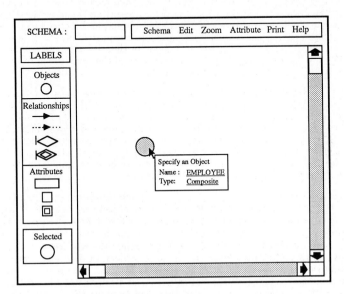

Figure 8: Specifying the Employee object

the object data type is set to "composite".

2. He then selects the rectangular *key attribute* icon. By default, the **Employee** object, as the last object manipulated by the user, becomes the owner of the attributes to be specified. The user creates the key attribute below the **Employee** object and a line is drawn from the created rectangle to the object. The user enters the name "ID" and selects the type "text". (Figure 9)

3. Similarly, he creates the other four attributes.

4. By Figure 10, he has used the *hide attribute of...* command on the **Employee** object, and has created, using the above steps, the object **Project** and hidden all its attributes as well.

5. The user specifies the **Works for** relationship by first clicking on **Employee**, then selecting the *many-to-many temporal relationship* icon, then clicking on **Project** to give Figure 11.

6. The **Department** and **Manager** objects and their attributes, as well as their relationships with the other objects are specified in a similar fashion. This gives the schema shown in Figure 3.

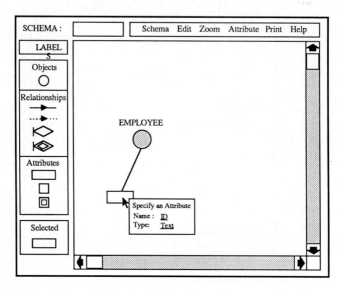

Figure 9: After specifying the ID key attribute

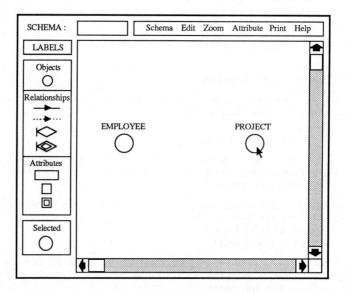

Figure 10: After hiding the attributes of the Project object

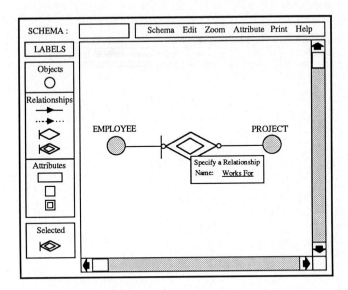

Figure 11: After specifying the Works For relationship

5 The Browser

We come now to the second part of **VILD** that deals with the schema of a database —
the Browser. The Browser allows a user to examine, at a comfortable level of detail,
the structure of the database. The user should be familiar with the MOTAR data
model. However, a naive user can easily learn the meanings of the various symbols in
the schema representation from the Help screen.

5.1 The Browser Interface

The Browser has only two regions: a command and information area at the top of the
screen and a display area taking up the rest of the window.

5.1.1 The Command and Information Area

This is laid out identically to the same region in the ODL, except that it displays the
name of the database being browsed rather than the schema being defined, and that
the command menus and options differ. In the Browser, these are:

Database The *Load* command specifies a database to be browsed, and the *Quit*
command ends the Browser. The *Save* command stores the current configuration
of the database being browsed – this is termed the *subschema* – which the user
may *Reload* at a later point.

Select These commands allow the user to select what information he wishes to examine. The *Select...* command chooses the schema items the user wants, and the
Discard... command chooses the items the user doesn't want. The *Discard...*
command works immediately – the items that are discarded disappear from the
screen. The *Select...* command takes effect only when the Browse is started.

At that point, any relationships between *select*-ed objects will be made *selected*, and objects of a *selected* relationship will also be made *select*-ed. After that, all objects and attributes not *select*-ed will automatically be *discard*-ed. The *Restore* command returns the display to the state before any *select* or *discard* commands were invoked. This is normally done before starting a new Browse session (on the same database) or in the case of an error. The *Undo* command un-*select*-s or un-*discard*-s the last *select*-ed or *discard*-ed item respectively.

Zoom This is identical to the **Zoom** menu of the ODL.

Attribute This too is identical to the corresponding menu in the ODL.

Browse The *Browse* command starts the browsing. The *next...* and *previous...* commands gets the next or previous instance of the specified object to be browsed, respectively. These commands seem rather troublesome to use as pull down menus but this is because these commands are meant to be invoked from the mouse and are present here only for completeness. Once the Browse has started, if the mouse is on an object, pressing the left mouse button gets the next instance, and pressing the right mouse button gets the previous instance. This object-oriented mousing is more thoroughly explained in Section 5.2.

Help The help is organized in the same way as in the ODL.

5.1.2   The Display Area

This is similar to the definition area of the ODL (including scrollbars and other features). It is used to display the representation of the schema to the user, and also to display the information retrieved about a browsed object or relationship. The schema representation uses the same icons as in the ODL, and is initially displayed in a reduced form ie, with all the attributes hidden. This makes it easier for the user to see the relationships between objects. Information retrieved is displayed depending on its type. Single occuring text attribute values are displayed in a small box overlapping the icon representing it in the schema. If the text is longer than the box, double-clicking on the text box will pop up a large window that will display the entire value of the attribute (Figure 12a). Non-text attributes will have a representative icon

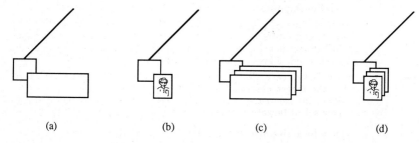

(a)   (b)   (c)   (d)

Figure 12: Displaying attributes in the Browser

displayed overlapping the schema icon. This icon may be double-clicked to pop up a large window to display, in the correct form, the value of the attribute (Figure 12b). Multiply occuring attribute values are displayed as a series of overlapping boxes or icons depending on type (Figure 12c/d). Lastly, the cardinality of the set of object instances retrieved is indicated within the icon corresponding to that object. The form is n/m where m is the cardinality and n is the position of the current object instance eg, 2/12 means the second of twelve instances.

5.2 The Browsing Process

There are four main browsing mechanisms. The user interface in all four are the same, and the different mechanisms may coexist or even be active one within another. Once the *Browse* command has started, the entire browsing process is under the control of the mouse while within the display area. In the command area, of course, the mouse is used to manipulate the menus. The following are the different browse mechanisms.

1. The first is the simplest – just a single object with its attributes. When the Browse is started, the object is retrieved from the database, and the first instance is displayed as described above. The mouse may be left pointing to the object. If the left (right) button is clicked, the next (previous) instance is retrieved.

2. Then we have multiply-occuring attributes. This is a feature of MDBMS and also a necessary consequence of temporal data. This information may be independently scrolled within an object. The mechanism using the mouse is the same. If the information is also grouped (recall the Facets of a Slot approach of MDBMS), then scrolling a slot attribute value will automatically scroll the facet values as well.

3. Next, we have a single object and a relationship. An example of this could be a user wanting to know the number of hours an employee has worked – which is an attribute of the relationship bf Works for – without caring what project it was for. This is obtained by either discarding all the attributes of the related object (**Project**), or hiding its attributes. So while we have two objects (**Employee** and **Project**) in the display area, one of them (**Project**) becomes a dummy. This roundabout process is necessary as once an object is discarded, then so are all of its relationships. The dummied object has no control, and may not be scrolled. So control is only from the remaining object (**Employee**). The relationship information will change to stay consistent with the scrolling of this object.

4. Lastly, we have two objects and a relationship. This gives rise to the following possible relationships:

   one-to-one This is simple, if either object is scrolled, then the other object, and the relationship information is also scrolled to remain consistent.

   one-to-many The "many" object may be scrolled independently within the "one" object, and the relationship information will be scrolled accordingly. If the "one" object is scrolled, however, then a new set of "many" objects has to be retrieved. These, in turn, may be independently scrolled.

   many-to-many In this case, the reference object in the relationship takes precedence over the target object. The target object may be scrolled independently within the reference object, but once the reference object changes, a whole new set of target objects is retrieved.

These mechanisms may be active one within the other, so an object in a many-to-one relationship may have temporal attributes, etc. Also, a single object may be involved in more than one relationship at a time. There are some exceptions eg, where two objects are related by two different relationships, and each is the reference object of the other. In this and any other ambiguous case, the user will be prompted to identify the dominant relationship.

5.3 Browsing the Example Database

Consider a user wishing to browse the database to find out what employees are doing. He will take the following steps:

1. The user is initially presented with the reduced form of the schema. He decides
   that he is not interested in either the **Department** or the **Manager** information, and uses the *discard* command to get rid of them (Figure 13).

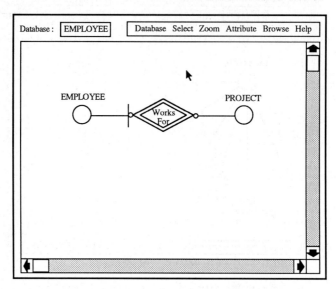

Figure 13: After discarding the unwanted objects

2. He selects *Show attribute of. . .* and clicks on both **Employee** and **Project** to
   show all their attributes. He then *selects* only the Name, Picture, and salary fields
   in **Employee** and the ID field in **Project**. These fields are highlighted, and by
   default their objects are also selected and highlighted (Figure 14).

3. Then the user selects *Browse*. The **Works For** relationship is automatically
   selected, but since its attributes were not shown, they are discarded. The rest of
   the unselected attributes are also discarded. The **Employee** object is identified
   as the reference object in the many-to-many relationship, so it is retrieved first.
   The **Project** information corresponding to the first instance of **Employee** is
   also fetched. The information is displayed as in Figure 15.

4. The user is presented with the employee information for Tom Smith. By clicking
   on the Picture icon, he sees an image of Smith in a new window. Tracing through
   the relationship, he sees that Smith is working for the OA project. Clicking
   repeatedly with the left button on the **Project** icon, he scans through the list of
   projects that Smith is involved in. He then clicks on the **Employee** object icon
   with the left mouse button. The window containing Smith's image is closed, and
   the next instance of employee information is presented.

5. He continues in this manner until he is satisfied, then selects the *Restore* command to start again.

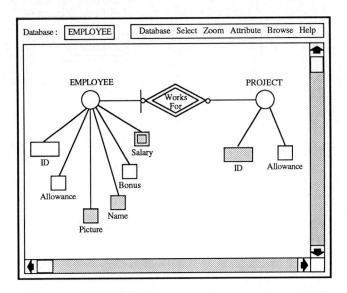

Figure 14: After selecting the desired fields

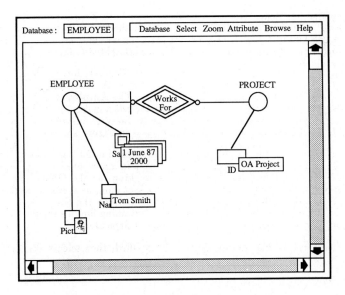

Figure 15: Browsing the Example database

6   The Query Language

The Query Language is the third part of **VILD** that deals with the schema. It may be viewed as an enhancement of the Browser. Where the Browser is good for a user who has no fixed subset of the data in mind, the Query Language allows a user to focus his attention on a specifiec subset of the data. The Browser allows the structure of the database to be constrained to best suit the user's requirements, the Query Language additionally allows the instances of one or more objects to be similarly constrained. Also, the Query Language allows the user to choose between two ways of looking at the selected and constrained data.

6.1   The Query Language Interface

The Query Language Interface is laid out in the same fashion as the Browser. There is an identical Display Area occupying most of the window. The top of the window is the Command and Information Area. Most of the commands present in the Browser are present in the Query Language. The **Browse** menu has been replaced with a **Query** menu, the *Discard...* command in the **Select** menu has been removed, and two menus have been added:

Database The *Save* and *Reload* commands here not only allow the subschema to be saved, but also allow queries to continue across multiple sessions.

Query This starts the query after the required fields have been selected, and the appropriate constraints put on the objects to be retrieved. The *next* and *previous* commands are the same as in the Browser.

Select This is the same as the Browser except that the *Discard...* command has been removed. This is because the entire schema may be required for specifying constraints, and so may not be erased from the screen. Both explicitly and implicitly *select*-ed schema items remain highlighted throughout the constrain process. Only when the *Query* command is run, will any items not selected or constrained be discarded.

Constrain The *Constrain...* command puts a series of constraints on a selected object. The constraints take the form of *conditions* on attributes of an object or a relationship. The *Union* command combines the instances defined by different constraints for a single display. This command is further explained in section 6.2.

Display These options control the way information is returned to the user. The *Object Display* option is the way described in the Browser. The *Table Display* option returns the information in the form of heirachical tables. The attributes will form the columns of the table, and instances of the object or relationship will form rows within the table. There is a default size for a table display (ie, number of rows of data) and if the amount of data returned exceeds the size, then the *Expand...* command allows the specified table to take over as much of the screen as possible to display as much data as possible at one time. The *Contract...* command reverses the *Expand...* command.

The mouse is now also used to specify the constraints on an object. For *Object Display*, the mouse functions exactly as in the Browser. For *Table Display*, the mouse can be used to scroll a table, normally vertically, but, if required, also horizontally (The table subwindow is similar to the display subwindow layout). Additionally, the mouse may be clicked within a cell[7] of a table to do one of the following:

---

[7]A cell is a field in the table specified by a particular row and column.

- If the column is a multiply-occuring attribute, then a new table window is created to display the various values. This subtable is closed by any other command.

- If the column is a non-text attribute, or an attribute which is very long, then a subwindow is created to display the data in the proper form. This window is also closed by any other command.

6.2 The Constraint

In any query language, there are several levels of complexity in specifying constraints. In **VILD**, the user interface at all levels remain the same ie, mouse based and object oriented. Before we describe these levels, we clarify what we mean by a constraint on an object or relationship.

Since **VILD** is object-oriented, we have decided that a constraint will basically describe a single subset of an object (or relationship). Thus a condition like *all round objects OR all blue objects*, where *round* and *blue* are values of different attributes, describe a union of two subsets and cannot be specified as a single constraint. Such a condition must be expressed as separate constraints, which can be linked by the *Union* command. This command takes the union of the subsets defined by separate constraints so that they may all be displayed in a single session.[8] We may do this since the structure of each subset is identical, having been specified by the same *Select* command. There is the unfortunate side-effect, however, that whenever the *Union* command is invoked, the last constraint is assumed to be fully specified. Additionally, each constraint is independent, so common conditions between constraints have to be respecified each subsequent time. So, specifying compound constraints may be tedious; however, it may also help a user structure his query in a more logical and manageable fashion, since each constraint necessarily returns a precise, well-defined set.[9] The main reason for defining a constraint this way is the resultant simplicity in specifying conditions. All the conditions may be specified using the mouse to select a schema item, and the keyboard to enter a value if required. Compare this with the visual complexity of either the templates in Larson's browser or the predicate worksheet in ISIS.

Multiple conditions may be specified on the same attribute. Obviously, since an attribute may not have more than one value, these conditions are inclusive disjuncts. Specification of conditions on different attributes is equivalent to taking the intersection of the subsets resulting from satisfying individual attribute conditions.

Formally then, a **VILD** constraint on an object or relationship is a set of conditions in Conjunctive Normal Form, with the restriction that all predicates in a conjunct apply only to one attribute, and no attribute occurs in more than one conjunct. The **VILD** query then is the (possibly trivial) union of the subsets of objects or relationships defined by each constraint.[10]

---

[8] We recommend that the *Union* command be used as little as possible since the resultant set may no longer be well-defined (see the next footnote). We include the *Union* command only because most query languages allow the users to mix and match the data to be retrieved. We hope to remove this command in future either by finding a more elegant procedure to specify compound constraints, or by educating users to look at a single well-defined set at a time.

[9] We say well-defined in the sense that if a condition, say *colour=green* is given, then we can be confident that every object in the set is green. Of course, once there is a *Union* of two or more sets, each of which may have been defined by different parameters, we can no longer be sure of the colour of the objects.

[10] Actually, this is not correct as the mapping between nested conditions and the formal CNF notation has not been clarified. We will be addressing this, and other issues (including incremental queries, temporal queries, and the power of the query language), in a forthcoming paper.

6.3 Levels of Constraints

The levels of constraints correspond to the complexity of a query. In **VILD**, we have identified three levels.

6.3.1 The Simple Query

The simplest level is like an un-nested query in a non-visual query language. The constraint on an attribute is done by selecting the *Constrain...* command and clicking on the appropriate attribute icon. The user may then enter a conditional and a value using the keyboard. If the selected schema item and the constrained item are the same, then the query proceeds straight-forwardly. If the two are not the same, and are not related, then the query fails. If they are related, then that relation is assumed to be a necessary part of the constraint. For example, if **Employee** attributes Name and Allowance are selected, and the constraint is put on a **Project** attribute eg, *ID = OA project* (Figure 16), then the Query Language will return the attributes of the employees that work for the OA project (Figure 17).

6.3.2 The Relationship-Reflexive Query

The second level of query has no correspondence in most languages, being possible only under an object-oriented environment. We term it a *relationship-reflexive* query. It is best illustrated with an example: The user wants all employees that work for the same project as Tom Smith. In most languages, even visual ones (eg, Campbell's), this is an explicit nested query. In **VILD**, the user selects the required **Employee** attributes, then selects the **Works For** relationship. Now if a constraint was put on either the relationship or on a **Project** attribute, it becomes a simple query. But the user puts the constraint back on the **Employee** object (hence the *reflexive* part) by specifying *Name = Tom Smith* (Figure 18). The Query Language will recognize this unusual pattern, and return the required instances (Figure 19).

This is possible because **VILD** is object-oriented. In relational systems, reflexivity exists only at an attribute level. In an object-oriented system, there is reflexivity at the object/relationship level. This thus provides sufficient semantics for the system to recognize the relationship-reflexive nature of such a query. Additionally, the graphical nature of **VILD** allows specific relationships to be explicitly depicted and hence selectable, in contrast with relational systems where relationships are arbitrary and which may occur between any two compatible attributes.

It does not matter how many conditions are put on the constrained object, nor whether the relationship is one-to-many, many-to-many, or whatever. It is also independent of which is the reference object and which is the target object in the relationship. The Query Language knows the primary key of the related object (the object related to the constrained object) and can use this to determine the subset of unique instances that is related to the constrained object set. This condition is then added to the constraint of the selected set, and the query is executed. All this, of course, is transparent to the user.

So in our example, the Query Language will extract the primary key of all the objects in **Project** for which Tom Smith works for. This happens to be the unary set, ID = OA Project. Since there are no other conditions on **Employee**, the Query Language uses *Works for OA Project* as the condition to select the required employees.

6.3.3 The Nested Query

And of course, the last level would be nested queries. This is done by popping up another level of schema to the user, but only of the schema items that are involved in the nested conditions. The nesting may extend to an arbitrary level, depending on system limitations. This is because **VILD** actually evaluates each nested query individually so that the results of each nested query is available to the user if the user

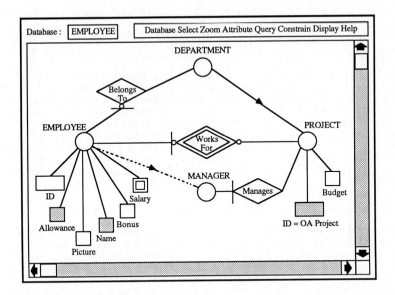

Figure 16: Specifying a simple query

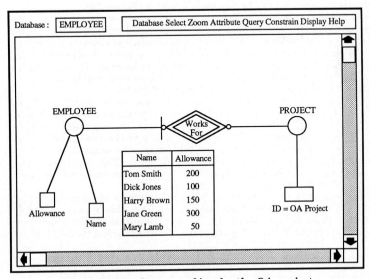

Figure 17: Employees working for the OA project

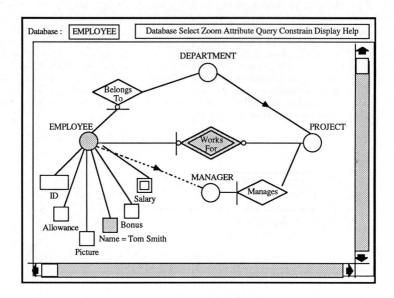

Figure 18: **Specifying a relationship-reflexive query**

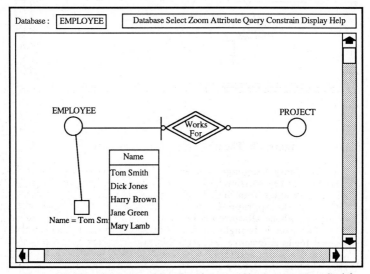

Figure 19: **Employees working for the same project as Tom Smith**

wishes to scroll through the nesting levels after the query has been executed. This is also to allow the user to incrementally continue his query (eg, specify an additional constraint at some nested level) or to amend the existing one (eg, change the operator in a conditional from *less than* to *equals*).

Consider the example: The user wants the name of all employees whose allowance is less than Tom Smith's bonus. The user is interested only in the **Employee** object, so he zooms in on it. He selects the required **Name** attribute. Then he adds the constraints by clicking on **Allowance**, but after adding the conditional *less than*, instead of typing in a value, he clicks on the attribute **Bonus**. This procedure signifies a nested query, and a new window is created with the schema of **Employee** in it. The user is prompted to specify a constraint on this object (Figure 20).

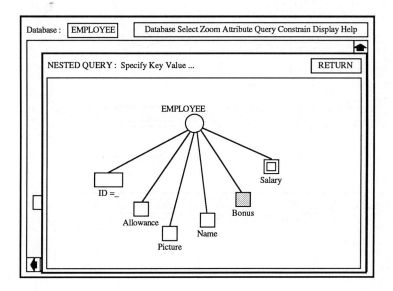

Figure 20: The nested query schema window

By default, the Query Language expects the Bonus to be uniquely qualified, so it expects a value for the key attribute **ID**. The user has three choices: he may nest the query further, he may enter Tom Smith's ID,[11] or he may choose not to qualify bonus. The second choice is the appropriate one for our example. The third choice would return all employees whose allowance is less than their own bonus. By clicking on a *Return* button, The user is brought back to the main schema, where the condition on **Allowance** now reads *Allowance less than (*Bonus)* (Figure 21). The asterisk and paranthesis indicate nesting, and the mouse can be clicked on the word to display the nested level. Choosing the *Query* command will execute the query and return the required information (Figure 22).

---

[11] The user may, of course, repeatedly enter several values for the **ID** as in a normal disjunctive condition

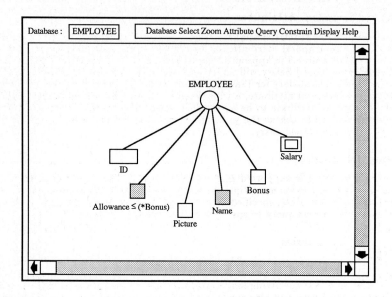

Figure 21: The primary query schema window

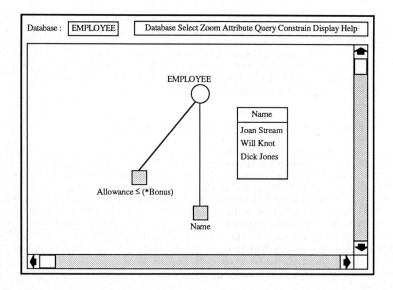

Figure 22: Employees whose allowance is less than Tom Smith's bonus

6.4   Temporal, Incremental, and More Complex Queries[12]

Querying Temporal Attributes

Temporal attributes require special handling (See [SS87]). From [Nar88], we see that the definition of temporal attributes in MOTAR automatically defines at least one additional field to store the appropriate temporal portion of the data. For example, the definition of Annual Salary will imply two subfields (facets in MDBMS) that will store the year and the salary for that year respectively. Therefore, when a condition is specified on a temporal attribute, a window will pop up that will allow the temporal qualification of the attribute to be given eg, if we specify *Annual Salary > 2000*, the window will pop up to ask us the year. If no year is specified, then the default is to take the temporally latest entry.

Incremental Queries

Incremental querying is supported in a variety of ways. The *Save* and *Reload* commands allow a query to span multiple sessions. The ability to add new constraints or amend existing constraints, specified in section 6.3.3, allow users to make use of data retrieved in the current query to specify a further query.

More Complex Queries

The VILD query language is capable of handling much more complex queries. The interface is straight forward, but as we mentioned before, occasionally tedious. Users will probably find that specifying long difficult queries incrementally would reduce the complexity of the query and also result in a clearer understanding of the information desired.

7   The VILD Implementation

We have just gone through the description of the **VILD** language system in some detail. This system is being built on top of the MDBMS database. The MDBMS functions and structures required by **VILD** have been completed. The OML is also finished except for the integration of the Chinese language editor, which is in progress. The ODL has been completed, and the Browser has been designed and is being built. It is expected to be ready by end-1988. The Query Language enhancements on the Browser have not yet been scheduled for implementation.

8   Summary and Future Directions

We have described the visual language system **VILD** implemented on top of the object-oriented multi-media database system, MDBMS. **VILD** is object oriented, both in the structure of the data it handles, and in its user interface. It handles multi-media information, and supports temporal attributes and relationships in all its four language parts. These four parts of **VILD** show how modularity can allow for easy enhancement of the language (such as adding security to the OML), and how consistency of presentation allows the information provider (in the ODL) to easily give the semantics of the data (via the schema) to the information user (in the Browser and the Query Language). Finally, though **VILD** has a slightly tedious way of specifying compound constraints, we have seen how this lets us have a visual object-oriented query language that handles simple queries, relationship-reflexive queries, and complex queries with equal ease.

---

[12]See footnote 10.

Let us now look at some future directions for **VILD**. On the processing side, we would like to improve the response time. We hope that this will come automatically when MDBMS leaves the prototype stage and becomes a full-fledged database system. More importantly, we would like to see several enhancements to the **VILD** interface. The first is the inclusion of simple one-word speech recognition to replace the menus and commands currently selected by the mouse. Then replace the mouse-pointing with finger indexical references, using a touch-screen or similar method. And finally, add in speech recognition and coordination with indexical references to the extent that, with pointing to the screen, we can literally say to the computer, "I want to know this, this, and all this about employees that earn less than two thousand dollars a month", and get what we want.

Acknowledgements

We acknowledge the help of Boon-Siong Choo, Chun-Hong Kok, and Jyh-Jang Lim in the implementation of various portions of **VILD**.

References

[CEC87]   Douglas M. Campbell, David W. Embley, and Bogdan Czejdo. Graphical query formulation for an entity-relationship model. *Data & Knowledge Engineering*, 2, 1987.

[CLN87]   S.C. Chan, H.B. Low, and T.M. Ng. Intelligent chinese language input system for casual users. In *International Conference on Chinese Information Processing*, 1987.

[GGKZ85] Kenneth J. Goldman, Sally A. Goldman, Paris C. Kanellakis, and Stanley B. Zdonik. ISIS: interface for a semantic information system. In *ACM SIGMOD Conference Proceedings*, 1985.

[Ham81]   Michael Hammer. Database description with SDM: a semantic database model. *ACM Transactions on Database Systems*, 6(3), 1981.

[Her80]   Christopher F. Herot. Spatial management of data. *ACM Transactions on Database Systems*, 5(4), 1980.

[Hir88]   Fumiyasu Hirano. Hypermedia-based documentation system for the office environment. In *RIAO 88 Conference on User-Oriented Content-Based Text and Image Handling*, 1988.

[IoSS]   National University of Singapore Institute of Systems Science. System specs for IPIS – prototype I.

[JD86]   William P. Jones and Susan T. Dumais. The spatial metaphor for user interfaces: experimental tests of reference by location versus name. *ACM Transactions on Office Information Systems*, 4(1), 1986.

[Kan88]   Alex Kang. *IPIS User Interface Toolkit Documentation Release 1*. Institute of Systems Science, National University of Singapore, April 1988.

[KK86]   Robert R. Korfhage and Margaret A. Korfhage. Criteria for iconic languages. In *Visual Languages*, Plenum Press, 1986.

[KKS87] Kazuya Kosaka, Kouichi Kajitani, and Masaki Satoh. An experimental mixed-object database system. In *Proceedings of 1987 IEEE-CS Symposium on Office Systems*, 1987.

[KKS88] Hyoung-Joo Kim, Henry F. Korth, and Avi Silberschatz. Picasso: a graphical query language. *SOFTWARE — PRACTICE AND EXPERIENCE*, 18(3), March 1988.

[Lar86] James A. Larson. A visual approach to browsing in a database environment. *IEEE Computer*, June 1986.

[Mot86] Amihai Motro. Baroque: a browser for relational databases. *ACM Transactions on Office Information Systems*, 4(2), 1986.

[Nar88] A.D. Narasimhalu. *A Data Model for Object-Oriented Databases with Temporal Attributes and Relationships*. Technical Report, Institute of Systems Science, National University of Singapore, 1988.

[NKO*88] A.D. Narasimhalu, Nancy Karta, B.C. Ooi, M.K. Leong, Rosanne Price, Juliana Lim, K.T. Loh, and I.F. Chang. An object oriented multimedia DBMS for public information systems. 1988. In preparation.

[NLH*87] T.M. Ng, L.L. Lim, H.K.Tan, L.E. Tan, and H.Y. Wong. Towards an implementation of a computer aided chinese input system for casual users. In *1987 International Conference on Chinese and Oriental Language Computing*, 1987.

[OMA*87] Masataka Ohta, Mamoru Maekawa, Takashi Arano, Kiyokuni Kawachiya, and Keiichi Noguchi. *The Implementation and Experience of Multimedia Workstation – PIE*. Technical Report 87-04, Department of Information Science, Faculty of Science, University of Tokyo, January 1987.

[ONWC86] B. C. Ooi, A. D. Narasimhalu, K. Y. Wang, and I. F. Chang. A multimedia file server using optical disks for office applications. In *Proceedings of IEEE Symposium on Office Automation*, 1986.

[PLKN88] Rosanne Price, M.K. Leong, Nancy Karta, and Desai Narasimhalu. Experiences in the implementation of a multimedia DBMS. 1988. To be presented at IT Works '88, Singapore.

[Sno87] R. Snodgrass. The temporal query language TQuel. *ACM Transactions on Database Systems*, 12(2), 1987.

[SS87] Arie Segev and Arie Shoshani. Logical modelling of temporal data. In *Proceedings of the 1987 SIGMOD Conference*, 1987.

[WKL86] Darrel Woelk, Won Kim, and Willis Luther. An object-oriented approach to multimedia databases. In *Proceedings of ACM SIGMOD Conference 1986*, 1986.

Visual Database Systems
T.L. Kunii (Editor)
Elsevier Science Publishers B.V. (North-Holland)
© IFIP, 1989

IMAGE MANAGEMENT IN A MULTIMEDIA DATABASE SYSTEM

Klaus MEYER-WEGENER, Vincent Y. LUM, and C. Thomas WU

Naval Postgraduate School
Department of Computer Science
Code 52
Monterey, CA 93943
U.S.A.

This paper introduces a general concept for the representation of multimedia data by unformatted and formatted data in a new way to allow users to perform contents-search. It is used in a basic-function approach to the design and development of multimedia database systems, that exploits the extension of a relational database management system with new attribute types. Raster (bitmap) images are used as an example to actually define the structure of multimedia data values and a basic set of operations for access and manipulation. Going beyond the capabilities of most image database systems, contents-oriented search is supported by text descriptions that are integrated with the images. The special character of these descriptions makes it possible to use advanced query specification and search techniques that combine DBMS and information retrieval capabilities very efficiently. The integration into a query language like SQL is straightforward and yields a powerful instrument to store and retrieve images that can be associated with other objects in the database. Further, the approach can be applied to other types of multimedia data as well. The paper finally sketches a prototype implementation on top of an existing relational database management system (INGRES).

Klaus Meyer-Wegener's permanent address is: Universitaet Kaiserslautern, Fachbereich Informatik, Postfach 30 49, 6750 Kaiserslautern, West Germany. The work described in this paper has been sponsored by the Naval Oceans System Center (NOSC), San Diego, under project no. RC32510.

1. INTRODUCTION

As database applications become more and more diversified, the capabilities of the current commercial database management systems (DBMS) developed on the basis of handling formatted data become less and less satisfactory. In many of the newer applications, handling of *multimedia data* such as text, graphics, images, voices, sound, and signal data is important and must be dealt with. Such are the cases of managing engineering and office data. However, storing data of this kind is one thing; organizing a large amount of them for efficient search and retrieval is quite another [LWH87]. Research to develop multimedia DBMS has been initiated few years ago [Ma87, Ch86, Gi87, WKL86]. Some prototypes have been implemented.

Unfortunately, because of the complexity in managing multimedia data, there are no generally accepted solutions at this time. In fact, it can be said that there is not yet a good general solution. Most projects adopted the approach of developing a *specialized system* for a special application to reduce complexity (e.g. office environment or engineering environment). While this is definitely one approach we can try to solve our problems, one can also take a different direction as well.

The approach in this paper illustrates an alternative in finding a solution. It is to develop a basic functional DBMS that can handle multimedia for *any* application, analogous to the way how one constructs a normal DBMS for handling formatted data. That is to say, we shall concentrate on developing a DBMS with the basic functions for retrieving, searching, and managing multimedia data as we do in handling formatted data. Among these functions, searching is the most challenging. In fact, to this date there are hardly any proposals that allow users to do *contents-search* of the multimedia data in a similar manner as done with formatted data. Simply applying relational technology in this environment is not a solution at all. The observation is well substantiated by the fact that users of CAD, CAM, CIM, etc. do not use DBMS to manage their data which generally contain much graphics and diagrams. The proposals to enhance a DBMS to include user-defined abstract data types [OFS84, St86, SR86] and object-orientation [Di87, KCB88] are some concrete steps in appropriate directions. They do not, however, suggest specific methods to process multimedia data like images, and none talks about processing contents of multimedia data at all. This is the area that we want to cover. However, in order for us to be successful with this approach, it is necessary for us to find a way to reduce the complexity of handling multimedia data. Thus, first we shall discuss a little on the complexity issue of multimedia data handling.

The fundamental difficulty in handling multimedia data lies in the problem of handling the *rich semantics* that is contained in the multimedia data. In traditional DBMS, data is always formatted. The semantics that can be associated with the formatted data is very restrictive. For example, if the attribute is age with the unit to be year, then a storage of 34 in the data for this attribute can mean only 34 years of age, and nothing more. Further semantics in the interpretation of the data can be done, but would be at a different level. This, in fact, gives rise to the research in semantic data modeling, which after many years of research is still in its infantile stage. This problem is difficult and complex. No pat solution is expected in the near future.

Unfortunately multimedia data is intrinsically tied to a very rich semantics. Consequently, a simple extension from formatted data into textual data, for example, already brings us much difficulty. Information retrieval scientists have spent a number of years trying to solve this problem with some good success. Extending into other kind of media such as image is much more difficult. To illustrate such a difficulty, one only need to look at a simple image of ships. Given such a picture, how is the system to know what kind of ships they are? Are they destroyers? cruisers? aircraft carriers? passenger ships? freighters? oil tankers? or whatever? Or, given a picture of a dog and a cat, both running, how is the system to know if the dog is chasing the cat or vice versa? Or are they simply playing with each other?

To answer queries posed on images, a person must draw from a very rich experience one has encountered in life. Further, the person must also perform integration, analysis, synthesis, and even extrapolation of his or her knowledge to derive a good answer. One must have a very sophisticated technique to analyze the content of the images to get the semantics of many, many different things. This kind of capability is generally referred to as *intelligence*. As a result, persons with limited experience and knowledge, such as a child or someone who has not been exposed to the various kinds of ships, will not be able to give good answers to queries on the contents of images.

To expect systems to have this kind of capability to answer multimedia queries is definitely not possible in today's systems. Technology has not been developed to this level thus far. Hence, we cannot develop a DBMS to be able to handle the multimedia data to the same extent we know how to handle formatted data.

We can, however, do the next best thing. As the proverb says, "a picture is worth a thousand words". This also means vice versa that we can describe a picture or an image by a thousand words, although one would never have exactly the same thing, feeling- or meaning-wise. A thousand words, more or less, is not so important. What is important is that we can *abstract the content* of the image data, sound data, or other forms *into words or text*. Right now, a human user can do a much better job on providing a contents description than any machine, and text is the most convenient form of entering it. Once we have the text description, we can say that we have the "equivalent" of the original multimedia data, at least for searching and analysis purposes. Through parsing we can turn the text into some kind of *knowledge representation* that makes way for the application of advanced information retrieval methods based on artificial intelligence. Please note that this kind of description does not in any way restrict the domain of the application. It can be used for x-rays, press photos, satellite photos, and portraits with the same benefit. Hence, it adds significantly to the search capacity of the envisioned multimedia DBMS.

The resulting basic concept is that each media object will be represented by three parts: registration data, description data, and raw data. Raw data is a bit string of the data. For example, in image data, it can be the bitmap of the image. Registration data is the data related to the physical aspect of the raw data for the device to display the raw data. For example, it includes the color intensity and the colormap for an image. Description data relates to the content of the multimedia data entered by the users. It is in the form of formatted data or natural language description. For example, the image may show "a battleship docked at the San Diego harbor". This part of the data will be used for content search on multimedia data in the system.

Naturally the integration in such a way requires the definition of a new query interface to allow the users to store, search and manipulate their multimedia data. Such an interface must have the broad capability and flexibility, as available in a DBMS interface for formatted data, to satisfy its users. It must be broadly usable without restrictions to the kind of applications the system serves.

To the best of our knowledge, the use of such a technique to represent and search multimedia data has not been proposed before, although registration data and raw data have been used. It is the definition and integration of the description data that allow us to do the complicated and complex content search of multimedia data that has been elusive to this date. By combining the techniques of database and information retrieval disciplines, and enhancing them further to fit into our environment, we will be able to handle multimedia data in similar ways as one does in handling formatted data. We can extend the relational structure and the query interface to allow us to construct a broadly capable multimedia database system for various applications. Operations for such a system will be described. However, the architecture and internal structure of the system go beyond the scope of this paper and will not be discussed.

Readers of this paper should have no problem to see that there are many alternatives for the internal structure.

In section 2 we introduce a general concept of multimedia data management that can be supported by such a DBMS. Section 3 concentrates on images that are used as a representative type of multimedia data during prototype development. This makes it necessary to review image databases briefly. In section 4 three different relation schemas for the modelling of images and their related data are discussed, and the details of the attribute type image are presented. This section also outlines the interface to handle image data, and the operations to manipulate the various tasks in the integrated environment of relational and image data. Section 5 sketches the architecture of the prototype being developed, and section 6 concludes with an outlook on future work in this field.

2. DATA ORGANIZATION FOR MULTIMEDIA

Multimedia data are also referred to as unformatted data. More precisely this means that their values consist of a variable-length list of many small items the meaning of which is not associated with database processing: characters in the case of text, pixels in images, line segments and areas in graphics, and so on. There are usually higher-level structures as well (sentences, paragraphs, 2D objects, scenes), but again they may not be known to the DBMS when the data are stored. Invariably, multimedia data are accompanied by some standard formatted data called *registration data*. For text this could be something like document number, name and affiliation of the author, the wordprocessor used, delimiters, etc. For images it could be resolution, pixel depth, source, date of capture, and colormap. The important issue of the registration data is that they are mandatory if anything is to be done with the multimedia data at all, either to interpret them for replay or display, or to identify them and distinguish them from others. Registration data can easily be stored in the attributes and tuples of standard relational database systems, thus making the full power of query languages available to retrieve and manipulate them.

While the registration is indispensable, other formatted (or unformatted) data describing the contents of multimedia data generally are not on hand. This so-called *description data* are per se redundant, because they repeat information already present in the image, text, or sound. However, because of the complexity and the depth of the information content, there is hardly any chance to perform efficiently a contents-oriented search on the unformatted raw data themselves. It is much easier to create the description that may even be structured as formatted data, so that the power of a query language can be applied. It is very difficult and time-consuming to derive the description automatically (this is called *feature and content extraction),* although the areas of natural language understanding, image analysis, and pattern recognition have developed a number of techniques and algorithms. With these techniques, we have limited success in feature extraction. But we are nowhere near the success of achieving automatic information content extraction. As mentioned in the introduction, such kind of work requires much too much intelligence in a system than we know how to provide today. Thus, it is much easier and more effective to let a human user provide the description, just as an author provides abstract and keywords with an article. In either case the database should hold the result of the extraction, i.e. the description, and link it to the multimedia data. It is the purpose of a multimedia database system to provide long-term storage for the multimedia data as well as their description.

The description can be fairly rich and complicated, due to the amount of information embodied in an image or a signal. It is well known that the relational model, though powerful, lacks the power to define the semantics associated with its data [Co79, Ke79, KCB88]. It is in recognition of this fact that many researchers in recent years have been searching for a better data model to allow its users to define more semantics with their data. However, while the lack of capability to specify more semantics in the relational model is a deficiency in a way, its inherent simplicity and flexibility to accommodate different applications and enhancements are some of the strong points of this model and should be exploited. In cases where the relational model is not sufficient to capture the semantics of multimedia data, attachment of plain text offers great improvement at limited cost. Text can be entered by users without special skills, and it can be used to search for multimedia data: All the well-known techniques of information retrieval can be applied [Sh64, LF73, SM83]. In doing so, one type of multimedia data (e.g. image) is in fact described with the help of another type of multimedia data (text) that is easier to handle. This is not unusual: graphics can be used to describe aspects of an image, and voice can partly be represented by text. However, it should be noted that this is almost always accompanied by a loss of information.

The representation of media objects in terms of raw data, registration data, and description data helps to classify the operations, as sketched in fig. 1. Any access to the raw data must go "through" the registration data to make sure that the raw data are interpreted correctly. *Editing* operations on the raw data including filtering, clipping, bitmap operations for images, stripping of layout commands and control characters for text, etc. are permitted. *Special operators* that are applied to the description data can be distance and volume calculations on geometric data [CF80], or the addition of synonyms in the case of keywords. These operators can actually do a lot of processing without ever

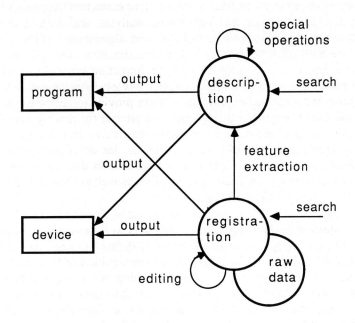

FIGURE 1
Groups of Operations on Multimedia Data
and on the Associated Formatted Data

touching the raw data. In fact, it is expected that most of the processing, except the editing of the raw data, will be done outside the raw data. Some of these operators cannot be implemented with commands of the query language only. They need the features of a general-purpose programming language. New data models will allow them to be incorporated into the database as "procedures" or "methods".

To make the following discussion more explicit, we shall concentrate on *images* as a representative type of multimedia data. This allows us to define registrations, descriptions, and operations in more detail. We plan to do similar things for the other types of multimedia data as well.

3. IMAGE DATABASE SYSTEMS

There is quite a tradition of database support for image management and image analysis [CK81, TY84]. Some of the approaches concentrate on the description data, while others address the raw data and registration data first. Many implicitly restrict the type of images stored to satellite photos and introduce specific descriptions and operations for them [LC80, CF81, RFS88]. None has been found to address raw data, registration data, and description data in any thorough fashion.

Raw image data consist of a matrix of *pixels* (picture elements). Each pixel indicates the color or greyness of a small (atomic) portion of the image. It can be encoded by a single bit to indicate black or white. Alternatively, several bits can be used to encode a pixel, e.g. 8 or 24. The number of bits per pixel is called the *pixel depth*. As the size of the image (the number of pixels in rows and columns) as well as the depth can vary, the raw data appear just as a string of bits that can only be interpreted if the size and the depth are known. Hence, size (also called resolution) and depth are first examples of registration data.

Pixels either define a color/greyness value directly or index a so-called *colormap*. A typical colormap contains 256 entries each of which specifies the particular intensities of the three basic colors red, green, and blue, or defines a certain color in another way. To display an image on a particular device, special storage segments or registers assigned to the device must be loaded with the colormap. The colormap can have a variable length, thus it is debatable whether it belongs to the raw data or to the registration data. Because it is needed to interpret and reproduce the image and because its size is rather limited, we classify it as registration data.

If the pixels consist of 8 bits each, up to 256 colors can be used in that image. If there are 24 bits per pixel, each 8-bit portion addresses a different entry in the colormap: The first one is used to obtain the intensity of red only, the second and third are used for green and blue respectively. Thus 2^{24} colors can be used in the image.

The use of a colormap is to save storage. Instead of repeating the definition of a color in thousands of pixels, it is done only once in the table entry where it can occupy several bytes. However, this indirection has more advantages: Instead of using the basic colors red, green, and blue (RGB) the encoding in the colormap could as well be done in terms of "intensity, hue, and saturation" (IHS) or the "YIQ" defined by the National Television Systems Committee. This can be required for the output on certain types of monitors. Formulae are available to calculate one color definition from the other [Ni86, BB82]. The translation is limited to the 256 entries of the colormap and does not touch the 10000 or more pixels of the image. Finally, modifying the colors of an image can be used to highlight minimal color changes and thus to make visible hidden shapes on an image, or to perform some simple animations.

Some image *identification* should also be part of the registration data to be able to distinguish images properly. Depending on the application this could be merely an arbitrary number, a combination of source (camera, satellite) and time, or other similar schemes.

How are raw data and registration data integrated into a database system? Some systems simply put them in files, e.g. EIDES [TM77, Ta80b] and IMDB [LU77, LH80]. This means that they do not offer a data model, but only a set of operations (subroutines) to access and manipulate the image files. Others have moved the registration data to a relational database system and linked them to the raw data in the files, e.g. REDI/IMAID [CF79, CF81] and GRAIN [CRM77, LC80]. They use special relations in which each tuple stands for one image. Display and editing operations can be applied to the tuples of these relations. However, as G.Y. Tang pointed out in [Ta80a], it is not clear what the semantics of the standard relational operators should be when they are applied to those image relations. Especially when two image tuples are joined, which of the images is represented by the result? Both of them?

For this reason, Tang proposed that the raw data should be conceptually represented in the data model as attribute values. This does not imply anything for the storage structures. Internally, images can still be kept in separate files, but they are now accessible through the query language. The display and editing operators are applied to the attribute, not to the tuple. Joining two tuples with image attributes yields a tuple with more than one image attributes which can be handled easily.

Tang himself and Grosky [Gr84] have designed data models based on this approach, but neither of them has reported a successful implementation. The IBM Tokyo Scientific Center has in fact implemented a system called ADM (Aggregate Data Manager) that is based on System R and uses SQL as a query language [TII79]. Some of the registration data are handled in the form of type information, i.e. there are different domains used for binary and grey-tone images. Using SQL queries, images can be retrieved as attributes in relations and tuples and can then be moved to a workspace, where a variety of editing operations can be applied to them. The resulting image can be reinserted into the database. Unfortunately, the program interface is not explained in the paper; it is expected to be some modification of the SQL embedding. However, this approach seems more appropriate than that of [Ta80a]. We shall adopt the ADM concept as a starting point for our system and develop it to more detail. The authors of the ADM model themselves have suggested the extension of their system to other types of multimedia data [TII79], but we could not find out whether they have actually pursued that goal.

Other image DBMS like IMAID and GRAIN have put much more emphasis on the image description data. They are stored in relations with a special structure (e.g. attributes holding geometric coordinates) that can be used as input to pictorial operators. A more recent approach, PSQL, makes use of more advanced database concepts like abstract data types [RFS88]. The geometric description data, i.e. points, line segments, and regions, are not represented by tuples, but also by attribute values that belong to new domains and have special operations defined with them. However, in all these systems the description data as well as the operations are based on the assumption that they deal with a special class of images, namely satellite photographs. Lines detected almost immediately resemble objects like highways, rivers, or city boundaries. There is hardly any need for a textual description. This is different from analyzing arbitrary photographs of three-dimensional objects, where it is much harder to relate a line to an object. We do not want to restrict ourselves to an application area, and therefore concentrate on the basic "intra-domain operators" that are mentioned, but not discussed in [RFS88]. This is to satisfy the storage and retrieval requirements of satellite photos as well as x-rays, newspaper photos, and other images. Applications that make use of the specific properties of a class of images can be build on top of our system, and thus benefit from the data abstraction already provided by it.

4. EXTENDING THE RELATIONAL MODEL WITH THE DATA TYPE IMAGE

Introducing new data types into the relational model has been an issue for quite a while. For instance, an extension mechanism has been proposed for INGRES [OFS84, St86] and is also being implemented in its successor POSTGRES [SR86]. It provides a framework for the definition of new data types, but does not include the actual definition of the IMAGE data type. Our intension is to close this gap and to define the data type in detail, with all its functions. It should be clear by now that the simple handling of images ist not sufficient. We have to examine ways of incorporating contents-search in the system as well. We shall therefore need to both define techniques for contents-search and the appropriate interface for such operations. We want to check how useful they can be in the formulation of various queries that evolve in image capture, display, and processing. Once we know what functions are needed, they can be included into POSTGRES or any other extensible database system.

To find out what could be done with image attributes, we begin with a look at some modelling issues of assigning images to objects and vice versa, which have not been addressed by the papers cited in the last section.

4.1. The Relationship of Objects and Images

IMAGE is a *new* attribute domain, i.e. an image is supposed to be an attribute of some object or entity (a ship or an aircraft, for instance). Usually it is an attribute of the object shown on the picture, but that need not be the case. Making image an attribute does not prevent the treatment of pictures as stand-alone objects (see relation schema type 3 below). The simplest way of assigning an image to an object leads to a relation schema like this:

OBJECT (<u>O-ID</u> , ... , O-IMAGE)

OBJECT is the name of the relation such as SHIP, CAR, or PERSON, followed by a list of attributes. The object identifier O-ID is underlined to indicate that it is the primary key. We denote this as the *relation schema type 1*. Its advantage is that access to the tuple describing an object fetches the image, too. More than one attribute of type IMAGE can be defined for a relation. However, it may often be the case that the number of images per object varies. If first normal form is required, such repeating groups can only be modelled by a separate relation. Hence, there is a *relation schema type 2:*

OBJECT (<u>O-ID</u> , ...)
OBJECT-IMAGE (<u>O-ID, O-IMAGE</u>)

In the relation OBJECT-IMAGE the O-ID alone cannot serve as a key, because there may be several images of one object, leading to several tuples with the same O-ID. Thus O-IMAGE has to be included to make the key unique. The fact that an attribute of type IMAGE is part of the primary key might lead to severe implementation problems, but we do not consider them here (introducing an image identifier can help). Access to an image is not as simple as it was with schema type 1, for a natural or outer join is required. If the tuple of the object is available, a selection on the OBJECT-IMAGE relation must be performed, using the given object identifier.

Another problem with the two approaches discussed so far is that a picture showing several objects must be stored redundantly, i.e. the same image is repeated in the relation for the number of different objects "having" (shown on) this image. The database system treats the copies as different images. To avoid this, a *relation schema type 3* has to be used:

OBJECT (<u>O-ID</u> , ...)
IMAGE-OBJECT (<u>I-ID</u> , I-IMAGE)
IS-SHOWN-ON (<u>O-ID, I-ID</u> , COORDINATES, ...)

The COORDINATES can be used to give the approximate position of the object on the image. Please note that we do not distinguish the statement "object x has an image y" from "object x is shown on image y", but represent both by the same modeling concept. Now it becomes even more complicated to find the images of an object:

$$\text{NATJOIN } (\text{SELECT}_{\text{O-ID=object1}} (\text{IS-SHOWN-ON}),$$
$$\text{IMAGE-OBJECT})$$

NATJOIN stands for the natural join of two relations, i.e. the equi-join on the attributes with the same name (IS-SHOWN-ON.I-ID = IMAGE-OBJECT.I-ID). Each image is stored only once, regardless of how many objects it shows. It is possible now to start with an image and to retrieve the depicted objects:

$$\text{NATJOIN (OBJECT, SELECT}_{\text{I-ID=image1}} (\text{IS-SHOWN-ON}))$$

One could even define a window on the image, use it to restrict the coordinates, and thus retrieve only the objects shown in the window. Hence, the third type of relation schema is a little bit unwieldy, but it provides the highest degree of freedom in modelling and processing (even images with unknown contents can be stored).

The three schema types are depicted in fig. 2. The dotted line indicates a primary-key-foreign-key relationship (one-to-many). A relational database system extended by image attributes supports all of them. The choice depends on the application. If there is at most one image per object and each image shows only one object (e.g. a database of employees), then type 1 is most appropriate.

There is one problem with schema type 3 that has not been mentioned yet: There may be different types of objects, e.g. ships, aircrafts, and submarines, each represented by a different relation. In this case different IS-SHOWN-ON relations are needed as well, for the domain of the O-ID part of the key cannot be the union of the domains of all the object identifiers. This makes the path from a picture to the shown objects really awkward. The introduction of a generalization hierarchy with a superclass 'object' is a solution, but that goes beyond the relational model.

4.2. The IMAGE Data Type

As indicated earlier, not all the operations of the relational algebra can be performed directly on the data type IMAGE. They treat an IMAGE value as a

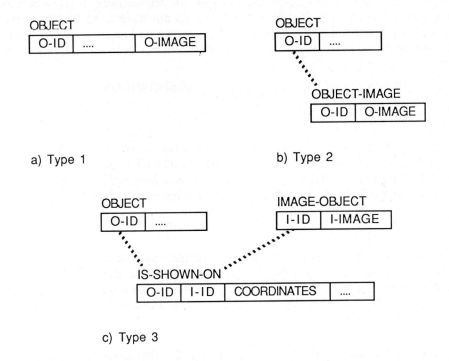

FIGURE 2

The Three Relation Schema Types for Storing Images

whole, i.e. projection either drops it completely or keeps it in the result. The comparisons needed in selections and joins cannot be performed on the whole image. Even the definition of equality is rather complex for images, whereas it is easy to see what the condition "pixel_depth (I-IMAGE) = 8" means. Hence, IMAGE should be regarded as an *abstract data type* with its own set of operators or functions, some of which map the complex domain IMAGE to standard domains like number or string. The result of these functions can be used in selections and joins without problems. To identify the functions, we have to take a closer look at the structure of an IMAGE value. It will have the three parts introduced before, namely raw data, registration, and description. Raw data and the registration are intrinsically tied together, so they will both be covered in the next subsection, while description data are discussed separately after that.

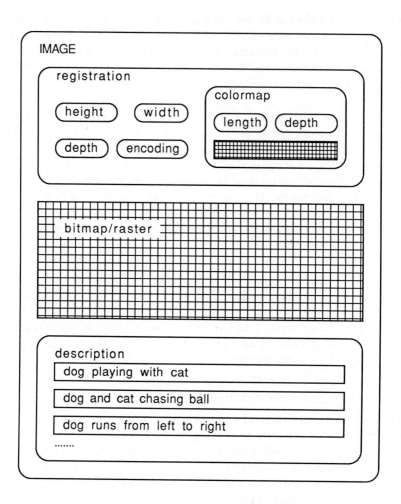

FIGURE 3
Conceptual View of an Instance of the Abstract Data Type IMAGE

4.2.1. Raw Data and Registration Data

The registration data could be stored in normal attributes next to the IMAGE attribute, but then it would be the user's responsibility to define them, and the display of an image could be impossible, if the user forgot some of them. Hence, to make sure that they are available for every IMAGE attribute, those required to interpret the pixel matrix are made part of the IMAGE value, as shown in fig. 3. They can be seen as internal or hidden attributes, and they are accessed through operators of the IMAGE data type. This is almost as easy as the access to the other attributes. The registration data identifying an image are application-dependent and thus are kept in ordinary attributes (compare the O-ID and the I-ID in the schema examples of the last section).

The internal attribute named "encoding" specifies the way the colors are defined in the colormap, or in the pixels if no colormap is used. Possible values may be "RGB" or "IHS", but it must also indicate how the values of the three components are encoded, i.e. integer or real, and how many bits they use (8, 24, 32). This, of course, must be consistent with the depth of the colormap or the depth of the pixels. If a colormap is used, its size must further be consistent with the depth of the pixels. However, the depth may sometimes be set to 8 bits, although less than 256 colors are used, in which case the pixel values have to be consistent with the size of the colormap.

To read an attribute of type IMAGE from the database into a program, one could use a very complex, variable-length record structure in the program. It seems more convenient to make the components of an IMAGE value accessible only through functions. This has the additional advantage that the program is even more independent of the storage structures and data encodings used by the DBMS. For instance, the function

CONSTRUCT_IMAGE (height, width, pixel_depth, encoding, colormap_size, colormap_depth, colormap, pixel_matrix)

produces a (transient) value of type IMAGE that cannot be assigned to program variables, but can only be used in INSERT and UPDATE statements of the query language. It reads a number of input parameters (variables or results of other functions) and combines their values into a single value of type IMAGE. To illustrate this, we show how the CONSTRUCT_IMAGE function could be used in the query language SQL [Ch76] (cf. relation schema type 3 above):

UPDATE IMAGE-OBJECT
SET I-IMAGE = CONSTRUCT_IMAGE ($height, $width, $depth,
                                RGB_REAL_32, 256, ...)
WHERE I-ID = 1234;

INSERT (4567, CONSTRUCT_IMAGE ($height, $width, 24,
                                IHS_INT_8, 0, ...))
INTO IMAGE-OBJECT;

Identifiers with a leading dollar sign represent program variables, whereas parameters with capital letters indicate named constants.

It should be clear at this point that this kind of command notation may be appropriate for the programmer, but not for the end-user. The interface for the latter should offer menus and icons to specify the source of the image to be stored. Even if only text input is possible, functions like READ_CAMERA (device_id) should be used in place of CONSTRUCT_IMAGE. The program that actually implements the user interface with the help of the query language could utilize this to avoid unnecessary copying of the large pixel matrix: It replaces the parameter variable in the internal CONSTRUCT_IMAGE call by a function call that reads the camera input (usually part of the driver software that is delivered with a camera):

CONSTRUCT_IMAGE (..., READ_RGB_CAMERA ($camera_id), ...)

Avoiding intermediate storage and unnecessary copying is a very important design issue in multimedia databases. We shall return to this in section 5.

Retrieving attribute values of type IMAGE from the database into program variables uses another set of functions like:

HEIGHT (IMAGE attribute) : integer;
WIDTH (IMAGE attribute) : integer;
DEPTH (IMAGE attribute) : integer;
ENCODING (IMAGE attribute) : encoding_type;
COLORMAP_DEPTH (IMAGE attribute) : integer;
COLORMAP_LENGTH (IMAGE attribute) : integer;
COLORMAP (IMAGE attribute) : array [0:cm_depth*cm_length]
                                              of char;
PIXELMATRIX (IMAGE attribute) : array [0:height*width*depth]
                                              of bit;
etc.

Each function has a specific output type. Different functions can be defined to produce different output types for the same component of an IMAGE attribute. A query may look like this:

SELECT PIXELMATRIX (I-IMAGE), COLORMAP (I-IMAGE)
INTO $rgb_screen, $rgb_colormap
FROM IMAGE-OBJECT
WHERE I-ID = 35;

Instead of copying the image into program variables, it should again be possible to send it to an output device directly. To do so, the DBMS might be required to perform some transformation on the colormap and the pixel matrix, e.g. change the RGB encoding to IHS. It has not been decided yet how the syntax for that should look like. One could also think of many other access functions like WINDOW, ZOOM, etc. [LH80, TII79]. The system is planned in a way that it is easy to add those functions when it seems appropriate.

4.2.2. Description Data

Some contents of an image can be represented by linking it to the objects it shows (fig. 2). That is not enough if we want to use the description data instead of the raw data whenever possible, especially in search. It does not say anything about *how* the objects are shown on the image. For instance, a ship could be shown in a harbor, out on the sea, in a storm, or in a convoy. None of these circumstances are likely to be represented by tuples in some relations of the DB. The same is true for the interrelation or interaction of the objects shown on the same image.

We have already pointed out why a text description seems to be most appropriate. In general, text can also cause some problems: it can be imprecise, it depends on the capabilities of the author, and it can be ambiguous. In this context however, we need a special type of text that differs from the intended general multimedia data type TEXT in several aspects:

- it is not self-content, but refers to other data
- it has a very simple structure (one paragraph)
- it is explicitly determined to support search.

Therefore, we have decided to tie the image and its description together, that is, we enhance the IMAGE type with a description part. It consists of a *set of phrases or sentences* that characterize the contents of the image (fig. 3). The set notion implies that each phrase or sentence is independent of all the others, which necessarily leads to some repetitions (of nouns, for example), but makes it much easier for the search mechanisms to grasp the meaning - or at least the important phrases. A typical example would be:

dog chases cat;
cat is running from left to right;
a house in the background;
front door of house is open;

This is still easy to enter and easy to read for human beings, but it also gives the system much more opportunity to distinguish images and to locate the ones that fit to a query.

The description part can be empty, if an image is entered into the database that nobody has looked at yet. To add the description later, a function will be provided that takes an IMAGE value as input, expands the set of description phrases by the given new ones, and produces a new IMAGE value that can be assigned to an IMAGE attribute:

    UPDATE IMAGE-OBJECT
    SET I-IMAGE = ADD_DESCRIPTION (I-IMAGE,
                    { dog playing with cat,
                    dog and cat chasing ball,
                    dog runs from left to right,
                    cat runs from right to left,
                    ball is between dog and cat,
                    ball bounces up in the air,
                    dog and cat are in the backyard of a house })
    WHERE I-ID = 1122;

This suits particularly well to situations where someone examines an image and adds his or her observations to those that others have entered before, thereby making the new knowledge available to all the other users of the system.

In case the contents of an image are already known when it is stored, the two functions can be combined in the INSERT command:

    INSERT (4387, ADD_DESCRIPTION (CONSTRUCT_IMAGE (...),
                    { USS Enterprise in the South Pacific on the way to ... }))
    INTO IMAGE-OBJECT;

Other functions can be defined to read the set of descriptions or to delete elements from it. The most important operator is the one used in search: SHOWS (IMAGE attribute, search phrase). The simplest form of a search phrase is just a word, and SHOWS yields true, if any of the phrases in the description contains that word. The search phrase may be more complicated, containing several words that must appear in an arbitrary or given order, or specifying "wild cards" for unknown parts of a word. Many access paths and indexing methods are available to support this kind of retrieval [Fa85, KW81, KSW79].

To give an impression of how the description can be used in the retrieval of images, consider a relation schema type 2 with ships as objects. The following query tries to find out whether the database holds some photos of a sinking destroyer:

    SELECT SHIP.S-ID, HEIGHT (S-IMAGE), ...
    INTO $ship_id, $height, ...
    FROM SHIP, SHIP-IMAGE
    WHERE SHIP.CLASS = "destroyer"
    AND SHIP.S-ID = SHIP-IMAGE.S-ID
    AND SHOWS (SHIP-IMAGE.S-IMAGE, "sinking");

As another example consider the image of a cat and a dog playing as given above, and a relation schema of type 3. If we want to find all the pictures that show a dog playing with a cat, and both are chasing after a ball, we can a query like the following:

```
SELECT WIDTH (I-IMAGE), ...
INTO $width, ...
FROM IMAGE-OBJECT
WHERE SHOWS (I-IMAGE,
                "cat I play* I dog",
                "dog & chas* & ball",
                "cat & chas* & ball" );
```

The I symbol between two given words requests that both words appear in the same sentence, but in an arbitrary sequence. The & symbol means that between the two words there may be other words that are ignored in the selection process. The * symbol finally matches strings of arbitrary length (not containing spaces), usually part of a single word like prefix or suffix. Hence, if the sentence "a black cat plays with a brown dog running in the backyard" is used to describe the contents of a picture, this satisfies the first search pattern in the SELECT query, and so does the phrase "dog playing with cat" entered in the example UPDATE operation above.

The details of the syntax for search phrases or templates are still to be determined. It is desirable to have Boolean operations. For instance, the given example assumes a logical conjunction (and) between the three search patterns. That means, each search pattern must be satisfied by at least one of the phrases, for the image to be selected. Naturally, one would also like to specify a disjunction (or), a negation (not), or combinations of all.

The pattern matching approach described so far is purely syntactical. In fact, there are better ways. The concept of the START system developed at the MIT AI Lab [Ka88] looks very promising for search on our description data, too. So-called *T-expressions* (ternary expressions) are extracted from sentences in natural language and are stored in a knowledge base. They consist of subject, relation, and object in a reduced form, i.e. without tenses, adverbs, attributes, etc. (these are stored separately). A single sentence may yield a couple of T-expressions. In our example we get:

```
<dog play cat>
<dog chase ball>
<cat chase ball>
etc.
```

The search phrase in the SHOWS predicate is parsed in the same way as the description phrases, and the resulting T-expressions are matched with the T-expressions in the knowledge base. This makes the specific syntax of the search phrase much less important. "The dog is chasing the ball" and "the ball is chased by the dog" are both reduced to <dog chase ball> and thus both select the image. The meaning of a search phrase is now completely different from the pattern matching approach: instead of specifying characters it now gives words and relations. For the treatment of complex noun phrases, embedded sentences, and some semantic rules see [Ka88]. The subject of defining contents-search in queries, either syntactically or semantically, is much more complex than we can discuss in this paper and is an on-going process in our research. This short description should only serve to indicate that there are concepts that can be exploited for our purposes.

Apart from registration data and description data there are some other issues about images that a multimedia DBMS should support, e.g. the management of *subimages* [Ta80a, Gr84]. The relation schema type 3 with the coordinates in the IS-SHOWN-ON relation already provides a way to define subimages, but it is rather cumbersome to extract them for display (WINDOW function). Instead we want to access a subimage as easily as the full image - without storing the pixels redundantly. There are several ways to do this, and we have not yet decided about it. However, it seems clear that the system has to support two different concepts: First, subimages can be derived from other images by selecting rectangular subsections. Second, several images can be combined to form a larger image. The latter is particularly useful for Landsat photographs. Ideally, both concepts can be handled by the same mechanism. This might add another item to the list of problems with the relational data model that we will summarize in the next section.

4.3. Shortcomings of the Relational Data Model

So far, we have defined a new domain IMAGE with an abstract view of the internal structure of its values and a set of functions to access them. We have shown how this could be embedded in a relational database system, and there are systems under development that will make such an embedding relatively easy (e.g. POSTGRES [SR86]). To our knowledge, there is no experience yet about how applications that make use of such a system might look like. We are convinced that this should be tried before moving from the relational data model to some more advanced data model.

However, we already came across some shortcomings of the relational model that we will summarize now. First, there is no generalization concept. This means that it is rather cumbersome to link an image to a number of objects it shows, when these objects are represented by different relations. In addition to that, generalization could also be very helpful in managing different types of images, e.g. x-rays, satellite photos, and portraits. They all have in common the functions we defined for images in general, but they may have some special functions for editing and feature extraction. A generalization concept would allow us to define a class image with the general functions and subclasses with added special functions. This is supported by the Multimedia Information Manager (MIM) of the ORION DBMS [WK87].

The management of subimages also causes problems in the relational model. It leads to the notion of complex objects [HL82, KCB88]. As long as subimages are only cut-out portions of larger images, the scheme is strictly hierarchical (one-to-many), i.e. the the complex objects representing large images and their subimages are disjunct. If images can also be composed of other images, they may share components (overlapping maps of satellite photos). This leads to a many-to-many relationship that can only be handled by special relations, and we need two joins to collect all the components of an images. There is no way to treat the large image just as any other image, nor even for display.

Another shortcoming is query formulation and performance. In the example queries of section 4.1 a number of joins were needed. They are known to be expensive. Again the notion of complex objects could help a lot by allowing to treat the images as - possibly shared - components of the objects they show. This eliminates the need for joins.

Despite these shortcomings of the relational data model, we do not intend to define yet another extensible or object-oriented data model. Rather it is our idea to add to the requirements for such systems by investigating the objects and the operations needed for multimedia applications. In that sense we want to influence the development of such systems and be ready to use them once they become available. The framework of ORION already looks promising, although the actual implementation of the Multimedia Information Management seems to require a significant amount of programming to create all the different methods [WK87]. A lot of work is spent on the representation of input/output devices in the database systems which further adds to the programming of methods. Experience will show whether this is necessary to achieve the performance needed in multimedia environments.

As the proposals in [OFS84] and [St86] indicate, the addition of new data types fits into the relational model rather smoothly. Hence, we do not regard this as a shortcoming. The reason why we take a different approach in the prototype sketched in the next section is that the commercially available version of INGRES does not offer this facility (only the University version does).

5. ARCHITECTURE OF A PROTOTYPE

The prototype is intended to cope only with the management of images, including storage organization, query and browsing facilities, and presentation issues. To keep the effort limited and to make the functionality of the envisioned system available as soon as possible, it is being built around an existing relational DBMS (INGRES [RTI85, RTI87]). That implies that performance will not be an issue in the first version. The high-level architecture is shown in fig. 4.

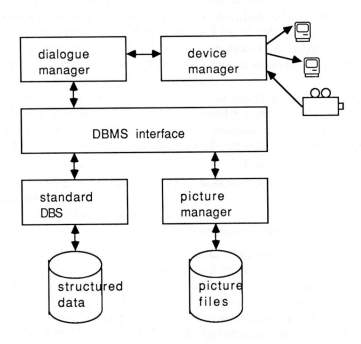

FIGURE 4
Architecture of the Prototype

The *dialogue manager* can be regarded as the main program. It calls the device manager to perform the exchange of the data with the user, employing a variety of input/output devices. It also calls the DBMS interface to store and retrieve the data, and maintains the state of the dialogue with the user. The *device manager* is to hide the specific details of the different I/O devices (cameras, monitors, VCRs) and to provide the dialogue manager with a more abstract view on their capabilities (comparable to the HIOMM in [WLK87]).

The *DBMS interface* implements the query language sketched in section 4.2. It gives the dialogue manager (and other applications) the illusion of using a DBMS with integrated image management facilities. In fact it engages two different systems, a standard relational DBMS for the structured data and a picture manager. The *picture manager* is responsible for storing all the images in standard files. Each image will be given a unique identifier (e.g. the file name) that is used by the relational database to refer to the image.

All the interfaces must be defined in detail. To do so, we have to investigate the different ways to encode images and the transformations required during input (capture) and output (display). How does the actual signal read from a camera through a video board look like? What has to be sent to the various types of monitors? And what is a suitable standard format that can cover both and thus avoid redundant storage of pictures?

Implementing the interfaces should take into account that we have to avoid copying the whole picture whenever possible. A good idea might be to *pipe* the data read from the database through the transformation process into the monitor driver. To do this the dialogue manager should be written in the style of functional programming:

```
DISPLAY (TRANSFORM (DB-ACCESS   (attribute,
                                 db-access-parameters)
                    transformation-parameters)
         display-parameters)
```

The analogous solution can be used for data capture. This gives the implementation the freedom not to copy the data but to hand over pointers instead. The only main memory copy of an image will then probably reside in the DBMS interface. Of course, this is only possible in a single-site database system. We have not yet thought about a network of multimedia workstations connected to a central database server, although this is definitely a long-term goal to keep in mind.

6. OUTLOOK AND FUTURE WORK

As presented in this paper, a new approach to represent multimedia data with formatted and unformatted data to allow contents-search is discussed. An outline of a low-level interface combining DBMS and information retrieval techniques and their enhancements to form the operations for processing image data in an extended relational DBMS environment is given. With this new approach, users of such a system will have much greater querying and manipulation power of multimedia data than what is available today.

Design and implementation along the presented line have begun. A simple
version of the prototype handling images is expected to be operational at the
end of 1988. There are four major areas of continuing development:

- investigation in the various search issues on description data
- other attribute domains like text and sound
- integration with an object-oriented data model
- user interfaces and applications

The management of the description data is a central issue in our proposal, and
syntax and semantics of the search expressions as well as the internal organization (indexing) have to be designed carefully. To support the full range of
multimedia applications, the database system must offer data types like text
and sound as well. They will be included in the query language in a way similar to that of IMAGE. However, their access functions will be different. Especially the proper treatment of sound relies on some real-time features of the
DBMS: When a recorded sound sequence is to be heard through a speaker, the
DBMS must deliver the data fast enough to guarantee uninterrupted and timely
replay. At the same time, the volume of data increases drastically. Investigations about this special data type are about to begin.

Once all the new data types and their access functions have been tested
thoroughly, it is time to think about their integration into an object-oriented
data model. This should be much easier than with the relational model. It
should also be easier to design and implement new applications using the
object-oriented DBMS. The user interface can be enhanced with sophisticated
query and browsing facilities. In addition to that applications can be built to
provide higher-level objects like documents or hypertext to the user - including
the operations to access and manipulate them. Enough experience should be
available then to discuss new storage methods and devices, such as optical
disk, that may be more appropriate for multimedia data than the standard magnetic disk, for their integration into the new DBMS.

ACKNOWLEDGEMENT

We would like to thank the anonymous referees for their comments that were very helpful
in improving the paper.

REFERENCES

BB82   Ballard, D.H., and Brown, C.M., *Computer Vision,* Prentice-Hall, Englewood
        Cliffs, 1982.

CF79   Chang, N.S., and Fu, K.S., "Query-by-pictorial-example," in *Proc. COMPSAC 79*
        (Chicago, IL, 1979), pp. 325-330, also *IEEE Trans. on Software Engineering,* vol.
        SE-6, 1980, pp. 519-524.

CF80   Chang, N.S., and Fu, K.S., "A Query Language for Relational Image Database Systems," in *Proc. IEEE Workshop on Picture Data Description and Management* (Asilomar, CA, Aug. 1980), IEEE Computer Society, catalog no. 80CH1530-5, pp. 68-73.

CF81   Chang, N.S., and Fu, K.S., "Picture Query Languages for Pictorial Information Systems," *IEEE Computer,* vol. 14, no. 11, Nov. 1981, pp. 23-33.

Ch76   Chamberlin, D.D., et al., "SEQUEL2: A Unified Approach to Data Definition, Manipulation and Control," *IBM Journal of Research and Development,* vol. 20, 1976, pp. 560-575.

Ch86   Christodoulakis, S., Theodoridou, M., Ho, F., Papa, M., and Pathria, A., "Multimedia Document Presentation, Information Extraction, and Document Formation in MINOS: A Model and a System," *ACM Trans. on Office Information Systems,* vol. 4, no. 4, Oct. 1986, pp. 345-383.

CK81   Chang, S.-K., and Kunii, T.K., "Pictorial Data-Base Systems," *IEEE Computer,* vol. 14, no. 11, Nov. 1981, pp. 13-19.

Co79   Codd, E.F., "Extending the Database Relational Model to Capture More Meaning," *ACM Trans. on Database Systems,* vol. 4, no. 4, Dec. 1979, pp. 397-434.

CRM77   Chang, S.K., Reuss, J., and McCormick, B.H., "An Integrated Relational Database System for Pictures," in *Proc. IEEE Workshop on Picture Data Description and Management,* (Chicago, IL, Apr. 1977), IEEE Computer Society, catalog no. 77CH1187-4C, pp. 49-60.

Di87   Dittrich, K.R., "Object-Oriented Database Systems," in *Entity-Relationship Approach,* ed. S. Spaccapietra, North-Holland, Amsterdam 1987, pp. 51-66.

Fa85   Faloutsos, C., "Access Methods for Text," *ACM Computing Surveys,* vol. 17, no. 1, March 1985, pp. 49-74.

Gi87   Gibbs, S., Tsichritzis, D., Fitas, A., Konstantas, D., and Yeorgaroudakis, Y., "Muse: A Multimedia Filing System," *IEEE Software,* vol. 4, no. 2, March 1987, pp. 4-15.

Gr84   Grosky, W.I., "Toward a Data Model for Integrated Pictorial Databases," *Computer Vision, Graphics, and Image Processing,* vol. 25, no. 3, March 1984, pp. 371-382.

HL82   Haskin, R., and Lorie, R., "On Extending the Functions of a Relational Database System," in *Proc. ACM SIGMOD Conf.* (June 1982), pp. 207-212.

Ka88   Katz, B., "Using English for Indexing and Retrieval," in *Proc. RIAO 88* (Cambridge, MA, March 1988), pp. 314-332.

KCB88   Kim, W., Chou, H.-T., and Banerjee, J., "Operations and Implementation of Complex Objects," *IEEE Trans. on Software Engineering,* vol. 14, no. 7, July 1988, pp. 985-996.

Ke79   Kent, W., "Limitations of Record-Based Information Models," *ACM Trans. on Database Systems,* vol. 4, no. 1, Jan. 1979, pp. 107-131.

KSW79   Kropp, D., Schek, H.-J., and Walch, G., "Text Field Indexing," in *Datenbanktechnologie,* ed. J. Niedereichholz, Teubner, Berichte des German Chapter of the ACM, vol. 2, Stuttgart 1979, pp. 101-115.

522   *K. Meyer-Wegener et al.*

KW81   Kropp, D., and Walch, G., "A Graph Structured Text Index," *Information Processing and Management,* vol. 17, no. 6, 1981, pp. 363-376.

LC80   Lin, B.S., and Chang, S.K., "GRAIN - A Pictorial Database Interface," in *Proc. IEEE Workshop on Picture Data Description and Management* (Asilomar, CA, Aug. 1980), IEEE Computer Society, catalog no. 80CH1530-5, pp. 83-88.

LF73   Lancaster, F.W., and Fayen, E.G., *Information Retrieval On-Line,* Melville Publ. Comp., Los Angeles, CA, 1973.

LH80   Lien, Y.E., and Harris, S.K., "Structured Implementation of an Image Query Language," in *Pictorial Information Systems,* eds. S.K. Chang and K.S. Fu, Springer-Verlag, Lecture Notes in Computer Science, vol. 80, pp. 416-430.

LU77   Lien, Y.E., and Utter, D.F., "Design of an Image Database," in *Proc. IEEE Workshop on Picture Data Description and Management* (Chicago, IL, Apr. 1977), IEEE Computer Society, catalog no. 77CH1187-4C, pp. 131-136.

LWH87   Lum, V.Y., Wu, C.T., and Hsiao, D.K., "Integrating Advanced Techniques into Multimedia DBMS," report no. NPS52-87-050, Naval Postgraduate School, Monterey, CA, Nov. 1987.

Ma87   Masunaga, Y., "Multimedia Databases: A Formal Framework," in *Proc. IEEE CS Office Automation Symposium* (Gaithersburg, MD, April 1987), IEEE CS Press, Washington, pp. 36-45.

Ni86   Niblack, W., *An Introduction to Digital Image Processing,* Prentice/Hall Intern., Englewood Cliffs, 1986.

OFS84   Ong. J., Fogg, D., and Stonebraker, M., "Implementation of Data Abstraction in the Relational Database System INGRES," *ACM SIGMOD Record,* vol. 14, no. 1, March 1984, pp. 1-14.

RFS88   Roussopoulos, N., Faloutsos, C., and Sellis, T., "An Efficient Pictorial Database System for PSQL," ul IEEE Trans. on Software Engineering, vol. 14, no. 5, May 1988, pp. 639-650.

RTI85   Relational Technology Inc., *INGRES Reference Manual,* Version 3.0, UNIX, October, 1985.

RTI87   Relational Technology Inc., *INGRES/Embedded SQL User's Guide,* Release 5.0, UNIX, 1987

Sh64   Sharp, H.S. (ed.), *Readings in Information Retrieval,* The Scarecrow Press, New York & London 1964.

SM83   Salton, G., and McGill, M.J., *Introduction to Modern Information Retrieval,* McGraw-Hill, New York 1983.

SR86   Stonebraker, M., and Rowe, L.A., "The Design of POSTGRES," in *Proc. ACM SIGMOD '86* (Washington, DC, May 1986), ed. C. Zaniolo, pp. 340-355.

St86   Stonebraker, M., "The Inclusion of New Types in Relational Database Systems," in *Proc. 2nd Int. Conf. on Database Engineering* (Los Angeles, CA, Feb. 1986), IEEE CS Press, Washington 1986, pp. 262-269.

Ta80a   Tang, G.Y., "A Logical Data Organization for the Integrated Database of Pictures and Alphanumerical Data," in *Proc. IEEE Workshop on Picture Data Description and Management* (Asilomar, CA, Aug. 1980), IEEE Computer Society, catalog no. 80CH1530-5, pp. 158-166.

Ta80b   Tamura, H., "Image Database Management for Pattern Information Processing Studies," in *Pictorial Information Systems,* eds. S.K. Chang and K.S. Fu, Springer-Verlag, Lecture Notes on Computer Science, vol. 80, Berlin 1980, pp. 198-227.

TII79   Takao, Y., Itoh, S., and Iisak, J., "An Image-Oriented Database System," in *Database Techniques for Pictorial Applications,* ed. A. Blaser, Springer-Verlag, Lecture Notes in Computer Science, vol. 81, Berlin 1979, pp. 527-538.

TM77   Tamura, H., and Mori, S., "A Data Management System for Manipulating Large Images," in *Proc. IEEE Workshop on Picture Data Description and Management* (Chicago, IL, April 1977), IEEE Computer Society, catalog no. 77CH1187-4C, pp. 45-54, extended version in *Int. Journal on Policy Analysis and Information Systems,* vol. 1, no. 2, Jan. 1978.

TY84   Tamura, H., and Yokoya, N., "Image Database Systems: A Survey," *Pattern Recognition,* vol. 17, no. 1, 1984, pp. 29-44.

WKL86   Woelk, D., Kim, W., and Luther, W., "An Object-Oriented Approach to Multimedia Databases," in *Proc. ACM SIGMOD '86 Int. Conf. on Management of Data* (Washington, D.C., May 1986), ed. C. Zaniolo, *ACM SIGMOD Record,* vol. 15, no. 2, pp. 311-325.

WK87   Woelk, D., and Kim, W., "Multimedia Information Management in an Object-Oriented Database System," in *Proc. 13th Int. Conf. on VLDB* (Brighton, England, Sept. 1987), eds. P.M. Stocker and W. Kent, Morgan Kaufmann Publishers, Los Altos, CA, 1987, pp. 319-329.

WLK87   Woelk, D., Luther, W., and Kim, W., "Multimedia Applications and Database Requirements," in *Proc. IEEE CS Office Automation Symposium* (Gaithersburg, MD, Apr. 1987), IEEE CS Press, order no. 770, Washington, 1987, pp. 180-189.

Visual Database Systems
T.L. Kunii (Editor)
Elsevier Science Publishers B.V. (North-Holland)
© IFIP, 1989

A VISUAL SYSTEM OF PLACING CHARACTERS
APPROPRIATELY IN MULTIMEDIA MAP DATABASES [†]

Hiromi AONUMA, Hiroshi IMAI and Yahiko KAMBAYASHI

Department of Computer Science & Communication Engineering
Kyushu University
Fukuoka, JAPAN

In multimedia databases, there arise problems of manipulating interactions between different media. Automatic character placing function is a user interface to handle such interactions between characters and graphics data, where these characters give names of or explain objects in figures. This function automatically places characters in figures at some appropriate place nicely so that meanings of the corresponding object becomes visually apparent. This paper investigates this function in multimedia geographical databases, and discusses algorithms for it, which are based on the methods of computational geometry.

1. Introduction

As needs of database users are becoming increasingly sophisticated, multimedia databases have been studied extensively in recent years. However, most of the attention has been directed towards methods for storing and retrieving each of multimedia, such as sound, images, graphics, characters, etc., rather separately. That is, most of existing multimedia databases are just a direct sum of databases for each medium, and hence do not have enough power to cope with those sophisticated needs. An ideal multimedia database system should handle different media interactively, although such new problems on many kinds of interactions between different media have not yet been fully considered.

In this paper we discuss the interaction of graphics data and character data, and describe a user interface which beautifully and neatly displays a drawing by combining them automatically. Here, characters should be placed in appropriate positions so that names or some explanations of the corresponding object in graphics data become visually obvious. The interaction problem is then to place characters fast with satisfying the requirement. We call this user interface an "*automatic character placing function*" (ACPF, in short). ACPF receives graphic and character data and integrates them to realize the interface (Fig.1.1). This kind of user interface has been introduced by Kambayashi and Arikawa [11] in a more general setting where modeling the multimedia database has been investigated extensively. This paper gives an algorithmic approach to it.

It is very useful to manage drawings, such as geographical maps for various purposes, logic circuit diagrams, equipment layout in plants or powerstations, etc., by multimedia databases with such user interfaces. For example, in

---

[†] Part of this work was supported by the Grant in Aid for Scientific Research of the Ministry of Education, Science and Culture of Japan.

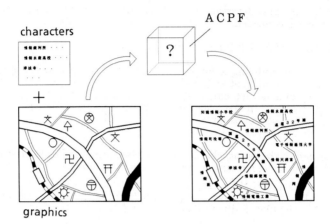

Fig.1.1 Automatic character placing function (ACPF)

multimedia geographical databases, it is now possible to display a map of any specified region. When displaying a certain prefecture, some small parts of neighboring prefectures would appear simultaneously, and prefecture names of each of those parts should be shown in those small parts automatically. Also, in treating layouts in plants or powerstation, the layouts are often updated. If characters in them can be automatically handled accordingly, maintaining such layouts becomes much easier.

Although such a user interface is really useful, it is a rather difficult task in terms of both time and labor to incorporate characters, which describe parts of the image, into these drawings.

In this paper, we focus on maps as particularly interesting multimedia objects. This is because the amount of picture data is huge, and its distribution on the plane is not uniform, so that geographical maps appear to be a subject general enough for implementing ACPF.

This paper proceeds as follows. In Section 2, we will describe the background and examine the role of ACPF in map databases in detail, then, considering the role and the way to use it, enumerate the specifications required for ACPF.
In Section 3, we first classify constructive elements of a map into three: points, polygonal lines and regions. Then this section presents algorithms to find an appropriate place (or places) of characters for a constructive element in each of three classes. The algorithms are called "fundamental algorithms", and do not consider interactions between places of characters of different elements, which will be considered in the next section.
In Section 4, making use of the layout made by fundamental algorithms, we will show some idea for an overall algorithm. The algorithm integrates the individual placement, where, the algorithm tries to find intersections of characters, and avoiding them in some way. We call this algorithm a "global algorithm". In this paper, we mainly discuss a basic idea of the global algorithm for points. This idea can be generalized to other cases.

2. The necessity of ACPF

In this section we first describe the background of this research, and then the reason why ACPF is needed.

2.1 Background of ACPF for map databases

In recent years, visualizing a large amount of scientific data becomes a very popular field (McCormick, et al. [17]). A map includes much more information in a compact way and is also easier to recognize compared with a collection of numbers or strings. In geographical information processing (GIP), many databases that process maps have been realized. These systems deal with characters using the following methods:

* by scanning the maps, characters are also stored and displayed as part of the image (Kato, Kanai and Yamashita [13], Inaba [9]),

* each character of the string is at a fixed location in a world-coordinate system, and is displayed using the terminal font (Roussoupoulos, et al. [21], Tanaka [22], Fujitsu [5]), or as vector picture,

* using windows, characters are isolated from picture or image (Kidode, Tsunekawa [15], Uryu, et al. [24])

and so on. In most systems, it seems that methods to deal with characters in a flexible and visually understandable way are not fully considered. We will describe why these methods by themselves are not sufficient for intelligent visual map databases in Section 2.2.

Other researchers have considerd the question of what language and data structures are necessary for a database to dynamically create a map from a user query (Roussoupoulos, et al. [21], Orenstein [19]). These authors just mentioned that the object names should be displayed on the picture to assist the user in visualizing their correspondence, but gave no algorithms for that purpose.

In other fields, there are some "ACPF-like" functions. These are:
* an application program to place atomic names to crystallographic (Cambrudge [2]),
* a browser for directed graphs (Lawrence, et al. [16]),
* design capture for CAD (IBM [6], Sumitomo [23]),

etc., however not for maps. We are also considering ACPF in implementing SOVF in multimedia database systems, and our approach is general enough to apply to other multimedia systems.

2.2 Specifications required for ACPF

In the following we describe two main reasons why ACPF is necessary in map databases:
   (1) for automating geographical information processing,
   (2) for building an interactive map system,
and then consider what is required for ACPF.

<Role of ACPF>

(1)Automating geographical information processing

In geographical information processing (GIP), data sources such as maps or photographs of remote sensing devices are first digitized. GIP then stores and transforms the data, and finally produces outputs offering useful information. In the past, the main object of GIP was to produce printed maps, but now carto-graphic databases are being designed to answer various advanced queries by users. Even now, however, placing characters on a map is done by hand, as it requires special sense and skill. Since this is very costly, it is desirable to automate the process to make maps to be stored in database (Nagy, Wagle [18]). Thus, in this case, graphic data and character data are first given to ACPF, then ACPF places the characters nicely and outputs a map. (In the following

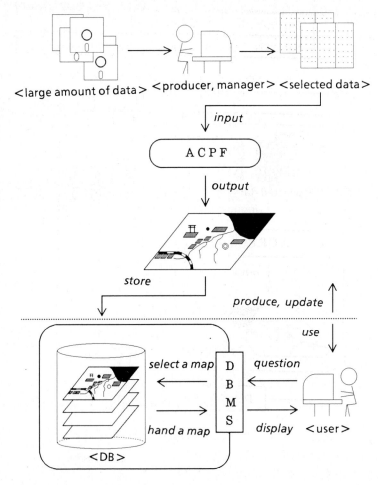

Fig.2.1 Role of ACPF in geographical information processing

process or usage of the database, this new information is dealt with as attributes of each character.) As the last step, they index each of the maps made at the second step, and store them in the databases, together with the local information of characters. After producing a database, when a user wants to see a map, the database selects one of those maps and displays it. Moreover, adding to this preprocessing, ACPF can be used in updating maps. See Fig.2.1.

(2)Building an interactive map system

The second reason why ACPF is necessary is that it is used in an interactive map system with a "*semantic overview function* (SOVF)" (Kambayashi, Arikawa

name	location	height	Importance
Mt. Fuji	Lat. *OO*N, Long. *OO*E	3776	1
Mt. Aso	Lat. *XX*N, Long. *XX*E	1024	3

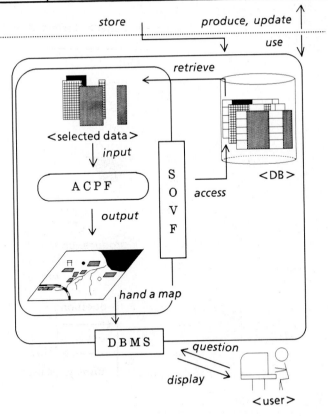

Fig.2.2 Role of ACPF in the semantic overview function

[11]). In general, conventional map systems in GIP only retrieves stored data. SOVF, on the other hand, responds to users dynamically, and constructs an appropriate answer from partially processed data. The information to be displayed is selected according to various requirements of users (namely a certain district, magnification factor, and purpose). So placing different characters and graphics data each time requires an ACPF. See Fig.2.2.

For example, it does *"semantic reduction / magnification"* explained below. If a map is reduced simply geometrically, there occur many troubles as follows:

* The characters or symbols may become too small to read. (by reduction)
* The drawing may become very complicated. (by reduction)
* The time to display a map may be too long, because of the large quantity of data in a map. (by reduction)
* The map may be very sparse. (by magnification)
* The characters may be so big as having no sense. (by magnification)

Consider the map shown in Fig.2.3(a). Fig.2.3(b) shows a map obtained by geometric reduction of Fig.2.3(a). In this figure characters are very hard to read. In order to keep the character size we have to handle the intersection problem as shown in Fig.2.3(c).

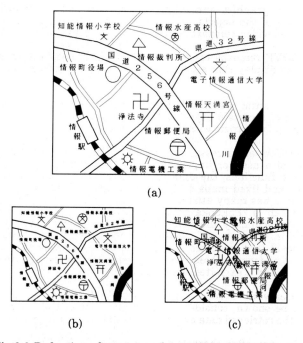

(a)

(b)   (c)

Fig.2.3 Reductions from (a) to (b), (c): (b) geometric reduction, (c) reduction with maintaining the size of characters

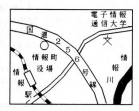

Fig.2.4 Semantic reduction

On the other hand, at the semantic reduction / magnification, the information is selected according to the reduced scale, purpose, and so on (Fig.2.4). To be concrete, at a semantic reduction/magnification, SOVF does following processes:

* The characters and symbols are kept in a certain size.

* The threshold of Importance to display or not is set by the reduction scale or the purpose. For example, in a drive map, even less important roads must be displayed.

* The data of graphics are approximated according to the reduction scale.

* The size of graphics and characters are determined according to the Importance of the objects. For example, the more important roads are represented wider, compared with the less important one.

In this way, SOVF removes complicated parts, and then the map can be a readable one and displayed in a moderate time, even if reduced or magnified by any factor.

Adding to the semantic reduction/magnification, SOVF does emphasization or characterization of a certain object, say making a map for drivers with traffic facilities or a map for tourists with many sightseeing spots.

All of these functions are necessary for making a map that is easy to read and fit to the purpose of a user, or implementing interactive response. In order to implement these functions, the data in database are "half processed" (unlike fully processed and fixed maps as (1)) which means that each object in the geographical data has many attributes attached to it. For example, the object the name of which is "Fukuoka city" has attributes as the name, the sets of coordinates of the boundary, the population in it, the address of the city hall, and so on. In addition, "Importance" is associated with each object. "Importance" is, literally, the level that indicates how important the class to which the object belongs is in the real world. This may be represented in partially ordered tree as shown in Fig.2.5, and is exploited in the selection step of SOVF.

Every time a user wants to see a specified map, SOVF, using the DBMS, selects what object to be shown, considering the importance of each object, and then ACPF accepts the retrieved data and composes them into a map.

Contrary to (1), even after characters are inputted in ACPF and formed into a map, characters will have no fixed location. Maps are formed, displayed and then "abandoned" every time.

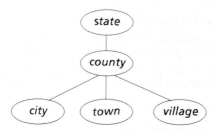

Fig.2.5 Importance graph of administrative districts

<specifications required for ACPF>

Considering the role and the circumstance, ACPF for (1) has to do minute layout, on the other hand ACPF for (2) should do a fast processing. Apparently, the case of (2) - interactive map systems - is the more sophisticated and interesting visual database, so that our main purpose is fairly directed towards making ACPF for (2). Then the speed of the algorithms is also very important, even if the information in a map is relatively less.

In the following, we discuss the function, assuming that the data are already selected, and then the job is to combine them into a map. We first try to express mathematically what is the beautiful and neat placement for each symbol. After that, we examine the way to avoid the intersections between character - character, or character - graphics. Our algorithms are based on the methods of computational geometry.

3. Fundamental algorithms

We will construct ACPF by combining following two kinds of algorithms.

  1. fundamental algorithm ······determines an initial position of characters
  for each constructive element.

  2. global algorithm ·············avoids the intersections among characters
  placed by fundamental algorithms.

Here, a "constructive element" means a unit of graphics (e.g., a polygon that represents a prefecture, a symbol that represents a school), and it represents an object (e.g., a prefecture, a river, a public institution) in the real world. A constructive element is a minimal element of graphics that can make sense.

Constructive elements are divided into three types according to the geometry of the objects as follows.

  Point: the signs of public institutions, small circles that represent where
            the place names indicate, and so on.

  Line: the sequences of line segments, that represent rivers, rails, and
            roads, and so on.

  Region: the polygons that represent administrative districts, coast lines of
            islands, and so on.

To make fundamental algorithms, we determine the strategies to place characters for each constructive element as follows.

for Point: To place the string "near" the Point.

for Line: To place each of characters individually "along" a part of the Line, that part verges on a straight line.

for Region: To place the characters approximately around the "center" of the Region in human sense, and if possible, "inside" the Region.

We adopt these strategies taking account of the possibility that characters can be placed in appropriate positions so that names or explanations of the corresponding object in graphics data becomes visually obvious. Actually, it looks that many published maps were made under these strategies (Keates [14], Imhof [8], Robinson [20]).

Fundamental algorithms implement the placement strategies by some mathematical computation considering only one corresponding constructive element. In other words, fundamental algorithms give some candidates orderly where to place characters to the constructive element, and then a general algorithm selects one among these candidates taking account of interactions.

In the following, we will describe fundamental algorithms for Region, Line, and Point.

3.1 Fundamental algorithm for Region

At first we consider about Region. Here, we consider a Region as a polygon, and a string as a rectangle (mostly with sides parallel to the axis) the lengths of which vertical and horizontal segments are A and B, respectively. To implement the strategy mentioned above, we come up with the following methods for a fundamental algorithm.

(1) Compute the "central point of the polygon" such as

(1-a) the center of gravity

(1-b) the geodestic center

and make it the center of the string. Here, the geodestic center of a simple polygon is a point inside the polygon which minimizes the maximum internal distance to any point in the polygon. The center of gravity is not necessarily contained in the polygon, while the geodestic center is contained by the definition, and might be preferable as a representative point.

(2) Enclose the polygon with a rectangle, for example,

(2-a) rectangle with sides parallel to the axis (Fig.3.1(a))

(2-b) rectangle with minimum width (Fig.3.1(b))

(2-c) rectangle with minimum area

and let the center of the rectangle that of the string.

(3) Find the maximum rectangle contained in the polygon, such that the ratio of that vertical segments to horizontal segments is A to B, then use the center of the maximum rectangle as the center of the string (from now on, we call such a rectangle an "A-B rectangle" in short). See Fig.3.1(c).

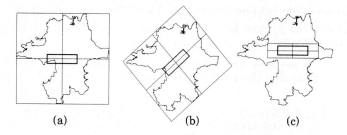

(a)　　　　　　　(b)　　　　　　　(c)

Fig.3.1　Placing characters to a Region

Let n be the number of points of the polygon. Then algorithms are known to compute (1-a) and all of (2) in $O(n)$ time, and (1-b) in $O(n \log n)$ time (e.g., see [10]).

In these methods, (3) might be better, because it seems to place the string of characters near the center of the polygon in human sense. What is even better, it guarantees that the strings are always placed in the polygon if possible, and that the strings in the same level (e.g., the names of prefectures) then do not intersect one another. In addition, we can make the strings of the same level Region, the uniform size as the smallest Region.

The outline of the algorithm for (3) is as follows.

step 1. (transforming the polygon)

We first transform the polygon by a scaling mapping f

$$f: (x, y) \rightarrow (Ax/B, y)$$

For example, in Fig.3.2, the polygon R is transformed into R'. The rectangle for the string is transformed into a square.

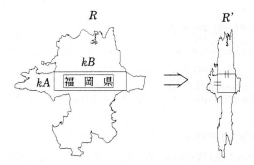

Fig.3.2　Transformation $R \rightarrow R'$

step 2. (finding the maximum empty square)

By the transformation in step 1, we have only to find the maximum square contained in the polygon R' with sides parallel to the axis (we will call this square the maximum empty square), which corresponds to the maximum A-B rectangle in R.

step 3. (recovering the polygon R' to R, and placing the rectangle)

Transform again the polygon by $(f)^{-1}$ then place the string in the center of the maximum A-B rectangle.

step 1 and **step 3** are easy and to perform in $O(n)$ time. Therefore in the following, assuming that the polygon is already transformed by f, we focus on **step 2**.

In order to do step 2 efficiently, we use $L\infty$ Voronoi diagram of line segments. So in the following, we first introduce $L\infty$ Voronoi diagram, then investigate the properties of it, and finally consider how to make it.

(After this paper was accepted, the authors noticed a paper by Fortune [4], in an oral communicatrion with him, which solved this problerm in a more general setting before. Our result was obtained independently, but we should also note that it is based on the previous work of Fortune [3]. Here, to make the paper complete and since we are interested in a simple case of locating a maximum empty square, we will briefly describe the result below.)

3.1.1 L∞Voronoi diagram of line segments

<L∞-distance of two points>
The $L\infty$-distance $d\infty(P_1, P_2)$ of two points $P_1 = (x_1, y_1)$ and $P_2 = (x_2, y_2)$ in the plane is defined by

$$d\infty(P_1, P_2) = \max(|x_1 - x_2|, |y_1 - y_2|)$$

Throughout this section, $L\infty$-distance is denoted by distance.

<L∞-distance between a line and a point>
The $L\infty$-distance $d\infty(l, P)$ between a line segment l and a point P is defined by

$$d\infty(l, P) = \min\{d\infty(l, Q)\} \quad (Q : \text{point on } l)$$

It is equal to the length of the edge of a square whose vertex is on P, and that touches l.

<L∞Voronoi diagram of line segments>
For a set of n line segments l_i $(i=1,..,n)$ (to be called generators in the following) in the plane, the Voronoi region of l_i in the $L\infty$-distance is defined by

$$Vn(l_i) = \cap_{j \neq i}\{P \mid d\infty(l_i, P) < d\infty(l_j, P)\}$$

The planar skeleton Vn formed by the boundaries of $Vn(l_i)$ $(i=1,..,n)$ is called the Voronoi diagram. Voronoi points are points equidistant to at least three generators.

3.1.2 Maximum empty square and Voronoi diagram

The Voronoi point (P) of the Voronoi diagram of three segments l_1, l_2, l_3 is equidistance to the three generators, then P is the center of the square that touches the three generators, and does not contain them.

It is readily seen that the maximum empty square in a polygon must touch at least three edges. If we construct a Voronoi diagram in a polygon, considering the n edges as generators (Fig.3.3), we see that the Voronoi points are the candidates for the center of the maximum empty square, because a square that touches three genarators but does not have the corresponding Voronoi point necessarily contains other generator(s). The number of Voronoi points in a polygon with n edges is $O(n)$, which follows from Euler's formula. Thus, if the Voronoi diagram is at hand, we can get the maximum empty square in $O(n)$ time, by investigating the all Voronoi points in the polygon. Hence, the complexity to compute the Voronoi diagram dominates the complexity to get a maximum empty square.

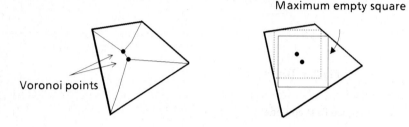

Fig.3.3 Voronoi diagram in a polygon

3.1.3 How to compute a Voronoi diagram

Now, we will describe how to compute a Voronoi diagram, first for two generators, next for n generators.

The locus of the points equidistant from two segments l_1, l_2 is called the bisector B_{12}. It is derived by tracing the center point of a square that touches l_1 and l_2 (Fig.3.4). A bisector consists of three segments and two lines (Fig.3.5).

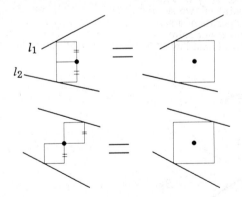

Fig.3.4 Points equidistant from two segments

A Voronoi diagram is computed by handling the overlap of B_{ij} ($i \neq j$). For n generators, there exist $n(n-1)/2$ bisectors. So the problem becomes how we can treat them efficiently. We can execute this in $O(n \log n)$ time by using the sweepline algorithm (Fortune [3]).

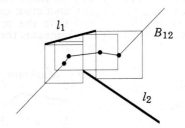

Fig.3.5 Bisector of two segments

In this algorithm, we first consider a mapping $* : R^2 \to R^2$ defined by

$$* \, (x, y) = (x, y + d_\infty((x, y), l))$$

where $d_\infty((x, y), l)$ means the minimum distance between point (x, y) and all generators.$*$ maps a bisector B_{ij} to B^*_{ij}, and does Voronoi region $Vn(l_i)$ to $Vn^*(l_i)$, fixing all generators as they are.

Vn^* and B^*_{ij} keep some good properties, that are necessary to apply the sweepline algorithm of Fortune for Euclidean Voronoi diagram of lines. What is better, a bisector in L_∞-Voronoi diagram consists of lines and segments, so that it is easier to compute a Voronoi diagram, compared with a bisector consisting of lines and parabolas in Euclidean Voronoi diagram.

The nice property of B^*_{ij} is that any point in B^*_{ij} is not lower than the highest-lower-endpoint of two segments l_i, l_j, where lower-endpoint means the lower one of two endpoints of a segment, and highest-lower-endpoint means the higher one of two lower-endpoints of two segments. So any point in transformed Voronoi region $Vn^*(l_i)$ is not lower than the lower-endpoint of l_i.

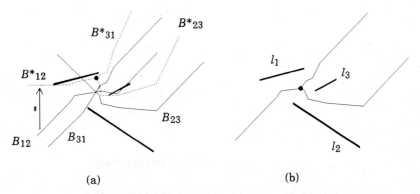

(a)   (b)

Fig.3.6 (a) Bisectors and transformed bisectors
(b) Voronoi diagram

Scanning the plane from bottom to top, we consider the bisector B_{ij} when the sweepline hits a lower-endpoint of l_i, where l_j is a neighboring generator. At this

time we take the intersections with other bisectors, then on the scanning
investigate where these are actually transformed Voronoi points or not.

Because a transformed Voronoi diagram has the same incidence structure as a
Voronoi diagram, we can get Voronoi points from this diagram.

Fig.3.6(a) shows segments l_1, l_2, l_3 and their bisectors, broken lines in (a) are the
transformed bisectors. (b) shows the Voronoi diagram of the three segments.

3.2 Fundamental algorithm for Line and Point

We now consider the other two elements, Line and Point. First, consider the case
of Line. Considering a Line as digitized curve, and a string of characters as
regular squares, the number of which is the same as the number of the
characters. We adopt the following method to implement the strategy: Cover a
portion of the Line with the rectangles with a specified length, and find the part
covered with the thinnest rectangles. The outline of the algorithm is as follows.

step 1. Considering the number and size of characters, calculate the length L of
the covering rectangle. Here, L represents the length needed for placing the
characters (Fig.3.7).

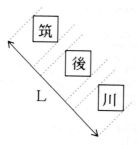

Fig.3.7 The length needed to place characters

step 2. Cover the digitized curve with the rectangle of length L, and find the part
that can be covered with the thinnest rectangle (Fig.3.8).

step 3. Let the part covered with the thinnest rectangle be the first candidate,
and the second one the second candidate, and so on.

After finding the appropriate part to place characters, put regular squares along
the part. We can execute this algorithm in $O(n^2 \log n)$ time, using a convex-hull
algorithm.

Placing the string for Point is simple. We just adopt the (right, left, upper,
lower) rectangle touching to the Point, as the candidates of positions for the
string in this order (Yoeli [25]). This process can be executed in a constant time.

The details of the above algorithms are shown in [1].

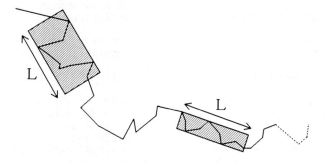

Fig.3.8 Covering Line by rectangles

4. Global algorithms for a point set

The fundamental algorithms mentioned in Section 3 are, so to speak, "fragments of algorithms" or "tools for ACPF", because they do not take it into consideration, the interaction with other strings or constructive elements. In the following sections, we will design "global algorithms". A global algorithm is constructed by compiling fundamental algorithms under some strategy, considering the interaction with other strings and constructive elements. In that process, it may have to do some selection of objects to display in order to avoid intersections.

To begin with, we will consider the problem of character layout adapted to a point set. Such an algorithm is effective for "town maps" with a reduced scale 1/10000, which display mainly the names of buildings, if the intersections are not considered with graphics as roads, rails, certain boundary, and so on [26]. Our algorithm is based on graph theory and computational geometry. At the end of this section we mention extensions of this approach to other objects.

In Section 4.1, we describe some terms of graph theory used in the algorithm. In Section 4.2, we will show an algorithm to determine whether all the strings can be placed under the condition that the degree of freedom for a string given to a Point is 2, where this condition means that, for example, the string to each point can be placed either its right side or its left side. We will call this version of the problem "checking the placing possibility with 2-freedoms." In Section 4.3, we will suggest a measure against the cases such that it is impossible to place all strings with 2-freedoms.

4.1 Intersection graph and an independent set of maximally possible size

We first describe some terms used in the algorithm.

<intersection graph>
An intersection graph of objects in the plane is obtained by identifying each object with a vertex, and connecting two vertices by an edge iff their corresponding objects intersect. Fig.4.1(a) shows a graph consisting of only vertical and

horizontal lines. The graph in Fig.4.1(b) consists of vertices corresponding to these lines and edges indicating their intersection.

<matching>
In a graph $G=(V, E)$ (V: set of vertex, E: set of edges), a subset X of E is called a matching in G if no two edges in X share a common vertex in G (the bold lines in Fig.4.1(b)).

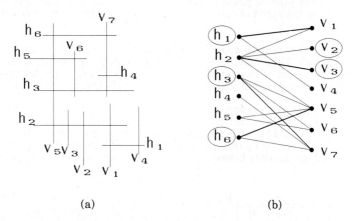

(a)   (b)

Fig.4.1 Intersection graph, matching, independent set: bold lines denote a matching and circles an independent set

<independent set>
In a graph $G=(V, E)$, a subset S of V is called an independent set of G if no two vertices of S are adjacent in G (the vertices with cicles in Fig.4.1(b)).

<an independent set of maximally possible size>
Let $G=(V, E)$ be a graph with n vertices. Let X be a matching of G. For each $u \in V$, we define mate(u) to be v if there is an edge $\{u,v\} \in X$ and to be nil otherwise. A vertex u with mate(u)=nil is called unmatched. Apparently, the size of a maximum independent set of G is at most $n-|X|$. Further, if there is an independent set S of G of size $n-|X|$, then, for each edge $\{u,v\} \in X$, exactly one of $\{u,v\}$ is an element of S (Imai, Asano [7]).

4.2 Placing with 2-freedoms

Originally, the candidates where to place characters exist continuously around the Point, and the number of candidates is infinite. But in order to deal the maps with computers efficiently, we may make the problem discrete by limiting possible positions for each string of characters. Typical possible positions would be right, left, upper, lower sides of the Point as well as upper-right, upper-left, lower-right, lower-left sides of the Point. This case consists of 8 possible positions. We may avoid intersections by moving the characters placed at one of these positions infinitesimally, but we will not consider such continuous movements and restrict ourselves in a discrete setting. However, even if the problem is restricted to this discrete version, it is still too difficult to choose one position among several candidates for each string without making any intersections because of combinatorial explosions.

Hence we further limit the candidates to the highest two, say "right" and "left", because the problem to check the placing possibility with 3-freedoms is demonstrated to belong NP-complete (Kato, Imai [12]). Of course, restricting possible positions of each string to two, choices are limited and it becomes harder to place all the characters without intersections. But, due to this restriction, we can determine the placing possibility efficiently as described below (the readers should note that the speed of executing ACPF is very important as described in Section 2.2).

In this examination, at first we make an intersection graph of $2n$ strings (n: the number of Points). Then making use of the algorithm to determine the existence of an independent set of maximally possible size (e.g., see Imai, Asano[7]), we examine the placing possibility at high speed. We now describe the details.

<how to make the intersection graph>
As shown in Fig.4.2, the rectangle L and R are the "box" for Point P_k, in one of them the string should be placed. Then we consider rectangles L_k and R_k as the candidates for P_k, where L_k includes L and P_k, and R_k does R and P_k. This is to avoid intersections not only between string - string but also string - Point.

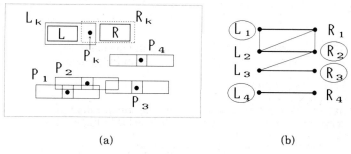

(a)   (b)

Fig.4.2 Intersection graph of strings for a point set

Assuming two candidates for each Point, identify each candidate with a vertex, and connect two vertices by an edge, iff their corresponding candidates intersect. Further, match the sets of two candidates L_k, R_k that belong to the same Point.

<determining the placing possibility>
Let $G=(V, E)$ be the intersection graph of $2n$ rectangles L_k and R_k. The number of vertices of G is $2n$, and the size of matching X is n. The size of a maximum independent set of G is at most $2n-|X|=n$. The two vertices corresponding to the same Point are matched, and the two vertices the corresponding rectangles intersect are connected by an edge. Considering these facts and the condition for the existence of an independent set of maximally possible size, if there is an independent set of size n, it means that we can adopt exactly one candidate for every Point. Namely, we can place strings for all n Points, right or left side of them, respectively, without any intersections.

Fig.4.2(b) shows the intersection graph for the drawing of Fig.4.2(a). The vertices circled are the member of the independent set of maximally possible size. Then, it can be seen that we can place names for all Points in Fig.4.2.

The problem of placing possibility with 2-freedoms can be converted to that of 2-satisfiability in logic. We explain this by an example. Assume the drawing is like Fig.4.2(a). Define a logical variable x_i as follows: When the rectangle L_i is used, x_i is defined to be true (or, 1) and when the rectangle R_i is used x_i is false (0; or, x_i is true). We consider that L_i and R_i corresponds to x_i and x_i, respectively. Since the two intersecting rectangles should not be adopted at the same time, for each pair of intersecting rectangles, at most one of two corresponding variables is true. Hence, one of two rectangles for each Point can be placed without intersections if the following is true for some assignment to x_1, x_2, x_3 (note that each term in the brackets corresponds to an edge of the intersection graph):

$$(\overline{x_1 \wedge x_2}) \wedge (\overline{\overline{x_1} \wedge x_2}) \wedge (\overline{\overline{x_1} \wedge \overline{x_2}}) \wedge (\overline{\overline{x_2} \wedge x_3}) \qquad (1)$$

(1) can be transformed to

$$(\overline{x_1} \vee \overline{x_2}) \wedge (x_1 \vee \overline{x_2}) \wedge (x_1 \vee x_2) \wedge (x_2 \vee \overline{x_3}) \qquad (2)$$

The 2-satisfiability problem is to decide whether there exists an assignment x_k ($x_k = 1$, or 0 ; $k = 1,2,...m$) to make the value of (2) 1. This decision corresponds to whether we can place all the strings for each Point in the drawing. In general, the boolean expression of the satisfiability problem is given like

$$E = E_1 E_2 .... E_m$$

If E_i ($i = 1,2,...m$) contains at most two literals which are variables or their negations, the problem is called "2-satisfiability", and the number of literals is three 3-satisfiability. It is well known that the problem of 2-satisfiability can be solved in polynomial time (and hence we can solve the problem on the intersection graph in a similar way).

<complexity of determining the possibility at 2-freedoms>
We have mentioned that the placing possibility with 2-freedoms can be checked in polynomial time on the intersection graph. Especially in this case, we can solve the problem faster, using the geometric characteristics. Imai, Asano [7] have shown an algorithm to determine the existence of an independent set of maximally possible size in $O(n (\log n)^2)$ time by making the intersection graph implicitly with a geometric data structure. Applying the algorithm, this problem also can be computed in the same time complexity.

4.3 Selections to avoid intersections

Once it is observed to be impossible to place strings for all n Points under the condition that the degree of freedom of each string is 2, we must select which characters are to be displayed. For this selection, there are two principles to solve:

    (1) display as much strings as possible

    (2) display the more important one of two intersecting strings

We must solve the maximum independent set problem on the intersection graph to solve (1), and that is one of NP-complete problems well known. On the other hand, to solve (2) means to solve the lexicographically maximum independent set problem on the intersection graph, that can be solved in polynomial time. Of course a map made on principle(2) is much more useful and easy to recognize. Hence we should take account of the Importance among the objects, and delete some strings.

In the following, we present an algorithm to select strings based on principle(2), using repeatedly the checking placing possibility algorithm mentioned above. Suppose that n objects in the map are sorted in the order of Importance; object(1) is the most important object in the map (e.g., the name of prefecture), and object(2) the second, and so on. Also Rects(i) denote the two candidates where to place strings of object(i). Vertices(i) denotes the two vertices in the intersection graph corresponding to Rects(i). S is the list of i where the name of object(i) can be placed. We also consider three procedures which work as follows:

MAKE($G(i)$) makes intersection graph $G(i)$ among Rects(i) and Rects(k) ($k \in S$), that is, add Vertices(i) and all edges incident upon Vertices(i) to intersection graph $IG(i-1)$ at the $(i-1)$-th stage in the process of the algorithm.

CHECK($G(i)$) returns "true" if $G(k)$ has an independent set of maximally possible size, and otherwise does "false."

DELETE(i) deletes Vertices(i) and all edges incident upon them from $G(i)$.

Algorithm   Select strings to display

```
        begin
            S := ∅
            Do  i = 1  to  n
                begin
                    MAKE(G(i))
                    if CHECK(G(i)) = true then
                        add i to S
                    else
                        DELETE(i)
                    IG(i) := G(i)
                end
        end
```

After this selection, we display the names of object(i) at one of Rects(i) corresponding to the vertices that are the member of independent set of $IG(n)$.

In this algorithm, the intersention graph is updated step by step, and the "impossible" rectangles Rects(i), which can not be located at the i-th stage, are no longer investigated. Since the k-th step can be done in $O(k \log^2 k)$ time, entirely it costs

$$\sum_{k=1}^{n} O(k \log^2 k) = O(n^2 \log^2 n) \quad (n: \text{number of points})$$

time. Since the graph is updated from $IG(i-1)$ to $G(i)$ locally as above, we may utilize this fact to enhance the practical efficiency of the algorithm.

In the remaining part of this section, we briefly discuss how the global algorithm can be also applied to Lines and Regions.

To apply the algorithm discussed above to general maps, we make intersection graph including Lines and Regions. We must limit the candidates to the highest two for each Line and Region, the same as a Point, assuming those candidates are already computed by fundamental algorithms. What we have to do in making the intersection graph are :

At a Region: Deal the two rectangles of string in the same way as that of Points.

At a Line: The string are decomposed to each character. Then we investigate the intersection on every regular square, while representing the group of regular squares as one vertex in the intersection graph.

In this way, the 2-freedom algorithm can be applied to Line and Region similarly. Fig.4.3 shows a drawing and its intersection graph. We can place names at the candidates corresponding to the encircled vertices.

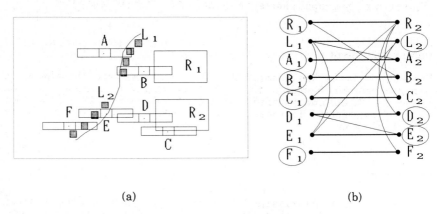

(a)   (b)

Fig.4.3 Intersection graph of strings

5. Concluding remarks

In this paper, we have focused the problem of automatically placing characters into a map that arises in multimedia database, and discussed how to manage it. Changing the fundamental algorithm appropriately, this method can be applied to many subjects, for example, naming the lines or gates in logic circuits scheme, identifying the equipments in plants design, making flow chart maps, etc.

By limiting the candidates to the highest two, ACPF can be executed in high speed, and also the algorithm can reflects the order of priority of candidates, namely, only the objects, one of whose highest two candidates can be placed, are displayed.

Our approach to the automatic character placing function lays stress on the speed of the algorithm as it is used to realize the semantic overview function in multimedia databases. But, in some cases, we may consider the trade-off between minuteness and fastness according to the purpose.

Now we are developing an interactive map system that realizes SOVF. In it, data is stored in a relational database system (SQL/DS) and retrieved according to queries of users. Especially, pictorial data is expressed in a vector form and is stored in the relational database system which can handle variable length data. Retrieved data is handled by ACPF, and finally displayed using a graphic tool (graPHIGS). The computer system is IBM 4341, and the program is written in PL/I.

Our final objective is to realize an entire geographical database system in which SOVF is combined as a powerful view system. Thus our research also covers the following topics.

* the input-output man - machine interface

* how to store the data for general purpose

* how to deal with relations for various scale factors

* appropreate approximation of polygonal lines

This advanced geographical database system will be reported elsewhere.

Acknowledgment

The authors would like to thank Mr. Masatoshi Arikawa, Mr. Masatomo Arimatsu and Mr. Nobuhiko Kojiro for their valuable discussions on the problem. IBM Co. Ltd. provided us with a computer system IBM 4341. The degitized Geographical Information is supplied by the Geographical Survey Institute of Japan.

References

[1] H. Aonuma: Automatic Character Displaying in Geographical Information Processing, *Graduation Thesis, Department of Computer Science and Communication Engineering, Kyushu University*, 1988 (in Japanese).

[2] Cambridge Crystallographic Database, Pratical Guide to Search Retrieval Analysis and Display, *Cambridge Crystallographic Data Centre, University Chemical Laboratory, Lensfield Road, Cambridge CB2 IEW, England*, 1979.

[3] S. Fortune: A Sweepline Algorithm for Voronoi Diagram, *Proc. 2nd ACM, Symp. on Comp. Geom*, pp. 313-322, 1986.

[4] S. Fortune: A Fast Algorithm for Polygon Containment by Translation, *Automata, Languages and Programming, in Springer-Verlag Lecture Notes in Computer Science*, Vol. 194, pp. 189–198, 1985.

[5] Fujitsu: An Introduction to ARISPLAN, 1988 (in Japanese).

[6] IBM: Computer-Integrated Electrical Design Series (CIEDS) *Command Reference Manual* Vol. 1, 1986.

[7] H. Imai and T. Asano: Efficient Algorithms for Geometric Graph Search Problems, *SIAM Journal on Computing*, Vol. 15, No. 2, pp. 478–494, 1986.

[8] E. Imhof: Positioning Names on Maps, *The American Cartographer*, Vol. 2, No. 2, pp. 128-144, 1975.

[9] N. Inaba: A Mapping system with high-speed scrolling, *NE report, Nikkei Electronics*, No. 451, pp. 98-99, 1988.

[10] M. Iri, T. Koshizuka, et al.: Computational Geometry and Geographical Information Processing, *bit supplement*, 1986 (in Japanese).

[11]   Y. Kambayashi and M. Arikawa: An Overview Function on Pictorial Databases and Its Realization. *Special Interest Group Notes Information Processing Society, Japan*, 86-DB-54-10, 1986 (in Japanese).

[12]   K. Kato and H. Imai: The NP-completeness of the character Placing problem of 2 or 3 degrees of freedom, *Record of Joint Conference of Electrical and Electronics Engineers in Kyushu*, 1138, 1988 (in Japanese).

[13]   T. Kato, H. Kanai and K. Yamashita: Mapping Information Data Management System, *Toshiba Review* Vol. 43, No. 1, pp. 45-48, 1988 (in Japanese).

[14]   J. S. Keates: Lettering, *Cartographic Design and Production, Longman Group Limited, London*, pp. 201-211, 1973.

[15]   M. Kidode and S. Tsunekawa (Toshiba R & Center): Multi-Media Database on Image Processing, *Journal of Information Processing Society of Japan*, Vol. 28, No. 6, 1987.

[16]   Lawrence, A. R. Michael, et al.: A Bowser for Directed Graphs, *Software-Practice and Experience*, Vol. 17(1), pp. 61-76, January 1987.

[17]   B. H. McCormick, T. A. DeFanti and M. D. Brown: Visualization in Scientific Computing (ViSC), *ACM SIGGRAPH - Computer Graphics*, Vol. 21, No. 6, 1987.

[18]   G. Nagy and S. Wagle: Geographical Data Processing, *ACM Computing Surveys*, Vol. 11, No. 2, pp. 139–181, 1979.

[19]   J. A. Orenstein: Spatial Query Processing in an Object-Oriented Database System, *Proc. ACM SIGMOD*, pp. 326-336, May 1986.

[20]   A. H. Robinson, et al.: Element of Cartography, *John Wiley & Sons*, 1978.

[21]   N. Roussopoulos, C. Faloutsos and T. Sellis: An Efficient Pictorial Database System for PSQL, *IEEE Transactions on Software Engineering*, Vol. 14, No. 5, pp. 639-650, May 1988.

[22]   K. Tanaka: A Map Information System begins to be put to practice, *Nikkei Computer Graphics*, pp. 79-86, July 1988 (in Japanese).

[23]   Sumitomo Electric Industries, Ltd.: U-GAL *User's Manual* Vol. 1, 1986 (in Japanese).

[24]   K. Uryu, N. Terasaki, et al.: Power Appatus Management System Using Visual Maps, *Annual Convention, Institute of Electronics, Information and Communication Engineers of Japan*, 4R-5, 1988 (in Japanese).

[25]   P. Yoeli: The Logic of Automated Map Lettering, *The Cartographic Journal*, 9, pp. 99-108, 1972.

[26]   T. Yoshii, T. Agui and M. Nakajima: A Setting Method of Characters on City Maps. *Annual Convention, Institute of Electronics, Information and Communication Engineers of Japan*, 110, 1987 (in Japanese).

3